Global Value Chains and Development

Over the past half century globalization has transformed how nations, firms, and workers compete in the international economy. The chapters in this book, authored by one of the founders of the global value chains (GVC) approach, trace the emergence of the most influential paradigm used to analyze globalization and its impact by academics and policy makers alike. In the mid-1990s, Gary Gereffi introduced the notion that offshore production was fuelled by buyer-driven and producer-driven supply chains, which highlighted the role of giant retailers, global brands, and manufacturers to orchestrate complex networks of suppliers in low-cost developing economies around the world. The GVC framework was built around the twin pillars of 'governance' (how global supply chains are controlled and organized) and 'upgrading' (how countries and firms try to create, capture, and retain high-value niches in GVCs). This book contains the seminal writings used to launch the GVC framework, along with in-depth case studies that explain how Mexico, China, and other countries emerged as prominent exporters in the world economy. As the social dimension of globalization became more pronounced, Gereffi and colleagues elaborated the concept of 'social upgrading' and a new paradigm of 'synergistic governance' based on the coordinated efforts of private, civil society, and public-sector actors. During the 2000s, the rise of large emerging economies like China, India, Brazil, and South Africa transformed the structure and dynamics of GVCs in the direction of greater regionalization. Today new challenges are looming in resurgent economic nationalism and populism. Large international organizations such as the WTO, World Bank, and ILO, policymakers in national economies, development practitioners, and academics continue to be guided by insights from the GVC approach.

Gary Gereffi is Professor of Sociology and Director of the Global Value Chains Center at Duke University, Durham, USA. He has published numerous books and articles on globalization, industrial upgrading, and social and economic development, and is one of the originators of the GVC framework.

Development Trajectories in Global Value Chains

Globalization is characterized by the outsourcing of production tasks and services across borders, and the increasing organization of production and trade through global value chains (GVCs), global commodity chains (GCCs), and global production networks (GPNs). With a large and growing literature on GVCs, GCCs, and GPNs, this series is distinguished by its focus on the implications of these new production systems for economic, social, and regional development.

This series publishes a wide range of theoretical, methodological, and empirical works, both research monographs and edited volumes, dealing with crucial issues of transformation in the global economy. How do GVCs change the ways in which lead firms and suppliers shape regional and international economies? How do they affect local and regional development trajectories, and what implications do they have for workers and their communities? How is the organization of value chains changing and how are these emerging forms contested? How does the large-scale entry of women into value-chain production impact gender relations? What opportunities and limits do GVCs create for economic and social upgrading and innovation? In what ways are GVCs changing the nature of work and the role of labor in the global economy? And how might the increasing focus on logistics management, financialization, and social standards and compliance shape the structure of regional economies?

This series includes contributions from all disciplines and interdisciplinary fields related to GVC analysis and is particularly supportive of theoretically innovative and informed works grounded in development research. Through their focus on changing organizational forms, governance systems, and production relations, volumes in this series contribute to on-going conversations about development theories and policy in the contemporary era of globalization.

Series editors

Stephanie Barrientos is Professor of Global Development at the Global Development Institute, University of Manchester.

Gary Gereffi is Professor of Sociology and Director of the Global Value Chains Center, Duke University.

Dev Nathan is Visiting Professor at the Institute for Human Development, New Delhi, and Visiting Research Fellow at the Global Value Chains Center, Duke University.

John Pickles is Earl N. Phillips Distinguished Professor of International Studies at the University of North Carolina, Chapel Hill.

Titles in the Series

1. Labour in Global Value Chains in Asia
   Edited by *Dev Nathan, Meenu Tewari and Sandip Sarkar*

2. The Sweatshop Regime: Labouring Bodies, Exploitation, and Garments *Made in India*
   Alessandra Mezzadri

3. The Intangible Economy: How Services Shape Global Production and Consumption
   Edited by *Deborah K. Elms, Arian Hassani and Patrick Low*

4. Making Cars in the New India: Industry, Precarity and Informality
   Tom Barnes

5. Development with Global Value Chains: Upgrading and Innovation in Asia
   Edited by *Dev Nathan, Meenu Tewari and Sandip Sarkar*

'The concept of global value chains has become a mainstay of research in international trade over several decades. This concept owes much to the pioneering work of Gary Gereffi. In this lucid volume he describes how global value chains arise and differ across various industries and countries, and how they have evolved over time in response to economic and political forces, right up to the recent calls for protection.'

Robert Feenstra, C. Bryan Cameron Distinguished Professor in International Economics, University of California, Davis

'GVCs drive productivity growth, investment, technology transfer and job creation. For more than 20 years, Gary Gereffi has led the world in understanding the governance, upgrading and evolution of GVCs. In *Global Value Chains and Development* he brings together his most relevant work while providing insights on the evolving trade and technology landscape transforming GVCs. This is a must-read book for policy makers, practitioners and academics committed to economic development.'

Anabel Gonzalez, Former Senior Director of the World Bank Global Practice on Trade and Competitiveness and former Costa Rica Minister of Trade

'Gary Gereffi explains the organization of the global economy better than anyone. This book reaffirms his importance as the founder and still leading theorist of global value chains, and is essential reading for all those who wish to understand the complexity of manufacturing in the 21st century.'

Gary Hamilton, Professor Emeritus, University of Washington

'Gary Gereffi is a pioneer in the analysis of global value chains and their implications for economic development policy and governance. This volume brings together his key contributions and is required reading for all students of trade and development.'

Bernard Hoekman, European University Institute, Florence

'Gary Gereffi's work over the past 25 years has changed how we understand capitalism. This brilliant collection of essays shows that capitalism today can be understood in its global form by an array of production networks that generate profits, employment and wage income, and that economic development itself is deeply molded by these networks. Gereffi's analysis of global value changes has spearheaded a generation of scholars and has influenced policy makers from around the world. He effectively defined the field and then continued to move the thinking forward as the world evolved – with the growth of services trade and telecommunications, with economic booms in East Asia and busts in Latin America, and most recently with a riveting account of the shifting politics of industrial policy and protectionism. Gereffi is the gold standard: the writing is clear, data are illuminating and the analysis is sharp and relevant. This book is essential reading for anyone seeking to understand globalization and economic development.'

William Milberg, Dean and Professor of Economics, New School for Social Research

'Global value chains are a key feature of the global economy in the 21st century. By providing the essentials of the GVC framework, unpacking the key concepts of governance and upgrading, and exploring the relevant policy implications – this collection of writings from the founder of this field is an essential companion to academics, policy makers, activists and business leaders interested in understanding present-day capitalism.'

Stefano Ponte, Professor of International Political Economy, Copenhagen Business School

Global Value Chains and Development

Redefining the Contours of 21st Century Capitalism

Gary Gereffi

CAMBRIDGE
UNIVERSITY PRESS

CAMBRIDGE
UNIVERSITY PRESS

University Printing House, Cambridge CB2 8BS, United Kingdom

One Liberty Plaza, 20th Floor, New York, NY 10006, USA

477 Williamstown Road, Port Melbourne, vic 3207, Australia

314 to 321, 3rd Floor, Plot No.3, Splendor Forum, Jasola District Centre, New Delhi 110025, India

79 Anson Road, #06–04/06, Singapore 079906

Cambridge University Press is part of the University of Cambridge.

It furthers the University's mission by disseminating knowledge in the pursuit of education, learning and research at the highest international levels of excellence.

www.cambridge.org
Information on this title: www.cambridge.org/9781108471947

© Gary Gereffi 2018

First published 2018

Printed in India by Rajkamal Electric Press

A catalogue record for this publication is available from the British Library

ISBN 978-1-108-47194-7 Hardback

ISBN 978-1-108-45886-3 Paperback

To Pela,
My inspiration, best friend,
and loving spouse for this entire journey

Contents

List of Tables   *xiii*

List of Figures and Boxes   *xv*

Foreword   *xvii*

Acknowledgments   *xix*

Sources   *xxi*

1. The Emergence of Global Value Chains: Ideas, Institutions, and
   Research Communities   1

Part I: Foundations of the Global Value Chain Framework

2. The Organization of Buyer-Driven Global Commodity Chains: 43
   How US Retailers Shape Overseas Production Networks

3. International Trade and Industrial Upgrading in the Apparel   72
   Commodity Chain

4. The Governance of Global Value Chains   108
   (*with John Humphrey and Timothy J. Sturgeon*)

**Part II: Expanding the Governance and Upgrading Dimensions in
       Global Value Chains**

5. The Global Economy: Organization, Governance, and Development   137

6. Local Clusters in Global Chains: The Causes and Consequences   176
   of Export Dynamism in Torreon's Blue Jeans Industry
   (*with Jennifer Bair*)

7. Development Models and Industrial Upgrading in China and Mexico   205

8. Economic and Social Upgrading in Global Production Networks: 228
   A New Paradigm for a Changing World
   (*with Stephanie Barrientos and Arianna Rossi*)

9. Regulation and Economic Globalization: Prospects and Limits   253
   of Private Governance
   (*with Frederick Mayer*)

10. Economic and Social Upgrading in Global Value Chains and Industrial
Clusters: Why Governance Matters   276
(with Joonkoo Lee)

Part III: Policy Issues and Challenges

11. Global Value Chain Analysis: A Primer (Second Edition)   305
(with Karina Fernandez-Stark)

12. Global Value Chains, Development, and Emerging Economies   343

13. Risks and Opportunities of Participation in Global Value Chains   381
(with Xubei Luo)

14. Global Value Chains in a Post-Washington Consensus World   400

15. Protectionism and Global Value Chains   429

Co-authors   453

Index   455

Tables

2.1 Sales of Leading US Retailers, 1987–1992   54
2.2 Net Income and Return on Revenues of Leading US Retailers, 1987–1991   55
2.3 Types of Retailers and Main Global Sourcing Areas   59
3.1 Trends in US Apparel Imports by Region and Country   84
3.2 The Triangle Sourcing Networks of the Top 10 US Retail Buying Offices in Taiwan, 1992   98
3.3 Regional Trade Patterns in World Exports of Textiles and Clothing   100
4.1 Key Determinants of Global Value Chain Governance   117
4.2 Some Dynamics of Global Value Chain Governance   119
5.1 Comparison of Varieties of Capitalism and Global Production Networks   153
6.1 Apparel Industry Indicators for Torreon /La Laguna   183
6.2 Main Clients for Torreon Apparel Exports   187
6.3 Top 10 Apparel Manufacturers in Torreon, Mexico—July 2000   192
6.4 Interviews in Torreon, 1998 and 2000   204
7.1 Foreign Direct Investment in China and Mexico, 1995–2015   211
7.2 Mexico's and China's Competing Exports to the United States, 2000–2014   215
7.3 US Imports in Which Mexico and/or China Hold 40% or More of the US Market, 2014   216
8.1 Key Drivers of Economic and Social Upgrading and Downgrading, by Type of Work   241
10.1 Types of Governance in Clusters and Global Value Chains by Scope and Actor   285
10.2 Key Drivers, Mechanisms, and Actors of Social Upgrading   293
11.1 Types of Work in Global Value Chains   325
11.2 Firms in Costa Rica's Medical Devices Sector   333
12.1 Seven Selected Emerging Economies in Comparative Perspective, 2013   361
12.2 Export Profiles of Emerging Economies, 2000–2013   362
14.1 Use of Global Value Chain Analysis in Selected International Organizations   415

Figures and Boxes

Figures

2.1 The Organization of Producer-Driven and Buyer-Driven
Global Commodity Chains   45
2.2 Production Frontiers for Global Sourcing by US Retailers:
The Apparel Industry   60
3.1 The Organization of Producer-Driven and Buyer-Driven
Global Commodity Chains   76
3.2 Shifts in the Regional Structure of US Apparel Imports,
1986–1996   89
4.1 Five Global Value Chain Governance Types   118
5.1 Industrial Upgrading in the Asian Apparel Value Chain   158
6.1 Pre-NAFTA Maquila Networks in Torreon   188
6.2 Post-NAFTA Full-Package Networks in Torreon   189
6.3 US–Torreon Apparel Commodity Chain Activities and Location 190
7.1 Composition of Mexico's Exports to the World Market, 1990–2014 213
7.2 Composition of China's Exports to the World Market, 1990–2014 213
7.3 China's Supply-Chain Cities in Apparel   220
8.1 Typology of Workforce Composition across Different GPNs   238
8.2 Possible Social Upgrading Trajectories   245
10.1 The Confluence of Actors in GVC and Cluster Governance   287
11.1 Six Dimensions of GVC Analysis   307
11.2 Fruit and Vegetables Global Value Chain Segments   308
11.3 Fruit and Vegetables Global Value Chain   309
11.4 Five Global Value Chain Governance Types   312
11.5 Upgrading Stages of Selected Countries in the Fruit and Vegetables
Value Chain   313
11.6 US–Torreon Apparel Value Chain: Activities and Location   314
11.7 Smile Curve of High-Value Activities in Global Value Chains 315
11.8 Model for Sustainable Smallholder Inclusion in High-Value
Agro-food Chains   317
11.9 Four Pillars Model for SME Participation in GVCs   318

11.10 The Offshore Services Global Value Chain   321
11.11 Examples of Upgrading Trajectories in the Offshore
       Services Value Chain   323
11.12 Workforce Composition Across Different GVCs   327
11.13 Examples of Workforce Development Initiatives in the Offshore
       Services Value Chain   328
11.14 Costa Rica Medical Exports by Product Category, 1998–2011   332
11.15 Offshore Services Industry in Costa Rica: MNC Participation
       by Segment, 2011   334
11.16 Offshore Services Industry in Costa Rica: US Exports and Number
       of Employees by Segment, 2011   335
11.17 Policy Recommendations: Medical Devices and Offshore Services   336
12.1   Five Types of Global Value Chain Governance   348
12.2   Curve of Value-Added Stages in the Apparel Global Value Chain:
       Nicaragua   354
13.1   Industry Groups, GVCs, and Economic Upgrading   390
13.2   Different Pathways to Social Upgrading   391
14.1   Five Types of Global Value Chain Governance   404
14.2   US Bilateral Trade Balance with China for One Unit of iPhone4   411
15.1   The Architecture of the Digital Economy   441

Box

13.1   From One Shock to Another: The 2011 Earthquake in Japan
       Rattled the Auto Industry Worldwide   386

Foreword

The themes covered in this book resonate with a distinction I made often between the old world of trade and the new world of trade when I was Director–General of the World Trade Organization. In the old world of trade, production was national, most trade occurred within countries, and the job of trade negotiators was to remove obstacles to trade that protected producers, such as tariffs and subsidies, so that international trade could flourish. In the new world of trade, production of both goods and services is transnational, organized in global supply chains where a product could be made in up to 10 to 12 countries, and trade increased greatly as intermediate inputs crossed borders many times in the process of making final products. This new world of trade involved value addition at every stage of the chain, and the obstacles to trade were increasingly about non-tariff barriers such as regulatory standards, consumer protection, intellectual property and data privacy, the purpose of which is to protect consumers.

A big part of my job at the WTO was to try to get people who negotiate trade agreements to make the transition from thinking about trade in traditional terms to the new realities of global supply chains. After lots of discussion with business people who were familiar with fully integrated systems of production where goods were largely produced in Asia and sold in the West, I launched the WTO's 'Made in the World' initiative, and shortly thereafter, we began to partner with the research unit at the OECD to elaborate ways to measure 'trade in value added'. This helped us drive home the point that it was no longer the volume of trade per se that mattered, but rather whether and how countries were connected to increasingly pervasive global value chains.

I first learned of Gary Gereffi's pioneering work on this topic in the context of these WTO efforts to create a new narrative on global trade and development. In a couple of international conferences organized by the WTO in Geneva, such as the Global Forum on Trade Statistics in February 2011 and the Fourth Global Review of Aid for Trade on 'Connecting to Value Chains' in July 2013, Professor Gereffi made key presentations that illustrated how the global economy was changing and why this was relevant to policy makers. Then in the fall of 2014, Gary and his colleague Frederick Mayer invited me to present a keynote address at the Global Value Chain Summit that they were organizing at Duke University as a forum to promote high-level dialogue between top international organizations who were using the value chain framework and leading academics also working on these issues.

The chapters in this book offer a panoramic perspective on the sweeping changes that have transformed the global economy in recent decades. I would summarize the import of this book in three overarching impressions. First is its historical sweep. The chapters chart in admirable detail the shift from a nation-state-centered global economy in the early postwar decades to the intricate division of labor and continuously evolving supply chains that we see today. Early chapters in the book dealing with the apparel industry in Asia and North America bring to life the old world of trade, in which production and trade networks were adjusting to continuously shifting tariffs and quota systems. Middle chapters of the book capture the impact of the rise of emerging economies as well as the 2008 economic crisis on the international trading system, while the final chapter on 'Protectionism and Global Value Chains' offers an up-to-date interpretation of what's old and what's new in US President Trump's trade disputes with his NAFTA neighbors and China.

A second takeaway from the book is the clarity of the analysis, couched in a language that is equally accessible to business leaders, development practitioners, policy makers, and scholars. Although the book covers a very broad spectrum of industries, countries and regions, its actor-centered approach provides a largely jargon-free discussion of national development models, technology trends, industrial transformation, and policy options for developing and developed economies. Multinational corporations and international business networks are center stage in the global value chains framework laid out in this book, but it is also clear that development goals encompass a much bigger agenda than just trade and investment. The theme of governance is a particularly rich concept in this book, since it embraces not just the organization of supply chains by lead firms and top suppliers, but also the role of public authorities and civil society groups in promoting various kinds of social, environmental, and economic upgrading at the country level.

A final reflection on this book stems from my conviction that we need a new narrative that not only brings together the old and new worlds of trade, but also helps to bridge the divides that threaten to fracture the international system of trade and development into completing blocs with no common agenda or goals. Change is inevitable, and this book analyzes dramatic shifts in the world economy that have altered the fortunes of large and small, and industrial and agrarian economies alike. An open question is how the international system that helped to establish and adjudicate the rules of the game in the late 20th century will respond to these shifts in the early 21st century. Countries are very heterogeneous in their collective preferences and development situations, but in the search for common ground, we need inclusive frameworks that address the interests of citizens, businesses and consumers, practitioners and policy makers, and other diverse constituencies. This book has the breadth, quality and analytical tools to contribute to this much-needed dialogue.

Pascal Lamy
Former Director-General of the World Trade Organization
June 6, 2018

Acknowledgments

This book brings together research that spans several decades and I have been fortunate to be at Duke University for this entire period. Duke has been an ideal intellectual and institutional base for my work because it embraced both international and interdisciplinary scholarship, and it encouraged entrepreneurial teaching and research programs. The Sociology Department was my faculty home, and it supported multiple conferences and workshops I organized at Duke. The Center for Latin American and Caribbean Studies and Duke's Asian/Pacific Studies Institute contributed in multiple ways to create a vibrant atmosphere for faculty and students alike who are working within and across both regions.

I am particularly proud of the innovative, dedicated and policy-relevant scholarship carried out at Duke's Center for Globalization, Governance and Competitiveness that I founded in 2005, which was renamed the Duke Global Value Chains Center in 2017. The researchers and doctoral students associated with the Center have been amazingly committed and talented development scholars, who applied and extended the ideas and frameworks discussed in this book in virtually all regions of the world. Special thanks go to Mike Hensen, the managing director of the Center since its early years, and Tom Nechyba, director of the Social Science Research Institute, the Center's main institutional sponsor at Duke.

A number of the chapters in this book are co-authored, and I appreciate and value the intellectual and collegial contributions of my co-authors, which in most cases go well beyond the particular chapters that appear in the book. Within Duke, I have worked especially closely with Fritz Mayer, a faculty colleague in the Sanford School of Public Policy, on multiple projects related to global value chains and international development. Fritz and Will Goldsmith, who completed his Ph.D in the History Department at Duke, helped me document the history of the GVC approach and the role of international organizations in promoting and disseminating the GVC framework. Some of these ideas appear in Chapter 1.

Finally, a very deep sense of gratitude goes to my family. International research is exceptionally demanding in terms of the amount of time required for traveling and working abroad, and this has been true in my case as well. Fortunately, my wife, Pela, and my daughters, Emily and Karen, not only accepted these difficulties, but actually shared in many of the international travels and experiences that made my scholarly work around the world much more enjoyable and rewarding. For this reason and many others, this book is dedicated to Pela.

Sources

Chapter 2   Gereffi, Gary. 1994. 'The Organization of Buyer-Driven Global
Commodity Chains: How U.S. Retailers Shape Overseas Production
Networks.' In *Commodity Chains and Global Capitalism*, edited by Gary
Gereffi and Miguel Korzeniewicz, 95–122. Westport, CT: Praeger.
Copyright © 1993, CCC Republication. Reprinted with permission.

Chapter 3   Gereffi, Gary. 1999. 'International Trade and Industrial Upgrading in
the Apparel Commodity Chain.' *Journal of International Economics* 48(1):
37–70. Copyright © 1999, Elsevier. Reprinted with permission.

Chapter 4   Gereffi, Gary, John Humphrey and Timothy J. Sturgeon. 2005. 'The
Governance of Global Value Chains.' *Review of International Political
Economy* 12(1): 78–104. www.tandfonline.com. Reprinted with permission.

Chapter 5   Gereffi, Gary. 2005. 'The Global Economy: Organization, Governance,
and Development.' In *The Handbook of Economic Sociology*, 2nd edition,
edited by Neil J. Smelser and Richard Swedberg, 160–182. Princeton,
NJ: Princeton University Press and Russell Sage Foundation. Copyright
© 2005 by Russell Sage Foundation. Reprinted with permission.

Chapter 6   Bair, Jennifer and Gary Gereffi. 2001. 'Local Clusters in Global Chains:
The Causes and Consequences of Export Dynamism in Torreon's Blue
Jeans Industry.' *World Development* 29(11): 1885–1903. Copyright © 2001,
Elsevier. Reprinted with permission.

Chapter 7   Gereffi, Gary. 2009. 'Development Models and Industrial Upgrading in
China and Mexico.' *European Sociological Review* 25(1): 37–51. Reprinted
with permission.

Chapter 8   Barrientos, Stephanie, Gary Gereffi and Arianna Rossi. 2011. 'Economic
and Social Upgrading in Global Production Networks: A New Paradigm
for a Changing World.' *International Labour Review* 150(3–4): 319–340.
Copyright © The authors 2011 Journal compilation © International
Labour Organization 2011. Reprinted with permission.

Chapter 9   Mayer, Frederick and Gary Gereffi. 2010. 'Regulation and Economic
Globalization: Prospects and Limits of Private Governance.' *Business and
Politics* 12(3), Article 11. Copyright © V.K. Aggarwal 2010 and published
under exclusive license to Cambridge University Press.

Chapter 10   Gereffi, Gary and Joonkoo Lee. 2016. 'Economic and Social Upgrading in Global Value Chains: Why Governance Matters.' *Journal of Business Ethics* 133(1): 25–38. Copyright © 2014, Springer Nature. Reprinted with permission.

Chapter 11   Gereffi, Gary and Karina Fernandez-Stark. 2016. 'Global Value Chain Analysis: A Primer' (Second Edition). Available at https://gvcc.duke.edu/wp-content/uploads/Duke_CGGC_Global_Value_Chain_GVC_Analysis_Primer_2nd_Ed_2016.pdf. Printed with permission.

Chapter 12   Gereffi, Gary. 2015. 'Global Value Chains, Development and Emerging Economies.' UNIDO/UNU-MERIT Working Paper Series #2015-047. Available at https://www.merit.unu.edu/publications/working-papers/abstract/?id=5885. Printed with permission.

Chapter 13   Gereffi, Gary and Xubei Luo. 2015. 'Risks and Opportunities of Participation in Global Value Chains.' *Journal of Banking and Financial Economics* 2(4): 51–63. (Originally published as World Bank Policy Research Working Paper 6847, April 2014.) Reprinted with permission.

Chapter 14   Gereffi, Gary. 2014. 'Global Value Chains in a Post-Washington Consensus World.' *Review of International Political Economy* 21(1): 9–37. www.tandfonline.com. Reprinted with permission.

The Emergence of Global Value Chains
Ideas, Institutions, and Research Communities

The chapters in this book were written during the past 25 years and the ideas in them evolved over a considerably longer period. This era spans dramatic changes in the global economy: the forging of the US-led Bretton Woods system to rebuild the postwar international economy in the 1950s and 1960s; the rise of offshore outsourcing and far-flung global supply chains in the 1970s and 1980s; the dismantling of the Soviet Union and the emergence of the BRICs[1] in the 1990s; the surge of China as an export power following its admission to the World Trade Organization (WTO) in 2001; the wrenching disruptions of the global recession of 2008–2009; the waning influence of the 'Washington Consensus' policy regime; and the surprising turn in the mid-2010s to a virulent economic nationalism and xenophobic populism in the United States and Europe that reject many of the principles of the post-World War II Pax Americana (Buruma, 2016). How can we make sense of such fundamental transformations in global capitalism? What are the determinants of this reorganization of the international economy, and how do we link these global shifts to their national and local consequences? Who are the winners and losers along the way? This book addresses these questions.

By nature, the analytical task at hand is international, interdisciplinary and also highly personal. Legions of scholars and pundits have addressed these topics from varied perspectives and geographic vantage points. Providing a coherent interpretation of the evolving events, however, reflects one's unique intellectual identity based on specific experiences and influences. In my case, I was trained in graduate school at Yale University as a development and economic sociologist, and I spent two years in Mexico doing interview-based field research for my doctoral dissertation on the Mexican pharmaceutical industry. Although my background at Yale was highly interdisciplinary involving coursework in sociology, political science and economics, I had an even more intense exposure to the interplay of academic and policy-engaged work during a three-and-a-half year stint at the Center for International Affairs at Harvard University in the late 1970s. During this period, I also did extensive consulting and contract research for the United Nations Centre on Transnational Corporations in New York and the Pan American Health Organization in Washington, DC. Through these and related institutional experiences after I joined the Sociology Department at Duke University in 1980, my worldview reflects the imprint of multiple professional and research communities. Thus, this introductory chapter includes elements of intellectual autobiography, sociology of knowledge, and the institutional underpinnings of the research communities that helped define the ideas and paradigms developed in this book.

The structure of the chapter is as follows. First, I highlight several contending perspectives on the international economy and development in the 1970s and 1980s that set the stage for the emergence of the global commodity chain (GCC) and global value chain (GVC) approaches. Modernization theory, dependency theory and world-systems theory were popular paradigms in academic circles that had dramatically different prescriptions for national development in general, and contrasting assessments of the role of multinational corporations (MNCs), the main agent for economic globalization, in particular. Second, I will discuss four building blocks that were instrumental to the emergence of the GVC framework in the 2000s: (1) the centrality of power and MNC lead firms in the GCC and GVC frameworks; (2) the analysis of 'global industries' as a complement to development research at the national and local levels; (3) the role of the state and contrasting regional development strategies in the global economy; and (4) the institutionalization of the GVC research community. Third, and finally, I will introduce each chapter of the book in terms of its core ideas and novel contributions to the emerging field of GVC studies.

Contending Perspectives on the International Economy and Development

In the early decades following the Second World War, modernization theory and dependency theory offered diametrically opposed proposals for developing economies and newly emergent post-colonial societies in the so-called Third World. Modernization theorists explicitly modeled their prescriptions for development on the historical legacy and institutional features of the advanced industrial democracies of the West. One of the best-known economic books in this genre was Walt W. Rostow's *The Stages of Economic Growth* (1960), which postulated that all countries pass through five stages of economic development[2] with identical content regardless of when these nations started out on the road to industrialization. Notwithstanding the widely criticized Eurocentric bias of the modernization approach (Bendix, 1967; Gusfield, 1967; Huntington, 1971; Portes, 1973), a key recommendation was close economic, political and social ties between developing economies and the Western capitalist democracies they were encouraged to emulate.

Dependency theory, by contrast, highlighted the exploitative potential of increased contact between the 'core' countries and the 'periphery' in the international capitalist system. Andre Gunder Frank, one of the most widely read Marxist dependency authors, claimed that asymmetric ties of economic and political dependency between core and peripheral economies promote 'the development of underdevelopment' (Frank, 1967), and citing evidence from Latin America and Africa, dependency writers argued that links to the center were the source of many of the Third World's problems, rather than a solution (see also Amin, 1973; Dos Santos, 1970). The dependency school, while unified in its critique of the ahistorical and apolitical assumptions of modernization theory, had significant internal differences in theoretical and research orientations with varying prognoses for capitalist development in the periphery (see Gereffi, 1983, chapter 1; Gereffi, 1994a).

Dependency theory altered its initial claims with a new wave of research in the 1970s and 1980s. Diverging sharply from the 'stagnationist' views of writers like Frank, Dos Santos and Amin, which declared that dependency could only lead to underdevelopment and socialist revolution, a number of authors promoted the notion of 'dependent development' (Cardoso and Faletto, 1979), which asserted that structural dependency on foreign capital and external markets might constrain and distort but is not necessarily incompatible with capitalist economic development in the more advanced countries of the Third World, such as Brazil (Evans, 1979), Chile (Moran, 1974), Nigeria (Biersteker, 1978), Taiwan (Gold, 1981), South Korea (Lim, 1985), India (Encarnation, 1989) and Kenya (Bradshaw, 1988).

A related and at the time novel research agenda was pursued by dependency scholars who focused on industries rather than countries. This approach often employed a 'bargaining perspective' that analyzed the interaction between the state, MNCs and national business elites in shaping local outcomes in relatively dynamic manufacturing industries. Sectors included in the initial set of studies were pharmaceuticals (Gereffi, 1978; 1983), automobiles (Bennett and Sharpe, 1979; 1985), computers (Grieco, 1984), and the electrical, tractor, tire, and food-processing industries (Newfarmer, 1985). This bargaining framework sparked a vigorous debate about the limits of dependency, hypothesis testing, counterfactual analysis and the possibilities for dependency reversal (Caporaso, 1978; Becker, 1983; Encarnation, 1989).

The research methodologies of these early country and especially industry case studies of dependency are a clear forerunner of the GCC studies that emerged in the mid-1990s (Gereffi and Korzeniewicz, 1994). Like the GCC and subsequent GVC approach, dependency analysis involved extensive and detailed field research, with the authors typically spending one to two years in their chosen countries gathering relevant secondary materials and meeting local informants. These studies relied heavily on in-depth or 'strategic' interviews[3] with government officials in charge of both macro and industry-specific policies, as well as firm-level managers and other stakeholders for the industries in question. Multinational corporations were a central actor in virtually all dependency research, whether of the case-study variety or in quantitative, cross-national studies intended to 'test dependency theory.'[4] The main issues analyzed in the country or industry studies of dependency revolved around the kinds of power being exercised by MNCs at the national level, the transnational structure and strategies of MNCs, and the roles played by national governments, local firms, workers and other industry actors in defending perceived national interests vis-à-vis the domestic and global goals of MNCs.

Against this backdrop, world-systems theory had a very different intellectual agenda. World-systems theory, which drew heavily on earlier critical perspectives of imperialism and capitalist exploitation, has been closely associated with the work of Immanuel Wallerstein (1974; 1979; 1980; 1989). This approach establishes a hierarchy of core, semiperipheral and peripheral zones in which upward or downward mobility is conditioned by the resources and obstacles associated with a country's mode of incorporation in the capitalist world-economy. Leaving one structural position implies taking on a new role in the international division of labor, rather than escaping from the system; thus, the possibilities for autonomous paths of development are quite limited.

The semiperiphery, a main category in world-systems theory, identifies an intermediate stratum between the core and peripheral zones that promotes the stability and legitimacy of the three-tiered world-economy. The diverse countries within the contemporary semiperipheral zone, such as South Korea and Taiwan in East Asia, Mexico and Brazil in Latin America, India in South Asia, and Nigeria and South Africa in Africa, purportedly have the capacity to resist peripheralization, but not to move into the upper tier (Wallerstein, 1974; Arrighi and Drangel, 1986). While world-systems theory takes a long-run historical view of cycles of change in the capitalist world-economy that cuts across all regions, it is not well suited to analyze the specific development trajectories of countries and regions that are similarly situated in the hierarchical structure, but respond differently to external economic challenges.[5]

For development scholars working on global industries, the general categories of core, semiperipheral and peripheral zones in world-systems theory were viewed as structural contexts in the world economy, shaped by both world-historic forces and the technological features of key industries (Henderson, 1989; Doner, 1991) as well as by the economic strategies of countries seeking to move toward higher-value-added activities in GCCs (Gereffi and Korzeniewicz, 1990; 1994). While the 'commodity chain' concept was originally introduced as part of the world-systems approach by Hopkins and Wallerstein (1977), and defined simply as 'a network of labor and production processes whose end result is a finished commodity' (Hopkins and Wallerstein, 1986: 159), it became the central theme of the co-edited volume by Gereffi and Korzeniewicz (1994), *Commodity Chains and Global Capitalism*. For reasons to be explored in greater detail below, this book actually marked a sharp break between world-systems theory and the GCC approach, which sought to link the macro-level issues related to the structure of the world-economy with the meso-level characteristics of national development strategies, and the micro-level emphasis on the inter-firm networks and related political and social consequences of local embeddedness (Gereffi, 1994a: 214).

Building Blocks in the Emergence of the GVC Paradigm

Given this brief overview of the contending theoretical perspectives on the international economy and development in the 1970s and 1980s, we turn to several cross-cutting themes that cumulatively began to distinguish the GCC and GVC research communities from their peers: (1) the centrality of MNCs and power dynamics in development studies; (2) the analysis of 'global industries' as a complement to national case studies of dependency and the parallel work on local industrial clusters; (3) reconceptualizing the role of the state and regional development strategies in East Asia and Latin America; and (4) institutionalizing the GVC research agenda through the support of foundations and university-affiliated research centers.

MNCs and Power in the Global Economy

While there was a great deal of popular interest in the power and global reach of MNCs in the 1970s (e.g., Barnet and Müller, 1974; Sampson, 1973; 1975), the study of multinational enterprises was still a neophyte field from an academic point of view. To the neoclassical economists of the 1950s and 1960s, the postwar world economy was defined by international capital flows, which were viewed at the country level as foreign direct investment (FDI). The United States was the main source of outward FDI, and the first national studies of US FDI were carried out by Dunning (1958) on the United Kingdom and Safarian (1966) on Canada. Both of these authors were interested in the public policy question of the contributions that US FDI had for a host economy (Rugman 1999), and thus they did not really think about MNCs as an institutional actor.

The Multinational Enterprise Project at Harvard Business School, which began in 1965 under the direction of Raymond Vernon and lasted for 12 years, tried to remedy the relative neglect of MNCs. In his most popular book, *Sovereignty at Bay*, Vernon (1971) posed the question: To what extent have MNCs supplanted the national autonomy of governments? Despite being out of step with his academic brethren in economics departments and business schools who were using general equilibrium models and rational choice to study the properties of efficient markets, Vernon's approach emphasized the strategies and activities of MNCs as both a political and economic force, rather than just another form of international capital movement (Vernon, 1999). Furthermore, empirical studies of MNCs underscored their large size, whether measured in sales or by more sophisticated calculations of value added, which showcased the concentrated power of vertically integrated MNCs that were bigger in economic terms than many countries.[6]

In applying to graduate programs in sociology, I was interested in international development and preferred programs that encouraged interdisciplinary scholarship. Yale fit the bill on both counts. I received a fellowship in a comparative sociology project that focused on inequality systems in five nations, and Yale had strong area studies programs in multiple regions with particular strengths in Latin America, Africa and Europe.[7] Among my sociology mentors, Louis Wolf Goodman worked on MNCs in Chile and political scientist Alfred Stepan was a noted Brazilianist who had close personal ties with Fernando Henrique Cardoso, one of the early pioneers of dependency theory.[8] In economics, there was also a very strong group of Latin American scholars, including Carlos Diaz-Alejandro, Gus Ranis, and Jorge Katz, among others. My exposure to dependency theory came largely through courses with Stepan and Goodman, who co-chaired my dissertation committee. I developed a proposal to work on MNCs in Mexico, and I received funding for a two-year Foreign Area Fellowship from the Social Science Research Council (SSRC) in New York.

While MNCs and dependency theory were both popular topics, there was considerable controversy about how to combine them in a dissertation project. In my case, I was fortunate that the SSRC took a pro-active stance in fostering a research community to help address a number of theoretical and operational challenges in this emergent field. In 1976, the SSRC created the 'Continuing Working Group on Multinational Corporations in Latin America' that brought junior and senior researchers together for periodic meetings in New York in the late 1970s and early 1980s to discuss their projects, methods and preliminary findings.[9] All members of the working group were studying MNCs in different countries and industries across Latin America, and exploring how dependency on MNCs in particular sectors shaped national development outcomes. In the early 1980s, Richard Newfarmer joined the working group. Trained as an industrial organization economist at the University of Wisconsin, Newfarmer helped to create a much-needed structural perspective on how global industries were organized. Using the tools of conventional industrial organization theory (such as Bain, 1968; Scherer, 1980), Newfarmer edited a book with chapters from all members of the working group that related the market power of MNCs in each industry to the conduct and performance of overseas affiliates and domestic firms (Newfarmer, 1985).[10] This model was a precursor to the governance structure dimension that later appeared in GCC and GVC studies.

My own dissertation project focused on MNCs in the pharmaceutical industry in Mexico (Gereffi, 1980). After two years of field research in Mexico (1975–1976), Raymond Vernon invited me to write my dissertation at Harvard, where I could interact with members of his Multinational Enterprise Project team as well as scholars at Harvard's Center for International Affairs, which Vernon was directing. My stay at Harvard extended from January 1977 through June 1980, and my work on MNCs evolved in several directions. In terms of my dissertation research on Mexico, I developed my central arguments in an article (Gereffi, 1978) for a special issue of the journal *International Organization* on 'Dependence and Dependency in the Global System,' (Caporaso, 1978). Although my analysis was a single-country case study, I was pushed by Vernon and others to develop falsifiable hypotheses related to dependency reversal, including a 'counterfactual analysis' that extrapolated from the experience of relevant comparative cases how national firms in Mexico might have performed better than MNCs in terms of national welfare (defined as local industry growth) and global consumer welfare (defined as identical products at lower prices).

Beyond my dissertation, I had the opportunity to initiate different kinds of policy-related studies of MNCs in the global pharmaceutical industry: one project involved the UN Centre on Transnational Corporations in New York, and a second looked at the viability of 'essential drugs' programs in Latin America for the Pan-American Health Organization (PAHO) in Washington, DC. In both cases, I was asked to analyze the structure and strategies of top MNCs in the global pharmaceutical industry, which was a key (and missing) complement to the bottom-up perspective of my Mexican case study on the steroid hormone industry. In retrospect, learning how to study a global industry from the perspective of MNCs and link it to the experience of national economies was critical to framing the governance structure and industrial upgrading pillars of the GCC and GVC paradigms in subsequent decades. However, in the late 1970s and 1980s these were uncharted waters.

Studying Global Industries

One of the major limitations of dependency theory was the absence of an integrated global perspective on MNCs. Most of the historical-structural authors in the dependency tradition assessed the development implications of peripheral capitalism by focusing on the class structure in the peripheral country, the alliances formed by local business and political elites with international capital, and the role of the state in shaping and managing the national, foreign and class forces that propel or constrain development within countries (Cardoso and Faletto, 1979; Evans, 1979). For dependency theorists, not the whole country but only a selected portion of it is integrated into the international economy (Sunkel, 1973), which does not fit classic power-dependence models that view dependence as a dyadic asymmetrical relationship between pairs of nation-states or other unitary actors (Emerson, 1962; Duvall, 1978).

For those dependency scholars who focused on industries rather than countries or regions, MNCs became a logical focal point for research because these companies embodied the power asymmetries entailed by a peripheral economy's integration into the international capitalist system. However, in US academic circles, there was a great deal of pressure to develop methodological strategies that would treat dependency not merely as a holistic structural 'situation' but rather as a relational 'variable' that could be measured and tested in falsifiable propositions about MNCs and other key actors (Caporaso, 1978; Gereffi, 1978; Moran, 1978; Bennett and Sharpe, 1979).[11] Notwithstanding this uptick of interest in analyzing MNCs through an industry lens, dependency theory still looked at the world from the bottom up, i.e., from the perspective of peripheral economies. There was little systematic empirical information about international industries viewed from the top down.

World-systems theory had the advantage of a more intrinsically global perspective on the historical evolution of the capitalist system, but the broad tripartite classification of core, semiperipheral and peripheral zones used in this approach created an agency problem in terms of not clearly specifying the concrete actors and mechanism of change in the system. In their influential study of the semiperipheral zone in the world-economy, Arrighi and Drangel (1986: 11) critiqued the dependent development literature for acknowledging 'the possibility that development in general and industrialization in particular might occur within states while still reproducing a structure of dependence.' Among the weaknesses of dependent development from a world-systems stance is that national or regional economies do not simply occupy an intermediate position between 'center' and 'periphery' in the world-economy; rather, a systemic view emphasizes the structural significance of each stratum or group of states (core, semiperipheral, peripheral), and not the rise or fall of individual economies. This three-tiered structure of the world-economy is assumed to be 'more or less constant throughout the history of the capitalist world-economy' and 'to play a key role in promoting the legitimacy and stability of the system' (Arrighi and Drangel, 1986: 12–13).[12]

In world-systems theory, commodity-chain dynamics are closely linked to world-system position. Core-periphery relations comprise 'economic activities structured in commodity chains that cut across state boundaries': 'core' countries are countries where 'core' activities are located, and 'core activities are those that command a larger share of the total surplus produced within a commodity chain and peripheral activities are those that command little or no such surplus' (Arrighi and Drangel, 1986: 11–12).[13] In other words, there is something about core status that enables firms (called 'core capital') to generate the highest returns or secure the most rent. But world-systems theory does not specify what those mechanisms are in any detail, so the formulation ends up being tautological.[14] If indeed commodity chains link all three tiers of the world-economy and are a key to reproducing this hierarchical system, we need to know more about the kinds of firms (state-owned, foreign and domestic) and industries that make up these chains, and how state policy can shape their contribution to surplus generation in zones like the semiperiphery (Gereffi and Evans, 1981).

These theoretical debates among dependency and world-systems scholars reaffirmed the importance of a core-periphery system, but did little to address the empirical question of how to analyze the global industries that actually make up the world economy. This became a practical mandate for the newly formed UN Centre on Transnational Corporations (UNCTC) in the late 1970s. Although UNCTC is probably best known for its unfilled quest to draft a code of conduct to govern the activities of transnational companies[15] in the wake of political scandals in the early 1970s,[16] it also did important work in commissioning comprehensive empirical studies of MNCs.

One of the initial priorities was a study of the global pharmaceutical industry, which had received a lot of attention because of controversial practices related to transfer pricing, differential drug labeling across countries, and the role of essential drugs programs in the developing world (Lall, 1973; 1975; 1978). Given my ongoing dissertation research on the pharmaceutical industry in Mexico (Gereffi, 1978; 1980), I was commissioned by UNCTC in 1977 to write a report on the structure and strategies of the top 50 pharmaceutical MNCs worldwide. This was followed by a second report on how the structure, conduct and performance of these pharmaceutical MNCs was good or bad for economic and health outcomes in developing countries, including various industry stakeholders such as consumers, domestic drug firms and local innovation systems (UNCTC, 1979; 1981).

The scale of this project was unlike anything I had undertaken before. Even more daunting, there were no guidelines offered by UNCTC staff because there were no research models of what a report on MNCs in a global industry should look like. Drawing on a wide variety of industry-specific source materials and numerous consultations with academic and business experts on the sector, I drafted the initial report focusing on the 50 largest pharmaceutical MNCs in the world. After listing the biggest companies in terms of their annual sales, the MNCs were classified by nationality and information was gathered on their position in distinct 'therapeutic markets' within the pharmaceutical sector (e.g., antibiotics and vaccines, cardiovascular, respiratory, autoimmune diseases, pain, etc.) in order to establish the main competitors in each market segment. The global reach of the top pharmaceutical firms was estimated by their sales distribution across major geographic regions. While the methodological and empirical difficulties in compiling such a report were formidable, the toughest hurdle was handling the intense political scrutiny and stakeholder interests attached to a UN study of pharmaceutical MNCs.[17] The official report (UNCTC, 1979) was widely circulated in UN circles and it became a reference point for how subsequent global industry studies could be carried out.[18]

The UNCTC report on MNCs in the global pharmaceutical industry complemented the national focus in my dissertation on the Mexican steroid hormone industry (Gereffi, 1980). In my book on *The Pharmaceutical Industry and Dependency in the Third World* (Gereffi, 1983), I added a couple of chapters that used the UNCTC studies to put the Mexican case in a broader international perspective. In the early 1980s, the Pan American Health Organization, the regional arm of the World Health Organization, commissioned me to prepare a policy paper and several national case studies evaluating the scope and effectiveness of 'essential drags' programs in various Latin American countries, including Mexico, Brazil and Peru (PAHO, 1984; Gereffi, 1988).

These early studies of global industries foreshadow several important themes in the subsequent GCC and GVC literature. First, a focus on specific industries has obvious policy relevance. Often, the demand for industry studies comes from those most interested in designing or implementing effective regulation.[19] Second, the organization of global industries reflects the power dynamics of their leading firms. This insight led directly to the concept of 'governance structures,' which is a mainstay in the GCC and GVC frameworks.[20] Third, the organization of global industries shapes the potential 'upgrading' pathways available to developing economies. The structures and strategies of MNCs present both opportunities and obstacles for how countries can link up with the international economy and build domestic industries.[21] Fourth, a detailed understanding of the role of MNCs in global industries allows us to 'map the activities' associated with efforts to create, capture and retain value, which are essential to economic growth and development.[22]

Development Strategies in Latin America and East Asia

East Asia has been the most dynamic region in the world since the 1990s and it played a major role in the emergence of the GCC and GVC paradigms. Dependency theory dealt primarily with developing economies in Latin America and Africa, and neither it nor world-systems theory had the analytical tools nor temporal focus to explain the impact of the rapid ascent of East Asia in the post-World War II era. Scholars who worked on East Asia believed that dependency theory had little, if any, relevance to their part of the world, where dynamic economic growth and social progress occurred without a number of the drawbacks typical of the Latin American experience (Amsden, 1979; Barrett and Whyte, 1982; Berger, 1986). Instead, East Asian political and economic elites managed to use external economic linkages effectively and selectively to promote domestic development.[23]

The import-substituting industrialization (ISI) model of growth had been well established in Latin America, Eastern Europe and a few other areas since the 1950s, and indeed, it was the preferred national development strategy recommended by the UN Economic Commission for Latin America, directed by Raúl Prebisch. It argued that industrialization could be the solution to Latin America's economic problems, which were rooted in both limited export markets due to the Great Depression and declining terms of trade (whereby the prices of the region's agricultural goods exports fell more rapidly than manufactured imports). However, this would require an active industrial policy by Latin American governments willing to entice foreign investors to produce major consumer goods locally in return for protected domestic markets (Love, 1980). Although the accuracy of Prebisch's empirical claims of declining terms of trade was challenged, the ISI policy became widely adopted throughout most of Latin America from the 1950s through the 1970s.

In East Asia, Japan and the newly industrializing economies of South Korea, Taiwan, Hong Kong and Singapore were dubbed 'miracle economies' because of their unparalleled accomplishments in the latter half of the twentieth century (World Bank, 1993). They registered record economic growth rates not only during the prosperous 1960s when international trade and investment were expanding rapidly, but they sustained their dynamism through the 1970s and 1980s in the face of several oil price hikes, a global recession, and rising protectionism in their major export markets. In contrast to Latin America's inward-oriented ISI policies, the East Asian economies pursued a very different outward model known as export-oriented industrialization (EOI). When one examines the details of East Asia's EOI, though, there is considerable disagreement over its generalizability as a development model to other parts of the world.

The World Bank (1993) adopted a 'market friendly' view of East Asian success that attributed its economic growth in large measure to functional intervention in market 'fundamentals' such as stable macroeconomic policies, high investments in human capital (especially education), secure financial systems, limited price distortions, and openness to foreign technology and trade. A widely held alternative 'statist' interpretation, however, criticized the World Bank's adherence to doctrinaire market fundamentalism, and emphasized instead pervasive state intervention and the critical role played by selective industrial policies in promoting the sustained and diversified patterns of export growth exhibited by these high-performing Asian economies (Johnson, 1982; Amsden, 1989; Wade, 1990).

To better understand the relevance of the Latin American and East Asian experiences to other newly industrializing countries, scholars elaborated cross-regional comparisons of their development strategies (Gereffi and Wyman, 1990; Haggard, 1990; Deyo, 1987). One of the earliest studies in this vein was *Manufacturing Miracles: Paths of Industrialization in Latin America and East Asia* (Gereffi and Wyman, 1990), which compared the development strategies of four of the most successful newly industrializing economies: Mexico, Brazil, South Korea and Taiwan. The core concept of *Manufacturing Miracles* was 'development strategies,' defined as 'sets of government policies that shape a country's relationship to the global economy and that affect the domestic allocation of resources among industries and major social groups' (Gereffi and Wyman, 1990: 23). This meso-level approach, in contrast to the macro focus of world-systems theory or the micro analysis of industrial clusters, highlighted the role of state policies in promoting desired local development outcomes, and it made the inward- or outward-oriented nature of industrial production a subject of both comparative and historical interest.

A central finding of *Manufacturing Miracles* was that, contrary to prevailing stereotypes, the distinction typically made between Latin America and East Asia as representing inward- and outward-oriented development models, respectively, was oversimplified. Each of the regional pairs pursued both inward and outward strategies of industrialization, although their timing and duration varied by region. In the early phases of development, all four economies adopted commodity export and 'primary' ISI strategies. The main divergence occurred after the initial ISI phase: Mexico and Brazil followed a strategy of ISI deepening or 'secondary' ISI (mid-1950s through the early 1980s), while Taiwan and South Korea shifted to 'primary' EOI (1960–1972) and then pursued 'secondary' ISI[24] (1973–1979) and 'secondary' EOI[25] (1980s onward) (Gereffi, 1989: 515–519).

One of the key messages from the cross-regional analysis of development strategies was that regions like Latin America could not simply emulate the East Asian experience, given significant differences in both historical patterns of international economic and geopolitical engagement as well as domestic institutions. East Asia, in particular, had unique circumstances associated with regional conflicts (the Communist Chinese Revolution and the Korean War) and subsequent Cold War tensions that led to very distinct patterns of international economic engagement than found in Latin America. These differences sparked a new view of global commodity chains and their governance structures in the 1990s.

The Emergence of the GCC and GVC Paradigms

To challenge widely held but misleading stereotypes of development patterns in Latin America and East Asia, a new knowledge network willing to rethink the commonalities and differences within and between the two regions was needed. Often this is most readily carried out in a university context. The institutional setting for the discussions and workshops that led to *Manufacturing Miracles* was the University of California at San Diego (UCSD), which had strong programs in both Latin America and Asia–Pacific Studies. I spent a one-year sabbatical at UCSD's Center for US–Mexican Studies in 1983–1984, and worked closely with my colleague Donald L. Wyman[26] to organize two workshops on Latin America and East Asia that led to our co-edited volume. The initial workshop brought together experts on each region to define themes of greatest relevance for the volume, and the second workshop discussed draft chapters where individual authors or pairs of authors addressed the same topic in both regions to make the bases for the comparative analysis more explicit and realistic.

Global Commodity Chains

The origins of the GCC framework are also linked to university-based research communities, conferences and subsequent publications that reframed and expanded earlier world-systems work on commodity chains. Immanuel Wallerstein founded the Fernand Braudel Center at Binghamton, State University of New York in 1976, which became the intellectual hub for the development of world-systems theory in the United States. Wallerstein sponsored an annual Political Economy of the World-System (PEWS) conference series, which brought together scholars around world-systems topics to present papers subsequently published in conference volumes.[27] The concept of commodity chains was first introduced by Hopkins and Wallerstein (1977; 1986) as a heuristic to study the operation of global capitalism and the reproduction of a stratified and hierarchical world-system beyond the territorial confines of the nation-state. By contrast, the introduction of the 'global' commodity chain[28] perspective in the early 1990s focused on the organization of contemporary global industries and how power asymmetries of MNC lead firms affected the prospects for national development. This led to a split with traditional world-systems theory (Bair, 2005; 2009).

The first publication that explicitly utilized the GCC framework was a study of the footwear industry by Gereffi and Korzeniewicz (1990). The paper was presented at one of the annual PEWS conferences on 'Semiperipheral States in the World-Economy,'[29] and my co-author was Miguel Korzeniewicz,[30] a doctoral student in the Sociology Department at Duke University. The research question that motived our study was why Argentina, Miguel's home country, had very high-quality leather exports but lacked a strong footwear industry, while neighboring Brazil had extensive shoe exports but limited leather inputs. Since Brazil and Argentina were both in the semiperiphery of the current world-system, the paper examined how export niches were created in the footwear commodity chain during the initial phases of economic globalization (1967–1987). The rapid growth of exports from the semiperiphery in footwear involved high levels of specialization, which shaped patterns of upward and downward mobility among the main footwear-exporting countries.[31] Creating export niches in the footwear commodity chain was partly a story of how and why the previous industry leaders allowed new capabilities for the emergent exporters,[32] and how intermediaries (like trading agents) linked small producers to global markets.[33]

The analysis of a contemporary global industry using the commodity chain concept generated spirited controversy[34] and a lot of interest among participants at the 1989 PEWS conference. Wallerstein suggested to Miguel and me that Duke University might like to host a subsequent PEWS conference on commodity chains, looking at both historical and contemporary cases. We accepted the invitation. The 16th annual PEWS conference on 'Commodity Chains and Global Capitalism' was held at Duke in April 1992, and it resulted in our edited volume on this topic[35] (Gereffi and Korzeniewicz, 1994).

While building on the original definition provided by Hopkins and Wallerstein (1986: 159), which views a commodity chain as 'a network of labor and production processes whose end result is a finished commodity,' the *Commodity Chains and Global Capitalism* book broke with several core precepts of world-systems analysis.

Whereas research on commodity chains from a world-systems perspective focused on the reconstruction of industries during the long sixteenth century, most chapters in our volume used the GCC concept to analyze contemporary industries.[36] The introductory chapter to the *Commodity Chains* volume describes the GCC framework as 'a nuanced analysis of world-economic spatial inequalities in terms of differential access to markets and resources' (Gereffi et al., 1994: 2). In addition, a critical contention of the GCC approach was that the internationalization of production in contemporary globalization reflected a novel process of economic organization – i.e., 'governance structures' that could be characterized as 'producer-driven' and 'buyer-driven' commodity chains (Gereffi, 1994b; 1996). This fueled a debate about 'whether globalization is better understood as a contemporary phenomenon enabled by increasingly integrated production systems, or as a process beginning with the emergence of capitalism in the long sixteenth century' (Bair, 2005: 157).

This 'developmentalist turn' in commodity chain research shared with the world-systems framework the notion that mobility is possible as individual countries move up or down between different tiers of the world-economy. For world-systems theorists, however, this is a zero-sum process; what is relevant is the reproduction of a hierarchically structured global capitalist economy (Wallerstein, 1974; Arrighi and Drangel, 1986). Hence, national development as a generalized goal is not deemed possible; it is simply a 'developmentalist illusion' (Arrighi, 1990).[37] Actually, the GCC approach was open to the option that commodity chains do not necessarily reproduce hierarchy and inequality in every case, and it assumed power asymmetries are rooted in the organization of global industries. Thus, commodity chain dynamics indeed are essential to the prospects for upgrading or downgrading in the global economy.[38] Notwithstanding these controversies, the GCC approach gained considerable popularity because of the detailed insights it provided in the analysis of contemporary industries and upgrading/downgrading trajectories of countries and firms within them, and it became a foundation for the elaboration of the closely related GVC framework.

The Global Value Chains Initiative

In September 1999, the Institute of Development Studies (IDS) at the University of Sussex in Brighton, UK hosted a workshop on 'Spreading the Gains from Globalization.'[39] Two broad research communities were invited. One set of scholars focused primarily on the local dynamics of industrial clusters to understand how small firms in both developed[40] and developing[41] economies could improve their export competitiveness in the global economy. A second set of researchers emphasized the changing organizational features of global industries,[42] and how new strategies by powerful lead firms were altering international and domestic production networks and opportunities for upgrading by developing economies.[43] The workshop's goals were threefold: (1) to bring these disparate research communities together for fruitful dialogue; (2) to establish direct communication between the researchers and the policy-making and policy-implementing communities; and (3) to promote a new research agenda that could identify implementable policies to help reduce growing inequality within and between countries and the impoverishing aspects of globalization.[44]

These two communities saw the challenges of economic globalization from opposite vantage points. Industrial cluster researchers had a bottom-up, country-level perspective, built around numerous small exporters that sought to leverage local advantages to enter global markets. Global industry researchers, by contrast, tended to adopt a top-down international perspective, where the drivers of change were multinational manufacturers and global buyers (retailers and brands) whose international production and sourcing networks imposed new rules of the game that determined winners and losers in the globalization era. The core challenge posed at the IDS workshop was to forge an integrated research framework that could link the macro (global), meso (industry and country) and micro (firm and community) levels of analysis, and generate novel findings and evidence-based policy proposals. To achieve these goals, a new type of policy-oriented, multidisciplinary and international research initiative was necessary, and it required an institutional backer with a long-term vision and a shared agenda.

The Rockefeller Foundation, one of the participants at the IDS meeting, met all these criteria. Rockefeller supported a five-year Global Value Chains Initiative (2000–2005),[45] which provided funding for a committed network of scholars to create an integrated research paradigm to address both the knowledge gaps and the policy gaps created by globalization. At the initial meeting in Bellagio in September 2000,[46] discussion centered around what to call the new framework. This decision was complicated because a variety of overlapping terms had been used to describe the network relationships that made up the global economy (Gereffi et al., 2001: 3; Sturgeon, 2001). The GVC Initiative adopted the term 'global value chains'[47] for various reasons, including: the association of 'commodity' with undifferentiated primary products (such as agricultural commodities, crude oil or unprocessed minerals), leaving out manufactured goods and services; potential confusion with the world-systems theory usage of commodity chain; and the term 'value' aligned closely with the concept of 'value-added,' which focused attention on the process of creating, capturing and sustaining value in global supply chains (Sturgeon, 2009: 117).[48]

The proceedings of the first Bellagio meeting appeared in a special issue of the *IDS Bulletin* on 'The Value of Value Chains' (Gereffi and Kaplinsky, 2001).

Core areas of concern like governance (Humphrey and Schmitz, 2001), upgrading (Dolan and Tewari, 2001; Fleury and Fleury, 2001), gender (Barrientos, 2001) and rents (Fitter and Kaplinsky, 2001) were introduced, and agriculture and apparel were among the industry cases studied.[49] In subsequent contributions, Humphrey and Schmitz (2002) elaborated the contrast between cluster and GVC approaches to governance and upgrading. Also, Gereffi, Humphrey and Sturgeon (2005) expanded the initial governance structure of producer-driven and buyer-driven chains used in the GCC approach (Gereffi, 1994b) into a fivefold typology that included three forms of network governance (captive, relational and modular) between the more conventional modes of markets and hierarchies (vertically integrated firms).[50] Along with annual meetings,[51] which brought together researchers, practitioners, members of the business community and policy makers, and support for academic publications, another contribution of the GVC Initiative was the creation of a public website to maintain an inventory of GVC-related publications and researchers.[52]

The evolution of ideas and research communities that contributed to the GCC and GVC paradigms provides a useful backdrop for the chapters that make up this book. There is a continuity of concern with the changing contours of globalization and the dynamic yet uneven nature of economic development in contemporary capitalism. Various theoretical traditions have grappled with these questions, including the modernization, dependency and world-systems authors and critics discussed in this chapter. However, a history of ideas alone is not enough to understand the communities of practice that underlie the conceptual advances and novel findings needed to challenge extant paradigms.

Thus, I have also emphasized the institutional underpinnings of the research communities that shaped and sustained the GCC and GVC frameworks. Universities and foundations provide relatively stable and tangible sources of support for these initiatives. Equally consequential are the more transitory knowledge communities forged by edited volumes and special issues of academic journals, as well as the conferences and workshops that often precede these publications.

The Chapters in This Volume: Context and Content

There are three sections of this book: Part I – Chapters 2–4 provide the foundations of the GVC framework; Part II – Chapters 5–10 examine the governance and upgrading dimensions of GVC analysis; and Part III – Chapters 11–15 explore specific policy issues associated with the GVC approach. For each chapter, I will provide contextual background and then briefly note its main substantive contributions.

Part I: Foundations of the Global Value Chain Framework

The three chapters in this section of the book are the most highly cited contributions in the GCC/GVC literature.[53] They introduce key concepts, typologies and empirical findings that will be building blocks for later chapters in the book.

Chapter 2: The Organization of Buyer-Driven Global Commodity Chains: How US Retailers Shape Overseas Production Networks

The book on *Commodity Chains and Global Capitalism* (Gereffi and Korzeniewicz, 1994) launched the GCC paradigm, and this chapter introduced the notion of governance structures into the GCC literature with the distinction between producer-driven and buyer-driven commodity chains. Governance structures are defined in terms of the power exercised by different types of lead firms (manufacturers, retailers and brands), and the apparel commodity chain is used to illustrate the dynamics of buyer-driven chains. The concept of buyer-driven chains has been extended to cover a wide range of labor-intensive, consumer-goods industries linking developing country exporters and advanced industrial end markets in the GVC literature. This chapter also discusses the role of state policies in GCCs, and stresses the affinity between the ISI development strategy and producer-driven chains, and the EOI development strategy and buyer-driven chains.

Chapter 3: International Trade and Industrial Upgrading in the Apparel Commodity Chain

This chapter was included in a special issue of the *Journal of International Economics* on 'Business and Social Networks in International Trade' co-edited by Robert C. Feenstra and James E. Rauch, both prominent trade economists. The chapter establishes a network-based concept of industrial upgrading that has become widely used in the GCC and GVC literatures. Focusing on the apparel industry in the newly industrializing economies of East Asia (Hong Kong, Taiwan and South Korea), industrial upgrading is defined in terms of several sequential stages: assembly; original equipment manufacturing (OEM); original brand manufacturing (OBM); and original design manufacturing (ODM). Organizational learning and triangle manufacturing are identified as key mechanisms in the evolution of East Asia's export roles.

Chapter 4: The Governance of Global Value Chains (co-authored with John Humphrey and Timothy J. Sturgeon)

This has become the classic theoretical formulation of the GVC governance paradigm, and it poses an alternative to the producer-driven and buyer-driven governance typology introduced in Chapter 2.[54] The chapter draws on three streams of literature – transaction cost economics, production networks, and technological capability and firm-level learning – to generate a theory of five types of GVC governance: hierarchy, captive, relational, modular and market. It highlights the dynamic nature of GVC governance with four brief industry case studies, and indicates how changes in any of the three key variables in the theory (complexity of information, codifiability of transactions, and capabilities in the supply base) would alter GVC governance structures.

Part II: Expanding the Governance and Upgrading Dimensions in Global Value Chains

Governance and upgrading are the two main analytical pillars of the GVC framework: governance structures and the organization of global industries look at the global economy from the top down (with a focus on international industries and MNCs), while industrial upgrading looks at the global economy from the bottom up (with a focus on countries, industrial clusters and local suppliers). The chapters in Part II of the book differentiate and unpack these master concepts.

Chapter 5: The Global Economy: Organization, Governance, and Development

This chapter appeared in *The Handbook of Economic Sociology*, 2nd edition (Smelser and Swedberg, 2005), and it is one of the very few chapters dealing with global topics in that influential volume.[55] It offers a comprehensive review of the conceptual frameworks used by scholars to analyze changes in the global economy over the past several decades. Particular emphasis is given to the role of transnational corporations and the emergence of global production networks and GVCs in the reorganization of production and trade in the global economy. Various governance perspectives are covered as well, including a comparison of the varieties of capitalism and global production network paradigms. The concept of industrial upgrading is defined and illustrated empirically.

Chapter 6: Local Clusters in Global Chains: The Causes and Consequences of Export Dynamism in Torreon's Blue Jeans Industry (co-authored with Jennifer Bair)

This chapter was one of the first to explicitly link the GCC framework with the study of local industrial clusters. It highlights how the establishment of the North American Free Trade Agreement (NAFTA) in 1994 allowed Torreon's blue jeans export industry to shift from a producer-driven chain led by US blue jeans manufacturers to a buyer-driven chain supplying US retailers and brand marketers.

Thus, a policy variable (the initiation of NAFTA) prompted the change in GCC governance structures, which in turn sparked an export surge in blue jeans from Mexico to the United States. Cluster networks in Torreon tended to be hierarchical and involved low trust, in contrast to the horizontal and cooperative networks typical in much of the cluster literature. Nonetheless, Torreon's boom cycle became a bust with the slowdown in the US economy after 2000. This highlights the likelihood of both downgrading and' upgrading outcomes when cluster dynamics are linked to the behavior of foreign buyers and external markets.[56]

Chapter 7: Development Models and Industrial Upgrading in China and Mexico

This chapter compares and contrasts the export-oriented economic development strategies pursued by China and Mexico in the global economy. While Mexico has been the paradigm for the neoliberal ('Washington Consensus') development model associated with foreign direct investment, extensive privatization and open markets, China has attained record levels of foreign capital inflows and export growth utilizing a more strategic, statist approach to its development. One of the keys to China's success has been a unique form of industrial organization called supply-chain cities, which has permitted it to achieve both economies of scale and scope in GVCs. Because China and Mexico depend heavily on the US market for their export growth, their development models are very susceptible to disruptions caused by US economic downturns as well as rising protectionism.

Chapter 8: Economic and Social Upgrading in Global Production Networks: A New Paradigm for a Changing World (co-authored with Stephanie Barrientos and Arianna Rossi)

This chapter was part of a special feature on 'Decent Work in Global Production Networks' in the International Labor Organization's journal, *International Labour Review*. A key challenge in promoting decent work worldwide is how to improve the position of both firms and workers in value chains and global production networks driven by lead firms. This chapter analyzes the linkages between the economic upgrading of firms and the social upgrading of workers. Drawing on studies that indicate firm upgrading does not necessarily lead to improvements for workers, with a particular focus on the Moroccan garment industry, it outlines different trajectories and scenarios of the tradeoffs involving economic and social upgrading. The framework outlined in this chapter was the basis for a multiyear international research program called 'Capturing the Gains,' which has been one of the most productive collaborations emanating from the GVC approach.[57]

Chapter 9: Regulation and Economic Globalization: Prospects and Limits of Private Governance (co-authored with Frederick Mayer)

Appearing in a special issue of *Business and Politics* on 'Private Regulation in the Global Economy' edited by Tim Büthe, this chapter focuses on the corporate codes of conduct, product certifications, process standards, and other voluntary, non-governmental forms of private governance that have proliferated in recent decades. Private governance has notable successes, but there are clear limits to what it alone can accomplish. This chapter hypothesizes that the effectiveness of private governance depends on four main factors: (1) the structure of the particular GVC in which production takes place; (2) the extent to which demand for a firm's products relies on its brand identity; (3) the possibilities for collective action by consumers, workers, or other activists to exert pressure on producers; and 4) the extent to which commercial interests of lead firms align with social and environmental concerns. Taken together, these hypotheses suggest that private governance will flourish in only a limited set of circumstances.

Chapter 10: Economic and Social Upgrading in Global Value Chains: Why Governance Matters (co-authored with Joonkoo Lee)

This chapter appeared in a special section of *Journal of Business Ethics* on 'Industrial Clusters and Corporate Social Responsibility in Developing Countries,' co-edited by Peter Lund-Thomsen, Adam Lindgreen, and Joelle Vanhamme. It examines the role played by corporate social responsibility (CSR) in both industrial clusters and GVCs. With geographic production and trade patterns in many industries becoming concentrated in the global South, lead firms in GVCs have been under growing pressure to link economic and social upgrading in more integrated forms of CSR. A new paradigm of 'synergistic governance' is outlined based on a confluence of private governance (corporate codes of conduct and monitoring), social governance (civil society pressure on business from labor organizations and non-governmental organizations), and public governance (governmental policies to support gains by labor groups and environmental activists).

Part III: Policy Issues and Challenges

The GVC community has elaborated the policy implications of its work since its inception, which reflects in part the role played by IDS researchers in the Global Value Chains Initiative. In addition, the Duke University Global Value Chains Center was created in 2005 to help institutionalize and extend the GVC perspective as an outgrowth of the GVC Initiative. The chapters in this section highlight the ongoing policy relevance of the GVC framework.

Chapter 11: Global Value Chain Analysis: A Primer (Second Edition) (co-authored with Karina Fernandez-Stark)

This is the second edition of the popular GVC Primer, which was created at the Duke GVC Center to introduce a range of policy actors (national governments, non-governmental organizations, development banks, bilateral and multilateral donors, etc.) to the key features of the GVC framework. This chapter provides a conceptual and methodological primer for practitioners and policy makers, defining and illustrating the core concepts in the GVC toolkit. It offers up-to-date examples of how the GVC framework is being utilized, especially in studies carried out by Duke University's Global Value Chains Center, a premier university-based research unit for GVC analysis.

Chapter 12: Global Value Chains, Development, and Emerging Economies

This chapter was a background paper for the United Nations Industrial Development Organization's *Industrial Development Report 2016* (UNIDO, 2015). It highlights the significant and diverse roles that emerging economies are playing in GVCs. During the 2000s, they were simultaneously major exporters of intermediate and final manufactured goods (China, South Korea, and Mexico) and primary products (Brazil, Russia, and South Africa). However, market growth in emerging economies has also led to shifting end markets in GVCs (Staritz et al., 2011) as more trade has occurred between developing economies (often referred to as South–South trade in the literature), especially since the 2008–09 economic recession (Cattaneo et al., 2010). China has been the focal point of both trends: it is the world's leading exporter of manufactured goods and the world's largest importer of many raw materials, thereby contributing to the primary product export boom for selected commodities and regions. Emerging economies are at the forefront of efforts to redefine their development models to incorporate their large domestic economies more fully in their upgrading strategies (Gereffi and Sturgeon, 2013).

Chapter 13: Risks and Opportunities of Participation in Global Value Chains (co-authored with Xubei Luo)

The chapter highlights the risks and opportunities that firms and their workers face in GVCs. It examines the risk-sharing mechanisms that firms provide from the national and global perspectives; it assesses the new opportunities and challenges both firms and individuals confront in the global arena; it discusses the role of economic and social upgrading, and it evaluates how governments can help people manage risks and reap the benefits of participating in GVCs.

Chapter 14: Global Value Chains in a Post-Washington Consensus World

This chapter appeared in a special issue of *Review of International Political Economy* on 'Global Value Chains and Global Production Networks in the Changing International Political Economy,' co-edited by Jeffrey Neilson, Bill Pritchard and Henry Wai-chung Yeung. The chapter looks at GVCs in the current post-Washington Consensus era, with an emphasis on several new trends: the organizational streamlining of GVCs; the geographic consolidation of GVCs, with particular attention to the emerging economies; new patterns of strategic coordination among value chain actors; the rise of South–South trade and the growing importance of new end markets; and the rapid uptake of the GVC framework by international organizations. All of these trends are pushing toward a reformulation of established development paradigms. The chapter also highlights the key role played by international organizations in the diffusion of the GVC paradigm.[58]

Chapter 15: Protectionism and Global Value Chains

This chapter is an original contribution to this volume. It provides an historical perspective to analyze recent manifestations of economic nationalism and calls for protectionism to curb the trade and investment imbalances associated with GVCs. One instance of the current protectionist threat is President Trump's statements that he may install a border tax on US imports from Mexico and substantially renegotiate or dismantle the North American Free Trade Agreement between the United States, Mexico, and Canada. Evidence is presented to show that since NAFTA went into effect in 1994, it has promoted a complex ecosystem of regional trade and cross-border investment that significantly benefits manufacturers, jobs and value-added trade on both sides of the US–Mexico border. In terms of the even larger US trade dispute with China, the chapter argues that this reflects a much deeper strategic competition between these two economic superpowers linked to the rise of the digital economy and a technological revolution that will deeply affect the future of manufacturing, jobs and innovation in the 21st century.

Conclusion

This chapter addresses the question: Where does the idea of global value chains come from? As we have seen, it is not a simple or a linear story. In part, it has roots in debates over development theory stretching back to the early formulations of center and periphery in the modernization and dependency paradigms of the 1960s and 1970s. It also reflects the controversy over the nature of globalization, and whether it should be traced back to the origins of capitalism in the long sixteenth century, as world-systems theorists claim, or whether we should focus on the novel features of contemporary globalization in the postwar era, especially the genesis of international production networks in the 1970s and 1980s and their rapid acceleration in the 1990s and beyond. Ideas about the global economy struggled to keep pace with the startling changes facilitated by the ever greater connectedness of the world and the geopolitical realignments brought by the end of the Cold War.

Another vantage point is how the GVC framework has been shaped by the many knowledge and research communities traced in this chapter. While ideas tend to flow easily once established, paradigm shifts are much harder to explain. Based on my own experience, the evolution of the GVC approach has drawn upon diverse groups of scholars with institutional support from numerous universities, foundations and professional associations. The account provided in this chapter is far from exhaustive; it identifies multiple strands in the story and it suggests how my views were influenced by the knowledge networks and research communities I participated in. Often these communities were purposive and oriented to a collective goal, such as the Global Value Chains Initiative supported by the Rockefeller Foundation or SSRC's Continuing Working Group on Multinational Corporations in Latin America. In other instances, the supporting institutions had more specific and instrumental objectives, such as the UNCTC's commissioned study on the top 50 pharmaceutical MNCs or the 'Capturing the Gains' research network funded by DFID.

A final point worth highlighting is the role played by temporary research communities, such as edited volumes and special issues of academic journals to promote innovative and interdisciplinary scholarship. Financial support from foundations and universities is a tangible and much appreciated contribution to research communities. Even more pervasive are the opportunities provided by collective publications to bring together scholars from diverse disciplinary backgrounds and settings to generate knowledge around a particular theme, and frequently for audiences that have not been exposed to these ideas before.[59] Together, all the influences outlined in this chapter contributed in significant ways to the emergence and dissemination of the GVC framework.

Notes

1. Brazil, Russia, India, and China.
2. Rostow's five basic stages were: traditional society; transitional society; take-off; drive to technological maturity; and high mass consumption.
3. For a brief description of strategic interviews in GCC studies, see Gereffi (1995: 51–53) and Bair and Gereffi (2001), Appendix A.
4. These quantitative studies generally related indicators of dependency (operationalized as foreign direct investment, foreign aid, and/or foreign trade) to separate indicators of national development or well-being (usually measured by the rate of economic growth per capita and/or the degree of inequality within countries). The measures of dependency are treated as the independent variables in regression models, and development or national welfare is the dependent variable (e.g., Chase-Dunn, 1975; Rubinson, 1976; Bornschier et al., 1978). For a critique of this approach, see Cardoso (1977).
5. For other evaluations and critical discussions of Wallerstein and world-systems theory, see Brenner (1977), Skocpol (1977), Chirot and Hall (1982) and Ragin and Chirot (1984).
6. UNCTAD's *World Investment Report, 2002* contained a table of the 100 largest 'economies' in the world in 2000, using a value-added measure for firms deemed comparable to the gross domestic product (GDP) calculation used for countries. There were 29 MNCs in the top 100 entries on the combined list of countries and nonfinancial corporations. The largest MNC was ExxonMobil, whose $63 billion of value added in 2000 ranked 45th on the country-company list, similar to the GDP of Chile or Pakistan (UNCTAD, 2002: 90–91).
7. My personal experience resonated with many of these topics. Prior to graduate school, I spent a year traveling with one of my college roommates (John C. Rudolf) through Mexico, Central America, Switzerland, Spain and Africa. The highlight of our trip was hitchhiking across the Sahara Desert from Algiers to Niamey, Niger. From Niger, I made my way to Lagos, Nigeria, where I taught high school, and John ventured to Kenya. In the fall of 1971, we both entered graduate programs in sociology; I went to Yale and John to Columbia University.
8. Of course, Cardoso also had a notable political career, serving as president of Brazil from 1995 to 2003.
9. The SSRC working group was co-chaired by Lou Goodman and Al Stepan from Yale and Peter Evans at Brown University, whose Ph.D. thesis at Harvard had analyzed Brazil from a dependency perspective (Evans, 1979). Regular members of the SSRC working group included: Douglas C. Bennett, Gary Gereffi, Rhys Jenkins, David Martin, David Moore, Richard Newfarmer, Kenneth Sharpe, Phillip Shepherd, Peter West, and Van Whiting, Jr.
10. The industries covered in the book included: automobiles, tires, cigarettes, food-processing, pharmaceuticals, iron and steel, tractors, and electric power.
11. The special issue of *International Organization* on 'Dependence and Dependency in the Global System' (Caporaso, 1978) was a breakthrough publication because it contained a number of articles that addressed both the theoretical and methodological challenges

highlighted by this debate. Albert Hirschman (1978) offered a broader historical reflection based on his 1945 book, *National Power and the Structure of Foreign Trade*, which he portrays as an intellectual harbinger of dependency theory and some of its shortcomings. For a more detailed review of variations in dependency theory and their empirical implications, see Gereffi (1980, chapters 2 and 3).

12. In Wallerstein's own words: 'Over time the loci of economic activities keep changing… Hence some areas "progress" and others "regress." But the fact that particular states change their position in the world-economy, from semiperiphery to core say, or vice versa, does not in itself change the nature of the system. These shifts will be registered for individual states as "development" or "regression." The key factor to note is that within a capitalist world-economy, all states cannot "develop" simultaneously *by definition*, since the system functions by virtue of having unequal core and peripheral regions' (Wallerstein, 1979: 60–61; emphasis in the original).

13. Activities in commodity chains are defined in an abstract and functional way, with little attention to the nature and strategies of firms that carry out these activities: 'All states enclose within their boundaries both core and peripheral activities. Some (core states) enclose predominantly core activities and some (peripheral states) enclose predominantly peripheral activities. As a consequence, the former tend to be the locus of world accumulation and power and the latter the locus of exploitation and powerlessness. The legitimacy and stability of this highly unequal and polarizing system are buttressed by the existence of semiperipheral states defined as those that enclose within their boundaries a more or less even mix of core-peripheral activities. Precisely because of the relatively even mix of core-peripheral activities that fall within their boundaries, semiperipheral states are assumed to have the power to resist peripheralization, although not sufficient power to overcome it altogether and move into the core' (Arrighi and Drangel, 1986: 12).

14. I am indebted to Jennifer Bair for this insight.

15. In this chapter, transnational corporations and MNCs are treated as synonyms.

16. UNCTC was created in New York in 1974 amidst rampant criticism in the wake of the 1972 revelations that the International Telephone and Telegraph Company (ITT) plotted with the US Central Intelligence Agency in 1970 to block the presidential election of Salvador Allende in Chile (Sampson, 1973). For nearly two decades, from 1975 to 1992, the UNCTC struggled to fashion a code of conduct to govern MNC activities and it ultimately failed to achieve consensus (Moran, 2009: 92–93; Bair, 2015). UN Secretary General Boutros-Boutros Ghali dismantled UNCTC, and in 1993 shifted the United Nations' work on MNCs to the UN Conference on Trade and Development (UNCTAD) in Geneva. Renamed the Division of Investment, Technology and Enterprise Development, the unit was assigned responsibility for producing what would become UNCTAD's flagship publication, *The World Investment Report*.

17. Every three months, I went to New York for meetings with UNCTC staff and representatives of the Pharmaceutical Manufacturers Association and the International Federation of Pharmaceutical Manufacturers and Associations, where I was grilled on all aspects of my research methodology and provisional findings. Drafts of the report were reviewed, critiqued and defended line by line.

18. Given the favorable reception of my initial report on pharmaceutical MNCs (UNCTC, 1979), the UNCTC commissioned a second report highlighting the role of developing countries in the global pharmaceutical industry (UNCTC, 1981).

19. In the case of the pharmaceutical industry, UNCTC had broad concerns over controversial MNC practices in terms of the high prices of medicines, tax avoidance through transfer pricing, misleading drug advertising, and the impact of patents on local innovation, while PAHO wanted to evaluate and strengthen an important social initiative, essential drugs programs in Latin America.

20. In addition to the general governance typologies like producer-driven and buyer-driven chains (Gereffi, 1994b) and the fivefold typology of GVC governance in Gereffi et al. (2005), most detailed empirical studies of GVCs identify the leading MNCs involved in governing the chains they are analyzing. Industry examples include: apparel (Bair and Gereffi, 2001; Gereffi and Memodovic, 2003); automotive (Humphrey and Memodovic, 2003; Sturgeon et al., 2009); electronics (Sturgeon, 2002; Sturgeon and Kawakami, 2011); offshore services (Fernandez-Stark et al., 2011); and cocoa (Fold, 2002).

21. There is a voluminous literature on this topic. For a few examples, see Gereffi (1999), Schmitz (2004) and Staritz et al. (2011).

22. In contrast to the abstract treatment of core and peripheral activities in the world-systems discussion of commodity chains (e.g., Arrighi and Drangel, 1986), 'value chain mapping' involves a detailed analysis of specific activities carried out by MNCs in different geographic locations and across diverse GVC segments. For examples, see Gereffi and Fernandez-Stark (2016) and Frederick (forthcoming).

23. An assessment of four types of transnational economic linkages – foreign aid, foreign trade, foreign direct investment and foreign loans—shows that historically FDI and foreign loans were most important in Latin American newly industrializing economies, while export trade and foreign aid have been the main forms of East Asian linkage to the international economy (Gereffi, 1989: 519–522). Dependency is a particularly thorny issue in Latin America in part because FDI tends to create more friction than other types of foreign capital in Third World economies.

24. This was also known as 'heavy and chemical industrialization' in both cases, following the Japanese path.

25. In the 'commodity export' phase, the output was usually unrefined or semi-processed raw materials. In 'primary' ISI and EOI, firms were making basic consumer goods (e.g., textiles, clothing, footwear, food) for the domestic and export markets, respectively. In 'secondary' ISI and EOI, there was a focus on consumer durables (e.g., automobiles), intermediate goods (e.g., petrochemicals and steel), and capital goods (e.g., heavy machinery).

26. Wyman received his Ph.D. in history from Harvard University and specialized in Mexican economic history and US policies toward Mexico. Don was associate director of the Center for US-Mexican Studies since 1981, where he initiated a campus-wide research program on the Pacific Basin. He became associate dean for the newly created Graduate School of International Relations and Pacific Studies at UCSD in 1986, whose founding director was Peter Gourevitch. Sadly, Don died prematurely in March 1987

following an extended illness before the collaborative project that we planned came to fruition.

27. For a listing of the PEWS annual conference volumes, see http://asapews.org/annuals.html.

28. In the GCC lexicon, the term 'global' does not necessarily refer to the geographic scope of commodity chains since many commodity chains are regional and vary in their geography over time. Rather, it builds on the distinction introduced by Dicken (1992) between 'internationalization' and 'globalization': the former refers simply to the spread of economic activities across international boundaries, while the latter requires significant functional integration between these geographically dispersed activities (Gereffi, 1994b: 96).

29. This was the 13th annual PEWS conference, organized at the University of Illinois in Champagne-Urbana in April 1989.

30. Miguel's elder brother, Roberto Patricio Korzeniewicz, was in the Ph.D. program in sociology at SUNY/Binghamton at the time, and he helped spark Miguel's interest in world-systems theory. Since 1993, Roberto has been a member of the Sociology Department at the University of Maryland.

31. During the late 1960s and early 1970s, Japan, Spain and Italy were the main exporters of shoes to the US market, which was the largest in the world. In 1971, they accounted for two-thirds of the $760 million in US footwear imports. By the late 1980s, these three economies were displaced by Taiwan, South Korea and Brazil, which represented two-thirds of American shoe imports totaling $7.6 billion in 1987, a tenfold increase in the size of the US import market since 1971 (Gereffi and Korzeniewicz, 1990: 51, 53).

32. East Asian footwear exports in the mid-1960s originated in the decision of Mitsubishi (the leading Japanese trading company dealing in footwear) to relocate plastic sandals production for the US market from Kobe, Japan to Taiwan, and to move the manufacture of rubber shoes to South Korea, given Korea's prior experience in making rubber shoes during the Japanese occupation. The Brazilian footwear export industry took advantage of growing US demand for leather shoes in the early 1970s and the inability of Italy and Spain to fully meet that demand (Gereffi and Korzeniewicz, 1990: 59–60).

33. Small export traders were particularly important for the Taiwanese and Brazilian footwear industries. These trading agents played two main roles: (1) they parceled big orders from large overseas buyers among many suppliers, therefore allowing exporters to remain relatively small; and (2) they helped local producers adapt to fashion and marketing changes in core footwear markets.

34. At the same PEWS conference where Miguel and I presented our paper on the footwear commodity chain, Arrighi (1990) presented a paper on 'The Developmentalist Illusion' that argued against the 'developmentalist turn' in commodity chain research.

35. Miguel received his Ph.D. in sociology from Duke in 1990, and joined the Sociology Department at the University of New Mexico. Shortly after the Duke commodity chains conference, Miguel was involved in a severe automobile accident in August 1992 that left him a quadriplegic. After battling his injuries for many years and continuing to contribute to the GCC field, Miguel passed away in August 2002.

36. The only exceptions were the studies of the shipbuilding (Özveren, 1994) and grain flour (Pelizzon, 1994) commodity chains, which covered the period 1590–1790. The other industries in the volume included: apparel, athletic footwear, automobiles, fresh fruit and vegetables, business services, and cocaine.

37. For a critique of *Commodity Chains and Global Capitalism* on these grounds, see Dunaway and Clelland (1995); and for a rejoinder, Korzeniewicz et al. (1996). An effort to link the GCC and world income inequalities literatures is provided by Brewer (2011), who sees an 'upgrading' paradox in the discontinuity between the 'sub-systemic' unit of commodity chains and the stable patterns of income inequality at the world-systemic level. This purportedly creates an 'adding up' problem because GVC upgrading at the national level cannot redress enduring global income inequality. However, GCC/GVC scholars do not claim upgrading could eliminate global inequalities. Their meso-level approach analyzes the linkages between GVC governance and upgrading (or downgrading) at the sectoral level, and in this respect departs from the exclusive macro focus of world-systems theory.

38. For a perceptive review of the world-system, GCC and GVC approaches to commodity chains, see Bair (2009: 7–14).

39. IDS was established in 1966 as Britain's first national institute of development studies. The workshop was organized by senior IDS researchers, including Raphael Kaplinsky, Hubert Schmitz and John Humphrey, among others. It was held on September 15–17, 1999 with around 60–70 participants. For more details on the IDS meeting, see http://www.ids.ac.uk/ids/global/conf/globwks.html#sum.

40. Among developed economies, Italian 'industrial districts' were a cornerstone of Piore and Sabel's *The Second Industrial Divide* (1984), a pioneering work that translated the experience of small firms in craft-based regions like the Third Italy into a new 'flexible specialization' model that represented an alternative to the Fordist system of mass production geared to making identical, inexpensive goods.

41. IDS researchers edited two special issues of *World Development*, a leading multidisciplinary journal, which highlighted the key themes related to industrial clusters and globalization, and indeed laid the groundwork for subsequent collaboration with GVC scholars (see Humphrey, 1995; Nadvi and Schmitz, 1999). Similar topics were addressed in the edited volume by Schmitz (2004).

42. This includes the work of GCC researchers discussed previously, such as Gereffi and Korzeniewicz (1994). In addition, the Alfred P. Sloan Foundation in New York launched its Industry Studies program in 1990 to foster a closer interaction between academia and industry so that researchers could learn first-hand about the markets, firms and institutions in the industries they sought to examine. The Sloan program grew to include 26 centers at US universities. For several years, the Sloan Foundation also established a Globalization Workshop for Junior Scholars, with an emphasis on the globalization of industries and its impact on employment. The first Sloan Junior Scholars workshop was held at Duke University on April 24–25, 1998 and it was co-organized by Richard Florida, Gary Gereffi and Martin Kenney. Participating scholars were: Yuko Aoyama, Jennifer Bair, Edmund Egan, Eun Mie Lim, Greg Linden, Teresa Lynch, Layna Mosley, Seán O'Riain, Mei-Lin Pan, Balaji Pathasarathy, John Richards, Jennifer Spencer, and Tim Sturgeon.

43. This included scholars affiliated with the Berkeley Roundtable on the International Economy (BRIE), which looked at 'international production networks' (e.g., Ernst and Ravenhill, 1999; Borrus et al., 2000; Sturgeon, 2002).

44. The format of the three-day meeting was results oriented. The workshop began with presentations by leaders from government, business, international organizations, and civil society. On the second and third days, researchers and funders discussed how the policy challenges and knowledge gaps laid out on the first day might translate into an agenda that could integrate both the micro and macro research themes, and maintain a close dialogue with policy makers.

45. Rockefeller later provided supplemental funding for 2006–2008.

46. The first GVC workshop in Bellagio took place on Sept. 25-Oct. 1, 2000. The participants included: Catherine Dolan, Afonso Fleury, Gary Gereffi, Peter Gibbon, John Humphrey, Raphael Kaplinsky, Ji-Ren Lee, Dorothy McCormick, Katherine McFate (Rockefeller Foundation), Mike Morris, Florence Palpacuer, Hubert Schmitz, Timothy J. Sturgeon, and Meenu Tewari (institutional affiliations are listed in Gereffi and Kaplinsky, 2001: 8).

47. Although Michael Porter of Harvard Business School developed a value-chain framework that he applied at the level of individual firms (Porter, 1985) and as one of the bases for determining the competitive advantage of nations (Porter 1990), Porter did not use it to highlight the changing organizational structure of global industries or to address the impact of GVCs on the upgrading dynamics of developing economies as GVC researchers did.

48. There was also discussion of whether to replace the *chain* metaphor with less linear terms like networks or webs. Ultimately, the metaphor was retained because it embodied the familiar input-output structure of a production network where value is added as goods are transformed along a supply chain.

49. All of these topics are covered in the forthcoming *Handbook on Global Value Chains*, co-edited by Gary Gereffi, Stefano Ponte and Gale Raj-Reichert, which provides an excellent review of progress made over the past two decades, especially in core areas like GVC governance (Ponte et al., forthcoming), economic upgrading (Gereffi, forthcoming), and measurement (Sturgeon, forthcoming).

50. See Sturgeon (2009) for a more extensive analysis of the GCC and GVC approaches to governance. As noted in Bair (2009: 13–14, 26–27), the shift from GCC to GVC governance structures implies a conceptual reorientation from 'drivenness' to 'coordination' that remains relevant for researchers, in particular for those who want to retain the power dimension of the GCC approach (e.g., Appelbaum and Gereffi, 1994).

51. While Rockefeller sponsored most of the events, a GVC Initiative workshop held at Rockport, Massachusetts on 'Globalization, Employment and Economic Development' in June 2004 was supported by the Alfred P. Sloan Foundation – see http://www.soc.duke.edu/sloan_2004/.

52. About 1,050 publications and 780 researchers appear on the Global Value Chains Initiative website (https://globalvaluechains.org/publications) as of July 27, 2018. The website is hosted and maintained by the Global Value Chains Center at Duke University (see https://gvcc.duke.edu/).

53. The Google Scholar citation counts (as of October 6, 2018) are: Chapter 2 – 3,300 citations; Chapter 3 – 4,211 citations; and Chapter 4 – 6,220 citations (available at https://scholar.google.com/citations?hl=en&user=2Kd61F0AAAAJ&view_op=list_works).

54. There are various discussions of the relationship between the GCC and GVC governance typologies presented in Chapters 2 and 4 (see Gibbon et al., 2008; Bair, 2009: 19–28; Sturgeon, 2009). A particularly instructive formulation is the distinction between three approaches to GVC governance: governance as 'driving,' 'linking' and 'normalizing' (Ponte and Sturgeon, 2014). The producer-driven versus buyer-driven formation in Chapter 2 is 'governance as driving', while the fivefold typology in Chapter 4 is governance as 'linking' or 'coordinating'.

55. More generally, the new economic sociology popularized by a number of US scholars pays very little attention to globalization (Hamilton and Gereffi, 2009: 140–143).

56. This was a central conclusion of Schmitz (1999), whose research on the Sinos Valley footwear cluster in Brazil highlighted the limitations of focusing solely on the local level and ignoring the behavior of foreign buyers.

57. The Capturing the Gains research program (2009–2012) focused on economic and social upgrading in global production networks and it was funded primarily by the UK's Department for International Development (DFID) and the Swiss Agency for Development and Cooperation. It was administered by Stephanie Barrientos and housed at the Brooks World Poverty Institute at the University of Manchester, UK. The research targeted the apparel, agro-food, mobile telecommunication, and tourism sectors with a primary geographic focus on Sub-Saharan Africa. It assembled an international network of experts from North and South to research and promote strategies for fairer trade and decent work, and it culminated in a global summit in Cape Town, South Africa on Dec. 3–5, 2012. For more information, see http://www.capturingthegains.org.

58. For a more detailed discussion of this topic, see Mayer and Gereffi (forthcoming).

59. There are many examples of this in relation to the GCC and GVC fields, including special issues of *International Organization, Journal of International Economics, Journal of Business Ethics*, and *International Labour Review* mentioned above. See also the article on GVCs commissioned by the *Journal of Supply Chain Management* for its Discussion Forum on Global Supply Chains (Gereffi and Lee, 2012).

References

Amin, Samir. 1973. *Unequal Development: An Essay on the Social Formations of Peripheral Capitalism*. New York: Monthly Review Press.

Amsden, Alice H. 1979. 'Taiwan's Economic History: A Case of Etatisme and a Challenge to Dependency Theory.' *Modern China* 5(3): 341–380.

————. 1989. *Asia's Next Giant: South Korea and Late Industrialization*. New York: Oxford University Press.

Appelbaum, Richard P. and Gary Gereffi. 1994. 'Power and Profits in the Apparel Commodity Chain.' In *Global Production: The Apparel Industry in the Pacific Rim*, edited by Edna

Bonacich, Lucie Cheng, Norma Chinchilla, Nora Hamilton and Paul Ong, 42–62. Philadelphia, PA: Temple University Press.

Arrighi, Giovanni. 1990. 'The Developmentalist Illusion: A Reconceptualization of the Semiperiphery.' In *Semiperipheral States in the World-Economy*, edited by William Martin, 11–42. Westport, CT: Greenwood Press.

Arrighi, Giovanni and Jessica Drangel. 1986. 'The Stratification of the World-Economy: An Exploration of the Semiperipheral Zone.' *Review* 10(1): 9–74.

Bain, Joe. 1968. *Industrial Organization*. New York: John Wiley and Sons.

Bair, Jennifer. 2005. 'Global Capitalism and Commodity Chains: Looking Back, Going Forward.' *Competition & Change* 9(2): 153–180.

———. 2009. 'Global Commodity Chains: Genealogy and Review.' In *Frontiers of Commodity Chain Research*, edited by Jennifer Bair, 1–34. Stanford, CA: Stanford University Press.

———. 2015. 'Corporations at the United Nations: Echoes of the New International Economic Order?' *Humanity* 6(1): 159–171.

Bair, Jennifer and Gary Gereffi. 2001. 'Local Clusters in Global Chains: The Causes and Consequences of Export Dynamism in Torreon's Blue Jeans Industry.' *World Development* 29(11): 1885–1903.

Barnet, Richard J. and Ronald E. Müller. 1974. *Global Reach: The Power of the Multinational Corporations*. New York: Simon and Schuster.

Barrett, Richard E. and Martin King Whyte. 1982. 'Dependency Theory and Taiwan: Analysis of a Deviant Case.' *American Journal of Sociology* 87(5): 1064–1089.

Barrientos, Stephanie. 2001. 'Gender, Flexibility and Global Value Chains.' *IDS Bulletin* 32(3): 83–93.

Becker, David. 1983. *The New Bourgeoisie and the Limits of Dependency: Mining, Class and Power in 'Revolutionary' Peru*. Princeton, NJ: Princeton University Press.

Bendix, Reinhard. 1967. 'Tradition and Modernity Reconsidered.' *Comparative Studies in Society and History* 9(3): 292–346.

Bennett, Douglas C. and Kenneth E. Sharpe. 1979. 'Agenda Setting and Bargaining Power: The Mexican State vs. Transnational Automobile Corporations.' *World Politics* 32(1): 57–89.

———. 1985. *Transnational Corporations Versus the State: The Political Economy of the Mexican Auto Industry*. Princeton, NJ: Princeton University Press.

Berger, Peter L. 1986. *The Capitalist Revolution*. New York: Basic Books.

Biersteker, Thomas J. 1978. *Distortion or Development? Contending Perspectives on the Multinational Corporation*. Cambridge, MA: MIT Press.

Bornschier, Volker, Christopher Chase-Dunn, and Richard Rubinson. 1978. 'Cross-National Evidence of the Effects of Foreign Investment and Aid on Economic Growth and Inequality: A Survey of Findings and a Reanalysis.' *American Journal of Sociology* 84(3): 651–683.

Borrus, Michael, Dieter Ernst, and Stephan Haggard, eds. 2000. *International Production Networks in Asia: Rivalry or Riches?* London: Routledge.

Bradshaw, York W. 1988. 'Reassessing Economic Dependency and Uneven Development: The Kenyan Experience.' *American Sociological Review* 53(5): 693–708.

Brenner, Robert. 1977. 'The Origins of Capitalist Development: A Critique of Neo-Smithian Marxism.' *New Left Review* 104: 25–92.

Brewer, Benjamin D. 2011. 'Global Commodity Chains and World Income Inequalities: The Missing Link of Inequality and the "Upgrading" Paradox.' *Journal of World-Systems Research* 17(2): 308–327.

Buruma, Ian. 2016. 'The End of the Anglo-American Order.' *New York Times*, November 29.

Caporaso, James. 1978. 'Introduction to the Special Issue of *International Organization* on Dependence and Dependency in the Global System.' *International Organization* 32(1): 1–12.

Cardoso, Fernando Henrique. 1977. 'The Consumption of Dependency Theory in the United States.' *Latin American Research Review* 12(3): 7–24.

Cardoso, Fernando Henrique and Enzo Faletto. 1979. *Dependency and Development in Latin America*. Berkeley, CA: University of California Press.

Cattaneo, Olivier, Gary Gereffi, and Cornelia Staritz, eds. 2010. *Global Value Chains in a Post-Crisis World: A Development Perspective*. Washington, DC: World Bank.

Chase-Dunn, Christopher. 1975. 'The Effects of International Economic Dependence on Development and Inequality: A Cross-National Study.' *American Sociological Review* 40(6): 720–738.

Chirot, Daniel and Thomas D. Hall. 1982. 'World System Theory.' *Annual Review of Sociology* 8: 81–106.

Deyo, Frederic C., ed. 1987. *The Political Economy of the New Asian Industrialism*. Ithaca, NY: Cornell University Press.

Dicken, Peter. 1992. *Global Shift: The Internationalization of Economic Activity*, 2nd edition. New York: Guilford Press.

Dolan, Catherine S. and Meenu Tewari. 2001. 'From What We Wear to What We Eat: Upgrading in Global Value Chains.' *IDS Bulletin* 32(3): 94–104.

Doner, Richard F. 1991. *Driving a Bargain: Automobile Industrialization and Japanese Firms in Southeast Asia*. Berkeley, CA: University of California Press.

Dos Santos, Theotonio. 1970. 'The Structure of Dependence.' *American Economic Review* 60(2): 231–236.

Dunaway, Wilma A. and Donald A. Clelland. 1995. Review of 'Commodity Chains and Global Capitalism.' *Journal of World-Systems Research* 1(1): 415–422.

Dunning, John H. 1958. *American Investment in British Manufacturing Industry*. London: Allen and Unwin.

Duvall, Raymond D. 1978 'Dependence and Dependencia Theory: Notes Toward Precision of Concept and Argument.' *International Organization* 32(1): 51–78.

Emerson, Richard M. 1962. 'Power-Dependence Relations.' *American Sociological Review* 27(1): 31–41.

Encarnation, Dennis. 1989. *Dislodging Multinationals: India's Strategy in Comparative Perspective*. Ithaca, NY: Cornell University Press.

Ernst, Dieter and John Ravenhill. 1999. 'Globalization, Convergence, and the Transformation of Iinternational Production Networks in Electronics in East Asia.' *Business and Politics* 1(1): 35–62.

Evans, Peter B. 1979. *Dependent Development: The Alliance of Multinationals, State and Local Capital in Brazil*. Princeton, NJ: Princeton University Press.

Fernandez-Stark, Karina, Penny Bamber, and Gary Gereffi. 2011. 'The Offshore Services Value Chain: Upgrading Trajectories in Developing Countries.' *International Journal of Technological Learning, Innovation and Development* 4(1–3): 206–234.

Fitter, Robert and Raphael Kaplinsky. 2001. 'Who Gains from Product Rents as the Coffee Market Becomes More Differentiated? A Value Chain Analysis.' *IDS Bulletin* 32(3): 69–82.

Fleury, Afonso and Maria Tereza Fleury. 2001. 'Alternatives for Industrial Upgrading in Global Value Chains: The Case of the Plastics Industry in Brazil.' *IDS Bulletin* 32(3): 116–126.

Fold, Niels. 2002. 'Lead Firms and Competition in "Bi-Polar" Commodity Chains: Grinders and Branders in the Global Cocoa-chocolate Industry.' *Journal of Agrarian Change* 2(2): 228–247.

Frank, Andre Gunder. 1967. *Capitalism and Underdevelopment in Latin America: Historical Studies in Chile and Brazil*. New York: Monthly Review Press.

Frederick, Stacey. Forthcoming. 'Mapping Global Value Chains.' In *Handbook on Global Value Chains*, edited by Gary Gereffi, Stefano Ponte, and Gale Raj-Reichert. Cheltenham, UK: Edward Elgar Publishing.

Gereffi, Gary. 1978. 'Drug Firms and Dependency in Mexico: The Case of the Steroid Hormone Industry.' *International Organization* 32(1): 237–286.

———. 1980. *'Wonder Drugs' and Transnational Corporations in Mexico: An Elaboration and Limiting-Case Test of Dependency Theory*. Ph.D. dissertation, Yale University, New Haven, CT.

———. 1983. *The Pharmaceutical Industry and Dependency in the Third World*. Princeton, NJ: Princeton University Press.

———. 1988. 'The Pharmaceuticals Market.' In *Health Care in Peru: Resources and Policy*, edited by Dieter K. Zschock, 165–196. Boulder, CO: Westview Press.

———. 1989. 'Rethinking Development Theory: Insights from East Asia and Latin America.' *Sociological Forum* 4(4): 505–533.

———. 1994a. 'The International Economy and Economic Development.' In *The Handbook of Economic Sociology*, edited by Neil J. Smelser and Richard Swedberg, 206–233. Princeton, NJ: Princeton University Press.

———. 1994b. 'The Organization of Buyer-Driven Global Commodity Chains: How U.S. Retailers Shape Overseas Production Networks.' In *Commodity Chains and Global Capitalism*, edited by Gary Gereffi and Miguel Korzeniewicz, 95–122. Westport, CT: Praeger.

———. 1995. 'Contending Paradigms for Cross-Regional Comparisons: Development Strategies and Commodity Chains in East Asia and Latin America.' In *Latin America in Comparative Perspective: New Approaches to Methods and Analysis*, edited by Peter H. Smith, 33–58. Boulder: Westview Press.

———. 1996. 'Global Commodity Chains: New Forms of Coordination and Control among Nations and Firms in International Industries.' *Competition & Change* 1(4): 427–439.

———. 1999. 'International Trade and Industrial Upgrading in the Apparel Commodity Chain.' *Journal of International Economics* 48(1): 37–70.

————. Forthcoming. 'Economic Upgrading in Global Value Chains.' In *Handbook of Global Value Chains*, edited by Gary Gereffi, Stefano Ponte, and Gale Raj-Reichert. Cheltenham, UK: Edward Elgar Publishing.

Gereffi, Gary and Peter Evans. 1981. 'Transnational Corporations, Dependent Development and State Policy in the Semiperiphery: A Comparison of Brazil and Mexico.' *Latin American Research Review* 16(3): 31–64.

Gereffi, Gary and Karina Fernandez-Stark. 2016. 'Global Value Chain Analysis: A Primer,' Second edition. Durham, NC: Duke University, Center on Globalization, Governance and Competitiveness. Available at: https://gvcc.duke.edu/wp-content/uploads/Duke_CGGC_Global_Value_Chain_GVC_Analysis_Primer_2nd_Ed_2016.pdf.

Gereffi, Gary, John Humphrey, Raphael Kaplinsky, and Timothy J. Sturgeon. 2001. 'Introduction: Globalisation, Value Chains and Development.' *IDS Bulletin* 32(3): 1–8.

Gereffi, Gary, John Humphrey, and Timothy J. Sturgeon. 2005. 'The Governance of Global Value Chains.' *Review of International Political Economy* 12(1): 78–104.

Gereffi, Gary and Raphael Kaplinsky, eds. 2001. Special Issue on 'The Value of Value Chains: Spreading the Gains from Globalisation.' *IDS Bulletin* 32(3).

Gereffi, Gary and Miguel Korzeniewicz. 1990. 'Commodity Chains and Footwear Exports in the Semiperiphery.' In *Semiperipheral States in the World-Economy*, edited by William Martin, 45–68. Westport, CT: Greenwood Press.

————, eds. 1994. *Commodity Chains and Global Capitalism*. Westport, CT: Praeger.

Gereffi, Gary, Miguel Korzeniewicz, and Roberto P. Korzeniewicz. 1994. 'Introduction: Global Commodity Chains.' In *Commodity Chains and Global Capitalism*, edited by Gary Gereffi and Miguel Korzeniewicz, 1–14. Westport, CT: Praeger.

Gereffi, Gary and Joonkoo Lee. 2012. 'Why the World Suddenly Cares About Global Supply Chains.' *Journal of Supply Chain Management* 48(3): 24–32.

Gereffi, Gary and Olga Memodovic. 2003. 'The Global Apparel Value Chain: What Prospects for Upgrading by Developing Countries.' Vienna: United National Industrial Development Organization.

Gereffi, Gary, Stefano Ponte, and Gale Raj-Reichert, eds. Forthcoming. *Handbook on Global Value Chains*. Cheltenham, UK: Edward Elgar Publishing.

Gereffi, Gary and Timothy J. Sturgeon. 2013. 'Global Value Chain-Oriented Industrial Policy: The Role of Emerging Economies.' In *Global Value Chains in a Changing World*, edited by Deborah K. Elms and Patrick Low, 329–360. Geneva: World Trade Organization, Fung Global Institute and Temasek Foundation Centre for Trade & Negotiations.

Gereffi, Gary and Donald L. Wyman, eds. 1990. *Manufacturing Miracles: Paths of Industrialization in Latin America and East Asia*. Princeton, NJ: Princeton University Press.

Gibbon, Peter, Jennifer Bair, and Stefano Ponte. 2008. 'Governing Global Value Chains: An Introduction.' *Economy and Society* 37(3): 315–338.

Gold, Thomas B. 1981. *Dependent Development in Taiwan*. Ph.D. dissertation, Harvard University, Cambridge, MA.

Grieco, Joseph. 1984. *Between Dependency and Autonomy: India's Experience with the International Computer Industry*. Berkeley, CA: University of California Press.

Gusfield, Joseph R. 1967. 'Tradition and Modernity: Misplaced Polarities in the Study of Social Change.' *American Journal of Sociology* 72(4): 351–362.

Haggard, Stephan. 1990. *Pathways from the Semiperiphery: The Politics of Growth in the Newly Industrializing Countries.* Ithaca, NY: Cornell University Press.

Hamilton, Gary G. and Gary Gereffi. 2009. 'Global Commodity Chains, Market Makers, and the Rise of Demand-Responsive Economies.' In *Frontiers of Commodity Chain Research,* edited by Jennifer Bair, 136–161. Stanford, CA: Stanford University Press.

Henderson, Jeffrey. 1989. *The Globalisation of High Technology Production: Society, Space and Semiconductors in the Restructuring of the Modern World.* New York: Routledge.

Hirschman, Albert O. 1978. 'Beyond Asymmetry: Critical Notes on Myself as a Young Man and on Some Other Old Friends.' *International Organization* 32(1): 45–50.

Hopkins, Terence K. and Immanuel Wallerstein. 1977. 'Patterns of Development in the Modern World-System.' *Review* 1(2): 111–145.

———. 1986. 'Commodity Chains in the World-Economy Prior to 1800.' *Review* 10(1): 157–170.

Humphrey, John, ed. 1995. Special Issue on 'Industrial Organization and Manufacturing Competitiveness in Developing Countries.' *World Development* 23(1).

Humphrey, John and Olga Memodovic. 2003. 'The Global Automotive Industry Value Chain: What Prospects for Upgrading by Developing Countries.' Vienna: United National Industrial Development Organization.

Humphrey, John and Hubert Schmitz. 2001. 'Governance in Global Value Chains.' *IDS Bulletin* 32(3): 19–29.

———. 2002. 'How Does Insertion in Global Value Chains Affect Upgrading in Industrial Clusters?' *Regional Studies* 36(9): 1017–1027.

Huntington, Samuel P. 1971. 'The Change to Change: Modernization, Development and Politics.' *Comparative Politics* 3(3): 283–322.

Johnson, Chalmers. 1982. *MITI and the Japanese Miracle: The Growth of Industrial Policy, 1925–1975.* Stanford, CA: Stanford University Press.

Korzeniewicz, Miguel E., Gary Gereffi, and Roberto Patricio Korzeniewicz. 1996. 'Response to Wilma A. Dunaway and Donald A. Clelland.' *Journal of World-Systems Research* 2(1): 578–584.

Lall, Sanjaya. 1973. 'Transfer-Pricing by Multinational Manufacturing Firms.' *Oxford Bulletin of Economics and Statistics* 35(3): 173–195.

———. 1975. 'Major Issues in Transfer of Technology to Developing Countries: A Case Study of the Pharmaceutical Industry.' Geneva: United Nations Conference on Trade and Development. (TD/B/C.6/4).

———. 1978. 'Growth of the Pharmaceutical Industry in Developing Countries: Problems and Prospects.' Vienna: United Nations Industrial Development Organization. (United Nations publication, Sales No. E.78.II.B.4).

Lim, Hyun-Chin. 1985. *Dependent Development in Korea, 1963–1979.* Seoul: Seoul National University Press.

Love, Joseph L. 1980. 'Raúl Prebisch and the Origins of the Doctrine of Unequal Exchange.' *Latin American Research Review* 15(3): 45–72.

Mayer, Frederick and Gary Gereffi. Forthcoming. 'International Development Organizations and Global Value Chains.' In *Handbook of Global Value Chains*, edited by Gary Gereffi, Stefano Ponte, and Gale Raj-Reichert. Cheltenham, UK: Edward Elgar Publishing.

Moran, Theodore H. 1974. *Multinational Corporations and the Politics of Dependence: Copper in Chile*. Princeton, NJ: Princeton University Press.

———. 1978. 'Multinational Corporations and Dependency: A Dialogue for Dependentistas and Non-Dependentistas.' *International Organization* 32(1): 79–100.

———. 2009. 'The United Nations and Transnational Corporations: A Review and a Perspective.' *Transnational Corporations* 18(2): 91–112.

Nadvi, Khalid and Hubert Schmitz, eds. 1999. Special Issue on 'Industrial Clusters in Developing Countries.' *World Development* 27(9).

Newfarmer, Richard, ed. 1985. *Profits, Progress and Poverty: Case Studies of International Industries in Latin America*. Notre Dame, IN: University of Notre Dame Press.

Özveren, Eyüp. 1994. 'The Shipbuilding Commodity Chain, 1590–1790.' In *Commodity Chains and Global Capitalism*, edited by Gary Gereffi and Miguel Korzeniewicz, 20–34. Westport, CT: Praeger.

PAHO (Pan American Health Organization). 1984. 'Policies for the Production and Marketing of Essential Drugs.' Scientific Publication No. 462. Washington, DC: PAHO.

Pelizzon, Sheila. 1994. 'The Grain Flour Commodity Chain, 1590–1790.' In *Commodity Chains and Global Capitalism*, edited by Gary Gereffi and Miguel Korzeniewicz, 34–47. Westport, CT: Praeger.

Piore, Michael J. and Charles F. Sabel. 1984. *The Second Industrial Divide: Possibilities for Prosperity*. New York: Basic Books.

Ponte, Stefano and Timothy J. Sturgeon. 2014. 'Explaining Governance in Global Value Chains: A Modular Theory-Building Effort.' *Review of International Political Economy* 21(1): 195–223.

Ponte, Stefano, Timothy J. Sturgeon, and Mark Dallas. Forthcoming. 'Governance and Power in Global Value Chains.' In *Handbook of Global Value Chains*, edited by Gary Gereffi, Stefano Ponte, and Gale Raj-Reichert. Cheltenham, UK: Edward Elgar Publishing.

Porter, Michael. 1985. *Competitive Advantage*. New York: Free Press.

———. 1990. *The Competitive Advantage of Nations*. New York: Free Press.

Portes, Alejandro. 1973. 'Modernity and Development: A Critique.' *Studies in Comparative International Development* 8(3): 247–279.

Ragin, Charles and Daniel Chirot. 1984. 'The World System of Immanuel Wallerstein: Sociology and Politics as History.' In *Vision and Method in Historical Sociology*, edited by Theda Skocpol, 276–312. New York: Cambridge University Press.

Rostow, Walt W. 1960. *The Stages of Economic Growth: A Non-Communist Manifesto*. 2nd edition. Cambridge: Cambridge University Press.

Rubinson, Richard. 1976. 'The World-Economy and the Distribution of Income within States: A Cross-National Study.' *American Sociological Review* 41(4): 638–659.

Rugman, Alan M. 1999. 'Forty Years of the Theory of the Transnational Corporation.' *Transnational Corporations* 8(2): 51–70.

Safarian, A. Edward. 1966. *Foreign Ownership of Canadian Industry.* Toronto: McGraw-Hill.

Sampson, Anthony. 1973. *The Sovereign State of ITT.* New York: Stein and Day.

————. 1975. *The Seven Sisters: The Great Oil Companies and the World They Shaped.* New York: Viking.

Scherer, Frederic M. 1980. *Industrial Market Structure and Economic Performance.* Chicago: Rand McNally.

Schmitz, Hubert. 1999. 'Global Competition and Local Cooperation: Success and Failure in the Sinos Valley, Brazil.' *World Development* 27(9): 1627–1650.

————, ed. 2004. *Local Enterprises in the Global Economy: Issues of Governance and Upgrading.* Cheltenham, UK: Edward Elgar.

Skocpol, Theda. 1977. 'Wallerstein's World Capitalist System: A Theoretical and Historical Critique.' *American Journal of Sociology* 82(5): 1075–1090.

Smelser, Neil J. and Richard Swedberg, eds. 2005. *The Handbook of Economic Sociology*, 2nd edition. Princeton, NJ: Princeton University Press and Russell Sage Foundation.

Staritz, Cornelia, Gary Gereffi, and Olivier Cattaneo, eds. 2011. 'Shifting End Markets and Upgrading Prospects in Global Value Chains.' *International Journal of Technological Learning, Innovation and Development* 4(1–3).

Sturgeon, Timothy J. 2001. 'How Do We Define Value Chains and Production Networks?' *IDS Bulletin* 32(3): 9–18.

————. 2002. 'Modular Production Networks: A New American Model of Industrial Organization.' *Industrial and Corporate Change* 11(3): 451–496.

————. 2009. 'From Commodity Chains to Value Chains: Interdisciplinary Theory Building in an Age of Globalization.' In *Frontiers of Commodity Chain Research*, edited by Jennifer Bair, 110–135. Stanford, CA: Stanford University Press.

————. Forthcoming. 'Measuring Global Value Chains.' In *Handbook of Global Value Chains*, edited by Gary Gereffi, Stefano Ponte, and Gale Raj-Reichert. Cheltenham, UK: Edward Elgar Publishing.

Sturgeon, Timothy J. and Momoko Kawakami. 2011. 'Global Value Chains in the Electronics Industry: Characteristics, Crisis, and Upgrading Opportunities for Firms from Developing Countries.' *International Journal of Technological Learning, Innovation and Development* 4(1–3): 120–147.

Sturgeon, Timothy J., Olga Memodovic, Johannes Van Biesebroeck, and Gary Gereffi. 2009. 'Globalisation of the Automotive Industry: Main Features and Trends.' *International Journal of Technological Learning, Innovation and Development* 2(1–2): 7–24.

Sunkel, Osvaldo. 1973. 'Transnational Capitalism and National Disintegration in Latin America.' *Social and Economic Studies* 22(1): 132–176.

UNCTAD (United Nations Conference on Trade and Development). 2002. *World Investment Report: Transnational Corporations and Export Competitiveness.* New York: United Nations.

UNCTC (United Nations Centre on Transnational Corporations). 1979. *Transnational Corporations and the Pharmaceutical Industry.* New York: UNCTC. (United Nations publication, Sales No. E.79.II.A.3).

————. 1981. *Transnational Corporations and the Pharmaceutical Industry in Developing Countries*. New York: UNCTC. (E/C.10/85).

UNIDO (United Nations Industrial Development Organization). 2015. *Industrial Development Report 2016*. Vienna: UNIDO.

Vernon, Raymond. 1971. *Sovereignty at Bay: The Multinational Spread of U.S. Enterprises*. New York: Basic Books.

————. 1999. 'The Harvard Multinational Enterprise Project in Historical Perspective.' *Transnational Corporations* 8(2): 35–49.

Wade, Robert. 1990. *Governing the Market: Economic Theory and the Role of Government in East Asian Industrialization*. Princeton, NJ: Princeton University Press.

Wallerstein, Immanuel. 1974. *The Modern World-System I: Capitalist Agriculture and the Origin of the European World-Economy in the Sixteenth Century*. New York: Academic Press.

————. 1979. *The Capitalist World-Economy*. New York: Cambridge University Press.

————. 1980. *The Modern World-System II: Mercantilism and the Consolidation of the European World-Economy, 1600–1750*. New York: Academic Press.

————. 1989. *The Modern World-System III: The Second Era of Great Expansion of the Capitalist World-Economy, 1730–1840*. New York: Academic Press.

World Bank. 1993. *The East Asian Miracle: Economic Growth and Public Policy*. New York: Oxford University Press.

Part I

Foundations of the Global Value Chain Framework

The Organization of Buyer-Driven Global Commodity Chains

How US Retailers Shape Overseas Production Networks

Global industrialization is the result of an integrated system of production and trade. Open international trade has encouraged nations to specialize in different branches of manufacturing and even in different stages of production within a specific industry. This process, fueled by the explosion of new products and new technologies since World War II, has led to the emergence of a global manufacturing system in which production capacity is dispersed to an unprecedented number of developing as well as industrialized countries (Harris, 1987; Gereffi, 1989b). The revolution in transportation and communications technology has permitted manufacturers and retailers alike to establish international production and trade networks that cover vast geographical distances. While considerable attention has been given to the involvement of industrial capital in international contracting, the key role played by commercial capital (i.e., large retailers and brand-named companies that buy but don't make the goods they sell) in the expansion of manufactured exports from developing countries has been relatively ignored.

This chapter will show how these 'big buyers' have shaped the production networks established in the world's most dynamic exporting countries, especially the newly industrialized countries (NICs) of East Asia. The argument proceeds in several stages. First, a distinction is made between producer-driven and buyer-driven commodity chains, which represent alternative modes of organizing international industries. These commodity chains, though primarily controlled by private economic agents, are also influenced by state policies in both the producing (exporting) and consuming (importing) countries.

Second, the main organizational features of buyer-driven commodity chains are identified, using the apparel industry as a case study. The apparel commodity chain contains two very different segments. The companies that make and sell standardized clothing have production patterns and sourcing strategies that contrast with firms in the fashion segment of the industry, which has been the most actively committed to global sourcing. Recent changes within the retail sector of the United States are analyzed in this chapter to identify the emergence of new types of big buyers and to show why they have distinct strategies of global sourcing.

Third, the locational patterns of global sourcing in apparel are charted, with an emphasis on the production frontiers favored by different kinds of US buyers. Several of the primary mechanisms used by big buyers to source products from overseas are outlined in order to demonstrate how transnational production systems are sustained and altered by American retailers and branded apparel companies. Data sources include in-depth interviews with managers of overseas buying offices, trading companies, manufacturers, and retailers in East Asia and the United States, plus relevant secondary materials at the firm, industry, and country levels.[1]

Producer-Driven versus Buyer-Driven Commodity Chains

Global commodity chains (GCCs) are rooted in production systems that give rise to particular patterns of coordinated trade. A 'production system' links the economic activities of firms to technological and organizational networks that permit companies to develop, manufacture, and distribute specific commodities. In the transnational production systems that characterize global capitalism, economic activity is not only *international* in scope; it also is *global* in its organization (Ross and Trachte, 1990; Dicken, 1992). While 'internationalization' refers simply to the geographical spread of economic activities across national boundaries, 'globalization' implies a degree of functional integration between these internationally dispersed activities. The requisite administrative coordination is carried out by diverse corporate actors in centralized as well as decentralized economic structures.

Large firms in globalized production systems simultaneously participate in many different countries, not in an isolated or segmented fashion but as part of their global production and distribution strategies. The GCC perspective highlights the need to look not only at the geographical spread of transnational production arrangements, but also at their organizational scope (i.e., the linkages between various economic agents—raw material suppliers, factories, traders, and retailers) in order to understand their sources of stability and change (see Gereffi and Korzeniewicz, 1990).

Global commodity chains have three main dimensions: (1) an input-output structure (i.e., a set of products and services linked together in a sequence of value-adding economic activities); (2) a territoriality (i.e., spatial dispersion or concentration of production and distribution networks, comprised of enterprises of different sizes and types); and (3) a governance structure (i.e., authority and power relationships that determine how financial, material, and human resources are allocated and flow within a chain).

The governance structure of GCCs, which is essential to the coordination of transnational production systems, has received relatively little attention in the literature (an exception is Storper and Harrison, 1991). Two distinct types of governance structures for GCCs have emerged in the past two decades, which for the sake of simplicity, are called 'producer-driven' and 'buyer-driven' commodity chains (see Figure 2.1).

Figure 2.1 The Organization of Producer-Driven and Buyer-Driven Global Commodity Chains

1. Producer-Driven Commodity Chains

(Industries such as automobiles, computers, aircraft, and electrical machinery)

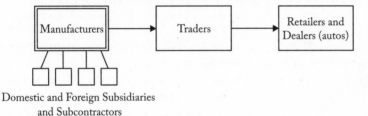

Domestic and Foreign Subsidiaries
and Subcontractors

2. Buyer-Driven Commodity Chains
(Industries such as garments, footwear, toys, and housewares)

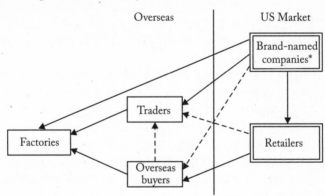

*These design-oriented, national brand companies, such as Nike, Reebok, Liz Claiborne, and Mattel Toys, typically own no factories. Some, like The Gap and The Limited, have their own retail outlets that only sell private-label products.

Source: Author.

Note: Solid arrows are primary relationships; dashed arrows are secondary relationships.

Producer-driven commodity chains refer to those industries in which transnational corporations (TNCs) or other large integrated industrial enterprises play the central role in controlling the production system (including its backward and forward linkages). This is most characteristic of capital- and technology-intensive industries like automobiles, computers, aircraft, and electrical machinery. The geographical spread of these industries is transnational, but the number of countries in the commodity chain and their levels of development are varied. International subcontracting of components is common, especially for the most labor-intensive production processes, as are strategic alliances between international rivals. What distinguishes 'producer-driven' production systems is the control exercised by the administrative headquarters of the TNCs.

Hill (1989) analyzes a producer-driven commodity chain in his comparative study of how Japanese and US car companies organize manufacturing in multilayered production systems that involve thousands of firms (including parents, subsidiaries, and subcontractors). Doner (1991) extended this framework to highlight the complex forces that drive Japanese automakers to create regional production schemes for the supply of auto parts in a half-dozen nations in East and Southeast Asia. Henderson (1989), in his study of the internationalization of the US semiconductor industry, also supports the notion that producer-driven commodity chains have established an East Asian division of labor.

Buyer-driven commodity chains refer to those industries in which large retailers, brand-named merchandisers, and trading companies play the pivotal role in setting up decentralized production networks in a variety of exporting countries, typically located in the Third World. This pattern of trade-led industrialization has become common in labor-intensive, consumer-goods industries such as garments, footwear, toys, consumer electronics, housewares, and a wide range of hand-crafted items (e.g., furniture, ornaments). International contract manufacturing again is prevalent, but production is generally carried out by independent Third World factories that make finished goods (rather than components or parts) under original equipment manufacturer (OEM) arrangements. The specifications are supplied by the buyers and branded companies that design the goods.

One of the main characteristics of firms that fit the buyer-driven model, including athletic footwear companies like Nike, Reebok, and L. A. Gear (Donaghu and Barff, 1990) and fashion-oriented clothing companies like The Limited, The Gap, and Liz Claiborne (Lardner, 1988), is that frequently these businesses do not own any production facilities. They are not 'manufacturers' because they have no factories.[2] Rather, these companies are 'merchandisers' that design and/or market but do not make the branded products they sell. These firms rely on complex tiered networks of contractors that perform almost all their specialized tasks. Branded merchandisers may farm out part or all of their product development activities, manufacturing, packaging, shipping, and even accounts receivables to different agents around the world.

The main job of the core company in buyer-driven commodity chains is to manage these production and trade networks and make sure all the pieces of the business come together as an integrated whole. Profits in buyer-driven chains thus derive not from scale economies and technological advances as in producer-driven chains, but rather from unique combinations of high-value research, design, sales, marketing, and financial services that allow the buyers and branded merchandisers to act as strategic brokers in linking overseas factories and traders with evolving product niches in their main consumer markets (see Rabach and Kim, 1994; also Reich, 1991).

The distinction between producer-driven and buyer-driven commodity chains bears on the debate concerning mass production and flexible specialization systems of industrial organization (Piore and Sabel, 1984). Mass production is clearly a producer-driven model (in our terms), while flexible specialization has been spawned, in part, by the growing importance of segmented demand and more discriminating buyers in developed country markets. One of the main differences between the GCC and flexible specialization perspectives is that Piore and Sabel deal primarily with the organization of production in domestic economies and local industrial districts, while the notion of producer-driven and buyer-driven commodity chains focuses on the organizational properties of global industries. Furthermore, a buyer-driven commodity chain approach would explain the emergence of flexibly specialized forms of production in terms of changes in the structure of retailing, which in turn reflect demographic shifts and new organizational imperatives. Finally, while some of the early discussions of flexible specialization implied that it is a 'superior' manufacturing system that might eventually displace or subordinate mass production, buyer-driven and supplier-driven commodity chains are viewed as contrasting (but not mutually exclusive) poles in a spectrum of industrial organization possibilities.

Our analysis of buyer-driven commodity chains will focus on the main companies that coordinate these economic networks: large US retailers. Whereas in producer-driven forms of capitalist industrialization, production patterns shape the character of demand, in buyer-driven commodity chains the organization of consumption is a major determinant of where and how global manufacturing takes place. However, the economic agents of supply and demand do not operate in a political vacuum. They, in turn, respond to political pressures from the state.

The Role of State Policies in Global Commodity Chains

National development strategies play an important role in forging new production relationships in the global manufacturing system (Gereffi and Wyman, 1990).

Conventional economic wisdom claims that Third World nations have followed one of two alternative development strategies: (1) the relatively large, resource-rich economies in Latin America (e.g., Brazil, Mexico, and Argentina), South Asia (e.g., India and Bangladesh), and Eastern Europe have pursued import-substituting industrialization (ISI) in which industrial production was geared to the needs of sizable domestic markets; and (2) the smaller, resource-poor nations like the East Asian NICs adopted the export-oriented industrialization (EOI) approach that depends on global markets to stimulate the rapid growth of manufactured exports. Although the historical analysis of these transitions tends to have been oversimplified, today it is abundantly clear that most economies have opted for an expansion of manufactured or non-traditional exports to earn needed foreign exchange and raise local standards of living. The East Asian NICs best exemplify the gains from this path of development.

An important affinity exists between the ISI and EOI strategies of national development and the structure of commodity chains. Import substitution occurs in the same kinds of capital- and technology-intensive industries represented by producer-driven commodity chains (e.g., steel, aluminum, petrochemicals, machinery, automobiles, and computers). In addition, the main economic agents in both cases are TNCs and state-owned enterprises. Export-oriented industrialization, on the other hand, is channeled through buyer-driven commodity chains where production in labor-intensive industries is concentrated in small to medium-sized, private domestic firms located mainly in the Third World. Historically, the export-oriented development strategy of the East Asian NICs and buyer-driven commodity chains emerged together in the early 1970s, suggesting a close connection between the success of EOI and the development of new forms of organizational integration in buyer-driven industrial networks.

State policy plays a major role in GCCs. In EOI, governments are primarily facilitators; they are condition-creating and tend not to become directly involved in production. Governments try to generate the infrastructural support needed to make export-oriented industries work: modern transportation facilities and communications networks; bonded areas like export-processing zones (including China's special economic zones); subsidies for raw materials; customs drawbacks for imported inputs that are used in export production; adaptive financial institutions and easy credit (e.g., to facilitate the obtaining of letters of credit by small firms); etc. In ISI, on the other hand, governments play a much more interventionist role. They use the full array of industrial policy instruments (such as local content requirements, joint ventures with domestic partners, and export-promotion schemes), while the state often gets involved in production activities, especially in upstream industries.

In short, the role of the state at the point of production tends to be facilitative in buyer-driven commodity chains and more interventionist in producer-driven chains. However, there is an important caveat for buyer-driven chains. Since these are export-oriented industries, state policies in the consuming or importing countries (like the United States) are also highly significant. This is where the impact of protectionist measures such as quotas, tariffs, and voluntary export restraints comes in to shape the location of production in buyer-driven chains. If one compares the global sourcing of apparel (where quotas are prevalent) and footwear (no quotas),[3] one sees that far more countries are involved in the production and export networks for clothes than for shoes. This is basically a quota effect, whereby the array of Third World apparel export bases continually is being expanded to bypass the import ceilings mandated by quotas against previously successful apparel exporters. Therefore, the globalization of export production has been fostered by two distinct sets of state policies: Third World efforts to promote EOI, coupled with protectionism in developed country markets.

The Apparel Commodity Chain

The textile and apparel industries are the first stage in the industrialization process of most countries. This fact, coupled with the prevalence of developed country protectionist policies in this sector, has led to the unparalleled diversity of garment exporters in the Third World. The apparel industry thus is an ideal case for exploring the organization and dynamics of buyer-driven commodity chains. The apparel commodity chain is bifurcated along two main dimensions: (1) textile versus garment manufacturers and (2) standardized versus fashion-oriented segments in the industry (see Taplin, 1994, for a diagram incorporating both of these dimensions). A complete analysis must also take account of how backward and forward linkages are utilized in the apparel commodity chain to protect the profitability of leading firms.

Textile versus Garment Producers

Textile manufacturers and garment producers inhabit different economic worlds. Textile companies are frequently large, capital-intensive firms with integrated spinning and weaving facilities. The major textile manufacturers 'finish' woven fabrics into a variety of end products, including sheets, towels, and pillowcases. While the US fiber industry is composed of TNCs that make synthetic as well as natural fibers, fabric producers are more diverse in size, including numerous small businesses along with industrial giants like Burlington Mills.

The apparel industry, on the other hand, is the most fragmented part of the textile complex, characterized by many small, labor-intensive factories. Two primary determinants explain shifts in the geographical location and organization of manufacturing in the apparel sector: the search for low-wage labor and the pursuit of organizational flexibility. Although apparel manufacturing depends on low wages to remain competitive, this fact alone cannot account for dynamic trends in international competitiveness. Cheap labor is what Michael Porter calls a 'lower-order' competitive advantage, since it is an inherently unstable basis on which to build a global strategy. More significant factors for the international competitiveness of firms are the 'higher-order' advantages such as proprietary technology, product differentiation, brand reputation, customer relationships, and constant industrial upgrading (Porter, 1990: 49–51). These assets allow enterprises to exercise a greater degree of organizational flexibility and thus to create as well as respond to new opportunities in the global economy.

Standardized versus Fashion Segments

A second major divide in the apparel commodity chain is between the producers of standardized and fashion-oriented garments. In the United States, the majority of the 35,000 firms in the textile-apparel complex are small clothing manufacturers (Mody and Wheeler, 1987). For standardized apparel (such as jeans, men's underwear, brassieres, and fleece outerwear), large firms using dedicated or single-purpose machines have emerged. Companies that make standardized clothing include the giants of the American apparel industry, like Levi Strauss and Sara Lee (both $4 billion companies), VF Corporation (a $2.6 billion company with popular brands such as Lee and Wrangler jeans and Jantzen sportswear), and Fruit of the Loom (a $1.6 billion firm that is the largest domestic producer of underwear for the US market). These big firms tend to be closely linked with US textile suppliers, and they manufacture many of their clothes within the United States or they ship US-made parts offshore for sewing.[4]

The fashion-oriented segment of the garment industry encompasses those products that change according to retail buying seasons. Many of today's leading apparel firms like Liz Claiborne have six or more different buying seasons every year (Lardner, 1988). These companies confront far greater demands for variation in styling and materials, and they tend to utilize numerous overseas factories because of their need for low wages and organizational flexibility in this labor-intensive and volatile segment of the apparel industry.

It is the fashion-oriented segment of the apparel commodity chain that is most actively involved in global sourcing. In 1990, imports accounted for 51% of US consumer expenditures on apparel. Of the $75 billion spent on US apparel imports (in a total US market of $148 billion), $25 billion corresponded to the foreign-port value of imported clothing, $14 billion to landing, distribution, and other costs, and $36 billion to the retailers' average markup of 48% on imported goods (*AAMA*, 1991: 3). The consumer's retail price thus amounts to three times the overseas factory cost for imported clothing. Meanwhile, the wholesale value of domestic apparel production totaling $73 billion in 1990 was $39 billion, with another $34 billion going to the retailers' net markup of 46%. In other words, the global sourcing of apparel by major retailers and brand-named companies is big business in the United States and it is growing bigger every year. This is why the organization of global sourcing merits close attention.

The Impact of Backward and Forward Linkages

The severe cost pressures endemic in the labor-intensive segments of the garment industry highlight the interdependence between different economic agents in buyer-driven commodity chains. Throughout the 1980s, US garment companies were demanding lower prices and faster delivery from their overseas (principally Asian) suppliers, as well as their largely immigrant core and secondary contractors in New York City and Los Angeles, who in turn, squeezed their workers for longer hours and lower wages (Rothstein, 1989). But the intensity of these pressures has varied over time. Why do the garment manufacturers pressure their contractors more at some times than at others? In a related vein, how can we explain differences in the level and location of profits in this industry over time?

The answers to these questions lie in an analysis of the apparel industry's backward and forward linkages. Garment manufacturers are being squeezed from both ends of the apparel commodity chain. Textile firms in the United States have become larger and more concentrated as they turned to highly automated production processes. This allowed them to place greater demands on the domestic garment manufacturers for large orders, high prices for inputs, and favorable payment schedules (Waldinger, 1986). One response has been for US garment companies to find more competitive overseas suppliers of textiles and fabrics. Since this option is constrained by quotas that limit the extent of US textile imports, many apparel makers had little choice but to accede to the demands of their main domestic textile suppliers.

At the other end of the apparel commodity chain, US retailers went through a merger movement of their own (Bluestone et al., 1981). A number of prominent retail companies have gone into bankruptcy, been bought out, or have faced economic difficulties.[5] Those 'big buyers' that remain are becoming larger, more tightly integrated, organizationally and technologically, and frequently more specialized. This has put increasing pressure on merchandise manufacturers to lower their prices and improve their performance.[6] The result is that garment firms again are squeezed, with negative consequences (e.g., lower purchase prices, increased uncertainty) for their domestic and overseas contractors and the affiliated workers who actually make the clothes.

These illustrations show the importance of considering the full array of backward and forward linkages in the production process, as the GCC framework does, rather than limiting our notion of transnational production systems to manufacturing alone. Industrial organization economics tells us that profitability is greatest in the more concentrated segments of an industry characterized by high barriers to the entry of new firms. Producer-driven commodity chains are capital- and technology-intensive. Thus manufacturers making advanced products like aircraft, automobiles, and computer systems are the key economic agents in these chains not only in terms of their earnings, but also in their ability to exert control over backward linkages with raw material and component suppliers, as well as forward linkages into retailing.

Buyer-driven commodity chains, on the other hand, which characterize many of today's light consumer goods industries like garments, footwear, and toys, tend to be labor-intensive at the manufacturing stage. This leads to very competitive and globally decentralized factory systems. However, these same industries are also design- and marketing-intensive, which means that there are high barriers to entry at the level of brand-named companies and retailers that invest considerable sums in product development, advertising, and computerized store networks to create and sell these products. Therefore, whereas producer-driven commodity chains are controlled by core firms at the point of production, control over buyer-driven commodity chains is exercised at the point of consumption.

In summary, our GCC approach is historical since the relative strength of different economic agents in the commodity chain (raw material and component suppliers, manufacturers, traders, and retailers) changes over time; it is also comparative because the structural arrangements of commodity chains vary across industrial sectors as well as geographical areas. Finally, contemporary GCCs have two very different kinds of governance structures: one imposed by core manufacturers in producer-driven commodity chains, and the other provided by major retailers and brand-named companies in the buyer-driven production networks. These have distinct implications for national development strategies and the consequences of different modes of incorporation into the world economy.

The Retail Revolution in the United States

In order to gain a better understanding of the dynamics of the governance structure in buyer-driven commodity chains, we need to take a closer look at the US retail sector, whose big buyers have fueled much of the growth in consumer goods exports in the world economy. Changes in America's consumption patterns are one of the main factors that have given rise to flexible specialization in global manufacturing.

For the past two decades, a 'retail revolution' has been under way in the United States that is changing the face of the American marketplace. A comprehensive study of US department stores showed that the structure of the industry became more oligopolistic during the 1960s and 1970s as giant department stores swallowed up many once-prominent independent retailers (Bluestone et al., 1981). The growth of large firms at the expense of small retail outlets was encouraged by several forces, including economies of scale, the advanced technology[7] and mass advertising available to retail giants, government regulation, and the financial backing of large corporate parent firms. Ironically, despite the department store industry's transformation into an oligopoly, the price competition between giant retailers became more intense, not less (Bluestone et al., 1981: 2).[8]

In the 1980s, the department store in turn came under siege. In their heyday, department stores were quintessential middle-class American institutions.[9] These retailers offered a broad selection of general merchandise for 'family shopping', with 'the mother as "generalist" buying for other family members' (Legomsky, 1986: R62).[10] While this format typically met the needs of the suburban married couple with two children and one income, by 1990 less than 10% of American households fit that description. Today the generalist strategy no longer works. The one shopper of yesterday has become many different shoppers, with each member of the family constituting a separate buying unit (Sack, 1989).

The breakup of the American mass market into distinct, if overlapping, retail constituencies has created a competitive squeeze on the traditional department stores and mass merchandisers,[11] who are caught between a wide variety of specialty stores, on the one hand, and large-volume discount chains, on the other.[12] The former, who tailor themselves to the upscale shopper, offer customers an engaging ambience, strong fashion statements, and good service;[13] the latter, who aim for the lower-income buyer, emphasize low prices, convenience, and no-frills merchandising.

Tables 2.1 and 2.2 show the varied performance levels of some of the major US retail chains in the 1980s and 1990s. In 1990, both Wal-Mart and Kmart surpassed Sears as the largest US retailers in terms of sales (see Table 2.1). Wal-Mart, Kmart, and Target (a division of Dayton Hudson) now control over 70% of the booming discount-store business in the United States. Wal-Mart and the leading specialty stores also have far better earnings than the department stores and mass merchandise chains. The 10-year compounded growth rates in net income for Wal-Mart (34.5%) and the two leading specialty retailers in apparel, The Gap (34.6%) and The Limited (33.5%),[14] are the highest of any of the stores listed. In addition, the specialty stores tend to have the top rate of return on revenues of any US retailers between 1987 and 1991 (see Table 2.2).

Table 2.1 Sales of Leading US Retailers, 1987–1992

	1987	1988	1989	1990	1991	1992
Discounters						
Wal-Mart	16.0	20.6	25.8	32.6	43.9	55.5
Kmart	25.6	27.3	29.5	32.1	34.6	37.7
Mass Merchandisers						
Sears	28.1	30.3	31.6	32.0	3L4	32.0
Dayton Hudson	10.7	12.2	13.6	14.7	16.1	17.9
Woolworth	7.1	8.1	8.8	9.8	9.9	10.0
Department Stores						
J. C. Penney	16.4	15.9	17.1	17.4	17.3	19.1
May Department Stores	10.3	8.4	9.4	10.1	10.6	11.2
Specialty Stores						
Melville	5.9	6.8	7.6	8.7	9.9	10.4
The Limited	3.5	4.1	4.6	5.3	6.1	6.9
The Gap	1.1	1.3	1.6	1.9	2.5	3.0
Toys 'R' Us	3.3	4.0	4.8	5.5	6.1	7.2

Source: Standard and Poor's Industry Surveys, 'Retailing: Current Analysis', April 20, 1989, R79; May 2, 1991, R80; May 13, 1993, p. R80; and company annual reports.

Wal-Mart appears to be in a much stronger position for future growth than its leading challenger, Kmart. In 1990, Wal-Mart cleared $2 billion before taxes compared to Kmart's $1 billion on basically the same volume of sales (Saporito, 1991: 54). The performance of companies like Kmart,[15] J. C. Penney, and Woolworth have been hindered by their major corporate restructurings over the past several years. Although the specialty stores are considerably smaller than other types of US retailers, the former have the highest ratio of sales per retail square footage of any US retail establishments and they have a reputation for more fashionable and higher quality merchandise.

Unlike the earlier 'retail revolution' when department stores became oligopolies, the current surge of specialty and discount formats is less a function of the evolution of retail institutions than of overriding demographic and life-style changes in American society. 'The fragmentation of the American marketplace … reflects the expanding ranks of single-person households, the greater proportion of two-income families, and the sharp rise in the number of working women' (Legomsky, 1986: R62).[16] Furthermore, there has been a widening of the gap between the rich and the poor in the United States.[17] The retail sector has mirrored this dichotomy—stores have either gone upscale or low-price, with middle-income consumers pulled in both directions.

Table 2.2　Net Income and Return on Revenues of Leading US Retailers, 1987–1991

Company	Net Income[a] (millions of dollars)					Compound Growth Rate (%)			Return on Revenues[b] (%)		
	1987	1988	1989	1990	1991	1-yr.	5-yr.	10-yr.	1987	1989	1991
Discounters											
Wal-Mart	628	837	1076	1291	1608	24.6	29.0	34.5	3.9	4.2	3.7
Kmart	692	803	323	756	859	13.6	8.5	14.6	2.7	1.1	2.5
Mass Merchandisers											
Sears	1649	1032	1446	829	1279	43.4	-1.1	7.0	3.4	2.7	2.2
Dayton Hudson[c]	228	287	410	410	301	-26.6	3.4	6.6	2.1	3.0	1.9
Woolworth	251	288	329	317	-53	NM	NM	NM	3.5	3.7	NM
Department Stores											
J. C. Penney	608	807	802	577	264	-54.2	-13.0	-3.8	3.8	4.7	1.5
May Department Stores[d]	444	503	515	500	515	3.0	6.2	15.1	4.2	5.4	4.9
Specialty Stores											
Melville[e]	285	354	398	385	347	-10.0	7.8	9.8	4.8	5.3	3.5
The Limited[f]	235	245	347	398	403	1.2	12.1	33.5	6.7	7.3	6.4
The Gap[f]	70	74	98	144	230	59.1	27.5	34.6	6.6	6.2	9.1
Toys 'R' Us[g]	204	268	321	326	340	4.2	17.4	21.4	6.5	6.7	5.5

Source: Standard and Poor's Industry Surveys, 'Retailing: Comparative Company Analysis', May 13, 1993: R104–R107.

Notes: [a] 'Net income' refers to profits derived from all sources after deduction of expenses, taxes, and fixed charges, but before any discounted operations, extraordinary items, and dividend payments (preferred and common).
[b] Net income divided by operating revenues.
[c] Dayton Hudson stores include: Target, Mervyn's, Marshall Field's, and Hudson.
[d] May Department Stores Company includes: Lord and Taylor, Filene's, Hecht's, Foley's, Kaufmann's, Robinson-May, Famous-Barr, and Meier and Frank, among others. May also owns the discount footwear chain of Payless ShoeSource stores.
[e] Shoes.
[f] Garments.
[g] Toys.
NM = not meaningful.

This segmentation of the American market creates numerous opportunities for specialized retail formats. Just as the era of mass production is giving way to flexible manufacturing in the productive sphere, the renowned American mass market is becoming more customized and personalized. This has paved the way for increased trans-Atlantic competition by European and other foreign-based retailers, such as Benetton in Italy and Laura Ashley in the United Kingdom.

According to Lester Thurow, professor of economics and management at the Massachusetts Institute of Technology, 'The American economy died about 10 years ago, and has been replaced by a world economy ... [American retailers] are going to face an international challenge' (Legomsky, 1986: R61).

Department stores and other mass merchandisers in the United States have tried to develop effective counterstrategies to these trends. Some retailers like J. C. Penney have sought to upgrade their status from mass merchandiser to department store by adding higher-priced apparel, and to increase profitability by emphasizing higher-margin merchandise that has a faster turn-around time (Sack, 1989: R80). Other firms have begun to diversify their appeal by establishing their own specialty retail outlets (like the Foot Locker stores, which are owned by Woolworth Corporation).[18] On the international front, retailers and manufacturers alike are acquiring large importers to shore up their position in global sourcing networks,[19] while unique organizational forms such as member-owned retail buying groups are being used in overseas procurement.[20]

In summary, the transformation of the retail sector in the United States has remained fast-paced throughout the 1980s and 1990s. This reflects not only the changing demography and purchasing power of American society, but as we will see in the next sections, it also proves to be a significant determinant of production patterns within the global economy.

The Economic Agents in Buyer-Driven Commodity Chains

Big buyers are embedded in GCCs through the export and distribution networks they establish with overseas factories and trading companies. In order to understand the structure and dynamics of this relationship, we must first identify the economic agents in buyer-driven commodity chains (retailers, traders, overseas buyers, and factories), and then look at the impact of the main coordinating group (large retailers) on global production patterns.

Retailers

The organization of consumption in the United States is stratified by retail chains that target distinct income groups in the population. There are several types of retailers: large-volume, low-priced discount stores; mass merchandisers; department stores; and 'fashion' or upper-end specialized retailers that deal exclusively with national brand-named products. These stores vary in their mixes of nationally branded, store-branded, and unbranded products.[21] The different categories of retailers also establish distinctive relationships with importers and overseas manufacturers. As one moves down this list of retailers, the quality and price of the goods sold increase and the requirements for their international contractors become more stringent.

Traders

Trading companies have evolved from the global juggernauts that spanned the British, Dutch, and Japanese empires in centuries past to the highly specialized organizations that exist today. As recently as 25 years ago, there were no direct buying offices set up by US retailers in Asia.[22] Originally, American retailers bought from importers on a 'landed' basis, i.e., the importer cleared the goods through US customs.[23] In the late 1970s, importing began to be done on a 'first-cost' basis. The buyer opened a letter of credit directly to the factory and paid the importer (or buying agent) a commission to get the goods to the export port. The buyer handled the shipping and distribution in the United States. Before retailers established direct buying offices overseas, importers were the key intermediaries between retailers and their foreign contractors. There still is a broad array of specialized importers that deal in particular industries[24] or even in specific product niches within an industry.[25] While the importers handle production logistics and often help to develop new product lines, the leading apparel companies control the marketing end of the apparel commodity chain through their exclusive designs and brand-named products.[26]

Overseas Buyers

There is a symbiotic relationship between the overseas buying offices of major retail chains and the role played by importers and exporters. The direct buying offices of major retailers purchase a wide assortment of products, typically grouped into 'soft goods' (like garments and shoes) and 'hard goods' (such as lighting fixtures, kitchenware, appliances, furniture, and toys). Obviously, it is difficult for these buyers to develop an intimate knowledge of the supplier networks and product characteristics of such a diverse array of items. As a result, retail chains depend heavily on the specialized importers and trading companies that continuously develop new product lines with the local manufacturers and that provide retailers with valuable information about the hot items and sales trends of their competitors.

In general, the US-based buyers for American retailers tend to work with importers and trading companies in the fashion-oriented and new-product end of consumer-goods industries, while their overseas buying offices purchase the more standardized, popular, or large-volume items directly from the factories in order to eliminate the importer's commission. Large retailers usually have their own product development groups and buying offices in the United States for their most popular or distinctive items.

Factories

The factories that produce the consumer products that flow through buyer-driven commodity chains are involved in contract manufacturing relationships with the buyers who place the orders. Contract manufacturing (or specification contracting) refers to the production of finished consumer goods by local firms, where the output is distributed and marketed abroad by trading companies, branded merchandisers, retail chains, or their agents.[27] This is the major export niche filled by the East Asian NICs in the world economy.

In 1980, for example, Hong Kong, Taiwan, and South Korea accounted for 72% of all finished consumer goods exported by the Third World to OECD countries, other Asian nations supplied another 19%, while just 7% came from Latin America and the Caribbean. The United States was the leading market for these consumer products with 46% of the total (Keesing, 1983: 338–339). East Asian factories, which have handled the bulk of the specification contracting orders from US retailers, tend to be locally owned and vary greatly in size—from the giant plants in South Korea to the myriad small family firms that account for a large proportion of the exports from Taiwan and Hong Kong.[28]

Locational Patterns of Global Sourcing

Big retailers and brand-named merchandisers have different strategies of global sourcing, which in large part are dictated by the client bases they serve (see Table 2.3 and Figure 2.2). Fashion-oriented retailers that cater to an exclusive clientele for 'designer' products get their expensive, nationally branded goods from an inner ring of premium-quality, high-value-added exporting countries (e.g., Italy, France, Japan). Department stores and specialty chains that emphasize 'private label' (or store brand) products as well as national brands source from the most established Third World exporters (such as the East Asian NICs, Brazil, Mexico, and India), while the mass merchandisers that sell lower-priced store brands buy from more remote tiers of medium- to low-cost, mid-quality exporters (low-end producers in the NICs, plus China and the Southeast Asian countries of Thailand, Malaysia, the Philippines, and Indonesia). Large-volume discount stores that sell the most inexpensive products import from the outer rings of low-cost suppliers of standardized goods (e.g., China, Indonesia, Bangladesh, Sri Lanka, Mauritius, the Dominican Republic, Guatemala). Finally, smaller importers serve as industry 'scouts'. They operate on the fringes of the international production frontier and help develop potential new sources of supply for global commodity chains (e.g., Vietnam, Myanmar, Saipan).

Table 2.3 Types of Retailers and Main Global Sourcing Areas

Type of Retailer	Representative Firms	Main Global Sourcing Areas[a]	Characteristics of Buyer's Orders
Fashion-oriented companies	Armani, Donna Karan, Polo/ Ralph Lauren, Hugo Boss, Gucci	First and second rings	Expensive 'designer' products requiring high levels of craftsmanship; orders are in small lots.
Department stores, specialty stores, and brand-named companies	Bloomingdale's, Sales Fifth Avenue. Neiman-Marcus, Macy's, Nordstrom, The Gap, The Limited, Liz Claiborne, Calvin Klein	Second, third, and fourth rings	Top quality, high-priced goods sold under a variety of national brands and private labels (i.e., store brands); medium to large-sized orders, often coordinated by department-store buying groups (such as May Department Stores Company and Federated Department Stores).
Mass merchandisers	Sears Roebuck, Montgomery Ward, J. C. Penney, Woolworth	Second, third, and fourth rings	Good quality, medium-priced goods predominantly sold under private labels; large orders.
Discount chains	Wal-Mart, Kmart, Target	Third, fourth, and fifth rings	Low-priced, store-brand products; giant orders.
Small importers		Fourth and fifth rings	Pilot purchases and special items; sourcing done for retailers by small importers who act as 'industry scouts' in searching out new sources of supply; orders are relatively small at first, but have the potential to grow rapidly if the suppliers are reliable.

Source: Author.

Note: [a]For the countries in each of these rings, see Figure 2.2.

Several qualifications need to be mentioned concerning the schematic, purposefully oversimplified locational patterns identified in Table 2.3 and Figure 2.2. These production frontiers represent general trends that can vary by industry, by specific products, and by time period. More detailed analyses that trace the global sourcing of particular products over time are required to explore the factors that lead to shifts in these linkages. Two examples will illustrate the complexity of these arrangements.

The first example focuses on large-volume discount stores such as Kmart and Wal-Mart. According to Table 2.3, they should source primarily from the three outer rings of the production frontiers, but our direct research indicates that these discounters also are prominent buyers in the second ring of East Asian NICs. Why?

The reason is twofold. Apparel factories in relatively high-wage countries like Taiwan and South Korea work with anywhere from five to 20 clients (buyers) in a year. Although Kmart and Wal-Mart pay much less than department stores and specialty retailers like Macy's or Liz Claiborne, the factories use these discounters' large-volume orders to smooth out their production schedules so they don't have gaps or downtime. The other side of the equation is the discounter's vantage point. Kmart and Wal-Mart tend to source their most expensive, complicated items in the second-ring countries (e.g., infant's wear with a lot of embroidery). Thus, they are using the more expensive and skilled workers in the NICs to produce relatively high-quality merchandise.

Figure 2.2 Production Frontiers for Global Sourcing by US Retailers: The Apparel Industry

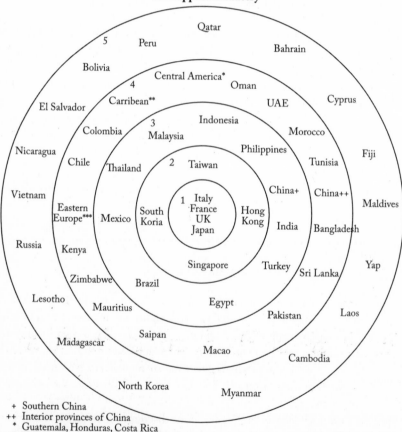

+   Southern China
++   Interior provinces of China
*   Guatemala, Honduras, Costa Rica
**   Dominican Republic, Jamaica, Haiti
***   Poland, Hungary, Czechoslovakia, Bulgaria

Source: Author.

A second illustration deals with the upper-end retailers. Large apparel retailers like The Limited and The Gap, and brand-named companies like Phillips-Van Heusen and Levi Strauss, tend to source heavily in the second and third rings of Figure 2.2, but they also buy from countries located in the fourth and even the fifth rings. The reason they are positioned in the outer reaches of the production frontiers is that these companies engage in 'price averaging' across their different manufacturing sites. A company like Phillips-Van Heusen, the number-one seller of men's dress shirts in the United States, is confident that its quality control procedures will allow it to produce identical dress shirts in its factories in the United States, Taiwan, Sri Lanka, or El Salvador. This also permits these companies to keep some of their production in, or close to, the United States for quick response to unexpectedly high demand for popular items as well as to gain the goodwill of the American consuming public.

Figure 2.2 highlights some methodological difficulties raised by the commodity chains perspective. Nation-states are not the ideal unit of analysis for establishing global sourcing patterns, since individual countries are tied to the world economy through a variety of export roles (Gereffi, 1989a, 1992). Production actually takes place in specific regions or industrial districts *within countries* that have very different social and economic characteristics (Porter, 1990). Where commodity chains 'touch down' in a country is an important determinant of the kind of production relationships that are established with retailers. Thus there can be several forms of international sourcing within a single nation.[29]

In the People's Republic of China, for example, Guangdong Province has very substantial investments from Hong Kong and Taiwan, while Fujian Province has a natural geographical and cultural affinity for Taiwanese investors. These two provinces in China are part of a Greater China Economic Region that includes Hong Kong and Taiwan (see Chen, 1994). Thus China falls within both the third and the fourth rings of Figure 2.2: the quality and price of the products made in southern China (third ring) in affiliation with its East Asian NIC partners tend to be higher than for the goods produced in the interior provinces of China (fourth ring), where state enterprises are more prevalent.

Despite these qualifications, several generalizations can be made about the production frontiers identified in Figure 2.2. As one moves from the inner to the outer rings, the following changes are apparent: the cost of production decreases; manufacturing sophistication decreases; and the lead time needed for deliveries increases. Therefore, there is a strong tendency for the high-quality, multiple-season 'fashion' companies, as well as the more upscale department stores and specialty stores, to source their production from the three inner rings, while the price-conscious mass merchandisers and discount chains are willing to tolerate the lower quality and longer lead times that characterize production in the two outer rings. The 'industry scout' role played by certain importers is particularly important for this latter set of buyers, since these importers are willing to take the time needed to bring the new, low-cost production sites located in the fourth and fifth rings into global sourcing networks.

Triangle Manufacturing in Global Commodity Chains

How do the countries in the inner rings of our global sourcing chart deal with the maturing of their export industries? What mechanisms are utilized to ensure a smooth transition to higher-value-added activities? One of the most important adjustment mechanisms for maturing export industries in East Asia is the process of triangle manufacturing, which came into being in the 1970s and 1980s.

The essence of triangle manufacturing is that US (or other overseas) buyers place their orders with the NIC manufacturers they have sourced from in the past (e.g., Hong Kong or Taiwanese apparel firms), who in turn shift some or all of the requested production to affiliated offshore factories in one or more low-wage countries (e.g., China, Indonesia, or Vietnam). These offshore factories may or may not have equity investments by the East Asian NIC manufacturers: they can be wholly owned subsidiaries, joint-venture partners, or simply independent overseas contractors. The triangle is completed when the finished goods are shipped directly to the overseas buyer, under the import quotas issued to the exporting nation. Payments to the non-NIC factory usually flow through the NIC intermediary firm.[30]

Triangle manufacturing thus changes the status of the NIC manufacturer from a primary production contractor for the US buyers to a 'middleman' in the buyer-driven commodity chain. The key asset possessed by the East Asian NIC manufacturers is their long-standing link to the foreign buyers, which is based on the trust developed over the years in numerous successful export transactions. Since the buyer has no direct production experience, he prefers to rely on the East Asian NIC manufacturers he has done business with in the past to assure that the buyer's standards in terms of price, quality, and delivery schedules will be met by new contractors in other Third World locales. As the volume of orders in new production sites like China, Indonesia, or Sri Lanka increases, the pressure grows for the US buyers to eventually bypass their East Asian NIC intermediaries and deal directly with the factories that fill their large orders.

The process of third-party production began in Japan in the late 1960s, which relocated numerous plants and foreign orders to the East Asian NICs (often through Japanese trading companies or *sogo shosha*).[31] Today, the East Asian NICs, in turn, are transferring many of their factories and orders to China and a variety of Southeast Asian countries. Initially, triangle manufacturing was the result of US import quotas that were imposed on Hong Kong, Taiwan, South Korea, and Singapore in the 1970s. These quotas led to the search for new quota-free production sites in the region. Then in the late 1980s the move to other Asian and eventually Caribbean factories occurred because of domestic changes—increased labor costs, labor scarcity, and currency appreciations—in the East Asian NICs. The shift toward triangle manufacturing has been responsible for bringing many new countries into these production and export networks, including Sri Lanka, Vietnam, Laos, Mauritius, small Pacific islands (like Saipan and Yap), Central America, and Caribbean nations.

The importance of triangle manufacturing from a commodity chains perspective is threefold. First, it indicates that there are repetitive cycles as the production base for an industry moves from one part of the world to another. An important hypothesis here is that the 'window of opportunity' for each new production base (Japan – East Asian NICs – Southeast Asian countries – China – Vietnam – the Caribbean) is growing progressively shorter as more new entrants are brought into these global sourcing networks. The reasons include the fact that quotas on new exporting countries in apparel are being applied more quickly by the United States,[32] and technology transfer from the East Asian NICs is becoming more efficient.

The second implication of triangle manufacturing is for social embeddedness. Each of the East Asian NICs has a different set of preferred countries where they set up their new factories. Hong Kong and Taiwan have been the main investors in China (Hong Kong has taken a leading role in Chinese production of quota items like apparel made from cotton and synthetic fibers, while Taiwan is a leader for non-quota items like footwear,[33] as well as leather and silk apparel); South Korea has been especially prominent in Indonesia, Guatemala, the Dominican Republic, and now North Korea; and Singapore is a major investor in Southeast Asian sites like Malaysia and Indonesia. These production networks are explained in part by social and cultural networks (e.g., ethnic or familial ties, common language), as well as by unique features of a country's historical legacy (e.g., Hong Kong's British colonial ties gave it an inside track on investments in Jamaica).

A final implication of the GCC framework is that triangle manufacturing has allowed the East Asian NICs to move beyond OEM production. Most of the leading Hong Kong apparel manufacturers have embarked on an ambitious program of forward integration from apparel manufacturing into retailing. Almost all of the major Hong Kong apparel manufacturers now have their own brand names and retail chains for the clothing they make. These retail outlets began selling in the Hong Kong market, but now there are Hong Kong-owned stores throughout East Asia (including China), North America, and Europe.[34] These cycles of change for East Asian manufacturers suggest the need for more elaborated product life cycle theories of Third World industrial transformation.

Conclusion

The role of the main economic agents in buyer-driven commodity chains is far from static. The sources of change are rooted in economic and political factors, plus the shifting organizational patterns of the distinct segments of GCCs. Several trends are particularly noteworthy. First, there has been an increased concentration of buying power in the leading US retail chains. This has been the result of spectacular growth strategies by a few companies (especially the large-volume discount stores like Wal-Mart in the 1980s and Kmart in the 1970s), slumping performance by several established retail leaders (such as Sears Roebuck and Montgomery Ward), and many bankruptcies in the small- and large-firm retail sector.

Second, at the same time as there has been a consolidation in the buying power of major retail chains, there has been a proliferation of overseas factories (especially in Asia) in most consumer-goods industries. In several notable cases, like garments and shoes, there is currently a substantial excess production capacity worldwide that will lead to numerous plant closings or consolidations in major exporting countries, such as the People's Republic of China. This combination of concentrated buying power in the retail/wholesale sector and excess capacity in overseas factories has permitted the big buyers in GCCs to simultaneously lower the prices they are paying for goods and dictate more stringent performance standards for their vendors (e.g., more buying seasons, faster delivery times, and better quality) in order to increase their profits.

Third, big buyers are acutely sensitive to political factors that can affect global supply networks and they currently are in a position to alter overseas production patterns accordingly. For example, during the recent debate in the United States about renewing the People's Republic of China's most-favored-nation (MFN) status, several large retailers and importers decided to diversify or curtail their purchases from China.[35] This led overseas suppliers to scramble to set up production facilities in nations perceived to relatively 'safe' in terms of domestic political stability (such as Indonesia, Thailand, and Malaysia). In quota-restricted industries like garments, retailers and importers also have taken the lead in encouraging production in countries that have favorable quota arrangements with their main export markets in North America and Europe. In other words, quotas drive overseas investment decisions and thus help shape global commodity chains.

Fourth, the recent recession in the world economy has placed a premium on low-priced goods in developed-country markets. This has strengthened the position of the large-volume discount chains in the retail sector and led retailers and manufacturers alike to look for new ways to cut costs. This further enhances the impact of retailers on overseas production networks.

One trend we might look for in the future is the establishment of consolidated factory groups (perhaps involving linkages between manufacturers and trading companies) to counter the increased leverage of the large buying groups. These could be coordinated by manufacturers in the East Asian NICs, who continue to be the nexus for many of the orders placed by US big buyers. Exporters in the East Asian nations have accounted for much of the technology transfer to lower-cost production sites, they have access to export networks through their established contacts with the US buyers, and they still handle much of the quality control, financing, and shipping needed to get goods to their destination markets in a timely fashion.

Finally, despite the fact that the East Asian NICs have managed to move beyond OEM production through forward as well as backward integration in the apparel commodity chain, the implications of triangle manufacturing for downstream exporters in Southeast Asia, Latin America, and Africa are not so promising. Genuine development in these countries is likely to be truncated by the vulnerabilities implied by their export-processing role in global sourcing networks. The main assets that Third World exporters possess in buyer-driven commodity chains are low-cost labor and abundant quotas. These are notoriously unstable sources of competitive advantage, however.

Few countries in the world have been able to generate the backward and forward linkages, technological infrastructure, and high levels of local value added of the East Asian NICs. Even the obvious job creation and foreign exchange benefits of export-oriented industrialization for Third World nations can become liabilities when foreign buyers or their East Asian intermediaries decide because of short-term economic or political considerations to move elsewhere. Triangle manufacturing is most advantageous to the overseas buyers and intermediaries in buyer-driven commodity chains. The long-run benefits for Third World countries occur only if exporting becomes the first step in a process of domestically integrated development.

Notes

The research for this chapter was funded by grants from the Chiang Ching-Kuo Foundation for International Scholarly Exchange (United States), based in Taiwan, as well as the University Research Council at Duke University. I gratefully acknowledge these sources of support. I also appreciate the research assistance of Jeffrey Weiss at Duke, and the detailed comments provided by Phyllis Albertson, Bradford Barham, Miguel Korzeniewicz, Stephen Maire, and Karen J. Sack on earlier drafts of this chapter.

1. The linkages between big buyers and their strategies of global sourcing were derived from numerous interviews carried out by the author in East Asia and the United States. A wide variety of trading companies, direct buying offices, and factories in

Taiwan, Hong Kong, South Korea, and the People's Republic of China were visited in August–October 1991 and September–December 1992. Interviews were also conducted in the headquarters of major US retailers and apparel firms in New York City and Los Angeles during the summers of 1991 and 1992.

2. The absence of factories also characterizes a growing number of US semiconductor houses that order customized as well as standard chips from outside contractors (Weber, 1991).

3. Orderly marketing agreements were imposed by the United States on footwear exporters in Taiwan and South Korea in 1977, but these were rescinded in 1981.

4. This used to be known as 807-production in the Caribbean and the Far East, and *maquiladora* assembly in Mexico. Now there is a new US tariff classification system called the Harmonized Tariff Schedule that replaces the 807 section with a 9802 tariff code. The basic idea in this system is to allow a garment that has been assembled offshore using US-made and -cut parts to be assessed a tariff only on the value added by offshore labor.

5. The much-publicized bankruptcy of R. H. Macy & Company in 1992 is a recent example of the competitive problems that have affected the traditional department store (Strom, 1992).

6. Garment manufacturers have been required to add more buying seasons, offer a greater variety of clothes, agree to mandatory buy-back arrangements for unsold merchandise, provide retailer advertising allowances, and so on.

7. These new technologies include: electronic data interchange (EDI), which is a system for communicating to the retailer what is selling well and what needs to be replenished; computerized point-of-service inventory control; merchandising processing systems that monitor cash flows from order placement to shipping to billing and payment; and electronic mail hook-ups for every online store in worldwide networks of retail outlets.

8. Enhanced price competition is compatible with oligopoly because the economies of scale and scope of large-volume discount chains lead to high concentration levels in the retail sector, at the same time as the discounters stimulate considerable price competition because of their low-income customer base.

9. Many department stores carry familiar household names: Macy's, Bloomingdale's, Jordan Marsh, Mervyn's, Nordstrom, Dillard, Filene's, Kaufmann's, Saks Fifth Avenue. Numerous American retail chains today are owned by holding companies, such as the May Department Stores Company, Federated Department Stores, and Dayton Hudson. In Europe, where consumers were more inclined to shuttle from store to store for their individual apparel and accessory needs, the department store never developed into the prominent retailing institution that it has in the mass market of the United States.

10. General merchandise retailers provide a broad selection of 'soft goods' (including apparel and home furnishings) and 'hard goods' (appliances, hardware, auto, and garden supplies, etc.).

11. The best-known mass merchandising chains are Sears Roebuck & Co., Montgomery Ward, and Woolworth Corporation. These stores are a notch below the department stores in the quality of their merchandise and their prices, but they offer more service and brand-name variety than the large-volume discount retailers. In terms of their overall position in American retailing, though, department stores and mass merchandisers face similar competitive environments.

12. The three most prominent discount chains today are Wal-Mart, Kmart, and Target. Discount chains may focus on a specific product, such as shoes (Payless ShoeSource, Pic 'n Pay, and the 550-store Fayva Shoes retail chain owned by Morse Shoe). Historically, discount retail chains differed from department stores because the former carried broader assortments of hard goods (e.g., auto accessories, gardening equipment, housewares) and they relied heavily on self-service.

13. Department stores have tried to simulate a specialty-store ambience through the creation of 'store-within-a-store' boutiques, each accommodating a particular company (like Liz Claiborne or Calvin Klein) or a distinct set of fashion tastes. Similarly, Woolworth Corporation has shed its mass merchandising image by incorporating dozens of specialty formats in its portfolio of 6,500 US stores, including Foot Locker, Champs Sports, Afterthoughts accessories, and The San Francisco Music Box Co. Specialty stores now account for about half of Woolworth's annual revenue, up from 29% in 1983 (Miller, 1993).

14. The Gap, one of the most popular and profitable specialty clothing chains in American retailing today, only sells clothes under its own private label. In 1991, The Gap surpassed Liz Claiborne Inc. to become the second-largest clothes brand in the United States after Levi Strauss (Mitchell, 1992). The Limited is another major force in specialty apparel. It is regarded as the world's largest retailer of women's clothing. The Limited is composed of 17 divisions (such as Victoria's Secret, Lerner, Lane Bryant, and Structure), more than 4,100 stores, 75,000 employees, and 1991 sales of $6.3 billion.

15. Kmart's net income in 1990 recovered to $756 million, after its nosedive to $323 million in 1989. One of the areas where Kmart has been lagging, however, is its electronic data interchange (EDI) systems. In 1990 it embarked on a six-year store modernization program. Kmart management hopes that point-of-sale systems, a satellite network, and automated replenishment combined with just-in-time merchandise delivery will improve the performance of its 2,400 general merchandise stores. Kmart also has 2,000 specialty retail stores, including Waldenbooks, Payless Drug Stores, and PACE Membership Warehouse.

16. At the end of 1985, nearly 60% of mothers with children under 18 were working, according to Labor Department figures, up nearly 5% from one year earlier,

17. Between 1977 and 1989, the richest 1% of American families reaped 60% of the growth in after-tax income of all families and an even heftier three-fourths of the gain in pre-tax income, while the pre-tax income of the bottom 40% of American families declined (Nasar, 1992). Similarly, a detailed study on family income prepared by the House Ways and Means Committee of the US Congress found that from 1979 to 1987 the standard of living for the poorest fifth of the American population fell by 9%, while the living standard of the top fifth rose by 19% (Harrison and Bluestone, 1990: xi).

18. The 18-year-old Foot Locker chain, with 1,500 US stores and $1.6 billion in annual sales, has generated an entire family of spin-offs, including Kids Foot Locker, Lady Foot Locker, and now World Foot Locker. Woolworth, which already garners 40% of its sales in foreign countries, plans to add 1,000 Foot Locker stores in Western Europe by the end of the decade (Miller, 1993).

19. For example, Payless Shoe Source International, the largest US footwear importer, is owned by May Department Stores; and Meldisco, a division of Melville Corporation,

handles the international purchasing of shoes for Kmart. Pagoda Trading Co., the second biggest US shoe importer, was acquired three years ago by Brown Shoe Co., the largest US footwear manufacturer.

20. Associated Merchandising Corporation (AMC) is the world's largest retail buying group. It consolidates the overseas purchasing requirements of 40 member department stores, and it sources products from nearly 70 countries through its extensive network of buying offices in Asia, Europe, and Latin America.

21. Many brand-named companies like Liz Claiborne and Nike don't allow their products to be sold by discount stores or mass merchandisers, which has prompted the proliferation of 'private label' merchandise (i.e., store brands).

22. Sears Roebuck, Montgomery Ward, and Macy's were the first US companies to establish direct buying offices in Hong Kong in the 1960s. However, the really big direct orders came when Kmart and J. C. Penney set up their Hong Kong buying offices in 1970; within the next couple of years, these sprawling merchandisers had additional offices in Taiwan, South Korea, and Singapore. By the mid-1970s, many other retailers such as May Department Stores, AMC, and Woolworth jumped on the direct buying bandwagon in the Far East.

23. The early importers with offices in the Far East were Japanese and American companies like Mitsubishi/CITC (a Japanese-US joint venture), C. Itoh, Manow, and Mercury.

24. For example, Payless ShoeSource International, Pagoda, and E. S. Originals are large importers that deal exclusively in footwear.

25. There are different importers for women's shoes versus men's shoes, dress shoes versus casual footwear, women's dresses versus men's suits, adult versus children's clothes, and so on.

26. Nike, Reebok, and L. A. Gear are the major brand-named companies in athletic footwear, while Armani, Polo/Ralph Lauren, and Donna Karan are premium labels in clothes. However, all of these companies have diversified their presence in the apparel market and put their labels on a wide range of clothes, shoes, and accessories (handbags, hats, scarves, belts, wallets, etc.).

27. 'Contract manufacturing' is more accurate than the commonly used terms 'international subcontracting' or 'commercial subcontracting' (Holmes, 1986) to describe what the East Asian NICs have excelled at. Contract manufacturing refers to the production of finished goods according to full specifications issued by the buyer, while 'subcontracting' actually means the production of components or the carrying out of specific labor processes (e.g., stitching) for a factory that makes the finished item. Asian contract manufacturers (also known as contractors or vendors) have extended their production networks to encompass domestic as well as international subcontractors.

28. Taiwan and Hong Kong have multilayered domestic subcontracting networks, including large firms that produce key intermediate inputs (like plastics and textiles), medium-sized factories that do final product assembly, and many small factories and household enterprises that make a wide variety of components.

29. In Mexico, for instance, there is a vast difference between the *maquilada* export plants along the Mexico-US border that are engaged in labor-intensive garment and electronics assembly, and the new capital- and technology-intensive firms in the automobile and computer industries that are located further inland in Mexico's northern states. These

latter factories use relatively advanced technologies to produce high-quality exports, including components and subassemblies like automotive engines. They pay better wages, hire larger percentages of skilled male workers, and use more domestic inputs than the traditional *maquiladora* plants that combine minimum wages with piecework and hire mostly unskilled women (Gereffi, 1991).

30. Typically, this entails back-to-back letters of credit: the overseas buyer issues a letter of credit to the NIC intermediary, who then addresses a second letter of credit to the exporting factory.

31. The industries that Japan transferred to the East Asian NICs are popularly known as the 'three Ds': dirty, difficult, and dangerous.

32. This may change if a new General Agreement on Tariffs and Trade is signed.

33. After controls were relaxed on Taiwanese investments in the People's Republic of China in the late 1980s, around 500 footwear factories were moved from Taiwan to China in less than two years. Although China recently passed Taiwan as the leading footwear exporter to the United States (in terms of pairs of shoes), it is estimated that nearly one-half of China's shoe exports come from Taiwanese owned or managed firms recently transferred to the mainland (author interviews with footwear industry experts in Taiwan).

34. A good example of this is the Fang Brothers, one of the principal suppliers for Liz Claiborne, who now have several different private-label retail chains (Episode, Excursion, Jessica, and Jean Pierre) in a variety of countries including the United States.

35. During an October 1991 interview in the Hong Kong office of one of the largest US footwear importers, I was told that the American headquarters of the company ordered 25% of the importer's purchases from the People's Republic of China to be shifted to Indonesia within one year to avoid the supply disruptions that would occur if China's MFN Status were denied.

References

AAMA (American Apparel Manufacturers Association). 1991. *FOCUS: 1991.* Washington, DC: AAMA.

Bluestone, Barry, Patricia Hanna, Sarah Kuhn, and Laura Moore. 1981. *The Retail Revolution: Market Transformation, Investment, and Labor in the Modern Department Store.* Boston: Auburn House Publishing Company.

Chen, Xiangming. 1994. 'The New Spatial Division of Labor and Commodity Chains in the Greater South China Economic Region.' In *Commodity Chains and Global Capitalism*, edited by Gary Gereffi and Miguel Korzeniewicz, 165–186. Westport, CT: Praeger.

Dicken, Peter. 1992. *Global Shift: The Internationalization of Economic Activity*, 2nd edition. New York: Guilford Publications.

Donaghu, Michael T. and Richard Barff. 1990. 'Nike Just Did It: International Subcontracting and Flexibility in Athletic Footwear Production.' *Regional Studies* 24(6): 537–552.

Doner, Richard F. 1991. *Driving a Bargain. Automobile Industrialization and Japanese Firms in Southeast Asia.* Berkeley: University of California Press.

Gereffi, Gary. 1989a. 'Rethinking Development Theory: Insights from East Asia and Latin America.' *Sociological Forum* 4(4): 505–533.

————. 1989b. 'Development Strategies and the Global Factory.' *Annals of the American Academy of Political and Social Science* 505: 92–104.

————. 1991. 'The 'Old' and 'New' Maquiladora Industries in Mexico: What is their Contribution to National Development and North American Integration?' *Nuestra Economía* 2(8): 39–63.

————. 1992. 'New Realities of Industrial Development in East Asia and Latin America: Global, Regional, and National Trends.' In *States and Development in the Asian Pacific Rim*, edited by Richard P. Appelbaum and Jeffrey Henderson, 85–112. Newbury Park, CA: Sage.

Gereffi, Gary and Miguel Korzeniewicz. 1990. 'Commodity Chains and Footwear Exports in the Semiperiphery.' In *Semiperipheral States in the World-Economy*, edited by William G. Martin, 45–68. Westport, CT: Greenwood Press.

Gereffi, Gary and Donald L. Wyman, eds. 1990. *Manufacturing Miracles: Paths of Industrialization in Latin America and East Asia*. Princeton, NJ: Princeton University Press.

Harris, Nigel. 1987. *The End of the Third World*. New York: Penguin Books.

Harrison, Bennett and Barry Bluestone. 1990. *The Great U-Turn: Corporate Restructuring and the Polarizing of America*. New York: Basic Books.

Henderson, Jeffrey. 1989. *The Globalisation of High Technology Production: Society, Space and Semiconductors in the Restructuring of the Modern World*. New York: Routledge.

Hill, Richard C. 1989. 'Comparing Transnational Production Systems: The Automobile Industry in the USA and Japan.' *International Journal of Urban and Regional Research* 13(3): 462–480.

Holmes, John. 1986. 'The Organizational and Locational Structure of Production Subcontracting.' In *Production, Work, and Territory: The Geographical Anatomy of Industrial Capitalism*, edited by Allen J. Scott and Michael Storper, 80–106. Boston, MA: Allen & Unwin.

Keesing, Donald B. 1983. 'Linking Up to Distant Markets: South to North Exports of Manufactured Consumer Goods.' *American Economic Review* 73(2): 338–342.

Lardner, James. 1988. 'The Sweater Trade-I.' *The New Yorker*, January 1, 39–73.

Legomsky, Joanne. 1986. 'The Europeanization of American Retailing.' *Standard & Poor's Industry Surveys*, April 3, R61–R65.

Miller, Annetta. 1993. 'A Dinosaur No More: Woolworth Corp. Leaves Dime Stores Far Behind.' *Newsweek*, January 4, 54–55.

Mitchell, Russell. 1992. 'The Gap: Can the Nation's Hottest Retailer Stay on Top?' *Business Week*, March 9, 58–64.

Mody, Ashoka and David Wheeler. 1987. 'Towards a Vanishing Middle: Competition in the World Garment Industry.' *World Development* 15(10/11): 1269–1284.

Nasar, Sylvia. 1992. 'The 1980's: A Very Good Time for the Very Rich.' *New York Times*, March 5, 1A.

Piore, Michael J. and Charles F. Sabel. 1984. *The Second Industrial Divide*. New York: Basic Books.

Porter, Michael E. 1990. *The Competitive Advantage of Nations*. New York: Free Press.

Rabach, Eileen and Eun Mee Kim. 1994. 'Where Is the Chain in Commodity Chains? The Service Sector Nexus.' In *Commodity Chains and Global Capitalism*, edited by Gary Gereffi and Miguel Korzeniewicz, 123–141. Westport, CT: Praeger.

Reich, Robert B. 1991. *The Work of Nations*. New York: Alfred A. Knopf.

Ross, Robert J. S. and Kent C. Trachte. 1990. *Global Capitalism: The New Leviathan*. Albany, NY: State University of New York Press.

Rothstein, Richard. 1989. *Keeping Jobs in Fashion: Alternatives to the Euthanasia of the US Apparel Industry*. Washington, DC: Economic Policy Institute.

Sack, Karen J. 1989. 'Department Stores: Avoiding the Way of the Dinosaur.' *Standard and Poor's Industry Surveys*, April 20, R77–R82.

Saporito, Bill. 1991. 'Is Wal-Mart Unstoppable?' *Fortune*, May 6, 50–59.

Storper, Michael and Bennett Harrison. 1991. 'Flexibility, Hierarchy and Regional Development: The Changing Structure of Industrial Production Systems and their Forms of Governance in the 1990s.' *Research Policy* 20(5): 407–422.

Strom, Stephanie. 1992. 'Department Stores' Fate: Bankruptcies Like Macy's Overshadowing Strong Consumer Loyalty, Experts Assert.' *New York Times*, February 3, C1.

Taplin, Ian M. 1994. 'Strategic Reorientations of US Apparel Firms.' In *Commodity Chains and Global Capitalism*, edited by Gary Gereffi and Miguel Korzeniewicz, 205–222. Westport, CT: Praeger.

Waldinger, Roger. 1986. *Through the Eye of the Needle: Immigrants and Enterprise in New York's Garment Trades*. New York: New York University Press.

Weber, Samuel. 1991. 'A New Endangered Species: Mulling a Fabless Future.' *Electronics* 64(7): 36–38.

3

International Trade and Industrial Upgrading in the Apparel Commodity Chain

Globalization has altered the competitive dynamics of nations, firms, and industries. This is most clearly seen in changing patterns of international trade, where the explosive growth of imports in developed countries indicates that the center of gravity for the production and export of many manufactures has moved to an ever expanding array of newly industrializing economies (NIEs) in the Third World. This shift is central to the 'East Asian Miracle', which refers to the handful of high-performing Asian economies that have attained lofty per capita growth rates, relatively low income inequality, high educational attainment, record levels of domestic saving and investment, and booming exports from the 1960s to the mid-1990s (World Bank, 1993). Regardless of whether the growth is due to productivity gains or to capital accumulation (Krugman, 1994; Young, 1994, 1995), their economic achievement is largely attributed to the adoption of export-oriented industrialization as the region's main development strategy.

This view of international trade as the fulcrum for sustained economic growth in East Asia, while unassailable in its macroeconomic basics, nonetheless leaves a number of critical questions unanswered in terms of the microinstitutional foundations supporting East Asian development. Why were Japan and the East Asian NIEs (South Korea, Taiwan, Hong Kong, and Singapore) so successful in exporting to distant Western markets, given the formidable spatial and cultural distances that had to be bridged? How were these East Asian nations able to *sustain* their high rates of export-oriented growth over three to four decades, in the face of a variety of adverse economic factors such as oil price hikes, rising wage rates, labor shortages, currency appreciations, a global recession, and spreading protectionism in their major export markets? Under what conditions can trade-based growth become a vehicle for genuine industrial upgrading, given the frequent criticisms made of low-wage, low-skill, assembly-oriented export activities? Do Asia's accomplishments in trade-led industrialization contain significant lessons for other regions of the world?

This chapter will address these questions using a global commodity chains framework. A commodity chain refers to the whole range of activities involved in the design, production, and marketing of a product. A critical distinction in this approach is between buyer-driven and producer-driven commodity chains. Japan in the 1950s and 1960s, the East Asian NIEs during the 1970s and 1980s, and China in the 1990s became world-class exporters primarily by mastering the dynamics of buyer-driven commodity chains, which supply a wide range of labor-intensive consumer products such as apparel, footwear, toys, and sporting goods. The key to success in East Asia's buyer-driven chains was to move from the mere assembly of imported inputs (traditionally associated with export-processing zones) to a more domestically integrated and higher value-added form of exporting known alternatively as full-package supply or OEM (original equipment manufacturing) production.[1] Subsequently, Japan and some firms in the East Asian NIEs pushed beyond the OEM export role to original brand-name manufacturing (OBM) by joining their production expertise with the design and sale of their own branded merchandise in domestic and overseas markets.

From a global commodity chains perspective, East Asia's transition from assembly to full-package supply derives in large measure from its ability to establish close linkages with a diverse array of lead firms in buyer-driven chains. Lead firms are the primary sources of material inputs, technology transfer, and knowledge in these organizational networks. In the apparel commodity chain, different types of lead firms use different networks and source in different parts of the world. Retailers and marketers tend to rely on full-package sourcing networks, in which they buy ready-made apparel primarily from Asia, where manufacturers in places like Hong Kong, Taiwan, and South Korea have historically specialized in this kind of production. As wage levels in those countries have gone up, East Asian manufacturers have tended to develop multilayered global sourcing networks where low-wage assembly can be done in other parts of Asia, Africa, and Latin America, while the NIE manufacturers play a critical coordinating role in the full-package production process. Branded manufacturers, by contrast, tend to create production networks that focus on apparel assembly using imported inputs. Whereas full-package sourcing networks are generally global, production networks established by branded manufacturers are predominantly regional. US manufacturers go to Mexico and the Caribbean Basin, European Union firms look to North Africa and Eastern Europe, and Japan and the East Asian NIEs look to lower-wage regions within Asia.

Industrial upgrading, from this perspective, involves organizational learning to improve the position of firms or nations in international trade networks (Gereffi and Tam, 1998). Participation in global commodity chains is a necessary step for industrial upgrading because it puts firms and economies on potentially dynamic learning curves. There are many obstacles, however, to moving up these chains from labor-intensive activities like export-oriented assembly, to more integrated forms of manufacturing like OEM and OBM production, to the most profitable and/or skill-intensive economic activities such as breakthrough innovations in new goods and services, design, marketing, and finance. Therefore, we need to address not only *why* industrial upgrading occurs in global commodity chains, but also *how* it occurs. A commodity chains framework that attempts to link international trade and industrial upgrading must specify: the *mechanisms* by which organizational learning occurs in trade networks; typical *trajectories* among export roles; and the *organizational conditions* that facilitate industrial upgrading moves such as the shift from assembly to full-package networks.

The economic theory of industrial upgrading is that as capital (both human and physical) becomes more abundant relative to labor and the endowments of other countries, nations develop comparative advantages in capital- and skill-intensive industries (Porter, 1990). This chapter will show, however, that upgrading does not occur to a random set of capital- or skill-intensive industries or activities, but rather to products that are organizationally related through the lead firms in global commodity chains.

The microfoundations of this upgrading pattern involve both forward (marketing) and backward (sourcing) linkages from production, and the kind of learning that occurs across these segments. With regard to marketing, countries that are upgrading within commodity chains have already identified the buyers for their products within the chains. The implication is that marketing outside the chain is more difficult due to search costs and the fact that foreign buyers provide access to information that assists local suppliers in their export and marketing efforts (Rhee et al., 1984). For sourcing linkages, both technological and tacit knowledge exists about how and where to establish new export capacity for finished products. There is a clear pattern of organizational succession in buyer-driven chains, however, whereby foreign buyers that occupy distinct positions (or price points) in the retail sectors of their home markets source from each of the major Asian exporting nations in distinctive cycles or sequences (Gereffi, 1994). This succession mechanism drives the geographical expansion of global sourcing networks, as buyers for less expensive goods are pushed into lower-cost production sites, and it is also crucial for industrial upgrading because the higher price points of fashionable retailers reflect more complicated products and differentiated styles.

Our empirical focus will be the apparel industry, with an emphasis on Asia. This selection is justified on multiple grounds. Apparel is one of the oldest and largest export industries in the world. Most nations produce for the international textile and apparel market (Dickerson, 1995: 6), making this one of the most global of all industries. Apparel is the typical 'starter' industry for countries engaged in export-oriented industrialization, and it played the leading role in

East Asia's early export growth. The apparel industry is a prototypical buyer-driven commodity chain because it generates a highly aggressive pattern of global sourcing through a variety of organizational channels, including giant cost-driven discount chains (Wal-Mart, Kmart, or Target), upscale branded marketers (Liz Claiborne, Tommy Hilfiger, Nautica), apparel specialty stores (The Limited, The Gap), and burgeoning private label programs among mass-merchandise retailers (J. C. Penney, Sears). Finally, apparel embodies two contrasting production systems characteristic of buyer-driven chains: the assembly and the OEM models. Whereas the assembly model is a form of industrial subcontracting in which manufacturers provide the parts for simple assembly to garment sewing plants, the OEM model is a form of commercial subcontracting in which the buyer–seller linkage between foreign merchants and domestic manufacturers allows for a greater degree of local learning about the upstream and downstream segments of the apparel chain.

The organization of the chapter is as follows. First, the global commodity chains framework will be outlined, with an emphasis on the structure and dynamics of buyer-driven chains. Second, the role of each of the big buyers (retailers, marketers and manufacturers) in forging global sourcing networks in the apparel commodity chain will be highlighted. Third, an industrial upgrading framework is introduced to help account for the most significant trade shifts among global apparel exporters. The organizational basis for upgrading is associated with different kinds of buyer-seller links, and distinct patterns of organizational succession among foreign buyers in exporting nations. Fourth, from a commodity chains perspective, industrial upgrading is associated with the process of building, extending, coordinating and completing integrated production and trade networks in Asia. These networks are resilient forms of social capital that are a valuable competitive asset in the global economy. Fifth, we will assess the implications of the Asian experience for the sourcing of apparel in North America. The United States currently is importing garments from Mexico and the Caribbean Basin countries that have been assembled using US inputs. Our analysis of industrial upgrading in Asia suggests that Mexico will have to move beyond assembly production and establish a full-package or OEM model in order to promote an integrated North American commodity chain. If full-package supply does succeed in Mexico, however, it will utilize very different kinds of networks than those found in Asia because of inter-regional variations in the industrial and spatial organization of the apparel commodity chain.

Producer-Driven and Buyer-Driven Global Commodity Chains

In global capitalism, economic activity is not only international in scope, it is also global in organization. 'Internationalization' refers to the geographic spread of economic activities across national boundaries. As such, it is not a new phenomenon; indeed, it has been a prominent feature of the world economy since at least the 17th century when colonial empires began to carve up the globe in search of raw materials and new markets for their manufactured exports. 'Globalization' is much more recent than internationalization because it implies the functional integration and coordination of internationally dispersed activities.

Industrial and commercial capital have promoted globalization by establishing two distinct types of international economic networks: 'producer-driven' and 'buyer-driven' commodity chains (Figure 3.1). Producer-driven commodity chains are those in which large, usually transnational, manufacturers play the central roles in coordinating production networks (including their backward and forward

Figure 3.1 The Organization of Producer-Driven and Buyer-Driven Global Commodity Chains

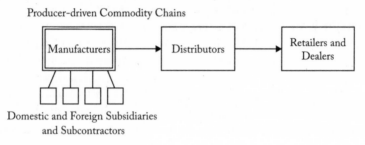

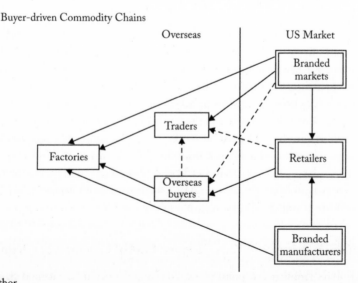

Source: Author.

Note: Solid arrow are primary relationship; dashed arrows are secondary relationships.

linkages). This is characteristic of capital- and technology-intensive industries such as automobiles, aircraft, computers, semiconductors, and heavy machinery. The automobile industry offers a classic illustration of a producer-driven chain, with multilayered production systems that involve thousands of firms (including parents, subsidiaries and subcontractors). The average Japanese automaker's production system, for example, comprises 170 first-tier, 4,700 second-tier, and 31,600 third-tier subcontractors (Hill, 1989: 466). Florida and Kenney (1991) have found that Japanese automobile manufacturers actually reconstituted many aspects of their home-country supplier networks in North America. Doner (1991) extends this framework to highlight the complex forces that drive Japanese automakers to create regional production schemes for the supply of auto parts in a half-dozen nations in East and Southeast Asia. Henderson (1989) and Borrus (1997) also support the notion that producer-driven commodity chains have established an East Asian division of labor in their studies of the internationalization of the US and Japanese semiconductor industries.

Buyer-driven commodity chains refer to those industries in which large retailers, branded marketers, and branded manufacturers play the pivotal roles in setting up decentralized production networks in a variety of exporting countries, typically located in the Third World. This pattern of trade-led industrialization has become common in labor-intensive, consumer goods industries such as garments, footwear, toys, housewares, consumer electronics, and a variety of handicrafts. Production is generally carried out by tiered networks of Third World contractors that make finished goods to the specifications of foreign buyers.

Profitability is greatest in the relatively concentrated segments of global commodity chains characterized by high barriers to the entry of new firms. In producer-driven chains, manufacturers making advanced products like aircraft, automobiles, and computers are the key economic agents not only in terms of their earnings, but also in their ability to exert control over backward linkages with raw material and component suppliers, and forward linkages into distribution and retailing. The transnationals in producer-driven chains usually belong to global oligopolies. Buyer-driven commodity chains, by contrast, are characterized by highly competitive, locally owned, and globally dispersed production systems. Profits in buyer-driven chains derive not from scale, volume, and technological advances as in producer-driven chains, but rather from unique combinations of high-value research, design, sales, marketing, and financial services that allow the retailers, branded marketers, and branded manufacturers to act as strategic brokers in linking overseas factories with evolving product niches in the main consumer markets. Thus, whereas producer-driven commodity chains are controlled by industrial firms at the point of production, the main leverage in buyer-driven chains is exercised by retailers, marketers, and manufacturers through their ability to shape mass consumption via strong brand names and their reliance on global sourcing strategies to meet this demand.

The leading firms in producer-driven and buyer-driven commodity chains use barriers to entry to generate different kinds of 'rents' (broadly defined as returns from scarce assets) in global industries. These assets may be tangible (as with machinery), intangible (brands), or intermediate (as in marketing skills). Adapting and extending the typology of rents in Kaplinsky (1998), producer-driven chains rely primarily on *technology rents*, which arise from asymmetrical access to key product and process technologies; and *organizational rents*, which refer to a form of intra-organizational process know-how that originated in Japan, and is particularly significant in the transition from mass production to mass customization (or flexible production), involving a cluster of new organizational techniques such as just-in-time production, total quality control, modular production, preventive maintenance, and continuous improvement.

Buyer-driven chains are most closely tied to *relational rents*, which refer to several families of inter-firm relationships, including the techniques of supply-chain management that link large assemblers with small and medium-size enterprises, the construction of strategic alliances, and small firms clustering together in a particular locality and manifesting elements of collective efficiency associated with OEM production;[2] *trade-policy rents*, understood as the scarcity value created by protectionist trade policies like apparel quotas; and *brand-name rents*, which refer to the returns from the product differentiation techniques used to establish brand-name prominence in major world markets.

In the apparel commodity chain, entry barriers are low for most garment factories, although progressively higher as one moves upstream to textiles and fibers; brand names and stores are alternative competitive assets firms can use to generate significant economic rents. The lavish advertising budgets and promotional campaigns required to create and sustain global brands, and the sophisticated and costly information technologies employed by today's mega-retailers to develop 'quick response' programs[3] that increase revenues and lower risks by getting suppliers to manage inventory, illustrate recent techniques that have allowed retailers and marketers to displace traditional manufacturers as the leaders in many consumer goods industries.

Big Buyers and Global Sourcing

A fundamental restructuring is underway in the retail sector in the United States and other developed economies. The global retailing industry is dominated by large organizations that are moving toward greater specialization by product (the rise of specialty stores that sell only one item, such as clothes, shoes, or office supplies) and price (the growth of high-volume, low-cost discount chains). Furthermore, the process of filling the distribution pipeline is leading these retailers to develop strong ties with global suppliers, particularly in low-cost countries (Management Horizons, 1993). Nowhere are these changes more visible than in apparel, which is the top merchandise category for most consumer goods retailers. Between 1987 and 1991, the five largest softgoods chains in the United States increased their share of the national apparel market from 35% to 45% (Dickerson, 1995: 452). By 1995, the five largest US retailers—Wal-Mart, Sears, Kmart, Dayton Hudson,[4] and J. C. Penney—accounted for 68% of all apparel sales in publicly held retail outlets. The next top 24 retailers, all billion-dollar corporations, represented an additional 30% of these sales (Finnie, 1996: 22). The two top discount giants, Wal-Mart and Kmart, by themselves control one-quarter of all apparel (by unit volume, not value) sold in the United States.

Although the degree of market power that is concentrated in large US retailers may be extreme, owing to the recent spate of mergers and acquisitions in this sector, a similar shift in power from manufacturers to retailers and marketers appears to be underway in most developed nations. Retailing across the European Union has been marked by substantial concentration in recent years. In Germany, the five largest clothing retailers (C&A, Quelle, Metro/Kaufhof, Kardstadt, and Otto) in 1992 accounted for 28% of the EU's largest national economy, while the United Kingdom's two top clothing retailers (Marks and Spencer and the Burton Group) controlled over 25% of the UK market in 1994 (OETH, 1995: 11–13). Marks and Spencer, Britain's largest and most successful retailing firm with over 260 stores in the United Kingdom plus stores in other parts of Europe and Canada, itself buys about 20% of all the clothing made in Britain (Dickerson, 1995: 472). In both France and Italy, the role of independent retailers in the clothing market has declined since 1985, while the share of specialty chains, franchise networks, and hypermarkets is rising rapidly. In Japan, the 1992 revision of the Large Retail Store Law, which liberalized restrictions on the opening of new retail outlets, has caused a rapid increase in the number of large-volume retailers and suburban chain stores. The Japanese government predicts there will be 20% fewer retailers in Japan in the year 2000 than in 1985, mainly due to attrition among the small and medium retail stores (*Japan Textile News*, 1996).

From the vantage point of buyer-driven commodity chains, the major significance of growing retailer concentration is its tendency to augment global sourcing. As each type of organizational buyer in the apparel commodity chain has become more actively involved in offshore sourcing, the competition between retailers, marketers, and manufacturers has intensified, leading to a blurring of the traditional boundaries between these firms and a realignment of interests within the chain.

Retailers

In the past, retailers were the apparel manufacturer's main customers, but now they are increasingly becoming their competitors. As consumers demand better value, retailers have increasingly turned to imports. In 1975, only 12% of the apparel sold by US retailers was imported; by 1984, retail stores had doubled their use of imported garments (*AAMA*, 1984). According to unpublished data in the US Customs Service's Net Import File, retailers accounted for 48% of the total value of imports of the top 100 US apparel importers in 1993 (who collectively represent about one-quarter of all 1993 apparel imports); US apparel marketers, which perform the design and marketing functions but contract out the actual production of apparel to foreign or domestic sources, represented 22% of the value of these imports; and domestic producers made up an additional 20% of the total[5] (Jones, 1995: 25–26). The picture in Europe is strikingly similar. European retailers account for fully one-half of all apparel imports, and marketers or designers add roughly another 20% (Scheffer, 1994: 11–12).

In the 1980s, many retailers began to compete directly with the national brand names of apparel producers and marketers by expanding their sourcing of 'private label' (or store-brand) merchandise. This is sold more cheaply than the national brands but it also is more profitable to the retailers since they eliminate some of the middlemen in the chain. Private-label programs have led a growing number of merchants to take on the entrepreneurial functions of normal apparel manufacturers, such as product design, fabric selection and procurement, and garment production or sourcing. Private label goods, which constituted about 25% of the total US apparel market in 1993 (Dickerson, 1995: 460), can curtail the business of both manufacturers and well-known designer lines.

Take the case of J. C. Penney, which like Sears, has repositioned itself as primarily a softgoods retailer, and within softgoods has traded up from the mass merchandiser image to higher-cost product lines to lure the traditional department store customer. Squeezed between discounters and fashionable specialty stores, Penney initially tried to move upscale in the early 1980s, but it was snubbed by well-known women's brands like Liz Claiborne, Estée Lauder, and Elizabeth Arden, who turned their noses up at Penney's stodgy, middle-brow image. So Penney concentrated on converting its own private labels—such as Hunt Club, Worthington, Stafford, St. John's Bay, Arizona jeans, and Jacqueline Ferrar—into high-quality brand names, which began to pay considerable dividends at home and abroad. Today, J. C. Penney's private-label lines account for up to 60% of the women's apparel volume and they are the fastest growing portion of the chain's product mix (Dickerson, 1995: 460). Penney's house brands now form the backbone of its thriving overseas business, which includes J. C. Penney stores in Canada and Mexico, sales of its private label apparel in 300 department stores owned by Aoyama Trading, Japan's largest retailer of men's suits, plus licensing agreements in Portugal, Greece, Singapore, Indonesia, Chile, and Middle East locations like United Arab Emirates and Dubai (Ortega, 1994; Warfield et al., 1995: 46–47).

Branded Marketers

One of the most notable features of buyer-driven chains is the creation since the mid-1970s of prominent marketers whose brands are extremely well known, but that carry out no production whatsoever. These 'manufacturers without factories' include companies like Liz Claiborne, Nike, and Reebok, who literally were 'born global' since their sourcing has always been done overseas. As pioneers in global sourcing, branded marketers were instrumental in providing overseas suppliers with knowledge that later allowed them to upgrade their position in the apparel chain.

The cumulative and diffused aspect of this learning is reflected in the remarks of Jerome Chazen, one of the founders of Liz Claiborne, who comments on his company's early years in Asian apparel sourcing (Chazen, 1996: 42):

> Sourcing overseas seems commonplace nowadays. When we started our company in 1976, nobody in our price category did any sourcing overseas … But the [overseas] manufacturers with whom we dealt back then had little or no experience servicing the United States market. Thus, we had to train and develop them by supplying technical help, trim, findings, and virtually all components. While we counted on them for their labor, we had to tell them exactly how to use the basic skills of their people and we had to watch them carefully, every step of the way. Our manufacturers learned quickly, however. We tested some products with the first company we used in Taiwan, and we found we could deliver better products and better fabric at a better price than the competition and make a respectable margin. Everybody was happy … We were very much the leaders as importers of high-end merchandise. We sailed in uncharted waters, made our share of mistakes, and attained an enormous competitive advantage.
>
> The competition (both retail and wholesale) that followed us started from a different plateau. They demanded and received more from their manufacturers who, by this time, were much improved. It is as if many of Liz Claiborne's competitiors 'leapfrogged' us.

In order to deal with the influx of new competition, branded marketers like Liz Claiborne are adopting several strategic responses that will alter the content and scope of their global sourcing networks: they are discontinuing certain support functions (such as pattern grading, marker making, and sample making), and reassigning them to contractors; they are instructing the contractors where to obtain needed components, thus reducing their own purchase and redistribution activities; they are shrinking their supply chains, using fewer but more capable manufacturers; they are adopting more stringent vendor certification systems to improve performance; and they are shifting the geography of their sourcing configuration from Asia to the Western Hemisphere (see Chazen, 1996). In essence, marketers now recognize that overseas contractors have the capability to manage all aspects of the production process, which restricts the competitive edge of marketers to design and brands.

Branded Apparel Manufacturers

Given that foreign production can often provide similar quantity, quality, and service as domestic producers, but at lower prices, apparel manufacturers in developed countries have been caught in a squeeze. They are responding in several different ways. In the United States and Europe, an 'If you can't beat them, join them' attitude has evolved among many smaller and mid-sized apparel firms, who feel they can not compete with the low cost of foreign-made goods and thus they are defecting to the ranks of importers.

The decision of many larger manufacturers in developed countries, however, is no longer *whether* to engage in foreign production, but *how* to organize and manage it. These firms supply intermediate inputs (cut fabric, thread, buttons, and other trim) to extensive networks of offshore suppliers, typically located in neighboring countries with reciprocal trade agreements that allow goods assembled offshore to be re-imported with a tariff charged only on the value added by foreign labor. This kind of international subcontracting system exists in every region of the world. It is called the 807/9802 program or 'production sharing' in the United States (USITC, 1997), where the sourcing networks of US manufacturers are predominantly located in Mexico, Central America, and the Caribbean; in Europe, this is known as outward processing trade (OPT), and the principal suppliers are located in North Africa and Eastern Europe (OETH, 1995); and in Asia, manufacturers from relatively high-wage economies like Hong Kong have outward processing arrangements (OPA) with China and other low-wage nations (Birnbaum, 1993).

A significant countertrend is emerging among established apparel manufacturers, however, who are de-emphasizing their production activities in favor of building up the marketing side of their operations by capitalizing on both brand names and retail outlets. Sara Lee Corporation, one of the largest apparel producers in the United States, whose stable of famous brand names includes L'eggs hosiery, Hanes, Playtex, Wonderbras, Bali, and Coach leather products, to name a few, recently announced its plans to 'de-verticalize' its consumer-products divisions, a fundamental reshaping that would move it out of making the brand-name goods it sells. 'As the world opens up to do business,' according to a Sara Lee spokeswoman, 'the operating model for today's exemplary companies no longer needs to include significant manufacturing assets ... We've determined that we no longer need to own all the assets needed in manufacturing the products we sell' (Miller, 1997: A3). Other well-known apparel manufacturers like Phillips-Van Heusen and Levi Strauss and Co. are also emphasizing the need to build global brands, frequently through acquisitions of related consumer products lines, while many of their production facilities are being closed or sold to offshore contractors.

The strengthening of brand names has led to a new focus on 'concept stores' that typically feature all the products offered by manufacturers and marketers, such as Levi Strauss, Nike, Disney, and Warner Bros. These stores provide a direct link between manufacturers and consumers, bypassing the traditional role of retailers. Levi Strauss, the largest apparel company in the United States, had 126 Levi's retail stores in 1993, all operated by a retail specialist, Designs Inc. Over half of Levi Strauss's profits in 1993 were generated from overseas operations, which included about 900 franchised Levi's shops in 30 countries in Europe, Asia, and Latin America (Warfield et al., 1995: 80–81). Thus, a de-verticalization of production co-exists with a re-verticalization of brands and stores.

Trade Shifts and Industrial Upgrading in the Apparel Commodity Chain in Asia

The world textile and apparel industry has undergone several migrations of production since the 1950s and they all involve Asia. The first migration of the industry took place from North America and Western Europe to Japan in the 1950s and early 1960s, when Western textile and clothing production was displaced by a sharp rise in imports from Japan. The second supply shift was from Japan to the 'Big Three' Asian apparel producers (Hong Kong, Taiwan, and South Korea), which permitted the latter group to dominate global textile and clothing exports in the 1970s and 1980s. During the past 10–15 years, there has been a third migration of production—this time from the Asian Big Three to a number of other developing economies. In the 1980s, the principal shift was to mainland China, but it also encompassed several Southeast Asian nations and Sri Lanka. In the 1990s, the proliferation of new suppliers included South Asian and Latin American apparel exporters, with new entrants like Vietnam waiting in the wings (Khanna, 1993; Gereffi, 1996).

This most recent shift is seen in sharp relief in Table 3.1, which looks at apparel imports to the United States, the world's largest market. In 1983, the Asian 'Big Three' (Hong Kong, Taiwan, and South Korea), plus China, were responsible for

Table 3.1 Trends in US Apparel Imports by Region and Country

Country source	1983 value US$ million	(%)	1986 value US$ million	(%)	1990 value US$ million	(%)	1993 value US$ million	(%)	1995 value US$ million	(%)	1997 value US$ million	(%)
Northeast Asia												
China	759		1661		3439		6187		5895		7450	
Hong Kong	2249		3392		3977		4019		4342		4028	
Taiwan	1800		2621		2489		2332		2157		2166	
South Korea	1685		2581		3342		2539		1841		1665	
Macao	132		229		417		483		757		930	
Total	6625	68	10483	60	13663	54	15558	46	14991	38	16239	33
Southeast Asia												
Indonesia	75		269		645		1114		1359		1789	
Philippines	319		473		1083		1361		1633		1650	
Thailand	125		213		483		943		1172		1468	
Malaysia	93		257		604		973		1199		1244	
Singapore	193		386		621		517		424		290	
Total	806	8	1598	9	3436	13	4907	14	5787	15	6440	13

Cont'd.

Cont'd.

Country source	1983 value US$ million	(%)	1986 value US$ million	(%)	1990 value US$ million	(%)	1993 value US$ million	(%)	1995 value US$ million	(%)	1997 value US$ million	(%)
South Asia												
India	220		344		636		1079		1263		1508	
Bangladesh	7		154		422		740		1072		1442	
Sri Lanka	126		257		426		834		970		1242	
Pakistan	32		92		232		442		620		705	
Total	385	4	847	5	1716	7	3094	9	3924	10	4897	10
Central America and the Caribbean												
Dominican Republic			287		723		1443		1753		2234	
Honduras	20		32		113		510		934		1688	
El Salvador	7		11		54		251		583		1052	
Guatemala	4		20		192		552		691		976	
Costa Rica	64		142		384		653		757		851	
Jamaica	13		99		235		388		531		471	
Other CBI	142		207		284		218		239		392	
Total	389	4	797	5	1985	8	4015	12	5486	14	7665	16
Mexico	199	2	331	2	709	3	1415	4	2876	7	5350	11
All other countries	1328	14	3283	19	4009	16	4914	14	6595	17	7664	16
Total apparel	9731	100	17341	100	25518	100	33904	100	39660	100	48492	100

Source: Compiled from official statistics of the US Department of Commerce, US imports for consumption, customs value. Data before 1989 are estimated.

two-thirds of US apparel imports; by 1997, this share had dropped to one-third. During the past 15 years, we see two main trends in US apparel imports: (1) a shift within Asia from the 'Big Three' to the growing importance of successive waves of exporters: first China, followed by capitalist Southeast Asia, South Asia, and now socialist Southeast Asia (Vietnam, Laos, and Cambodia); and (2) a growth in non-Asian sources of apparel supply, especially the importance of Central America and the Caribbean as a region (which doubled its share of US apparel imports from 8% in 1990 to 16% in 1997) and, most notably, Mexico (which nearly quadrupled its share of US apparel imports from 3% to 11% in the same period).

How can we explain these trade shifts in the apparel commodity chain? A simple market explanation is that the most labor-intensive segments of the apparel commodity chain will be located in countries with the lowest wages. This account is supported by the sequential relocation of textile and apparel production from the United States and Western Europe to Japan, the Asian Big Three, and China, given that each new tier of entrants to the production hierarchy had significantly lower wage rates than their predecessors. The cheap-labor argument does not hold up as well, however, when we get to the proliferation of new Asian and Caribbean suppliers, whose US market share expanded even though their wage rates are often considerably higher than China's. Furthermore, although the share of US apparel exports represented by Hong Kong, South Korea, and Taiwan has declined during the past decade, these NIEs still rank among Asia's top apparel exporters to the United States in 1997, despite having the highest apparel labor costs in the region, excluding Japan (ILO, 1995: 35–36)

Exchange rates and trade policies help to explain some of these discrepancies. A critical factor in the sharp decline of Taiwan's and South Korea's apparel exports in the late 1980s was not only their rising wage rates, but the sharp appreciation of their local currencies vis-à-vis the US dollar after the Plaza Agreement was signed in 1985. Between 1985 and 1987, the Japanese yen was revalued by close to 40%, the New Taiwan dollar by 28%, and from 1986 to 1988 the Korean won appreciated by 17% (Bernard and Ravenhill, 1995: 180). The most important policies that shape US apparel imports from Asia, the Caribbean, and elsewhere, however, are quotas and preferential tariffs. Since the early 1970s, quotas on apparel and textile items were regulated by the Multi-Fiber Arrangement (MFA). The MFA has been used by the United States, Canada, and various European nations to impose quantitative import limits in a wide variety of product categories.

Although the clear intent of these policies was to protect developed country firms from a flood of low-cost imports that threatened to disrupt major domestic industries, the result was exactly the opposite. Protectionism heightened the competitive capabilities of developing country manufacturers, who learned to make sophisticated products that were more profitable than simple ones. Protectionism by the industrialized nations also diversified the scope of foreign competition, as an ever widening circle of exporters was needed to meet booming North American and European demand. In recent years, the creation of the European Union and the North American Free Trade Agreement (NAFTA) has led to preferential tariffs in these trade blocs, and promoted a growing consolidation of supply chains within regions.

The ability of the East Asian NIEs to sustain their export success over several decades, and to develop a multilayered sourcing hierarchy within Asia, is only partially related to wage rates and state policies. From a commodity chain perspective, East Asia must be viewed as part of an interrelated regional economy. The apparel export boom in the less developed southern tier of Asia has been driven to a significant extent by the industrial restructuring of the northern tier East Asian NIEs. As Northeast Asian firms began moving their production offshore, they devised ways to coordinate and control the sourcing networks they created. Ultimately, they focused on the more profitable design and marketing segments within the apparel commodity chain to sustain their competitive edge. This transformation can be conceptualized as a process of industrial upgrading, based in large measure on building various kinds of economic and social networks between buyers and sellers.

Industrial upgrading is a process of improving the ability of a firm or an economy to move to more profitable and/or technologically sophisticated capital- and skill-intensive economic niches. Industrial upgrading operates at several different levels of analysis: (1) *within factories*—upgrading involves moving from cheap to expensive items, from simple to complex products, and from small to large orders; (2) *within inter-firm enterprise networks*—upgrading involves moving from mass production of standardized goods to the flexible production of differentiated merchandise; (3) *within local or national economies*—upgrading involves moving from simple assembly of imported inputs to more integrated forms of OEM and OBM production, involving a greater use of forward and backward linkages at the local or national level; and (4) *within regions*—upgrading involves shifting from bilateral, asymmetrical, inter-regional trade flows to a more fully developed intra-regional division of labor incorporating all phases of the commodity chain from raw material supply, through production, distribution, and consumption.

While the national and international dimensions of industrial upgrading will be analyzed in the following sections of this chapter, the organizational basis for industrial upgrading within factories and enterprises will be outlined here. At the organizational level, industrial upgrading in East Asia's apparel commodity chain was produced by the information flows and learning potential associated with the buyer-seller links established by different types of lead firms (retailers, marketers, and manufacturers), and also by a distinctive pattern of organizational succession among these lead firms, who placed varied kinds of demands on their overseas suppliers.

The retailers, marketers, and manufacturers involved in global sourcing play similar structural roles as big buyers in the apparel commodity chain because they are all major garment importers. What differs across the production and sourcing networks they set up is not the role of these companies as organizational buyers, but rather the kind of information that is transmitted and thus the kind of local learning that can take place, given the position of each of the buyers in the chain. Manufacturers engaged in production-sharing arrangements, for example, require the lowest level of expertise from their apparel suppliers: the assembly of cut parts into finished garments. The knowledge gained is relevant only to the production segment of the commodity chain. Retailers and marketers, however, need suppliers with the capability to make garments and the logistical know-how to find all the parts needed in the finished product.[6]

Thus, they require more advanced full-package or OEM companies who, in turn, may subcontract out parts of these orders to other local firms. Besides learning how to organize production networks, full-package companies also learn about the marketing side of the business. It is this learning that allows the Asian suppliers to move from the OEM to the OBM export roles.

A second key mechanism for the industrial upgrading of apparel suppliers in Asia is the pattern of organizational succession among different kinds of buyers, who contribute in unique ways to the geographic expansion and industrial upgrading of these buyer-driven chains. There is a clear status hierarchy among US retailers that affects where and how they engage in global sourcing (Gereffi, 1994: 110–113). Fashion-oriented retailers that cater to an exclusive clientele for 'designer' products get their expensive, nationally branded goods from a small group of premium-quality apparel exporters (e.g., Italy, France, Japan). Department stores and specialty chains that emphasize private-label products source primarily from the East Asian NIEs and more established Third World apparel exporters. The large-volume discount stores that sell the most inexpensive products import from the lowest-cost suppliers, which frequently make relatively simple or standardized goods.

Organizational succession in the apparel commodity chain refers to the fact that different types of foreign buyers pass through each tier in the global sourcing matrix (see Figure 3.2 for an illustration), as the countries in that tier develop their export capability. Discount chains like Kmart and mass merchandisers like J. C. Penney, for example, frequently were the first buyers to open up the capabilities for volume production in new export sites in Asia. When department stores or specialty stores willing to pay significantly more money for higher quality versions of the same garments came along, the discounters and mass merchandisers were 'pushed out' of these factories. They either had to move to less experienced factories in the same country or to less expensive countries. The process was repeated as higher status buyers came in and gained factory space for more expensive merchandise. Generally some large-volume orders were retained, along with high-value but smaller orders, so that factories could smooth out their production schedules. This succession of foreign buyers thus permitted manufacturers to upgrade their facilities as they met buyer demands for more sophisticated products.[7]

Figure 3.2 Shifts in the Regional Structure of US Apparel Imports, 1986–1996

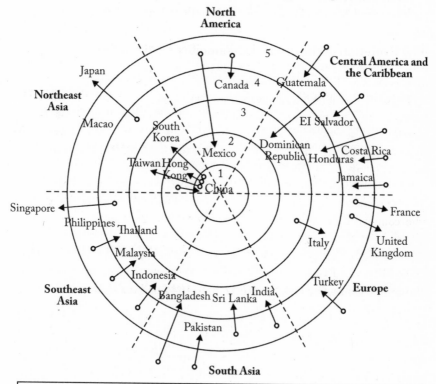

The rings indicate the share of total US imports in US dollars by partner country:
(1) 10%+   (2) 6.0%–9.9%   (3) 4.0%–5.9%   (4) 2.0%–3.9%   (5) 1.0%–1.9%
Total value of US clothing imports was $17.3 billion in 1986 and $41.7 billion in 1996.

Source: Compiled from official statistics of the US Department of Commerce, US imports for consumption, customs value.

Note: [1]The 1996 position corresponds to the ring where the country's name is located; the 1986 position, if different, is indicated by a small circle. The arrow represents the magnitude and direction of change over time.

Small trading companies operate as 'industry scouts' on the fringes of the international production frontier in order to help develop potential new sources of supply for the apparel commodity chain in places like Saipan, Yap, and Myanmar.

The difficult role of industry scouts is captured in the poignant remark of a long-time Asian sourcing specialist: 'Amateurs dream of traveling to the ends of the earth to produce garments. Professionals have already been to the ends of the earth, and they know the pressing there is not good' (Birnbaum, 1993: 139). With this conceptual backdrop to the organizational foundations of production and trade networks in buyer-driven commodity chains, we can now look more closely at the evolution of apparel trade patterns and industrial upgrading in Asia.

The Evolution of the Apparel Commodity Chain in Asia

Industrial upgrading within the apparel commodity chain in Asia involves the use of networks to create new sources of national and regional competitive advantage. We trace this process through four stages: the building of locally integrated manufacturing and marketing networks, involving close ties with foreign buyers; the internationalization of the apparel commodity chain to encompass new tiers of low-cost suppliers in Asia, in response to a combination of supply-side constraints and external pressures; the coordination of these buyer-driven chains through different types of trade networks; and the completion or regionalization of the apparel commodity chain within Asia. This industrial upgrading cycle in Asia is locally rooted, but it has important repercussions on how the apparel industry is organized in other regions of the world, such as North America and Europe.

Building Commodity Chains: OEM and OBM in East Asia

The East Asian NIEs are generally taken as the archetype for industrial upgrading among developing countries. They made a rapid transition from the initial assembly phase of export growth (typically utilizing export-processing zones located near major ports) to a more generalized system of incentives that applied to all export-oriented factories in their economies. The next stage for Taiwan, South Korea, Hong Kong, and Singapore was OEM production. The OEM model has the following features: the supplying firm makes a product according to the design specified by the buyer; the product is sold under the buyer's brand name; the supplier and buyer are separate firms; and the supplier lacks control over distribution. East Asian firms soon became full-range package suppliers for foreign buyers, and thereby forged an innovative entrepreneurial capability that involved the coordination of complex production, trade, and financial networks (Gereffi, 1995).

The OEM export role has many advantages. It enhances the ability of local entrepreneurs to learn the preferences of foreign buyers, including international standards for the price, quality, and delivery of export merchandise. It also generates substantial backward linkages in the domestic economy because OEM contractors are expected to develop reliable sources of supply for many inputs. Moreover, expertise in OEM production increases over time and it spreads across different types of activities. The OEM supplier learns much about the downstream and upstream segments of the apparel commodity chain from the buyer. This tacit knowledge can later become a powerful competitive weapon.

Particular places such as the East Asian NIEs thus retain an enduring competitive edge in export-oriented development. However, East Asian producers confront intense competition from lower-cost exporters in various parts of the Third World, and the price of their exports to Western nations has been further elevated by sharp currency appreciations during the past decade. Under these circumstances, it is advantageous to establish forward linkages to developed-country markets, where the biggest profits are made in buyer-driven commodity chains. Therefore, a number of firms in the East Asian NIEs that pioneered OEM are now pushing beyond it to the original brand-name manufacturing (OBM) role by integrating their manufacturing expertise with the design and sale of their own branded merchandise.

South Korea is the most advanced of the East Asian NIEs in OBM production, with Korean brands of automobiles (Hyundai), electronic products (Samsung), and household appliances (Samsung and Goldstar), among other items, being sold in North America, Europe, and Japan.[8] Taiwanese companies have pursued OBM in computers, bicycles, sporting equipment, and shoes, but not in apparel. In Hong Kong, clothing companies have been the most successful in making the shift from OEM to OBM. The women's clothing chain Episode, controlled by Hong Kong's Fang Brothers Group, one of the foremost OEM suppliers for Liz Claiborne in the 1970s and 1980s, has stores in 26 countries, only a third of which are in Asia. Giordano, Hong Kong's most famous clothing brand, has added to its initial base of garment factories 200 stores in Hong Kong and China, and another 300 retail outlets scattered across Southeast Asia and Korea. Hang Ten, a less-expensive line, has 200 stores in Taiwan, making it the largest foreign-clothing franchise on the island (Granitsas, 1998).

There have been significant reversals in the OBM experience, however. Mitac Corporation, the main competitor to Acer in Taiwan's personal computer market, reduced its own-brand computers from 70% of its total sales in 1990 to 40% in 1993 (Selwyn, 1993). Daewoo, Korea's third-largest appliance and consumer-electronics company (after Samsung and Goldstar), moved from years of brand-building back to the OEM game (*Asiaweek*, 1995).

Why has the OEM role proved so resilient? To a large degree, the answer lies with core competencies and networks. C. S. Ho, the president of Mitac, says that his firm was more profitable when it concentrated on its core competencies: 'We asked ourselves: What functions are we best at? Our strengths are in R&D, design and manufacturing. We are now focusing on designing and supplying products and key components for major OEM customers, whose brands are better-known but which have withdrawn from fully integrated manufacture' (Selwyn, 1993: 24). S. H. Bae, Chairman and Chief Executive Officer of Daewoo, says, 'Our strength is in manufacturing. If our margins are adequate, we don't mind making products for others' (*Asiaweek*, 1995: 56). Bae expects a shakeout in appliances and consumer electronics by the year 2000, and concludes that companies will have to become dominant producers in core products.

To keep OEM profitable under conditions of intense wage competition among developing countries and protectionism in Western markets, East Asian NIE companies have set up elaborate offshore production networks. Daewoo, for example, has 16 offshore plants in China, Vietnam, Central Asia, Europe and Mexico. Through worker-training programs, Bae claims that '[Daewoo's] Vietnam plant is almost as efficient as local ones' (*Asiaweek*, 1995: 57). Thus, the key to profitability in OEM production for East Asian NIEs seems to be manufacturing expertise (including substantial spending in research and development), and learning how to flexibly manage overseas production networks. This can be seen in Hong Kong's apparel manufacturers, Taiwan's footwear companies, and Singapore's computer firms. Network flexibility thus has become one of the major organizational assets utilized by the NIEs in their internationalization strategies.

Internationalizing Commodity Chains: Offshore Sourcing by the East Asian NIEs

In each of the East Asian NIEs, a combination of domestic supply-side constraints (labor shortages, high wages, and high land prices) and external pressures (currency revaluation, tariffs, and quotas) led to the internationalization of the textile and apparel complex by the late 1980s and early 1990s. Typically, the internationalization of production was sparked first by quotas, but the process was greatly accelerated as supply-side factors became adverse. Quotas determined *when* the outward shift of production began, while preferential access to overseas markets and social networks determined *where* the firms from the East Asian NIEs went. In this international division of labor, skill-intensive activities were retained in East Asia[9] and labor-intensive activities were relocated.

Hong Kong

The internationalization of Hong Kong's firms was triggered by textile import restrictions imposed by the United Kingdom in 1964, which led Hong Kong manufacturers in the late 1960s to shift production to Singapore, Taiwan, and Macao. The Chinese population in these three countries had cultural and linguistic affinities with Hong Kong investors. In addition, Macao benefited from its proximity to Hong Kong, while Singapore qualified for Commonwealth preferences for imports into the United Kingdom. In the early 1970s, Hong Kong apparel firms targeted Malaysia, the Philippines, and Mauritius. This second round of outward investments again was prompted by quota restrictions, coupled with specific host-country inducements. For example, Mauritius established an export-processing zone in an effort to lure Hong Kong investors, particularly knitwear manufacturers who directed their exports to European markets that offered preferential access in terms of low tariffs.

The greatest spur to the internationalization of Hong Kong's textile and apparel companies was the opening of the Chinese economy in 1978. At first, production was subcontracted to state-owned factories, but eventually an elaborate outward processing arrangement with China was set up that relied on a broad assortment of manufacturing, financial, and commercial joint ventures. The relocation of industry to the Chinese mainland led to a hollowing out of Hong Kong's manufacturing sector during the late 1980s and early 1990s. In 1991, 47,000 factories were employing 680,000 workers in Hong Kong, a figure 25% below the peak of 907,000 manufacturing jobs recorded in 1980 (Khanna, 1993: 19). The decline was particularly severe in textiles and apparel. Employment in the Hong Kong textile industry fell from 67,000 in 1984 to 36,000 in 1994—a drop of 47%. Meanwhile, Hong Kong's clothing jobs plummeted from 300,000 in 1984 to 137,000 in 1994—a decrease of 56% in a single decade (De Coster, 1996a: 65).

While manufacturing declined, trading activities in Hong Kong grew to encompass approximately 70,000 firms and 370,000 jobs in 1991, a fivefold increase in the number of firms and a fourfold increase in the number of workers in the trading sector compared to 1978 (Khanna, 1993: 19). Thus, trading companies to a large extent have replaced factories as the key economic agent in Hong Kong's export-oriented growth.

In 1995, Hong Kong entrepreneurs operated more than 20,000 factories employing an estimated 4.5–5 million workers in the Pearl River Delta alone in the neighboring Chinese province of Guangdong (De Coster, 1996b: 96). Considering that total employment in Hong Kong industry had shrunk to 386,000 in 1995, or just over 15% of the Hong Kong workforce (Berger and Lester, 1997: 9), Hong Kong manufacturers in effect increased their domestic labor force well over tenfold through their outward processing arrangement with China.

This extreme reliance of Hong Kong apparel manufacturers on low-cost Chinese labor has several sources of vulnerability that may undermine the viability of this model in the future (Berger and Lester, 1997: 158–162). First, although Guangdong province was once a zone of low wages and an abundant workforce, both wages and land costs have been rising rapidly. As costs in Guangdong go up, Hong Kong manufacturers who wish to retain this Chinese-based production system will have to move their facilities deeper and deeper inland into China, where they will once again encounter bad roads, inadequate water and power systems, and lack of commercial infrastructure. Second, as production moves inland, it will be increasingly difficult to maintain an adequate supply of Hong Kong managers. Rather than trying to replicate the Pearl River Delta pattern on a large scale further inland, it probably would be better to try to upgrade the operations in the Guangdong plants. Third, new low-cost apparel exporting nations are emerging in Asia—Indonesia, Sri Lanka, India, Myanmar, Vietnam, and others—while Mexico and the Caribbean Basin economies loom as cheap production sites with closer proximity to the large US market. Hong Kong has no special advantages in many of these locations, which suggests that it should avoid being locked into low-wage offshore manufacturing networks and instead take fuller advantage of the global trend toward service-enhanced manufacturing where Hong Kong retains a strong competitive edge.

South Korea

As in Hong Kong, the internationalization of South Korea's and Taiwan's apparel producers began as a response to quota restrictions. Korean garment firms lacking sufficient export quotas initially set up offshore production in quota-free locations like Saipan, a US territory in the Mariana Islands. More recent waves of internationalization have been motivated by the domestic constraints of rising wages and worker shortages. The low-wage regions that have attracted the greatest number of South Korean companies are Latin America, and Southeast and South Asia. The preference of Korean firms for investment in Latin America (Guatemala, Honduras, the Dominican Republic, etc.) is stimulated by its proximity to the US market and easy quota access. The pull of Asian nations such as Indonesia, Sri Lanka and Bangladesh comes mainly from their wage rates, which are among the lowest in the world.

Taiwan

When Taiwanese firms moved offshore in the early 1980s, they also confronted binding quotas. While Taiwan's wages in the late 1970s and early 1980s were still relatively low, quota rents were high. Firms had to buy quotas (whose value in secondary markets fluctuated widely) in order to be able to expand exports, thereby causing a decrease in profitability for firms without sufficient quota (Appelbaum and Gereffi, 1994). This led to a growing emphasis on non-quota markets by Taiwan's textile and apparel exporters. Quota markets (the United States, the European Community, and Canada) accounted for over 50% of Taiwan's textile and apparel exports in the mid-1980s, but this ratio declined to 43% in 1988 and fell further to 35% in 1991. The United States, which had been Taiwan's largest export market for years, claimed one-quarter of Taiwan's textile and apparel exports in 1991; the European Community 8%; and Canada just 2%. The main non-quota markets, which absorbed nearly two-thirds of Taiwan's textile and apparel exports in the early 1990s, were Hong Kong (30%), Japan (6%), and Singapore (3%) (Khanna, 1993: 29–30). Hong Kong, now Taiwan's leading export market, is mainly a conduit for shipping yarns, fabrics, and clothing to China for further processing and re-export.

Coordinating Commodity Chains: Triangle Manufacturing and Overseas Buying Offices

One of the most important mechanisms facilitating the geographical expansion and the shift to higher value-added activities for mature export industries like apparel in East Asia is the process of 'triangle manufacturing'. The essence of triangle manufacturing, which was initiated by the East Asian NIEs in the 1970s and 1980s, is that US buyers place their orders with the NIE manufacturers they have sourced from in the past, who in turn shift some or all of the requested production to affiliated offshore factories in low-wage countries (e.g., China, Indonesia, or Vietnam). The triangle is completed when the finished goods are shipped directly to the foreign buyer under the US quotas issued to the exporting nation. Triangle manufacturing thus changes the status of NIE manufacturers from established suppliers for US retailers and marketers to middlemen in buyer-driven commodity chains that can include as many as 50–60 exporting countries (Gereffi, 1994).

Triangle manufacturing networks are historically and socially embedded. The early traders in Asia established long-distance supply routes that relied heavily on social ties between Asian producers and their export markets. The Japanese *sogo shosha* were involved in transferring textile, apparel and footwear production from Japan to Hong Kong, Taiwan, and Korea during the 1950s. They mainly handled the logistics of providing machinery, intermediate goods, and working capital to East Asian apparel and footwear exporters. The British merchant houses, originally founded as intermediaries for trade between China and the West, were instrumental in the transition of Hong Kong from an entrepôt to a manufacturing-based economy. They gave Hong Kong's industrial enterprises the knowledge and logistical support needed for exports to distant countries, and they helped to establish confidence and goodwill for Hong Kong products among foreign buyers. But as markets for Hong Kong garments diversified following the Second World War to include North American and other European countries, Chinese-owned companies became an increasingly important channel of exports from the mid-1950s onward. These Chinese merchants played a crucial intermediary role because most of the first-generation Chinese manufacturers in Hong Kong did not speak English and thus could not communicate effectively with foreign buyers or merchants. Less well-known but also crucial for the early development of Hong Kong's garment industry were the Indian trading companies, who were part of a network of Indian merchants scattered in Asia and Africa who specialized in exports to the Middle East and Africa (Leung, 1997: Chapter 5).

Today, each of the East Asian NIEs has a different set of preferred countries where they set up their new factories. Hong Kong and Taiwan have been the main investors in China and Southeast Asia; South Korea has been especially prominent in Indonesia, Guatemala, the Dominican Republic, and North Korea; and Singapore is a leading force in nearby Malaysia and Indonesia. These production networks are explained in part by social and cultural factors (e.g., ethnic or familial ties, common language), as well as by unique features of a country's historical legacy (e.g., Hong Kong's British colonial ties gave it an inside track on investments in Mauritius and Jamaica). However, as the volume of orders expands in new low-wage production sites, the pressure grows for the large US buyers to eventually bypass their East Asian intermediaries and deal directly with the factories that fill their orders.

The most direct link between US buyers and their Asian suppliers are the overseas buying offices of the major US retailers, which join the seasonal orders[10] coming from US headquarters with the output from their offshore supply networks that include as many as 200–400 factories. The organizational capabilities of these buying offices began to expand as retailers got more heavily involved in product development to supply their growing collections of private-label merchandise. Prior to the formation of offshore buying offices, importers were the main link between US retailers and foreign factories. However, as the volume and range of imported products began to grow, retailers decided to initiate direct purchases offshore not only to save the commission paid to importers, but also to have a greater degree of control over the quantity, quality, and timing of their orders. Sears, Montgomery Ward, and Macy's were the first American companies to establish buying offices in Hong Kong in the 1960s, mainly to purchase hard goods (such as household appliances, lighting fixtures, furniture, kitchenware, and toys). The really big apparel orders came when Kmart and J. C. Penney set up their Hong Kong offices in 1970, quickly followed by branch offices in Taiwan, Korea, and Singapore. By the mid-1970s many other retailers, such as the May Department Stores Company, Associated Merchandising Corporation (AMC), and Woolworth, had jumped on the direct-buy bandwagon in the Far East (Gereffi and Pan, 1994).

Table 3.2 provides a detailed look at the top 10 US retailer buying offices in Taiwan in 1992. Kmart and Wal-Mart, the two biggest US retailers, did the largest volume of business in Taiwan, with annual orders in 1992 of $500 million and $300 million, respectively. J. C. Penney, AMC (a member-owned group buying office for 40 different US stores), Mast Industries (the major overseas sourcing arm of The Limited), Montgomery Ward, and Woolworth all purchased between $100 million and $200 million in merchandise through their Taiwan offices, while Sears, May Department Stores, and Macy's did $50 to $75 million in business. Note that these amounts refer to the value of *orders* placed with the retail buying offices in Taiwan by their US headquarters, not to the volume of *shipments* from Taiwan. Generally, a substantial portion of the orders placed in Taiwan in the early 1990s were transferred to lower-cost countries by the Taiwanese manufacturers, via the process of triangle manufacturing described above. Taiwan nonetheless served as the logistical center for filling the orders that were moved offshore, typically through the supply of fabric and other intermediate materials still made in Taiwan,[11] and the coordination of a variety of needed services, such as quality control inspections, shipping, and the transfer of funds for letters of credit.

The proportion of apparel orders placed with the Taiwanese buying offices of US retailers that were actually sourced domestically is also shown in Table 3.2. There is wide variation in company strategies. Whereas three retail buying offices (Kmart, Montgomery Ward, J. C. Penney) gave just 25–35% of their orders to local factories, six others sourced 70% or more of their apparel orders in Taiwan, and Mast Industries, the largest apparel sourcer from Taiwan, placed 100% of its orders with Taiwanese factories. The reasons for these differences in company strategy reflect a range of factors, including quota availability in Taiwan for the types of products ordered, the retailer's preference for low cost or high quality, and the speed with which the order must be filled. Mast Industries, which specializes in 'speed sourcing' and is reputed to have the fastest turnaround time in the business (30–40 days from order to shipment), filled all its orders in Taiwan because local factories there were the only option that allowed Mast to meet its short lead times.

Finally, we see in Table 3.2 the main countries to which Taiwan's US retail buying offices transferred the offshore portion of their orders. In many of the countries on this list, there is a sizable overseas Chinese business community that supplies the Taiwanese firms with political contacts, a business infrastructure, and the local knowledge necessary for lowering risks in an offshore operation. Thus, social ties shape sourcing networks.

Company	Value of orders placed in Taiwan (US$ millions)	Types of merchandise		Sourcing channels for apparel		Source of apparel shipments[c] (main countries)
		Softlines[a] (%)	Hardlines (%)	Taiwan[b] (%)	Offshore (%)	
Kmart	500	45	55	35	65	Indonesia, United Arab Emirates, Philippines, plus ten additional countries
Wal-Mart[d]	300	30	70	50	50	People's Republic of China, Indonesia, Thailand, Sri Lanka
J. C. Penney	200	50	50	25	75	Philippines, Indonesia, Thailand, Bangladesh
Associated Merchandising Corporation (AMC)[e]	180	65	35	70	30	Philippines, Singapore, Malaysia, Indonesia, Thailand, People's Republic of China
Mast Industries[f]	140	100	0	100	0	None
Montgomery Ward	135	35	65	33	67	Indonesia, Thailand, Philippines, Chile
Woolworth	110	46	54	75	25	People's Republic of China, Indonesia, Sri Lanka, Bangladesh, Vietnam, Lesotho
Sears	75	40	60	92	8	Bangladesh, Philippines
May Department Stores	70	65	35	80	20	Indonesia, Singapore, Philippines
R. H. Macy and Company	50	73	27	85	15	Philippines, Indonesia

Source: Interviews in Taiwan by the author.

Notes: [a] The softlines percentages are exclusively apparel, with the following exceptions: Kmart—apparel, handbags, and home fashions; Wal-Mart—apparel (70%) and footwear (30%); and Montgomery Ward—apparel and footwear (minimal).

[b] The Taiwan percentage refers to the proportion of each retail buying office's orders that are made in and shipped from Taiwan.

[c] Offshore shipments refer to orders given by the retail buying offices to local manufacturers in Taiwan, who in turn transfer the orders to affiliated offshore factories for production and export under the quota of the designated countries. Offshore sources are listed in their relative order of importance to Taiwan's buying offices.

[d] Wal-Mart's sole sourcing agent in Taiwan, and much of the rest of Asia as well, is Pacific Resources Export Limited (PREL). Although registered as a Hong Kong trading company, PREL is owned by Indonesia's Salim Group, one of the biggest industrial conglomerates in Asia.

[e] Associated Merchandising Corporation is a group buying office that serves about 40 different stores in the United States, including Dayton-Hudson, Federated Department Stores, Target, and Bradlees.

[f] Mast industries is the main overseas sourcing arm and a wholly owned subsidiary of The Limited.

Completing Commodity Chains: From Export Platform to Branded Marketing in Asia

Two trends—the shift from OEM to OBM, and the growing importance of non-quota markets for the NIEs—point to an important fact: production and trade networks in the apparel commodity chain are becoming increasingly concentrated in Asia. There has been a sharp decline in Asian clothing exports to North America (from 27% of the global total in 1984 to 16% in 1996), a drop in Asian apparel exports to Western Europe (down to 11% of global trade), and a striking increase in intra-Asian trade in apparel (from 4.3% in 1980 to 12.3% in 1996). This rise in intra-Asian trade is even stronger in textiles, where it increases from 13% of the world total in 1980 to nearly 28% in 1996 (see Table 3.3).

Asia's growing prominence as a market for its own textile and apparel output, and the continuing migration of production to low-cost supply sites around the world, suggest a general restructuring may be underway that is leading to parallel processes of regionalization of the apparel commodity chain within Asia, North America, and Europe. The emerging supply relationships that are being fashioned with nearby low-cost producers in each area (South Asia and Vietnam in Asia, Central America and the Caribbean vis-à-vis North America, and North Africa and Eastern Europe for the European Union) are likely to strengthen intra-regional trade and production networks in the apparel chain, thereby giving rise to new forms of economic coordination and competition among local as well as global firms.

Implications of the Asian Experience for North America

Our analysis of the apparel commodity chain in Asia suggests two main hypotheses for the future of the textile and apparel sector in North America. First, the relative decline of finished apparel exports from the East Asian NIEs is producing a 'supply gap' in the North American apparel commodity chain. This is partly due to the greater geographical distances and logistical complexity involved in managing Asia's triangle manufacturing networks, as well as the tendency for more direct marketing in Asia as local manufacturers shift from OEM to OBM. Second, since Asian apparel supply to the United States has primarily been oriented to filling the OEM orders of US retailers and branded marketers, apparel manufacturers in North America will need to develop the capability to carry out full-package supply. Previously this had only been done by the East Asia NIEs for the US mass market, or in the fashion centers of Europe for high couture. An interpretive sketch that offers a tentative response to these two hypotheses will be outlined in the remainder of this chapter.

Table 3.3　Regional Trade Patterns in World Exports of Textiles and Clothing

	1980	1984	1987	1990	1993	1996
Textiles						
World (US$ billions)	55.6	53.9	80.2	104.8	115.4	150.2
World (percentages)	100.0	100.0	100.0	100.0	100.0	100.0
Intra-Western Europe	40.1	34.9	40.0	41.4	32.8	30.0
Intra-Asia	13.1	17.4	18.2	20.6	26.6	27.6
Asia to Western Europe	1.6	4.6	5.9	5.6	5.8	5.3
Western Europe to C./E. Europe/ Baltic States/CIS[a]	NA	NA	NA	2.3	3.1	4.4
Asia to North America	2.9	5.4	4.9	3.6	4.3	3.5
Asia to the Middle East	NA	NA	NA	2.2	3.0	2.8
Western Europe to Asia	1.6	2.4	2.0	3.0	2.6	3.1
Western Europe to North America	1.6	3.2	2.9	2.4	2.3	2.0
Other	39.1	32.1	26.1	18.9	19.5	21.3
Clothing						
World (US$ billions)	41.8	48.2	81.9	106.4	133.0	163.3
World (percentages)	100.0	100.0	100.0	100.0	100.0	100.0
Intra-Western Europe	36.6	29.3	33.7	35.2	28.7	28.1
Asia to North America	14.8	26.8	22.5	19.5	19.6	15.8
Intra-Asia	4.3	6.2	6.0	8.8	10.5	12.3
Asia to Western Europe	14.4	11.0	13.2	12.9	13.6	11.0
Latin America to North America	1.7	2.1	2.3	2.4	3.9	5.1
C./E. Europe/Baltic States/CIS[a] to Western Europe	NA	NA	NA	NA	NA	4.1
Africa to Western Europe	1.9	1.2	2.1	NA	3.0	NA
Other	26.3	23.4	20.2	21.1	20.7	23.6

Sources: GATT, *International Trade*, and WTO, *Annual Report*, various years.

Notes: [a] Includes Central and Eastern Europe, the Baltic States, and the Confederation of Independent States.
NA = Not available.

Figure 3.2 reveals significant shifts in the regional patterns of US apparel sourcing between 1986 and 1996. During this 10-year period, US apparel imports rose from $17.3 to $41.7 billion. The five rings correspond to different levels of importance by the supplying nations: those in the central circle each account for 10% or more of the total value of clothing imports in 1995, while each of those in the outer ring makes up only 1.0–1.9% of total imports. In other words, as we move from the inner rings to the outer ones in this sourcing chart, the relative importance of the clothing suppliers decreases.

Several key aspects of the direction and magnitude of change in US apparel sourcing are revealed in Figure 3.2. First, there are striking regional differences in the pattern of US apparel imports. West European suppliers, as well as the NIEs in Northeast Asia, are becoming less important in US apparel sourcing, while Southeast Asia, South Asia, Central America and the Caribbean, and Mexico are all becoming more significant. Second, despite considerable mobility within the past decade, there is a strong core–periphery pattern that dominates the geography of export activity in the US apparel sourcing matrix.[12] Only four economies (Hong Kong, Taiwan, South Korea, and China) were core US suppliers (i.e., a US apparel import share of 10% or greater) during the past decade, and only China currently holds that distinction. There is a wide dispersion of apparel suppliers in the outer two rings (indicating 1–4% shares of the US apparel market). Only six nations are in the inner three rings. Third, while for most countries (19 of 27) the degree of change from 1986 to 1996 has been relatively modest (they changed their position by one ring or not at all), other nations have shown more substantial degrees of advancement (Mexico, the Dominican Republic, Honduras, and Bangladesh) or decline (South Korea, Taiwan, Japan, and Singapore). Nonetheless, inward shifts of even one ring may be quite significant for smaller economies, given the substantial overall growth of US apparel imports in the past ten years.

Two other very important features of US apparel sourcing are not revealed by this chart, however. First, there are two contending production systems reflected in US apparel sourcing: export-processing assembly (production sharing) and full-package supply (OEM production). The countries that have penetrated the US apparel market most deeply either have been experts at OEM supply (Hong Kong, Taiwan, and South Korea) or they are currently trying to develop full-package capabilities (China and Mexico). All of the other countries on this list are relegated to production sharing. Second, different kinds of networks are involved in these export success stories, and these networks link the countries on this chart in different ways. We have already discussed the triangle manufacturing scheme in East Asia, but we still need to consider the networks relevant to the North American sourcing mix.

If one envisions the complete apparel commodity chain as encompassing raw materials, yarn and synthetic fibers, textiles, apparel, and the distribution of apparel to retailers (Appelbaum and Gereffi, 1994), then the Mexican and US commodity chains are quite distinct. Mexico has several large, reasonably successful synthetic fiber companies, a multitude of maquiladora firms that export apparel products to the United States, and an emergent retail sector that is fashioning a number of strategic alliances with their US counterparts. The weakest link in the Mexican production chain, by far, is the textile segment. The vast majority of Mexico's textile companies are undercapitalized, technologically backward and inefficient, and they produce goods of poor quality. By contrast, the United States is very strong in synthetic fibers, textiles and retailing, but limited in its garment production capability, especially for women's and children's apparel. The Mexican apparel chain thus appears to be strongest where the US chain is relatively weak: garment production.[13]

This picture becomes more complex when we consider the differentiated nature of apparel production systems, and if we expand the borders of North America to include Central America and the Caribbean.[14] Export-oriented assembly in Latin America is centered in Mexico and the Caribbean Basin because of this area's low wages and proximity to the US market, where over 90% of their exports are sold. The maquiladora sector has benefitted most dramatically from Mexico's opening to trade in 1988. Between 1990 and 1997, total US imports of apparel assembled from US parts (under the 807/9802 production sharing program) rose from $2.4 billion to $11.7 billion. Mexico has been the star performer in the 1990s. Its apparel exports to the United States from Mexican maquiladora plants increased sevenfold from just over $600 million in 1990 to $4.4 billion in 1997. Assembly trade predominates in the North American garment sector, accounting in 1997 for 82% of US apparel imports from Mexico and 84% of those from the Caribbean and Central America (Gereffi and Bair, 1998: 28).

From a regional perspective, Mexico competes for the US market most directly with the Caribbean Basin Initiative (CBI) countries. In 1997, the total apparel exports (*maquila* and non-*maquila* trade combined) from CBI countries were almost 50% higher than Mexico's total ($7.7 billion vs. $5.4 billion, respectively). The leading CBI apparel exporter was the Dominican Republic ($2.2 billion), which actually had a higher level of garment exports than Mexico in the early 1990s before Mexico pulled ahead in 1994. The other leading CBI apparel exporters in 1997 are: Honduras ($1.7 billion), El Salvador ($1.1 billion), Guatemala ($980 million), Costa Rica ($850 million), and Jamaica ($470 million) (see Table 3.1). However, the lack of NAFTA parity for the Caribbean Basin has severely truncated the growth of export-oriented apparel assembly in these smaller economies. In 1995 and 1996, more than 150 apparel plants closed in the Caribbean and 123,000 jobs have been lost 'as a direct result of trade and investment diversion to Mexico', according to the Caribbean and Apparel Institute in Kingston, Jamaica (Rohter, 1997).

Given the power shifts that are occurring among North American textile, apparel and retail firms, the key question is: Who will be the main 'organizing agents' in modernizing Mexico's apparel commodity chain? The notion of organizing agents is used here to refer to those firms, foreign and domestic, that could enhance the competitiveness of the apparel commodity chain in Mexico through backward or forward linkages with major producers and retailers. Potential organizing agents, located in every segment of the commodity chain, have already begun to undertake major investments in Mexico: fibers (Celanese Mexicana, Cydsa, DuPont); textiles (Burlington Industries, Guilford Mills, Cone Mills, Grupo Kalach, Grupo Saba); apparel (Sara Lee, VF Corporation, Levi Strauss); and retailers (J. C. Penney, Sears, Kmart-Liverpool, Wal-Mart-Cifra). There are substantial differences in the scope and content of these varied attempts at vertical and horizontal integration in the Mexican economy (Gereffi and Bair, 1998).

The creation of new production and trade networks between the United States and Mexico in textiles and apparel is linking the US South and the northern and central regions of Mexico ever more tightly together. The US South is in a position to become the coordinating hub of the North American apparel commodity chain. North Carolina and Texas are the nerve centers of the manufacturer-centered US-Mexico networks. North Carolina is of central importance because it is the headquarters for most of the big US textile plants, many of which are making new investments in Mexico. When NAFTA becomes fully implemented, US textile companies expect to be able to supply Mexican apparel plants duty free from textile production centers located inside Mexico.

The lead firms in these manufacturer-centered and retailer-centered networks in the North American apparel commodity chain are in a position to play a direct role in upgrading Mexican domestic industry. US textile manufacturers are entering into production joint ventures with Mexican counterparts to build large textile complexes in northern and central Mexico to supply local apparel plants. US apparel manufacturers can provide both the technology and incentives for their Mexican affiliates to meet international competition. The next step would be for the US retailers that are going into Mexico to play a similar role in upgrading local supplier networks.

In contrast to the evolution of the apparel commodity chain in Asia, which utilized East Asian NIE apparel manufacturers as the hubs of triangle manufacturing networks that knit together suppliers from countries at different levels of development throughout the region, the coordinating agents in the North American apparel commodity chain are likely to be large US firms located in each of the main segments of the chain (fibers, textiles, apparel production, marketing, and retailing). The main reasons for such a different outcome are various. First, Mexico and the CBI countries are both geographically and culturally closer to the United States than are Asian suppliers. This allows US firms to play a far more dominant role in the North American chain. Second, the role of trade policies is an important factor here. The NAFTA pact provides Mexico at least a temporary edge over CBI suppliers, who thus far have not been granted NAFTA parity with Mexico. Even if parity is granted, Mexico has a big edge in developing a full-package supply capability because textile production in Central America and the Caribbean is virtually nonexistent. Finally, we would predict that sourcing intermediaries will emerge in Mexico to perform the same kind of 'full package' services that trading companies and integrated manufacturers provided in East Asia. Although the apparel commodity chain in North America remains buyer-driven, suppliers are likely to form rival networks across supply-chain segments to compete for large orders.

Notes

1. Throughout this chapter, OEM production will be used as a synonymous term for relational contracting, specification contracting, and full-package supply.

2. Although organizational and relational rents are closely related, they differ in that the former is intra-organizational, and the latter is inter-plant, inter-firm, and inter-institutional (e.g., research institutes or training programs with public-private sector support). The rent element arises from the fact that all these organizational features are tacit, cumulative and systemic. Adoption is a matter of degree. Some economies and firms are better at utilizing these techniques than others, giving rise to uneven diffusion and consequently to scarcity and rent (Kaplinsky, 1998).

3. An estimated 72% of a sample of large US apparel and textile manufacturers had quick response (QR) programs with their customers in 1995, up from 60% the year before (Jones, 1995: 26). These QR programs can reduce the typical production cycle of fashion merchandise from as much as nine months to a few weeks, although the apparel firms that lead in QR adoption tend to have strong brand-name identification and consumer loyalty, and the retailers initiating these programs are quite big.

4. Dayton Hudson Corporation owns Target, Mervyn's, Dayton's, Hudson's, and Marshall Field.

5. These figures do not include the production-sharing activities of US apparel firms in Mexico and in the Caribbean Basin, which also have been expanding very rapidly (USITC, 1997).

6. Some large retailers or designers, like The Limited or Liz Claiborne, also purchase fabric for their overseas contractors and participate in the quality control inspections for finished goods. However, they typically leave all other aspects of the sourcing process to the offshore garment makers.

7. This pattern of upgrading is well illustrated in the following quote about Thailand from a 25-year veteran of Asian apparel sourcing: 'Thailand has evolved the way of Korea, Taiwan and Hong Kong, in that manufacturers only cater to high quality, high price branded product. In prior days, I bought merchandise there to sell to the mass market retailers. Today, this is almost impossible to do. I visited the factory of a close friend of mine who has a completely vertical operation. He knits, dyes and sews knit tops. Before, he only did promotional shirts for mass market discounters. Today, he only manufactures for brands such as Polo, Tommy Hilfiger, and Donna Karan, and makes the same amount of units he did 20 years ago, except he has more than doubled his making charges. This is the true reality of manufacturing in Thailand today' (Bresky, 1997).

8. In a survey of approximately 100 South Korean export firms carried out in 1976, more than two-thirds reported that some or all of their exports to foreign markets consisted of their own brand name products (Rhee et al., 1984: 123).

9. In the apparel sector, the activities associated with OEM production that tended to remain in the NIEs were jobs such as product design, sample making, quality control, packing, warehousing, transportation, quota transactions, and local financing through letters of credit. These provided relatively high gross margins or profits.

10. Nowadays the fashion year is split up into at least six to eight seasons.

11. Between 1985 and 1996, Taiwan's exports of clothing declined from 56% to 20% of its textile and apparel total, while the share represented by intermediate goods (textile fibers, yarn, and fabrics) rose from 44% to 80% (Gereffi and Pan, 1994: 130, supplemented by more recent data from the Taiwan Textile Federation).

12. Borrowing from Krugman (1991: Chapter 1), the core–periphery pattern resulting from geographic concentration in US apparel imports can be related to the demand externalities and dynamics of imperfect competition in buyer-driven commodity chains.

13. Empirical support for this argument is provided in OTA (1992: Chapter 9) and Gereffi (1997).

14. Canada is at best a niche player in the North American apparel sector. Canada's considerable textile strengths are oriented to the home furnishings market (upholstery, rugs and curtains). Within apparel, Canada's main export niche to the United States is wool suits.

References

AAMA (American Apparel Manufacturers Association). 1984. *Apparel Manufacturing Strategies.* Arlington, VA: AAMA.

Appelbaum, Richard P. and Gary Gereffi. 1994. 'Power and Profits in the Apparel Commodity Chain.' In *Global Production: The Apparel Industry in the Pacific Rim* edited by Edna Bonacich et al. Philadelphia, PA: Temple University Press.

Asiaweek. 1995. 'What's in a Name? After Years of Building a Brand, Daewoo's Back to the OEM Game.' May 12, 56–57.

Berger, Suzanne and Richard K. Lester. 1997. *Made by Hong Kong.* New York: Oxford University Press.

Bernard, Mitchell and John Ravenhill. 1995. 'Beyond Product Cycles and Flying Geese: Regionalization, Hierarchy, and the Industrialization of East Asia.' *World Politics* 47(2): 171–209.

Birnbaum, David. 1993. *Importing Garments Through Hong Kong.* Hong Kong: Third Horizon Press.

Borrus, Michael. 1997. 'Left for Dead: Asian Production Networks and the Revival of US Electronics.' In *The China Circle: Economics and Technology in the PRC, Taiwan, and Hong Kong,* edited by Barry Naughton, 139–163. Washington, DC: Brookings Institution Press.

Bresky, Bart. 1997. 'Thai Sourcing Scene Much Changed.' *Bobbin* 38(12): 40.

Chazen, Jerome A. 1996. 'Notes from the Apparel Industry: Two Decades at Liz Claiborne.' *Columbia Journal of World Business* 31(2): 40–43.

De Coster, Jozef. 1996a. 'Hong Kong and China: The Joining of Two Giants in Textiles and Clothing.' *Textile Outlook International* 68: 63–79.

———. 1996b. 'Productivity: A Key Strategy of the Hong Kong Textile and Clothing Industry.' *Textile Outlook International* 68: 80–97.

Dickerson, Kitty G. 1995. *Textiles and Apparel in the Global Economy*, 2nd edition. New Jersey: Prentice Hall.

Doner, Richard F. 1991. *Driving a Bargain: Automobile Industrialization and Japanese Firms in Southeast Asia*. Berkeley, CA: University of California Press.

Finnie, Trevor A. 1996. 'Profile of Levi Strauss.' *Textile Outlook International* 67: 10–37.

Florida, Richard and Martin Kenney. 1991. 'Transplanted Organizations: The Transfer of Japanese Industrial Organization to the United States.' *American Sociological Review* 56(3): 381–398.

Gereffi, Gary. 1994. 'The Organization of Buyer-driven Global Commodity Chains: How US Retailers Shape Overseas Production Networks.' In *Commodity Chains and Global Capitalism*, edited by Gary Gereffi and Miguel Korzeniewicz, 95–122. Wesport, CT: Praeger.

———. 1995. 'Global Production Systems and Third World Development.' In *Global Change, Regional Response: The New International Context of Development*, edited by Barbara Stallings, 100–142. New York: Cambridge University Press.

———. 1996. 'Commodity Chains and Regional Divisions of Labor in East Asia.' *Journal of Asian Business* 12(1): 75–112.

———. 1997. 'Global Shifts, Regional Response: Can North America Meet the Full-package Challenge?' *Bobbin* 39(3): 16–31.

Gereffi, Gary and Jennifer Bair. 1998. 'US Companies Eye NAFTA's Prize.' *Bobbin* 39(7): 26–35.

Gereffi, Gary and Pan Mei-Lin. 1994. 'The Globalization of Taiwan's Garment Industry.' In *Global Production: The Apparel Industry in the Pacific Rim*, edited by Edna Bonacich et al., 42–62. Philadelphia, PA: Temple University Press.

Gereffi, Gary and Tony Tam. 1998. 'Industrial Upgrading through Organizational Chains: Dynamics of Rent, Learning, and Mobility in the Global Economy.' Paper presented at the 93rd Annual Meeting of the American Sociological Association, San Francisco, August 21–25.

Granitsas, Alkman. 1998. 'Back in Fashion: Hong Kong's Leading Garment Makers are Going Global — Learning to Add Value and High Technology.' *Far Eastern Economic Review* 21: 52–54.

Henderson, Jeffrey. 1989. *The Globalisation of High Technology Production: Society, Space and Semi-conductors in the Restructuring of the Modern World*. New York: Routledge.

Hill, Richard C. 1989. 'Comparing Transnational Production Systems: The Automobile Industry in the USA and Japan'. *International Journal of Urban and Regional Research* 13(3): 462–480.

ILO (International Labour Organization). 1995. 'Recent Developments in the Clothing Industry.' Report I. Geneva: ILO.

Japan Textile News. 1996. 'Japan's Distribution and Retail Industry.' *JTN Quarterly* 2(2): 14–30.

Jones, Jackie. 1995. 'Forces Behind Restructuring in US Apparel Retailing and its Effect on the US Apparel Industry.' *Industry, Trade, and Technology Review* (March): 23–27.

Kaplinsky, Raphael. 1998. 'Globalisation, Industrialisation and Sustainable Growth: The Pursuit of the nth Rent.' IDS Discussion Paper 365. Brighton: Institute of Development Studies, University of Sussex.

Khanna, Sri Ram. 1993. 'Structural Changes in Asian Textiles and Clothing Industries: The Second Migration of Production.' *Textile Outlook International* 49: 11–32.

Krugman, Paul. 1991. *Geography and Trade*. Cambridge: MIT Press.

————. 1994. 'The Myth of Asia's Miracle'. *Foreign Affairs* 73(6): 62–78.

Leung, Hon-Chu. 1997. 'Local lives and global commodity chains: Timing, Networking, and the Hong Kong-based Garment Industry, 1957–1993.' Unpublished Ph.D. Dissertation, Department of Sociology, Duke University.

Management Horizons, 1993. Global Retailing 2000, Management Horizons Division of Price Waterhouse, Columbus, OH.

Miller, James P. 1997. 'Sara Lee Plans "Fundamental Reshaping".' *Wall Street Journal*, September 15. A3, A10.

OETH (L'Observatoire Europe'en du Textile et de l'Habillement). 1995. *The EU Textile and Clothing Industry 1993/94*. Brussels: OETH.

Ortega, Bob. 1994. 'Penney Pushes Abroad in Unusually Big Way as it Pursues Growth.' *Wall Street Journal*, February 1, A1, A6.

OTA (Office of Technology Assessment). US Congress. 1992. 'US–Mexico Trade: Pulling Together or Pulling Apart?' ITE-545. Washington, DC: US Government Printing Office.

Porter, Michael E. 1990. *The Competitive Advantage of Nations*. New York: Free Press.

Rhee, Yung W., Bruce Ross-Larson, and Gary Pursell. 1984. *Korea's Competitive Edge: Managing the Entry into World Markets*. Baltimore, MD: Johns Hopkins University Press.

Rohter, Larry. 1997. 'Impact of NAFTA Pounds Economies of the Caribbean, Jobs Flowing to Mexico.' *New York Times*, January 30, 1.

Scheffer, Michael. 1994. *The Changing Map of European Textiles: Production and Sourcing Strategies of Textile and Clothing Firms*. Brussels: OETH.

Selwyn, M. 1993. 'Radical Departures.' *Asian Business* (August): 22–25.

USITC (United States International Trade Commission). 1997. *Production Sharing: Use of US Components and Materials in Foreign Assembly Operations, 1992–1995*. Washington, DC: USITC Publication 3032.

Warfield, Carol, Mary Barry, and Dorothy Cavendar. 1995. 'Apparel Retailing in the USA — Part 1.' *Textile Outlook International* 58: 37–91.

World Bank. 1993. *The East Asian Miracle*. New York: Oxford University Press.

Young, Alwyn. 1994. 'Lessons from the East Asian NICs: A Contrarian View.' *European Economic Review* 38(3–4): 964–973.

————. 1995. 'The Tyranny of Numbers: Confronting the Statistical Realities of the East Asian Growth Experience.' *Quarterly Journal of Economics* 110(3): 641–680.

The Governance of Global Value Chains

Gary Gereffi, John Humphrey, and Timothy J. Sturgeon

The world economy has changed in significant ways during the past several decades, especially in the areas of international trade and industrial organization. Two of the most important new features of the contemporary economy are the globalization of production and trade,[1] which have fueled the growth of industrial capabilities in a wide range of developing countries, and the vertical disintegration of transnational corporations, which are redefining their core competencies to focus on innovation and product strategy, marketing, and the highest value-added segments of manufacturing and services, while reducing their direct ownership over 'non-core' functions such as generic services and volume production. Together, these two shifts have laid the groundwork for a variety of network forms of governance situated between arm's length markets, on the one hand, and large vertically integrated corporations, on the other. The purpose of this chapter is to generate a theoretical framework for better understanding the shifting governance structures in sectors producing for global markets, structures we refer to as 'global value chains'. Our intent is to bring some order to the variety of network forms that have been observed in the field.[2]

The evolution of global-scale industrial organization affects not only the fortunes of firms and the structure of industries, but also how and why countries advance—or fail to advance—in the global economy. Global value chain research and policy work examine the different ways in which global production and distribution systems are integrated, and the possibilities for firms in developing countries to enhance their position in global markets. We hope that the theory of global value chain governance that we develop here will be useful for the crafting of effective policy tools related to industrial upgrading, economic development, employment creation, and poverty alleviation.

Fragmentation, Coordination, and Networks in the Global Economy

For us, the starting point for understanding the changing nature of international trade and industrial organization is contained in the notion of a value-added chain, as developed by international business scholars who have focused on the strategies of both firms and countries in the global economy. In its most basic form, a value-added chain is 'the process by which technology is combined with material and labor inputs, and then processed inputs are assembled, marketed, and distributed. A single firm may consist of only one link in this process, or it may be extensively vertically integrated ...' (Kogut, 1985: 15). The key issues in this literature are which activities and technologies a firm keeps in-house and which should be outsourced to other firms, and where the various activities should be located.

Trade economists are also concerned with how global production is organized. Arndt and Kierzkowski (2001) use the term 'fragmentation' to describe the physical separation of different parts of a production process, arguing that the international dimension of this separation is new. Fragmentation allows production in different countries to be formed into cross-border production networks that can be within or between firms. Feenstra (1998) takes this idea one step further by explicitly connecting the 'integration of trade' with the 'disintegration of production' in the global economy. The rising integration of world markets through trade has brought with it a disintegration of multinational firms, since companies are finding it advantageous to 'outsource' an increasing share of their non-core manufacturing and service activities—both domestically and abroad. This has led to a growing proportion of international trade occurring in components and other intermediate goods (Yeats, 2001).[3]

If production is increasingly fragmented across geographic space and between firms, then how are these fragmented activities coordinated? For Arndt and Kierzkowski, the options are clear: 'Separability of ownership is an important determinant of the organizational structure of cross-border production sharing. Where separation of ownership is not feasible, multinational corporations and foreign direct investment are likely to play a dominant role. Where it is feasible, arm's length relationships are possible and foreign direct investment is less important' (Arndt and Kierzkowski, 2001: 4).

This binary view of how global production might be organized, either through markets or within transnational firms, is explained by transaction costs economics in terms of the complexity of inter-firm relationships and the extent to which they involve investments specific to a particular transaction—asset specificity (Williamson, 1975). Arm's-length market relations work well for standard products because they are easily described and valued. Coordination problems are reduced not only because their ease of description makes contracts simple to write, but also because standard products can be produced for stock and supplied as needed. At the same time, because standard products are made by a variety of suppliers and bought by a variety of customers, problems arising from asset specificity are low.

Conversely, the transaction costs approach offers various reasons why firms will bring certain activities in-house. First, the more customized the product or service, the more likely it is to involve transaction-specific investments. This raises the risk of opportunism, which either rules out out-sourcing altogether, or makes it more costly because safeguards have to be put in place. Second, even without opportunism, transaction costs increase when inter-firm relationships require greater coordination. For example, non-standard inputs and integrated product design architectures involve more complex transfers of design information and therefore intense interactions across enterprise boundaries. Integral product architectures are more likely to require non-standard inputs, and changes in the design of particular parts tend to precipitate design changes in other areas of the system (Fine, 1998; Langlois and Robertson, 1995). Similarly, coordination costs increase for parts whose supply is time-sensitive, as separate processes have to be better coordinated in order to synchronize the flow of inputs through the chain.

Nevertheless, recognizing the importance of transaction costs need not lead to the conclusion that complex and tightly coordinated production systems always result in vertical integration. Rather, asset specificity, opportunism, and coordination costs can be managed at the inter-firm level through a variety of methods. Network actors in many instances control opportunism through the effects of repeat transactions, reputation, and social norms that are embedded in particular geographic locations or social groups. Network theorists (e.g., Jarillo, 1988; Lorenz, 1988; Powell, 1990; Thorelli, 1986) argue that trust, reputation, and mutual dependence dampen opportunistic behavior, and in so doing they make possible more complex inter-firm divisions of labor and interdependence than would be predicted by transaction costs theory.

Furthermore, the literature on firm capabilities and learning, which has its roots in the resource view of the firm pioneered by Penrose (1959), provides other reasons why firms are prepared to buy key inputs in the face of asset specificity, and therefore, construct relatively complex inter-firm relationships. According to Penrose, how and whether firms can capture value depends, in part, on the generation and retention of competencies (that is, resources) that are difficult for competitors to replicate. In practice, even the most vertically integrated firms rarely internalize all the technological and management capabilities that are required to bring a product or service to market. Transaction cost economics acknowledges this fact by employing the variable of frequency. If an input, even an important one, is required infrequently, then it will likely be acquired externally. This is essentially an argument about scale economies. The literature on firm capabilities and learning, by contrast, argues that the learning required to effectively develop the capability to engage in certain value chain activities may be difficult, time-consuming, and effectively impossible for some firms to acquire, regardless of frequency or scale economies. Thus, firms must in certain instances depend on external resources. The doctrine of 'core competence' takes this a step further, arguing that firms which rely on the complementary competencies of other firms and focus more intensively on their own areas of competence will perform better than firms that are vertically integrated or incoherently diversified (Prahalad and Hamel, 1990).

These issues, while often discussed at the local or national level, or in the context of 'a dense network of social relations' (Granovetter, 1985: 507), can equally be applied to the structuring of global-scale production and distribution. The recent work of geographers such as Hughes (2000), Henderson et al. (2002), and Dicken et al. (2001) has emphasized the complexity of inter-firm relationships in the global economy. The key insight is that coordination and control of global-scale production systems, despite their complexity, can be achieved without direct ownership.

The theories of industrial organization discussed here, when considered cumulatively, suggest that different ways of dealing with the problem of asset specificity, and different motivations for constructing complex firm-to-firm relationships in the face of asset specificity, result in three modes of industrial organization: market, hierarchy, and network. But empirical observation tells us that not all networks are alike. In the next section, we develop a theory that can help to specify and explain this variation.

Types of Governance in Global Value Chains

If a theory of global value chain governance is to be useful to policy makers, it should be parsimonious. It has to simplify and abstract from an extremely heterogeneous body of evidence, identifying the variables that play a large role in determining patterns of value chain governance while holding others at bay, at least initially. Clearly, history, institutions, geographic and social contexts, the evolving rules of the game, and path dependence matter; and many factors will influence how firms and groups of firms are linked in the global economy. Nevertheless, a simple framework is useful because it isolates key variables and provides a clear view of fundamental forces underlying specific empirical situations that might otherwise be overlooked. Our intention is to create the simplest framework that generates results relevant to real-world outcomes.

In the 1990s, Gereffi and others developed a framework, called 'global commodity chains', that tied the concept of the value-added chain directly to the global organization of industries (see Gereffi and Korzeniewicz, 1994). This work not only highlighted the importance of coordination across firm boundaries, but also the growing importance of new global buyers (mainly retailers and brand marketers) as key drivers in the formation of globally dispersed and organizationally fragmented production and distribution networks. Gereffi (1994) used the term 'buyer-driven global commodity chain' to denote how global buyers used explicit coordination[4] to help create a highly competent supply-base upon which global-scale production and distribution systems could be built without direct ownership.

By highlighting explicit coordination in dis-integrated chains and contrasting them to the relationships contained within vertically integrated, or 'producer-driven' chains, the global commodity chains framework drew attention to the role of networks in driving the co-evolution of cross-border industrial organization. However, the global commodity chains framework did not adequately specify the variety of network forms that more recent field research has uncovered. While research on the horticulture industry (Dolan and Humphrey, 2000) and the footwear industry (Schmitz and Knorringa, 2000) reinforced Gereffi's notion that global buyers (retailers, marketers, and traders) can and do exert a high degree of control over spatially dispersed value chains even when they do not own production, transport, or processing facilities, recent research on global production has highlighted other important forms of coordination.

Work on the electronics industry and contract manufacturing by Sturgeon (2002) and by Sturgeon and Lee (2001) contrasted three types of supply relationships, based on the degree of standardization of product and process: (1) the 'commodity supplier' that provides standard products through arm's length market relationships, (2) the 'captive supplier' that makes non-standard products using machinery dedicated to the buyer's needs, and (3) the 'turn-key supplier' that produces customized products for buyers and uses flexible machinery to pool capacity for different customers. This analysis emphasized the complexity of information exchanged between firms and the degree of asset specificity in production equipment. Sturgeon (2002) referred to production systems that rely on turn-key suppliers as 'modular production networks' because highly competent suppliers could be added and subtracted from the global production arrangements on an as-needed basis. Around the same time, Humphrey and Schmitz (2000, 2002) distinguished between suppliers in quasi-hierarchical relationships with buyers, whose situation corresponds to 'captive suppliers', and network relationships between firms that cooperate because they possess complementary competences.[5] Humphrey and Schmitz emphasized the role of supplier competence in determining the extent of subordination of suppliers to buyers. If global buyers needed to invest in supplier competence, they would need both to specify the product and process parameters to be followed by suppliers and to guard this investment in the supplier by remaining the dominant, if not exclusive, customer.[6]

Using the approaches outlined above and empirical reference points taken from many studies of global value chains,[7] we propose a more complete typology of value-chain governance. We acknowledge, as do most other frameworks that seek to explain industry organization—from transactions costs to global commodity chains to organizational theory—that market-based relationships among firms and vertically integrated firms (hierarchies) make up opposite ends of a spectrum of explicit coordination, and that network relationships comprise an intermediate mode of value chain governance. What we add to this conceptualization is an extension of the network category into three distinct types: modular, relational, and captive. Thus, our typology identifies five basic types of value chain governance. These are analytical, not empirical, although they have been in part derived from empirical observation. They are:

1. *Markets:* Market linkages do not have to be completely transitory, as is typical of spot markets; they can persist over time, with repeat transactions. The essential point is that the costs of switching to new partners are low for both parties.

2. *Modular value chains:* Typically, suppliers in modular value chains make products to a customer's specifications, which may be more or less detailed. However, when providing 'turn-key services', suppliers take full responsibility for competencies surrounding process technology, use generic machinery that limits transaction-specific investments, and make capital outlays for components and materials on behalf of customers.

3. *Relational value chains:* In these networks, we see complex interactions between buyers and sellers, which often create mutual dependence and high levels of asset specificity. This may be managed through reputation, or family and ethnic ties. Many authors have highlighted the role of spatial proximity in supporting relational value chain linkages, but trust and reputation might well function in spatially dispersed networks where relationships are built up over time, or are based on dispersed family and social groups (see for example, Menkhoff, 1992).

4. *Captive value chains:* In these networks, small suppliers are transactionally dependent on much larger buyers. Suppliers face significant switching costs and are, therefore, 'captive'. Such networks are frequently characterized by a high degree of monitoring and control by lead firms.

5. *Hierarchy:* This governance form is characterized by vertical integration. The dominant form of governance is managerial control, flowing from managers to subordinates, or from headquarters to subsidiaries and affiliates.

A Theory of Value Chain Governance

Having laid out this typology, our next step is to develop an operational theory of global value chain governance. Under which conditions would we expect market, modular, relational, captive, or vertically integrated global value chain governance to arise? Building on the work cited above, we will identify and discuss three key determinants of value chain governance patterns: complexity of transactions; codifiability of information; and capability of suppliers. In so doing, we acknowledge the problem of asset specificity as identified by transaction cost economics, but also give emphasis to what have been termed 'mundane' transaction costs—the costs involved in coordinating activities along the chain. It has been argued that these coordination, or mundane, transaction costs rise when value chains are producing non-standard products, products with integral product architectures, and products whose output is time sensitive (Baldwin and Clark, 2000).

Lead firms increase complexity when they place new demands on the value chain, such as when they seek just-in-time supply and when they increase product differentiation. However, lead firms also adopt strategies to reduce the complexity of these transactions. One important way of doing this is through the development of technical and process standards. The complexity of information transmitted between firms can be reduced through the adoption of technical standards that codify information and allow clean hand-offs between trading partners. Where in the flow of activities these standards apply goes a long way toward determining the organizational break points in the value chain. When standards for the hand-off of codified specifications are widely known, the value chain gains many of the advantages that have been identified in the realm of modular product design, especially the conservation of human effort through the re-use of system elements, or modules, as new products are brought on-stream (Langlois and Robertson, 1995; Schilling and Steensma, 2001; Sturgeon, 2002). In the realm of value chain modularity, suppliers and customers can be easily linked and de-linked, resulting in a very fluid and flexible network structure. While the dynamics are market-like, the system remains qualitatively different because of the large volumes of non-price information flowing across the inter-firm boundary, albeit in codified form. Furthermore, a high-level of product differentiation can be accommodated with limited information exchange as long as differentiation is defined by a set of unambiguous and widely accepted parameters. Institutions, both public and private, can both define grades and standards, and (in some cases) certify that products comply with them.[8] The development of process standards and certification in relation to quality, labor, and environmental outcomes perform similar functions.[9]

At the same time, the integration of new suppliers into global value chains also increases coordination challenges. Keesing and Lall (1992) argue that producers in developing countries are expected to meet requirements that frequently do not (yet) apply to their domestic markets. This creates a gap between the capabilities required for the domestic market and those required for the export market, which raises the degree of monitoring and control required by buyers.

These considerations lead us to construct a theory of value chain governance based on three factors:

A. The *complexity* of information and knowledge transfer required to sustain a particular transaction, particularly with respect to product and process specifications;

B. The extent to which this information and knowledge can be *codified* and, therefore, transmitted efficiently and without transaction-specific investment between the parties to the transaction; and

C. The *capabilities* of actual and potential suppliers in relation to the requirements of the transaction.

If these three factors are allowed only two values—high or low—then there are eight possible combinations, of which five are actually found.[10]

1. *Markets:* When transactions are easily codified, product specifications are relatively simple, and suppliers have the capability to make the products in question with little input from buyers, asset specificity will fail to accumulate and market governance can be expected. In market exchange, buyers respond to specifications and prices set by sellers. Because the complexity of information exchanged is relatively low, transactions can be governed with little explicit coordination.

2. *Modular value chains:* When the ability to codify specifications extends to complex products, value chain modularity can arise. This can come about when product architecture is modular[11] and technical standards simplify interactions by reducing component variation and by unifying component, product, and process specifications, and also when suppliers have the competence to supply full packages and modules, which internalizes hard to codify (tacit) information, reduces asset specificity and therefore a buyer's need for direct monitoring and control. Linkages based on codified knowledge provide many of the benefits of arm's-length market linkages—speed, flexibility, and access to low-cost inputs—but are not the same as classic market exchanges based on price. When a computerized design file is transferred from a lead firm to a supplier, for example, there is much more flowing across the inter-firm link than information about prices. Because of codification, complex information can be exchanged with little explicit coordination, and so, like simple market exchange, the cost of switching to new partners remains low.

3. *Relational value chains:* When product specifications cannot be codified, transactions are complex, and supplier capabilities are high, relational value chain governance can be expected. This is because tacit knowledge must be exchanged between buyers and sellers, and because highly

competent suppliers provide a strong motivation for lead firms to outsource to gain access to complementary competencies. The mutual dependence that then arises may be regulated through reputation, social and spatial proximity, family and ethnic ties, and the like. It can also be handled through mechanisms that impose costs on the party that breaks a contract, as discussed in Williamson's analysis of credible commitments and hostages (Williamson, 1983). The exchange of complex tacit information is most often accomplished by frequent face-to-face interaction and governed by high levels of explicit coordination, which makes the costs of switching to new partners high.

4. *Captive value chains:* When the ability to codify—in the form of detailed instructions—and the complexity of product specifications are both high but supplier capabilities are low, then value chain governance will tend toward the captive type. This is because low supplier competence in the face of complex products and specifications requires a great deal of intervention and control on the part of the lead firm, encouraging the build-up of transactional dependence as lead firms seek to lock in suppliers in order to exclude others from reaping the benefits of their efforts. Therefore, the suppliers face significant switching costs and are 'captive'. Captive suppliers are frequently confined to a narrow range of tasks—for example, mainly engaged in simple assembly—and are dependent on the lead firm for complementary activities such as design, logistics, component purchasing, and process-technology upgrading. Captive inter-firm linkages control opportunism through the dominance of lead firms, while at the same time providing enough resources and market access to the subordinate firms to make exit an unattractive option.

5. *Hierarchy:* When product specifications cannot be codified, products are complex, and highly competent suppliers cannot be found, then lead firms will be forced to develop and manufacture products in-house. This governance form is usually driven by the need to exchange tacit knowledge between value chain activities as well as the need to effectively manage complex webs of inputs and outputs and to control resources, especially intellectual property.

The five global value chain governance types, along with the values of the three variables that determine them, are listed in Table 4.1. These five types of global value chain governance arise from ascribing different values to the three key variables: (1) complexity of inter-firm transactions; (2) the degree to which this complexity can be mitigated through codification; and (3) the extent to which suppliers have the necessary capabilities to meet the buyers' requirements. Each governance type provides a different trade-off between the benefits and risks of outsourcing. As shown in the last column of Table 4.1, the governance types comprise a spectrum running from low levels of explicit coordination and power asymmetry between buyers and suppliers, in the case of markets, to high levels of explicit coordination and power asymmetry between buyers and suppliers, in the case of hierarchy.

Table 4.1 Key Determinants of Global Value Chain Governance

Governance type	Complexity of transactions	Ability to codify transactions	Capabilities in the supply-base	Degree of explicit coordination and power asymmetry
Market	Low	High	High	Low
Modular	High	High	High	↑
Relational	High	Low	High	
Captive	High	High	Low	↓
Hierarchy	High	Low	Low	High

Source: Authors.

Note: There are eight possible combinations of the three variables. Five of them generate global value chain types. The combination of low complexity of transactions and low ability to codify is unlikely to occur. This excludes two combinations. Further, if the complexity of the transaction is low and the ability to codify is high, then low supplier capability would lead to exclusion from the value chain. While this is an important outcome, it does not generate a governance type *per se*.

The fact that the governance types developed here can be used to illuminate how power operates in global value chains merits elaboration. In captive global value chains, power is exerted directly by lead firms on suppliers, which is analogous to the direct administrative control that top management at headquarters might exert over subordinates in an offshore subsidiary or affiliate of a vertically integrated firm (or 'hierarchy' in our framework). Such direct control suggests a high degree of explicit coordination and a large measure of power asymmetry with the lead firm (or top management) being the dominant party. In relational global value chains, the power balance between the firms is more symmetrical, given that both contribute key competences. There is a great deal of explicit coordination in relational global value chains, but it is achieved through a close dialogue between more or less equal partners, as opposed to the more unidirectional flow of information and control between unequal partners as in captive global value chains and within hierarchies. In modular global value chains, as in markets, switching customers and suppliers is relatively easy. Power asymmetries remain relatively low because both suppliers and buyers work with multiple partners.

Figure 4.1 illustrates much of the above discussion in graphic form, showing the five global value chain types arrayed along the dual spectrums of explicit coordination and power asymmetry. The small line arrows represent exchange based on price while the larger block arrows represent thicker flows of information and control, regulated through explicit coordination. This includes instructions coming from a more powerful buyer (or manager) to a less powerful supplier (or subordinate), as in captive global value chains or within the confines of a hierarchy, as well as social sanctions regulating the behavior of more or less equal partners, as in relational global value chains. In the case of modular global value chains, thick information flows are narrowed down to a codified hand-off at the inter-firm link, leaving each partner to manage tacit information within its own firm boundaries, or perhaps by combining some other form of global value chain governance, such as captive or market-based, for part of the chain. While relationships between the relational and modular suppliers and the firms providing their material inputs and components are displayed as market-based in the figure, they could equally take other forms.

Figure 4.1 Five Global Value Chain Governance Types

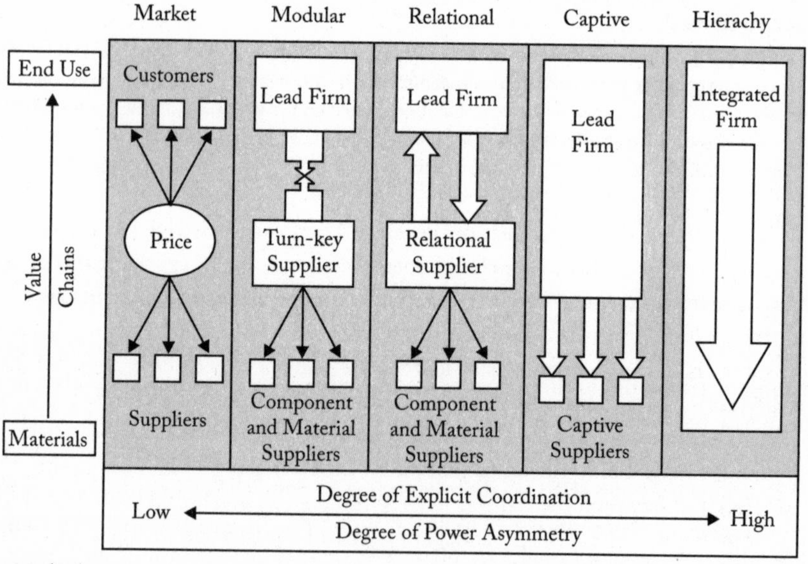

Source: Authors.

Dynamic Value Chain Analysis: Sectoral Cases

Identifying the main types of global value chain governance, and providing a theoretical explanation for why they arise, are important steps and hopefully this work will lead us to a better understanding of the contemporary world economy. Nonetheless, to make it a useful tool for policy, a theory of global value chain governance should allow us to do more than just generate different forms of inter-firm coordination; we must try to anticipate *change* in global value chains. Case studies, in particular, clearly show us how governance structures evolve over time. In the following section, we highlight how global value chain governance structures have evolved in four distinct industries: bicycles, apparel, fresh vegetables, and electronics. Some trajectories of change are identified on Table 4.2, and we refer to these trajectories as we discuss each of the cases.

Table 4.2 Some Dynamics of Global Value Chain Governance

Governance type	Complexity of transactions	Ability to codify transactions	Capabilities in the supply-base
Market	① Low ②	High	High
Modular	High	③ High ④	High
Relational	High	Low	⑤ High ⑥
Captive	High	High	Low
Hierarchy	High	Low	Low

Source: Authors.

Note: Dynamics of changes in governance:
① Increasing complexity of transactions also reduces supplier competence in relation to new demands.
② Decreasing complexity of transactions and greater ease of codification.
③ Better codification of transactions.
④ De-codification of transactions.
⑤ Increasing supplier competence.
⑥ Decreasing supplier competence.

The Bicycle Industry: From Hierarchy to Market-Based Coordination

The evolution of the bicycle industry in the twentieth century provides a good example of how hierarchies can evolve toward inter-firm governance that relies primarily on market mechanisms.[12] It shows how market governance is enabled not only by low transaction costs—particularly costs associated with coordination of component design with final product design—and the economies of scale and production enabled by the rise of industry standards, but also by the development of specialist competencies among suppliers (trajectories numbers 3 and 5 in Table 4.2).

In the early years of the bicycle industry (the 1890s), vertically integrated firms manufactured bicycles, but production soon became fragmented. Today, there are large firms within each segment of the value chain, such as Shimano in drive-train components and several large branded bicycle manufacturers, but very few firms that span more than one segment (Galvin and Morkel, 2001: 40). The different bicycle components require different competencies, which limits economies of scope. An integrated bicycle manufacturer would require many different technological competences, or would need to explicitly coordinate the activities of many different firms. After the initial stage of the industry's development, specialist firms became more competitive than vertically integrated companies that made complete bicycles. Well-defined interfaces between various components mean that specialist manufacturers have the advantages of scale through demand pooling. To the extent that economies of scale occur upstream in the value chain, there are strong incentives for market coordination and the development of the institutional mechanisms to make this possible. The specialist knowledge of the suppliers also gives them a greater capacity to innovate within their specific product ranges, as long as this does not require changes in other components. Where these specialists dominate a market segment (for example, Shimano in drive systems), they can innovate within this area more successfully than others, and if extremely successful, may establish a new *de facto* standard applicable across the industry.

The industry standards required to make such specialization and divisions of labor work can arise in a variety of ways. They can be imposed by a dominant firm, as in the case of Shimano in bicycles and IBM in personal computers; they can arise informally through inter-firm networks, as with the emergence of regional standards in the early days of the bicycle industry; they can be managed by industry associations; or they can be regulated by international agencies and negotiations, as in the case of the development of new standards for mobile phones. The establishment of standards is often contentious and part of the competitive positioning of firms.

The Apparel Industry: From Captive to Relational Value Chains

The apparel industry has been characterized by global production and trade networks since at least the middle of the twentieth century, and the expansion and growing capabilities of its global supply-base have permitted it to move rapidly from captive to more complex relational value chains over the span of just a few decades. The epicenter of export-oriented apparel production has been East Asia, as Japan in the 1950s and 1960s, Hong Kong, South Korea, and Taiwan during the 1970s and 1980s, and China in the 1990s emerged sequentially as world-class textile and apparel exporters (Bonacich et al., 1994). The key to East Asia's success was to move from captive value chains—i.e., the mere assembly of imported inputs, typically in export-processing zones—to a more domestically integrated and higher value-added form of exporting broadly known in the industry as full-package supply.[13] Whereas the assembly-oriented captive model required explicit coordination in the form of cut fabric and detailed instructions, full-package production involved the more complex forms of coordination, knowledge exchange, and supplier autonomy typical of relational value chains.

Unlike captive networks, in which foreign firms take responsibility for supplying all the component parts used by local contractors, full-package production requires offshore contractors to develop the capability to interpret designs, make samples, source the needed inputs, monitor product quality, meet the buyer's price, and guarantee on-time delivery. From a development perspective, the main advantage of the full-package export role, compared to simple assembly, is that it allows local firms to learn how to make internationally competitive consumer goods and generates substantial backward linkages to the domestic economy. Increasing supplier competence has been the main driver behind the shift from captive to relational value chains in the apparel industry (trajectory number 5 in Table 4.2). The establishment of overseas buying offices and frequent international travel supported the intense interaction required for exchanging tacit information and building personal relationships between buyers and suppliers.

Trade rules have had an important impact on global value chain governance in the apparel industry, and this provides just one example of how variables, other than the three we have identified, work to shape the architecture of cross-border economic activity. US import quotas established by the Multi-Fiber Arrangement fueled the spread of global production networks in apparel beginning in the early 1970s. The existence of quotas prompted the rise of value-chain intermediaries, including East Asian trading companies such as Hong Kong's Li and Fung and manufacturers such as the Fang Brothers, to coordinate the flow of orders from US and European buyers to a large numbers of apparel factories established around the world in places with available quota (Gereffi, 1999: 60–63; Magretta, 1998). When the MFA is mostly phased out in 2005 in accordance with the World Trade Organization's Agreement on Textiles and Clothing, global apparel production is likely to become far more concentrated among the most capable firms in a handful of low-cost production sites, including China, India, Indonesia, Mexico, and Turkey (Gereffi and Memodovic, 2003: 12). Such concentration could well undermine the position of intermediary firms. Still, the variables we have highlighted in this chapter continue to be important. To the extent that the ability to codify transactions is increased by this concentration process, and supplier capabilities continue to improve, we would expect the relational value chains in apparel to become more modular (trajectory number 3 in Table 4.2).

Fresh Vegetables: From Market Coordination to Explicit Coordination

The changing nature of fresh vegetables trade between Kenya and the United Kingdom highlights a shift from market-based global value chain governance to more explicit coordination, and it reveals the importance of the competitive strategies of UK supermarkets in driving this change.[14] Beginning in the mid-1980s

UK supermarkets began to use the quality and variety of their produce offerings as a main source of competitive differentiation, and in doing so generated several distinct forms of governance at different stages in the chain.

Until the mid-1980s, the fresh vegetables trade was handled through a series of arm's-length market relationships. Traders in Kenya bought produce in wholesale markets or at the farm gate and exported it to the United Kingdom, where it was sold in wholesale markets. However, as supermarket chains in the United Kingdom gradually took an increasing share of fresh food sales and therefore became more powerful actors, they began to introduce more explicit coordination in the chain. Supermarkets saw fresh produce (fruit and vegetables) as strategic because it was one of the few product lines that could persuade consumers to shift from one supermarket chain to another. In order to attract customers, the supermarkets introduced new items, emphasized quality, provided consistent year-round supply, and increased the processing of products to provide fresh produce that required little or no preparation prior to cooking or eating. At the same time, the supermarkets were forced to respond to an increasingly complex regulatory environment related to food safety, particularly pesticide residues and conditions for post-harvest processing, as well as environmental and labor standards.

Supermarkets pursued these strategic goals by increasing explicit coordination in the value chain. Instead of purchasing through wholesale markets, they developed closer relationships with UK importers and African exporters, and moved to renewable annual contracts with suppliers whose capabilities and systems were subject to regular monitoring and audit. Supermarkets began to inspect suppliers prior to incorporation in the chain, and made regular spot checks at all points in the chain, right down to the field. The interaction of the firms in the chain also became more complex and relational. Suppliers and buyers worked together on product development, logistics, quality, and the like. This created new value chain relationships and competencies. Over time, relationships between supermarkets and UK importers took new forms, with the recent trend moving value chain governance in the direction of modularity. The supermarkets have reduced the number of UK suppliers/importers for each product range and given the remaining suppliers greater responsibility for supply chain management, product development, and consumer research. These importers work for a range of UK supermarkets and food retailers, although the three largest supermarket chains (Tesco, Asda, and Sainsbury) do try to avoid using the same suppliers.

Further back along the chain, organizational fragmentation has decreased and inter-organizational relationships have become relational. The risks of this have been contained by the development of exclusive bilateral relationships. A Kenyan exporter will only deal with one UK importer, although it may sell to other markets through other channels, and a UK importer will only have one Kenyan supplier.

There has even been some forward and backward integration between African exporters and UK importers, with outright ownership or equity participation. This bilateral dependence of African exporters and UK importers has not created captive relationships. First, importers and exporters do change partners from time to time. Second, there is a situation of mutual dependence and power symmetry. Exporters need an outlet to the UK market, but importers also need an assured supply of produce. Third, the exporters have become increasingly sophisticated and competent, as additional processing functions were transferred to Africa where costs are lower (trajectory number 5 in Table 4.2). In Kenya, the industry has become much more concentrated as the investment costs of processing have risen.

Within Kenya, the largest exporter of fresh vegetables from Africa to the United Kingdom, increasing requirements have led leading exporters to increase own-farm production at the expense of purchasing vegetables from both smallholders and large contract farmers. This can be seen as a case of increasing complexity leading to vertical integration when it is not accompanied by either codification or higher supplier competence.

The US Electronics Industry: From Hierarchy to Modular Value Chains and Beyond

For most of the twentieth century, the electronics industry in the United States has been dominated by large, vertically integrated firms, first in the telephone industry (ATT) and then the radio industry (RCA), out of which grew other consumer electronics sectors such as television and eventually, computers (e.g., IBM). In the 1960s and 1970s, with the push for better semiconductors for military and aerospace applications, an independent, or 'merchant', components industry (e.g., Texas Instruments) gathered steam with the Air Force and the National Aeronautics and Space Administration playing the role of 'lead firm'. In the 1980s, as the civilian electronics industry began to grow rapidly with the personal computer, a range of other value chain functions were outsourced, beginning with production equipment for both semiconductor fabrication and circuit-board assembly, and then spreading to specialized sub-components such as disk drives and monitors, and most recently to the manufacturing process itself in a practice called 'contract manufacturing'.[15]

During the 1990s, nearly all major North American product-level electronics firms, and several important European companies as well, made the decision to get out of manufacturing. Plants were closed or sold off to contract manufacturers, driving a significant share of the world's electronics production capacity into a handful of huge globally operating contract manufacturers. The contract manufacturer Solectron, for example, grew from a single Silicon Valley location with 3,500 employees and $256 million in revenues in 1988 to a global powerhouse with more than 80,000 employees in 50 locations and close to $20 billion in revenues in 2000. During the same period, Solectron extended its service offerings beyond circuit-board assembly to include, among other things, product (re)design-for-manufacturability, component purchasing and inventory management, test routine development, final product assembly, global logistics, distribution, and after-sales service and repair. Global contract manufacturers such as Solectron introduce a high degree of modularity into value chain governance because the large scale and scope of their operations create comprehensive bundles, or modules, of generic value chain activities that can be accessed by a wide variety of lead firms. Standardized protocols for handing-off computerized design files and highly automated and standardized process technologies made it easy for lead firms to switch and share contractors, and inhibited the build-up of specific assets.

Today, as contractors seek new sources of revenue by providing additional inputs to lead-firm design and business processes, and new circuit-board assembly technologies appear on the scene, such as those for boards with optical components, the hand-off of design specifications is becoming more complex and less standardized, making it harder for lead firms to switch and share suppliers. Closer collaboration in the realm of product design requires contractors to receive fully blown computer-aided-design files for their customer's new products; files that can contain core intellectual property. As contractors take over more distribution functions, lead firms must reveal critical knowledge about end-customer requirements and pricing. All of these interactions are being embedded in elaborate information technology systems that span the organizations of lead firms and their key contractors, creating new areas of risk for lead firms in the areas of intellectual property leakage and buyer-supplier lock-in. Shared information technology systems are evolving in two directions simultaneously: toward proprietary systems that increase asset specificity and lock-in, but better protect key intellectual property; and toward open standards (e.g., RosettaNet) and/or third-party systems that better support value chain modularity but that leave the door open for intellectual property leakage. The question of which direction the industry will take—toward proprietary systems and relational value chains, or toward commonly used standards and modular value chains—is still open, and its answer will help to determine the future shape of the electronics industry.

The electronics case shows value chain modularity is enabled by the codification of complex information (for example, through computerized product design and automated process technologies) because codification simplifies the hand-off at the inter-firm link. But the case also shows that modularity can be undermined by 'de-codification' (trajectory number 4 in Table 4.2), spurred either by technological change, as in the case of the emergence of optical circuit-board assembly technology, or by the bundling of supplier activities in such a way that suppliers reach across the codified link to assist with lead firm activities that remain tacit or are highly proprietary, or both, such as product design and customer contact.

The Dynamics of Global Value Chains

The case studies presented in this section are meant to highlight the dynamic and overlapping nature of global value chains. Value chain governance patterns are not static or strictly associated with particular industries. They depend on the details of how interactions between value chain actors are managed, and how technologies are applied to design, production and the governance of the value chain itself. Nor are value chain governance patterns monolithic. Even in a particular industry in a particular place and time, governance patterns may vary from one stage of the chain to another. While we believe that this dynamism and variation can largely be accounted for by the three explanatory variables presented in this chapter, more work will be needed to fully understand their dynamic characteristics. How and why do the complexity of information, the ability to codify information, and supplier competence change?

We can at this stage offer only a partial answer. First, information complexity changes as lead firms seek to obtain more complex outputs and services from their supply-base. This can reduce the effective level of supplier capabilities as existing capabilities may not meet the new requirements (trajectory number 1 in Table 4.2). Alternatively, reduced complexity may increase the ability to codify transactions (trajectory 2 in Table 4.2). Second, within industries there is a continuing tension between codification and innovation (trajectories numbers 3 and 4 in Table 4.2). As Storper (1995) and David (1995) have both pointed out, new technologies can restart the clock on the process of codification. Third, supplier competence changes over time: increasing as suppliers learn, but falling again as buyers introduce new suppliers into value chains, as new technologies come on-stream, or as lead firms increase the requirements for existing suppliers (trajectories numbers 5 and 6 in Table 4.2).

When we look broadly at the evidence provided by global value chain research across a variety of industries and time periods, it is tempting to make generalizations about trends in the global economy. In all of the case studies presented here, and many other industries as well, increasing capabilities in the supply-base have helped to push the architecture of global value chains away from hierarchy and captive networks and toward the relational, modular, and market types. Value chain modularity seems to be especially likely when suppliers offer lead firms greater levels of value chain bundling (e.g., turn-key and full-package services), which has the advantages of internalizing tacit knowledge and pooling capacity utilization for greater economies of scale. However, organizational fragmentation will not lead to value chain modularity if codification is extremely difficult. For example, a strong shift toward fragmentation in the organization of the US motor vehicle industry beginning in the mid-1980s has resulted in value chains with strong relational elements. This can be partly explained by the difficulty of codifying complex mechanical systems (Fine, 1998), which has inhibited the rise of industry-wide standards and kept the complexity of the transactions between lead firms and suppliers high even as the capabilities of suppliers, driven in part by the consolidation of first tier suppliers, has increased dramatically (Humphrey, 2003; Sturgeon and Florida, 2004).

As standards, information technology, and the capabilities of suppliers improve, the modular form appears to be playing an increasingly central role in the global economy.[16] Again, the general shift toward value chain fragmentation has been driven by the cost and risk advantages of outsourcing (assuming that a solution to the problem of asset specificity can be developed). When we take relational networks as our starting point, however, a shift to modular—and perhaps eventually to market—forms can be expected as standards and codification schemes improve because more fluid value chains offer additional decreases in cost and risk.

Still, we resist the overly simplistic notion that global value chains are evolving along a single trajectory. First, the standards that enable the codification of product and process specifications are different across industries and are constantly evolving. Second, standards for codifying product and process specifications can become obsolete as technologies change or when there is a drive to bundle value chain activities in new ways. This can drive market and modular relationships, as we may be seeing in the case of the electronics industry today, back toward relational governance, and if the problem of asset specificity becomes severe enough, the hierarchical form. Third, knowing the standard and adopting the protocol may not be straightforward, inexpensive, or immediately possible for all actors in an industry, and there may be competing standards in use that make choosing and investing difficult and risky. Since standards and protocols are dynamic, major advantages accrue to those actors that actively participate in the rule-setting process, which favors established actors and locations (Sturgeon, 2003). Finally, there is clearly no single best way to organize global value chains. In some product categories, where integral product architecture makes it difficult to break the value chain, vertical integration may be the most competitive approach to value chain governance. Sony and Samsung's success in consumer electronics has come despite, or perhaps, because of high levels of vertical integration. In the garment industry, Zara's success with extremely rapid product cycles—bi-weekly in some cases—has been supported by the company's in-house textile manufacturing subsidiary and captive sewing workshops (Bonnen, 2002).

Conclusion

In this chapter we have developed a typology of global value chain governance and presented some theoretical justifications for why these patterns might occur. We argue that the structure of global value chains depends critically upon three variables: the complexity of transactions, the ability to codify transactions, and the capabilities in the supply-base. These variables are sometimes determined by the technological characteristics of products and processes (some transactions are inherently more complex and difficult to codify than others, for example) and they often depend on the effectiveness of industry actors and the social processes surrounding the development, dissemination, and adoption of standards and other codification schemes. It is the latter set of determinants, in particular, that opens the door for policy interventions and corporate strategy.

The global value chains framework focuses on the nature and content of the inter-firm linkages, and the power that regulates value chain coordination, mainly between buyers and the first few tiers of suppliers. However, it is important not to ignore the actors at both ends of the value chain. On the upstream end, component and equipment suppliers can wield a great deal of power. For example, in the personal computer industry two firms, Intel and Microsoft, set parameters that most other value chain actors must adjust to. The power of such 'parameter-setting' firms, such as Shimano in bicycles and Applied Materials in semiconductors, is not exerted through explicit coordination, but through their market dominance in key components and technologies. On the downstream end of the chain, highly knowledgeable users can play a significant role in determining the attributes and innovative trajectory of the products and services that global value chains churn out, as they do in many complex service industries such as enterprise computing. Even average consumers are far from passive, as Leslie and Reimer (1999) point out. Consumer culture, whether it emerges from the home, street, school, or park, can subvert the original intention of producers by altering and ascribing meaning to products in ways that designers and marketers never intended.

Our primary concern in this chapter is with organizational structures that span international borders and particularly those that have a global reach. Nonetheless, local and national structures and institutions also matter. Geographers and planners have provided us with insights into how the spatial and social propinquity of local industrial agglomerations work to buoy organizationally disaggregated, and often highly innovative, economic activities (e.g., Storper and Scott, 1988; Storper and Walker, 1989). This work has usefully stressed the spatial embeddedness of tacit knowledge and the importance of tight interdependencies between geographically clustered firms (Maskell and Malmberg, 1999; Storper, 1995). We acknowledge these points, and have argued elsewhere that such agglomerations are the places where the most relational portions of global value chains might be found (Sturgeon, 2003). The varieties of capitalism literature, coming largely from political science (e.g., Berger and Dore, 1996; Soskice, 1999; Streeck, 1992), similarly argues that national-level rules and institutions (e.g., in finance, corporate governance, and education and training) profoundly affect the character of industries. Other studies (Borrus et al., 2000; Florida and Kenney, 1993; Lynch, 1998) show that many geographically rooted characteristics are carried abroad, as foreign direct investment projects local and national models onto the global stage. These variations can and do have profound effects on value chain governance. For example, even when the underlying conditions for emergent organizational forms such as value chain modularity are well established, as they are in the Japanese personal computer industry, large-scale outsourcing might be antithetical to long-standing corporate strategies and institutions, such as lifetime employment in large firms, which make radical industry reorganization extremely difficult and slow.

It is also clear that global-scale regulations, the 'rules of the game' as it were, have a profound effect on the shape and direction of change in global value chains. In a wide range of industries, from electronics to apparel to household goods, selective exemptions for duties on value added in particular locations, such as section 807 and most-favored-nation status for the United States and outward processing arrangements for Europe, have encouraged the geographical fragmentation of global value chains, as we have seen in the apparel case study. Yet political pressures in both developed and developing nations to retain (or gain) apparel jobs, and managerial desires to spread risk through geographical diversification, are likely to keep the apparel value chain more fragmented than it would be if production decisions were based on economic criteria alone.

While there is a multitude of factors that affect the evolution of the global economy, we feel confident that the variables internal to our model influence the shape and governance of global value chains in important ways, regardless of the institutional context within which they are situated. The governance framework that we propose takes us part of the way toward a more systematic understanding of global value chains, but much remains to be done.[17] One of the most pressing areas is the development of policy tools for industrial upgrading that are consistent with the framework. One of the key findings of value chain studies is that access to developed country markets has become increasingly dependent on participating in global production networks led by firms based in developed countries. Thus, the governance of global value chains is essential for understanding how firms in developing countries can gain access to global markets, what the benefits of access and the risks of exclusion might be, and how the net gains from participation in global value chains might be increased. While the search for paths of sustainable development in the global economy is an inherently difficult and elusive objective, our task is greatly facilitated by having a clearer sense of the various ways in which global value chains are governed, and the key determinants that shape these outcomes.

Acknowledgments

The authors wish to thank the Rockefeller Foundation for its generous support of the Global Value Chains Initiative (see http://www. globalvaluechains.org). In preparing this chapter, we have drawn upon discussions at workshops on value chains held in Bellagio, Italy, in September 2000 and April 2003 and in Rockport, Massachusetts, in April 2002. However, any errors or shortcomings remain our own.

Notes

1. While 'internationalization' refers to the geographic spread of economic activities across national boundaries, 'globalization' implies the functional integration and coordination of these internationally dispersed activities (Dicken, 2003: 12).
2. We do not suggest that the theory developed in this chapter can explain all governance patterns observed in global value chains. The theory should be used as a complement to, not a substitute for, the rich detail and complexity that can be observed in global value chains, especially their historical, geographical, and sectoral specificity.
3. Similarly, Hummels et al. (1998: 80–81) use the term 'vertical-specialization-based-trade' to refer to the amount of imported inputs embodied in goods that are exported. 'Vertical specialization' of global trade occurs when a country uses imported intermediate parts to produce goods it later exports.
4. 'Explicit coordination' is a term used by Clemons et al. (1993) to refer to non-market forms of coordination of economic activity.
5. This work drew on the analysis of Palpacuer (2000) on core and complementary competences in value chains.
6. Work on the apparel industry (Gereffi, 1999) and on commodity exports from Africa (Gibbon, 2001) also showed a variety of contracting arrangements.
7. An indication of the range of studies is provided by the collection edited by Gereffi and Kaplinsky (2001).
8. For a discussion of grades and standards in the food industry, see Reardon et al. (2001). For a more general discussion of modular product architectures and its implications for industry structure, see Baldwin and Clark (2000).
9. The development of product and process standards and their implications for value chain governance are discussed by Nadvi and Wältring (2002).
10. Low informational complexity without codification generates two combinations that are unlikely to occur regardless of supplier competence, high or low. Furthermore, if there is low complexity and a high possibility for codification, and suppliers still do

not have the capabilities to meet the requirements of buyers, then it is likely that they will be excluded from the chain. While this does not generate a global value chain type, *per se*, it is a situation that is quite common, and with requirements for suppliers increasing, perhaps increasingly likely to occur (Sturgeon and Lester, 2004). This case is important insofar as it opens up a discussion of the problems facing developing country suppliers and policies for industrial upgrading.

11. Product architectures generally vary from integral to modular. In integral product architectures, the functional elements of a product are tightly linked and optimised for a particular configuration. In modular product architectures, by contrast, the physical building blocks (or sub-systems) of a product are loosely coupled and designed to be relatively independent of one another because of standardized interfaces and visible design rules, which permit some components and sub-systems to be disaggregated and recombined into a large number of product variations (see Baldwin and Clark, 2000; Schilling and Steensma, 2001; Ulrich, 1995).

12. This discussion is based on Galvin and Morkel (2001).

13. In the Asian context, the full-package model was also known as original equipment manufacturing (OEM).

14. Kenya is the largest exporter of fresh peas and beans from Africa to the European Union and by far the most important supplier to the UK market. This section is based on the work of Dolan and Humphrey (2000, 2004).

15. This discussion is based on Sturgeon (2002).

16. This process is not driven solely by the efforts of suppliers. Value chain actors clearly co-evolve. Lead firm strategies to simultaneously increase outsourcing and consolidate their supply-chains have created a set of highly capable suppliers that, in turn, make outsourcing more attractive for lead firms that have yet to take the outsourcing plunge (Sturgeon and Lee, 2001). Similarly, the evolution of global value chains emanating from one national or local context, especially if successful, provides an example that often generates a reaction in value chains rooted in other places.

17. A high priority for the future will be the development of methods for measuring the key variables in the model. Effective proxies for transactional complexity, level of codification, and supplier competence must be identified and tested in the field.

References

Arndt, Sven W. and Henryk Kierzkowski. 2001. 'Introduction.' In *Fragmentation: New Production Patterns in the World Economy*, edited by Sven W. Arndt and Henryk Kierzkowski, 1–16. Oxford: Oxford University Press.

Baldwin, Carliss Y. and Kim B. Clark. 2000. *Design Rules*. Cambridge, MA: MIT Press.

Berger, Suzanne and Ronald Dore, eds. 1996. *National Diversity and Global Capitalism*. Ithaca, NY: Cornell University Press.

Bonacich, Edna, Lucie Cheng, Norma Chinchilla, Nora Hamilton, and Paul Ong, eds. 1994. *Global Production: The Apparel Industry in the Pacific Rim*. Philadelphia, PA: Temple University Press.

Bonnen, Arturo R. 2002. 'The Fashion Industry in Galicia: Understanding the "Zara" Phenomenon.' *European Planning Studies* 10(4): 519–527.

Borrus, Michael, Dieter Ernst, and Stephen Haggard, eds. 2000. *International Production Networks in Asia*. London and New York: Routledge.

Clemons, Eric K., Sashidhar P. Reddi, and Michael C. Row. 1993. 'The Impact of Information Technology on the Organization of Economic Activity: The "Move to the Middle" Hypothesis.' *Journal of Management Information Systems* 10(2): 9–35.

David, Paul A. 1995. 'Standardization Policies for Network Technologies: The Flux Between Freedom and Order Revisited.' In *Standards, Innovation and Competitiveness: The Politics and Economics of Standards in National and Technical Environments*, edited by Richard Hawkins, Robin Mansell, and Jim Skea, 15–35. Aldershot, UK: Edward Elgar.

Dicken, Peter. 2003. *Global Shift: Reshaping the Global Economic Map in the 21st Century*, 4th edition. London: Sage.

Dicken, Peter, Philip F. Kelly, Kris Olds, and Henry Wai-chung Yeung. 2001. 'Chains and Networks, Territories and Scales: Towards a Relational Framework for Analysing the Global Economy.' *Global Networks* 1(2): 89–112.

Dolan, Catherine and John Humphrey. 2000. 'Governance and Trade in Fresh Vegetables: The Impact of UK Supermarkets on the African Horticulture Industry.' *Journal of Development Studies* 37(2): 147–176.

————. 2004. 'Changing Governance Patterns in the Trade in Fresh Vegetables between Africa and the United Kingdom.' *Environment and Planning A* 36(3): 491–509.

Feenstra, Robert C. 1998. 'Integration of Trade and Disintegration of Production in the Global Economy.' *Journal of Economic Perspectives* 12(4): 31–50.

Fine, Charles H. 1998. *Clockspeed: Winning Industry Control in the Age of Temporary Advantage*. Reading, MA: Perseus.

Florida, Richard and Martin Kenney. 1993. *Beyond Mass Production: The Japanese System and its Transfer to the US*. New York: Oxford University Press.

Galvin, Peter and Andre Morkel. 2001. 'The Effect of Product Modularity on Industry Structure: The Case of the World Bicycle Industry.' *Industry and Innovation* 8(1): 31–47.

Gereffi, Gary. 1994. 'The Organization of Buyer-Driven Global Commodity Chains: How US Retailers Shape Overseas Production Networks.' In *Commodity Chains and Global Capitalism*, edited by Gary Gereffi and Miguel Korzeniewicz, 95–122. Westport, CT: Praeger.

————. 1999. 'International Trade and Industrial Upgrading in the Apparel Commodity Chain.' *Journal of International Economics*. 48(1): 37–70.

Gereffi, Gary and Raphael Kaplinsky, eds. 2001. 'The Value of Value Chains.' *IDS Bulletin* 32(3) Special Issue.

Gereffi, Gary and Miguel Korzeniewicz, eds. 1994. *Commodity Chains and Global Capitalism*. Westport, CT: Praeger.

Gereffi, Gary and Olga Memodovic. 2003. 'The Global Apparel Value Chain: What Prospects for Upgrading by Developing Countries?' United Nations Industrial Development Organization, Sectoral Studies Series. Available at http://www.unido.org/doc/12218.

Gibbon, Peter. 2001. 'Upgrading Primary Products: A Global Value Chain Approach.' *World Development* 29(2): 345–363.

Granovetter, Mark. 1985. 'Economic Action and Social Structure: The Problem of Embeddedness.' *American Journal of Sociology* 91(3): 481–510.

Henderson, Jeffrey, Peter Dicken, Martin Hess, Neil Coe, and Henry Wai-chung Yeung. 2002. 'Global Production Networks and the Analysis of Economic Development.' *Review of International Political Economy* 9(3): 436–464.

Hughes, Alex. 2000. 'Retailers, Knowledges and Changing Commodity Networks: The Case of the Cut Flower Trade.' *Geoforum* 31(2): 175–190.

Hummels, David, Dana Rapoport, and Kei-Mu Yi. 1998. 'Vertical Specialisation and the Changing Nature of World Trade.' *Federal Reserve Bank of New York Economic Policy Review* 4(2): 79–99.

Humphrey, John. 2003. 'Globalisation and Supply Chain Networks: The Auto Industry in Brazil and India.' *Global Networks* 3(2): 121–141.

Humphrey, John and Hubert Schmitz. 2000. 'Governance and Upgrading: Linking Industrial Cluster and Global Value Chain Research.' IDS Working Paper 120. Brighton: Institute of Development Studies, University of Sussex.

———. 2002. 'How Does Insertion in Global Value Chains Affect Upgrading in Industrial Clusters?' *Regional Studies* 36(9): 1017–1027.

Jarillo, Carlos J. 1988. 'On Strategic Networks.' *Strategic Management Journal* 9(1): 31–41.

Keesing, Donald B. and Sanjaya Lall. 1992. 'Marketing Manufactured Exports from Developing Countries: Learning Sequences and Public Support.' In *Trade Policy, Industrialisation and Development*, edited by Gerald K. Helleiner, 176–193. Oxford: Oxford University Press.

Kogut, Bruce. 1985. 'Designing Global Strategies: Comparative and Competitive Value-Added Chains.' *Sloan Management Review* 26(4): 15–28.

Langlois, Richard N. and Paul L. Robertson. 1995. *Firms, Markets and Economic Change*. London: Routledge.

Leslie, Deborah and Suzzane Reimer. 1999. 'Spatializing Commodity Chains.' *Progress in Human Geography* 23(3): 401–420.

Lorenz, Edward H. 1988. 'Neither Friends nor Strangers: Informal Networks of Subcontracting in French Industry.' In *Trust-Making and Breaking Cooperative Relations*, edited by Diego Gambetta, 194–209. Oxford: Basil Blackwell.

Lynch, Teresa. 1998. 'Leaving Home: Three Decades of Internationalization by US Automotive Firms.' IPC Working Paper: 98–007. Cambridge, MA: MIT Industrial Performance Center.

Magretta, Joan. 1998. 'Fast, Global and Entrepreneurial: Supply Chain Management, Hong Kong Style—An Interview with Victor Fung.' *Harvard Business Review* 76(5): 103–140.

Maskell, Peter and Anders Malmberg. 1999. 'Localised Learning and Industrial Competitiveness.' *Cambridge Journal of Economics* 23(2): 167–185.

Menkhoff, Thomas. 1992. 'Xinyong or How to Trust Trust? Chinese Non-Contractual Business Relations and Social Structure: The Singapore Case.' *Internationales Asienforum* 23(1–2): 261–288.

Nadvi, Khalid and Frank Wältring. 2002. 'Making Sense of Global Standards.' INEF Report 58. Duisburg: Institut für Entwicklung und Frieden, Gerhard-Mercator University.

Palpacuer, Florence. 2000. 'Competence-Based Strategies and Global Production Networks: A Discussion of Current Changes and their Implications for Employment.' *Competition and Change* 4(4): 353–400.

Penrose, Edith. 1959. *The Theory of the Growth of the Firm.* Oxford: Basil Blackwell.

Powell, Walter W. 1990. 'Neither Market nor Hierarchy: Network Forms of Organization.' *Research in Organizational Behaviour* 12: 295–336.

Prahalad, Coimbatore K. and Gary Hamel. 1990. 'The Core Competence of the Corporation.' *Harvard Business Review* 68(3): 79–91.

Reardon, Thomas, Jean-Marie Codron, Lawrence Busch, James Bingen, and Craig Harris. 2001. 'Global Change in Agrifood Grades and Standards: Agribusiness Strategic Responses in Developing Countries.' *International Food and Agribusiness Management Review* 2(3): 421–435.

Schilling, Melissa A. and H. Kevin Steensma. 2001. 'The Use of Modular Organizational Forms: An Industry-Level Analysis.' *Academy of Management Journal* 44(6): 1149–1168.

Schmitz, Hubert and Peter Knorringa. 2000. 'Learning from Global Buyers.' *Journal of Development Studies* 37(2): 177–205.

Soskice, David. 1999. 'Divergent Production Regimes: Coordinated and Uncoordinated Market Economies in the 1980s and 1990s.' In *Continuity and Change in Contemporary Capitalism,* edited by Herbert Kitschelt, Peter Lange, Gary Marks, and John D. Stephens, 101–134. Cambridge: Cambridge University Press.

Storper, Michael. 1995. 'The Resurgence of Regional Economies, Ten Years Later.' *European Urban and Regional Studies* 2(3): 191–221.

Storper, Michael and Allen J. Scott. 1988. 'The Geographical Foundations and Social Regulation of Flexible Production Complexes.' In *The Power of Geography,* edited by Jennifer Wolch and Michael Dear, 21–40. Boston, MA: Allen and Unwin.

Storper, Michael and Richard Walker. 1989. *The Capitalist Imperative: Territory, Technology and Industrial Growth.* Oxford: Basil Blackwell.

Streeck, Wolfgang. 1992. *Social Institutions and Economic Performance.* London: Sage.

Sturgeon, Timothy J. 2002. 'Modular Production Networks: A New American Model of Industrial Organization.' *Industrial and Corporate Change* 11(3): 451–496.

———. 2003. 'What Really Goes on in Silicon Valley? Spatial Clustering Dispersal in Modular Production Networks.' *Journal of Economic Geography* 3(2): 199–225.

Sturgeon, Timothy J. and Richard Florida. 2004. 'Globalization, Deverticalization and Employment in the Motor Vehicle Industry.' In *Creating Global Advantage,* edited by Martin Kenney and Richard Florida, 52–81. Stanford, CA: Stanford University Press.

Sturgeon, Timothy J. and Ji-Ren Lee. 2001. 'Industry Co-Evolution and the Rise of a Shared Supply-Base for Electronics Manufacturing.' Paper Presented at Nelson and Winter Conference, Aalborg, Denmark.

Sturgeon, Timothy J. and Richard K. Lester. 2004. 'The New Global Supply-base: Challenges for Local Suppliers in East Asia.' In *Global Production Networking and Technological Change in East Asia,* edited by Shahid Yusuf, M. Anjum Altaf, and Kaoru Nabeshima, 35–87. New York: Oxford University Press.

Thorelli, Hans. 1986. 'Networks: Between Markets and Hierarchies.' *Strategic Management Journal* 7(1): 37–51.

Ulrich, Karl. 1995. 'The Role of Product Architecture in the Manufacturing Firm.' *Research Policy* 24: 419–440.

Williamson, Oliver E. 1975. *Markets and Hierarchies*. New York: Free Press.

————. 1983. 'Credible Commitments: Using Hostages to Support Exchange.' *American Economic Review* 73(4): 519–540.

Yeats, Alexander J. 2001. 'Just How Big Is Global Production Sharing?' In *Fragmentation: New Production Patterns in the World Economy*, edited by Sven W. Arndt and Henryk Kierzkowski, 108–143. Oxford: Oxford University Press.

Part II

Expanding the Governance and Upgrading Dimensions in GVCs

The Global Economy
Organization, Governance, and Development

The global economy has changed in significant ways during the past several decades, and these changes are rooted in how the global economy is organized and governed. These transformations affect not only the flows of goods and services across national borders, but also the implications of these processes for how countries move up (or down) in the international system. The development strategies of countries today are affected to an unprecedented degree by how industries are organized, and this is reflected in a shift in theoretical frameworks from those centered around the legacies and actors of nation-states to a greater concern with supranational institutions and transnational organizations. Policy makers, managers, workers, social activists, and many other stakeholders in developed as well as developing nations need a firm understanding of how the contemporary global economy works if they hope to improve their position in it, or forestall an impending decline.

The topic of the global economy is inherently interdisciplinary. No single academic field can encompass it or afford to ignore it. Because of its vast scope, pundits who focus on the global economy are likely to be classified as academic interlopers; they run the risk of being too simplistic if they advance forceful hypotheses and too eclectic if they try to capture the full complexity of their topic. Scholars in this field thus have to master what economist Albert Hirschman has popularized as 'the art of trespassing' (Hirschman, 1981; Foxley et al., 1986).

The global economy can be studied at different levels of analysis. At the *macro* level are international organizations and regimes that establish rules and norms for the global community. These include institutions like the World Bank, the International Monetary Fund, the World Trade Organization, and the International Labor Organization, as well as regional integration schemes like the European Union and the North American Free Trade Agreement. These regimes combine both rules and resources, and hence they establish the broadest parameters within which the global economy operates.

At the *meso* level, the key building blocks for the global economy are countries and firms. Those scholars who take countries as their main analytical unit (as in the varieties of capitalism literature) provide an *institutional* perspective on the main, enduring features of national economies. The global economy is seen as the arena in which countries compete in different product markets. An alternative approach is to focus on firms and interfirm networks as the central units of analysis, and analyze these actors in a global industry or sectoral framework (as in the global commodity chains or industrial districts approaches). These scholars typically take a more *organizational* approach. In both the institutional and the organizational perspectives on the global economy, we tend to get a top-down focus on leading countries and firms as drivers of change.

Institutionalists like those in the varieties of capitalism school tend to focus on developed or industrialized countries. Alternatively, one can take a development-oriented perspective with regard to countries, and ask how the economic prospects of developing nations are shaped by their position in the global economy. These questions help to bridge the concerns of economic sociologists and development specialists because the theories of industrial upgrading that have emerged in the last couple of decades have been shaped very closely by several of the organizational and institutional theories mentioned above.

At a *micro* level, there is a growing literature on the resistance to globalization by consumer groups, activists, and transnational social movements (such as those dealing with labor issues and environmental abuses). This research is relevant to a chapter titled 'The Global Economy' because the very same perspectives used to understand how the global economy is organized are being employed by social and environmental activists to challenge the existing order.

Many theories related to economic sociology incorporate the global economy in their frameworks, but they differ in the degree to which it is conceptualized as a system that shapes the behavior and motivation of actors inside it, or as an arena where nationally determined actors meet, interact, and influence each other (Therborn, 2000). This chapter identifies how the global economy has been constructed analytically by a wide range of social scientists. The first task is to define what is really 'new' about the global economy in the last half of the twentieth century, which is the main temporal focus of this chapter. The increasingly seamless web of international production and trade networks that girdle the globe appears to be a distinctive feature of the last several decades, and it requires a new kind of organizational perspective that has been growing rapidly. The second section of this chapter takes a closer look at how and why production and trade have been reorganized in the global economy in the contemporary era. Research by a diverse group of scholars from economics, business schools, sociology, and economic geography, among other fields, has contributed to a reconceptualization of the key actors that make up the global economy, and to a realization that the integration of trade and the disintegration of production on a global scale are fundamentally altering our ideas about what connects national economies, firms, places, and people. The third section reviews selected institutional and organization perspectives on the global economy. We will highlight the competing and complementary claims of various approaches, such as the varieties of capitalism literature, national business systems, and global commodity chains.

The last two sections of the chapter offer 'bottom-up' perspectives on the global economy to complement the 'top-down' views on the reorganization of global industries. The fourth section takes a country perspective, and asks how a focus on global production networks allows us to understand the process of industrial upgrading, whereby economic actors try to move to higher-value activities in the global economy. The fifth and concluding section of the chapter examines several of the emerging challenges and dilemmas for governance and development in the contemporary global economy.

How New Is the Global Economy?

Much of the globalization debate has been fueled by different conceptions of what is happening 'out there' in the global economy, and whether it really represents something new. We need to distinguish the process of *internationalization*, which involves the mere extension or geographic spread of economic activities across national boundaries, from *globalization*, which is qualitatively distinct because it involves the functional integration of internationally dispersed activities (Dicken, 2003: 12). How functional integration occurs is a topic that we will deal with in more detail below in terms of the governance structures in the global economy. However, one of the key actors that distinguishes the global economy of the latter half of the twentieth century from its predecessors is the transnational corporation (TNC), which we will discuss in this section.[1]

The origins of a global economy can be traced back to the expansion of long-distance trade during the period of 1450–1640, which Wallerstein (1979) has labeled as the 'long sixteenth century'. From the fifteenth century onward, a number of chartered trading companies emerged in Europe, such as the East India Company and the Hudson's Bay Company, which created vast international trading empires. Although their activities were worldwide in scope, their main purpose was trade and exchange, rather than production. The development of a world trading system over a period of several centuries helped to create the tripartite structure of core, semiperipheral, and peripheral economic areas. According to world-systems theory, the upward or downward mobility of nations in the core, semiperiphery, and periphery is determined by a country's mode of incorporation in the capitalist world-economy, and these shifts can only be accurately portrayed by an in-depth analysis of the cycles of capitalist accumulation in the *longue durée* of history (Wallerstein, 1974, 1980, 1989; Arrighi, 1994).

The dynamics of the capitalist world-system laid the foundation for a process of industrialization and new international divisions of labor on a global scale. Originally, as defined by the eighteenth-century political economist Adam Smith ([1776] 1976), 'division of labor' referred simply to the specialization of workers in different parts of the production process, usually in a factory setting. Quite early in the evolution of industrial economies, the division of labor also acquired a geographical dimension. Different areas began to specialize in particular types of economic activity. At the global scale, the 'classic' international division of labor was between the industrial countries producing manufactured goods, and the non-industrialized economies that supplied raw materials and agricultural products to the industrial nations and that became a market for basic manufactures. This relatively simple pattern no longer applies. During the decades following the Second World War, trade flows have become far more complex, and so have the relationships between the developed and developing nations of the global economy.

The foundations of the contemporary economic order were established in the late 1940s by the system of financial and trade institutions that were set up at an international conference in Bretton Woods, New Hampshire, in 1944. The principal institutions that constitute the Bretton Woods system are the International Monetary Fund (IMF), the International Bank for Reconstruction and Development (later renamed the World Bank), and the General Agreement on Tariffs and Trade (GATT) (see Held et al., 1999: chapters 3 and 4). Unlike the classical gold standard system, which collapsed during the First World War, the Bretton Woods financial system required that every currency had a fixed exchange rate vis-à-vis the US dollar, with the dollar's value pegged to gold at $35 an ounce. In practice, Bretton Woods became a dollar system because the United States was the leading economy and the only major creditor nation in the first 25 years following the Second World War. While the rise of the Eurocurrency market in the 1960s placed increasing strain on the Bretton Woods financial order, its actual demise came on August 15, 1971, when President Nixon announced that the US dollar was no longer freely convertible into gold, effectively signaling the end of fixed exchange rates.

Notwithstanding these changes, the legacy of the Bretton Woods system remained powerful throughout the latter decades of the twentieth century. The IMF has policed the rules of the international financial order, and intervened in national economies (especially in developing countries) to impose stabilization programs when balance-of-payments crises were deemed structural rather than cyclical. Following the post-war reconstruction of Europe and Japan, the World Bank increasingly became a development agency for third world nations (Ayres, 1983). Its policy recommendations were closely tied to those of the IMF, especially after the neoliberal agenda (dubbed the Washington Consensus) became established in the 1980s (Gore, 2000). GATT, a multilateral forum for trade negotiations, became the primary international trade agency by default when the International Trade Organization, provided by the 1947 Havana Charter, was abandoned by President Truman after it was staunchly opposed in the US Congress. In 1995, the GATT was superseded by the much more powerful World Trade Organization (WTO), which sought to reduce or eliminate a whole range of non-tariff barriers and uneven trading conditions between countries.

Distinctive Features of the Contemporary Global Economy, 1960s to the Present

There is considerable controversy over how to characterize the distinctive aspects of the global economy in the postwar period. Wallerstein (2000: 250) argues that the period from 1945 to the present corresponds to a typical Kondratieff cycle of the capitalist world-economy, which has an upward and a downward swing: an A-phase of economic expansion from 1945 to 1967–1973, and a B-phase of economic contraction from 1967–1973 to the present day. While the evolution of the capitalist world-economy stretches from 1450 to the contemporary era, in world-systems theory it is marked by periods of genesis, normal development, and the current phase of 'terminal crisis' (Wallerstein, 2000, 2002).

From a trade perspective, the level of economic integration in the latter half of the twentieth century is not historically unprecedented. The decades leading up to 1913 were considered a golden age of international trade and investment. This was ended by the First World War and the Great Depression, when most of the world's economies turned inward. Merchandise trade (imports and exports) as a share of world output did not recover its 1913 level until sometime in the mid-1970s (Krugman, 1995: 330–331).[2] If we take 1960 as the baseline, interconnectedness through trade has vastly increased in recent decades, and furthermore trade has grown consistently faster than output at the world level. Among the OECD[3] nations (the 24 richest industrial economies), the ratio of exports to gross domestic product (GDP) roughly doubled from 1960 to 1990, rising from 9.5% to 20.5% in this period, and world merchandise trade grew at an average of one and a half times the rate of growth of world GDP from 1965 to 1990 (Wade, 1996: 62).

International trade, investment, and finance have become the hallmarks of economic globalization. Global interconnectedness through foreign direct investment grew even faster than trade during the 1980s, and the most dynamic multinationalization of all has come in finance and in technology. Flows of foreign direct investment grew three times faster than trade flows and almost four times faster than output between 1983 and 1990 (Wade, 1996: 63), and according to one estimate, TNCs control one-third of the world's private sector productive assets (UNCTAD, 1993: 1). Globalization appears to have gone furthest in the area of finance. The stock of international bank lending (cross-border lending plus domestic lending, denominated in foreign currency) rose from 4% of the GDP of OECD countries in 1980 to an astonishing 44% in 1990, and foreign exchange (or currency) trading was 30 times greater than and quite independent of trade flows in the early 1990s (Wade, 1996: 64). Global financial flows accelerated in considerable measure because of the growing popularity in the 1980s and 1990s of new financial instruments, such as international bonds, international equities, derivatives trading (futures, options, and swaps), and international money markets (Held et al., 1999: 205–209).

This quantitative assessment of the growth in international trade, investment, and financial flows is one side of the story, but it is challenged by the notion that the nature of global economic integration in the recent era is qualitatively different than in the past. Before 1913, the world economy was characterized by *shallow integration* manifested largely through *trade* in goods and services between independent firms and through international movements of portfolio capital. Today, we live in a world in which *deep integration*, organized primarily by TNCs, is pervasive and involves the *production* of goods and services in cross-border, value-adding activities that redefine the kind of production processes contained within national boundaries (UNCTAD, 1993: 113). There is little consensus, however, over what kind of framework to use in analyzing the contemporary global economy because of the breadth and rapidity of change, and the fact that countries, firms, workers, and many other stakeholders in the global economy are affected by these shifts.

A global manufacturing system has emerged in which production and export capabilities are dispersed to an unprecedented number of developing as well as industrialized countries. Fröbel et al. (1980) likened the surge of manufactured exports from labor-intensive export platforms in low-wage economies to a 'new international division of labor' that used advanced transport and communication technologies to promote the global segmentation of the production process. The OECD coined the term *newly industrializing countries* and reflected the concern of advanced capitalist nations that the expanding share of these emergent industrializers in the production and export of manufactured goods was a threat to slumping Western industrial economies (OECD, 1979). World-systems theorists argued that the gap between core and periphery in the world economy had been narrowing since the 1950s, and by 1980 the semiperiphery not only caught up with but also overtook the core countries in their degree of industrialization (Arrighi and Drangel, 1986: 54–55; Arrighi et al., 2003).

In retrospect, the assembly-oriented export production in the newly industrializing countries was merely an early stage in the transformation of the global economy into 'a highly complex, kaleidoscopic structure involving the *fragmentation* of many production processes, and their *geographical relocation* on a global scale in ways which slice through national boundaries' (Dicken, 2003: 9). Expanded niches for labor-intensive segments have been created by splitting the production of goods traditionally viewed as skill-, capital-, or technology-intensive and putting the labor-intensive pieces of the value chain in low-wage locations.

In Mexico, for example, the booming export-oriented maquiladora program[4] has engaged in more sophisticated kinds of manufacturing operations over time. First-generation maquiladoras were labor-intensive with limited technology, and they assembled export products in industries like apparel using imported inputs provided by US clients (Sklair, 1993). In the late 1980s and early 1990s, researchers began to call attention to so called second- and third-generation maquiladoras. Second-generation plants are oriented less toward assembly and more toward manufacturing processes that use automated and semi-automated machines and robots in the automobile, television, and electrical appliance sectors. Third-generation maquiladoras are oriented to research, design, and development, and rely on highly skilled labor such as specialized engineers and technicians. In each of these industries, the maquiladoras have matured from assembly sites based on cheap labor to manufacturing centers whose competitiveness derives from a combination of high productivity, good quality, and wages far below those prevailing north of the border (Shaiken and Herzenberg, 1987; Carrillo and Hualde, 1998; Bair and Gereffi, 2001; Cañas and Coronado, 2002).

A cover story in the February 3, 2003, issue of *Business Week* highlighted the impact of global outsourcing over the past several decades on the quality and quantity of jobs in both developed and developing countries (Engardio et al., 2003). The first wave of outsourcing began in the 1960s and 1970s with the exodus to developing countries of jobs making shoes, clothes, cheap electronics, and toys. After that, simple service work, like processing credit-card receipts and airline reservations in back-office call centers, and writing basic software code, went global. Today, driven by digitization, the Internet, and high-speed data networks that circle the world, all kinds of 'knowledge work' that can be done almost anywhere are being outsourced.

Global outsourcing reveals many of the key features of contemporary globalization: it deals with international competitiveness in a way that inherently links developed and developing countries; a huge part of the debate centers around jobs, wages, and skills in different parts of the world; and there is a focus on value creation in different parts of the value chain. There are enormous political as well as economic stakes in how global outsourcing evolves in the coming years, particularly in well-endowed and strategically positioned economies like India, China, the Philippines, Mexico, Costa Rica, Russia, parts of eastern Europe, and South Africa—that is, countries loaded with college grads who speak Western languages and can handle outsourced information-technology work. India seems particularly well positioned in this area.

However, these shifts reveal a sobering globalization paradox: the dramatic expansion of production capabilities reflected in global outsourcing across a wide range of industries does not necessarily increase levels of development or reduce poverty in the exporting nations. As more and more countries have acquired the ability to make complex as well as standard manufactured goods, barriers to entry have fallen and competitive processes at the production stage of value chains have increased. This has resulted in a pattern that Kaplinsky (2000: 120), following Bhagwati's (1958) original use of the term, has dubbed 'immiserizing growth,' in which economic activity increases in terms of output and employment, but economic returns fall. The emergence of China and, to a lesser extent, India has expanded the global labor force so significantly that the likely consequence of globalization is to bid down living standards not only for unskilled work and primary products, but increasingly for skilled work and industrial products as well (Kaplinsky, 2001: 56). The only way to counteract this process is to search for new sources of dynamic economic rents (i.e., profitability in excess of the competitive norm), which are increasingly found in the intangible parts of the value chain where high-value, knowledge-intensive activities like innovation, design, and marketing prevail (Kaplinsky, 2000).

These trends raise fundamental questions about winners and losers in the global economy, and also about the forces and frameworks needed to understand why these changes are occurring, and what their impact is likely to be. In the next section of this chapter, we will review how and why new patterns of international production and trade are emerging. In the subsequent section, we will examine some of the major theoretical perspectives in economic sociology and related fields that seek to account for these institutional and organization features of the global economy.

The Reorganization of Production and Trade in the Global Economy

The Role of Transnational Corporations

While the post-war international economic order was defined and legitimized by the United States and the other core powers that supported it in terms of the ideology of free trade, it was the way in which TNCs linked the production of goods and services in cross-border, value-adding networks that made the global economy in the last half of the twentieth century qualitatively distinct from what preceded it. Transnational corporations have become the primary movers and shakers of the global economy because they have the power to coordinate and control supply-chain operations in more than one country, even if they do not own them (Dicken, 2003: 198). Although they first emerged in the late nineteenth and early twentieth centuries in the natural resource (oil, mineral, and agricultural) sectors, TNCs did not play a central role in shaping a new global economic system until after the Second World War.

To the neoclassical economists of the 1950s, the post-war world economy was constituted by international capital flows, which were viewed at the country level as foreign direct investment (FDI). The United States was the main source of outward FDI, and the first empirical studies of US FDI at the country level were carried out by Dunning (1958) on the United Kingdom and Safarian (1966) on Canada. Both of these studies were interested in the public policy question of the benefits that US FDI had for a host economy (Rugman, 1999), and thus they did not really think about transnational corporations as an institutional actor. The Multinational Enterprise Project at Harvard Business School, which began in 1965 under the direction of Raymond Vernon and lasted for 12 years, tried to remedy the economists' relative neglect of TNCs. Despite being out of step with its academic brethren in economics departments and business schools, who were using general equilibrium models and rational choice to study the properties of efficient markets, the Harvard Multinational Enterprise Project was distinguished by its emphasis on the strategies and activities of TNCs at the micro level of the firm, rather than as merely one more form of international capital movement (Vernon, 1999).

In the 1960s and 1970s, the key players in most international industries were large, vertically integrated TNCs, whose use and abuse of power in the global economy were chronicled by numerous authors (e.g., Sampson, 1973; Barnet and Müller, 1974). The overseas activities of these firms were primarily oriented toward three main objectives: the search for raw materials; finding new markets for their products; and tapping offshore sources of abundant and relatively low-cost labor (Vernon, 1971).[5] In developing countries, which were attractive to TNCs for all three of these reasons, the predominant model of growth since the 1950s was import-substituting industrialization. This development strategy used the tools of industrial policy, such as local-content requirements, joint ventures, and export-promotion schemes, to induce foreign firms that had established local subsidiaries inside their borders to transfer the capital, technology, and managerial experience needed to set up a host of new industries. In return, TNCs could make and sell their products in the relatively protected domestic markets of Latin America, Asia, and Africa, and even in the socialist bloc connected with the former Soviet Union (Bergsten et al., 1978; Newfarmer, 1985).

By the mid-1980s, several significant shifts were transforming the organization of the global economy. First, the oil shock of the late 1970s and the severe debt crisis that followed it were the death knell for import-substituting industrialization in many developing countries, especially in Latin America. The import-substitution approach had found no way to generate the foreign exchange needed to pay for increasingly costly imports, and escalating debt service payments led to a net outflow of foreign capital that crippled economic growth.[6] Second, the 'East Asian Miracle', based on the rapid economic advance of Japan and the so-called East Asian tigers (South Korea, Hong Kong, Taiwan, and Singapore) since the 1960s, highlighted a contrasting development model: export-oriented industrialization. Buttressed by the neoliberal thrust of the Reagan and Thatcher governments in the United States and the United Kingdom, respectively, export-oriented development soon became the prevailing orthodoxy for developing economies around the world.[7] Third, the transition from import-substituting to export-oriented development strategies during the 1980s in many industrializing countries was complemented by an equally profound reorientation in the strategies of TNCs. The rapid expansion of industrial capabilities and export propensities in a diverse array of newly industrializing economies in Asia and Latin America allowed TNCs to accelerate their own efforts to outsource relatively standardized activities to lower-cost production locations worldwide.

One of the central questions that generated great interest in TNCs was this: To what extent have TNCs supplanted national governments, and in what areas? The attitude of many researchers was that TNCs had the power, the resources, and the global reach to thwart the territorially based objectives of national governments in both developed and developing countries (see Bergsten et al., 1978; Barnet and Müller, 1974). This was a key tenet of dependency theory, one of the most popular approaches in the 1970s, which argued that TNCs undercut the ability of nation-states to build domestic industries controlled by locally owned firms (Sunkel, 1973; Evans, 1979; Gereffi, 1983). Even the most balanced scholarly approaches reflected the challenge to national autonomy captured by the title of Raymond Vernon's best-known book, *Sovereignty at Bay* (1971). The large size of TNCs, whether measured in sales or by more sophisticated calculations of value added, still leads to the conclusion that many TNCs are bigger than countries.[8] However, the concentrated power of vertically integrated, industrial TNCs has been diminishing for the past couple of decades as a result of the tendency toward both the geographic and the organizational outsourcing of production. Thus, the original concern with how TNCs affect the sovereignty and effectiveness of national governments needs to be reframed in light of the current shift to a more network-centered global economy, which will be discussed below.

The Emergence of International Trade and Production Networks

The growth of world trade has probably received the most attention in the globalization literature because of its direct relevance to employment, wages, and the rising number of free trade agreements around the world. The most common causes usually given to explain expanding world trade are technological (improvements in transportation and communication technologies) and political (e.g., the removal of protectionist barriers, such as tariffs, import quotas, and exchange controls, which had restricted world markets from 1913 until the end of the Second World War).[9] It is also important to acknowledge that the volume of international trade depends to a considerable degree on how boundaries are drawn, both for different geographies of production[10] and according to whether trade covers final products only or whether it also includes intermediate inputs. However, even though the share of trade in world output surpassed its 1913 peak in the 1980s and 1990s, the sheer volume of trade is probably not sufficient to argue for a qualitative break with the past.

Of far greater significance are several novel features in the *nature* of international trade that do not have counterparts in previous eras. These suggest the need for a new framework to understand both patterns of competition among international firms and the development prospects of countries that are trying to upgrade their position in diverse global industries. The three new aspects of modern world trade relevant here are: (1) the rise of intra-industry and intra-product trade in intermediate inputs; (2) the ability of producers to 'slice up the value chain,' in Krugman's (1995) phrase, by breaking a production process into many geographically separated steps; and (3) the emergence of a global production networks framework that highlights how these shifts have altered governance structures and the distribution of gains in the global economy.

Intraindustry Trade in Parts and Components

Arndt and Kierzkowski (2001) use the term *fragmentation* to describe the international division of labor that allows producers located in different countries and often with different ownership structures to form cross-border production networks for parts and components. Specialized 'production blocks' are coordinated through service links, which include activities such as transportation, insurance, telecommunications, quality control, and management specifications. Yeats (2001), analyzing detailed trade data for the machinery and transport equipment group

(SITC 7),[11] finds that trade in components made up 30% of total OECD exports in SITC 7 in 1995, and that trade in these goods was growing at a faster pace than the overall SITC 7 total. Similarly, Hummels et al. (1998: 80–81) argue that the 'vertical specialization' of global trade, which occurs when a country uses imported intermediate parts to produce goods it later exports, accounted for about 14.5% of all trade among OECD countries in the early 1990s. Vertical specialization captures the idea that countries link sequentially in production networks to produce a final good, although vertical trade itself does not require the vertical integration of firms.

Feenstra (1998) takes this idea one step further, and explicitly connects the 'integration of trade' with the 'disintegration of production' in the global economy.[12] The rising integration of world markets through trade has brought with it a disintegration of the production process of multinational firms,[13] since companies are finding it profitable to outsource (domestically or abroad) an increasing share of their non-core manufacturing and service activities. This represents a breakdown of the vertically integrated mode of production—the so-called Fordist model, originally exemplified by the automobile industry—on which US industrial prowess had been built for much of the twentieth century (Aglietta, 1980). The success of the Japanese model of 'lean production' in the global economy since the 1980s, pioneered by Toyota in automobiles, reinforces the central importance of coordinating exceptionally complex interfirm trading networks of parts and components as a new source of competitive advantage in the global economy (Womack et al., 1990; Sturgeon and Florida, 2000).

Slicing Up the Value Chain

The notion of a value-added chain has been a useful tool for international business scholars who have focused on the strategies of both firms and countries in the global economy. Bruce Kogut (1984: 151), a professor at the Wharton School of Business, University of Pennsylvania, was one of the first to argue that value chains are a key element in the new framework of competitive analysis that is needed because of the globalization of world markets: 'The formulation of strategy can be fruitfully viewed as placing bets on certain markets and on certain links of the value-added chain ... . The challenge of global strategy formulation is to differentiate between the various kinds of economies, to specify which link and which factor captures the firm's advantage, and to determine where the value-added chain would be broken across borders.' In a subsequent paper, Kogut (1985) elaborates the central role of the value-added chain[14] in the design of international business strategies, which are based upon the interplay between the comparative advantage of countries and the competitive advantage of firms. While the logic of comparative advantage helps to determine *where* the value-added chain should be broken across national borders, competitive (or firm-specific) advantage influences the decision on *what* activities and technologies along the value-added chain a firm should concentrate its resources in.[15]

Michael Porter of Harvard Business School also developed a value-chain framework that he applied both at the level of individual firms (Porter, 1985) and as one of the bases for determining the competitive advantage of nations (Porter, 1990). At the firm level, a value chain refers to a collection of discrete activities performed to do business, such as the physical creation of a product or service, its delivery and marketing to the buyer, and its support after sale.[16] On the basis of these discrete activities, firms can establish two main types of competitive advantage: low relative cost (a firm's ability to carry out the activities in its value chain at lower cost than its competitors); or differentiation (performing in a unique way relative to competitors). While competitive advantage is determined at the level of a firm's value chain, Porter argues, 'The appropriate unit of analysis in setting international strategy is the industry because the industry is the arena in which competitive advantage is won or lost' (1987: 29).

The pattern of competition differs markedly across industries: at one extreme are 'multidomestic' industries, in which competition in each country is basically independent of competition in other countries; and at the other end of the spectrum are 'global industries,' in which a firm's competitive position in one country is significantly impacted by its position in other countries. Since international competition is becoming the norm, Porter believes that firms must adopt 'global strategies' in order to decide how to spread the activities in the value chain among countries.[17] A very different set of scholars, studying the political economy of advanced industrial societies, highlighted the transformation from 'organized capitalism' to 'disorganized' or 'competitive' capitalism. This approach is based on dramatic shifts in the strategic and institutional contexts of the global economy in the 1980s toward deregulated national markets and unhampered international exchanges (Offe, 1985; Lash and Urry, 1987). According to Schmitter (1990: 12), sectors or industries are the key unit for comparative analysis in this setting because they represent a meso level where a number of changes in technology, market structure, and public policy converge.

Our review of the contemporary global economy thus far has highlighted two distinctive shifts: the unparalleled fragmentation and reintegration of global production and trade patterns since the 1970s; and the recognition by Kogut and Porter, among others,[18] of the power of value-chain or industry analysis as a basis for formulating global strategies that can integrate comparative (location-specific) advantage and competitive (firm-specific) advantage. However, the third transformation in the global economy that needs to be addressed as a precursor to the global value chain perspective is the remarkable growth of manufactured exports from low-wage to high-wage nations in the past several decades. This phenomenon has produced a range of reactions—from anxiety by producers in developed countries who believe they cannot compete with the flood of low-cost imports, to hope among economies in the South that they can catch up with their neighbors in the North by moving up the ladder of skill-intensive activities, to despair that global inequality and absolute levels of poverty have remained resistant to change despite the rapid progress of a relative handful of developing nations.

Production Networks in the Global Economy

In the 1990s, a new framework, called global commodity chains (GCC), tied the concept of the value-added chain directly to the global organization of industries (see Gereffi and Korzeniewicz, 1994; Gereffi, 1999, 2001). This work was based on an insight into the growing importance of global buyers (mainly retailers and brand companies, or 'manufacturers without factories') as key drivers in the formation of globally dispersed production and distribution networks. Gereffi (1994a) contrasted these buyer-driven chains to what he termed producer-driven chains. The latter are the production systems created by vertically integrated transnational manufacturers, while the former term recognizes the role of global buyers, highlighting the significance of design and marketing in initiating the activities of global production systems.[19] The GCC approach drew attention to the variety of actors that could exercise power within global production and distribution systems. It was the field-based methodology of GCC research, in particular, that provided new insights into the statistics showing an increase in trade involving components and other intermediate inputs. The trade data alone mask important organizational shifts because they differentiate neither between intra-firm and inter-firm trade nor between the various ways in which global outsourcing relationships were being constructed.

A variety of overlapping terms has been used to describe the complex network relationships that make up the global economy. Each of the contending concepts, however, has particular emphasis that are important to recognize for a chain analysis of the global economy:

- *Supply chains*: A generic label for an input-output structure of value-adding activities, beginning with raw materials and ending with a finished product.
- *International production networks:* A focus on the international production networks in which TNCs act as 'global network flagships' (Borrus et al., 2000).
- *Global commodity chains:* An emphasis on the internal governance structure of supply chains (especially the producer-driven vs. buyer-driven

distinction) and on the role of diverse lead firms in setting up global production and sourcing networks (Gereffi and Korzeniewicz, 1994).

- *French 'filière' approach:* A loosely knit set of studies that used the *filière* (i.e., channel or network) of activities as a method to study primarily agricultural export commodities such as rubber, cotton, coffee, and cocoa (Raikes et al., 2000).

- *Global value chains:* Emphasis on the relative value of those economic activities that are required to bring a good or service from conception, through the different phases of production (involving a combination of physical transformation and the input of various producer services), delivery to final consumers, and final disposal after use (Kaplinsky, 2000; Gereffi and Kaplinsky, 2001).

The 'value chain' concept has recently gained popularity as an overarching label for this body of research because it focuses on value creation and value capture across the full range of possible chain activities and end products (goods and services), and because it avoids the limiting connotations of the word *commodity*, which to some implies the production of undifferentiated goods with low barriers to entry. Like the GCC framework, global value chain (GVC) analysis accepts many of the observations made previously on geographical fragmentation, and it focuses primarily on the issues of industry (re)organization, coordination, governance, and power in the chain (Humphrey and Schmitz, 2001). Its concern is to understand the nature and consequences of organizational fragmentation in global industries. The GVC approach offers the possibility of understanding how firms are linked in the global economy, but also acknowledges the broader institutional context of these linkages, including trade policy, regulation, and standards.[20] More generally, the global production networks paradigm has been used to join scholarly research on globalization with the concerns of both policy makers and social activists, who are trying to harness the potential gains of globalization to the pragmatic concerns of specific countries and social constituencies that feel increasingly marginalized in the international economic arena.[21]

The next section of this chapter looks at different perspectives on governance at the meso level of the global economy, and it will be followed by a discussion of industrial upgrading, which analyzes the trajectories by which countries seek to upgrade their positions in the global economy.

Governance in the Global Economy: Institutional and Organizational Perspectives

Scholars who study the global economy at the meso level form distinct camps in terms of their units of analysis, theoretical orientations, and methodological preferences. The two main units of analysis at the meso level are countries and firms. In the 1970s and 1980s, political economy perspectives dealing with nations and TNCs in the global economy tended to predominate, fueled by dependency theory (Cardoso and Faletto, 1979; Evans, 1979), world-systems theory (Wallerstein, 1974, 1980, 1989), and statist approaches (Amsden, 1989; Wade, 1990; Evans, 1995), among others. During the last decade, however, research on the global economy has shifted toward institutional and organizational theories. The choice of countries or firms as empirical units has a striking affinity with the researcher's primary theoretical orientation: those who study countries tend to adopt institutional perspectives, while those who work with firms favor organizational frameworks.[22]

This paradigm divide at the meso level of the global economy is revealed by looking at two broad literatures, which we label 'varieties of capitalism' and 'global production networks'. The former is closely associated with institutional analysis, and the latter with diverse organizational perspectives. Both approaches tend to focus on governance structures in the global economy, but the scope and content of what is being governed differ greatly. The varieties of capitalism literature looks primarily at coordination problems and institutional complementarities in advanced industrial economies, where the nation-state is the explicit unit of analysis. This research is comparative, but not transnational, in orientation. By contrast, the research on global production networks highlights the linkages between developed and developing countries created by TNCs and interfirm networks. Governance in this context is typically exercised by lead firms in global industries, and one of the key challenges addressed is industrial upgrading—that is, how developing countries try to improve their position in the global economy, which is characterized both by power asymmetries and by opportunities for learning through networks. International and industry-based field research is a requisite in the study of global production networks because publicly available and detailed information at the level of firms is generally lacking. The main dimensions of this comparison are outlined in Table 5.1.

The institutionalist paradigm encompasses several related approaches that deal with the governance of modern capitalist economies, including regulation theory (Aglietta, 1980; Boyer, 1989), national systems of innovation (Lundvall, 1992; Nelson, 1993), social systems of production (Campbell et al., 1991; Hollingsworth et al., 1994; Hollingsworth and Boyer, 1997), and varieties of capitalism (Berger and Dore, 1996; Kitschelt et al., 1999; Hall and Soskice, 2001). All of the authors in this field focus on the 'institutional foundations of comparative advantage' in the advanced capitalist democracies, with an emphasis on topics like business-government relations, labor markets and collective bargaining, the welfare state, the internationalization of capital, and innovation systems.

A key unifying concept is institutional complementarity, which rests on 'multilateral reinforcement mechanisms between institutional arrangements: each one, by its existence, permits, or facilitates the existence of the others' (Amable, 2000: 656). Complementary institutions and other forms of path dependency lead most scholars in the varieties of capitalism genre to argue vociferously against convergence, given their belief that unique and valued institutions will sustain national diversities despite the withering pressures of international competition in an increasingly open global economy. Actually, the paradigm does allow for a limited form of convergence in the sense that advanced market economies are organized into three broad types: liberal market economies, which adopt laissez-faire, pro-business policies (United States, United Kingdom, Canada, and Australia); and coordinated market economies, with their corporatist (strong state—Germany and Japan) and welfare state (strong trade unions—Scandinavian and northern European) variants. However, there is no serious effort to extend this paradigm to address the varieties of capitalism in the vast majority of countries that are in the developing world.[23]

Table 5.1 Comparison of Varieties of Capitalism and Global Production Networks

Dimension	Varieties of Capitalism	Global Production Networks
Theoretical orientation	Institutional analysis	Organizational analysis
Unit of analysis	Countries	Interfirm networks
Empirical focus	Advanced industrial economies/ capitalist democracies	Linkages between developed and developing countries
Methodological preference	Rational actor; multivariate analysis	Comparative/historical analysis across industries, firms, and countries
Research style	Quantitative, cross-national; country case studies	International, industry-based field research; political economy interpretations
Ideal types	Liberal and coordinated market economies	Producer-driven and buyer-driven commodity chains
Main challenges/collective action problems	Coordination problems in developed countries	Industrial upgrading in developing countries
Key concepts	Institutional complementarities	Lead firms; economic rents; learning through networks

Source: Authors.

The global production networks paradigm provides a very different perspective on the global economy because its organizational lens focuses on transnational linkages between developed and developing nations. The central questions deal with the kinds of governance structures that characterize global industries, how these governance arrangements change, and what consequences these shifts have for development opportunities in rich and poor countries alike. International institutionals, such as trade and intellectual property regimes, clearly shape inclusion and exclusion of countries and firms in global production networks, but this approach tends to focus on the strategies and behavior of the players (firms), while the rules of the game (regulatory institutions) are taken as an exogenous variable.

Notwithstanding the potential complementarities between institutional and organizational perspectives on the global economy, there has been virtually no dialogue between these two literatures. They do not cite one another's research or engage in collaborative projects, despite the fact that both are concerned with the international forces shaping countries and firms in the global economy.

There are several hybrid approaches that seek to bridge this gap between organizational and institutional frameworks. One of these is the business systems perspective, pioneered by Whitley (1992a, 1992b). As defined by (Whitley, 1996: 412).

Business systems are particular forms of economic organization that have become established and reproduced in certain institutional contexts—local, regional, national, or international. They are distinctive ways of coordinating and controlling economic activities which developed interdependently with key institutions which constitute particular kinds of political, financial, labor, and cultural systems. The more integrated and mutually reinforcing are such institutional systems over a particular territory or population, the more cohesive and distinctive will be its business system.

While firms presumably are central to business systems, Whitley's framework shares the institutionalist paradigm's emphasis on institutional complementarities and cohesion, and national or culturally proximate regions. However, the business systems approach seems relatively ill-equipped to deal with the question, 'How do US, European, or Asian business systems respond to globalization?' While the business systems logic would lead us to expect that firms of the same nationality maintain their distinctive features in the face of international competition, findings from research on global production networks indicate that the competition among firms from different business systems in overseas markets tends to diminish the influence of national origins on firms' behavior (Gereffi, 1996: 433).[24]

Sociologists have looked at a range of other actors in the global economy. 'Business groups,' defined as a collection of firms bound together in persistent formal or informal ways, are a pervasive phenomenon in Asia, Europe, Latin America, and elsewhere (Granovetter, 1994; 2005). Business groups may encompass kinship networks, but they are not delimited by family boundaries because the goals of families can conflict with the principles of profit maximization that characterize firms in these groups. Business groups play a role in the global economy through their impact on national market structures, and on product variety and product quality in international trade (Feenstra et al., 1999). Transnational business networks based on family or ethnic ties are another form of economic organization that shapes global production and trade (Hamilton et al., 1989; Yeung, 2000). Japanese *sogo shosha*, British trading companies, and Chinese and Indian merchants laid the social groundwork for the long-distance supply routes between Asian producers and their export markets (Gereffi, 1999: 60–61). For Castells (1996), the universality of network society in the information age is a defining feature of the modern era. Others argue that the global system is now ruled by a transnational capitalist class, which is more interested in building hegemony than in domination and control (Sklair, 2001; Carroll and Fennema, 2002).

At a more micro level, phenomena within nation-states can also reflect globalization processes. Meyer (2000) defines modern actors on the global stage as entities with rights and interests that create and consult collective rules, that often enhance their legitimacy by adopting common forms, and that exercise agency through moral action. From Meyer's 'world society' perspective, the modern world is stateless; it is based on shared rules and models, and made up of strong, culturally constituted actors. Sassen (2000) also detaches sovereignty from the national state. She emphasizes the role of global cities as strategic sites for the production of specialized functions to run and coordinate the global economy, and posits that financial and investment deregulation are driving the geographic location of strategic institutions related to globalization deep inside national territories.

Industrial Upgrading and Global Production Networks

Major changes in global business organization during the last several decades of the twentieth century have had a significant impact on the upgrading possibilities of developing countries. This section will illustrate how the reorganization of international trade and production networks affects the capability of developing countries in different regions of the world to improve their positions in the value chains of diverse industries.

Industrial upgrading refers to the process by which economic actors—nations, firms, and workers—move from low-value to relatively high-value activities in global production networks. Different mixes of government policies, institutions, corporate strategies, technologies, and worker skills are associated with upgrading success. However, we can think about upgrading in a concrete way as linked to a series of economic roles associated with production and export activities, such as assembly, original equipment manufacturing (OEM), original brand name manufacturing (OBM), and original design manufacturing (ODM) (Gereffi, 1994b: 222–224). This sequence of economic roles involves an expanding set of capabilities that developing countries must attain in pursuing an upgrading trajectory in diverse industries. In the remainder of this section, we will look at evidence from several sectors to see how global production networks have facilitated or constrained upgrading in developing nations.

Apparel

The global apparel industry contains many examples of industrial upgrading by developing countries.[25] The lead firms in this buyer-driven chain are retailers (giant discount stores like Walmart and Target, department stores like J. C. Penney and Marks and Spencer, specialty retailers like The Limited and The Gap), marketers (who control major apparel brands, such as Liz Claiborne, Tommy Hilfiger, Polo/ Ralph Lauren, Nike), and brand-name manufacturers (e.g., Wrangler, Phillips-van Heusen). These lead firms all have extensive global sourcing networks, which typically encompass 300 to 500 factories in various regions of the world. Because apparel production is quite labor-intensive, manufacturing is typically carried out in countries with very low labor costs.

The main stages for firms in developing countries are first, to be included as a supplier (i.e., exporter) in the global apparel value chain; and then to upgrade from assembly to OEM and OBM export roles within the chain. Because of the Multi Fiber Arrangement (MFA) associated with the GATT, which used quotas to regulate import shares for the United States, Canada, and much of Europe, at least 50 to 60 different developing countries have been significant apparel exporters since the 1970s, many just assembling apparel from imported inputs using low-wage labor in local export-processing zones.

The shift from assembly to the OEM export role has been the main upgrading challenge in the apparel value chain. It requires the ability to fill orders from global buyers, which includes making samples, procuring or manufacturing the needed inputs for the garment, meeting international standards in terms of price, quality, and delivery, and assuming responsibility for packing and shipping the finished item. Since fabric supply is the most important input in the apparel chain, virtually all countries that want to develop OEM capabilities need to develop a strong textile industry. The OBM export role is a more advanced stage because it involves assuming the design and marketing responsibilities associated with developing a company's own brands.

East Asian newly industrializing economies (NIEs) of Hong Kong, Taiwan, South Korea, and Singapore, which are generally taken as the archetype for industrial upgrading among developing countries, made a rapid transition from assembly to OEM production in the 1970s. Hong Kong clothing companies were the most successful in making the shift from OEM to OBM production in apparel, and Korean and Taiwanese firms pursued OBM in other consumer goods industries like appliances, sporting goods, and electronics.[26] After mastering the OEM role, leading apparel export firms in Hong Kong, Taiwan, and South Korea began to set up their own international production networks in the 1980s, using the mechanism of 'triangle manufacturing' whereby orders were received in the East Asian NIEs, apparel production was carried out in lower-wage countries in Asia and elsewhere (using textiles from the NIEs), and the finished product was shipped to the United States or other overseas buyers using the quotas assigned to the exporting nation (Gereffi, 1999).

Thus, international production networks facilitated the upgrading of East Asian apparel firms in two ways: first, they were the main source of learning from US and European buyers about how to make the transition from assembly to OEM and OBM; and second, the East Asian NIEs established their own international production networks when faced with rising production costs and quota restrictions at home, and in order to take advantage of lower labor costs and a growing supply base in their region. Asian apparel manufacturers thus made the coordination of the apparel supply chain into one of their own core competences for export success.

Figure 5.1 presents a stylized model of industrial upgrading in the Asian apparel value chain. The main segments of the apparel chain—garments, textiles, fibers, and machinery—are arranged along the horizontal axis from low to high levels of relative value added in the production process. Countries are grouped on the vertical axis by their relative level of development, with Japan at the top and the least-developed exporters like Bangladesh, Sri Lanka, and Vietnam at the bottom.

Figure 5.1 reveals several important dynamics about the apparel value chain in Asia, and the GVC approach more generally. First, individual countries progress from low- to high-value-added segments of the chain in a sequential fashion over time. This reinforces the importance in GVC research of looking at the entire constellation of value-added steps in the supply chain (raw materials, components, finished goods, related services, and machinery), rather than just the end product, as traditional industry studies are wont to do. Second, there is a regional division of labor in the apparel value chain, whereby countries at very different levels of development form a multitiered production hierarchy with a variety of export roles (e.g., the United States generates the designs and large orders, Japan provides the sewing machines, the East Asian NIEs supply fabric, and low-wage Asian economies like China, Indonesia, or Vietnam sew the apparel). Industrial upgrading occurs when countries change their roles in these export hierarchies.[27]

Finally, advanced economies like Japan and the East Asian NIEs do not exit the industry when the finished products in the chain become mature, as the 'product cycle' model (Vernon, 1966, 1971, chapter 3) implies, but rather they capitalize on their knowledge of production and distribution networks in the industry and thus move to higher value-added stages in the apparel chain. This strategic approach to upgrading requires that close attention be paid to competition within and between firms occupying all segments of global value chains.

Figure 5.1   Industrial Upgrading in the Asian Apparel Value Chain

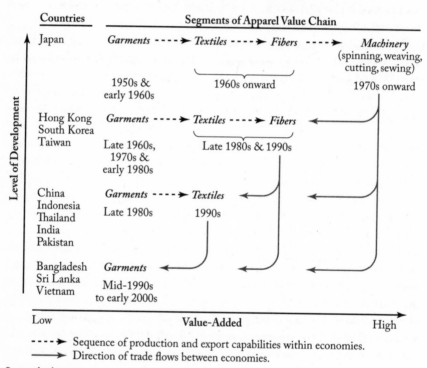

- - - -► Sequence of production and export capabilities within economies.
———► Direction of trade flows between economies.

Source: Authors.

Note: Dates refer to a country's peak years for exports of specific products.

It is important to note, in closing this section, the key role played by international regulation in the organization of the apparel value chain. The MFA and its apparel quotas will be eliminated in 2005 as a result of the Agreement on Textiles and Clothing in the WTO, and many of the smaller apparel exporters that only do assembly will probably be forced out of the world export market. This should greatly increase export concentration in the global apparel industry, with China likely to be the major winner, along with other large countries such as Mexico,

India, Turkey, Romania, and Vietnam that have developed considerable expertise in OEM production. Mexico's rapid move in the 1990s to the top of list as the leading apparel exporter to the United States owes a great deal to the passage of NAFTA in 1994, which allowed the creation of textile production and other backward linkages in Mexico, and thereby facilitated the entry of the US retailers and apparel marketers that previously shunned Mexico in order to import apparel from Asia. In addition, employment in the apparel export industry increased in Mexico from 73,000 in 1994 to nearly 300,000 in 2000, mainly because Mexico coupled its relatively low wage rates with its recently acquired ability to carry out 'full-package' (or OEM) production (Bair and Gereffi, 2001; Gereffi et al., 2002). However, China regained the lead from Mexico in 2001 and 2002, as Mexico has been unable to match the volume and low price of Chinese apparel exports, and because of the intense competition from new suppliers that continue to enter the US market.[28]

Electronics

Global production networks have been a central feature in the development and upgrading of Asia's large, dynamic electronics sector. In the case of electronics, there have been competing cross-border production networks set up by US, Japanese, and European firms, led by TNCs that span the entire value chain in various industries. For high-tech industries like electronics, these producer-driven chains must combine cost competitiveness with product differentiation and speed to market. Cross-border networks not only allow firms to combine these very different market demands effectively, but they also permit the integration of Asia's four distinct development tiers: Japan occupies the first tier; the East Asian NIEs are in the second tier; the major Southeast Asian countries of Malaysia, Thailand, the Philippines, and Indonesia are in the third tier; and the fourth tier contains China and late-late developers such as Vietnam. While the economic crisis of 1997 called East Asia's economic miracle into question, it appears that the structural changes associated with recovery from the crisis will reinforce and increase the opportunities for networked production, as the process of corporate restructuring leads firms to focus on core activities and supplement these with the increasingly specialized technology, skills, and know-how that are located in different parts of Asia (Borrus et al., 2000).

The diverse upgrading dynamics in Asian electronics can best be seen by contrasting the US and Japanese production networks. In the mid-1990s, US networks were considered to be relatively open and conducive to local development in host countries, while Japanese networks were perceived as closed and hierarchical with activities confined within affiliates that were tightly controlled by the parent company (Borrus, 1997). US electronics multinationals typically set up Asian networks based on a complementary division of labor: US firms specialized in 'soft' competencies (the definition of standards, designs, and product architecture); and the Taiwanese, Korean, and Singaporean firms specialized in 'hard' competencies (the provision of components and basic manufacturing stages). The Asian affiliates of US firms in turn developed extensive subcontracting relationships with local manufacturers, who became increasingly skilled suppliers of components, sub-assemblies, and even entire electronics systems. Japanese networks, by contrast, were characterized by market segmentation: electronics firms in Japan made high-value, high-end products, while their offshore subsidiaries in Asia continued to make low-value, low-end products.

In terms of Asian upgrading, the US production networks were definitely superior: US networks maximized the contributions from their Asian affiliates, and Japanese networks minimized the value added by their regional suppliers. Although there is some evidence that Japanese firms tried to open up their production networks in the late 1990s, at best there has been partial convergence, with persistent diversity (Ernst and Ravenhill, 2000).

Taiwan's achievements in electronics are especially notable for several reasons. During the 1990s, Taiwan established itself as the world's largest supplier of computer monitors, main boards, mouse devices, keyboards, scanners, and notebook personal computers (PCs), among other items. About 70% of the notebook PCs sold under OEM arrangements to American and Japanese computer companies, which resell them under their own logos, have been designed by Taiwanese firms. Acer, Taiwan's leading computer maker, is successful at both OEM and OBM production. Progress has been equally remarkable in the field of electronic components, and Taiwan also boasts one of the world's leading silicon foundry companies, the Taiwan Semiconductor Manufacturing Corporation (Ernst, 2000). What is especially impressive about these accomplishments is that small and medium enterprises have played a central role as a source of flexibility in Taiwan's production networks.

The role of small and medium enterprises as engines of growth and industrial transformation sets Taiwan apart from South Korea, which has relied extensively on huge, diversified conglomerates (*chaebol*) as the cornerstone of its electronics sector. The Taiwanese model in the computer industry draws on a combination of several factors: government policies that facilitated market entry and upgrading; strong linkages with large Taiwanese firms and business groups; and organizational innovations, such as the shift from relatively simple, production-based OEM to more complex 'turn-key production' arrangements that encompass a wide variety of high-end support services, including design and global supply chain management (Poon, 2002).

One of the most striking features of the electronics industry in recent years has been the rise of global contract manufacturers (Sturgeon, 2002). A significant share of the world's electronics manufacturing capacity is now contained in a handful of huge contractors, such as Solectron, Flextronics, and Celestica. These firms are pure manufacturers. They sell no products under their own brand names and instead focus on providing global manufacturing services to a diverse set of lead firms, such as Hewlett-Packard, Nortel, and Ericsson. All have operations that are truly global in scope, and all have grown dramatically since the early 1990s. Solectron, the largest contractor, expanded from a single Silicon Valley location with 3,500 employees and $256 million in revenues in 1988 to a global powerhouse with more than 80,000 employees in 50 locations and nearly $20 billion in revenues in 2000. Although they have global reach, all of the largest contract manufacturers are based in North America. Except for the personal computer industry, Asian and European contract manufacturers have not developed, and the few that did were acquired by North American contractors during their buying spree fueled by the inflated stock prices of the 1990s. Global contract manufacturers introduce a high degree of modularity into value chain governance because the large scale and scope of their operations create comprehensive bundles of standardized value chain activities that can be accessed by a variety of lead firms through modular networks.

Fresh Vegetables

A final example of the role of global production networks in promoting industrial upgrading involves the production of fresh vegetables in Kenya and Zimbabwe for export to UK supermarkets.[29] Africa has very few success stories in the realm of export-oriented development, but some countries of sub-Saharan Africa seem to have found a niche in the fresh vegetables market. Several factors tie this case to our previous examples. First, fresh vegetables are a buyer-driven value chain, albeit in the agricultural sector. As with apparel, there is a high level of concentration at the retail end of the chain. The largest UK supermarkets and other food retailers control 70% to 90% of fresh produce imports from Africa. These retailers have avoided direct involvement in production; they just specialize in marketing and in the coordination of their supply chains.

Second, a major stimulus for local upgrading in Africa comes from UK retailers ratcheting up the standards that exporters must meet. UK supermarkets have moved beyond compliance with product quality and legislative (or due diligence) requirements for how produce is grown, processed, and transported. They now are focusing on broader standards that exporters must meet, such as integrated crop management, environmental protection, and human rights. In addition, retailers are beginning to use third-party auditors paid for by producers to ensure compliance with these standards.

Third, more stringent UK requirements have led to a decline in the market share of smallholder production and small export firms, which have been excluded from the supermarket supply chain. The horticulture industry in sub-Saharan Africa is dominated by a few large exporters that source predominantly from large-scale production units. In both Kenya and Zimbabwe, the top five exporters controlled over three-quarters of all fresh vegetable exports in the late 1990s.[30]

Fourth, as in apparel and electronics, market power in the horticultural chain has shifted from those activities that lower production costs to those that add value in the chain. In fresh vegetables, the latter include investing in post-harvest facilities, such as cold storage; barcoding products packed in trays to differentiate varieties, countries, and suppliers; moving into high-value-added items such as ready-prepared vegetables and salads; and treating logistics as a core competence in the chain in order to reduce the time between harvesting, packing, and delivery. Pushing back these functions into Africa can reduce the cost for UK supermarkets because adding value to vegetables is labor-intensive and African labor is relatively cheap, but taken together these high-end services can become a new source of competitiveness and an opportunity to add value in Africa.

The Globalization Backlash: Dilemmas of Governance and Development

In recent decades, a strong anti-globalization movement has emerged. As markets have gone global, many people sense that globalization means greater vulnerability to unfamiliar and unpredictable forces that can bring economic instability and social dislocation, as well as a flattening of culture in the face of well-financed global marketing machines and 'brand bullies' (Rodrik, 1997; Klein, 2000; Ritzer, 2000). The so-called Battle of Seattle, the massive protest against WTO trade talks in late 1999, was triggered not only by a lack of accountability and transparency in the deliberations of dominant global economic institutions like the WTO and the IMF, but also by a sense of outrage that corporate-sponsored international liberalization was moving full steam ahead, while the social safety nets and adjustment assistance traditionally provided by national governments were being removed. The historic compromise of 'embedded liberalism', characterized by the New Deal in the United States and social democracy in Europe, whereby economic liberalization was rooted in social community, was being undone (Ruggie, 2002a).

A major problem is that the purported benefits of globalization are distributed highly unequally. The IMF's Managing Director, Horst Köhler, has conceded that 'the disparities between the world's richest and poorest nations are wider than ever'.[31] Of the world's 6 billion people, almost half (2.8 billion) live on less than two dollars a day, and a fifth (1.2 billion) live on less than one dollar a day, with 44% of them living in South Asia. In East Asia the number of people living on less than one dollar a day fell from 420 million to 280 million between 1987 and 1998, largely because of improvements in China. Yet the numbers of poor people continue to rise in Latin America, South Asia, and sub-Saharan Africa (World Bank, 2001: 3). What forces might be able to ameliorate these problems in both governance and development in the global economy?

In the 1990s, there was a sharp escalation in social expectations about the role of corporations in society, both in developed and developing nations (Ruggie, 2002b). One reason is that individual companies have made themselves, and in some cases entire industries, targets by engaging in abusive or exploitative behavior. As a result, trust in the corporate sector has been eroded. In addition, there is a growing imbalance in global rule-making: on the one hand, the rules favoring market expansion have become stronger and more enforceable (such as intellectual property rights for software and pharmaceutical companies, or the restrictions on local-content provisions and export-performance requirements in the WTO); on the other hand, rules that favor other valid social objectives, such as human rights, labor standards, environmental sustainability, or poverty reduction, are lagging behind. These perceived problems and others have provided the fuel for anti-corporate campaigns worldwide.

Government policy alone is inadequate to handle these grievances: they are transnational in scope, and they deal with social demands in areas where regulations are weak, ill-defined, or simply absent. A variety of new 'private governance' responses or certification institutions are emerging (Gereffi et al., 2001), such as individual corporate codes of conduct; sectoral certification schemes involving non-governmental organizations (NGOs), firms, labor, and other industry stakeholders; third-party auditing systems, such as SA 8000 for labor standards or the Forest Stewardship Council (FSC) certification for sustainable forestry practices; and the United Nations Global Compact, an initiative that encourages the private sector to work with the United Nations, in partnership with international labor and civil society organizations, to move toward 'good practices' in human rights, labor standards, and environmental sustainability in the global public domain. While skeptics claim there is little evidence to show that these codes have significant impact on corporate behavior (Hilowitz, 1996; Seidman, 2003), proponents generally argue that new systems of certification, enforced either by global consumers or by institutional actors such as the United Nations, can provide the basis for improved regulatory frameworks (Fung et al., 2001; Williams, 2000).

Although there is enormous variation in the character and purpose of different voluntary regulatory schemes—with some schemes created by activists in response to global concerns, and others implemented by corporations as a preemptive effort to ward off activist pressure—certification institutions have gained a foothold in both Europe and North America. In the apparel industry, a variety of certification and monitoring initiatives were established in the latter half of the 1990s.

- Clean Clothes Campaign (CCC), a consumer coalition in Europe that aims to improve working conditions in the worldwide garment industry.
- Social Accountability 8000 (or SA 8000), a code of conduct verification and factory certification program launched in October 1997 by the New York–based Council on Economic Priorities.
- Fair Labor Association (FLA), which includes major brand merchandisers such as Nike, Reebok, and Liz Claiborne.
- Worldwide Responsible Apparel Production (WRAP), an industry-initiated certification program designed as an alternative to the FLA and representing the large US apparel manufacturers that produce for the discount retail market.
- Workers Rights Consortium (WRC), developed by the United Students Against Sweatshops in cooperation with apparel unions, universities, and a number of human rights, religious, and labor NGOs (see Maquila Solidarity Network, 2002).

In Mexico, the FLA and WRC collaborated in settling a strike and gaining recognition for the workers' union in the Korean-owned Kukdong factory, which made Nike and Reebok sweatshirts for the lucrative US collegiate apparel market (Gereffi et al., 2001: 62–64). In the coffee sector, the Fair Trade movement has worked with small coffee growers in Costa Rica and elsewhere to get above-market prices for their organic and shade-grown coffees distributed by Starbucks and other specialty retailers (Fitter and Kaplinsky, 2001; Ponte, 2002).

Private governance in multistakeholder arrangements seeks to strengthen oversight in global supply chains by charting a course that goes beyond conventional top-down regulation based on uniform standards, on the one hand, and reliance on voluntary initiatives taken by corporations in response to social protest, on the other. Some argue that a continuous-improvement model based on 'ratcheting labor standards' upward would work well in a highly competitive, brand-driven industry such as apparel (Fung et al., 2001). Others propose a 'compliance-plus' model that pushes beyond the basic floor of minimum standards set by most codes, and seeks an 'inside-out' approach to ethical sourcing based on training and empowerment initiatives that address the needs and interests of factory-based stakeholders (Allen, 2002). In either instance, sustainable and meaningful change requires a shift in organizational cultures and expectations regarding improvement of social and environmental conditions.

Governance has become a central theoretical issue in the global economy. Institutional paradigms and local or regional frameworks centered on the nation-state are being superseded by approaches that emphasize transnational governance structures, with an emphasis on power, networks, and the uneven distribution of gains from globalization. Much still needs to be done in this area. The inability of the neoliberal agenda to redress the most serious development problems in the world is leading to fresh thinking on the role of the state and civil society institutions in developing nations (Wolfensohn, 1998; IDB, 1998, 2000; Garretón et al., 2003). Transnational corporations are being pressured to comply with a broad range of social objectives in multistakeholder institutions of private governance that can have an impact on public policies in the developed as well as the developing world. The challenge in research on the global economy is to create theory and carry out insightful empirical studies that provide tools to understand the constantly changing reality we seek to apprehend and change.

Notes

I am grateful to Giovanni Arrighi, Fred Block, Frank Dobbin, Mark Granovetter, Evelyne Huber, Larry King, Victor Nee, Gay Seidman, Neil Smelser, and Richard Swedberg for their helpful comments on an earlier draft of this chapter.

1. Another key actor in the contemporary global economy is the state. While the role of the state is an important aspect in many of the institutional perspectives we will review, a more comprehensive discussion of this topic can be found in Block and Evans (2005).

2. Because the services component of GDP in industrial countries has grown substantially relative to 'merchandise' trade like manufacturing, mining, and agriculture, the merchandise component of GDP is shrinking. Thus Feenstra (1998: 33–35) uses the ratio of merchandise trade to merchandise value-added to measure the significance of trade for industrial economies between 1890 and 1990. He finds that this ratio doubled for France, Germany, Italy, and Sweden between 1913 and 1990, and nearly tripled for the United States.

3. Organization for Economic Co-operation and Development.

4. The maquiladora program in Mexico, initially called the Border Industrialization Program, was created in 1965 after the United States terminated the bracero program, whose main objective had been to bring in Mexican workers to fulfil the demand for agricultural labor. The end of the bracero program left thousands of unemployed farm-workers in Mexican border cities, and the maquiladora program was set up to alleviate the resultant unemployment and growing poverty. The growth of the maquiladora program has been spectacular, especially in the 1990s. In 1991, Mexico's maquiladora industry generated $15.8 billion in exports and employed 466,000 Mexicans; by 2000, it had grown to $79.5 billion in exports with nearly 1.3 million employees. Around 15% of Mexico's GDP corresponded to maquiladora exports in 2001, and the main destination for these products is the United States (Cañas and Coronado, 2002).

5. These three motives for investing abroad subsequently became popularized as distinct forms of foreign direct investment: resource-seeking FDI, market-seeking FDI, and efficiency-seeking FDI (Beviglia Zampetti and Fredriksson, 2003: 406).

6. The debt crisis hit all of Latin America very hard. The high external debt burden required the allocation of 25% to 30% of the region's foreign-exchange proceeds merely to cover interest payments, which prompted scholars to refer to the 1980s as Latin America's 'lost development decade' (Urquidi, 1991).

7. The World Bank's (1993) overview of the East Asian development experience attributes the region's sustained international competitiveness largely to the application of market-friendly policies, including stable macroeconomic management, high investments in human capital (especially education), and openness to foreign trade and technology. For a critique of this 'Washington Consensus' model, see Gore, 2000. For a detailed comparison of the import-substituting and export-oriented development strategies in Latin America and East Asia, see Gereffi and Wyman (1990).

8. UNCTAD's *World Investment Report, 2002* contains a table of the largest 100 'economies' in the world in 2000, using a value-added measure for firms that is conceptually comparable to the GDP calculation used for countries. There were 29 TNCs in the top 100 entities on this combined list of countries and nonfinancial companies. The world's largest TNC was ExxonMobil, with an estimated $63 billion in value added in 2000; it ranked 45th on the country-company list, making the company approximately equal in size to the economies of Chile or Pakistan (UNCTAD, 2002a: 90–91).

9. For OECD countries, falling tariffs were twice as important as falling transport costs in explaining the growth of trade relative to income between 1958 and 1988 (Feenstra, 1998: 34).

10. The European Union is a case in point. Taken individually, European Union economies are very open, with an average trade share of 28% in 1990, but more than 60% of their trade is with each other. Taken as a unit, the European Union's merchandise trade with the rest of the world is only 9% of GDP, which is similar to that of the United States (Krugman, 1995: 340).

11. SITC refers to Standard International Trade Classification, which is the United Nations' system of trade categories. One-digit product groups, such as SITC 7, are the most general. Components are reported at the level of three-, four- and five-digit product groups.

12. Feenstra's focus on linkages between the integration of trade and the disintegration of production in the current trade-based era calls to mind a similar duality in Osvaldo Sunkel's classic article 'Transnational Capitalism and National Disintegration in Latin America.' Writing 25 years before Feenstra in a TNC-based world economy, Sunkel (1973) argued that vertically integrated TNCs were generating international polarisation as they used direct foreign investment (rather than trade) to integrate the global economy and simultaneously disintegrate national and regional economies. Thus, we have a curiously reversed image of TNCs moving from being highly integrated to disintegrated actors in the last quarter of the twentieth century, while the economic context shifts from transnational capitalism (based on closed domestic economies) in the 1970s to global value chains (based on specialized economic activities in relatively open economies) in the 1990s.

13. Actually, the disintegration of production through outsourcing of specific activities by large corporations itself leads to more trade, as intermediate inputs cross borders several times during the manufacturing process. This is part of the boundary problem in measuring international trade noted by Krugman (1995).

14. Kogut (1985: 15) defines the value-added chain as 'the process by which technology is combined with material and labor inputs, and then processed inputs are assembled, marketed, and distributed. A single firm may consist of only one link in this process, or it may be extensively vertically integrated.'

15. The main sources of a firm's competitive advantage that can be transferred globally are several economies that exist along and between value-added chains: economies of scale (related to an increase in market size); economies of scope (related to an increase in product lines supporting the fixed costs of logistics, control, or downstream links of the value-added chain); and learning (based on proprietary knowledge or experience). 'When these economies exist, industries are global in the sense that firms must compete in world markets in order to survive' (Kogut, 1985: 26).

16. A firm's value chain is nested in a larger stream of activities Porter calls a 'value system,' which includes the separate value chains of suppliers, distributors, and retailers (Porter, 1990: 40–43).

17. There are two distinct dimensions in how a firm competes internationally: the *configuration* of a firm's activities worldwide, which range from concentrated (performing an activity, such as research and development, in one location and serving the world from it) to dispersed (performing every activity in each country); and the *coordination* of value chain activities, which range from tight to loose structures (Porter, 1987: 34–38).

18. Reich (1991) says that core corporations in the United States at the end of the twentieth century have moved from high-volume production of standard commodities to high-value activities that serve the unique needs of particular customers. This requires an organizational shift from vertical coordination (represented as pyramids of power, with strong chief executives presiding over ever-widening layers of managers, atop an even larger group of hourly workers) to horizontal coordination (represented as webs of high-value activities connected by networks of firms).

19. The GCC approach adopted what Dicken et al. (2001: 93) call 'a network methodology for understanding the global economy.' The objective is 'to identify the actors in these networks, their power and capacities, and the ways through which they exercise their power through association with networks of relationships.'

20. One of the key findings of value chain studies is that access to developed country markets has become increasingly dependent on participating in global production networks led by firms based in developed countries. Therefore, how value chains function is essential for understanding how firms in developing countries can gain access to global markets, what the benefits from such access might be, and how these benefits might be increased. A GVC research network has formed to study these issues. See http://www.globalvaluechains.org.

21. Several international organizations have featured the global production networks perspective in recent reports, including UNIDO (2002, chapter 6), UNCTAD (2002a, chapter 5; 2002b, chapter 3), the World Bank (2003: 55–66), and the International Labour Organization's program 'Global Production and Local Jobs' (see the April 2003 issue of *Global Networks* for several articles from this project).

22. These distinctions are not ironclad. Often they reflect primary versus secondary research orientations. The scholars who adopt an institutional perspective at the national level can still look at the diversity of firm strategies within national contexts (e.g., Morgan et al., 2001). Similarly, those who use organizational perspectives to understand the evolution of firm strategies and inter-firm networks within global industries may ground their generalizations in diverse institutional contexts at the regional, national, and local levels of analysis (e.g., Bair and Gereffi, 2001; Gereffi et al., 2002).

23. Guillén (2001) offers a very insightful sociological perspective on the limits of convergence in his systematic comparison of organizational change in Argentina, South Korea, and Spain since 1950. Guillén uses a comparative institutional approach to show that 'the emergence of a specific combination of organizational forms in a given country enables it to be successful in the global economy at certain activities but not others' (2001: 16).

24. Indeed, companies from the *same* national business system may show contradictory patterns as they confront global markets. A careful study of seven German transnational companies in three of Germany's core industries— Hoechst, Bayer, and BASF in the chemical/pharmaceutical industries; Volkswagen, Mercedes-Benz, and BMW in the automobile industry; and Siemens in electrical/electronic engineering—reveals that strikingly different strategies exist within and between these industries, resulting from a mixture of traditional German ways of doing business and bold global moves (Lane, 2001). This departs markedly from Whitley's classification of firms in the German business system as 'collaborative hierarchies.'

25. This analysis of industrial upgrading in apparel draws mainly from Gereffi (1999) and Gereffi and Memodovic (2003).

26. However, a number of OBM companies have returned to OEM because it capitalises on East Asia's core competence in manufacturing expertise. Some East Asian companies pursue a dual strategy of doing OBM for the domestic and other developing country markets, and OEM production for the United States and other industrial country markets.

27. By contrast, the popular 'flying geese' model of Asian development assumes that countries industrialize in a clear follow-the-leader pattern (Akamatsu, 1961), and no attention is paid to the kind of international production networks that may emerge between the lead economies and their followers.

28. A prime example is sub-Saharan Africa, which, under the African Growth of Opportunity Act of October 2000, has been granted quota-free and duty-free access to the US market for products that meet specified rules of origin.

29. See Dolan and Humphrey (2000) for the facts relevant to this case.

30. The one exception to this high level of concentration is organic produce, for which there is both a price premium and a significant unmet market demand in the United Kingdom because local production is very fragmented. Smaller African exporters still have an opportunity to penetrate this market because organics do not presently require the scale and investment of more exotic forms of produce.

31. 'Working for a Better Globalization,' remarks by Horst Köhler at the Conference on Humanizing the Global Economy, Washington, DC, 28 January 2002. Cited in Ruggie 2002a: 3.

References

Aglietta, Michel. 1980. *A Theory of Capitalist Regulation*. London: New Left Books.

Akamatsu, Kaname. 1961. 'A Theory of Unbalanced Growth in the World Economy.' *Weltwirtschaftliches Archiv* 86(1): 196–217.

Allen, Michael. 2002. 'Analysis: Increasing Standards in the Supply Chain.' *Ethical Corporation*, October 15.

Amable, Bruno. 2000. 'Institutional Complementarity and Diversity of Social Systems of Innovation and Production.' *Review of International Political Economy* 7(4): 645–687.

Amsden, Alice H. 1989. *Asia's Next Giant: South Korea and Late Industrialization*. Oxford: Oxford University Press.

Arndt, Sven W. and Henryk Kierzkowski, eds. 2001. *Fragmentation: New Production Patterns in the World Economy*. Oxford: Oxford University Press.

Arrighi, Giovanni. 1994. *The Long Twentieth Century*. London: Verso.

Arrighi, Giovanni and Jessica Drangel. 1986. 'The Stratification of the World-Economy: An Exploration of the Semiperipheral Zone.' *Review* 10(1): 9–74.

Arrighi, Giovanni, Beverly J. Silver, and Benjamin D. Brewer. 2003. 'Industrial Convergence, Globalization, and the Persistence of the North-South Divide.' *Studies in Comparative International Development* 38(1): 3–31.

Ayres, Robert L. 1983. *Banking on the Poor: The World Bank and World Poverty*. Cambridge, MA: MIT Press.

Bair, Jennifer and Gary Gereffi. 2001. 'Local Clusters in Global Chains: The Causes and Consequences of Export Dynamism in Torreon's Blue Jeans Industry.' *World Development* 29(11): 1885–1903.

Barnet, Richard J. and Ronald E. Müller. 1974. *Global Reach: The Power of the Multinational Corporations*. New York: Simon and Schuster.

Berger, Suzanne and Ronald Dore, eds. 1996. *National Diversity and Global Capitalism*. Ithaca, NY: Cornell University Press.

Bergsten, C. Fred, Thomas Horst, and Theodore H. Moran. 1978. *American Multinationals and American Interests*. Washington, DC: Brookings Institution Press.

Beviglia Zampetti, Americo and Torbjörn Fredriksson. 2003. 'The Development Dimension of Investment Negotiations in the WTO: Challenges and Opportunities.' *Journal of World Investment and Trade* 4(3): 399–450.

Bhagwati, Jagdish. 1958. 'Immiserizing Growth: A Geometrical Note.' *Review of Economic Studies* 25(3): 201–205.

Block, Fred and Peter Evans. 2005. 'The State and the Economy.' In *The Handbook of Economic Sociology*, 2nd edition, edited by Neil J. Smelser and Richard Swedberg, 505–526. Princeton, NJ: Princeton University Press and Russell Sage Foundation.

Borrus, Michael. 1997. 'Left for Dead: Asian Production Networks and the Revival of US Electronics.' In *The China Circle*, edited by Barry Naughton, 139–163. Washington, DC: Brookings Institution Press.

Borrus, Michael, Dieter Ernst, and Stephan Haggard, eds. 2000. *International Production Networks in Asia*. London: Routledge.

Boyer, Robert. 1989. *The Regulation School: A Critical Introduction*. Translated by Craig Charney. New York: Columbia University Press.

Campbell, John L., Joseph R. Hollingsworth, and Leon N. Lindberg, eds. 1991. *Governance of the American Economy*. Cambridge: Cambridge University Press.

Cañas, Jesus and Roberto Coronado. 2002. 'Maquiladora Industry: Past, Present, and Future.' *Business Frontier*, Issue 2. El Paso Branch of the Federal Reserve Bank of Dallas.

Cardoso, Fernando Henrique and Enzo Faletto. 1979. *Dependency and Development in Latin America*. Translated by Marjory Mattingly Urquidi. Expanded edition. Berkeley and Los Angeles, CA: University of California Press.

Carrillo, Jorge and Alfredo Hualde. 1998. 'Third Generation Maquiladoras: The Delphi-General Motors Case.' *Journal of Borderlands Studies* 13(1): 79–97.

Carroll, William K. and Meindert Fennema. 2002. 'Is there a Transnational Business Community?' *International Sociology* 17(3): 393–419.

Castells, Manuel. 1996. *The Rise of the Network Society*. Oxford: Blackwell.

Dicken, Peter. 2003. *Global Shift: Reshaping the Global Economic Map in the 21st Century*, 4th edition. London: Sage.

Dicken, Peter, Philip F. Kelly, Kris Olds, and Henry Wai-chung Yeung. 2001. 'Chains and Networks, Territories and Scales: Towards a Relational Framework for Analysing the Global Economy.' *Global Networks* 1(2): 89–112.

Dolan, Catherine and John Humphrey. 2000. 'Governance and Trade in Fresh Vegetables: The Impact of UK Supermarkets on the African Horticulture Industry.' *Journal of Development Studies* 37(2): 147–175.

Dunning, John H. 1958. *American Investment in British Manufacturing Industry*. London: Allen and Unwin.

Engardio, Peter, Aaron Bernstein, and Manjeet Kripalani. 2003. 'Is Your Job Next?' *Business Week*, February 3, 50–60.

Ernst, Dieter. 2000. 'What Permits David to Grow in the Shadow of Goliath? The Taiwanese Model in the Computer Industry.' In *International Production Networks in Asia*, edited by Michael Borrus, Dieter Ernst, and Stephan Haggard, 110–140. London: Routledge.

Ernst, Dieter and John Ravenhill. 2000. 'Convergence and Diversity: How Globalization Reshapes Asian Production Networks.' In *International Production Networks in Asia*, edited by Michael Borrus, Dieter Ernst, and Stephan Haggard, 226–256. London: Routledge.

Evans, Peter B. 1979. *Dependent Development: The Alliance of Multinationals, State, and Local Capital in Brazil*. Princeton, NJ: Princeton University Press.

————. 1995. *Embedded Autonomy: States and Industrial Transformation*. Princeton, NJ: Princeton University Press.

Feenstra, Robert C. 1998. 'Integration of Trade and Disintegration of Production in the Global Economy.' *Journal of Economic Perspectives* 12(4): 31–50.

Feenstra, Robert C., Tzu-Han Yang, and Gary G. Hamilton. 1999. 'Business Groups and Product Variety in Trade: Evidence from South Korea, Taiwan, and Japan.' *Journal of International Economics* 48(1): 71–100.

Fitter, Robert and Raphael Kaplinsky. 2001. 'Who Gains from Product Rents as the Coffee Market Becomes More Differentiated? A Value-Chain Analysis.' *IDS Bulletin* 3(3): 69–82.

Foxley, Alejandro, Michael S. McPherson, and Guillermo O'Donnell, eds. 1986. *Development, Democracy, and the Art of Trespassing: Essays in Honor of Albert O. Hirschman.* Notre Dame, IN: University of Notre Dame Press.

Fröbel, Folker, Jürgen Heinrichs, and Otto Kreye. 1980. *The New International Division of Labour.* Cambridge: Cambridge University Press.

Fung, Archon, Dara O'Rourke, and Charles Sabel. 2001. 'Realizing Labor Standards: How Transparency, Competition, and Sanctions Could Improve Working Conditions Worldwide.' *Boston Review*, February–March.

Garretón, Manuel Antonio, Marcelo Cavarozzi, Peter Cleaves, Gary Gereffi, and Jonathan Hartlyn. 2003. *Latin America in the Twenty-First Century: Toward a New Sociopolitical Matrix.* Miami, FL: North-South Center Press.

Gereffi, Gary. 1983. *The Pharmaceutical Industry and Dependency in the Third World.* Princeton, NJ: Princeton University Press.

————. 1994a. 'The Organization of Buyer-Driven Global Commodity Chains: How US Retailers Shape Overseas Production Networks.' In *Commodity Chains and Global Capitalism*, edited by Gary Gereffi and Miguel Korzeniewicz, 95–122. Westport, CT: Praeger.

————. 1994b. 'The International Economy and Economic Development.' In *The Handbook of Economic Sociology*, edited by Neil J. Smelser and Richard Swedberg, 206–233. Princeton, NJ: Princeton University Press.

————. 1996. 'Global Commodity Chains: New Forms of Coordination and Control among Nations and Firms in International Industries.' *Competition and Change* 1(4): 427–439.

————. 1999. 'International Trade and Industrial Upgrading in the Apparel Commodity Chain.' *Journal of International Economics* 48(1): 37–70.

————. 2001. 'Shifting Governance Structures in Global Commodity Chains, with Special Reference to the Internet.' *American Behavioral Scientist* 44(10): 1616–1637.

Gereffi, Gary, Ronie Garcia-Johnson, and Erika Sasser. 2001. 'The NGO-Industrial Complex.' *Foreign Policy* 125: 56–65.

Gereffi, Gary and Raphael Kaplinsky, eds. 2001. 'The Value of Value Chains: Spreading the Gains from Globalisation.' Special Issue of the *IDS Bulletin* 32(3).

Gereffi, Gary and Miguel Korzeniewicz, eds. 1994. *Commodity Chains and Global Capitalism.* Westport, CT: Praeger.

Gereffi, Gary and Olga Memodovic. 2003. 'The Global Apparel Value Chain: What Prospects for Upgrading by Developing Countries?' Vienna: UNIDO, Strategic Research and Economy Branch.

Gereffi, Gary, David Spener, and Jennifer Bair, eds. 2002. *Free Trade and Uneven Development: The North American Apparel Industry after NAFTA.* Philadelphia, PA: Temple University Press.

Gereffi, Gary and Donald L. Wyman, eds. 1990. *Manufacturing Miracles: Paths of Industrialization in Latin America and East Asia.* Princeton, NJ: Princeton University Press.

Gore, Charles. 2000. 'The Rise and Fall of the Washington Consensus as a Paradigm for Developing Countries.' *World Development* 28(5): 789–804.

Granovetter, Mark. 1994. 'Business Groups.' In *The Handbook of Economic Sociology*, edited by Neil J. Smelser and Richard Swedberg, 453–475. New York: Russell Sage Foundation; Princeton, NJ: Princeton University Press.

————. 2005. 'Business Groups and Social Organization.' In *The Handbook of Economic Sociology*, 2nd edition, edited by Neil J. Smelser and Richard Swedberg, 429–450. New York: Russell Sage Foundation; Princeton, NJ: Princeton University Press.

Guillén, Mauro F. 2001. *The Limits of Convergence: Organization and Organizational Change in Argentina, South Korea, and Spain*. Princeton, NJ: Princeton University Press.

Hall, Peter A. and David Soskice, eds. 2001. *Varieties of Capitalism: The Institutional Foundations of Comparative Advantage*. Oxford: Oxford University Press.

Hamilton, Gary G., William Zeile, and Wan-Jin Kim. 1989. 'The Network Structure of East Asian Economies.' In *Capitalism in Contrasting Cultures*, edited by Stewart Clegg and Gordon Redding, 105–129. Berlin: Walter de Gruyter.

Held, David, Anthony McGrew, David Goldblatt, and Jonathan Perraton. 1999. *Global Transformations*. Stanford, CA: Stanford University Press.

Hilowitz, Janet. 1996. *Labelling Child Labour Products: A Preliminary Study*. Geneva: International Labour Organization.

Hirschman, Albert O. 1981. *Essays in Trespassing: Economics to Politics and Beyond*. Cambridge: Cambridge University Press.

Hollingsworth, Joseph R. and Robert Boyer, eds. 1997. *Contemporary Capitalism: The Embeddedness of Institutions*. Cambridge: Cambridge University Press.

Hollingsworth, Joseph R., Philippe Schmitter, and Wolfgang Streeck, eds. 1994. *Governing Capitalist Economies: Performance and Control of Economic Sectors*. Oxford: Oxford University Press.

Hummels, David, Dana Rapaport, and Kei-Mu Yi. 1998. 'Vertical Specialization and the Changing Nature of World Trade.' *Federal Reserve Bank of New York Economic Policy Review* 4(2): 79–99.

Humphrey, John and Hubert Schmitz. 2001. 'Governance in Global Value Chains.' *IDS Bulletin* 32(3): 19–29.

IDB (Inter-American Development Bank). 1998. *Facing Up to Inequality in Latin America: Economic and Social Progress in Latin America, 1998–99 Report*. Washington, DC: IDB.

————. 2000. *Development beyond Economics: Economic and Social Progress in Latin America, 2000 Report*. Washington, DC: IDB.

Kaplinsky, Raphael. 2000. 'Globalisation and Unequalisation: What can be Learned from Value Chain Analysis?' *Journal of Development Studies* 37(2): 117–146.

————. 2001. 'Is Globalization All It Is Cracked Up to Be?' *Review of International Political Economy* 8(1): 45–65.

Kitschelt, Herbert, Peter Lange, Gary Marks, and John D. Stephens, eds. 1999. *Continuity and Change in Contemporary Capitalism*. Cambridge: Cambridge University Press.

Klein, Naomi. 2000. *No Logo: Taking Aim at the Brand Bullies*. New York: Picador.

Kogut, Bruce. 1984. 'Normative Observations on the International Value-Added Chain and Strategic Groups.' *Journal of International Business Studies* 15(2): 151–167.

————. 1985. 'Designing Global Strategies: Comparative and Competitive Value-Added Chains.' *Sloan Management Review* 26(4): 15–28.

Krugman, Paul. 1995. 'Growing World Trade.' *Brookings Papers on Economic Activity* 1: 327–377.

Lane, Christel. 2001. 'The Emergence of German Transnational Companies: A Theoretical Analysis and Empirical Study of the Globalization Process.' In *The Multinational Firm:*

Organizing across Institutional and National Divides, edited by Glenn Morgan, Peer Hull Kristensen, and Richard Whitley, 69–96. Oxford: Oxford University Press.

Lash, Scott and John Urry. 1987. *The End of Organized Capitalism*. Oxford: Polity Press.

Lundvall, Bengt-Ake, ed. 1992. *National Systems of Innovation: Towards a Theory of Innovation and Interactive Learning*. London: Pinter.

Maquila Solidarity Network. 2002. 'Memo: Codes Update', No. 12, November.

Meyer, John W. 2000. 'Globalization: Sources and Effects on National States and Societies.' *International Sociology* 15(2): 233–248.

Morgan, Glenn, Peer Hull Kristensen, and Richard Whitley, eds. 2001. *The Multinational Firm: Organizing across Institutional and National Divides*. Oxford: Oxford University Press.

Nelson, Richard R., ed. 1993. *National Innovation Systems: A Comparative Analysis*. Oxford: Oxford University Press.

Newfarmer, Richard, ed. 1985. *Profits, Progress, and Poverty: Case Studies of International Industries in Latin America*. Notre Dame, IN: University of Notre Dame Press.

OECD (Organisation for Economic Cooperation and Development). 1995. *The Impact of the Newly Industrializing Countries on Production and Trade in Manufactures*. Paris: OECD.

Offe, Claus. 1985. *Disorganized Capitalism*. Cambridge: Polity Press.

Ponte, Stefano. 2002. 'The "Latte Revolution"? Regulation, Markets, and Consumption in the Global Coffee Chain.' *World Development* 30(7): 1099–1122.

Poon, Teresa Shuk-Ching. 2002. *Competition and Cooperation in Taiwan's Information Technology Industry: Inter-firm Networks and Industrial Upgrading*. Westport, CT: Quorum Books.

Porter, Michael E. 1985. *Competitive Advantage*. New York: Free Press.

————. 1987. 'Changing Patterns of International Competition.' In *The Competitive Challenge: Strategies for Industrial Innovation and Renewal*, edited by David J. Teece, 27–57. Cambridge, MA: Ballinger.

————. 1990. *The Competitive Advantage of Nations*. New York: Free Press.

Raikes, Philip, Michael Friis Jensen, and Stefano Ponte. 2000. 'Global Commodity Chain Analysis and the French *Filière* Approach: Comparison and Critique.' *Economy and Society* 29(3): 390–417.

Reich, Robert B. 1991. *The Work of Nations: Preparing Ourselves for 21ˢᵗ-Century Capitalism*. New York: Alfred A. Knopf.

Ritzer, George. 2000. *The McDonaldization of Society*. Thousand Oaks, CA: Pine Forge Press.

Rodrik, Dani. 1997. *Has Globalization Gone Too Far?* Washington, DC: Institute for International Economics.

Ruggie, John G. 2002a. 'Taking Embedded Liberalism Global: The Corporate Connection.' Paper presented at the 98th Annual Meeting of the American Political Science Association, Boston, August 26–September 1.

————. 2002b. 'The New World of Corporate Responsibility.' *Financial Times*, 25 October.

Rugman, Alan M. 1999. 'Forty Years of the Theory of the Transnational Corporation.' *Transnational Corporations* 8(2): 51–70.

Safarian, A. Edward. 1966. *Foreign Ownership of Canadian Industry*. Toronto: McGraw-Hill.

Sampson, Anthony. 1973. *The Sovereign State of ITT*. New York: Stein and Day.

Sassen, Saskia. 2000. 'Territory and Territoriality in the Global Economy.' *International Sociology* 15(2): 372–393.

Schmitter, Philippe C. 1990. 'Sectors in Modern Capitalism: Modes of Governance and Variation in Performance.' In *Labour Relations and Economic Performance*, edited by Renato Brunetta and Carlo Dell'Aringa, 3–39. New York: New York University Press.

Seidman, Gay. 2003. 'Monitoring Multinationals: Lessons from the Anti-apartheid Movement.' *Politics and Society* 31(3): 381–406.

Shaiken, Harley and Stephen Herzenberg. 1987. *Automation and Global Production: Automobile Engine Production in Mexico, the United States, and Canada*. La Jolla, CA: Center for US-Mexican Studies, University of California, San Diego.

Sklair, Leslie. 1993. *Assembling for Development: The Maquila Industry in Mexico and the United States*. La Jolla, CA: Center for US-Mexican Studies, University of California, San Diego.

⸻. 2001. *The Transnational Capitalist Class*. Oxford: Blackwell.

Smith, Adam. [1776] 1976. *An Inquiry into the Nature and Causes of the Wealth of Nations*, 2 volumes. Oxford: Clarendon Press.

Sturgeon, Timothy J. 2002. 'Modular Production Networks. A New American Model of Industrial Organization.' *Industrial and Corporate Change* 11(3): 451–496.

Sturgeon, Timothy J. and Richard Florida. 2000. 'Globalization and Jobs in the Automotive Industry'. Final report to the Alfred P. Sloan Foundation. International Motor Vehicle Program, Center for Technology, Policy, and Industrial Development, Massachusetts Institute of Technology.

Sunkel, Osvaldo. 1973. 'Transnational Capitalism and National Disintegration in Latin America.' *Social and Economic Studies* 22(1): 132–176.

Therborn, Göran. 2000. 'Globalizations: Dimensions, Historical Waves, Regional Effects, Normative Governance.' *International Sociology* 15(2): 151–179.

UNCTAD (United Nations Conference on Trade and Development). 1993. *World Investment Report: Transnational Corporations and Integrated International Production*. New York: United Nations.

⸻. 2002a. *World Investment Report: Transnational Corporations and Export Competitiveness*. New York: United Nations.

⸻. 2002b. *Trade and Development Report, 2002: Developing Countries in World Trade*. New York: United Nations.

UNIDO (United Nations Industrial Development Organization). 2002. *Industrial Development Report 2002/2003: Competing through Innovation and Learning*. Vienna: UNIDO.

Urquidi, Victor L. 1991. 'The Prospects for Economic Transformation in Latin America: Opportunities and Resistances.' *LASA Forum* 22(3): 1–9.

Vernon, Raymond. 1966. 'International Investment and International Trade in the Product Cycle.' *Quarterly Journal of Economics* 80(2): 190–207.

⸻. 1971. *Sovereignty at Bay: The Multinational Spread of US Enterprises*. New York: Basic Books.

⸻. 1999. 'The Harvard Multinational Enterprise Project in Historical Perspective.' *Transnational Corporations* 8(2): 35–49.

Wade, Robert. 1990. *Governing the Market: Economic Theory and the Role of Government in East Asian Industrialization*. Princeton, NJ: Princeton University Press.

————. 1996. 'Globalization and Its Limits: Reports of the Death of the National Economy Are Greatly Exaggerated.' In *National Diversity and Global Capitalism*, edited by Suzanne Berger and Ronald Dore, 60–88. Ithaca, NY: Cornell University Press.

Wallerstein, Immanuel. 1974. *The Modern World-System I: Capitalist Agriculture and the Origin of the European World-Economy in the Sixteenth Century*. New York: Academic Press.

————. 1979. *The Capitalist World-Economy*. Cambridge: Cambridge University Press.

————. 1980. *The Modern World-System II: Mercantilism and the Consolidation of the European World-Economy, 1600–1750*. New York: Academic Press.

————. 1989. *The Modern World-System III: The Second Era of Great Expansion of the Capitalist World-Economy, 1730–1840s*. New York: Academic Press.

————. 2000. 'Globalization or the Age of Transition? A Long-Term View of the Trajectory of the World System.' *International Sociology* 15(2): 249–265.

————. 2002. 'The Eagle Has Crash Landed.' *Foreign Policy* 131: 60–68.

Whitley, Richard. 1992a. *Business Systems in East Asia: Firms, Markets, and Societies*. London: Sage.

————. ed. 1992b. *European Business Systems*. London: Sage.

————. 1996. 'Business Systems and Global Commodity Chains: Competing or Complementary Forms of Economic Organisation?' *Competition and Change* 1(4): 411–425.

Williams, Oliver F., ed. 2000. *Global Codes of Conduct: An Idea Whose Time Has Come*. Notre Dame, IN: University of Notre Dame Press.

Wolfensohn, James D. 1998. 'The Other Crisis.' Speech by the President of the World Bank Group to the Board of Governors, October 6. Available at http://www.worldbank.org/html/extdr/am98/jdw-sp/am98-en.htm.

Womack, James P., Daniel T. Jones, and Daniel Roos. 1990. *The Machine That Changed the World*. New York: Macmillan.

World Bank. 1993. *The East Asian Miracle*. Oxford: Oxford University Press.

————. 2001. *World Development Report, 2000/2001: Attacking Poverty*. Oxford: Oxford University Press.

————. 2003. *Global Economic Prospects and the Developing Countries, 2003*. Washington, DC: World Bank.

Yeats, Alexander J. 2001. 'Just How Big is Global Production Sharing?' In *Fragmentation: New Production Patterns in the World Economy*, edited by Sven W. Arndt and Henryk Kierzkowski, 108–143. Oxford: Oxford University Press.

Yeung, Henry Wai-chung. 2000. 'Economic Globalization, Crisis, and the Emergence of Chinese Business Communities in Southeast Asia.' *International Sociology* 15(2): 266–287.

6

Local Clusters in Global Chains

The Causes and Consequences of Export Dynamism in Torreon's Blue Jeans Industry

Jennifer Bair and Gary Gereffi

Introduction

The decade of the 1980s witnessed the widespread adoption of export-led growth strategies and neoliberal policies prescribing open markets and privatization programs in much of the developing world. Development research in the 1990s focused primarily on the implications of these trends for the industrializing countries that are increasingly integrated into global markets. The abandonment of import-substituting strategies, which were influenced by the neo-marxist and dependency theories of the 1960s and 1970s, and the implementation of far-reaching reforms corresponding to a new economic model have led to a watershed in development studies. Researchers and policy makers alike confront the challenge of how to analyze the link between the global and the local. Latin America is a case in point. Spirited debates have arisen about the local development outcomes associated with the adoption of neoliberal reforms in the region and what theories and paradigms can best explain these outcomes (Dussel Peters, 2000; Reinhardt and Peres, 2000).

Our chapter contributes to this debate by focusing on one dynamic exporting cluster in Mexico, a country that has undergone a rapid and radical economic restructuring over the past decade. Across a wide variety of sectors, Mexico's exports have been booming since the implementation of the North American Free Trade Agreement (NAFTA) in 1994, increasing from $51.8 billion in 1993 to $166.4 billion in 2000 (SECOFI, 2001). Aside from impressive export growth, Mexico has also managed to achieve many of the other objectives associated with Latin America's new economic model: a stable currency, modest inflation, and plentiful direct foreign investment. Perhaps most important, the presidential election of July 2000, which saw the historic victory of opposition candidate Vicente Fox, provided evidence that Mexico's decades long transition to genuine democracy from one-party rule has been consolidated.

Despite the seeming abundance of good news, there is a growing sense that all is not well in Mexico. While the liberalization strategy that Mexico enthusiastically embraced in the 1990s has been successful in its own terms, critics have pointed out that Mexico's shift from an import-substituting industrialization strategy to an export-led growth model has been associated with a more unequal income distribution and falling real wages for the majority of the country's workers (De la Garza, 1994; Dussel Peters, 2000; Robinson, 1998–99).

The most dynamic sector of the Mexican economy in terms of exports and job creation is the maquila industry of in-bond plants, while small and medium enterprises have been hard hit by the country's rapid liberalization. NAFTA skeptics claim that the trade agreement, and the export-led growth model it represents, are leading to the '*maquilization* of Mexico', with the entire country becoming converted into an export-processing zone for low-value-added activities benefiting large corporations on both sides of the border. This position contends that the economic growth associated with the post-NAFTA era does not represent positive development outcomes for the majority of Mexican workers or firms.

In this chapter, we report on one of the most vibrant sectors within Mexico— the export-oriented apparel industry—and one of the most rapidly growing production centers within that industry, the region surrounding the city of Torreon in northern Mexico. In Section 2, we lay out the theoretical debates involving two main paradigms in developmental studies—the industrial districts and global commodity chains (GCC) perspectives—and we indicate how they frame our case. Section 3 explains why we have chosen Torreon as our empirical focus and addresses the relevance of the maquila sector for our study. Section 4 discusses our methodology and Section 5 analyzes our findings, focusing on the emergence of post-NAFTA, full-package networks for apparel production that link local manufacturers in Torreon to a new set of US customers. In Section 6, we examine the local developmental outcomes associated with the emergence of full-package networks in Torreon. In the final section, we reassess the industrial districts and GCC approaches in light of the data presented in this chapter. The industrial districts literature, which emphasizes the importance of local institutions and dynamics in promoting competitiveness, has been influential in shaping research on clusters in developing country contexts. We argue that studies of such clusters should be supplemented by a GCC perspective that privileges the dynamics of global industries and the role of foreign buyers in linking local firms into crossborder networks.

Clusters and Chains: Competing or Complementary Approaches to Understanding Development?

Throughout the late 1980s and 1990s, the industrial districts model generated significant enthusiasm in development circles. Using a Weberian ideal type based primarily on the experiences of small and medium enterprises in the Emilia-Romagna region of the so-called Third Italy, the industrial districts literature sought to explain how geographically bounded and sectorally specialized clusters of firms combined successful export performance of primarily labor-intensive, light manufacturing goods, such as footwear and apparel, with relatively high wages paid to a skilled work force (Sengenberger and Pyke, 1991). Although it emerged from a distinct social, cultural, and economic context, researchers wondered if the industrial districts model might provide clusters of firms in developing countries a 'high-road' to development as well.

A special issue of *World Development* (Humphrey, 1995a) was dedicated to this question. The focus on industrial districts was accompanied by a review of recent literature on Japanese manufacturing methods and the lean production model most closely associated with Toyota. The various contributors to the special issue examined the applicability of these two models—industrial districts and lean production—in developing-country contexts. What makes both models distinctive is their focus on inter-firm networks. While lean production involves reorganizing vertical inter-firm relationships along the supply chain, the industrial districts model emphasizes the importance of horizontal networks between firms located within the cluster:

> The crucial characteristic of an industrial district is its organization.... It is the firm as part of, and depending on, a collective network which perhaps more than anything else incapsulates the essence of the district's character (Pyke and Sengenberger, 1992: 1).

A second special issue of *World Development* (Schmitz and Nadvi, 1999a) devoted to the topic of industrial clusters in developing countries sought to 'specify the circumstances in which clustering boosts industrial growth and competitiveness' (Schmitz and Nadvi, 1999b: 1503). In the 1999 special issue, the earlier discussion of lean production as a phenomenon associated with Japanese manufacturing methods, such as Just-in-Time and Total Quality Management, was not reintroduced.[1] Similarly, there was a move away from the terminology and specificity of the industrial districts model in favor of a more inclusive and flexible approach to the study of clusters.[2] The strongest research finding to emerge from this second group of studies was the need to focus on linkages external to the cluster. While early formulations of the industrial districts model emphasized the importance of intra-cluster networks, the empirical work on clusters, particularly in developing countries, suggests that the way in which firms in clusters are linked to external actors has significant implications for the cluster's performance and local development.

Like several contributions to the second issue dealing with the impact of trade liberalization on developing-country clusters, Rabellotti (1999) examined the impact of Mexico's economic opening on one shoe cluster in Guadalajara. Focusing on the cooperative behavior of local firms, Rabellotti found that trade liberalization produced greater cooperation and increased horizontal and vertical linkages, and that this increased cooperation had a positive effect on firm performance. She also found that liberalization increased the heterogeneity within the cluster, and that exporting firms were favored by local suppliers. While only large manufacturers were able to develop direct links with US brokers because of the production volumes they require, the export dynamism generated by a few firms implied externalities for the cluster because production for export requires rapid access to quality inputs. This upgrading of the local supply-base, although it disproportionately benefited the large exporting firms that initiated it, was a positive consequence of liberalization. Rabellotti concluded that trade liberalization produces positive externalities for the cluster, while also increasing heterogeneity within it, mainly due to the bifurcation of market channels between firms serving the domestic market and a few large exporters.

Hubert Schmitz's analysis of the footwear cluster in Brazil's Sinos Valley showed how the arrival of foreign buyers that handled the higher value-added activities of product development, marketing, and quality control introduced new price pressures within the cluster. He notes that while the industrial districts model provided a useful framework for his study, it is weak in two areas: 'it emphasizes specialization, i.e., differentiation by size; [and] it is strong on linkages internal to the cluster but weak on external linkages' (Schmitz, 1995: 23). The importance of external linkages is sharply underscored in Schmitz's sequel to the Sinos Valley footwear case. His follow-up study showed that 'an ambitious upgrading project failed mainly because some of the leading and most influential entrepreneurs identified more with their main overseas customer than with their local colleagues' (Schmitz, 1999: 1647). This connection between local producers and global buyers is viewed as a central research question (Schmitz, 2000).

These two special issues of *World Development* examined the value, first, of the lean production and industrial districts models in industrializing countries, and second, the role of clusters more generally in developing country contexts. Several key conclusions emerge from this research trajectory:

- The initial formulation of the industrial districts model was too stagnant and culture-bound to capture the variety and heterogeneity of developing country experiences;

- clusters in developing countries generally have a pronounced mix of small and large enterprises, and the larger firms are likely to yield disproportionate influence in the cluster;
- particularly in the context of trade liberalization in industrializing countries, vertical cooperation is high or growing within clusters;
- despite the emphasis placed on cooperative competition in the early industrial districts literature, bilateral horizontal cooperation is low or decreasing; and
- growth trajectories, firm performance, and local development outcomes are all to some extent dependent on the external links that connect enterprises in the cluster to foreign companies and/or markets.

The importance of external linkages, and the limited empirical attention given to these linkages to date, are often noted in the literature on clusters in developing countries. A useful antidote to this problem is the work on global commodity chains (Gereffi and Korzeniewicz, 1994). The GCC perspective starts from the premise that analyzing the dynamics and structure of global industries is a useful way to understand the local consequences of globalization for firms and workers. Commodity chains are composed of links that represent discrete, though interrelated, activities involved in the production and distribution of goods and services. In the case of the apparel industry, which is the empirical focus of our chapter, the chain extends from raw materials (e.g., cotton or petrochemicals), to the production of natural or synthetic fibers and textiles, then to the design, cutting, assembly, laundering, and finishing of apparel, and, finally, to the distribution, marketing and retailing of garments (Appelbaum and Gereffi, 1994).

While the industrial districts approach tends to focus on the role of institutions in shaping local development outcomes, the commodity chains approach when applied to clusters focuses instead on firms, both in terms of foreign buyers and local producers. Each commodity chain is driven by lead firms that coordinate and control the organization of the production process. One of the key hypotheses of the commodity chains literature is that the type of lead firms that drive a commodity chain, and therefore the type of governance structure that characterizes it, will shape local development outcomes in those areas where the chains touch down (Gereffi, 1999). Thus, the extent to which export-oriented clusters in industrializing countries can achieve industrial upgrading objectives and positive developmental outcomes will depend on the way in which firms in these clusters become incorporated into global chains, who has power in particular chains, and how that power is exercised.

The value of the commodity chains framework to the research on clusters was identified by Humphrey, who called in the 1995 special issue of *World Development* for greater attention to the relationship between global chains and local development:

Whether or not insertions into a commodity chain will create development potential for a cluster will depend on both its position in the chain and the capacity of firms and institutions to make use of or create sources of competitive advantage and opportunities for upgrading (Humphrey, 1995b: 158).

The utility of the commodity chains framework was also underscored in a recent paper by Schmitz and Knorringa, who note that the GCC approach is useful in orienting studies of developing country clusters

> because it identifies the key feature of the context in which export manufacturers from developing countries tend to operate: they feed into chains which are organized by lead firms that source globally. However, this approach needs to be developed further in order to specify where local upgrading is facilitated or hindered by these global buyers (Schmitz and Knorringa, 1999: 23).

In this chapter, we use the commodity chains framework to analyze the firm strategies, upgrading opportunities, and development outcomes associated with the Torreon blue jeans cluster. Ours is a two-part analysis. In the first part, we show how the arrival of new lead firms, in particular US retailers and marketers, has changed the organization of the local industry in Torreon by developing full-package networks with several of the most advanced and innovative apparel manufacturers in the cluster. This part of the Torreon story, in which the US buyers serve as a catalyst for the emergence of full-package networks, shows the importance of external links in changing the organizational dynamics of a cluster.

The second part of our analysis examines how these full-package networks, now the independent variable, shape firm performance, intra-cluster dynamics, and local development outcomes in Torreon. The difference between pre-NAFTA maquila networks and post-NAFTA full-package networks in terms of development outcomes is underscored. We explain what kinds of local linkages and industrial upgrading opportunities full-package networks provide in Torreon, as well as how the full-package shift affects firms and workers. In short, our analysis shows: (a) how the arrival of a new set of foreign lead firms affects the organization of the Torreon cluster and allows for the emergence of full-package networks; and (b) how these networks shape intra-cluster dynamics and development outcomes.

The New Blue Jeans Capital of the World: More Than Maquilas?

Torreon is a dynamic industrial cluster of 500,000 people in the northern Mexican state of Coahuila, about four hours by car from the Texas portion of the US border. It is located in the heart of the Laguna region, which is well known for its cotton and dairy products. The apparel industry in Torreon straddles the nearby municipalities of Gomez Palacio and Lerdo in the neighboring state of Durango. Following an economic recession in the early 1990s, Torreon has been one of the main beneficiaries of Mexico's recent export boom. Although the area is also home to other export-oriented manufacturing sectors, such as autoparts and machinery, the apparel industry has been the most dynamic in terms of exports and job creation.

Torreon is one of several rapidly growing post-NAFTA apparel production clusters in Mexico, reflecting the increased importance of this industry to the country's overall export profile in recent years. Mexico has emerged as a world-class player among global textile and apparel exporters during the second half of the 1990s. In 1991, Mexico was the seventh largest exporter of apparel to the United States. By the decade's close, Mexico toppled China to gain the number one spot, with the value of Mexican apparel exports increasing from $1.2 billion in 1990 to $8.8 billion in 1999 (SECOFI, 2001).

While overall apparel exports from Mexico have increased dramatically over the past five years, we focus on the leading item in Mexico's garment export repertoire: blue jeans. In 1999, the United States imported more than $2.6 billion of trousers from Mexico, accounting for 34% of total apparel imports from its southern neighbor (USITC, 2001). Torreon specializes in denim blue jeans, which account for the lion's share of cotton trousers. In 2000, firms in the Torreon area were producing an average of six million garments a week, of which 90% were exported. Jeans accounted for 75% of the exported apparel, and thus the region made over four million pairs of jeans each week. In contrast, El Paso, Texas–Torreon's predecessor as the blue jeans capital of the world and a major manufacturing center for Levi Strauss and Co. before the company closed its last factories there in 1999—produced two million pairs of jeans a week at its peak in the early 1980s. To keep pace with this dramatic increase in output, employment in Torreon's 360 apparel factories has grown considerably from 12,000 jobs in 1993 to an estimated 75,000 in 2000. In addition, the proportion of Mexican denim used in Torreon's exported blue jeans increased from a negligible 1-2% in 1993 to 15% in 2000, and the piece rates paid to firms for blue jean assembly rose two- to threefold (see Table 6.1).

We have chosen Torreon as the empirical focus of our paper because it is a leading apparel production cluster in Mexico, and the dynamism of Mexico's apparel exports in recent years suggests that it has been one of the industries most strongly affected by NAFTA. Some of the earliest research in the now vast maquiladora literature examined in-bond sewing plants along the border as exemplars of two characteristics that would become closely associated with the maquilas: a young, predominantly female workforce with low education and skill levels; and a highly routinized, low-value-added manufacturing process that involved simple assembly of imported inputs.[3] Apparel plants outnumber all other maquila establishments and they employ more workers than any other maquila sector except electronics. In 1993, the year prior to NAFTA's implementation, there were 392 apparel maquilas with 64,000 workers. By 2000, there were 1,058 registered maquila plants in the apparel industry throughout Mexico, employing a total of 270,000 workers[4] (SECOFI, 2001).

Table 6.1 Apparel Industry Indicators for Torreon / La Laguna[a]

Variables	1993	1998	2000
Total output (garments per week)	500,000	4.0 million	6.0 million
Output per company (garments per week)	Max. 50,000	Max. 230,000	Max. 480,000
Mexican denim in export production	1–2%	5%	15%
Assembly price per piece	US$0.90–1.10	US$1.20–2.05	US$1.60–3.00
Employment	12,000	65,000	75,000

Source: Authors based on interviews carried out in Torreon (see Table 6.4).

Note: [a] Torreon is the center of La Laguna, a highly integrated economic region formed by two additional cities (Gomez Palacio and Lerdo) and several rural communities. Although each city is a distinct political entity, they form an integrated production zone.

If the industrial districts model provides a 'high road' to competitiveness, the maquiladora industry has long been associated with a 'low road' based on exploiting substantial wage differences between the United States and Mexico. The maquiladoras are in-bond factories that produce goods primarily from imported US inputs.[5] These goods are then re-exported for sale in the US market, with only a minimal duty paid on the value-added in Mexico. While proponents of the maquiladora regime assert that it is a valuable source of export revenue and job creation for Mexico, the program's critics claim that the maquila sector offers nothing but dead-end jobs, and traps developing countries into providing cheap labor for low value-added assembly operations. Because the vast majority of inputs are imported, it has been argued that the maquilas do not stimulate growth in the rest of the economy (Sklair, 1993). Furthermore, early work on the maquilas documented abusive or poor working conditions and suppression of workers' efforts to organize (Fernandez-Kelly, 1983; Iglesias Prieto, 1985).

The profile of the maquila sector has changed dramatically since it was established by the Border Industrialization Program in 1965. Although the maquilas were initially confined to the northern border, this geographical restriction was later relaxed and maquila plants now exist throughout the country. Recent studies contend that the maquiladoras have evolved from low-value-added assembly plants to factories capable of more sophisticated manufacturing operations. This revisionist perspective emerged in the late 1980s and early

1990s, when researchers began to call attention to so-called second- and even third-generation maquilas.

Although local inputs to the production process remain low, the mix of activities being performed by Mexican workers in the maquilas has become more diverse, expanding beyond the simple assembly operations associated with earlier plants. The sectoral focus of recent research includes autoparts production in northern Mexico, televisions and other electronics in Tijuana, and computers in Guadalajara. In each of these industries, the maquilas have matured from assembly sites based on cheap labor to manufacturing centers whose competitiveness derives from a combination of high productivity, good quality, and wages far below those prevailing north of the border (Carrillo, 1998; Gereffi, 1996, 2000; Shaiken and Herzenberg, 1987).

While the maquilas existed for almost three full decades prior to NAFTA, this in-bond sector of the Mexican economy has grown rapidly since NAFTA's passage. Over 400,000 maquila jobs were created during 1994–1998, the first four years after the implementation of NAFTA (Buitelaar and Padilla, 2000). Growth in the maquila sector was accelerated by the devaluation of the Mexican peso in December 1994. The devaluation had the effect of making Mexican labor even cheaper for US firms and it has resulted in a major export boom since 1995. The rapid growth of the maquila sector has generated widespread debate in Mexico, which reflects not only the importance of this sector of the economy, but also the concern generated by Mexico's shift to an export-led development strategy in the context of trade liberalization and regional integration.

Our study of Torreon provides an opportunity to contribute to this debate about Mexico's prospects for development in the NAFTA era, as well as to the literature on industrial clusters in developing countries. Does clustering and specialization in Torreon's apparel industry provide a 'high road' to development, where firms can compete on non-price factors such as quality and flexibility and the local workforce enjoys relatively high wages? Or does Torreon more closely resemble the old-style maquila model, where local production for export is confined to low-value-added assembly activities, there are minimal backward linkages to suppliers, few horizontal networks connect firms, companies compete only on the basis of price, and unskilled workers receive low wages? Our research suggests that there has been a significant shift beyond the traditional model of maquila production in the region, but the outcomes for local firms and workers are mixed.

Methodology

Our on-site research in Torreon was conducted during two trips, each of about two weeks in duration, in July 1998 and July 2000.[6] Supplemental fieldwork during this two-year period consisted of interviews with US textile and apparel manufacturers in the United States that provided us with information about their global and North American strategies. Most of these companies are located in the Piedmont region of North Carolina, one of the major textile manufacturing centers in the United States.[7] These interviews, carried out as part of an on-going, larger research project examining the restructuring of the North American apparel industry, provided an initial set of contacts in the Torreon region. The primary method of data collection consisted of open-ended strategic interviews with Mexican, US, and joint-venture firms, industry associations, and local government organizations, coupled with plant visits and factory tours. We also used secondary materials, including production and trade data and articles in local newspapers, to document recent changes in the industry. (For additional discussion of the strategic interviews we conducted, see Appendix A.)

Our 1998 sample included nine apparel companies and two textile mills. Of these 11 firms, two were subsidiaries of US multinational corporations, three were joint ventures between US and Mexican companies, and six were wholly-owned Mexican manufacturers. In our second visit to Torreon, we interviewed 10 apparel companies, including follow-up interviews with the six largest firms we talked with in 1998. This sample consisted of three subsidiaries of US apparel companies, one joint venture, and six wholly-owned Mexican companies. In both 1998 and 2000, we also interviewed the local branch of the national apparel industry association as well as officials in the local office of the federal government ministry concerned with commerce and industry. Given the disproportionate role played by foreign firms in the sector and our interest in understanding the power dynamics that exist in the industry, our study focused on the 10 largest apparel manufacturers in Torreon. Although about 360 different garment firms operate in the Laguna region, the 10 biggest companies in our sample in 2000 directly produced or coordinated about one-third of the total apparel output of the region. (See Appendix B for a list of the authors' interviews in Torreon.)

Interviews were conducted primarily in Spanish with the company's plant manager, director of foreign operations, or owner, and they lasted an average of two hours. The interviews were usually followed by a tour of the production facilities. In Torreon, these included the traditional sewing factory, textile mills, laundries, finishing plants (where the garments are pressed, inspected for quality, and packed), and a distribution center. In addition to providing an opportunity to evaluate the working conditions and industrial relations (as suggested by plant floor interactions between the workers and managerial staff), these tours also permitted us to speak with additional informants, such as production trainers and line supervisors, whose perspectives on the operation complement the data collected in the initial interview.

Torreon's NAFTA-Era Networks: The Arrival of New Lead Firms

The Laguna region where Torreon is located has long been a center for textile and apparel production. The presence in the region of one of the oldest textile companies in the country, Compañía Industrial de Parras, established the area early on as an important source of cotton-based textiles and apparel for the national market. From the beginning, firms in Torreon specialized in denim trousers, first as workwear for the area's growing industrial labor force and later as fashion apparel when blue jeans became a mainstream clothing staple. The early period of the cluster's development in the 1940s and 1950s coincided with an import-substituting industrialization strategy, protecting national companies in virtually every sector from foreign competition and essentially guaranteeing healthy profits to firms in the closed domestic market.

The opening of Mexico's economy with the country's accession to the General Agreement on Tariffs and Trade in 1986, along with major devaluations of the peso in 1982, 1985, and 1988, contributed to an extremely difficult period for apparel firms in Torreon and throughout the country. As the purchasing power of Mexican consumers decreased, they also faced a wide array of new and cost-competitive imported apparel products. Together these factors resulted in declining employment and output in Mexico's apparel and textile industries, with small and medium firms especially hard hit. While the domestic industry faced a period of crisis throughout the 1980s, the maquila sector of in-bond plants flourished, primarily along the border. Many of the local firms that had survived the leanest years in places like Torreon recognized that exporting was the only viable option for national producers, and so they too focused their attention on producing blue jeans for the US market.

The transition of many firms from domestic manufacturer to export producer transformed the Torreon cluster. While several local companies had developed and marketed their own lines of jeans in the Mexican market, they quickly discovered that they could not meet the quality or quantity standards demanded by US buyers. Thus, they exported through the only mechanism that was available to them: they became maquiladora plants assembling jeans for the US market. The implementation of NAFTA in 1994 coincided with a sharp devaluation of the Mexican peso in December of the same year, from 3.4 to 6.8 pesos to one dollar. The immediate effect of the devaluation was to lower the relative cost of Mexican labor, expand manufactured exports, and thereby boost the country's maquiladora sector.

As a result of NAFTA, the Torreon apparel cluster has experienced a qualitative change in the type of networks connecting local firms to export markets. This transition is associated with the arrival of a new set of foreign buyers whose sourcing needs are different than those of the apparel manufacturers that used to dominate the region's export-oriented apparel production. Table 6.2 highlights the magnitude of this shift. In 1993, the major US customers for the blue jeans made in Torreon were four large manufacturers: Levi Strauss, Wrangler, Farah, and Sun Apparel. By 2000, these companies were joined by the top US retail chains (J. C. Penney, Sears, Kmart, Wal-Mart, and Target), the two leading specialty retailers for apparel (Gap and Limited), and the marketers who sell a wide range of fashionable brands (such as Liz Claiborne, Donna Karan, Tommy Hilfiger, Calvin Klein, and Polo/Ralph Lauren).

Table 6.2 Main Clients for Torreon Apparel Exports[a]

Type of clients	1993	2000
Manufacturers	Farah (M) Sun Apparel (M)	Sun Apparel-Jones of NY (M) Aalfs (M) Kentucky Apparel (M) Grupo Libra (M) Siete Leguas (M) Red Kap (M)
Brand marketers	Levi's (BM, M) Wrangler (BM, M)	Levi's (BM, M) Wrangler (BM, M) Action West (BM, M) Polo (BM) Calvin Klein (BM) Liz Claiborne (BM) Old Navy (BM) Tommy Hilfiger (BM) Donna Karan (BM) Guess (BM) Chaps (BM)
Retailers		Gap (BM, R) The Limited (BM, R) K-Mart (R) Wal-Mart (R) J. C. Penney (R) Sears (R) Target (R)

Source: Authors based on interviews carried out in Torreon (see Table 6.4).
Note: [a]M: Manufacturers; BM: Brand Marketers; R: Retailers.

The contrast between manufacturers and other big buyers (retailers and marketers) in their capabilities and needs gives rise to the difference between assembly and full-package networks. Figure 6.1 shows the typical manufacturer-dominated assembly network, which was prevalent in Torreon from the mid-1980s to the mid-1990s. The assembly plants on the Mexican side of the border received cut parts from US manufacturers or brokers. In turn, these assembly plants often subcontracted out a portion of their production to smaller firms known as submaquilas. These cut parts were to be sewn into garments and then re-exported to the United States under the maquila/807 regime. The profile of foreign lead firms in Torreon at this time was undifferentiated—US manufacturers, most of whom had some production in their own plants north of the border—and there was no variation in the type of assembly networks these manufacturers established in the region.

Figure 6.1 Pre-NAFTA Maquila Networks in Torreon

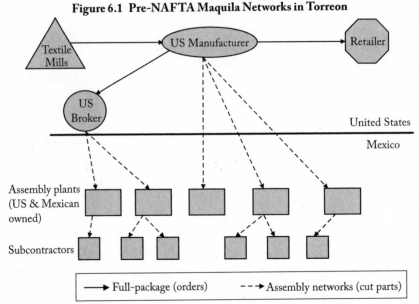

Source: Authors.

In Figure 6.2, the assembly networks typical of the maquila phase have diversified to include the full-package networks characteristic of buyer-driven commodity chains. In this full-package model, a local manufacturer receives detailed specifications for garments from the buyer and the supplier is responsible for acquiring the inputs and coordinating all parts of the production process: the purchase of textiles, cutting, garment assembly, laundry and finishing, packaging, and distribution.

Prior to NAFTA, the lead firms in the apparel commodity chain (retailers, marketers, and branded manufacturers) sourced primarily from East Asia because countries such as Hong Kong, South Korea, and Taiwan were home to contract manufacturers that could produce orders for finished apparel according to these buyers' specifications[8] (Gereffi, 1999). After NAFTA, retailers and marketers became eager to transfer as much of this business to Mexico as possible because NAFTA's rules of origin give apparel produced under full-package arrangements the same preferential access to the US market as apparel exported under the maquila/807 regime, as long as it is manufactured from North American textile inputs (Gereffi and Bair, 1998). Buyers placing orders for full-package apparel in Mexico generally do not have to worry about tariffs or quotas, as they do when importing from other apparel exporting countries.

Figure 6.2 Post-NAFTA Full-Package Networks in Torreon

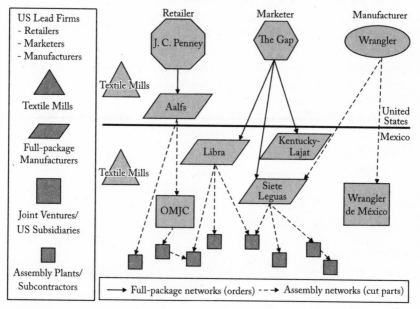

Source: Authors.

Upgrading Through Networks: Torreon's Success and Its Limitations

The arrival of a new set of foreign buyers changed the nature of Torreon's role in the apparel commodity chain: pure assembly networks typical of the maquila sector were replaced with a mix of assembly and full-package networks. In this section, we explain the relevance of these networks for local development outcomes, focusing on four areas: upgrading at the level of the industry; upgrading at the level of the firm; the hierarchical organization of Torreon's inter-firm networks; and the implications for labor.

Upgrading at the Industry Level

Upgrading is clearly occurring at the industry level in Torreon as a result of full-package networks established by new lead firms. Prior to NAFTA, the only link in the apparel commodity chain that was strong in Torreon's export-oriented blue jeans cluster was assembly, since this was the activity that the maquila/807 regime encouraged. As more US buyers began to change their sourcing and production networks to take advantage of new activities gradually liberalized under NAFTA's phase-in schedule, other activities in the chain began to touch down in the region. Figure 6.3 shows the expansion of the apparel commodity chain in Torreon over 1993–2000. In 1993, the only link on the Mexican side was assembly; by 1996, textile production as well as the post-assembly stage of laundering and finishing, one of the first production processes liberalized under NAFTA, were added. In 2000, the full range of production activities was taking place in Torreon. The other links of the chain that have been transferred to Torreon mean that more backward linkages and value are being added in the region beyond the assembly activities that were dominant prior to the emergence of full-package networks.

Figure 6.3 US–Torreon Apparel Commodity Chain Activities and Location

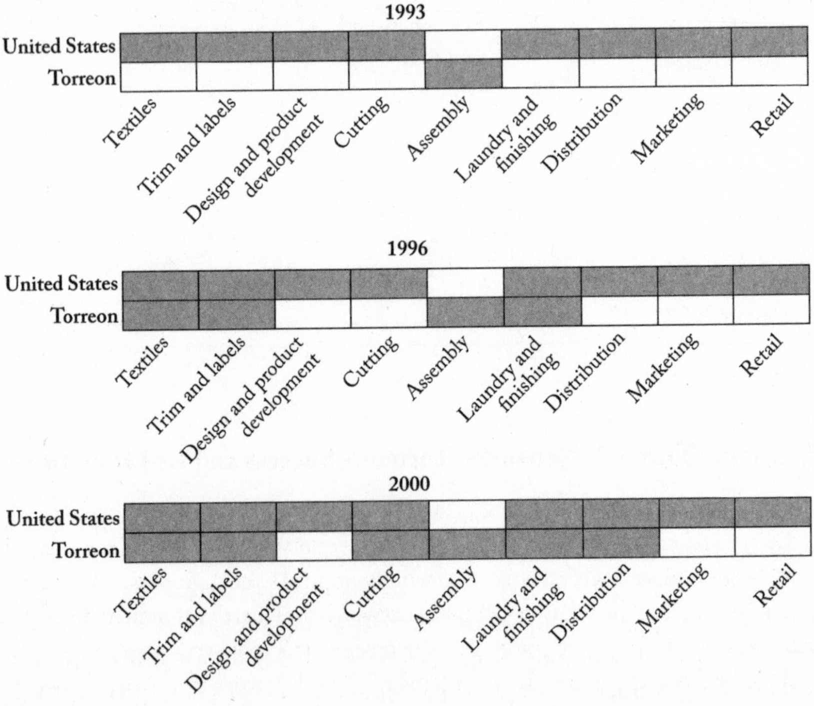

Source: Authors.

Figure 6.3 shows that three links in the apparel commodity chain—design and product development, marketing, and retail—have remained predominantly in the United States. These are the highest value-added activities in the chain, and they are also the ones with significant barriers to entry closely guarded by the foreign firms that control them. US lead firms—whether manufacturers, marketers, or retailers—view these links of the commodity chain as core competencies, and they see design and product development in particular as critical in terms of differentiating their fashions and styles from competitors. A number of the full-package manufacturers in Torreon that we interviewed have begun to work more closely with their clients on product development, but this is generally confined to translating the buyer's specifications into practical knowledge that is necessary for production.[9]

No manufacturer in Torreon markets its own apparel brands in the United States, although some companies still have a presence in the domestic market, and no Torreon producer of a US brand is able to sell its branded output directly in Mexico (everything is exported to the United States). One company that we interviewed planned in the future to launch its own line of apparel in the US market, but the amount of capital necessary to promote and market a new brand makes such endeavors risky. Strategies that local firms are considering in order to reduce these risks include marketing their products specifically to Mexican-American or Mexican consumers in the United States (whose fashion preferences are presumably closer to their own), and targeting regional retail chains and boutiques, which have lower volume needs and are less likely to choose their suppliers based solely on price.

Upgrading at the Firm Level

Upgrading is also occurring at the firm level in Torreon, although here the picture is more complex. A significant portion of full-package orders in Torreon is being handled by a small number of first-tier manufacturers with the capabilities and capital needed to coordinate full-package networks. Table 6.3 lists the top 10 firms in Torreon according to their production volume and the type of activities they perform. Four of these 10 firms are 'full-package' manufacturers, meaning that they receive an order from a client and deliver a finished product. Four more are what may be termed 'half-package' producers, meaning that they carry out all the production activities (cut, sew, and launder), but do not buy the fabric. The difference between full-package and half-package is indicated in Table 6.3, where the capabilities of some firms include an 'F' denoting that they purchase the fabric for the orders they fill, while others have only C, S, and W listed for cut, sew, and wash, respectively.

All four of these full-package manufacturers—Kentucky-Lajat, Libra, Siete Leguas, and Pafer Huichita—are Mexican-owned companies. The emergence of local full-package companies competing alongside a US-owned contractor like Maquilas Pami (the sixth-largest manufacturer in Torreon and a subsidiary of Jones Apparel of New York) is significant. Having gained experience through maquila production for US clients and having earned the trust of foreign buyers, Mexican firms are now developing direct links to export markets. These full-package firms are upgrading by eliminating middlemen like brokers or trading companies, which allows them to enjoy the higher profits full-package production offers as compared to maquila orders.

Table 6.3 Top 10 Apparel Manufacturers in Torreon, Mexico—July 2000

Rank	Firm	Capacity[a]	Employment	Capability[b]	Ownership
1	Wrangler	480,000	1,900	C, S, W	US subsidiary[c]
2	Kentucky-Lajat	400,000	5,500	F, C, S, W	Mexican[d]
3	Libra	400,000	5,000	F, C, S, W	Mexican
4	Siete Leguas	250,000	3,200	F, C, S, W	Mexican
5	Grupo Denim	245,000	3,300	C, S, W	Mexican
6	Maquilas Pami	240,000	3,800	C, S, W	US subsidiary[e]
7	Red Kap (RKI)	156,000	1,430	S	US subsidiary[f]
8	Pafer Huichita	150,000	2,450	F, C, S, W	Mexican
9	Grupo Impeccable	150,000	1,500	C, S,	Mexican
10	Original Mexican Jeans Co. (OMJC)	135,000	3,000	C, S, W	Joint venture[g]
	Total	2,606,000	31,080		

Source: Authors based on interviews carried out in Torreon (see Table 6.4).

Notes:

[a] Pairs of jeans per week.

[b] Capabilities: F: fabric, C: cutting, S: sewing, W: washing and finishing.

[c] Wrangler's parent company is the VF Corporation.

[d] Kentucky-Lajat was set up in 1995 as a joint venture between Kentucky Apparel, a US-based jeans manufacturer, and the Lajat Group in Mexico, but Lajat bought out its US partner in July 1999.

[e] Maquilas Pami is owned by Sun Apparel, which was purchased by Jones Apparel of New York in 1998.

[f] Red Kap is a division of VF Workwear, Inc.

[g] OMJC is a joint venture between Aalfs, a US-based jeans manufacturer, and the Martín Group in Mexico.

Vertical Network Structure and Hierarchical Organization of the Industry

While upgrading is occurring in Torreon, both at the level of the industry and for some specific firms, we are not sanguine about all the outcomes associated with the emergence of full-package networks in the region. Due to increasing concentration on both sides of the border, more orders are in the hands of fewer foreign buyers and they are being given to a relatively small number of Mexican suppliers. The social foundation of this concentration is revealed by the fact that six of the 10 firms listed in Table 6.3 are owned by family members related by blood or marriage.[10] This is particularly striking considering that three of the remaining four firms are subsidiaries of US corporations. Thus, the development of full-package networks in Torreon is primarily benefiting a wealthy domestic elite whose control over the local industry is being further strengthened by its exclusive access to the US customers placing orders in the region. While these orders are received by a few large, full-package manufacturers in Torreon, they are actually being filled by a burgeoning array of contractors and subcontractors organized into tiers of hierarchical networks controlled by the dominant firms in the cluster.

This hierarchical organization of the industry applies two sorts of pressures on local firms. First, the US buyers are benchmarking Mexican full-package manufacturers against other global suppliers. Consequently, these manufacturers are under pressure to reduce their production costs to a minimum in order to offer a competitive price. Second, these first-tier manufacturers then exert pressure on their subcontractors as they try to procure assembly services for the lowest possible price per piece. The end result of this vertical competitive dynamic is significant downward pressure on the manufacturers' profit margins, and consequently on workers' wages.

As noted in the previous section, several Mexican companies have emerged as leading full-package manufacturers in Torreon. To the extent that this puts ownership and control in local hands, it is a positive developmental outcome. But, these Mexican firms exert the same kinds of pressure and control on their local subcontractors as US-owned companies impose on them. From the perspective of the second- and third-tier suppliers in Torreon's assembly networks, the difference between receiving an order from a Mexican intermediary or a US buyer is probably negligible. To avoid being squeezed by the local full-package manufacturers, the obvious upgrading path for these subcontractors is to become full-package producers themselves, but this transition is difficult to make for two reasons. First, full-package business requires significant amounts of working capital to purchase piece goods (i.e., fabric), and credit is both scare and expensive in Mexico. Second, full-package manufacturers need direct links to US clients who are looking for their services, and access to this customer base is jealously guarded by the US and Mexican companies in Torreon that already have it.

Implications for Labor

How has the arrival of full-package networks coordinated by new US buyers affected workers in Torreon? We examined five main issues relating to the implications of this process for labor: (i) employment growth; (ii) skills upgrading of the local labor force; (iii) working conditions; (iv) unionization; and (v) wages. Dramatic employment growth in the apparel industry is the most obvious impact of Torreon's export boom on the local labor market. Apparel and textiles have become the major source of employment in the region. During 1993–98, apparel jobs increased 300%, while during the same period employment in commerce and services only grew 3%, construction 80%, and the auto industry 100%. In 1993, the area employed 12,000 workers in the apparel and textile industries; by 2000, the number had grown to 75,000 (see Table 6.1). It is equally important to note that activities associated with the deepening of the supply chain—such as textile production, laundering, and cutting—are bringing new types of jobs to the region to complement the growing number of sewing workers.

The development of full-package networks in the cluster has resulted in some upgrading of the local skills base, as jobs in Torreon's cutting rooms and laundries entail more training and better pay than is offered to the average sewing machine operator. The different levels of investment that firms make in the human capital of workers reveal not just the varying complexity of specific jobs, but also the way in which gender stratifies the local labor market. During our fieldwork in Torreon, we saw only men working in the laundries and cutting rooms. While management would attribute this to the physically strenuous nature of the work, sex segregation also reflects the reluctance of companies to invest in enhancing the skills of female employees. Women workers are expected to remain in the workforce only until they begin families, typically withdrawing from the labor market in their mid-20s.

Despite the fact that the ratio of male to female sewing machine operators in several of Torreon's larger plants is approaching 50%, the internal labor market within the factories continues to be stratified by gender in subtle ways. Male sewers are far more likely than female sewers to be promoted to higher-wage jobs in the cutting rooms or laundries, and often even the most difficult and best paying assembly line jobs, such as sewing the inseam in a jean, are given to men because supervisors believe they are more easily able to handle the heavy denim fabric.

Due to the tightness of the local labor market, turnover is high across every job category in Torreon's apparel industry. The average turnover rate in many of the sewing factories in Torreon was estimated at 10% per *week*. Thus, firms have little incentive to invest in training their workers. While there are more opportunities for skill upgrading than there would be in the absence of full-package networks, the boom in Torreon's apparel exports is characterized by very uneven development of the local labor force.

Our evidence from Torreon suggests that there has been an improvement in working conditions in the region associated with the arrival of US buyers that are sourcing their brand-name apparel locally. The presence in the region of widely recognized clients with upscale labels (such as Calvin Klein, Polo, and Tommy Hilfiger) has prompted an improvement in working conditions. Large retailers and marketers do not want their brands associated with the exploitation of workers or with unsafe working conditions. Companies such as Gap and J. C. Penney have issued Codes of Conduct related not only to the final quality of the product, but also to the work process itself. Any plant or company that fails to fulfill these requirements, including compliance with local labor laws, safety practices, and even the conditions of the bathrooms, is in danger of losing its contracts. In addition, since most factories have been constructed since 1994, they were designed with modern standards to provide a relatively safe working environment with proper ventilation, lighting, ergonomic equipment, etc. In general, the working conditions of many of these new Mexican plants are not only better than those offered by local competitors, but frequently better than those in comparable US apparel factories.

Currently the topic of sweatshops is receiving a great deal of attention in both the academic and popular press, thanks to a number of publicity campaigns sponsored by various consumer organizations, student groups, and organized labor (National Interfaith Committee for Worker Justice, 1998; Ross and Kernaghan, 2000). Activists have called attention to the abusive working conditions that prevail in many sewing factories, both in the United States and abroad, and they challenge leading companies in the industry to do a better job of ensuring their apparel is produced in a sweatfree environment. A commodity chains approach has been implicit in many of these campaigns, as activists demand that US firms take responsibility for the working conditions prevailing in any plant where apparel bearing their label is produced, including subcontractors in developing countries. Blatant sweatshop conditions were not evident in any of the large plants we visited. Most of the factories appeared clean, well lit and ventilated, and reasonably efficient. They had Codes of Conduct from their clients displayed where workers could see them, although in at least one case they were displayed in English. The visibility of these Codes in the plants that we visited increased between 1998 (when it was uncommon to see them posted in a factory) and 2000 (when posting them had become a standard practice).

Because we primarily studied large firms, additional research is necessary to evaluate working conditions in the numerous smaller contractors and sub-maquilas in the Torreon region. Limited evidence from Torreon and fieldwork conducted elsewhere in Mexico suggest that small, lower-tier subcontractors generally have worse working conditions and lower wages (Bair, 2000, 2001).

While the arrival of new buyers has created jobs in Torreon and appears to have improved working conditions in some factories, the evidence in terms of wages and industrial relations is disturbing. The status of organized labor in the

Torreon apparel industry mirrors the situation throughout Mexico. In tandem with the liberalization of the economy and in pursuit of the labor flexibility so prized by foreign firms, the Mexican government has reduced the power of unions to a minimum (Carrillo, 1994; De la Garza, 1994). The role of unions in the apparel industry in the Torreon region has been limited in many cases to helping the firms and their managers 'deal' with the workers. Effective representation and collective bargaining have virtually disappeared and here, as elsewhere in Mexico, 'protection contracts' (i.e., collective contracts signed with 'company-friendly unions,' often without the knowledge of workers, designed to prevent the entrance of a genuine union) are the norm. In the absence of effective representation, workers exercise their limited power by moving from one company to another fairly often. They use their mobility as a source of bargaining to obtain small wage increases and nonmonetary benefits, such as transportation, free lunch, classes, raffles, and prizes. This is a benefit contingent, however, upon a continued high demand for labor.

In terms of wages, the evidence is more mixed. Workers in the apparel industry are paid according to a piece-rate system whereby they receive a base wage, which is typically a multiple of the local minimum wage, plus additional earnings 'per piece' when they achieve certain productivity levels or fulfill set production quotas. It is widely agreed that Mexico's minimum wage, which varies by geographic region, is not a living wage, and consequently many companies pay a multiple of it, such as 1.5 times or two times the legally allowed minimum. When we completed our initial fieldwork in Torreon in July 1998, the local minimum wage was 182 pesos per week (US$21.00). Base wages in the companies we interviewed generally ranged between 220 and 280 pesos a week, but most workers earned more due to the piece-rate system. Maximum average salaries ranged from 500 pesos (US$ 57.50) to 750 pesos (US$86.20) a week.

By July 2000, average sewing wages had risen in Torreon to around 650 pesos (US$68.40) a week.[11] Several of the firms interviewed reported that good sewers with high productivity were earning as much as 800–1,000 pesos (US$84.20 to $105.30) a week.[12] Companies repeatedly told us that in Torreon's tight labor market no one works for 'minimum wage' and many of the sewers in the region's factories were earning well in excess of two times the legal minimum. Apparel wage increases in Torreon have generally been running ahead of inflation, which was about 12% in 1999. But real wages are only now returning to the levels reached prior to the 1994 devaluation, which has led some analysts to conclude that many Mexican workers have actually experienced a decline in their standard of living over the past five years (*The Economist*, 2000).

Although the high turnover and tight labor market in Torreon have been driving wages up in the region's apparel plants, this trend has not gone unnoticed by the factory's owners. High and persistent turnover was repeatedly cited in our interviews as the most pressing problem employers face. In the summer of 1998, the employers initiated discussions among themselves in an effort to find a 'solution' to the problem of rising wages as a result of Torreon's increasingly tight labor market. The employers particularly were concerned with the practice of companies pirating away each other's workers with wage increases. By July 2000, their efforts in this regard had not been successful. Some entrepreneurs in the local industry expressed resentment towards the foreign firms that arrived in Torreon after the passage of NAFTA. They complain that because foreign firms can afford to pay higher wages than their Mexican counterparts, they often hire away the better and more experienced workers whose skills the local companies have developed.

Lessons from Torreon: The Value of a Commodity-Chains Perspective for Research on Clusters

Our analysis of the blue jeans industry in Torreon shows how the types of links that connect local firms to global chains shape development outcomes in export-oriented manufacturing. Recent literature on manufacturing clusters in developing countries has argued that the local-global link, and in particular the role of foreign buyers, is not well understood. Our study is intended to help fill this gap. The global commodity chains framework that we applied to the case of Torreon allows us to explore how the structure of competition within a global industry affects the experiences of local firms and workers in specific production locales.

Many of the factors that the industrial districts literature would expect to be important in explaining local outcomes in clusters were not evident in Torreon. For example, we found that networks in Torreon tended to be hierarchical and vertical as opposed to cooperative and horizontal. During the course of our conversations with owners and managers, we learned that trust and collaboration between companies in Torreon is very uncommon. One of our informants described the networks between local firms as a 'cadena de disconfianza' or a chain of distrust: 'Information here is not shared. If you want to know how many jeans are being made across the street, you have to bribe someone.' Relations between companies often appear distant or even strained, not close and collaborative, despite the fact that several of the major firms are owned by relatives.

Several decades ago, researchers influenced by dependency theory claimed that transnational corporations had negative implications for local development in Latin America. They would not have been surprised by the low levels of trust, weak horizontal ties, and hierarchical networks that characterize Torreon's apparel exporting cluster. It is not accurate, however, to suggest that all foreign firms establish vertical networks that are uncooperative in nature, nor that all local companies build horizontal networks that promote collaboration and trust. The climate of distrust also affects relations among Mexican-owned firms. In fact, some of our informants spoke more favorably of the foreign clients they did business with on a regular basis than the local entrepreneurs with whom they competed for orders and workers. More research is needed to understand the boundaries of solidarity in clusters like Torreon, but it is clear that they are not determined solely by foreign versus domestic ownership, nor are they inevitably fostered by the existence of family ties.

Supporting institutions, such as trade associations and industry-specific educational/ training programs, apparently, have not played an important role in Torreon's emergence as a major blue jeans cluster. In the case of the local apparel industry association, its growth seems to have been more a response to Torreon's export boom than a cause of it. In short, the institutional environment characterizing the Torreon cluster is radically different from the stylized profile (e.g., trust and effective sanctions, strong socio-cultural ties) found in the industrial districts model. In his valuable discussion of upgrading in exporting clusters, Schmitz notes, 'Strategic response to global competitive pressures cannot just rely on private joint action but require public agencies as catalysts or mediators' (Schmitz, 2000: 15).

Our research in Torreon yielded little evidence of private collaboration in the form of joint action among local firms, and even less evidence to suggest that the cluster benefits from the support of public agencies capable of mediating relations between the companies that comprise it. We have argued that the arrival of new buyers in Torreon has resulted in upgrading, both at the industry and at the firm level. But the absence of an institutional environment that would help further diffuse the benefits of Torreon's export boom beyond the first tier of full-package firms means that there are limits to this process of upgrading, and they may have already been reached.

Recent events in Torreon indicate that links to the global economy can produce disruption as well as growth. A slowdown in the US economy has had a dampening effect on the export boom in Torreon at the end of 2000, and the effects have continued through the first half of 2001. Conversations with industry representatives in May 2001 revealed that 8,000 apparel jobs had been lost since October 2000, and production was down 20% as compared with the same period last year. A commodity chains approach would lead us to expect that job losses and plant closings will be concentrated among the small subcontractors located at the bottom tiers of the chain. Furthermore, we would expect that companies possessing the additional capabilities associated with full-package production are less negatively affected than the assembly-oriented maquilas. Evidence from Torreon confirms that the companies that have suffered most to date are smaller, locally owned subcontractors. The negative implications of the slowdown could spread beyond this group of firms, however, and the absence of institutional support mechanisms in Torreon means that the adjustment to a sustained economic downturn will be harder to manage given the heavy reliance on the US market as the source of export growth.

Both the commodity chains and industrial districts approaches address the issue of development, conceived largely as a process of industrial upgrading, and both can be used to draw policy implications about the best way to achieve local development and upgrading goals. The literature on clusters has shown that under a particular set of conditions, it is possible to use industrial policy and local institutions to promote the creation of industrial districts as a 'high road' to development.

In many developing countries, however, these conditions are not present. This is likely to be even more true in an era marked by the increasing (if contested) hegemony of the World Trade Organization and institutions such as the International Monetary Fund, which privilege the adoption of neoliberal programs that promote open trade and discourage industrial policy. It is in this environment, characterized by hyercompetition between industrializing countries pursuing export-led growth strategies, that the specter of competitive devaluations and immiserizing growth haunts poorer countries' dreams of development (Kaplinsky, 1999).

Given that the governments of industrializing countries have limited power to 'get the institutions right,' the question becomes how firms can use their participation in global commodity chains to pursue developmental goals. In the case of Torreon, foreign buyers have provided local firms with a full-package link to the US market that gives them better upgrading prospects. In the context of Mexico's export-oriented growth strategy, figuring out how local firms can improve their position within global industries is a preeminent topic for producers and policy makers alike.

Notes

1. More generally, there has been considerable research contributing to our understanding of the lean production model and its critique. See, for example, Harrison (1994), Boyer (1998), and Freyssenet (1998).

2. The need to adopt a more flexible approach to industrial districts was already recognized in Pyke and Sengenberger (1992). See, for example, Zeitlin's concluding chapter, which calls for 'a 'thin,' 'open' model capable of generating a variety of empirically observable forms' (Zeitlin, 1992: 285).

3. The word 'maquiladora' is used to refer to any factory in Mexico, owned by international or local capital, that has a permit from the Mexican government to import and export products under a special tariff and income tax regime. The term often evokes images typical of the first generation of maquiladoras—very large plants along the northern border owned by multinational companies. But, there is tremendous diversity within the maquila sector, ranging from giant, wholly owned subsidiaries of multinational corporations to small firms that export only a portion of their production under the maquila regime to supplement sales on the domestic market.

4. While this growth in the maquila sector is impressive, official statistics actually understate export-oriented apparel production and employment in Mexico since they reflect only those establishments that have registered as maquiladoras with the Mexican government. Traditionally, registering as a maquila provided a number of incentives, the most important being the ability to import duty-free foreign-made inputs. But, NAFTA changed the rules of the game for this kind of cross-border production sharing by introducing free trade between the three signatory countries. Materials can flow freely between Canada, the United States, and Mexico without duties as long as they meet the North American rules of origin established by NAFTA. Consequently, companies with cross-border production networks that are using North American inputs no longer have as strong of an incentive to register Mexican assembly plants as maquilas.

5. In the United States the analog of the maquila regime is the 807 program, so-named for the clause of US trade law that describes the status of goods assembled in export-processing factories like Mexico's maquilas. The relevant clause was later changed to 9802, so this type of production sharing is often referred to as 807/9802.

6. Martha A. Martínez, a graduate student in the Sociology Department at Duke University, collaborated on the first phase of our fieldwork in Torreon.

7. Major textile and apparel corporations headquartered in the Piedmont region of North Carolina include: Burlington Industries, Cone Mills Corporation, Sara Lee (which owns Hanes and several other well-known apparel brands), and VF Corporation (which manufactures and markets several lines of jeans, including Lee and Wrangler).

8. Although traditionally retailers have sold garments made by apparel companies, most retailers now have their own store brands called private labels. Examples of private label jeans include J. C. Penney's Arizona brand and Sears' Canyon River Blues line.

9. Schmitz and Knorringa (1999: 20) reported a similar finding from their interviews with global footwear buyers, who seemed more willing to assist their suppliers in acquiring the skills needed to 'translate designs into technical specifications' than with helping them develop new and innovative designs. Our analysis points to the same conclusion that these authors reached: buyer-supplier relationships can help developing country manufacturers upgrade their production activities, but they rarely offer manufacturers the opportunity to develop skills, such as design and marketing capabilities, that would elevate them from the status of supplier to potential competitors. Schmitz (2000) concludes that foreign buyers may assist local firms in process and product upgrading, but they do not encourage functional upgrading that involves moving into new stages of the value chain.

10. The owners of Libra and Grupo Impeccable are brothers, and cousins of the two brothers that own Siete Leguas and Grupo Denim. The families that own Kentucky Lajat and OMJC are also related by marriage. A full discussion of the family networks that crisscross the Torreon apparel cluster is beyond the scope of this chapter, but will be explored in future analyses.

11. The US$ exchange rate in Mexico increased from 8.7 pesos in 1998 to 9.5 pesos in 2000.

12. Wages in the apparel industry, and in the maquiladoras more generally, vary dramatically across Mexico. In Guanajuato, where growth in the maquila sector was dramatic under then-governor, now president, Vicente Fox, average weekly salaries ranged from 300 to 450 pesos (US$31.60 to US$47.40) in July 2000 (Martínez, 2000). In addition to abundant coverage in the Mexican press, the country's booming maquiladora program has been the subject of several recent articles in US newspapers. Examples include Thompson (2001), Dillon (2001) and Jordan (2000).

References

Appelbaum, Richard P. and Gary Gereffi. 1994. 'Power and Profits in the Apparel Commodity Chain.' In *Global production: The Apparel Industry in the Pacific Rim*, edited by Edna Bonanich et al., 42–62. Philadelphia, PA: Temple University Press.

Bair, Jennifer. 2000. 'Sewing up Development? Mexico's Apparel Industry in the Era of NAFTA.' Presented at 'Organisational Praxis.' 16th Annual European Group for Organizational Studies Colloquium, Helsinki School of Economics and Business Administration, Helsinki, Finland, July 2–4.

—————. 2001. 'Casos exitosos de pequeñas y medianas empresas en México: Lecciones de Aguascalientes de la industria de la confección.' In *Condiciones y retos de la pequeñas y medianas empresas en México: estudio de casos de vinculación de empresas exitosas y propuestas de política*, edited by Enrique Dussel Peters. Santiago: United Nations Economic Commission for Latin America and the Caribbean.

Boyer, Robert, ed. 1998. *Between Imitation and Innovation: The Transfer and Hybridization of Productive Models in the International Automobile Industry.* New York: Oxford University Press.

Buitelaar, Rudolf M. and Ramón Padilla Pérez. 2000. 'Maquila, Economic Reform and Corporate Strategies.' *World Development* 28(9): 1627–1642.

Carrillo, Jorge. 1994. 'Dos decadas de sindicalismo en la industria maquiladora de exportación: examen en las ciudades de Tijuana, Juárez, y Matamoros.' Mexico City, DF: Universidad Autónoma Metropolitana-Iztapalapa.

—————. 1998. 'Third Generation Maquiladoras? The Delphi-General Motors Sase.' *Journal of Borderlands Studies* 3(1): 79–97.

De la Garza, Enrique. 1994. 'The Restructuring of State-labor Relations in Mexico.' In *The Politics of Economic Restructuring*, edited by Maria L. Cook, Kevin J. Middlebrook, and Juan Molinar Horcasitas, 195–217. La Jolla, CA: Center for US-Mexican Studies, University of California, San Diego.

Dillon, Sam. 2001. 'Profits Raise Pressures on US-owned Factories in Mexican Border Zone.' *The New York Times*, February 15.

Dussel Peters, Enrique. 2000. *Polarizing Mexico: The Impact of Liberalization Strategy.* Boulder, CO: Lynn Reinner.

Fernandez-Kelly, Patricia. 1983. *For We Are Sold, I and My People: Women and Industry in Mexico's Frontier.* Albany, NY: State University of New York Press.

Freyssenet, Michel, ed. 1998. *One Best Way? Trajectories and Industrial Models of the World's Automobile Producers.* New York: Oxford University Press.

Gereffi, Gary. 1996. 'Mexico's "Old" and "New" Maquiladora Industries: Contrasting Approaches to North American Integration.' In *Neoliberalism Revisited: Economic Restructuring and Mexico's Political Future*, edited by Gerardo Otero, 85–105. Boulder, CO: Westview Press.

—————. 1999. 'International Trade and Industrial Upgrading in the Apparel Commodity Chain'. *Journal of International Economics* 48(1): 37–70.

—————. 2000. 'The Transformation of the North American Apparel Industry: Is NAFTA a Curse or a Blessing?' *Integration and Trade* 4(11): 47–95.

Gereffi, Gary and Jennifer Bair. 1998. 'US Companies Eye NAFTA's Prize.' *Bobbin* 39(7): 26–35.

Gereffi, Gary and Miguel Korzeniewicz, eds. 1994. *Commodity Chains and Global Capitalism.* Westport, CT: Praeger.

Harrison, Bennett. 1994. *Lean and Mean: The Changing Landscape of Corporate Power in the Age of Flexibility*. New York: Basic Books.

Humphrey, John. 1995a. Special Issue on 'Industrial Organization and Manufacturing Competitiveness in Developing Countries.' *World Development* 23(1).

————. 1995b. 'Industrial Re-organization in Developing Countries: From Models to Trajectories'. *World Development* 23(1): 149–162.

Iglesias Prieto, Norma. 1985. *La flor más bella de la maquiladora*. Tijuana: El Colegio de la Frontera Norte.

Jordan, Mary. 2000. 'Mexicans Reap NAFTA's Benefits.' *Washington Post*, 17 September.

Kaplinsky, Raphael. 1999. 'Is Globalization All It Is Cracked Up to Be?' *IDS Bulletin* 30(4): 106–116.

Martínez, Fabiola. 2000. 'Guanajuato: Empleo para casi todos, pero con bajos salarios.' *La Jornada* 10, July 31.

National Interfaith Committee for Worker Justice. 1998. 'Cross-border Blues: A Call for Justice for the Maquiladora Workers of Tehuacan.' July.

Pyke, Frank and Werner Sengenberger, eds. 1992. *Industrial Districts and Local Economic Regeneration*. Geneva: International Institute for Labour Studies.

Rabellotti, Roberta. 1999. 'Recovery of a Mexican Cluster: Devaluation Bonanza or Collective Efficiency?' *World Development* 27(9): 1571–1585.

Reinhardt, Nora and Wilson Peres. 2000. 'Latin America's New Economic Model: Micro Responses and Economic Restructuring.' *World Development* 28(9): 1543–1566.

Robinson, William I. 1998–99. 'Latin American and Global Capitalism.' *Race and Class* 40(2/3): 111–131.

Ross, Robert. J. S. and Charles Kernaghan. 2000. 'Countdown in Managua.' *The Nation*, 4–11 September.

Schmitz, Hubert. 1995. 'Small Shoemakers and Fordist Giants: Tale of a Supercluster.' *World Development* 23(1): 9–28.

————. 1999. 'Global Competition and Local Cooperation: Success and Failure in the Sinos Valley, Brazil.' *World Development* 27(9): 1627–1650.

————. 2000. 'Local Upgrading in Global Chains.' Presented at the International Conference, 'Local Production Systems and New Industrial Policies.' Rio de Janeiro, September.

Schmitz, Hubert and Peter Knorringa. 1999. 'Learning from Global Buyers.' *IDS Working Paper* 100. Brighton, UK: Institute for Development Studies, University of Sussex.

Schmitz, Hubert and Khalid Nadvi, eds. 1999a. Special Issue on 'Industrial Clusters in Developing Countries.' *World Development* 27(9).

————. 1999b. 'Clustering and Industrialization: Introduction.' *World Development* 27(9): 1503–1514.

SECOFI (Secretaría de Comercio y Fomento Industrial). 2001. Official Data of the Mexican Commerce and Industrial Development Ministry, now Secretaría de Económia. Available at www.economia-snci.gob.mx.

Sengenberger, Werner and Frank Pyke. 1991. 'Small Firms, Industrial Districts and Local Economic Regeneration.' *Labour and Society* 6(1): 1–25.

Shaiken, Harley and Stephen Herzenberg. 1987. 'Automation and Global Production: Automobile Engine Production in Mexico, the United States, and Canada.' Center for US-Mexican Studies, Monograph Series, 26. La Jolla, CA: University of California, San Diego.

Sklair, Leslie. 1993. 'Assembling for Development: The Maquila Industry in Mexico and the United States.' La Jolla, CA: Center for US-Mexican Studies, University of California, San Diego.

The Economist. 2000. 'Mexico's Trade Unions Stick to the Same Old Tune.' October 23, 35–36.

Thompson, Ginger. 2001. 'Chasing Mexico's Dream into Squalor.' *The New York Times,* Februrary 11.

USITC (United States International Trade Commission). 2001. Official Statistics from the Office of Textiles, US Department of Commerce. Available at www.usitc.gov.

Zeitlin, Jonathan. 1992. 'Industrial Districts and Local Economic Regeneration: Overview and Comment.' In *Industrial Districts and Local Economic Regeneration,* edited by Frank Pyke and Werner Sengenberger, 279–294. Geneva: International Institute for Labour Studies.

Appendix A
Strategic Interviews

Strategic interviews were carried out with corporate managers and other knowledgeable informants in the textile and apparel sector in the United States and Mexico in order to understand the diverse factors contributing to the restructuring of the North American apparel industry in the 1990s. These interviews include a mix of standard and open-ended questions, and thus they depart from traditional survey instruments that only ask a pre-determined set of closed questions and seek fixed responses. For our fieldwork in Torreon, we used a semi-structured protocol that listed key questions to ensure that critical issues were addressed with each respondent. Respondents were asked to provide a historical description of their firm (e.g., In what year was it founded? Did it serve the national market, and if so through what channels and with what products?), as well as a current profile (number of employees, number of customers, production volume, main clients, main suppliers). Our interviews typically lasted an average of two hours in length, and included questions regarding:

- The kind of link (direct or indirect, and if indirect, through what kind of intermediary) connecting the exporting firm to foreign markets;
- the type of production networks characterizing the firm and its relationship with clients and suppliers (e.g., maquila versus full-package relationships);
- the existence and nature of vertical and/or horizontal relationships with local firms and the role of local institutions, such as industry associations, in promoting the cluster;
- how the Torreon region and the experiences of local firms have changed since both Mexico's initial trade liberalization of the mid-1980s and the implementation of NAFTA; and
- a set of issues addressing industrial and human relations (average wage, turnover rate, training procedures, union presence in the plant), as well as

characteristics of the workforce (age, gender, marital status, previous work experience, educational background).

Appendix B
Interviews in Torreon, 1998 and 2000

In cases of multiple interviews per firm, the number is indicated in parentheses (see Table 6.4).

Table 6.4　Interviews in Torreon, 1998 and 2000

Firms[a]	Ownership	1998		2000	
Original Mexican Jean Company (OMJC)	Joint venture	X	(3)	X	(4)
Maquilas Pami	US subsidiary	X	(2)	X	(2)
Wrangler	US subsidiary	X		X	
Kentucky-Lajat[b]	Joint venture (1998); Mexican (2000)	X		X	
Libra	Mexican	X		X	
Siete Leguas	Mexican	X		X	
Grupo Denim	Mexican			X	(2)
Grupo Impecable	Mexican			X	
Pafer Huichita	Mexican			X	
Red Kap International	US subsidiary			X	
Parras Cone[c]	Joint venture	X			
Creaciones Lobo	Mexican	X			
Dustin	Mexican	X			
Fabricas de Ropa Manjai	Mexican	X			
Viesca 2000	Mexican	X			
Total number of firm interviews		14		15	
Other interviews					
Camara Nacional de la Industria del Vestido (CNIV) (Laguna branch)[d]		X		X	
Secretaría de Comercio y Fomento Industrial (SECOFI)[e]		X		X	
Fomento Económico de Laguna de Coahuila (FOMEC)[f]		X		X	

Source: Authors.

Notes:

[a] Additional information regarding the first 10 firms is provided in Table 6.3.

[b] In July 1998, Kentucky–Lajat was a US–Mexican joint venture that produced denim fabric as well as apparel. In December 1998, Kentucky–Lajat sold its denim mill to Parras, a Mexican textile firm. Then in July 1999, the Mexican Lajat Group bought out its US partner, Kentucky Apparel, and later that year expanded its operations to include apparel design as well as production in Mexico.

[c] Produces denim fabric only.

[d] The local branch of the national apparel industry association.

[e] The local office of the federal ministry of commerce and industrial promotion.

[f] A local development company in the Laguna region.

Development Models and Industrial Upgrading in China and Mexico*

Introduction

There are fundamental changes afoot in the global economy, and no simple answers for countries that want to improve or even maintain their levels of development. In recent decades, national and regional development models have come under increasing scrutiny, and countries are trying to determine what kinds of policies and institutions provide the best opportunities for long-term growth and prosperity.

This chapter will explore these issues through a comparative analysis that focuses on how international trade and foreign direct investment (FDI) have shaped the development trajectories of China and Mexico, two of the most dynamic emerging economies in the world. The first section provides a broad comparison of the development models in Latin America and China, with an emphasis on how each has changed in recent decades. The second section uses international trade data to examine industrial upgrading patterns in Mexico and China, with an emphasis on their competitive niches in the US market and why China is taking the lead in a number of different industries. The third and final section looks more closely at a new feature of China's industrial upgrading pattern known as supply chain cities. China's unique model of economic development is fascinating in its own right, but China's escalating importance as a supplier, a market, and recently as a source of outward direct investment makes many countries and regions in the world highly dependent on China's future economic performance.

Comparative Development Models

Since the mid-1980s, globalization has been associated with a neoliberal model of development that has produced rapid economic growth and improving standards of living in some parts of the world, most notably East Asia. In other regions,

---

* The data in Figures 7.1 and 7.2, Tables 7.1, 7.2, and 7.3 and corresponding text have been updated to 2014–2015 from the original article published in the *European Sociological Review* (February 2009).

like Latin America, neoliberalism has been marked by slow economic growth, large-scale unemployment, social deterioration, and political protest. Development models in both Latin America and East Asia, however, have evolved considerably during this period.

Within these regions, China and Mexico present particularly interesting cases because of notable contrasts as well as similarities in their development policies and economic trajectories. Mexico is the most diversified and export-oriented economy in Latin America, with an emphasis on manufactured exports to the United States. China is one of the world's fastest growing economies, with extensive diversification and growing exports to the world. Mexico and China compete head-to-head in many product categories in the US market. This section of the chapter will review the main features of the Latin American and Chinese development experiences, as prelude to a more detailed analysis of industrial upgrading trajectories in both Mexico and China.

The Latin American Development Model

The idea of a common Latin American development model is misleading for two main reasons. First, Latin America as a region is extremely diverse in terms of its geography, demographics, infrastructure, and culture, and its individual economies have diverged in the post-war era. Countries like Mexico have been at the forefront of the region's development, while others have lagged considerably. Second, Latin American development remains a topic of fierce debate within the region, leading to clashing opinions regarding its future development trajectory (IADB, 2006). Despite these differences, some clear trends in the history of Latin American development policy can be identified.

Import-Substituting Industrialization (ISI)

From World War II through the early 1980s, most Latin American countries pursued the import-substitution model, a set of policies that favored state-led industrialization and the protection of domestic industry, using a combination of support for publicly owned enterprises and extensive inflows of foreign investment (Thorp and Lowden, 1996). This approach was fueled by a conviction that certain Latin American characteristics—including its cultural values and institutional structure—made market-led mechanisms ineffective in the region, as well as a belief that the market would place further control over the economy in foreign hands.

Under ISI, the state played a central role in controlling the economy. Government made economic self-sufficiency and the development of domestic industry as its top priorities. Latin American governments valued industrial development over the region's traditional agricultural and primary-resource trade patterns, and many believed that the gradual accumulation of industrial capacity that ISI encouraged would enhance Latin America's position in the world economy.

As ISI policies advanced in the 1950s and 1960s, they displayed a set of common features: high tariff barriers against foreign goods, especially industrial items; overvalued currencies; and, after the 1950s, increasing provisions for the attraction of foreign capital. In the 1960s and 1970s, the leading Latin American economies moved from a phase of primary ISI, which focused on basic consumer goods (such as textiles, clothing, footwear, and food processing), to secondary ISI, which involved using domestic production to substitute for imports in a variety of more advanced products, such as consumer durables (e.g., automobiles), intermediate goods (e.g., petrochemicals and steel), and capital goods (e.g., heavy machinery) (Gereffi, 1994).

Like its Latin American counterparts, Mexico's ISI experience included a system of high tariff barriers, the formation of government-run monopolies in industries like petroleum and electricity, and government intermediation in the financing of Mexican businesses. The sustainability of these policies was aided by Mexico's political landscape, which was dominated by the Institutional Revolutionary Party (PRI). Under PRI leadership, Mexico posted solid growth from the 1950s to the 1970s, averaging about 6% per year while maintaining low levels of inflation (Portes, 1997; Fourcade-Gourinchas and Babb, 2002).

Latin America became heavily dependent upon international capital markets in the 1970s to finance its burgeoning state sector, and this debt bubble eventually burst. By the 1980s, ISI was in trouble throughout the region. Mexico's public announcement in August 1982 that it was unable to meet its debt requirements was the first in a series of government defaults, putting an end to ISI and leading to major changes in the region's economic structure.

Neoliberalism

In the 1980s, a series of economic issues—low growth, widening economic inequality, government balance-of-payments crises, and periodic hyperinflation—led to a more market-oriented approach, dubbed in the United States as the 'Washington Consensus' (Gore, 2000). This was facilitated by the rise of right-wing dictatorships in countries like Chile, Uruguay, and Brazil. Initially, neoliberal policies focused on reforming current and capital account flows, and controlling volatile inflation rates in the region. Later, reform spread to addressing and reshaping the role of the state in the economy (Weyland, 2004; Huber and Solt, 2004).

In Mexico, these reforms proceeded in stages. The first stage, lasting from 1982 to 1985, was directly linked to Mexico's negotiations with international monetary authorities after its debt crisis, and brought new controls on monetary and fiscal policy, including much lower state expenditures. The second stage, which began in 1985, saw more drastic changes, including widespread privatization, lowering of trade barriers, and liberalization of the regulations governing foreign investment. The third stage began in 1994 with the passage of the North American Free Trade Agreement (NAFTA), and has resulted in further structural reforms and the continued lowering of trade and investment barriers (Fourcade-Gourinchas and Babb, 2002).

The most important policies of economic neoliberalism in Latin America can be summarized in seven major actions (Portes, 1997: 238):

- opening to foreign trade
- privatizing state enterprises
- deregulating goods, services, and labor markets
- liberalizing capital markets, including privatized pension funds
- promoting fiscal discipline, based on deep cuts in public expenditures
- dismantling and downsizing state-supported social programs
- ending ISI-style industrial policy

Neoliberal reforms spread through Central and South America at different speeds. In nearly every country, however, reformers stressed an increased use of market mechanisms. In addition, national governments sought to adjust their currency valuations and dramatically lower both barriers to free trade (tariffs) and controls on foreign private capital (FDI restrictions). Under the neoliberal model, Latin America showed moderate economic growth in the early 1990s. Yet slower growth in the late 1990s and early 2000s generated renewed criticism of Latin America's development model, a controversy that continues today (Dussel Peters, 2000; Lora et al., 2004).

Current Situation

The general debate over Latin American development stems from the simple fact that the region's economic performance under neoliberalism was less than hoped for, and far less than promised. Although 'equitable economic growth' and 'economic justice' are priorities for most Latin Americans, economic inequality has grown markedly since 1990 and growth has lagged (Thorp and Lowden, 1996; Dussel Peters, 2000; Ellner, 2006). Many have criticized their governments' neoliberal policies as a front for the economic elite to get rich at the expense of the entire population, claiming—as Vargas Llosa (2005: 23) does—that:

Countries replaced inflation with new taxes on the poor, high tariffs with regional trading blocs, and, especially, state monopolies with government-sanctioned private monopolies. The courts were subjected to the whims of those in power, widening the divide between official institutions and ordinary people...

In academic and policy circles, there has been an ongoing controversy regarding the success—or failure—of the neoliberal model. Weyland (2004) chronicles the debate in academic circles, noting that Huber and Solt (2004) blame neoliberal reform itself for Latin America's economic problems, while Walton (2004) argues that shortcomings have been due to an inadequate implementation of reforms and deficiencies in the surrounding institutional framework. Within the government arena, the agenda ranges from adjusting present policies to proposing new paradigms for regional development (IADB, 2006).

Politically, the trends are clearer. Latin America has shifted sharply to the left in the last few years, with a more radical cohort of leaders elected in Argentina, Uruguay, Venezuela, Chile, Bolivia, and Brazil. Yet as many authors note, this 'leftward' shift is hardly uniform. Chile, for example, under socialists Ricardo Lagos and Michelle Bachelet, has retained an emphasis on free-market policies, despite being liberal on social issues. Argentina's Nestor Kirchner, in contrast, is far more critical of the international financial system and the policies of economic neoliberalism (Carlsen, 2004; Shifter, 2005; Vargas Llosa, 2005)

In recent years, the economic tide has been rising. Latin America's exports to the world increased by 11% in 2007, marking the fifth consecutive year of growth, and Latin America's intra-regional trade as a share of its total trade with the world reached 17.3% (IADB, 2007). The region's strong economic performance in recent years has been driven by two main factors: a robust US economy and exceptional demand from China for Latin America's primary product exports. While concerns about a slump in US economic activity are mounting (EIU, 2008), demand from China in the near future is expected to remain strong.

China's Development Model

China's reform efforts began in 1978 with the Third Plenum of the 11th National Party Congress, and reforms accelerated after Deng Xiaoping's 1992 'Southern Trip' and again after China's 2001 accession to the World Trade Organization (WTO) (Wang and Meng, 2004; Branstetter and Lardy, 2005). These changes have taken place amidst a second wave of economic globalization in which billions of people have joined the global economy, and in the midst of a broad dialogue among economists, politicians, and activists about the role of the market and how to utilize its power to promote healthy development.

Bai Gao (2006) highlights a number of key characteristics of the Chinese development model:

* government relies on the market as the driving mechanism behind economic growth
* government aggressively seeks to attract foreign capital
* government opens its domestic market to the outside world
* government uses low-cost labor to participate in the global economy
* government stresses harmony in the local economy, placing more emphasis on 'soft' supervision rather than inspection and control
* government values economic growth and upgrading, even at the expense of social stability.

China's economy has expanded at a phenomenal pace since 1978. Average annual gross domestic product has increased by 9% a year; exports grew by 12.4% annually in the 1990s and by more than 20% a year since 2000 (IADB, 2005). China's development model is premised on leveraging its domestic advantages, including the size of its potential market and the low cost of its factor inputs— chiefly labor, but also the cost of land, electricity, and raw materials. Over time, China has sought to add to these advantages by seeking to minimize its weaknesses (bureaucratic red tape, low quality of labor), upgrade its logistics capabilities, and move up the technology value chain.

However, the Chinese development model is also associated with its impressive ability to attract FDI. The annual FDI flows in China jumped from an average of $76 billion in 2005–2007 to $128 billion in 2014 and $136 billion in 2015. The total stock of FDI in China more than quadrupled from $272 billion in 2005 to $1,085 billion in 2014 and $1,221 billion in 2015, which vastly exceeded Mexico's FDI stock of $210 billion in 2005 and around $500 billion in 2014 and 2015 However, Mexico's reliance on FDI is far higher than China's as a share of gross domestic product (44.2% for Mexico versus 10.9% for China in 2015) and gross fixed capital formation (12.8% versus 2.8%, respectively) (see Table 7.1). FDI has brought both capital goods and high technology into the country, and helped to move China's export mix from 'unskilled' to 'skilled' labor-intensive activities, and has boosted China's exports in the capital- and technology-intensive sectors (Brandt and Rawski, 2005: 23).

From an upgrading perspective, China's openness is beginning to pay off. China has become a top destination for research and development (R&D), due to its crop of high-quality, low-cost engineers and to the size of its potential market (Hu and Jefferson, 2004). China's growth of R&D centers has been especially dramatic: whereas in 1997 China registered less than 50 multinational R&D centers, by 2004 the Chinese government registered over 600 multinational R&D facilities in the country, many from large US multinational corporations (MNCs) (Freeman,

2005: 8). In just one year, from June 2003 to June 2004, MNCs established 200 R&D centers in China (*Asia Times Online*, 2005).

Table 7.1 Foreign Direct Investment in China and Mexico, 1995–2015

FDI Flows (billions of US dollars)			2005–2007 (annual average)	2014	2015
China			76.2	128.5	135.6
Mexico			26.5	27.5	33.2
FDI Flows (as a percentage of gross fixed capital formation)			2005–2007 (annual average)	2014	2015
China			6.7	2.7	2.8
Mexico			12.7	10.1	12.8
FDI stock (billions of US dollars)	1995	2000	2005	2014	2015
China	101	193	272	1,085	1,221
Mexico	41	97	209	487	509
FDI stocks (as a percentage of gross domestic product)	1995	2000	2005	2014	2015
China	13.7	17.9	13.7	10.3	10.9
Mexico	12.0	16.7	27.3	37.5	44.2

Source: UNCTAD, *World Investment Report 2017* and earlier years.

This reliance on FDI and private property is generating an intense ideological debate within China over the merits of socialism versus capitalism and the future direction of the Chinese development model (Kahn, 2006). Criticisms of the current Chinese model highlight rampant corruption, widening income inequality, geographic polarization, the plight of rural migrants, and environmental issues as evidence that neoliberalism and openness have tarnished China's recent economic growth (Nolan, 2005). There are also concerns that foreign firms are dominating the Chinese market, especially in certain key products like automobiles, leaving less room for Chinese firms to compete and profit. Others, however, argue that the answers to these problems lie in further reform and a vigorous implementation of existing reforms. They blame market rigidities and entrenched political elites for many of China's vexing social issues, and claim that abandoning reform would be a mistake (Huang, 2006). Despite this defense of current policies, the voices of critics are growing increasingly loud and the debate is becoming more acrimonious.

Observers of India, Asia's other emerging economic powerhouse, point out that India's economic growth relies on home-grown entrepreneurs, while China may be tying its export-led manufacturing boom too closely to FDI, since foreign-invested firms account for over 60% of China's exports (Huang and Khanna, 2003). Given the 'external contradictions' of the Chinese development model, there are calls for a new 'domestic demand-led development strategy' (Palley, 2006).

Any comparative assessment of the development paths taken by Latin America and China rests heavily on institutional and historical factors. How have these models performed in practice? Has export-oriented development in countries like Mexico and China led to industrial upgrading in these countries over the past two decades? In the next section, we will use international trade data to explore these questions.

Industrial Upgrading in Mexico and China—An International Trade Perspective

Industrial upgrading is defined as 'the process by which economic actors—nations, firms, and workers—move from low-value to relatively high-value activities in global production networks' (Gereffi, 2005: 171). One of the ways that we can assess industrial upgrading for export-oriented economies like China and Mexico is to look at shifts in the technology content of their exports over time. We divide each country's exports into five product groupings, which are listed in ascending levels of technological content: primary products, resource-based manufactures, and low-, medium-, and high-technology manufactures.[1]

In Figure 7.1, we see that in 1990, nearly 50% of Mexico's total exports to the US market were primary products, the most important of which was oil. By 1993, one year prior to the establishment of NAFTA, both medium-technology manufactures (mainly automotive products) and high-tech manufactures (largely electronics items) moved ahead of raw materials in Mexico's export mix. In 2014, about two-thirds of Mexico's exports of $398 billion to the US market were in the high-technology (44%) and medium-technology (22%) product categories, followed by primary products (14%) and low-technology manufactures (such as textiles, apparel, and footwear) (9.4%). Thus, in 25 years, Mexico's export structure was transformed from one based on raw materials to one dominated by medium- and high-technology manufactured items.

In Figure 7.2, we see the composition of China's exports to the US market during the 1990–2014 period. Unlike Mexico, the leading product category in China's exports to the US market during the 1990s and early 2000s was low-technology manufactured goods. These were primarily made up of a wide variety of light consumer goods—apparel, footwear, toys, sporting goods, house wares, and so on. These products accounted for over one-half of China's overall exports to the United States in the early 1990s. By 2004, however, high-technology exports from China had pulled even with low-technology products at 32% of China's overall exports to the US market, and they passed low-tech exports for the top spot in China's export mix until 2014, when they again converged and accounted for just under two-thirds of China's total exports.

Figure 7.1 Composition of Mexico's Exports to the World Market, 1990–2014

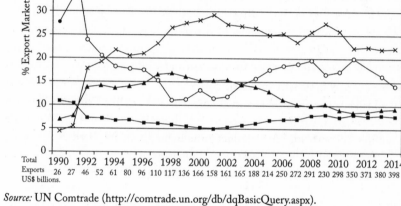

Source: UN Comtrade (http://comtrade.un.org/db/dqBasicQuery.aspx).

Figure 7.2 Composition of China's Exports to the World Market, 1990–2014

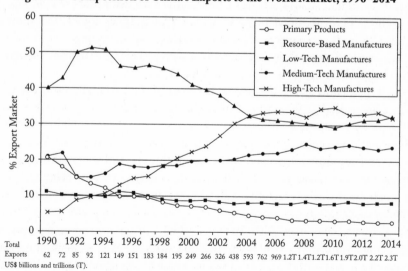

Source: UN Comtrade (http://comtrade.un.org/db/dqBasicQuery.aspx).

Thus, Mexico and China have a number of commonalities in their export trajectories to the US market during the past two decades. Both are diversified economies, with a range of different types of export products. In both cases, manufactured exports are more important than primary product or resource-based exports; within manufacturing, high- and medium-technology exports are displacing low-technology goods. While these export data have limitations as indicators of industrial upgrading,[2] both economies appear to be increasing the sophistication of their export structures.

A more detailed look at the international trade data, however, shows that since 2000, China has surpassed Mexico in head-to-head competition in the US market. Table 7.2 identifies six of the leading manufactured products in which China and Mexico are significant US suppliers. In five of these products, Mexico's share of the US market was greater than China's in 2000; by 2007, China had wrested the lead from Mexico in all but one of these items, and China increased its US market share in four of these five product categories by 2014. In automatic data processing machines (SITC 752), for example, China's share of US imports increased nearly sixfold from 11.3% in 2000 to 65.7% in 2014. In telecommunications equipment (SITC 764), China's market share again jumped by a factor of six from 10.3% to 58%; and in electrical machinery (SITC 778), it tripled from 11.9% to 33.2%. Only in auto parts and accessories (SITC 784) did Mexico maintain its substantial lead in the US market over China.

Table 7.3 shows the top US imports in which either Mexico or China accounted for 40% or more of the US import market in 2014. Mexico had five products that met this criterion in 2014, whereas China had 17 such items. For example, nearly two-thirds of all footwear imported to the United States comes from China, while China also accounts for 82% of toys, games and sporting goods, over 65% of imported office machines and automatic data processing machines, and more than half of US imports of textiles and apparel.

Why has China gained US market share over Mexico so rapidly and decisively? There are several factors. First, China has significantly lower labor costs than Mexico. In 2002, the US Bureau of Labor Statistics calculated China's average manufacturing compensation at $0.64 an hour,[3] compared with Mexico's US$2.48 (*Business Week*, 2004). It remains to be seen if this gap will widen, shrink, or be maintained in coming years. Persistent labor shortages are now being reported at hundreds of Chinese factories, a trend that is pushing up wages and leading a number of manufacturers to consider moving their factories to lower-cost countries like Vietnam (Goodman, 2005; Barboza, 2006).

Second, China has sought to leverage its huge economies of scale, and it has made major investments in infrastructure and logistics to lower transportation costs and to speed time to market for their export products. The growth of

Table 7.2 Mexico's and China's Competing Exports to the United States, 2000–2014

SITC Category	Product		2000		2007		2014		Change in market share 2000–2007	Change in market share 2007–2014
			Value (billions)	Share of US market	Value (billions)	Share of US market	Value (billions)	Share of US market		
752	Automatic Data Processing Machines	Mexico	6.4	11.5	5.6	9.6	13.5	16.6	-1.9	7.0
		China	6.3	11.3	28.6	49.3	53.3	65.7	38.0	16.4
		US Total	55.9		57.9		81.1			
764	Telecom Equipment	Mexico	9.1	20.6	10.8	13.6	12.1	10.2	-7.0	-3.4
		China	4.6	10.3	29.6	37.3	68.7	58.0	26.9	20.8
		US Total	44.3		79.5		118.4			
778	Electrical Machinery	Mexico	3.1	18.3	5.0	21.8	7.2	21.4	3.5	-0.4
		China	2.0	11.9	6.1	26.6	11.2	33.2	14.7	6.6
		US Total	17.1		23.1		33.7			
784	Auto Parts	Mexico	4.6	16.3	10.2	22.2	19.1	30.4	5.8	8.2
		China	0.4	1.5	3.6	7.8	8.3	13.2	6.2	5.4
		US Total	28.4		46.2		62.9			
821	Furniture	Mexico	3.2	16.9	4.6	13.6	7.6	18.3	-3.3	4.7
		China	4.5	23.6	16.2	47.7	19.2	46.3	24.1	-1.4
		US Total	18.9		33.9		41.5			
84	Apparel and Clothing	Mexico	8.7	13.6	4.7	5.8	4.0	4.4	-7.8	-1.4
		China	8.5	13.2	27.1	33.4	34.2	37.9	20.2	4.5
		US Total	64.3		81.2		90.2			

Source: US Department of Commerce (http://dataweb.usitc.gov). Downloaded on August 26, 2015.

Table 7.3 US Imports in Which Mexico and/or China Hold 40% or More of the US Market, 2014[1]

	Mexico					China			
Product	(SITC categories)	Import value (US billions)	% market share in USA	Absolute change in % market share, 2000–2014	Product	(SITC categories)	Import value (US billions)	% market share in USA	Absolute change in % market share, 2000–2014
783	Road motor vehicles, N.E.S.	6,858	89.5	75.5	894	Baby carriages, toys, games and sporting goods	23,444	81.9	17.3
782	Motor vehicles for the transport of goods and special purpose motor vehicles	19,005	81.0	49.4	697	Household equipment of base metal, N.E.S.	4,608	67.2	31.5
54	Vegetables, fresh, chilled, frozen or simply preserved; roots, tubers and other edible vegetable products, N.E.S., fresh or dried	5,126	62.0	1.1	831	Trunks, suitcases, vanity cases, binocular and camera cases, handbags, wallets, etc. of leather, etc.; Travel sets for personal toilet, sewing, etc.	7,274	66.2	16.3
773	Equipment for distributing electricity, N.E.S.	9,522	49.6	-11.1	752	Automatic data processing machines and units thereof; magnetic or optical readers; machines transcribing coded media and processing such data	53,339	65.8	54.5
761	TV receivers (including video monitors and projectors)	11,974	44.4	-19.0	851	Footwear	17,064	65.6	3.7
					813	Lighting fixtures and fittings, N.E.S.	6,104	64.3	6.0

Cont'd.

Cont'd.

Mexico					China			
Product (SITC categories)	Import value (US billions)	% market share in USA	Absolute change in % market share, 2000–2014	Product	(SITC categories)	Import value (US billions)	% market share in USA	Absolute change in % market share, 2000–2014
				759	Parts and accessories suitable for use solely or principally with office machines or automatic data processing machines	10,842	60.7	49.2
				764	Telecommunications equipment, N.E.S.; and parts, N.E.S., and accessories of apparatus falling within telecommunications, etc.	68,724	58.1	47.7
				775	Household type electrical and nonelectrical equipment, N.E.S.	9,778	54.9	17.7
				658	Made-up articles, wholly or chiefly of textile materials, N.E.S.	7,006	53.6	29.5
				848	Articles of apparel and clothing accessories of other than textile fabrics; headgear of all materials	3,689	51.5	6.7
				751	Office machines	9,182	48.4	19.2
				893	Articles, N.E.S. of plastics	10,218	48.1	17.2

Cont'd.

Cont'd.

Mexico				China			
Product (SITC categories)	Import value (US billions)	% market share in USA	Absolute change in % market share, 2000–2014	Product (SITC categories)	Import value (US billions)	% market share in USA	Absolute change in % market share, 2000–2014
				821	Furniture and parts thereof; bedding, mattresses,	19,213	46.3	22.7
				842	Women's or girls' coats, capes, jackets, suits, trousers, dresses, skirts, underwear, etc. of woven textiles (except swimwear and coated etc. apparel)	6,539	43.9	28.1
				761	TV receivers (including video monitors and projectors)	11,593	43.0	40.5
				771	Electric power machinery (other than rotating electric plant of power generating machinery) and parts thereof	5,577	40.2	18.4

Source: US International Trade Commission and US Department of Commerce (http://dataweb.usitc.gov). Downloaded on August 26, 2015.
1. Criteria: over **$3** billion in US imports from China or Mexico in 2014.
Note: N.E.S. means 'not elsewhere specified.'

China's 'supply-chain cities'—led by FDI-driven clusters in Guangdong (including Dongguan and Humen) and single-product clusters in Zhejiang (such as Anji and Datang)—is a perfect illustration of how China's governments and entrepreneurs are turning scale-driven specialization into a persistent competitive advantage for the country (Wang and Tong, 2002; Sonobe et al., 2002; Zhang et al., 2004).

Third, China has a coherent and multidimensional upgrading strategy to diversify its industrial mix and to add high-value activities. In their careful study of China's export performance, Lall and Albaladejo (2004) argue that China and its East Asian neighbors are developing high-technology exports in a regionally integrated fashion, based on complex networks of export production that link leading electronics MNCs and their first-tier suppliers and global contract manufacturers (Gereffi, 1996; Sturgeon and Lee, 2005; Gereffi et al., 2005). The export patterns for high-tech products reveal complementarity rather than confrontation between China and its mature East Asian partners (Japan, South Korea, Taiwan, and Singapore). China's role as a motor of export growth for the region, however, could change as China itself moves up the value chain and takes over activities currently carried out by its regional neighbors. Rodrik (2006) suggests that China is already exporting a wide range of highly sophisticated products, and he calculates that China's export bundle is similar to that of a country whose per capita income is three times higher than China's current level.

Fourth, China is using FDI to promote 'fast learning' in new industries and knowledge spillovers in its domestic market (Zhang and Felmingham, 2002; Wang and Meng, 2004). Despite restrictions imposed by the WTO against domestic performance requirements for MNCs, China's local market is sufficiently attractive for multinational manufacturers that they are willing to comply with the wishes of local, regional, and national government authorities, despite stringent technology transfer requirements.

A Note on China's Supply Chain Cities and Industrial Upgrading

The concept of 'supply chain cities' has been used in media reports and academic literature to highlight the growth of large-scale production in China and the agglomeration of multiple stages of the value chain in particular locales within China as a key to its upgrading success. Barboza (2004), for example, lays out in Figure 7.3 the incredible specialization and scale that characterizes China's diversified export success in the apparel industry, even before the phase-out of the Multi-Fibre Arrangement and apparel quotas by the WTO on 1 January 2005.

The term 'supply-chain cities' encompasses two distinct, but related, phenomena in China. The first usage refers to giant, vertically integrated *firm factories*. Appelbaum (2008), as well as a variety of textile journals and large textile/apparel

Figure 7.3 China's Supply-Chain Cities in Apparel

Made in China, Shipped Worldwide

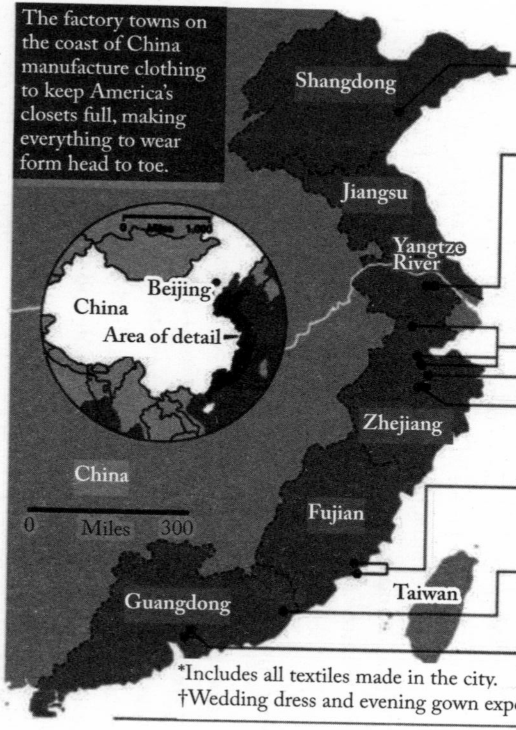

The factory towns on the coast of China manufacture clothing to keep America's closets full, making everything to wear form head to toe.

Factory orders, 2003	Production	Total Sales	US Exports
Men's wear *Zhucheng*	100 million pieces	$600 million	$100 million
Casual wear *Haiyu, Changshu*	160 million pieces	$260 million	$58 million
Down-filled products *Xintang, Hangzzhou, Xiaoshan*	26 million pieces	$470 million	$290 million
Ties *Shengzhou*	300 million pieces	$1.21 billion	$384 million
Socks *Datang, Zhuji*	9 billion pairs	$1.57 billion	$240 million
Underwear *Jinjiang, Shenhu*	969 million pieces	$360 million	$290 million
Wedding dresses, Evening gowns *Chaozhou*	510 million pieces	$950 million*	$640 million†
Jeans *Xintang, Zengcheng*	225 million pieces	$1.04 billion	$480 million

Shangdong

Jiangsu

Yangtze River

Zhejiang

Fujian

Taiwan

Guangdong

Beijing
China
Area of detail

China

0   Miles   300

*Includes all textiles made in the city.
†Wedding dress and evening gown exports only.

Source: Barboza, 2004.

companies like Luen Thai (2004), use 'supply chain city' to indicate a new breed of 'super-factory' that firms are constructing in China and in other parts of Asia (Kahn, 2004; Pang, 2004). These factories are company-specific, and are designed to bring together multiple parts of the firm's supply chain—designers, suppliers, and manufacturers—so as to minimize transaction costs, take advantage of economies of scale, and foster more flexible supply chain management. Luen Thai's factories in Guangdong Province (in Dongguan, Qingyuan, and Panyu) are the poster children for this approach.[4] Many of the firms actively establishing these giant factories are from Hong Kong and Taiwan.

A second usage of this term refers to so-called *cluster cities*. Barboza (2004) and others use 'supply-chain cities' when discussing the growing number of single-product industrial clusters that have sprung up in China's coastal regions. These areas have dramatically increased production of one specific product, and are churning out massive volumes, but are not limited simply to manufacturing firms. As these clusters have grown, they have attracted related and supporting businesses, including yarn dealers, sewers, pressers, packagers, and freight forwarders. These clusters also feature large sprawling factories, with factory buildings, dormitories, and limited amenities for workers, but the focus here is on the overall cluster of firms. Illustrative examples include Datang (socks) and Shengzhou (neckties) (Wang and Tong, 2002; Zhang et al., 2004; Wang et al., 2005; Kusterbeck, 2005).

What forces drive the formation of China's supply-chain cities? In addressing this question, bottom-up versus top-down metaphors offer a misleading dichotomy for China, simply because both characterizations are oversimplified. 'Top-down' implies that development patterns are directed closely by the central government, while 'bottom-up' implies that development patterns are determined purely by market forces. The reality in China lies somewhere in the middle.

(a) 'Supply-chain city' super-factories appear to be more bottom-up than top-down, since they result from individual sourcing decisions by private firms and are not directed by central government policy. The location of many of these factories is tied to existing manufacturing activities and the low cost of factor inputs (land, electricity, and labor), though local and provincial government has played a key role in providing a beneficial policy environment (tax incentives, streamlining bureaucratic red tape, etc.).

(b) As for the formation of clusters, this story is more complicated, and involves regional, technological, and industry factors. There is a growing body of scholarship—mostly in Chinese—on this topic, addressing the economic, policy, cultural, and historical reasons behind cluster formation.[5] At the risk of over-generalizing China's current situation, the major analytical divide in these clusters seems to be between clusters whose formation was driven initially by foreign capital, and those whose formation was initiated by domestic entrepreneurship.

The *foreign-led clusters* were founded first in the 1970s and 1980s as export-oriented production platforms, mainly in South China (Guangdong, Fujian). These began in low-cost manufacturing industries, including textiles and apparel, and have now expanded to include newer industries like electronics. Foreign investment was particularly important, with large investments coming from Hong Kong, Taiwan, and Macao; thus the central government's role in determining FDI policy was important. These clusters were founded in South China due to its low-cost labor and its relative proximity to both investors and major transportation centers. Guangdong (close to Hong Kong) and Fujian (across from Taiwan) were pioneers of this type of cluster, with larger cities in the Yangtze River Delta (Shaoxing, Hangzhou) developing at a later date (Zhang et al., 2004; Wang and Tong, 2005).

The *Chinese-led clusters* are mainly in Zhejiang and Jiangsu provinces, and began to grow more rapidly in the 1990s. These clusters are based on so-called town and village enterprises (TVEs) that were a major part of the government's push for economic development in the 1980s and 1990s, and are often in traditionally rural areas. In Zhejiang, many of these clusters were founded by chance—with a confluence of historical knowledge, individual entrepreneurship, networking, and pure luck—but continued to grow because of conscious local government policy. Thus, private entrepreneurship is critical, but the government had an important facilitative role (Sonobe et al., 2002; Zhang et al., 2004: 7–8; Wang et al., 2005: 12).

An additional question is whether these clusters are seeking to upgrade and move up the value chain. Again, it is helpful to separate our clusters into two groups.

- *South China:* The foreign-led cluster cities in Guangdong and Fujian seem to be further along in terms of fostering new, higher-tech industries, building firms with international brands, and feature a broader export mix in traditional industries. The growth of the electronics industry is a good example (Lüthje, 2004).
- *East China:* These cities lie at an earlier point on the development trajectory, and Chinese authors like Jici Wang have commented that these areas are still producing at the low end of the technology value chain. Even here, firms and government officials are increasingly conscious of their need to find new competitive advantages, especially in the face of rising labor costs and growing competition from other locations (Wang and Tong, 2002; Wang et al., 2005).

Conclusion

In the past several decades, China and Latin America have pursued very different economic trajectories. China's development model appears to have served it well, delivering steady levels of growth since 1978 and facilitating China's rise to economic prominence on the world stage. Latin America, in contrast, has displayed a far more uneven pattern of growth, and political observers have noted the shift to more radical leaders and leftist rhetoric. In both cases, however, international trade and FDI have played major roles in promoting industrial upgrading.

Yet, these two regions have much to learn from each other. Both China and Mexico currently face a host of new social and economic problems—corruption, environmental degradation, and income inequality—and are actively questioning the merits of a neoliberal, export-led growth model (Nolan, 2005). Each region faces criticism that previous paradigms of development have left parts of the economy vulnerable to foreign control or foreign pressure. In each case, reformers are calling for new social welfare programs to address their concerns, and they confront those who argue that only a fuller implementation of neoliberalism can address the problems of development.

In addition, China's growing economic links with Mexico and Latin America make this study a valuable one. Latin America has become an important source of raw material exports to China in the last decade, and a foreign policy priority as well, marked by major visits to the region by President Hu Jintao and Vice President Zeng Qinghong in recent years. In addition, Mexico and China are competing for US markets in a widening array of product lines, ranging from textiles/ apparel and furniture, to automotive and electronic products.

To understand China's development model and industrial upgrading experience, one must situate China within emerging intra-regional trade and production networks in East Asia, as well as to examine China's broader role in the global economy. Foreign direct investment has facilitated China's export diversification, but China is also pioneering new forms of domestic industrial organization in the form of supply-chain cities. The Chinese model is predicated on a clear value-chain strategy of giving high-value activities the most attention, and thus there is a growing emphasis on R&D, design, science and engineering education, and brands.

Both China and Mexico are trying to move beyond a simple cost-based approach to competitiveness (Farrell et al., 2005). Increasingly, the stakes are defined not as a race to the bottom, but as a quest to push the upgrading model beyond comparative advantages in raw materials, cheap labor, and manufacturing production to high-value niches in a broad range of global industries. China's current edge is its huge domestic market and its voracious appetite for raw materials and intermediate inputs from abroad to feed its soaring industrial growth. However, massive rural to urban migration, poor working conditions, acute labor shortages, and a deteriorating environment threaten to undermine the Chinese model if these problems are not ameliorated. While China and Mexico have made remarkable economic progress in recent decades, their development challenges continue to grow at least as fast as their accomplishments.

Notes

1. Sanjaya Lall (2000) developed this technological classification of exports based on 3-digit Standard International Trade Classification (SITC) categories. His article provides the detailed list of products under each category.
2. The main problem with these export data is that they are not sufficiently detailed to tell us about the process by which these products are made. Auto parts or electronic components, for example, could still be made in labor-intensive ways by relatively unskilled workers. Thus, industrial upgrading cannot be assured just by moving in the direction of medium- or high-technology finished products. However, it is probably true that the relative proportion of high-value activities goes up as we move from low-technology to medium- and high-technology export categories.
3. China's 30 million urban manufacturing workers on whom data could be found earned an average of US$1.06 an hour, while 71 million suburban and rural manufacturing workers earned 45 cents an hour, for a blended average of 64 cents (*Business Week*, 2004).
4. In Dongguan, in southern China, apparel maker Luen Thai Holdings Ltd boasts of a 'supply-chain city' that is a two-million square foot facility that includes a factory, dormitories for 4,000 workers, and a 300-room hotel (Kahn, 2004). Appelbaum (2008: 73–75) describes Hong Kong-based Yue Yuen—the world's largest footwear supplier—as a company that made nearly 160 million pairs of shoes for export in 2003, one-sixth of the world total of branded athletic and casual footwear. One of its four Dongguan factories employs as many as 70,000 workers.
5. My appreciation goes to Ryan Ong for his insights on this literature.

References

Appelbaum, Richard P. 2008. 'Giant Transnational Contractors in East Asia: Emergent Trends in Global Supply Chains.' *Competition and Change* 12(1): 69–87.

Asia Times Online. 2005. 'China Bucks Global Foreign Investment Trend.' February 15.

Barboza, David. 2004. 'In Roaring China, Sweaters are West of Sock City.' *New York Times*, December 24.

————. 2006. 'Labor Shortage in China May Lead to Trade Shift.' *New York Times*, April 3.

Brandt, Loren and Thomas G. Rawski. 2005. 'Chinese Industry after 25 Years of Reform.' In *China's Economy: Retrospect and Prospect*, edited by Loren Brandt, Thomas G. Rawski, and Gang Lin, 20–25. Asia Program Special Report, 129. Washington, DC: Woodrow Wilson International Institute for Scholars.

Branstetter, Lee and Nicholas Lardy. 2005. 'China's Embrace of Globalization'. In *China's Economy: Retrospect and Prospect*, edited by Loren Brandt, Thomas G. Rawski, and Gang Lin,

6–12. Asia Program Special Report, 129. Washington, DC: Woodrow Wilson International Institute for Scholars.

Business Week. 2004. 'Just How Cheap is Chinese Labor?' December 2.

Carlsen, Laura. 2004. 'Protest and Populism in Latin America.' Americas Program, Interhemispheric Resource Center, October 5. Available at http://americas.irc-online.org/am/836.

Dussel Peters, Enrique. 2000. *Polarizing Mexico: The Impact of Liberalization Strategy.* Boulder, CO: Lynne Rienner.

EIU (Economist Intelligence Unit). 2008. *Business Latin America,* January 7.

Ellner, Steve. 2006. 'Globalization, Macroeconomic Policies, and Latin American Democracy.' *Latin American Politics and Society* 48(1): 175–187.

Farrell, Diana, Antonio Puron, and Jaana K. Remes. 2005. 'Beyond Cheap Labor: Lessons for Developing Economies.' *The McKinsey Quarterly* 1: 99–109.

Fourcade-Gourinchas, Marion and Sarah L. Babb. 2002. 'The Rebirth of the Liberal Creed: Paths to Neoliberalism in Four Countries.' *American Journal of Sociology* 108(3): 533–579.

Freeman, Richard B. 2005. 'Does Globalization of the Scientific/Engineering Workforce Threaten US Economic Leadership?' National Bureau of Economic Research (NBER) Working Paper 11457. Available at http://www.nber.org/papers/w11457.

Gao, Bai. 2006. 'Neoliberal versus Classical: Chinese and Japanese Developmentalisms in Comparison.' *Sociological Research* (She hui xueyanjiu) 1: 116–141.

Gereffi, Gary. 1994. 'Rethinking Development Theory: Insights from East Asia and Latin America.' In *Comparative National Development: Society and Economy in the New Global Order,* edited by A. Douglas Kincaid and Alejandro Portes, 26–56. Chapel Hill, NC: University of North Carolina Press.

———. 1996. 'Commodity Chains and Regional Divisions of Labor in East Asia.' *Journal of Asian Business* 12(1): 75–112.

———. 2005. 'The Global Economy: Organization, Governance, and Development'. In *The Handbook of Economic Sociology,* 2nd edition, edited by Neil J. Smelser and Richard Swedberg, 160–182. Princeton, NJ: Princeton University Press and Russell Sage Foundation.

Gereffi, Gary, John Humphrey, and Timothy J. Sturgeon. 2005. 'The Governance of Global Value Chains.' *Review of International Political Economy* 12(1): 78–104.

Goodman, Peter S. 2005. 'China Ventures Southward: In Search of Cheaper Labor, Firms Invest in Vietnam.' *Washington Post,* December 6.

Gore, Charles. 2000. 'The Rise and Fall of the Washington Consensus as a Paradigm for Developing Countries.' *World Development* 28(5): 789–804.

Hu, Albert G. Z. and Gary H. Jefferson. 2004. 'Science and Technology in China.' Paper presented at the Conference 'China's Economic Transition: Origins, Mechanisms, and Consequences,' University of Pittsburgh, November 5–7.

Huang, Fuping. 2006. 'Only Progress in Reform Can Solve the New Problems Faced in Reform' (Gaigezhong mianlin de xin wenti, zhi neng yong jinyibu gaige lai jiejue). *Finance* 151.

Huang, Yasheng and Tarun Khanna. 2003. 'Can India Overtake China?' *Foreign Policy* 137: 74–81.

Huber, Evelyne and Fred Solt. 2004. 'Success and Failures of Neoliberalism.' *Latin American Research Review* 39(3): 150–164.

IADB (Inter-American Development Bank). 2005. *The Emergence of China: Opportunities and Challenges for Latin America and the Caribbean Basin.* Washington, DC: IADB.

————. 2006. *The Politics of Policies: Social and Economic Progress in Latin America, 2006 Report.* Washington, DC: IADB.

————. 2007. *Integration and Trade Sector Briefs: Latin American Annual Trade Estimates for 2007.* December. Washington, DC: IADB.

Kahn, Gabriel. 2004. 'Making Labels for Less: Supply-chain City Transforms Far-flung Apparel Industry.' *Wall Street Journal Online.* August 13.

Kahn, Joseph. 2006. 'In Beijing, New Debate on Socialism.' *New York Times,* March 12.

Kusterbeck, Staci. 2005. 'China Appeals to US Buyers with "Supply Chain Cities".' *Apparel Magazine,* August 1.

Lall, Sanjaya. 2000. 'The Technological Structure and Performance of Developing Country Manufactured Exports, 1985–1998.' *Oxford Development Studies* 28(3): 337–369.

Lall, Sanjaya and Manuel Albaladejo. 2004. 'China's Competitive Performance: A Threat to East Asian Manufactured Exports?' *World Development* 32(9): 1441–1466.

Lora, Eduardo, Ugo Panizza, and Ernesto H. Stein. 2004. 'A Decade of Development Thinking.' Inter-American Development Bank, Research Department. Washington, DC: IADB.

Luen Thai. 2004. Luen Thai Holdings Limited: Corporate Presentation, Interim Results 2004.

Lüthje, Boy. 2004. 'Global Production Networks and Industrial Upgrading in China: The Case of Electronics Contract Manufacturing.' East-West Center Working Paper 74. Available at www.eastwestcenter.org/stored/pdfs/ECONwp074.pdf.

Nolan, Peter H. 2005. 'China at the Crossroads.' *Journal of Chinese Economic and Business Studies* 3(1): 22.

Palley, Thomas I. 2006. 'External Contradictions of the Chinese Development Model: Export-led Growth and the Dangers of Global Economic Contraction.' *Journal of Contemporary China* 15(46): 69–88.

Pang, Carmen. 2004. 'Chain Reaction.' *Textile World Asia.*

Portes, Alejandro. 1997. 'Neoliberalism and the Sociology of Development: Emerging Trends and Unanticipated Facts.' *Population and Development Review* 23(2): 229–259.

Rodrik, Dani. 2006. 'What's So Special About China's Exports?' *China and World Economy* 14(1): 1–19.

Shifter, Michael. 2005. 'Don't Buy Those Latin American Labels'. *Los Angeles Times,* December 24.

Sonobe, Tetsuki, Keijiro Otsuka, and D. Hu. 2002. 'Process of Cluster Formation in China: A Case Study of a Garment Town.' *Journal of Development Studies* 39(1): 118–139.

Sturgeon, Timothy J. and Ji-Ren Lee. 2005. 'Industry Co-evolution: A Comparison of Taiwan and North American Electronics Contract Manufacturers.' In *Global Taiwan: Building Competitive Strengths in a New International Economy,* edited by S. Berger and R. K. Lester, 33–75. Armonk, NY: M. E. Sharpe.

Thorp, Rosemary and Pamela Lowden. 1996. 'Latin America's Development Models: A Political Economy Perspective.' *Oxford Development Studies* 24(2): 133–144.

UNCTAD (United Nations Conference on Trade and Development). 2017. *World Investment Report 2017: Investment and the Digital Economy.* Geneva: UNCTAD.

Vargas Llosa, Alvaro. 2005. 'The Return of Latin America's Left.' *New York Times*, March 22.

Walton, Michael. 2004. 'Neoliberalism in Latin America: Good, Bad or Incomplete?' *Latin American Research Review* 39(3): 165–183.

Wang, Jici and Xin Tong. 2002. 'Clustering in China: Alternative Pathways Towards Global-local Linkages.' In *Technological Innovation in China*, edited by Shulin Gu. Maastricht: United Nations University, Institute for New Technology.

Wang, Jici, Huasheng Xu, and Xin Tong. 2005. 'Industrial Districts in a Transitional Economy: The Case of Datang Sock and Stocking Industry in Zhejiang, China'. In *Proximity, Distance, and Diversity: Issues on Economic Interaction and Local Development*, edited by Arnoud Lagendjik and Päivi Oinas, 47–69. Burlington, VT: Ashgate.

Wang, Mark Y. and Xiaochen Meng. 2004. 'Global-local Initiatives in FDI: The Experience of Shenzhen, China.' *Asia Pacific Viewpoint* 45(2): 181–196.

Weyland, Kurt. 2004. 'Assessing Latin American Neoliberalism: Introduction to a Debate.' *Latin American Research Review* 39(3): 143–149.

Zhang, Qing and Bruce Felmingham. 2002. 'The Role of FDI, Exports and Spill-over Effects in the Regional Development of China.' *Journal of Development Studies* 38(4): 157–178.

Zhang, Zhiming, Chester To, and Ning Cao. 2004. 'How Do Industry Clusters Succeed? A Case Study in China's Textiles and Apparel Industries.' *Journal of Textile and Apparel Technology and Management* 4(2): 1–10.

Economic and Social Upgrading in Global Production Networks

A New Paradigm for a Changing World

Stephanie Barrientos, Gary Gereffi, and Arianna Rossi

A significant proportion of trade now takes place through coordinated value chains in which lead firms play a dominant role globally and locally. The outsourcing of production by Northern buyers has stimulated the growth of manufacturing, agriculture, and service industries in the South. It has promoted regional and global production networks (GPNs) that have opened up supply opportunities in new and expanding markets, including China, India, and Brazil. Firms engaged in GPNs have opportunities for economic upgrading through engaging in higher value production or repositioning themselves within value chains. However, they also face challenges meeting buyers' commercial demands and quality standards, which smaller and less efficient producers find hard to satisfy.

The expansion of global production in labor-intensive industries has been an important source of employment generation. Many of the new jobs have been filled by women and migrant workers who previously had difficulty accessing this type of wage employment, and they have provided new sources of income for poorer households (Raworth, 2004; Barrientos et al., 2003). Where such employment is regular and generates better rights and protection for workers, it can promote social upgrading and decent work. The demand for higher quality standards often requires skilling of at least some workers and provision of better employment conditions. But for many workers, this is not the outcome. Much GPN employment is insecure and unprotected, and ensuring decent work for more vulnerable workers poses significant problems.

Indeed, a key challenge is how to improve the position of both firms and workers within GPNs. This is particularly important in developing countries, where firms and workers are increasingly integrated into regional or global production systems involving many locations. Accordingly, this chapter explores the obstacles and opportunities for promoting decent work through economic and social upgrading in the context of GPNs. It draws on previous empirical studies in which we examined each type of upgrading/downgrading separately. Based on these insights, it aims to advance a more integrated analytical framework linking economic and social upgrading/downgrading. Rossi's (2011) case study of the Moroccan garment industry provides an early application of this framework, which can inform much-needed future research on the linkages between economic and social upgrading. This research indicates that firms' economic upgrading can, but does not necessarily, lead to improvements for workers. Therefore, the central question considered here is: under what circumstances can both firms and workers gain from a process of upgrading?

The remainder of this chapter is organized into five sections. The first examines the literatures on global value chains, production networks, and labor economics. It addresses the separation between the firm and worker levels of analysis in the context of GPNs, where production and employment decisions are influenced not only by local markets, but also by foreign buyers and their agents. The second section introduces the concepts of economic and social upgrading as means of assessing improvements for firms and workers engaged in GPNs. The third section develops a framework for assessing the linkages between economic and social upgrading based on type of value chain and type of work. It then examines some of the opportunities and challenges those linkages present, given that regular and irregular workers have very different levels of access to employer-based channels for promoting their rights, protection, and voice. The fourth section considers some of the trajectories (and mixed outcomes) that can be pursued through economic and social upgrading or downgrading. The fifth offers concluding remarks.

Changing Patterns of Trade, Production, and Employment

The rise of international outsourcing through global and regional production networks requires a shift in our analytical approach. Nowadays, expanded networks of firms and workers in Africa, Asia and Latin America are linked to the global economy. These range from large commercial factories and farms, through subcontractors and outgrowers, to smallholders and homeworkers. Global production and services account for a growing number of workers recruited into export-oriented industries in developing countries, such as apparel, footwear, and agriculture (Gereffi, 1999, 2006). These changing structures of trade, production, and employment have been defined in different ways, which should be addressed from the outset.

Global value chain (GVC) analysis initially focused on the commercial dynamics between firms in different segments of the production chain. A seminal distinction was made between producer-driven and buyer-driven commodity chains (Gereffi, 1994). In producer-driven chains, production was controlled by integrated transnational manufacturers in capital- and technology-intensive industries, such as automobiles and advanced electronics. Buyer-driven chains evolved as developed country firms set up global sourcing networks to procure labor-intensive consumer goods from low-cost suppliers in Asia, Latin America, and Africa. A novel feature of buyer-driven chains was that their lead firms were large retailers (such as Walmart and Tesco) and global brands or marketers (such as Nike and The Gap). They had no direct ownership of factories, but increasing control over production through their ability to set prices, product specifications, process standards and delivery schedules in their supply chains (Dolan and Humphrey, 2000, 2004). They also contributed to the institutionalization of demand-responsive economies with lead firms or agents based in developing countries, such as the Republic of Korea and Taiwan (China) (Hamilton and Gereffi, 2009). The expansion of GVCs has encompassed not only the agricultural and manufacturing sectors, but also global services, such as tourism, logistics, finance, and business process outsourcing located in diverse socio-economic contexts across countries (Gereffi et al., 2005; Staritz et al., 2011).

The growing complexity and pervasiveness of global production and trade led to diverse formulations. GVC analysis drew attention to the role of value creation, value differentiation, and value capture in a coordinated process of production, distribution and retail (Lee, 2010; Bair, 2009; Gereffi, 2005; Gereffi and Kaplinsky, 2001). A parallel literature around GPNs placed more emphasis on the institutional or social context of interconnected commercial operations (Henderson et al., 2002). GPN analysis examined not only the interaction between lead firms and suppliers, but also the whole range of actors that contribute to influencing and shaping global production, such as national governments, multilateral organizations, and international trade unions and nongovernmental organizations (NGOs) (Bair, 2009: 4; Hess and Yeung, 2006). A GPN approach also emphasizes the social and institutional embeddedness of production, and power relations between actors, which vary as sourcing is spread across multiple developing countries.

Consideration of workers in GPNs has so far been limited, particularly in academic studies (Pegler and Knorringa, 2007; Barrientos et al., 2003; Cumbers et al., 2008; Coe and Jordhus-Lier, 2011; Rossi, 2011). In the early GVC/GPN literature, the focus was on the firm, with labor treated primarily as an endogenous factor of production. Analysis of labor in value chains has largely been restricted to the aggregate number of workers at different nodes of the chain, with an occasional breakdown of employment by job category, skill, or sex. The exceptions have mainly been case studies examining conditions of employment, protection and the rights of workers in GPNs. These have included the study of female workers (Hale and Wills, 2005), homeworkers (McCormick and Schmitz, 2002), smallholders (ETI, 2005), social protection of informal workers (Barrientos and Barrientos, 2002) and trade unions (Miller et al., 2011; Cumbers et al., 2008). NGOs have also engaged in research on poor working conditions and lack of employment rights among workers in value chains as a basis for campaigns and advocacy in relation to high-profile global buyers and their suppliers (Raworth, 2004; Oxfam International, 2010; Action Aid International, 2005; Wilde and de Hann, 2006; CIVIDEP-India/SOMO, 2009; Clean Clothes Campaign, 2009; Raworth and Kidder, 2009). However, there has been a disjuncture in the literature between a 'firm focus' that treats labor as a factor of production, and a 'rights focus' on the conditions and entitlements of workers.

To bridge this divide between the economic and social analysis of labor, we seek to integrate workers as productive and social agents into the changing dynamics of GPNs in developing countries. Our aim is to gain a better understanding of how economic and social upgrading play out for firms and workers, and how strategies for upgrading that benefit both firms and workers can be enhanced. In order to capture the different dimensions of labor, we approach the analysis of labor in the context of GPNs from two perspectives. The first sees *labor as a productive factor*. Conventional economic theory views labor as a factor of production, based on the marginal productivity of labor and labor costs within individual firms or labor markets. An important assumption here is that firms need to produce at the lowest possible marginal cost to remain competitive. However, this does not fully take into account the role of labor within the context of GVCs/GPNs, where an important commercial driver is the need to meet both cost pressures and quality standards (Barrientos and Kritzinger, 2004). This affects the work intensity and skill levels of the labor required at different nodes within GPNs. In addition to the need to meet the requirements of lead firms and buyers, this is also determined by local labor market conditions (availability of different types of workers).

The second perspective sees *labor as socially embedded*. Viewing workers as social agents looks beyond their role as factors of production, highlighting them as human beings with capabilities and entitlements (Sen, 1999, 2000). Workers have rights under national legislation and international conventions, such as the core Conventions of the ILO. Wage laborers are indeed largely dependent on access to rights that enhance their well-being, and such access, in turn, can be affected either positively or negatively by participation in GPNs. Beyond the workplace, the well-being of workers and their dependants is affected by formal and informal social protection networks and strategies sustained by governments and communities.

The analysis of GPNs allows for examination of both the narrower commercial dimension of labor used within value chains and the broader, socially embedded dimension of work (often as a gendered process) in the globalization of production and services. However, the GPN context brings a number of challenges for the analysis of upgrading. First, the quantity and type of employment by individual supplier firms are affected not only by national labor market conditions, but also by requirements dictated by foreign agents or buyers (in relation to product quality, price, and delivery schedules). Second, the quality of employment is mediated not only by the national framework of labor legislation, inspection, and industrial relations, but also by the codes of conduct of large global buyers and a private system of monitoring and auditing.

In this context, the relationship between the quantity and quality of employment is poorly understood.[1] An important question is whether it is possible simultaneously to improve both the quantity and quality of employment in GPNs. And if so, under what circumstances might this occur, and what strategies could promote this? To examine further the linkages between the two, we now explore the concepts of economic and social upgrading and how they can contribute to a broader strategy of development.

Defining Economic and Social Upgrading

Upgrading has been identified as a move to higher value added activities in production, to improve technology, knowledge and skills, and to increase the benefits or profits deriving from participation in GPNs (Gereffi, 2005: 171–175). Initially, the GVC literature focused on labor-intensive manufacturing, such as garments, footwear, and toys. These industries exemplified the outsourcing of labor-intensive segments of production to low-wage countries; and their study used the concept of 'industrial upgrading' (Gereffi, 1999; Bair and Gereffi, 2001). However, GPNs have more recently widened beyond manufacturing to include sectors such as agro-food and services—e.g., call centers, tourism, and business-process outsourcing—where the term 'industrial upgrading' is less appropriate. The more generic concept used here is that of economic upgrading which applies across sectors.

There are four types of economic upgrading, each with different implications for skill development and jobs:

- *Process upgrading* involves changes in the production process with the objective of making it more efficient; this can be achieved by substituting capital for labor—i.e., higher productivity through automation—and thereby reducing skilled or unskilled work.
- *Product upgrading* occurs where more advanced product types are introduced, which often requires more skilled jobs to make an item with enhanced features.

- *Functional upgrading* occurs where firms change the mix of activities they perform towards higher-value-added tasks. In the apparel industry, for example, the inclusion of finishing, packaging, logistics, and transport can be done in at least two distinct ways: via vertical integration, which adds novel capabilities to a firm or an economic cluster; or via specialization, which substitutes one set of activities for another (e.g. an apparel firm that moves out of production and into brand marketing and design). In electronics, this can happen when firms move from simple assembly to contract manufacturing by engaging in full-package production or to original design manufacturing by developing their own design. Both involve new workforce skill sets linked to expanded firm capabilities.
- *Chain upgrading*—i.e., shifting to a more technologically advanced production chain—involves moving into new industries or product markets, which often utilize different marketing channels and manufacturing technologies. This may also require a different workforce or innovations that allow existing manufacturers to enter new industries as end markets (such as textile firms shifting from traditional fabrics, like denim for apparel, to specialty nanofibers and strong lightweight materials that can be used in the medical, defense or aircraft industries).

Each type of economic upgrading embodies a capital dimension and a labor dimension. The capital dimension refers to the use of new machinery or advanced technology. The labor dimension refers to skill development or to increased dexterity and productivity on the part of workers. In this formulation, labor is considered primarily as a productive factor determining the quantity and type of employment.

Social upgrading, by contrast, is the process of improvement in the rights and entitlements of workers as social actors, which enhances the quality of their employment (Rossi, 2011; Sen, 1999, 2000). This includes access to better work, which might result from economic upgrading (e.g., a worker who has acquired skills in one job is able to move to a better job elsewhere in a GPN). But it also involves enhancing working conditions, protection and rights. Improving the well-being of workers can also help their dependants and communities. The concept of social upgrading is framed by the ILO's Decent Work Agenda, which encompasses employment, standards and rights at work, social protection and social dialogue. This package promotes work performed under conditions of freedom, equity, security, and human dignity, in which rights are protected and adequate remuneration and social coverage are provided (ILO, 1999). Economists have long established methods for quantifying the upgrading of labor through measures of labor productivity and skill, but not all aspects of social upgrading are as easily quantifiable.

Social upgrading can be subdivided into two components: measurable standards and enabling rights (Elliott and Freeman, 2003; Barrientos and Smith, 2007). Measurable standards are those aspects of worker well-being that are more easily observable and quantifiable, including type of employment (regular or irregular), wage level, social protection, and working hours. They can also include data on sex and unionization, such as the percentage of female supervisors or the percentage of union members in the workforce. However, measurable standards are often the outcome of complex bargaining processes, framed by the enabling rights of workers. These are less easily quantified, such as freedom of association, the right to collective bargaining, non-discrimination, voice and empowerment. Lack of access to enabling rights undermines the ability of workers—or specific groups of workers, such as women or migrants—to negotiate improvements in their working conditions that can enhance their well-being.

It is often implicitly assumed that economic upgrading in value chains automatically translates into social upgrading through better wages and working conditions (Knorringa and Pegler, 2006). However, case studies provide a mixed picture. While social upgrading can be the outcome, it may be thwarted if the employment created is highly insecure and exploitative. A vivid but tragic example where apparent economic upgrading failed to translate into comparable social upgrading is that of the Foxconn factory in China, which became associated with multiple worker suicides. Since 2005, China has become the world's largest exporter and producer of mobile phones. Supplying Apple, Nokia, and other prominent global electronics brands, Foxconn, a Taiwanese contract manufacturer, has emerged as the largest private employer in China, with over one million workers across more than a dozen factories. The availability of jobs, however, has not necessarily led to social upgrading for Foxconn's workers. Excessive working hours, involuntary and often unpaid overtime work, lack of adequate safety measures, and military-style management practices led to growing discontent among young migrant workers, culminating in a series of suicide attempts that claimed 17 workers' lives during the first eight months of 2011 (SACOM, 2010). However, the links between economic and social upgrading/downgrading are often complex, with different workers experiencing different outcomes on the same production site, as shown by the example from the Moroccan garment industry reported below.

Framework for Linking Economic and Social Upgrading in GPNs

A number of factors can affect the economic and social upgrading (or downgrading) of firms and workers. These include their position within the value chain, the type of work performed, and the status of workers within a given category of work. This section provides a framework for identifying different types of work across GPNs, highlighting key elements of economic and social upgrading for each category. This schema will be used to analyze possible trajectories of economic and social upgrading in the next section.

Typology of Work in Agro-Food, Apparel, IT, and Services GPNs

When discussing upgrading from a GPN perspective, it is important to emphasize that the unit of analysis is not the individual country, firm or worker, but the value chain (linking primary production, processing, distribution and retail) within which firms and workers are located. GPNs are constituted by a mix of activities that require combinations of labor-intensive, low-skilled activities with knowledge- and technology-intensive higher-skilled activities. Different types of GPNs are likely to be composed of different ratios of both low-skill and high-skill production, therefore requiring a comprehensive typology of work. Here we outline different types of work performed within GPNs.

Small-Scale Household and Home-Based Work

Small-scale, household-based work is found in many GPNs with operations in developing countries. This type of work is typically performed by small-scale producers or outgrowers involved in agricultural production, and homeworkers in more labor-intensive or artisanal types of manufacturing. These workers usually have access to their own assets and means of subsistence, and are often (but not always) located in poorer countries and regions. Production takes place in or around the household residence, with limited separation between commercial productive activity (producing saleable goods) and unpaid reproductive activity (e.g., household subsistence and childcare). Small-scale production and home-based work involve both paid and unpaid family labor, often including child labor. Homeworkers and small-scale producers are linked into GPNs through very different types of commercial arrangements. In small-firm economies like Taiwan's, homeworking was often the initial stage in the development of what later became factory-based export production in buyer-driven commodity chains for consumer goods industries, such as garments, toys and, sporting goods (Hamilton and Gereffi, 2009; Feenstra and Hamilton, 2006; McCormick and Schmitz, 2002).

Low-Skilled Labor-Intensive Work

Labor-intensive production involving the use of wage labor in a formal factory setting is clearly distinct from household-based production. It involves a relationship based on wage employment between an employer (who may be the producer or an agent) and a worker (normally paid in cash, but sometimes in kind). Global brands and retailers have been able to reduce costs and spread their market reach through outsourcing to lower-cost developing countries. This stimulated the expansion of production and employment linked to GPNs. In manufacturing, since the first offshoring wave in the 1960s and 1970s, the nature of outsourced work has evolved. Whereas the first-generation *maquila* jobs based on the assembly of garments in Mexico were quite labor-intensive, subsequent generations oriented to the assembly of automotive parts and advanced electronics have often involved substantial automation. As one moves from apparel to auto-parts to electronics, the very nature of assembly work changes to second- and third-generation *maquila* work. This explains why workers in a given industrial district—e.g., Torreon, Tijuana or Ciudad Juarez in Mexico—often earn higher wages when they move from apparel to auto-parts to electronics (Bair and Gereffi, 2001; Carrillo, 1998).

China's phenomenal export success during the past two decades can also be linked to a variety of labor-intensive production arrangements—e.g., government-created Special Economic Zones and more locally rooted but highly specialized industrial districts—which have quite different implications for both economic and social upgrading. Recently, China has begun to adopt explicit policies to improve wages and working conditions in response to worker protests and growing uncertainty about the economic prospects for the country's huge migrant workforce, which could create a strong political mandate for linking economic and social upgrading (Zeng, 2010; Gereffi, 2009; Barboza and Tabuchi, 2010).

Medium-Skilled Mixed Production Technologies Work

This type of work is associated with full-package production, driven by the rise of global buyers whose preferred suppliers are required to coordinate all of the operations leading to the delivery of the final good, including design, inputs, production, pre-pricing, packaging and presentation (Gereffi, 1994, 2005; Dolan and Humphrey, 2000). While global buyers control the orders for full-package production, developing country suppliers coordinate the supply of inputs, make the final product and send it to the buyer. For developing country firms to fill full-package orders from global buyers, they need access to varied production technologies and skilled workers capable not only of making key components and finished products, but also of performing production-related service jobs like product design, quality control, packing, and logistics, which require a broad range of skills.

High-Skilled Technology-Intensive Work

High-skilled, technology-intensive work emerged in the 1980s and 1990s from a different set of offshore activities as lead firms in capital- and technology-intensive industries, such as automobiles and electronics, set up international production networks not only to assemble their finished goods, but also to develop a supply-base for key intermediate items and sub-assemblies. This form of production is reflected in the rise of global contract manufacturers in the electronics industry and 'mega suppliers' in the automotive industry. A dramatic but not atypical example from electronics is Celestica, which spun off from IBM in 1996. From two initial production locations in Canada and the United States, Celestica grew to nearly 50 factories across Asia, Europe, and the Americas by 2001 (largely via acquisitions), increasing its sales from $2 billion to $10 billion during this period (Sturgeon and Lester, 2004: 47–49). At the uppermost tiers of these production networks, the suppliers tend to be very large and technologically sophisticated, and they concentrate 'good' jobs in relatively few locations. However, as shown in the case of Foxconn above, global contract manufacturers may also hire large numbers of workers in highly labor-intensive jobs

Knowledge-Intensive Work

Knowledge-intensive work in GPNs is being driven by a new wave of offshoring in services (Gereffi and Fernandez-Stark, 2010). Although white-collar outsourcing started with simple service jobs like call centers and telemarketing, it now includes more advanced business services such as finance, accounting, software, medical services, and engineering. Knowledge-intensive service jobs are increasingly seen as an opportunity for developing economies to reap both economic and social benefits from technological learning, knowledge spillovers, and higher incomes. On average, however, the volume of employment in this work category is relatively small on account of its requirements for high skills and advanced degrees, mainly in science and engineering. Accordingly, the unskilled or less well-educated majority in many countries is excluded from the very desirable employment opportunities provided by knowledge-intensive work.

Based on a simplified typology identifying five GPNs that combine labor-intensive, low-tech manufacture, medium-tech manufacture, technology-intensive and knowledge-intensive activities, Figure 8.1 shows how different GPNs incorporate different types of work and skill levels. While all five types of work are represented in each GPN, there are significant differences in the proportions of each type of work across these sectors. Agro-food involves a relatively large proportion of small-scale and low-skill labor-intensive production, particularly at the farm level. Within manufacturing, if we compare industries that can be classified as relatively low-tech (apparel), medium-tech (automotive), and high-tech (electronics), the proportion of low-skilled and household-based types of work decreases, and the relative importance of knowledge-intensive and high-skilled work increases. This progression in the nature of the work involved is associated with economic upgrading: as we move to more technology- and knowledge-intensive GPNs, such as IT, labor-intensive production does not disappear but becomes relatively less prominent. However, there is no systematic connection between the proportion of labor-intensive work and social upgrading.

Figure 8.1 Typology of Workforce Composition Across Different GPNs

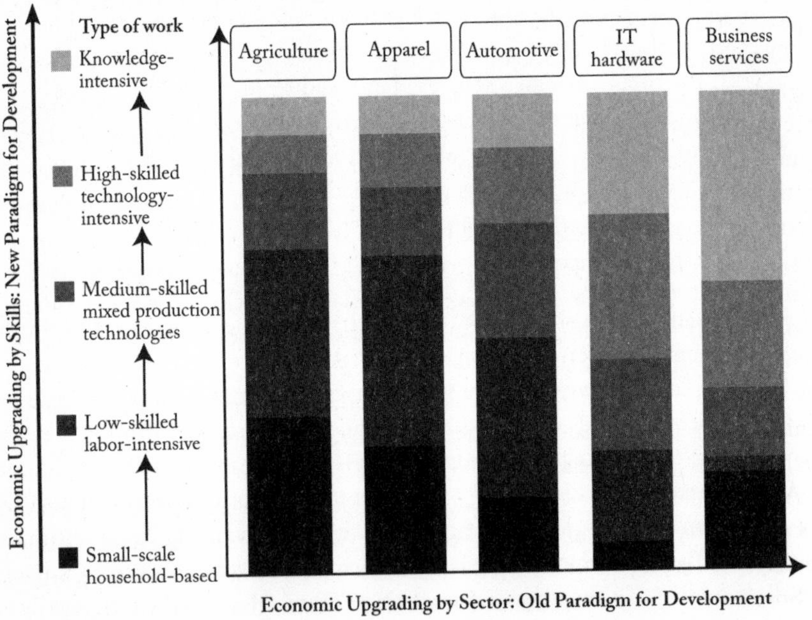

Source: Authors.

Status of Workers

The type of work undertaken at any point within a GPN has to be further unpacked. Here we draw on Rossi's (2011) case study of economic and social upgrading in the Moroccan garment industry to show that the status of workers can have important implications for their ability to benefit from or participate in economic and social upgrading. Empirical data collected through semi-structured manager interviews and focus group discussions with workers show that the workforce in supplier factories participating in garment GPNs is far from homogeneous.[2]

In response to lead-firm requirements in terms of low cost, short lead times, flexibility for last-minute changes in orders, and high quality, which characterize the fast-fashion buyers sourcing from Morocco,[3] supplier firms resort to employing two different categories of workers. The first consists of regular workers, who are senior and experienced, thereby guaranteeing high skills and good quality. They are usually employed on permanent contracts (albeit often oral contracts based on trust), and they are paid a premium over the minimum wage. The second category consists of irregular workers who are employed in the unskilled segments of the production chain, typically the most time-sensitive, such as packaging and loading trucks. These unskilled workers are usually young women, often internal migrants, who are frequently discriminated against, not covered by any formal contract, paid below the minimum wage, and not covered by any type of social protection.

These two categories of workers face very different opportunities for social upgrading. Regular workers with strong employer attachment can more easily access statutory employment protection and benefit from measurable labor standards. Their greater security of employment may increase their ability to participate in workplace-based trade union organizations and reduce their fear of reprisals, thus enhancing their enabling rights. Irregular workers, with their weak employer attachment, are less able to avail themselves of employer-based protection or measurable standards. Since irregular workers are over-represented among women and ethnic and migrant groups, they often face double discrimination on account of both their social and their employment status. Irregular workers in any type of job are therefore more likely to suffer a 'decent work deficit', which denies them access to enabling rights and undermines their relative ability to reap the benefits of economic and social upgrading.

A related but under-researched issue is the role of third-party labor contractors as a channel for recruiting and employing irregular workers in global production. Research by Barrientos (2011) on the garment industry in India and horticulture in South Africa and the United Kingdom indicates that such contracting is increasingly prevalent in the labor-intensive nodes of GPNs involving footloose or seasonal production, such as agro-food and apparel. Labor contracting can involve multiple types of relationship between the producing firm, the contractor, and the worker (e.g., payment by the number of workers where the contractor takes a percentage, or payment by task, such as clearing a field). Contractors move groups of workers between sites and locations depending on the season and shifts in demand for labor. They play an increasingly important role in matching 'the right type' of workers to tasks, in coordinating labor supply to firms on a 'just-in-time' basis (Rogaly, 2008), and in channelling migrant labor (internal and international) to production locations (Martin, 2006).

Labor contracting also allows firms to offset production or market risks and minimize labor costs (as well as associated human resource management needs). Such contracting can help workers enhance their continuity of employment between different producers and provide some form of protection in sectors where there are seasonality or 'just-in-time' pressures. But it can also open up space for unscrupulous agents who expose workers to high levels of exploitation both on and off site, thereby undermining decent work conditions (Barrientos and Kritzinger, 2004; Kuptsch, 2006; Theron and Godfrey, 2000; Theron et al., 2004). Barrientos (2011) finds that this can include new forms of bonded and forced labor at the heart of global production. Thus the role of labor contractors can significantly affect the relationship between economic and social upgrading, and their workers can be vulnerable to extreme forms of exploitation.

Factors Contributing to Economic and Social Upgrading or Downgrading

The different types of work and status of employment provide the context for social upgrading, highlighting the interplay between economic and social upgrading. Table 8.1 provides an initial overview of how the two are related in these different contexts. Social upgrading is mainly represented by measurable standards, although future work in this area should also utilize research tools to assess the existence and effectiveness of enabling rights. Case study evidence suggests that certain aspects of social upgrading/downgrading, such as flexibility, vulnerability, discrimination, voice, and empowerment, cut across the types of work and thus characterize household-based work and knowledge-intensive work alike.

A number of early case studies highlighted problems of poor working conditions and lack of access to decent work (Smith et al., 2004; Collins, 2003; Hale and Wills, 2005; Raworth, 2004). Conditions vary by sector and product, but mainly in relation to whether employment is regular or irregular. Labor conditions are consistently found to be better among permanent workers than among temporary and casual workers. Gender bias has also been found to play an important role: women are preferred by many employers for their perceived dexterity and 'nimble fingers' (Elson and Pearson, 1981). However, they tend to perform the insecure and low-paid work, often in temporary or seasonal employment arrangements (Barrientos and Kritzinger, 2004), while men typically occupy the better-paid and more skilled jobs. The position of workers in different nodes of GPNs also plays a role in their overall labor conditions. In manufacturing, for example, conditions are likely to be better in the factory of a preferred supplier that is regularly audited than in a subcontracted firm further down the chain that goes unmonitored (Locke et al., 2007).

Table 8.1 Key Drivers of Economic and Social Upgrading and Downgrading, by Type of Work

	Small-scale, household-based	Low-skilled, labor-intensive	Medium-skilled, mixed production technologies	High-skilled, technology-intensive	Knowledge-intensive
Economic upgrading/downgrading	(+) Allows poor workers and producers to engage in GPNs (+) Provides access to niche produce and labor skills, such as high plateau teas or handsewn embroidery (+/–) High dependence on intermediaries who can support or exploit (–) Difficulty meeting standards, hence exclusion from GPNs (–) Low value added (–) Often low value-capture within chain	(+) Good for ramping up output, exports, and foreign exchange (+) Helps to attract foreign investors and to meet international quality standards (–) Highly dependent on global buyers in control of inputs and orders (–) Minimal local linkages to host economy/local firms (–) Low value added (–) Vulnerable to buyers' purchasing decisions (–) Few opportunities for skill improvement	(+) Integrated production and control in final production, key inputs, even in finance, logistics, product development (+) A process of buyer-oriented upgrading (+) Stronger forward and backward linkages (+) Higher value added (–) More stringent performance standards and reduced margins procured by global buyers	(+) Higher capital- and technology-investment inflows (+) Increasing modularity (+) Technology learning and knowledge spillovers—supplier upgrading (+) Emerging 'global firms', e.g. in China and India (–) High entry barriers for local firms in lucrative segments and know-how	(+) Better income and export prospects (+) Technology learning and knowledge spillovers (+) Upgrading from simple service jobs (e.g., call centers) to more advanced business services (software, medical services, engineering) (+) Newest area: offshoring of design and innovation (R&D centers in developing countries) (–) Entry barriers in lucrative segments and know-how
Social upgrading/downgrading	(+) High quantity of jobs, especially for female workers (+) Women can balance productive and reproductive work (–) Likelihood of unpaid family labor, including child labor (–) Lack of contracts or security (–) Long or insecure working hours and poor conditions (–) Lack of social protection and rights	(+) High quantity of jobs, especially for female workers (–) Low quality, low wages; 'footloose' jobs (–) Operation of labor relations predominantly on a flexible, casual basis (–) Absence of fixed working hours (–) Lack of employment security and other benefits (–) No skill improvement (repetitive, scrappy work)	(+) Fair quantity of jobs (+) Relatively higher wages than assembly jobs (+/–) Relatively high job security in vertically integrated firms, but increased use of flexible employment (+) Layers of skills and jobs down the supply chain make it possible to retain core skills and outsource others to peripheral workers	(–) Relatively small volume of employment (+) High-quality jobs (higher wage than other manufacturing industries) (+) Relatively high job security (–) Flexible work arrangements on the rise (–) Concentration of 'good jobs' in advanced countries (+) Opportunity for skill improvement	(–) Small number of jobs (+) High wages and benefits by domestic standards (+) Continuous skill improvement (+) Flexible work arrangements not making employees vulnerable (+) Greater possibility of genderneutral work (–) High entry barriers, e.g., education, English language –'not inclusive' (+/–) High individualization of work

Source: Adapted from Gereffi and Güler, 2008, 2010.

Social upgrading may occur for some workers but not for others working in the same factory. Evidence from Morocco's garment industry shows that high-skilled workers—even those employed in factories in the cut-make-trim segment of the apparel GPN—may have opportunities for social upgrading, especially in terms of measurable standards, when lead firms are preoccupied with their brand reputation and require compliance with labor standards in their supplier factories. At the same time, unskilled workers may be largely excluded from social upgrading in order for the factory to remain cost-competitive and flexible in terms of last-minute changes in orders. The challenges of social upgrading remain significant for irregular workers even as factories shift their production towards higher value added items. Indeed, the new activities taken on by the factory as a result may well lead to social upgrading for regular workers—through the development of more skills and training for new capabilities—but irregular workers continue to be needed in order to respond to buyers' requirements in terms of low cost, short lead times, and high flexibility; their very status impedes their social upgrading.

Trajectories in Economic and Social Upgrading

As indicated previously, economic upgrading does not necessarily lead to social upgrading (Brown, 2007; Locke et al., 2007). Research (often by civil society organizations) has highlighted the adverse role company purchasing practices can play, with negative outcomes for the workers engaged in GPNs (Insight Investment/Acona, 2004; Raworth, 2004; Oxfam International, 2010; CAFOD, 2004; Barrientos and Kritzinger, 2004). However, this needs to be investigated further by exploring the conditions under which economic upgrading may lead to social upgrading or downgrading.

There are competing pressures for each of these two outcomes within GPNs as suppliers balance higher quality with lower cost. For example, if economic upgrading requires high and consistent quality standards that are best provided by a stable, skilled, and formalized labor force, then economic and social upgrading may be positively correlated, especially when they increase worker productivity. This is particularly true of process upgrading, which refers to improved efficiency of the production process, and is therefore closely linked to an efficient use of labor as a human resource. At the same time, pressures to reduce costs and increase flexibility might lead employers to combine economic upgrading with social downgrading (for example, by outsourcing employment to an exploitative labor contractor), although this raises questions about commercial sustainability if quality is to be assured.

Rossi's (2011) case study of GPN garment factories in Morocco led by fast-fashion buyers shows that functional upgrading brings about social upgrading and downgrading simultaneously, for regular and irregular workers, respectively. On the one hand, factories supplying a finished product and overseeing packaging, storage, and logistics for their buyers offer stable contracts and better social protection to their high-skilled workers to ensure a continuous relationship as well as full compliance with buyers' codes of conduct. On the other hand, in order to be able to respond quickly to buyers' frequently changing orders and to operate on short lead times, they simultaneously employ irregular workers on casual contracts, especially in the final segments of the production chain (such as packaging and loading), often imposing excessive overtime as well as discriminating against them on the basis of wages and treatment (Rossi, 2011).

To maintain or advance their position in GPNs, suppliers have to engage in a balancing act between maximizing quality (to meet buyers' standards) and minimizing costs/prices (to remain competitive to buyers). This has important implications for labor and the potential for social upgrading. In response to commercial pressures, suppliers' labor strategies can take a 'low road' involving economic and social downgrading, a 'high road' involving economic and social upgrading, or a mixed approach (see Milberg and Winckler, 2011). Those taking a low-road approach, based on worsening labor conditions, risk losing out on quality. Those taking a high-road approach, by improving wages and labor conditions, risk losing out on price competitiveness. Many producers, therefore, adopt a mixed approach of high-quality and low-cost employment which facilitates both standards and cost flexibility. This is reflected in the simultaneous use of regular and irregular workers on any given site.

Analyzing economic and social upgrading trajectories involves understanding that economic upgrading is not always the most appropriate strategy for long-term sustainability. Such strategic decision-making depends largely on the characteristics of the actors. One identified path of upgrading from integrated or 'full-package' production activities—also known as original equipment manufacturing (OEM)—to original design manufacturing (ODM) and original brand name manufacturing (OBM) has been very beneficial for some firms in GPNs, including a number of East Asian apparel companies (Gereffi, 1999). However, it cannot work for everyone because risk and competition are much higher in the more advanced segments of GPNs. Some firms choose to remain in their more secure niche of OEM without attempting to upgrade further. For these firms, economic 'downgrading' becomes a business strategy. In the computer industry of Taiwan (China), Acer decided it could upgrade by developing its own brand of computers, and was successful in doing so; its competitor, Mitac, initially opted to pursue an OBM strategy as well, but soon returned to OEM where the profits were lower, but more secure (Gereffi, 1995: 131–132).

Another example of tactical downgrading occurs in the highly competitive South African wine value chain, where some wine makers were shown to prefer a lower position on the price and quality pyramid for wines exported to the European market. Indeed, some strategies of product and functional 'downgrading'—such as selling higher volumes of basic quality or bulk wines rather than premium wines, vertical disintegration by moving away from the high fixed costs of grape growing, and reduced emphasis on premium brands—have enabled firms to maintain stable market shares and margins for mid-range or basic wines, especially during the economic crisis when cost cutting was necessary for survival in some segments of the industry (Ponte and Ewert, 2009). While these strategies have been associated with certain forms of social downgrading, such as reduced lead times and the increased casualization of labor, tactical downgrading in selected areas of the value chain can permit forms of upgrading when economic conditions improve. In short, suppliers in developing economies can adopt mixed strategies of moving up and down the value chain according to domestic and international conditions.

The garment industry in Eastern and Central Europe (ECE) provides an excellent example of how upgrading and downgrading trajectories have been intertwined. In the early 1980s, some of the ECE economies began to carry out outward-processing trade (OPT) for markets in western Europe, primarily with German buyers and contractors. Given their legacy of established industrialization, the emphasis on apparel exports might be considered economic downgrading. Within the apparel industry, more advanced economies like Slovakia's were able to move more quickly from OPT to full-package export production, and eventually to ODM and OBM, while less developed economies such as Bulgaria's had far more difficulty moving beyond basic OPT contracting. In the ECE economies, however, it was often easier to develop ODM and OBM upgrading strategies for the domestic retail market, than for the more discriminating fast-fashion markets of western Europe (Pickles et al., 2006; Evgeniev and Gereffi, 2008).

With regard to social upgrading, certain choices might be considered social 'downgrading' for some actors, but not for others. For example, in agriculture the choice to move from a smallholder job to wage employment in a farm might be regarded as an example of social downgrading, due to loss of independence and access to land. However, if the person making this choice is a woman who used to be an unpaid family worker, the move to wage employment can represent an improvement in terms of access to wages. Research on Senegal's horticultural industry found that some small-scale producers were able to comply with European supermarket standards, and that both they and wage workers on large estates received better incomes than small-scale producers unable to enter the supply chains (Maertens and Swinnen, 2009). In order to fully understand economic and social upgrading trajectories, it is important to keep in mind the social context and profile of the different actors involved, which can vary between countries and sectors.

Figure 8.2 illustrates implications for decent work by portraying three possible trajectories. The horizontal axis sets out the different types of work, from small-scale household-based production, through low- and medium-skilled jobs to high-skilled technology- and knowledge-intensive work. The vertical axis represents social upgrading, according to the measurable standards discussed above. Enabling rights are, by their very nature, not quantifiable in a chart of this form. Recognizing the limitations of Figure 8.2, being located below zero (the horizontal axis) in the diagram constitutes a 'decent work deficit' for any given type of work, while being above zero represents levels of 'decent work attainment' for any given type of work: the further above zero, the greater the social upgrading gains achieved.

Figure 8.2 Possible Social Upgrading Trajectories

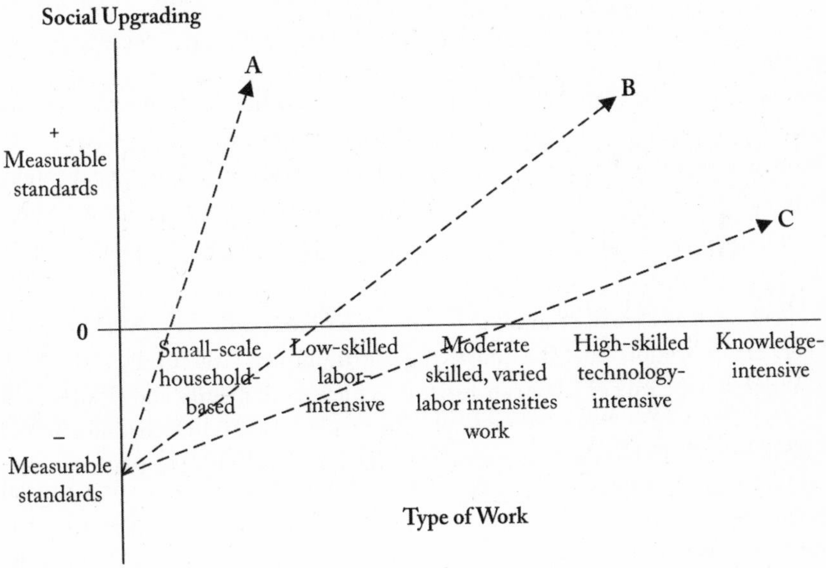

Source: Authors.

The social upgrading trajectories presented in Figure 8.2 depict a range of possible situations:

- *Small-scale worker upgrading* (trajectory A) occurs where workers remain within home-based production (agriculture or manufacturing), but are still able to enjoy improvements in their working conditions. For example, it is possible for improvements to occur for those working in small-scale horticulture in Africa, through the establishment of producer organizations and provision of more secure contracts, better pay and personal health and safety equipment.

- *Labor-intensive upgrading* (trajectory B) occurs where workers move to better types of labor-intensive work where they can also obtain better working conditions. In Bangladesh or Sri Lanka, for example, women who have migrated from subsistence farming to wage employment in the garment industry may be able to obtain jobs in factories that have implemented buyers' codes of labor practice.
- *Higher-skill upgrading* (trajectory C) occurs where workers move towards better types of paid employment associated with progressive social upgrading. For example, workers in India or China who have gained sufficient education and training can move from low-paid, low-skilled work into the IT sector and, at the same time, obtain higher-paid employment in firms where labor standards are improving.

Case study evidence suggests that a shift from lower- to higher-skilled types of work may directly lead to social upgrading, but not always. The challenge, therefore, is how to pursue strategies that will enhance labor standards for all workers in all types of work.

Research to date, including the findings from the garment industry in Morocco presented in this chapter, indicates that the main improvements generated by GPNs in terms of measurable standards and enabling rights tend to be limited to regular workers, i.e., those in stable, usually permanent jobs with a high degree of attachment to their employers. However, extending such improvements to irregular workers, such as casual, migrant and contract workers, poses serious challenges. There are indications that the underlying constraints are structurally embedded, as suppliers use a mix of labor categories to achieve both quality and flexibility of output as required by their buyers: employing regular workers to secure quality and consistency of production and irregular workers to cope with fluctuating orders and downward price/cost pressures.

Concluding Remarks

This chapter has sought to develop a more systematic framework for analyzing economic and social upgrading in GPNs, taking into account the different levels of integration of firms and workers that can exist across industries. Drawing on case studies in a variety of sectors has helped to highlight the issues, but their limitation is that they separately examine either economic or social upgrading/downgrading. Rossi's (2011) case study of the garment industry in Morocco sets out to address this gap by applying a framework for integrated analysis of economic and social upgrading in GPNs. Our approach reveals different economic and social upgrading opportunities, and downgrading risks. By analyzing the relationship between economic and social upgrading/downgrading more systematically, we hope to have laid the foundations for future research that incorporates both firms and workers as productive actors as well as social agents with rights.

An important aim is to better understand how and why economic upgrading does not automatically lead to social upgrading, thereby providing a more informed basis for designing and promoting interventions that will promote both (the so-called 'win-win' scenario). Such interventions—reviewed briefly in Barrientos et al. (2011) and Mayer and Pickles (2010)—can occur at different levels, including: independent trade union representation of workers; company-level initiatives (including buyer and multistakeholder codes of labor practice); government legislation; and multilateral initiatives (such as ILO and OECD guidelines). A key topic for future GPN research is how to design cross-border interventions that yield benefits for poor workers and firms linked through their involvement in the same GPN, but located in different countries.

Notes

1. On this point, see Milberg and Winkler (2011).
2. Interviews and focus group discussions were carried out in a sample of 19 factories in Casablanca, Rabat, Fez, and Tangiers in 2008 (Rossi, 2010, 2011).
3. The fast-fashion segment of the apparel GPN was pioneered by the Spanish brand Zara (which belongs to the Inditex group). The business strategy associated with fast fashion is based on extremely flexible production which follows the latest fashion trends. A garment is produced within two weeks of its design in Spain. Thanks to its proximity to Spain, Morocco has emerged as a key sourcing platform for Zara (Plank et al., 2011).

References

ActionAid International. 2005. *Power Hungry: Six Reasons to Regulate Global Food Corporations.* London: ActionAid. Available at https://www.actionaid.org.uk/_content/documents/%20 power_hungry.pdf.

Bair, Jennifer. 2009. 'Global Commodity Chains: Genealogy and Review.' In *Frontiers of Commodity Chain Research*, edited by Jennifer Bair, 1–34. Stanford, CA: Stanford University Press.

Bair, Jennifer and Gary Gereffi. 2001. 'Local Clusters in Global Chains: The Causes and Consequences of Export Dynamism in Torreon's Blue Jeans Industry.' *World Development* 29(11): 1885–1903.

Barboza, David and Hiroko Tabuchi. 2010. 'Power Grows for Striking Chinese Workers.' *New York Times*, June 8, B1.

Barrientos, Armando and Stephanie Barrientos. 2002. 'Extending Social Protection to Informal Workers in the Horticulture Global Value Chain.' Social Protection Discussion Paper 0216. Washington, DC: World Bank.

Barrientos, Stephanie. 2011. '"Labour Chains": Analysing the Role of Labor Contractors in Global Production Networks.' Brooks World Poverty Institute (BWPI) Working Paper 153. Manchester, UK: University of Manchester.

Barrientos, Stephanie, Catherine Dolan, and Anne Tallontire. 2003. 'A Gendered Value Chain Approach to Codes of Conduct in African Horticulture.' *World Development* 31(9): 1511–1526.

Barrientos, Stephanie and Andrienetta Kritzinger. 2004. 'Squaring the Circle: Global Production and the Informalization of Work in South African Fruit Exports.' *Journal of International Development* 16(1): 81–92.

Barrientos, Stephanie, Frederick Mayer, John Pickles, and Anne Posthuma. 2011. 'Decent Work in Global Production Networks: Framing the Policy Debate.' *International Labour Review* 150(3–4): 299–317.

Barrientos, Stephanie and Sally Smith. 2007. 'Do Workers Benefit from Ethical Trade? Assessing Codes of Labor Practice in Global Production Systems.' *Third World Quarterly* 28(4): 713–729.

Brown, Drusilla K. 2007. 'Globalization and Employment Conditions Study.' Social Protection Discussion Paper 0708. Washington, DC: World Bank.

CAFOD (Catholic Agency for Overseas Development). 2004. 'Clean Up Your Computer: Working Conditions in the Electronics Sector.' London: CAFOD. Available at http://www.cafod.org.uk/var/storage/original/application/phpYyhizc.pdf.

Carrillo, Jorge. 1998. 'Third-generation Maquiladoras? The Delphi-General Motors Case.' *Journal of Borderlands Studies* 13(1): 79–97.

CIVIDEP-India/SOMO. 2009. 'Corporate Geography, Labor Conditions and Environmental Standards in the Mobile Phone Manufacturing Industry in India.' Amsterdam, SOMO – Centre for Research on Multinational Corporations. Available at http://cividep.org/resources/reports.

Clean Clothes Campaign. 2009. 'Cashing In: Giant Retailers, Purchasing Practices, and Working Conditions in the Garment Industry.' Available at http://cleanclothes.org/resources/ccc/working-conditions/cashing-in.

Coe, Neil and David C. Jordhus-Lier. 2011. 'Constrained Agency? Re-evaluating the Geographies of Labour.' *Progress in Human Geography* 35(2): 211–233.

Collins, Jane Lou. 2003. *Threads: Gender, Labor and Power in the Global Apparel Industry.* Chicago, IL: Chicago University Press.

Cumbers, Andy, Corinne Nativel, and Paul Routledge. 2008. 'Labour Agency and Union Positionalities in Global Production Networks.' *Journal of Economic Geography* 8(3): 369–387.

Dolan, Catherine S. and John Humphrey. 2000. 'Governance and Trade in Fresh Vegetables: The Impact of UK Supermarkets on the African Horticulture Industry.' *Journal of Development Studies* 37(2): 147–176.

———. 2004. 'Changing Governance Patterns in the Trade in Fresh Vegetables between Africa and the United Kingdom.' *Environment and Planning A* 36(3): 491–509.

Elliott, Kimberly A. and Richard B. Freeman. 2003. 'The Role Global Labor Standards Could Play in Addressing Basic Needs.' In *Global Inequalities at Work: Work's Impact on the Health of Individuals, Families, and Societies,* edited by Jody Heymann, 229–327. New York: Oxford University Press.

Elson, Diane and Ruth Pearson. 1981. 'Nimble Fingers Make Cheap Workers: An Analysis of Women's Employment in Third World Export Manufacturing.' *Feminist Review* 7(1): 87–107.

ETI (Ethical Trading Initiative). 2005. 'ETI Smallholder Guidelines: Recommendations for Working with Smallholders.' London: ETI. Available at http://www.ethicaltrade.org/resources/key-eti-resources/eti-smallholder-guidelines-eng.

Evgeniev, Evgeni and Gary Gereffi. 2008. 'Textile and Apparel Firms in Turkey and Bulgaria: Exports, Local Upgrading and Dependency.' *Economic Studies* 17(3): 148–179.

Feenstra, Robert C. and Gary G. Hamilton. 2006. *Emergent Economies, Divergent Paths: Economic Organization and International Trade in South Korea and Taiwan.* New York: Cambridge University Press.

Gereffi, Gary. 1994. 'The Organization of Buyer-driven Global Commodity Chains: How US Retailers Shape Overseas Production Networks.' In *Commodity Chains and Global Capitalism*, edited by Gary Gereffi and Miguel Korzeniewicz, 95–122. Westport, CT: Praeger.

————. 1995. 'Global Production Systems and Third World Development.' In *Global Change, Regional Response: The New International Context of Development*, edited by Barbara Stallings, 100–142. New York: Cambridge University Press.

————. 1999. 'International Trade and Industrial Upgrading in the Apparel Commodity Chain.' *Journal of International Economics* 48(1): 37–70.

————. 2005. 'The Global Economy: Organization, Governance and Development.' In *Handbook of Economic Sociology*, 2nd edition, edited by Neil J. Smelser and Richard Swedberg, 160–182. Princeton, NJ: Princeton University Press and Russell Sage Foundation.

————. 2006. *The New Offshoring of Jobs and Global Development.* Geneva: ILO.

————. 2009. 'Development Models and Industrial Upgrading in China and Mexico.' *European Sociological Review* 25(1): 37–51.

Gereffi, Gary and Karina Fernandez-Stark. 2010. 'The Offshore Services Value Chain: Developing Countries and the Crisis.' World Bank Policy Research Working Paper 5262. Washington, DC: World Bank. Available at http://go.worldbank.org/K28XW86T40.

Gereffi, Gary and Esra Güler. 2008. 'Opportunities and Challenges of Participation in Global Production Networks for Decent Work: Evidence from Low- and High-Tech Industries in India and China'. Revised Version of Paper presented at the ILO workshop held in Bangalore, November 18–20, 2007.

————. 2010. 'Global Production Networks and Decent Work in India and China: Evidence from the Apparel, Automotive and Information Technology Industries. In *Labor in Global Production Networks in India*, edited by Anne Posthuma and Dev Nathan, 103–126. New Delhi: Oxford University Press.

Gereffi, Gary, John Humphrey, and Timothy J. Sturgeon. 2005. 'The Governance of Global Value Chains.' *Review of International Political Economy* 12(1): 78–104.

Gereffi, Gary and Raphael Kaplinsky, eds. 2001. *The Value of Value Chains: Spreading the Gains from Globalisation.* Special Issue of the *IDS Bulletin* 32(3).

Hale, Angela and Jane Wills, eds. 2005. *Threads of Labour.* Oxford: Blackwell.

Hamilton, Gary and Gary Gereffi. 2009. 'Global Commodity Chains, Market Makers, and the Rise of Demand-responsive Economies.' In *Frontiers of Commodity Chain Research*, edited by Jennifer Bair, 136–161. Stanford, CA: Stanford University Press.

Henderson, Jeffrey, Peter Dicken, Martin Hess, Neil Coe, and Henry Wai-chung Yeung. 2002. 'Global Production Networks and the Analysis of Economic Development.' *Review of International Political Economy* 9(3): 436–464.

Hess, Martin and Henry Wai-chung Yeung. 2006. 'Whither Production Networks in Economic Geography? Past, Present and Future.' *Environment and Planning A* 38(7): 1193–1204.

ILO (International Labour Organization). 1999. 'Decent Work.' Report of the Director-General to the 89th Session of the International Labour Conference, Geneva.

Insight Investment/Acona. 2004. 'Buying Your Way into Trouble? The Challenge of Responsible Supply Chain Management.' London. Available at http://www.acona.co.uk/reports/Buying+your+way+into+trouble.pdf.

Knorringa, Peter and Lee J. Pegler. 2006. 'Globalisation, Firm Upgrading and Impacts on Labour.' *Tijdschrift voor Economische en Sociale Geografie* 97(5): 470–479.

Kuptsch, Christiane, ed. 2006. *Merchants of Labour*. Geneva: International Institute for Labour Studies.

Lee, Joonkoo. 2010. 'Global Commodity Chains and Global Value Chains.' In *The International Studies Encyclopedia*, edited by Robert A. Denemark, 2987–3006. Oxford: Wiley-Blackwell.

Locke, Richard, Thomas Kochan, Monica Romis, and Fei Qin. 2007. 'Beyond Corporate Codes of Conduct: Work Organization and Labor Standards at Nike's Suppliers.' *International Labour Review* 146(1–2): 21–40.

Maertens, Miet and Joe Swinnen. 2009. 'Trade, Standards and Poverty: Evidence from Senegal.' *World Development.* 37(1): 161–178.

Martin, Philip. 2006. 'Regulating Private Recruiters: The Core Issues.' In *Merchants of Labour*, edited by Christiane Kuptsch, 13–25. Geneva: International Institute for Labour Studies.

Mayer, Frederick W. and John Pickles. 2010. 'Re-embedding Governance: Global Apparel Value Chains and Decent Work.' *Capturing the Gains* Working Paper 2010/1. Available at http://www.capturingthegains.org/pdf/ctg-wp-2010-01.pdf.

McCormick, Dorothy and Hubert Schmitz. 2002. *Manual for Value Chain Research on Homeworkers in the Garment Industry*. Brighton, UK: Institute of Development Studies, University of Sussex.

Milberg, William and Deborah Winkler. 2011. 'Economic and Social Upgrading in Global Value Chains: Problems of Theory and Measurement.' *International Labour Review* 150(3–4): 341–365.

Miller, Doug, Simon Turner, and Tom Grinter. 2011. 'Back to the Future? A Critical Reflection on Neil Kearney's Mature Systems of Industrial Relations Perspective on the Governance of Outsourced Apparel Supply Chains.' *Capturing the Gains* Working Paper 2011/08. Manchester, UK: University of Manchester. Available at http://www.capturingthegains.org/pdf/ctg-wp-2011-08.pdf.

Oxfam International. 2010. 'Better Jobs in Better Supply Chains.' Briefings for Business, 5. Oxford: Oxfam. Available at http://www.oxfam.org/sites/www.oxfam.org/files/b4b-better-jobsbetter-supply-chains.pdf.

Pegler, Lee J. and Peter Knorringa. 2007. 'Integrating Labor Issues in Global Value Chain Analysis: Exploring Implications for Labor Research and Unions'. In *Trade Union Responses to Globalisation: A Review by the Global Unions Research Network*, edited by Verena Schmidt, 35–51. Geneva: ILO.

Pickles, John, Adrian Smith, Milan Bucek, Poli Roukova, and Robert Begg. 2006. 'Upgrading, Changing Competitive Pressures, and Diverse Practices in the East and Central European Apparel Industry.' *Environment and Planning A* 38(12): 2305–2324.

Plank, Leonhard, Arianna Rossi, and Cornelia Staritz. 2011. 'Workers and Social Upgrading in "Fast Fashion": The Case of the Apparel Industry in Morocco and Romania.' Paper presented at the 'Better Work Research Conference – Workers, Businesses and Government: Understanding Labour Compliance in Global Supply Chains.' Washington, DC, 26–28 October.

Ponte, Stefano and Joachim Ewert. 2009. 'Which Way is "Up" in Upgrading: Trajectories of Change in the Value Chain for South African Wine.' *World Development* 37(10): 1637–1650.

Raworth, Kate. 2004. *Trading Away our Rights: Women Working in Global Supply Chains.* Oxford: Oxfam.

Raworth, Kate and Thalia Kidder. 2009. 'Mimicking 'Lean' in Global Value Chains: It's the Workers Who Get Leaned On.' In *Frontiers of Commodity Chain Research*, edited by Jennifer Bair, 165–189. Stanford, CA: Stanford University Press.

Rogaly, Ben. 2008. 'Intensification of Workplace Regimes in British Horticulture: The Role of Migrant Workers.' *Population, Space and Place* 14(6): 497–510.

Rossi, Arianna. 2010. 'The Impact of the Fibre Citoyenne Label on the Moroccan Garment Industry and its Workers'. Paper presented at the Conference on 'Social Labelling in the Global Fashion Industry', University of Northumbria, Newcastle, September 1–3.

————. 2011. 'Economic and Social Upgrading in Global Production Networks: The Case of the Garment Industry in Morocco.' DPhil Dissertation, Institute of Development Studies, University of Sussex, Brighton.

SACOM (Students and Scholars Against Corporate Misbehaviour). 2010. 'Workers as Machines: Military Management in Foxconn.' Hong Kong: SACOM. Available at http:// sacom.hk/archives/740.

Sen, Amartya. 1999. *Development as Freedom*. Oxford: Oxford University Press.

————. 2000. 'Work and Rights.' *International Labour Review* 139(2): 119–128.

Smith, Sally, Diana Auret, Stephanie Barrientos, Catherine Dolan, Karin Kleinbooi, Chosani Njobvu, Maggie Opondo, and Anne Tallontire. 2004. 'Ethical Trade in African Horticulture: Gender, Rights and Participation.' IDS Working Paper 223. Brighton, UK: Institute of Development Studies, University of Sussex.

Staritz, Cornelia, Gary Gereffi, Olivier Cattaneo, eds. 2011. 'Special Issue: Shifting End Markets and Upgrading Prospects in Global Value Chains.' *International Journal of Technological Learning, Innovation and Development* 4(1–3).

Sturgeon, Timothy J. and Richard K. Lester. 2004. 'The New Global Supply Base: New Challenges for Local Suppliers in East Asia.' In *Global Production Networking and Technological Change in East Asia*, edited by Shahid Yusuf, M. Anjum Altaf, and Kaoru Nabeshima, 35–87. Washington, DC: World Bank and Oxford University Press.

Theron, Jan and Shane Godfrey. 2000. 'Protecting Workers on the Periphery'. Cape Town: Institute of Development and Labour Law, University of Cape Town.

Theron, Jan, Shane Godfrey, Peter Lewis, and Mimi Pienaar. 2004. Labour Broking and Temporary Employment Services: A Report on Trends and Policy Implications of the Rise in Triangular Employment Arrangements. Labour and Enterprise Project, Institute of Development and labour Law, University of Cape Town.

Wilde, Joseph and Esther de Hann, 2006. The High Cost of Calling: Critical Issues in the Mobile Phone Industry. Amsterdam: SOMO – Centre for Research on Multinational Corporations. Available at http://somo.nl/html/paginas/pdf/High_Cost_of_Calling_ nov_2006_ EN.pdf.

Zeng, Douglas Zhihua, ed. 2010. *Building Engines for Growth and Competitiveness in China: Experience with Special Economic Zones and Industrial Clusters.* Washington, DC: World Bank.

Regulation and Economic Globalization
Prospects and Limits of Private Governance

Frederick Mayer and Gary Gereffi

Introduction

The last two decades have witnessed a remarkable burst of innovation in 'private governance', i.e., non-governmental institutions that 'govern—that is they enable and constrain—a broad range of economic activities in the world economy'.[1] These institutions serve functions that have historically been the task of governments, most notably that of regulating the negative externalities of economic activity.[2] Private governance takes many forms: standards governing a vast array of environmental, labor, health, product safety, and other matters; codes of conduct promulgated by corporations, industry associations, and non-governmental organizations (NGOs); labels that rely on consumer demand for 'green' and 'fair trade' products; and even self-regulation by corporations under the banner of corporate social responsibility (CSR).[3]

The move towards private governance is best seen as a response to societal pressures spawned by economic globalization and by the inadequacy of public governance institutions in addressing them. As firms, production networks, and markets transcended national boundaries, public (governmental) systems of economic governance built on the unit of the nation-state proved inadequate for regulating an increasingly fragmented and footloose global economy. In the language of Polanyi, markets became 'dis-embedded' from societal and state institutions (Polanyi, 1944. See also Evans, 1985; Ruggie, 1982). Logically, economic globalization demands global regulation, but at the international level regulatory standards are generally weak and there is little capacity to enforce them. In the developing world, where production is increasingly concentrated, many states lack the capacities of law, monitoring, and enforcement needed to regulate industry, even when they have strongly worded legislation on the books. The failure of public governance institutions to keep pace with economic globalization has, therefore, created a global 'governance deficit'.[4]

As Polanyi would predict, workers, environmentalists, human rights activists, and others in civil society have mobilized to demand new forms of governance. Part of this response focused on attempting to alter public policies—i.e., pushing back against neoliberal economic prescriptions or demanding that market opening be accompanied by regulatory measures. Frustrated with the perceived inability of governmental institutions to respond to the governance challenge, however, many social activists and labor groups also turned to pressure campaigns targeted at corporations and to other strategies designed to use market pressure to regulate the behavior of producers.

That such developments have had an impact is not in question. Fair Trade coffee, 'sweatshop free' collegiate apparel, and Forest Stewardship Council-certified lumber have all altered specific production practices. Even Walmart, the poster child of corporate malfeasance in the eyes of many activists, is now beginning to respond to social pressures for reform by stocking energy-efficient light bulbs, using environment-friendly packing materials, and so on (Gereffi and Christian, 2009). But the questions are: How far will this go? To what extent can private governance address the global governance deficit? Will private governance require complementary forms of public regulation, and where might this public regulation come from?

Much is happening, but there is no good overall assessment of whether these myriad private governance initiatives are anywhere close to sufficient to address the full range of labor, environmental, and other social concerns. Most research to date has been largely descriptive and anecdotal. Clearly, more is needed if we are to understand the impact of private regulatory governance. A necessary first step is to develop clearer theoretical propositions about the conditions under which various forms of private government are likely to succeed and, just as importantly, where they are unlikely to do so.

In this chapter, we offer six hypotheses about the conditions under which private governance is most likely to arise and to be effective, as well as for thinking about the interaction between private and public governance. Before turning to those hypotheses, it is necessary to consider the forces that underlie the move towards private governance, particularly those changes in the global economy that both created demand for new governance and also enabled its supply. Although we are largely concerned in this chapter with private governance, public and private governance interact. Indeed, it was a failure of public governance that led private modes of governance to emerge and proliferate. Ultimately, as we will argue, the limits of purely private governance will likely spur renewed attention to public governance and to new forms of public and private governance interaction.

The Demand for Governance: Economic Globalization and the Public Governance Deficit

Private governance arose in particular historical circumstances. In the world before globalization, although there was economic interdependence among advanced industrial countries (Keohane and Nye, 1977), large regions of the globe were not connected to the global market. In the mid-1980s, the Soviet Union, China, and Eastern and Central Europe still had centrally planned economies; high levels of protection and state ownership characterized most of Latin America; and boycotts isolated South Africa while the rest of sub-Saharan Africa barely registered. The last 25 years have witnessed a dramatic restructuring of economic activity around the globe, in large part because of changes in the policy environment. The collapse of communism in Europe and its transformation in China, the abandonment of import-substitution policies in Latin America and elsewhere (driven in no small measure by the International Monetary Fund (IMF)), and the expansion and deepening of the international trading rules in the World Trade Organization (WTO) and in ever more numerous regional and bilateral agreements, dramatically transformed the environment for global commerce.

The global economy that has emerged since the 1980s has two distinctive features with profound implications for public governance. First, a substantial portion of global manufacturing production—and increasingly of services as well—has shifted from the developed to the developing world (Dicken, 2007). Once largely outside the global production system, China, India, Brazil, Mexico, South Africa, and other big developing countries are now host to a very significant and rapidly growing portion of international manufacturing output. By 2000, half of all manufacturing production was in the developing world, and 60% of exports from developing countries to the industrialized world were no longer raw materials but manufactured goods (Held and McGrew, 2002).

Second, and equally important for governance, the organization of global production has changed dramatically. Historically, the vast majority of manufacturing production was carried out either by national companies and their suppliers within single countries or by multinational corporations (MNCs) based in developed economies that typically owned all or most of their foreign factories (Kaplinsky, 2005; Ocampo, 2010: 1–12). Today, the global economy is increasingly organized around international production networks in which large lead firms, often located in developed economies, control to a significant extent the production of suppliers, who are typically smaller and likely to be located in developing countries (Dicken, 2007). Variously referred to as global commodity chains (Bair, 2009), global value chains (Gereffi and Kaplinsky, 2001), and global production networks (Henderson et al., 2002), this new form of international industrial organization has allowed for production to be coordinated on transnational scales but with far greater flexibility than the older MNC model of direct ownership (Gereffi, 2005).

Key to understanding the implications of global production systems is the role of lead firms in these networks and chains. Producer-driven chains dominate capital- and technology-intensive industries such as automobiles, aircraft, and computers. Buyer-driven chains have become the new model of global sourcing in labor-intensive manufacturing industries like apparel, footwear, and toys, a development led by large US retailers, marketers, and 'manufacturers without factories' (Gereffi, 1999; Gereffi and Korzeniewicz, 1994). More recent studies point to the emergence of new drivers, such as large supermarkets and concentrated food processors (Dolan and Humphrey, 2004; Gereffi et al., 2009; Fuchs and Kalfagianni, 2010). In all of these cases, lead firms enjoy some measure of market power over suppliers and some ability, therefore, to affect their behavior.

Changes in the global economy have profound implications for public and private governance. On the one hand, they undermine public governance. When production largely involved national firms or vertically integrated MNCs based in developed countries, regulation—whether labor, environmental, health, or other—was undertaken by individual nation-states (roughly coordinated in a system characterized as 'embedded liberalism') (Ruggie, 1982). The shift to offshore outsourcing over the past several decades meant that much of global production was now beyond the reach of national governance institutions in the advanced industrial states, and extended beyond the international system of embedded liberalism that was largely confined to the industrialized world. Governments in those developing countries where production increasingly took place lacked the ability, and to some extent the will, to regulate production in their jurisdictions. The formerly centralized economies of China and Eastern Europe had no tradition of market governance, the newly opened economies of Latin America had little regulatory capacity, and most of sub-Saharan Africa had weak public governance of any form.

Moreover, initially at least, the interests of most developing countries lay in attracting investment, which meant that they tended to give relatively short shrift to regulatory concerns, and at the international level, public regulation remained very weak. International organizations such as the International Labor Organization (ILO), the United Nations Environmental Program (UNEP), and the United Nations Development Program (UNDP) have extremely limited powers, and are certainly less well developed than are market-facilitative organizations such as the WTO, the IMF, and the World Intellectual Property Organization (WIPO). Indeed, the relative strength of these facilitative forms of international public governance may well have inhibited certain forms of regulation and exacerbated unequal income distribution at the global level (Ocampo, 2010).

Changes in the international economy, therefore, can be seen as creating a vacuum or deficit of public regulation. But it is important to recognize that new patterns of industrial organization, notably the concentration of power in lead firms within global production networks, also created possibilities for private governance.

Social Responses and the Rise of Private Governance

As Polanyi would predict, the disembedding of markets from governance provoked a social response. Initially, the targets of social activism were international organizations associated with globalization—the IMF, the World Bank, and the WTO—but progress from the standpoint of the activists was extremely limited.[5] Frustrated by the lack of governmental response, many social activists began to shift to direct pressure on corporations to change their behavior (Vogel, 2010). Beginning in the early 1990s, demand for corporate codes of conduct, perhaps the most visible and widespread form of private governance, became the opening wedge in a 15-year campaign to bring some elements of social responsibility to international subcontracting networks (Gereffi et al., 2001). The genius of this approach was in recognizing that the industrial governance structures established by lead firms to manage their global supply chains could also be leveraged to achieve social and environmental objectives.

Many innovations in private governance began in the apparel sector, which was a forerunner of globalization in other manufacturing industries because of its labor-intensive production and relatively low barriers to entry. Levi Strauss, the American jeans maker, was one of the first MNCs to tout its own corporate code of conduct in 1991, using provisions against employing forced labor and child labor to justify its unwillingness to source from China (unlike many of its competitors, who already were making clothes there). Other multinationals in the apparel industry such as Liz Claiborne, Nike, Reebok, and The Gap soon followed suit, but these first-party codes had little external credibility because individual firms proclaimed and monitored their own rules.[6] While first-party codes became commonplace in certain industries, second-party codes of conduct were developed by trade associations to apply to their industry members (such as Responsible Care in the chemical industry) (Gereffi et al., 2001).

Second-party codes were soon followed by third-party certification arrangements, whereby an external group (often an NGO) monitored provisions adopted by particular firms or industries. While many argued that the early codes had no teeth and built-in conflicts of interest, these newer codes of conduct had stricter provisions and, most importantly, an independent monitoring mechanism that was not controlled by the firms whose behavior was being scrutinized (Kolk and van Tulder, 2004; Locke et al., 2007; Locke and Romis, 2007). This allowed domestic and international NGOs to play a significant role not only in detecting exploitative labor practices in global supply chains, but also to use well-coordinated campaigns to force leading multinationals with highly visible brands, such as Nike, Disney, and Starbucks, to improve working conditions in their global network of suppliers and to participate in equity-oriented programs like the Fair Trade movement (Esbenshade, 2004; Klein, 2000).

By the mid-2000s, a large number of multinational firms were publishing annual Corporate Social Responsibility reports (for example, Gap Inc., 2004) Furthermore, under pressure from a wide range of NGOs and labor groups, private governance regimes were becoming more pervasive: industry-wide codes of conduct proliferated and became more transparent (Kolk and van Tulder, 2005). The monitoring reports and complete lists of suppliers for well-known brands like Nike were made public, and instead of abandoning suppliers that violated the corporate codes, MNCs were pressured to get domestic suppliers to comply with the global codes.

Private governance has continued to evolve. The list of agricultural, craft, and other products in the Fair Trade line is expanding, as are organic and green-labeled goods. Examples abound of various types of socially responsible corporate practices. McDonald's recently tightened its procurement guidelines in response to the clear-cutting practices of Amazon soy producers and cattle ranchers who supplied the industry. Cadbury champions its commitment to the communities that grow its cocoa. Walmart has mandated energy savings throughout its supply chain. And in many sectors there are now jointly agreed upon codes and standards for such things as greenhouse gas emissions accounting (Green, 2010), sustainable timbering practices (Bartley, 2010), labor practices in apparel and footwear (Gereffi et al., 2001), electrical product safety standards (Büthe, 2010b), and many others.

Notwithstanding the impressive dynamism of private governance, however, it remains far from filling the public governance vacuum. For one thing, there is great variation in coverage. In some well-known sectors, private governance appears reasonably robust—apparel, for example—but even within that sector much production remains outside the private governance regime. Moreover, even when there are rules and standards in place, there is often less than meets the eye. The existence of a code does not guarantee that it will be observed or enforced.

Although there is a large and growing literature describing trends in private governance, to date there have been few attempts to develop propositions that would enable us both to explain the observed pattern of private regulation, and to predict its likely trajectory. Notable exceptions are Vogel (2008) and Mattli and Woods (2009a, 2009b), whose conceptualization of private governance as arising from the interplay of demand and supply factors provides a very useful starting point for further theorizing. Central to their thinking, and ours, is the interaction between private and public governance. Developments in each realm have implications for the other. Indeed, as Whytock (2010) convincingly demonstrates, it is often impossible to disentangle the two.

Six Hypotheses

Based on our review of the extant literature and our ongoing research on numerous supply chains, as well as our assessment of the evolving dynamic between public and private governance, we propose six hypotheses about when and where private governance is most likely to succeed. The first four hypotheses can be thought of as predicting the domain in which we expect to see the most established and effective forms of private governance. Hypotheses five and six deal more explicitly with the relationship between public and private governance and are more forward looking. Our primary objective in this chapter is the development of a coherent set of hypotheses rather than theory testing *per se*. Nevertheless, for each of our hypotheses, we provide not only the theoretical rationale but also offer illustrative examples in support of their plausibility.

Hypothesis 1: The more economic leverage large lead firms have over smaller suppliers in their value chains, the greater is the potential impact and scope of private governance.

The existence of lead-firm leverage magnifies the importance of private governance to smaller firms in its chain, although the impact of this leverage will depend on the specificity of the relationship (as outlined in Hypotheses 2–4 below) rather than the relative size of the actors *per se*. To a great extent, this is a matter of market concentration: firms with large market shares, whether marketers, retailers, or producers, usually have the option to source from many smaller suppliers, each of which may have few options other than doing business with the lead firm. As Fuchs and Kalfagianni (2010) observe in the case of private governance in food retail, 'the dominance of a few corporations fosters their ability to limit the choices available to other actors, specifically suppliers and labor, who desire entry'. Of course, it is possible that even a very large buyer might have little leverage if it is dependent on supply from a small but unique supplier, but this is less common. Given that they have a wider range of alternatives than their suppliers, lead firms tend to have considerable power in their supply chains.

The same leverage that can be used to demand lower prices and better quality from suppliers can also be used to press for better labor practices or greener production methods. This leverage is not simply a function of the lead firm's market share. Influence over supplier behavior may be limited by the relative transparency of practices, for instance. An implication of Auld et al.'s article on technological innovations is that some supplier practices are easier to monitor than others, and should be easier for lead firms to govern (Auld et al., 2010). Moreover, the larger the supplier, the more options it, too, is likely to have (to sell to other retailers or producers, for example), which limits the power a lead firm has in its chain. As Locke has pointed out in the apparel sector, for example, suppliers often have more options and lead firms less power than they might think. 'For most apparel suppliers, individual global brands constitute but a small fraction of their total business. In this context, it is not at all clear that global buyers have the ability/leverage (let alone credibility) to pressure these suppliers' (Locke et al., 2009: 12). It is no accident, therefore, that many of the most prominent cases of private regulatory governance involve very large lead firms with more-or-less captive suppliers. The success of the 'classic' forms of private governance in the apparel industry—codes of conduct adopted by lead firms such as Levi Strauss, Nike, and The Gap and imposed on their suppliers—depended on the power of those lead firms in their global value chains.

More recently, we have seen the adoption of private governance by a broader range of retailers. Walmart is perhaps the best publicized example. In the past few years, Walmart has launched a Sustainability Consortium through which it can use its considerable market power to demand certain environmental improvements by its suppliers (*GreenBiz*, 2010). Global supermarket chains have promoted new private standards for food quality and safety, including product and process specifications with labor and environmental implications (Memodovic and Sheperd, 2009). Many supermarkets have also established their own supply chains in cut flowers, which has created an opening for labor groups to press for better working conditions among suppliers (Dolan and Humphrey, 2004; Hughes, 2000; Reardon and Hopkins, 2006; Riisgaard, 2009; Riisgaard and Hammer, 2011). Powerful lead firms have also been important in pushing the adoption of new industry standards promoted by NGOs. For example, the decision by Home Depot and Lowes, the two largest home improvement retailers, to recognize the standards of the Forest Stewardship Council in the mid-1990s, led its major suppliers to adopt them as well (Bartley, 2010; Gereffi et al., 2001).

Hypothesis 2: Private governance is most likely for highly branded products and firms.

When demand for a product is less a function of observable utility than of constructed brand identity, firms are more vulnerable to societal pressure. (Also, of course, being a highly recognized brand makes a firm an easily identifiable target for groups demanding regulation; a point to which we will return with our next hypothesis.) It is for this reason that many of the first lead firms to promote private governance regimes in their value chains were highly visible consumer brands such as Nike and Starbucks, whose market niche depends more on marketing than on the intrinsic qualities of their product. A comparison with other large lead firms, less vulnerable to attack on their brand, is instructive. For example, ADM and Cargill have enormous leverage in their agricultural chains, but because they have almost no brand identity with consumers, they are less vulnerable to societal pressure (Gereffi and Christian, 2010). Similarly, Flextronics—a very large supplier in the electronics industry—shapes supplier standards in its chains, but it faces little social pressure to drive private governance (Sturgeon and Lester, 2004).

Increasingly, firms who once competed solely on price and product have begun to see themselves as vulnerable as well. Walmart, for example, historically used its considerable power in its supply chains primarily to drive prices down, sometimes to the detriment of workers and the environment. But in the last few years, even Walmart has concluded that it needs to protect its reputation from social critiques (Gereffi and Christian, 2009). Large firms in every sector are now taking steps to reduce risks to their brand. McDonald's, for example, faced with criticism about damage to Brazilian rainforests from clear-cutting for feed grains and cattle ranches, has compelled its suppliers to participate in a 'Sustainable Cattle Working Group' (Downie, 2007; McDonald's Corporation, 2009: 18).

Defensive considerations appear to have been the biggest factor in these cases, but firms may also be pro-active with respect to their brand identity. So far, this appears to be most common with smaller niche firms. For instance, the Body Shop promotes itself as a socially responsible company, featuring its 'Values and Campaigns' prominently on its webpage, and Patagonia's 'Footprint Chronicles' portray a positive image in terms of environmental sustainability in the making and sourcing of its products. Social labeling is a special case in which products are differentiated by their impact on workers or the environment, but follows a very similar logic. The increase in consumer demand for goods produced in socially responsible ways has made this new form of branding possible, as illustrated by the now-established market for 'fair trade' coffee, Forest Stewardship Council certified lumber, and the like.

It is important to recognize how hypotheses 1 and 2 interact. In chains with both powerful lead firm drivers and high brand vulnerability, we would expect, and indeed see, the greatest advances in private governance. The success of the classic forms of private governance in the apparel industry—codes of conduct adopted by lead firms such as Levi Strauss, Nike, and The Gap and imposed on their suppliers—depended on the market power of those lead firms in their global value chains, as well as these lead firms' vulnerability that resulted from being a highly recognized brand.

It is also useful to distinguish between firm-specific standards and those that are jointly adopted by several firms in the same sector in order to see how the former might evolve into the latter. In the apparel sector, once a critical mass of lead firms found it in their individual interests to adopt private codes, those firms had a collective interest in convergence on common standards—in part to minimize the compliance costs of suppliers who sold into more than one chain and in part because common standards allowed greater monitoring efficiency. The logic of this progression is very similar to that suggested by Büthe (2010a, 2010b) for the rise of the International Electrotechnical Commission and by Green (2010) in her discussion of the Greenhouse Gas Protocol, both instances in which industry-wide standards became focal points for coordinating the shared interests of firms in some common approach. Furthermore, once a common standard is established, first movers have a strong stake in persuading other competitors to adopt the standard, a dynamic that can also be observed in the apparel case.

Hypothesis 3: Effective private governance is most likely in the face of effective societal pressure, which, in turn, depends on the relative ease of mobilizing collective action.

Implicit in both Hypothesis 1 and Hypothesis 2 is the assumption that the ultimate driver of private governance is some form of external social pressure. Social pressure is necessary both in demanding new institutions of private governance—codes of conduct, for example—and, equally importantly, for ensuring that such regulations are actually observed (Vogel, 2010). Bartley's analysis of differences in the on-the-ground effectiveness of certification regimes for sustainably harvested timber and factory work conditions in Indonesia suggests the importance of sustained national and international pressure from civil society (Bartley, 2010). Such pressure, however, is far from inevitable, depending as it does on collective action, whether by individual citizens or organized groups such as NGOs and labor unions. Even when there is agreement about the desirability of some collective good, such as better labor conditions or environmental protection, to the extent that the accomplishment of that goal requires the coordinated efforts of many and the enjoyment of the good cannot be restricted to those who acted to procure it, the temptation to free ride creates a major obstacle to mobilizing collective action (Olson, 1965).

One determinant of successful collective action is the extent of prior organization relevant to an issue. The existence of environmental organizations and labor unions, for instance, significantly lowers the cost of collective action for their members.[7] When such organizations are present, we would expect to see greater social pressure on those issues on which they focus. Starobin and Weinthal's discussion of kosher food standards demonstrate the way in which existing social structures lower costs of collective action by reducing monitoring costs (Starobin and Weinthal, 2010). A related point made by Auld et al. (2010) is that technology may lower the costs of collective action.

A second factor in determining collective action might be called the inherent dramatic potential of the issue. As Bartley (2010) discusses with respect to the rise of private governance in Indonesia, public controversy regarding forest degradation and workplace conditions in footwear and apparel factories was essential. Drama may be related to the actual magnitude of a problem, but is far from identical to it. Some issues—abuses of children or the death of large marine mammals—are more emotive than others, and carry with them greater potential for both becoming an issue (because they are newsworthy) and spurring individuals to action.

The pattern of successful activism for private governance, as well as its absence when appropriate conditions are not met, appears to bear out our hypothesis. We see most mobilization when there are opportunity structures that lower the cost of cooperation and/or where the issue was successfully dramatized. The case of dolphin-safe tuna fishing methods illustrates the point. The death of dolphins at the hands of tuna fishermen became a cause célèbre in the late 1980s, in no small part because dolphins are such appealing animals. The prior existence of numerous environmental groups with memberships and communication channels, poised to seize upon the issue, also made a significant difference. Activism spawned by outrage over the practice has, over time, led to a 'dolphin safe' labeling regime and to decisions by large food retailers (including Walmart) to adopt the standard for their supply chains. Raising similar levels of awareness among activists and consumers for less easily dramatized practices has proven more difficult. Private governance has made only modest inroads in protecting other less glamorous fish.[8]

The 'anti-sweatshop' movement related to collegiate apparel also demonstrates the importance of drama in mobilizing social pressure. In this case, collective action was necessary on two levels: to organize students at multiple campuses and to coordinate a collective response by the universities. Well-publicized and extreme cases of exploitation provided a rallying point for college students, who were then able to pressure a consortium of universities to license only 'sweatshop free' collegiate apparel (Mandle, 2000).

In the case of activist campaigns, it may not be necessary to actually mount an attack if the threat is sufficiently credible. Regulation results from avoidance of possible activist campaigns targeted at embarrassing disclosures of poor practices. Many forms of private regulation are a form of risk management by skittish executives. The actions taken by McDonald's to address clear cutting of the Amazon forests by suppliers in its chain, for example, looks like a case in which the existence of environmental groups already actively working on deforestation, as well as a latent group of people ready to mobilize, created a very credible threat to McDonald's corporate image.

Before turning to our next hypothesis, it is useful to consider a related problem for collective action, that of failure in the market for information. The problem is that those who would demand accountability by corporations, whether in their role as consumers or as activists, cannot directly observe business practices. Such information is costly to obtain, and because it is a collective good, it is likely to be under-provided (Downs, 1957). Certification, as Starobin and Weinthal explore at some depth, is intended to solve the problem by providing an inexpressive signal, but the effectiveness of certification depends on the credibility of that signal. How, then, to certify the certifiers? In their analysis of kosher-food certification, the key is existing institutions. 'The success of kosher at a global scale derives from its continued reliance on the pre-existing social capital share among these tight-knit communities and the active participation of a vigilant consumer base in ongoing oversight' (Starobin and Weinthal, 2010).

Hypothesis 4: Private governance is most likely to be adopted when commercial interests align with social or environmental concerns.

It should not be surprising that the willingness of firms to adopt private regulatory measures, whether by lead firms driving their suppliers or adoption by the suppliers themselves, will depend in part on the cost of such measures. To the extent that standards can be met without incurring significant costs, or better yet, when they actually are cost-saving, they are much more likely to be adopted. Moreover, such measures will, in the long run, be most sustainable if there is a 'business model' for them, because they establish or protect consumer demand for the brand, hedge against risks of becoming a target of activism, or reduce production costs (Vogel, 2008).

There is some reason to believe that, for instance, improvements in environmental practices—'greening the value chain' in the current parlance—are more likely to be aligned with financial interests of firms than are upgrades in labor conditions. To some extent this may be a function of differences between the cost of compliance for environmental rather than labor provisions. Walmart's recent well-published efforts to replace lights in its stores with LED lighting illustrates the point. These actions are good for the environment, but they are also, in the long run, a cost-saving measure.

To summarize before turning to our last two hypotheses: pressure for private governance should be greatest when there is a powerful lead firm in a stable value chain, when that firm is highly branded and therefore vulnerable to shifts in consumer preferences, when there is potential for mobilizing social pressure, and when private governance is most consistent with commercial interests. These propositions are consistent with Vogel's assessment of the rise and potential for 'civil regulation', particularly his emphasis on the role of societal pressures that create demand for it. And, like Vogel, we distinguish between the existence of rules and their effectiveness. To a greater extent than Vogel, though, we emphasize the implications of industrial structure for the supply of private governance, and the factors that affect collective action on the demand side.

Notwithstanding the successes of private governance that we have been describing, our four hypotheses also suggest the limits to what it can accomplish. A great deal of global production does not meet one or more of our conditions. Much production takes place in chains and networks with no clear drivers. For every highly branded product vulnerable to consumer pressure, there are many unbranded products. And there remain considerable obstacles to collective action needed to mobilize and sustain social pressure on business. Moreover, when private regulation is costly and does not fit a firm's business model, firms are quite capable of resisting. Even in the best of cases, as Locke et al. (2007) have shown, the ability of suppliers to evade costly measures remains quite high (as is, perhaps, the willingness of lead firms to appear to be doing more than they are).

So far, our hypotheses have not addressed directly the relationship between public and private governance, although implicit throughout has been the assumption of a deficit or vacuum of public governance. But the trajectory of private governance cannot be addressed without simultaneously considering the trajectories of public governance. We suggest, therefore, two final hypotheses about the future direction of private governance that reflect more explicitly the interplay between private and public governance. These two hypotheses are somewhat different in character than the first four, in that they seek less to explain the current pattern than to predict the way in which private and public governance might co-evolve in the future.

Hypothesis 5: The more production becomes concentrated in the larger emerging economies, the more we should expect public governance in these countries to strengthen.

A recent World Bank study, *Global Value Chains in a Postcrisis World*, argues that the global crisis of 2008-2009 has not reversed globalization, but rather accelerated two long-term trends in the global economy: the consolidation of global value chains at both country and firm levels, and the growing salience of developing economies in the South as end markets for global production (Cattaneo et al., 2010). The consolidation of production in supply chains opens the door for a renewed emphasis on public governance. In an effort to reduce transaction costs and spread risk, lead firms are promoting rationalization of their global supply chains—with an emphasis on a smaller number of larger, more capable suppliers—in a handful of strategically selected countries. This can be seen in industries as diverse as apparel (Gereffi and Frederick, 2010), automobiles (Sturgeon et al., 2009), and electronics (Sturgeon and Kawakami, 2010; Sturgeon and Lester, 2004). In addition, some lead firms are returning to strategies of vertical integration, a reversal of the efficiency arguments that fostered the outsourcing and specialization of global supply chains in previous decades (Worthen et al., 2009).

As a result of these trends, production is increasingly consolidated a relatively small number of countries, most notably the large emerging economies of China, Brazil, and India. In the apparel industry, for example, China more than doubled its share of global apparel exports from 15.2% to 33.2% between 1995 and 2008; Turkey, Bangladesh, and India, the next three largest developing country apparel exporters, slightly improved their collective global market share from 8.9% to 9.8% between 2000 and 2008, while Mexico fell sharply from 4.4% of global apparel exports in 2000 to 1.4% in 2008 (Gereffi and Frederick, 2010: 8). Similarly, India has become a global leader in offshore services, with a peak 45% market share in 2008 (Gereffi and Fernandez-Stark, 2010: 20). Notwithstanding this growing concentration of production among a number of large emerging economies, most notably China and India, we also see continued outsourcing of production from large emerging economies to other lower-cost countries, such as Vietnam, Cambodia, and Bangladesh, as Chinese and Indian producers seek to climb the value chain to higher value and more skill-intensive activities.

Recall that private governance emerged to fill the void of public governance created by the diffusion of production across multiple governmental jurisdictions. To the extent that we now see consolidation of production in larger suppliers located in a handful of emerging economies, the ability of these governments to exercise control over production practices in their jurisdiction could be enhanced. Moreover, as China, India, Brazil, and other emerging economies grow, standards of living are more likely to rise, and with them societal expectations about labor, environment, health and safety standards (Inglehart, 1981, 2000). Unless actively checked by the state, those expectations may take the form of political pressure on the state to regulate such matters. Demand for greater public governance may also come from firms. This dynamic is evident in apparel value chains, for example, where Nike, The Gap, and other more socially conscious producers have an incentive to support government regulations that force their non-branded competitors to adopt similar practices in their supply chains.

There is growing evidence for a trend towards stronger public regulation in the large emerging economies. Most prominent, perhaps, have been the actions of the Chinese government, largely in response to growing pressure from domestic groups. On the labor front, for example, growing dissatisfaction with labor practices led in 2008 to passage of a new Chinese Contract Labor Law, which strengthened a variety of worker rights and gave greater standing to Chinese labor unions. By creating new contractual rights and a forum for presenting grievances, the Chinese labor law has enabled further activism. According to *The Economist*, by July 2010, more than 280,000 labor disputes had been handled by Chinese courts (*The Economist*, 2010). And in environmental policy, China has made significant strides in strengthening its policies and enforcement capacities.[9]

Similarly, Brazil has been moving in the direction of an increasingly mature public regulatory regime for some time. On labor, the government has pushed for increased formalization of work, improved its labor inspection capabilities, and raised minimum wages, among other policies (de Andrade Baltar et al., 2010). On the environment, as Hochstetler and Keck (2007) document, the rise of environmental activism in Brazil has translated into stronger state policy.

This trend towards greater public governance capacity is not limited to the large emerging economies. Bangladesh, which remains an extremely poor country, has recently adopted stronger labor regulations for its apparel sector, including a very large increase in the minimum wage, largely as a response to pressures from workers groups (*AFP*, 2010). Whether the new regulations will be observed is unclear, but notably, the changes were supported by many of the largest apparel buyers, including Walmart, Tesco, H&M, Zara, Carrefour, The Gap, Metro, J. C. Penney, Marks and Spencer, Kohl's, Levi Strauss, and Tommy Hilfiger, commitments that may give workers and their advocates a vehicle to hold employers accountable (*Just-Style*, 2010).

Hypothesis 6: Stronger public regulation in developing countries will reinforce rather than replace private governance, and will promote multi-stakeholder initiatives involving both public and private actors.

The rise of state governance does not imply the abandonment of private governance for various reasons. First, for the foreseeable future, the global economy will remain characterized by distributed production that spans national borders. National governments, therefore, will continue to face difficulties in regulating actors outside their jurisdictions. Second, states can use private governance to their ends. By relying on the power of lead firms, countries can condition access to their markets on lead-firm participation in monitoring their suppliers rather than rely on direct state regulation. Third, states and international organizations may find it expedient to reinforce certain types of private governance (see, in particular: Vogel, 2005). States can help overcome information market failures by providing information directly or by standardizing labeling practices, for example, as has been the case with organic foods.

Given these considerations, rather than a simple return of the state, we envision the emergence of multi-stakeholder governance in which public and private modes of governance interact and reinforce each other. Synergies between public and private governance are possible, not only at the national level but also internationally. International organizations such as the ILO and the International Finance Corporation are interested in promoting such ventures. For example, the ILO's Better Work program seeks to improve work conditions of textile workers in export-processing zones in Cambodia, Haiti, Jordan, Lesotho, and Vietnam, through a multi-stakeholder approach involving NGOs, labor groups, firms, and national governments (Lukas et al., 2010). And the United Nations Global Compact among firms, NGOs, and other entities in the United Nations system, has helped to give impetus to corporate social responsibility (Ruggie, 2002).

Bringing the State Back In: The Evolving Pattern of Public and Private Governance

Looking to the future, it is reasonable to expect some maturation of private governance regimes. Notwithstanding the impressive momentum of the private governance movement, however, there are significant limits to what we should expect from codes of conduct, corporate self-regulation, social labeling, and other such initiatives. Although there have been comprehensive efforts to extend and evaluate private governance schemes (Locke et al., 2009, 2007; Locke and Romis, 2007), there are also significant limits to what can be achieved by any non-governmental regime. In the highly competitive global economic environment, unless there is a sustainable competitive advantage associated with socially responsible behavior, it will be hard to sustain meaningful corporate self-regulation (Orsato, 2009). Most of the progress in this arena to date has come as a response to (or in anticipation of) social pressure. But sustaining social pressure poses a significant collective action problem for labor, environmental, and other social activists.

In addition to the theoretical reasons for limited expectations, the empirical record should also give pause to private governance enthusiasts. For example, those who have looked more closely at the actual effectiveness of codes and other forms of corporate social responsibility generally come away somewhat skeptical (Locke et al., 2009, 2007). Codes adopted by corporations are generally quite vague. Those promulgated by NGOs or international organizations are tougher but rarely complied with (Kolk and van Tulder, 2005). Similarly, effective labeling campaigns are rare and even the most successful have had limited impact to date. Despite the use of Fair Trade coffee as an exemplar of such campaigns, world market penetration of Fair Trade coffee remains very low (by one estimate just 1% in 2008 (Pay, 2009)) and the world's largest roasters remain resistant to the campaign (TransFair USA, 2005).

In our view, unless private governance is supplemented and reinforced by public institutions of governance, it cannot provide adequate governance capacity for the global economy. Differences of interest among advanced, developing, and least-developed nations, as well as continued resistance by states to limitations on their sovereignty, will likely continue to prevent stronger international rules and enforcement capacity. Greater progress is likely to come from building greater capacity in developing-country governments. As we have discussed, the consolidation of production in the larger emerging economies and the maturation of those societies create both opportunity and demand for greater public governance in those countries. In the end, as Ruggie (2008) and others have argued, international coordination may be less in the form of formal agreement than in an enlarged version of 'embedded liberalism' in which international commerce takes place among countries with comparable systems of national governance.

This shift back to public governance is to be welcomed for several reasons. First, many corporate codes of conduct merely commit corporations and their suppliers to adhere to local law. Obviously, having strong national laws becomes the crucial determinant in the stringency of such CSR regimes. Second, only national governments can enforce these laws. Since the monitoring and enforcement of codes is costly to corporations, which have limited incentive to enforce them, and NGOs have limited monitoring and no enforcement capacity, only governments have sufficient clout to ensure that codes are followed. Third, corporations lack incentives to include workers in the formulation and implementation of codes. Only governments can ensure that workers are adequately represented. Fourth, in more competitive industries, where producers have an incentive to avoid compliance, governments are best positioned to ensure that all producers adhere to common standards.

Moreover, it is not clear that we should want to substitute private governance for public, even if we could do it. In addition to basic questions about the legitimacy of governance systems controlled by institutions not accountable to the public, private governance regimes are frequently driven by Northern interests, i.e., by corporations, non-profits, and consumers in the developed world. Büthe's account of the evolution of the International Electrotechnical Commission, for example, demonstrates that 'the material costs of participation clearly created a bias in favor of commercially successful stakeholders from rich countries' (Büthe, 2010b). Similarly, Fuchs and Kalfagianni note that, in the food sector, the power and legitimacy of retailers as rule setters 'results primarily from the dominant ideational structures in developed countries and the political and economic elites of developing countries' (Fuchs and Kalfagianni, 2010). Although private regulation may be an important element of economic governance, it cannot and should not stand alone.

To a great extent, private governance is a second-best and partial solution to the governance challenge posed by globalization. Because cooperation at the international level has been so difficult, and because national governments in developing countries were initially slow to adapt, the social pressures triggered by globalization have focused more on private governance solutions than they otherwise would. As globalization progresses, particularly as the larger developing country economies mature, it is both likely and desirable that some significant part of the private governance innovations be institutionalized within the national governments of those countries. In the longer run, this would provide more effective, stable, and representative governance for the global economy.

Notes

1. Our use of 'private governance' is essentially synonymous with 'private regulation' as Büthe (2010a, 2010b) defines it, but we draw on a broader governance literature throughout this chapter.
2. Private governance may also serve functions other than regulation of externalities, including facilitating the formation and efficient functioning of markets and redressing the distributive consequences of market activities, but regulation has been the primary purpose of most private governance. The taxonomy of facilitative, regulatory and compensatory modes of market governance is addressed more fully in Gereffi and Mayer (2006).

3. Cafaggi and Janczuk (2010) do not include self-regulation in their definition of private regulation. We include it here on the grounds that corporations (or more precisely the people who run them) can internalize norms of appropriate corporate behavior that alter their behavior.

4. The phrase was first used by Peter Newell (Vogel, 2010). This line of argument is developed more fully in Gereffi and Mayer (2006).

5. In the North American Free Trade Agreement (NAFTA) negotiations, public opposition forced the Clinton Administration to add supplemental agreements on labor and environment (Mayer, 1998), and many bi-lateral and regional trade agreements have at least weak social clauses, but efforts to incorporate similar provisions at the global level have not been successful.

6. See Starobin and Weinthal (2010) for a discussion of the credibility problem in certification regimes.

7. In social movement theory, 'opportunity structures' are those institutions that facilitate collective action by lowering the costs of cooperation (see Tarrow, 1998).

8. The Monterey Bay Aquarium has, for example, led an effort to persuade restaurants and consumers to serve and buy only fish on its 'green' list and to shun those it lists as 'red,' categories that reflect its evaluation of the extent to which they are sustainably harvested. Whole Foods, the large organic food retailer, has now pledged to stop selling fish on the red list, but the major supermarkets have not adopted the standard and consumer awareness remains quite low.

9. See, for example, You and Huang (2009). It is also true that the number of reports of problems has increased, but it is much more likely that this increase reflects greater willingness to report than it does any increase in actual abuses.

References

AFP (Agence France-Presse). 2010. July 29. Available at http://www.google.com/hostednews/afp/article/ALeqM5ieRqjL0JDDmLXJwiGVFRq7GQyEKw.

Auld, Graeme, Benjamin Cashore, Cristina Balboa, Laura Bozzi, and Stefan Renckens. 2010. 'Can Technological Innovations Improve Private Regulation in the Global Economy?' *Business and Politics* 12(3).

Bair, Jennifer, ed. 2009. *Frontiers of Commodity Chain Research*. Palo Alto, CA: Stanford University Press.

Bartley, Tim. 2010. 'Transnational Private Regulation in Practice: The Limits of Forest and Labor Standards Certification in Indonesia.' *Business and Politics* 12(3).

Büthe, Tim. 2010a. 'Private Regulation in the Global Economy: A (P)Review.' *Business and Politics* 12(3).

————. 2010b. 'Engineering Uncontestedness? The Institutional Development of the International Electrotechnical Commission (IEC) as a Private Regulator.' *Business and Politics* 12(3).

Cafaggi, Fabrizio and Agnieszka Janczuk. 2010. 'Private Regulation and Legal Integration: The European Case.' *Business and Politics* 12(3).

Cattaneo, Olivier, Gary Gereffi, and Cornelia Staritz. 2010. 'Global Value Chains in a Postcrisis World: Resilience, Consolidation, and Shifting Markets.' In *Global Value Chains in a Postcrisis*

World: A Development Perspective, edited by Olivier Cattaneo, Gary Gereffi, and Cornelia Staritz, 3–20. Washington, DC: World Bank.

de Andrade Baltar, Paulo Eduardo, Anselmo Luis dos Santos, Jose Dari Krein, Eugenia Leone, Marcelo Weishaupt Proni, and Amilton Moretto. 2010. 'Moving Towards Decent Work. Labour in the Lula Government: Reflections on Recent Brazilian Experience.' Available at http://escholarship.org/uc/item/6w6062g2.

Dicken, Peter. 2007. *Global Shift: Mapping the Changing Contours of the World Economy*, 5th edition. New York: Guilford.

Dolan, Catherine and John Humphrey. 2004. 'Changing Governance Patterns in the Trade in Fresh Vegetables between Africa and the United Kingdom.' *Environment and Planning A* (36): 491–509.

Downie, Andrew. 2007. 'Amazon Harvest: Can European Pressure Stop the Creep of Soy Fields into Brazil's Rainforest.' *Nature Conservancy Magazine*. Available at http://www.nature.org/magazine/autumn2007/features/art21918.html.

Downs, Anthony. 1957. *An Economic Theory of Democracy*. New York: Harper.

Esbenshade, Jill. 2004. *Monitoring Sweatshops: Workers, Consumers, and the Global Apparel Industry*. Philadelphia, PA: Temple University Press.

Evans, Peter. 1995. *Embedded Autonomy: States and Industrial Transformation*. Princeton, NJ: Princeton University Press.

Fuchs, Doris and Agni Kalfagianni. 2010. 'The Causes and Consequences of Private Food Governance.' *Business and Politics* 12(3).

Gereffi, Gary. 1999. 'International Trade and Industrial Upgrading in the Apparel Commodity Chain.' *Journal of International Economics* 48(1): 37–70.

————. 2005. 'The Global Economy: Organization, Governance, and Development.' In *The Handbook of Economic Sociology*, edited by Neil J. Smelser and Richard Swedberg, 160–182. Princeton, NJ: Princeton University Press and Russell Sage Foundation.

Gereffi, Gary and Michelle Christian. 2009. 'The Impacts of Wal-Mart: The Rise and Consequences of the World's Dominant Retailer.' *Annual Review of Sociology* 35: 573–591.

————. 2010. 'Trade, Transnational Corporations and Food Consumption: A Global Value Chain Approach.' In *Trade, Food, Diet and Health*, edited by Corinna Hawkes, Chantal Blouin, Spencer Henson, Nick Drager, and Laurette Dubé, 91–110. Oxford: Wiley-Blackwell.

Gereffi, Gary and Karina Fernandez-Stark. 2010. 'The Offshore Services Value Chain.' Working Paper 5262, World Bank.

Gereffi, Gary and Stacey Frederick. 2010. 'The Global Apparel Value Chain, Trade and the Crisis: Challenges and Opportunities for Developing Countries.' Working Paper 5281, World Bank.

Gereffi, Gary, Ronie Garcia-Johnson, and Erika Sasser. 2001. 'The NGO-Industrial Complex.' *Foreign Policy* 125: 56–65.

Gereffi, Gary and Raphael Kaplinsky, eds. 2001. 'The Value of Value Chains: Spreading the Gains from Globalization.' Special Issue of *IDS Bulletin* 32(3).

Gereffi, Gary and Miguel Korzeniewicz, eds. 1994. *Commodity Chains and Global Capitalism*. Westport, CT: Praeger.

Gereffi, Gary, Joonkoo Lee, and Michelle Christian. 2009. 'US-Based Food and Agricultural Value Chains and Their Relevance to Healthy Diets.' *Journal of Hunger and Environmental Nutrition* 4(3): 357–374.

Gereffi, Gary and Frederick Mayer. 2006. 'Globalization and the Demand for Governance.' In *The New Offshoring of Jobs and Global Development*, edited by Gary Gereffi, 39–58. Geneva: International Labour Organization.

Green, Jessica F. 2010. 'Private Standards in the Climate Regime: The Greenhouse Gas Protocol.' *Business and Politics* 12(3).

GreenBiz. 2010. August 17. Available at: https://www.greenbiz.com/blog/2009/08/17/inside-walmarts-sustainability-consortium.

Held, David and Anthony McGrew, eds. 2002. *Governing Globalization: Power, Authority and Global Governance*. Cambridge: Polity Press.

Henderson, Jeffrey, Peter Dicken, Martin Hess, Neil Coe, and Henry Wai-chung Yeung. 2002. 'Global Production Networks and the Analysis of Economic Development.' *Review of International Political Economy* 9(3): 436–464.

Hochstetler, Kathryn and Margaret E. Keck. 2007. *Greening Brazil: Environmental Activism in State and Society*. Durham, London: Duke University Press.

Hughes, Alexandra. 2000. 'Retailers, Knowledges and Changing Commodity Networks: The Case of the Cut Flower Trade.' *Geoforum* 31(2): 175–190.

Inglehart, Ronald. 1981. 'Post-Materialism in an Environment of Insecurity.' *The American Political Science Review* 75(4): 880–900.

———. 2000. 'Globalization and Postmodern Values.' *The Washington Quarterly* 23(1): 215–228.

Just-Style. 2010. 'Continuing Protests Blight Bangladesh Pay Deal.' August 2. Available at http://www.just-style.com/comment/continuing-protests-blight-bangladesh-pay-deal_id108475.aspx.

Kaplinsky, Raphael. 2005. *Globalization, Inequality and Poverty*. Cambridge: Polity Press.

Keohane, Robert and Joseph Nye. 1977. *Power and Independence*. Boston, MA: Little, Brown and Company.

Klein, Naomi. 2000. *No Logo: Taking Aim at the Brand Bullies*. New York: Picador.

Kolk, Ans and Rob van Tulder. 2004. 'Ethics in International Business: Multinational Approaches to Child Labor.' *Journal of World Business* 39(1): 49–60.

———. 2005. 'Setting New Global Rules? TNCs and Codes of Conduct.' *Transnational Corporations* 14(3): 1–28.

Locke, Richard, Matthew Amengual, and Akshay Mangla. 2009. 'Virtue Out of Necessity? Compliance, Commitment, and the Improvement of Labor Standards in Global Supply Chains.' Working Paper 4719–08, MIT Sloan.

Locke, Richard, Fei Qin, and Alberto Brause. 2007. 'Does Monitoring Improve Labor Standards? Lessons from Nike.' *Industrial and Labor Relations Review* 61(1): 3–31.

Locke, Richard and Monica Romis. 2007. 'Improving Work Conditions in a Global Supply Chain.' *MIT Sloan Management Review* 48(2): 54–62.

Lukas, Karin, Leonhard Plank, and Cornelia Staritz. 2010. 'Securing Labour Rights in Global Production Networks: Legal Instruments and Policy Options.' Vienna: Chamber of Labour.

Mandle, Jay R. 2000. 'The Student Anti-Sweatshop Movement: Limits and Potential.' *The ANNALS of the American Academy of Political and Social Science* 570(1): 92–103.

Mattli, Walter and Ngaire Woods. 2009a. 'Introduction.' In *The Politics of Global Regulation*, edited by Walter Mattli and Ngaire Woods, ix–xvi. Princeton, NJ: Princeton University Press.

————. 2009b. 'In Whose Benefit? Explaining Regulatory Change in Global Politics.' In *The Politics of Global Regulation*, edited by Walter Mattli and Ngaire Woods, 1–43. Princeton, NJ: Princeton University Press.

Mayer, Frederick W. 1998. *Interpreting NAFTA*. New York: Columbia University Press.

McDonald's Corporation. 2009. Worldwide Corporate Responsibility Online Report. *The Values We Bring to the Table*. Available at http://www.aboutmcdonalds.com/mcd/csr/report/overview.RightParaContentTout-43872-ReportsLinkList-28982-File1.tmp/mcd052_2009report_v6.pdf.

Memodovic, Olga and Andrew Sheperd. 2009. 'Agri-Food Value-Chains and Poverty Reduction: Overview of Main Issues, Trends and Experiences.' Working Paper 12/2008. Research and Statistics Branch, UNIDO.

Ocampo, Jose A. 2010. 'Rethinking Global Economic and Social Governance.' *Journal of Globalization and Development* 1(1): 1–26.

Olson, Mancur. 1965. *The Logic of Collective Action; Public Goods and the Theory of Groups*. Harvard Economic Studies. Cambridge, MA: Harvard University Press.

Orsato, Renato J. 2009. *Sustainability Strategies: When Does It Pay to Be Green?* INSEAD Business Press Series. Basingstoke, NY: Palgrave Macmillan.

Pay, Ellen. 2009. 'The Market for Organic and Fair Trade Coffee.' Food and Agriculture Organization of the United Nations.

Polanyi, Karl. 1944. *The Great Transformation*. Boston: Beacon Press.

Reardon, Thomas and Rose Hopkins. 2006. 'The Supermarket Revolution in Developing Countries.' *European Journal of Development Research* 18(4): 522–545.

Riisgaard, Lone. 2009. 'Global Value Chains, Labor Organization and Private Social Standards: Lessons from East African Cut Flower Industries.' *World Development* 37(2): 326–340.

Riisgaard, Lone and Nikolaus Hammer. 2011. 'Prospects for Labour in Global Value Chains: Labour Standards in the Cut Flower and Banana Industries.' *British Journal of Industrial Relations* 49(1): 168–190. Available at http://onlinelibrary.wiley.com/doi/10.1111/j.1467-8543.2009.00744.x/abstract.

Ruggie, John. 1982. 'International Regimes, Transactions and Change: Embedded Liberalism in the Postwar Economic Order.' *International Organization* 36(2): 379–415.

————. 2002. 'Trade, Sustainability and Global Governance.' *Columbia Journal of Environmental Law* 27(2): 297–307.

————. 2008. 'Taking Embedded Liberalism Global: The Corporate Connection.' In *Embedding Global Markets: An Enduring Challenge*, edited by John Ruggie, 231–254. Aldershot, UK: Ashgate.

Starobin, Shana and Erika Weinthal. 2010. 'The Search for Credible Information in Social and Environmental Global Governance: The Kosher Label.' *Business and Politics* 12(3).

Sturgeon, Timothy J. and Momoko Kawakami. 2010. 'Global Value Chains in the Electronics Industry: Was the 2008-09 Crisis a Window of Opportunity for Developing Countries.' In

Global Value Chains in a Post-Crisis World, edited by Olivier Cattaneo, Gary Gereffi, and Cornelia Staritz, 245–301. Washington, DC: World Bank.

Sturgeon, Timothy J. and Richard Lester. 2004. 'The New Global Supply-Base: New Challenges for Local Suppliers in East Asia.' In *Global Production Networking and Technological Change in East Asia*, edited by Shahid Yusuf, M. Anjum Altaf, and Kaoru Nabeshima, 35–77. Washington, DC: World Bank and Oxford University Press.

Sturgeon, Timothy J., Olga Memedovic, Johannes Van Biesebroeck, and Gary Gereffi. 2009. 'Globalization of the Automotive Industry: Main Features and Trends.' *International Journal of Technological Learning, Innovation and Development* 2(1/2): 7–24.

Tarrow, Sidney. 1998. *Power in Movement: Social Movements and Contentious Politics*. Cambridge: Cambridge University Press.

The Economist. 2010. 'The Next China: China's Labour Market.' *The Economist Magazine*, July 29. Available at http://www.economist.com/node/16693397?story_id=16693397.

TransFair USA. 2005. *2005 Fair Trade Coffee: Facts and Figures*.

Vogel, David J. 2005. *The Market for Virtue*. Washington, DC: Brookings.

———. 2008. 'Private Global Business Regulation.' *Annual Review of Political Science* 11: 261–282.

———. 2010. 'The Private Regulation of Global Corporate Conduct.' *Business and Society* 49(1): 68-87.

Whytock, Christopher A. 2010. 'Public-Private Interaction in Global Governance: The Case of Transnational Commercial Arbitration.' *Business and Politics* 12(3).

Worthen, Ben, Cari Tuna, and Justin Scheck. 2009. 'Companies More Prone to Go "Vertical".' *Wall Street Journal*, December 1.

You, Mingqing and Ke Huang. 2009. 'Annual Review of Chinese Environmental Law Developments.' In *Environmental Law Reporter News and Analysis*, 10484. Washington, DC: Environmental Law Institute.

Economic and Social Upgrading in Global Value Chains and Industrial Clusters
Why Governance Matters

Gary Gereffi and Joonkoo Lee

Introduction

Upgrading through global value chains (GVCs), or moving to higher value activities, has become important for economic development and job creation in the global economy, where competition remains intense and production has become fragmented and geographically dispersed (Cattaneo et al., 2013). Linking lead firms in GVCs with small and medium suppliers in diverse local contexts is a major business challenge in different types of industries, whether characterized by producer-driven chains like automobiles, electronics, or shipbuilding for whom finding and nurturing technically capable local suppliers is a requisite of global supply chain management for manufacturers who play a leading role in determining what and how to produce (Contreras et al., 2012; Sturgeon, 2003; Sturgeon et al., 2008), or in buyer-driven chains like apparel and footwear, where low cost is a major driver and retail buyers govern how the chains work (Bair and Gereffi 2001; Schmitz, 2004, 2006), or fresh produce and food products, where safety and quality standards are of utmost concern for supermarkets and their customers (Humphrey and Memedovic, 2006).

In order to maintain good supplier relationships in all of these settings, GVC lead firms have developed more active strategies of corporate social responsibility (CSR) (van Tulder, 2009). While CSR is a multifaceted notion, it generally refers to 'the responsibility of enterprises for their impacts on society' (European Commission, 2011). It encompasses a wide range of efforts through which firms seek to integrate social, environmental, ethical, and human rights as well as consumer concerns into their core business practices. The goal is to maximize the benefit of shared value for a broad set of stakeholders, including owners, shareholders, and the wider society, while reducing potential negative impacts of corporate business practices to a minimum.

There is a growing concern, however, that economic upgrading—countries and firms moving to higher value activities in GVCs with improved technology, knowledge, and skills[1] (Gereffi, 2005: 161)—is no longer sufficient for sustainable CSR in global supply chains, given accumulating evidence and recent exposés about child labor, vulnerable workers, and abysmal working conditions in many export-oriented clusters located in developing countries (see Lund-Thomsen and Lindgreen, 2014; Lund-Thomsen and Nadvi, 2010a). Improving both economic and social conditions for workers and communities linked to GVCs is a vexing development problem, and it has attracted considerable attention by researchers, policy makers, and donor communities. Indeed, this was the central theme of the *Capturing the Gains* research program[2] carried out over a three-year period by a large group of development scholars: Under what conditions can economic and social upgrading be combined in GVCs? Social upgrading is defined as the process of improving the rights and entitlements of workers as social actors and enhancing the quality of their employment (Barrientos et al., 2011).

In the GVC framework, a key determinant of upgrading outcomes is the governance structure of global value chains. Governance structures are complex, and they include international as well as national regulations, and both public, private, and social forms of governance (Gereffi and Fernandez-Stark, 2011; Mayer and Gereffi, 2010). GVC scholars tend to focus on how external conditions and pressures, particularly by global buyers and through a variety of public and private governance processes, facilitate the diffusion of global standards and affect economic and social upgrading in developing countries (Gereffi et al., 2005); cluster scholars, by contrast, focus more on the social and cultural bonds and inter-firm learning and cluster institutions in local areas, which are considered critical for cluster upgrading (Lund-Thomsen and Pillay, 2012; Schmitz, 1995; Schmitz and Nadvi, 1999).

Notwithstanding an ongoing dialog between the GVC and cluster literatures (Bair and Gereffi, 2001; Chiarvesio et al., 2010; Humphrey and Schmitz, 2002; Schmitz, 2004), there is still a gap in understanding how GVCs and industrial clusters interact in terms of economic and social upgrading in developing countries. This chapter will review these literatures to identify the most fruitful bases for an integrated framework to better understand the governance conditions that allow economic and social upgrading in GVCs and clusters to be combined in a sustainable manner. This integrated framework has important implications for CSR, which is under pressure to move from transitory, ethical consumer-oriented public relations campaigns to 'sustainable development' concerns that involve a wide range of actors across GVCs and clusters, including not only global lead firms and cluster firms but also civil society actors like non-governmental organizations (NGOs), national and local governments, labor unions, and international organizations such as the International Labor Organization (ILO), and multilateral donors like the World Bank and regional development banks (Lund-Thomsen and Lindgreen, 2014).

This chapter aims to contribute to the existing industrial cluster and GVC literature by highlighting the following points: (1) economic and social upgrading in developing countries are affected by the interaction of both GVC and cluster actors, and the role of social and public actors has grown as more attention is paid to social upgrading; (2) the typologies of GVC and cluster governance need to be expanded to take into account both vertical and horizontal relationships and the complex interactions—tensions, conflicts, displacement, complementarity, and synergy—between public, social, and private forms of governance; and (3) depending on which types of governance and actors are involved, multiple paths for social upgrading are plausible. Six key trajectories are discussed: market, CSR, multi-stakeholder initiatives, labor, cluster, and governments. We focus more on social upgrading and different pathways that can accommodate it because social upgrading has lagged behind economic upgrading in most cases. Also, social gains are not necessarily accompanied by economic gains (Barrientos et al., 2011).

The organization of our chapter is as follows. The second and third sections review recent trends in the literature on industrial clusters and GVCs, respectively, and the fourth section explores how these approaches relate to economic and social upgrading. The fifth section proposes an integrated framework that shows how the increasingly diverse governance structures of GVCs and clusters are linked to different trajectories for social upgrading. The concluding section summarizes the implications for CSR of our integrated framework for industrial clusters and GVCs.

Industrial Clusters and Globalization

An industrial cluster consists of firms and related organizations within well-defined spatial boundaries engaging in similar sectorial activities (Porter, 1998; Pyke et al., 1990). Originating in Alfred Marshall's classical concept of industrial districts, the notion was popularized by Italian small- and medium-sized enterprises (SMEs) in industrial districts that were able to successfully compete in global industries (Piore and Sabel, 1984). The success was attributed to several key characteristics of industrial districts, i.e., geographic proximity and close-knit social relations, which helped to reduce transaction costs and nurture trust, and informal networks, which facilitate the flow of information, knowledge, and skills. While clusters are somewhat broader in scope than industrial districts (De Marchi and Grandinetti, 2014), the two are similar in that they are diversified production structures confined to local geographic spaces.

Since the early 1990s, the role of industrial clusters and SMEs in economic development has drawn a great deal of scholarly and policy interest in the context of developing economies (Altenburg and Meyer-Stamer, 1999; Ketels and Memedovic, 2008; Schmitz and Nadvi, 1999; see Lund-Thomsen and Lindgreen, 2014; Lund-Thomsen and Pillay, 2012 for reviews). The literature suggests that clusters matter for economic upgrading because, first, the agglomeration of productive activities generates economies of scale and scope external to individual firms but internal to the cluster, and second, it facilitates local joint actions by cluster firms and institutions to address common problems based on their interdependence. These benefits, or so-called 'collective efficiency' (Schmitz, 1995), are critical because SMEs in developing countries are typically too small in size and limited in resources to compete in global industries. Geographic proximity and dense social relations enable SMEs to develop a close network of suppliers and share a pool of skilled workers, information, and knowledge as well as the infrastructure necessary to collectively improve the efficiency of production activities (Sturgeon, 2003). Furthermore, cluster actors engage in joint actions to address common problems (Lund-Thomsen and Pillay, 2012). While cooperation among cluster firms is not easy because they often compete intensely with each other, it can be rewarding when they confront common upgrading challenges together. In organizing joint actions, the role of local cluster actors (e.g., industry associations) and institutions (e.g., trade fairs) is highlighted (Doner and Schneider, 2000; Schmitz and Nadvi, 1999).

In short, the industrial cluster literature highlights the importance of cluster governance operating horizontally between cluster firms and institutions in local contexts, be it learning and innovation for economic upgrading or implementing CSR measures for social upgrading. This horizontal governance can be contrasted with the vertical governance in GVCs that links global lead firms to both first-tier and local suppliers in international production networks (see below).

Cluster firms in developing economies often find themselves confronted by conflicting demands from global buyers, which seek lower labor costs while simultaneously requiring suppliers to comply with higher quality or social standards that would incur additional expenditures (Barrientos and Smith, 2007; Lund-Thomsen and Pillay, 2012). The fear of global buyers being 'foot-loose' can keep cluster actors from making sustained investments in infrastructure or workforce development, thereby hindering local joint action. Such anxiety has grown in the face of global economic recessions (Ruwanpura and Wrigley, 2011).

Clusters will have divergent responses to these challenges, depending not only on the characteristics and effectiveness of local institutions but also the form of global-local linkage and the nature of GVC governance regimes they have (Khara and Lund-Thomsen, 2012; Lund-Thomsen, and Nadvi, 2010a). Active upgrading efforts in industrial clusters increase the demand for high-skilled and better-paid workers as well as investment in advanced training and new skills such as product development and design (Posthuma, 2008). Yet, such upgrading may increase segmentation among cluster firms between mostly larger firms that have upgraded and smaller ones that fell behind (Suresh, 2010). The growing disparities can not only reduce the possibility of joint action and potential collective efficiency, but also differentiate social upgrading outcomes among the firms depending on their positions within the cluster as well as in GVCs and the end markets they are linked to (Nadvi and Barrientos, 2004). In the next section, we discuss the key recent trends in GVCs that affect global-local linkage and upgrading conditions for industrial clusters in developing countries.

Global Value Chains and Upgrading

The GVC framework was created to better understand how value is created, captured, sustained, and leveraged within all types of industries. The GVC approach provides a holistic view of global industries from two vantage points: governance and upgrading. The governance of GVCs focuses mainly on lead firms and the way they organize their supply chains on a global scale, while upgrading involves the strategies used by countries, regions, firms, and other economic stakeholders to maintain or improve their positions in the global economy (Gereffi, 2005). Both concepts have evolved considerably in recent years.

Governance is a centerpiece of GVC analysis. It shows how corporate power exercised by global lead firms actively shapes the distribution of profits and risks in an industry, and how this alters the upgrading prospects of firms in developed and developing economies that are included as well as excluded from the supply chains that constitute each industry (Gereffi and Lee, 2012). The role played by lead firms is highlighted in various typologies of GVC governance. The initial distinction between producer-driven and buyer-driven commodity chains was introduced to call attention to the rise of global buyers in the 1970s and 1980s. Unlike producer-driven chains where large manufacturers control much of the production process through direct ownership, retailers and brand marketers in buyer-driven chains began to set up international sourcing networks to procure consumer goods directly from offshore suppliers, mainly in East Asia (Gereffi, 1994, 1999).

However, the dichotomous categories of buyer-driven and producer-driven chains were too broad to capture the full complexity of GVC governance structures that were emerging in the world. To address this challenge, Gereffi et al. (2005) elaborated a fivefold typology of GVC governance structures, which sought both to describe and explain in a parsimonious way the main differences among various types of production networks. Between the two extremes of classic markets and hierarchies (i.e., vertical integration), three network forms of governance were identified: modular, relational, and captive (Gereffi et al., 2005; Sturgeon, 2009). In these network forms of GVC governance, the lead firm exercises varying degrees of power through the coordination of suppliers without any direct ownership of the firms.

Whereas the initial distinction between producer-driven and buyer-driven commodity chains conceptualizes governance as 'driving' and the more differentiated fivefold typology sees governance as 'coordinating', Ponte and Sturgeon (2014) introduce a third dimension: governance as 'normalizing'. Following Gibbon et al. (2008), their view of normalizing draws from convention theory, and means realigning a given practice to be compatible with a standard or a norm. In all of these conceptions of GVC governance, lead firms play a crucial role by defining the terms of supply chain membership, by incorporating or excluding other actors, and by shaping how, where, when, and by whom value is added. Thus, governing in global industries requires both buyer power (e.g., setting product specifications, standards, logistics, price, etc.) as well as normative power (e.g., shaping expectations of how businesses should be organized, how quality should be assessed, or the guidelines to be followed with respect to worker rights and factory conditions) (De Marchi et al., 2014).[3]

Several of the recent trends in GVCs have important implications for the role of local suppliers and the likelihood of economic and social upgrading in industrial clusters (Cattaneo et al., 2013; Gereffi, 2014): (1) organizational rationalization—the lead firms in these chains seek a much smaller number of big, technologically capable and strategically located suppliers (Gereffi, 2014: 15); (2) geographic consolidation—the production hubs of these supply chains are concentrating in large emerging economies, both because of their abundant supply of workers and local firms with manufacturing expertise and also because of expanding domestic markets (Gereffi and Sturgeon, 2013); and (3) a growth in South–South trade—this has surged especially since the 2008–2009 global economic recession, which dramatically slowed exports to advanced industrial markets.

Organizational rationalization tends to reinforce market dynamics and make it much harder for SMEs in industrial clusters to play a significant role in economic or social upgrading because they do not have the scale or scope to occupy the upper rungs of global supply chains. Geographic consolidation and the growth in South–South trade, on the other hand, both have the potential to support several of the trajectories of social upgrading for small firms and industrial clusters identified by Puppim de Oliveira (2008a). Geographic consolidation of production in sizeable emerging economies like China, Indonesia, Brazil, and South Africa has led to a revitalization of industrial policy (Gereffi and Sturgeon, 2013), which supports the role of public governance since national governments now have greater bargaining power to pressure foreign companies for changes to benefit local interests. When combined with multi-stakeholder initiatives, including labor unions and worker activism, along with the reputational pressure placed on GVC lead firms by CSR regimes, such as corporate codes of conduct and monitoring, sustainable improvements in working conditions in developing countries become far more likely.[4]

The shift in global demand from the North to the South, especially after the 2008–2009 recession, and the resultant growth of South–South trade have both positive and negative consequences for industrial clusters in developing economies (Kaplinsky et al., 2011). On the positive side, lower entry barriers and less stringent product and process standards in emerging markets can facilitate the participation of developing country firms in global supply chains. They can engage in higher value-added activities, such as product development and design, which they would have less chance to do in global chains. On the other hand, solely focusing on low-income markets could lock suppliers into slimmer margins and cut-throat competition.

The influence of GVCs on the upgrading of local clusters in developing countries has renewed an interest in institutions and their interaction with GVC governance. Quality conventions and standards as a governing device of GVCs play an increasing role in shaping upgrading opportunities for local clusters (Ponte and Gibbon, 2005). However, most of those measures are only applied to a selected group of firms inserted into GVCs and their regular employees, while a large majority of SMEs and temporary and migrant workers, who are more vulnerable, are frequently marginalized or excluded from these benefits of the measures (Lund-Thomsen and Lindgreen, 2014; Neilson and Pritchard, 2010). This has led to calls for a better understanding of place-based social and institutional contexts and their interaction with diversified, co-existing local production systems as well as with multiple forms of GVC governance (Palpacuer, 2008).

Economic and Social Upgrading in GVCs and Industrial Clusters

In order to more effectively link the GVC and cluster literatures to upgrading and the role of CSR, the definition of upgrading should be expanded to encompass both its economic and social dimensions. Economic upgrading is defined as a move to higher-value activities in production, to improved technology, knowledge and skills, and to increased benefits or profits deriving from participation in GVCs (Gereffi, 2005: 171). Within the GVC framework, four types of upgrading have been identified (Humphrey and Schmitz, 2002):

- *product upgrading*, or moving into more sophisticated product lines;
- *process upgrading*, which transforms inputs into outputs more efficiently by reorganizing the production system or introducing superior technology;

- *functional upgrading,* which entails acquiring new functions (or abandoning existing functions) to increase the overall skill content of the activities; and
- *chain upgrading,* where firms move into new but often related industries.

Social upgrading is defined as the process of improvement in the rights and entitlements of workers as social actors and the enhancement of the quality of their employment (Barrientos et al., 2011). The concept is anchored in the ILO Decent Work framework, which encompasses employment, standards and rights at work, social protection, and social dialog (ILO, 1999). Social upgrading not only includes access to better work, which might result from economic upgrading (for example, a worker that has acquired skills in one job is able to move a better job elsewhere in a GVC), but it also involves enhancing working conditions, protection and rights, thereby improving the overall well-being of workers as well as their dependents and communities.[5]

The social upgrading concept is related to, but more encompassing than, CSR. In recent decades, CSR initiatives by global lead firms were promoted as an effective way to improve labor conditions in GVCs that were predominantly buyer-driven (Jenkins et al., 2002). Leveraging their purchasing power vis-à-vis suppliers, global buyers tried to enforce codes of conduct within their supply chains in the hope that by complying with the codes, suppliers would address social and environmental concerns in their factories (Locke et al., 2009; van Tulder, 2009). Despite some progress, it has become clear that the CSR compliance model alone is woefully inadequate to fully address labor issues in global supply chains (Locke, 2013; Lund-Thomsen and Lindgreen, 2014), let alone encompassing broader concerns about sustainable development.[6] Also, while CSR compliance incurs significant costs to suppliers, the model generally does not allow suppliers and workers in developing countries to provide meaningful input although they are supposed to benefit from it (De Neve, 2014; Dolan and Opondo, 2005).

Social upgrading expands the scope of CSR by focusing not only on efforts by global companies to ameliorate labor conditions, but also other non-corporate measures initiated by NGOs and governments. It is less concerned about whether or not any specific CSR measure is effective, and shifts the question to 'under what conditions' social upgrading is more likely to occur, and how that relates to economic upgrading (Barrientos et al., 2011). It suggests that there may be several distinct, yet similarly effective, ways to achieve improvement, as we discuss below.

The existing literature on clusters and GVCs often implicitly assumes that economic upgrading will automatically translate into social upgrading through better wages and working conditions (Knorringa and Pegler, 2007; Puppim de Oliveira, 2008b). Case studies, however, provide a more variegated picture

(Bernhardt and Milberg, 2011; Nadvi and Barrientos, 2004; Posthuma and Nathan, 2010; Puppim de Oliveira, 2008a). Social upgrading can be affected by the type of economic upgrading that is pursued. When upgrading relies mainly on the 'low road' strategy of cutting labor costs, as illustrated in Indian leather clusters, the jobs created are often low-paid, informal ones with undesirable working conditions (Damodaran, 2010). Labor conditions are consistently found to be better among permanent workers in the cluster context, while temporary and casual workers are excluded from social upgrading and play a 'buffering' role for the factory to remain cost competitive and flexible in terms of last minute changes in orders, resulting in segmented social upgrading even within the same cluster (Suresh, 2010).

Gender bias has also been found to play an important role in industrial clusters and GVCs. Women workers tend to be engaged in insecure and low-paid work, often in temporary and seasonal employment arrangements (Barrientos and Kritzinger, 2004; Mezzadri, 2014). As clusters upgrade to the activities requiring a more highly skilled workforce, women and unskilled workers are often left out from social upgrading and become increasingly marginalized (Carr and Chen, 2004). Indeed, the CSR measures of global buyers are often only effective within a small pocket of 'regulatory enclaves' in their own supply chains (Posthuma, 2010), and smaller firms and marginal workers remain highly vulnerable (Suresh, 2010).

An Integrated Framework to Link Industrial Clusters to Governance and Upgrading

To understand how different forms of governance can affect economic and social upgrading, Table 10.1 outlines two distinct forms of governance in industrial clusters and GVCs. *Horizontal (cluster) governance* refers to locality-based coordination of the economic and social relations between cluster firms as well as institutions within and beyond the cluster. *Vertical (GVC) governance* operates along the value chain, linking a series of buyers and suppliers in different countries, each of which adds values toward the final product. GVC scholars generally focus on the vertical, cross-national dimension of governance and cluster researchers tend to stress the role of the horizontal, place-based form of governance. However, we need to take into account both types of governance and their interaction in order to fully understand the functioning of a global industry and its consequences to economic and social upgrading in industrial clusters (Lund-Thomsen and Nadvi, 2010a; Neilson and Pritchard, 2009).

Governance also differs by the kinds of actors involved, leading to discrete dimensions of private, public, and social governance. As more attention is paid to social upgrading, the role of public and social governance and relevant actors has grown. In clusters, *private governance* involves regulating economic transactions among cluster firms and with their external partners. In the cluster context, private governance is generally based on trust and mutual dependence among cluster firms and managers built around repetitive transactions and close interpersonal ties embedded in social relations within the cluster (Schmitz and Nadvi, 1999). It aims to achieve collective efficiency in order for cluster firms to overcome the constraints of their smallness and share resources with one another, often mediated by institutions like cluster associations or chambers of commerce (Schmitz, 1995). Joint action also could lower compliance costs for cluster firms while increasing compliance through collective monitoring and sanctions (Lund-Thomsen and Nadvi, 2010b).

Table 10.1 Types of Governance in Clusters and Global Value Chains by Scope and Actor

Actor	Scope	
	Horizontal (cluster) governance	Vertical (GVC) governance
Private governance	Collective efficiency (e.g., industrial associations, cooperatives)	GVC lead-firm governance (e.g., global buyers' voluntary codes of conduct)
Social governance	Local civil society pressure (e.g., workers, labor unions, NGOs for civil society, workers, and environmental rights; gender-equity advocates)	Global civil society pressure on lead firms and major suppliers (e.g., Fair Labor Association) and multi-stakeholder initiatives (e.g., Ethical Trading Initiative)
Public governance	Local, regional, and national government regulations (e.g., labor laws and environmental legislation)	International organizations (e.g., the ILO, WTO) and international trade agreements (e.g., NAFTA, AGOA)

Source: Authors.

In GVCs, private governance is driven by lead firms like global buyers, and often through private standards that dictate what products are to be made by whom and how (Lee et al., 2012). The key to GVC private governance lies in maximizing economic efficiency in making products whose quantity and quality are determined by lead firms in a decentralized production system. While private governance mainly pertains to economic transactions between firms in both cluster and GVC contexts, it can also involve social and environmental dimensions, such as working conditions or child labor (Khara and Lund-Thomsen, 2012; Nathan and Sarkar, 2011).

Public governance differs from private governance in that it is exercised by public actors, which include governments at various levels within nation-states, and supranational organizations. Public governance in the cluster context involves formal rules and regulations set by governments at local, regional, and national levels. They can facilitate or hinder social and economic upgrading, directly and indirectly. National labor laws, for instance, directly impact the conditions of workers in the cluster by regulating various aspects of labor conditions and standards. Other public governance measures, such as industrial policy, trade, and investment regulations or competition policy, do not intend to address labor concerns but can indirectly affect social upgrading outcomes, while they directly impact economic upgrading. Public governance in GVCs can also be exercised through bilateral or multilateral trade agreements, such as the North American Free Trade Agreement (NAFTA) and the African Growth and Opportunity Act (AGOA). For example, social clauses are integrated into trade agreements with an aim to apply core labor standards to international trade, which can have a significant impact on smaller firms and their workers in local clusters (Polaski, 2003). Relative to private standards which are voluntary, public governance, particularly government regulations, are mandatory and have a stronger legal basis. However, it is often incomplete in design and plagued by ineffective enforcement in many developing countries.

Finally, *social governance* is driven by civil society actors, such as NGOs and labor unions. It provides a more explicit means of regulating workers' rights and labor conditions. These include codes of conducts initiated by NGOs, and multi-stakeholder initiatives, such as the Ethical Trade Initiative (ETI) (Barrientos and Smith, 2007). In both GVCs and clusters, social governance can entail various forms of activism, such as boycotting, petitions, and protests (Selwyn, 2013). This form of governance is rarely mandatory, and generally relies on the action of private firms or governments that have direct power to enforce such codes or regulations. Partly for this reason, social governance often takes a multi-stakeholder form in which public, private, and civil society actors pursue their common goals through joint action (Dolan and Opondo, 2005; O'Rourke, 2006). This form of joint governance, as noted above, can be more effective than private, public, or social governance alone in achieving sustainable improvements of working conditions in developing countries (Locke, 2013; Mayer, 2014).

However, it may not always be feasible since collective action problems often arise. Who should bear the costs of compliance with respect to labor standards has been a contentious issue between global buyers and their suppliers, as well as among buyers, as illustrated in the recent tragic building collapse involving scores of Bangladesh garment factories (Greenhouse, 2013). The literature also points to the potential for free-rider problems as some firms in industrial clusters may not want to join or pay for collective actions, yet still benefit from them (Lund-

Thomsen and Pillay, 2012). Different interests and views among cluster firms can affect collective action outcomes, as seen in the Jalandhar cluster where football producers and the manufacturers of other sports equipment were divided by their own interests and perspectives regarding the child labor issue (Lund-Thomsen and Nadvi, 2010b).

Figure 10.1 illustrates the key actors in vertical and horizontal governance, and how different types of governance operate along the vertical and horizontal dimensions. As cluster firms are integrated to GVCs, they are positioned simultaneously on both dimensions, subject to governance pressure for social upgrading from vertical (GVC) or horizontal (cluster) dimensions.

Figure 10.1 The Confluence of Actors in GVC and Cluster Governance

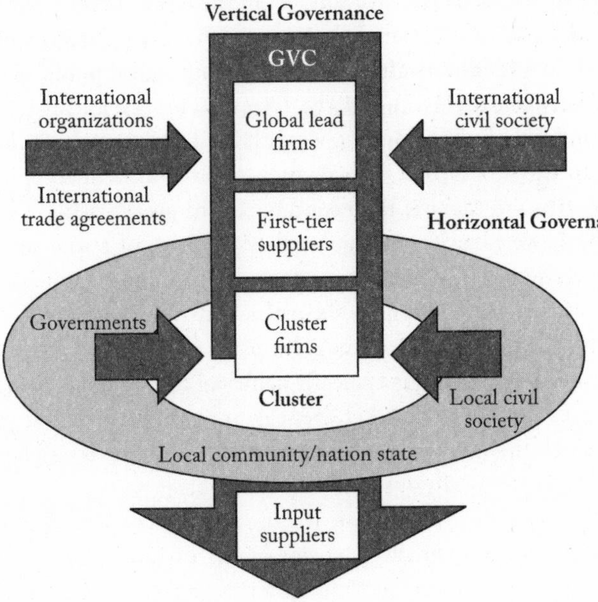

Source: Authors.

GVC and cluster governance can be in conflict, creating various kinds of tensions (Neilson and Pritchard, 2009). Child labor is an example. While many international NGOs, trade unions, and global buyers focus on abolishing child labor, their opposition to this practice confronts a very different viewpoint among some local firms and workers. They consider child labor as a form of job training for children who also can support their family's livelihood through work, particularly if formal schooling is not a viable option and other family members are not in a situation to get employed (Ruwanpura and Roncolato, 2006).

The GVC (vertical) and cluster (horizontal) forms of governance, however, can work together to generate upgrading outcomes. For example, confronting allegations of labor rights abuses, Kenyan producers and industry organizations set up a local program, called the Horticultural and Ethical Business Initiative (HEBI), which formulated its own social codes and trained auditors. These efforts were supported by vertical governance actors, notably the Ethical Trading Initiative (ETI), whose members included major retail buyers like Tesco (Dolan and Opondo, 2005). In the Cambodian garment sector, the Cambodian government and the Cambodian Garment Manufacturers Association (CGMA) worked with the ILO and the US government to improve labor conditions in the sector, while at the same time ensuring the access of the local producers in the US market (Polaski, 2006).

Such complementarity is found in other forms of vertical and horizontal governance. Many corporate codes of conduct (vertical private governance) require their suppliers to abide by national laws (horizontal public governance) (Kolk and van Tulder, 2004). The Better Work Program (vertical public governance), a partnership between the ILO and the International Financial Corporation, premises its 'conditionality' on compliance with local labor standards (local public governance).[7] In Cambodia, ILO's evaluation reports on firm compliance were used by private firms in making their sourcing decisions (Polaski, 2006).

In Table 10.2, we identify six potential trajectories of social upgrading in industrial clusters and GVCs, building upon and expanding Puppim de Oliveira's (2008a) distinctions. Each of these six paths is driven by the key actors and mechanisms that distinguish it from the other paths. These paths are not mutually exclusive and social upgrading is typically achieved through the engagement of multiple actors (O'Rourke, 2006). Yet, we seek to highlight different governance situations in which distinctive driving forces and leverage points play a critical role in advancing labor conditions and workers' rights.

1. *Market-driven path*: This refers to the situation in which market demand for goods produced with high social standards forces cluster firms to improve labor conditions in their factories or farms. The key driving force for this type of upgrading is cluster firms building up their market competiveness through product and process differentiation. Such efforts can be facilitated by mutual learning of market preferences by cluster firms, which may be supported by their national, regional, or global buyers (Schmitz and Knorringa, 2000). The key challenge in pursuing this trajectory is that market incentives do not always function well; the market frequently fails to reward firms that provide good working conditions and punish those who are exploitative to workers (Lund-Thomsen and Lindgreen, 2014; Ruwanpura and Wrigley, 2011). Furthermore, market incentives may be insufficient for cluster firms to

improve labor conditions if consumers they serve are unconcerned with social causes. This is likely to be the case in domestic markets, which many developing country clusters cater to (Kaplinsky and Farooki, 2010), although it is still unclear to what extent Southern consumers adhere less strongly to labor concerns relative to their Northern counterparts (Knorringa, 2011; Nadvi, 2014). Alternatively, market conditions may work to downgrade labor conditions. For example, the changing international demand for footballs involved a major reorganization of the Jalandhar football cluster in India, which had detrimental impacts on its competitiveness and the ability of women to participate in the workforce (Khara and Lund-Thomsen, 2012).

2. *CSR-driven path*: Cluster firms can improve the treatment of their workers to comply with global buyers' social codes of conduct (Lund-Thomsen and Nadvi, 2010a, 2010b; Puppim de Oliveira, 2008a). This path is driven by global buyers' explicit commitment to CSR, and corresponds to what is called the 'compliance' paradigm (Locke et al., 2009). While leading global brands need to avoid reputational damage that might be caused by the public disclosure of labor wrongdoings in their supply chains, cluster firms linked to the chains have the incentive to comply with the buyers' codes of conduct if it ensures access to global markets and differentiates them from other suppliers. Severe or repeated instances of non-compliance or violations of the codes could jeopardize such access (Lund-Thomsen and Nadvi, 2010b). Notwithstanding some success in certain areas of social upgrading, such as forced labor and health and safety, the compliance model confronts considerable limitations in further advancing social upgrading (Locke, 2013). The demands of the buyers often seem contradictory—e.g., they are forced to squeeze costs while simultaneously complying with the buyers' labor codes that provide little or no support for compliance costs (Barrientos, 2013). Furthermore, many clusters in developing countries serve the needs of domestic markets, or are linked to 'less visible' chains. In such clusters, CSR pressures may be weak and not adequately address the specific needs of the more disadvantaged actors (Neilson and Pritchard, 2010). Compliance pressures may come not only from vertical governance but also from diverse sets of local actors, including national media and local NGOs (Lund-Thomsen and Nadvi, 2010b), opening up other possible upgrading paths.

3. *Multi-stakeholder path*: The key momentum of this path comes from a multi-stakeholder initiative (MSI) to improve working conditions in SMEs in developing countries in a specific sector (e.g., Clean

Cloth Campaign in apparel) or across sectors (e.g., SA8000, the ETI) (Barrientos and Smith, 2007; O'Rourke, 2006). This model is distinctive from the CSR-driven compliance model. First, it is based on the cooperation of multiple (private and non-private) stakeholders, including national governments, cluster institutions, and local firms. Diversity and multivocality are the key to the model (Dolan and Opondo, 2005). Second, it combines compliance-monitoring with capability-building so that clusters can learn how to address labor issues on their own (Locke et al., 2009). The key driver is a broad-based coalition of various types of global and local actors—global lead brands, international and local NGOs, trade unions, cluster firms and industry associations—that cooperate in standard-setting, monitoring and sanctions, as well as capability-building. While the MSI model uses standardized codes of conduct and third-party accreditation (O'Rourke, 2006), local industries and clusters can generate collective responses, such as their own base codes and methodologies for audits, as Kenyan cut flower producers did (Dolan and Opondo, 2005). While local cluster firms and industry associations generally play a prominent role in 'less visible' chains, they can significantly contribute to social upgrading even in a 'highly visible' chain by organizing collective actions and enhancing the effectiveness and embeddedness of such activities in the local context (Lund-Thomsen and Nadvi, 2010b). Several challenges, however, are cited for the MSI model. For instance, stakeholders have different degrees of power, which affects how individual initiatives unfold (Dolan and Opondo, 2005). Also, the participation of Southern actors in MSI generally remains constrained (O'Rourke, 2006). Finally, capability-building may be limited to a few large cluster firms, not being spread across and beyond the cluster, as more hazardous jobs shift further down the supply chains or into the informal sectors (Lund-Thomsen and Lindgreen, 2014).

4. *Labor-centered path*: In some cases, the role of workers and labor unions is at least as significant as that of global buyers in promoting upgrading. Workers have increasingly been asserting their rights even in the places like China, where labor unions have traditionally been less effective (Gallagher, 2014). The advocates of this path criticize both CSR and MSI models for regarding workers as a passive subject with little agency (Carswell and De Neve, 2013; De Neve, 2014). Indeed, workers and trade unions are often active change agents in improving their own social conditions. Workers themselves can be the best monitors on the ground (O'Rourke, 2006). And in a tightly scheduled production system, workers' power to disrupt the supply chains with strikes or threats to do

so can be critical in their bargaining with employers. This is also the case for skilled workers where quality is emphasized in production, as in the horticulture sectors in Brazil and sub-Saharan Africa (Barrientos and Visser, 2012; Selwyn, 2013). One of the challenges for the labor-driven path is that in a segmented workplace, upgrading for one group of workers, for example, regular employees, often comes at the expense of other groups of workers, like women, migrant, casual, or temporary workers as well as those in the informal sectors. Employers can try to make up for their concession to one group with gains from others and use the latter as a buffer for their flexibility (Posthuma, 2010; Selwyn, 2013).

5. *Cluster-driven path*: This bottom-up path is initiated by cluster firms to improve working conditions within the cluster. Similar to workers, cluster actors tend to be portrayed as 'standard-takers' rather than 'standard-setters.' However, implementing externally driven labor codes often involves various kinds of tensions and conflicts with local institutions and practices (Lund-Thomsen and Nadvi, 2010a). Cluster-based initiatives, by contrast, take into account local contexts and perspectives. They also consider potential economic gains for cluster firms, which are often not the central concern in global buyers' CSR initiatives. The key mechanism of this model is cluster-based collective actions toward the improvement of labor conditions, facilitated by trust and mutual dependence between closely knit firms. Cluster institutions, such as business associations, chambers of commerce and cooperatives, play a key role by providing training and information on quality and social standards in external markets (Doner and Schneider, 2000; Puppim de Oliveira, 2008b). Even in the cases where cluster initiatives are prompted by pressures from global lead firms or international NGOs, local governance at the cluster level can play an important role by facilitating the effective implementation of collective actions (Lund-Thomsen and Nadvi, 2010b). These collective actions can lower compliance costs, promote the local ownership of social codes, improve the effectiveness of compliance-monitoring, and embed social goals in cluster norms and practices. The potential weakness of the model, however, is that local initiatives can be delayed or downscaled without sustained external pressures from global brands and independent scrutiny from NGOs, as often the case in 'less visible' chains (Lund-Thomsen and Nadvi, 2010b). For example, locally controlled child labor monitoring in Jalandhar, Pakistan was found weaker compared to a similar system in Sialkot, where well-known global brands are present (Lund-Thomsen and Nadvi, 2010a).

6. *Public-governance path*: Public regulations are important because they can make the most far-reaching impact on improving labor conditions involving all the suppliers under their jurisdiction, regardless of whether they are inside or out of a GVC or a cluster (Mayer and Gereffi, 2010). The role of the state is particularly important in 'enforcing the law' (Puppim de Oliveira, 2008a), preventing defections by individual firms, and resolving collective action problems among various stakeholders (Amengual, 2010). State power comes from various levels, including government ministries (Tewari and Pillai, 2005) and Supreme Courts (Crow and Batz, 2006) at a national level to labor inspectors at a local level (Coslovsky, 2014). The state's actions are prompted by workers' grievances and public discomfort with undesirable labor conditions as well as transnational campaigns demanding a stricter enforcement of labor laws and policing of labor abuses. Scholars have recently suggested that the state can go beyond its traditional deterrence-based regulations to take more innovative and experimental approaches by collaborating with private and civil actors, providing incentives such as technical assistance, supporting local capability-building initiatives, and closing off 'low-road' options[8] (Locke, 2013). The question, however, is whether national or local governments have the will to act to promote social upgrading in the face of business pressures not to drive away foreign investors. It is also unclear how much the state is capable of mediating the competing interests of different stakeholders. Despite some evidence of a proactive role of the state, it is unknown whether such models are applicable to a wide range of countries, different levels of government, and all sectors.

Table 10.2 summarizes key drivers, mechanisms, and actors involved in each of these social upgrading paths. In reality, social upgrading tends to be achieved through the engagement of multiple actors with distinctive capabilities and limitations (O'Rourke, 2006). For example, global standards are rarely implemented in a cluster without interacting with local contexts, creating various kinds of conflicts and tensions with existing local norms and institutions (Neilson and Pritchard, 2009). Consequently, what actually emerges is a form of governance 'co-produced' by global and local manifestations of public, social and private actors (Lund-Thomsen and Nadvi, 2010a).

When different types of governance coexist and interact, one possible outcome is displacement—i.e., one type of governance can pre-empt, displace, or crowd out other forms. Private governance like CSR, for instance, may replace public governance and weaken other forms of governance, such as local labor institutions or labor unions (Justice, 2005; O'Rourke, 2003). In criticizing fair and ethical trade initiatives for their limited scope, Neilson and Pritchard (2010) argue that the initiatives tend to 'supplant traditional regulatory formations anchored in the national state' (p. 1847). Bartley (2005) not only finds some empirical support for the displacement hypothesis in his study of the apparel sector, but also highlights that the rise of private labor regulations was highly contested and, as a result, the outcome is more complex than simple displacement.

Another possibility is that different forms of governance can complement each other (Amengual, 2010; Polaski, 2006) and, in some cases, lead to a 'hybrid system of regulation' (Amengual, 2010), or 'synergistic governance' (Mayer, 2014). Private and public governance can have comparative strengths and weaknesses that make them complementary (Rodríguez-Garavito, 2005).[9] Private auditing, for example, did not replace but rather complemented state regulations in the Dominican Republic's export processing zones by freeing up scarce government resources for monitoring and directing them to 'less visible' firms in the informal sector (Amengual, 2010). Furthermore, scholars are recently beginning to identify sets of conditions in GVCs and industrial clusters under which economic and social upgrading in global supply chains can come together and be mutually reinforcing (Barrientos et al., 2011; Mayer and Gereffi, 2010; Puppim de Oliveira, 2008b).

Table 10.2 Key Drivers, Mechanisms, and Actors of Social Upgrading

	Key drivers	Main mechanisms	Major actors
Market-driven path	Market competitiveness	Market supply and demand	Buyers; consumers; suppliers
CSR-driven path	Global buyer's reputation and purchasing power	Compliance to buyers codes; social audits	Global buyers
Multi-stakeholder path	A broad-based coalition for standard-setting, monitoring, capability-building and sanctions	Multiple, standardized, social standards; capability-building and cooperation	International NGOs; global buyers; local actors
Labor-centered path	Workers' grievances; exercise of bargaining power	Collective bargaining; strikes; sabotages	Workers; labor unions
Cluster-centered path	External CSR pressure; collective efficiency	Collective standard-setting, implementation, support	Cluster firms; industrial associations; cooperatives
Public-governance path	Public pressure; experimentalist approach to improve workers well-being	Strong labor law; law enforcement	National, regional, and local governments

Source: Authors.

Although private governance alone may not bring about sustainable changes in labor or environmental conditions, private voluntary standards appear to be most effective when they are layered on and blended with public mandatory regulations (Locke, 2013). Like corporate codes of conduct, CSR regimes may also have the greatest chance to succeed if they are combined with favorable market conditions, multi-stakeholder coalitions, government willingness and capacity to act, and sustained pressure from organized workers and other civic activists.

Conclusion

Global value chains and industrial clusters have been changing in significant ways in recent years. While the researchers who study these phenomena tend to focus on different levels of analysis—global and local, respectively—there is a need for more integrated frameworks that show how GVCs and clusters are connected through a variety of globalization processes, such as those outlined in this chapter. The linking of GVCs and clusters also offers some constructive recommendations for CSR, since GVC lead firms are under pressure to move beyond narrow cost-based models of competition in order to promote more sustainable development. This requires a shift from inactive or reactive CSR strategies, in which supply chain relationships are considered to be a liability of supply chain management, to more active and proactive CSR strategies, which highlight broader societal responsibilities related to local suppliers and communities (van Tulder, 2009).

This chapter proposes several building blocks for a more integrated CSR framework. First, economic and social upgrading should be linked in our GVC and cluster models, and we need to pursue research agendas that seek to identify the conditions under which economic and social upgrading can be mutually supportive (Barrientos et al., 2011, 2012, and the *Capturing the Gains* project highlighted in endnote 2). Second, we need to expand and integrate our typologies of GVC and cluster governance, which tend to focus on vertical and horizontal relationships, respectively, in order to take account of the different actors that are linked to private, public, and social forms of governance. Third, while we have highlighted six different pathways for social upgrading, we have suggested the importance of 'synergistic governance' as a way to advance more comprehensive and sustainable forms of upgrading, both economically and socially. Synergistic governance is not easy to achieve, but it offers a promising pathway to bringing together corporate, governmental, and civil society actors in a global setting to achieve joint objectives, where active collaboration among GVC and industrial cluster actors is required in order to simultaneously achieve economic and social gains.

Future research should make more explicit under what conditions complementary and synergistic forms of governance (or alliances among different governance actors) are likely to emerge, and what enables joint forms of governance to become institutionalized in the cluster (Amengual, 2010; Mayer and Gereffi, 2010). We also need to know how different paths or trajectories could accelerate social and economic upgrading in developing country clusters. To answer these questions, research projects that more explicitly link the cluster and GVC paradigms are needed.

Acknowledgments

The authors would like to thank Peter Lund-Thomsen and two anonymous reviewers for valuable feedback on earlier versions of this chapter. Lee's work was supported by the research fund of Hanyang University (HY-2012-2430). All errors of fact and interpretation are our responsibility.

Notes

1. There is an extensive discussion in the GVC literature that we review below about different ways to measure economic upgrading that involves a focus on both higher value products (e.g., product upgrading, often measured with unit values of exports) and various ways of contributing to higher value-added production, including greater levels of domestic content in exports.

2. *Capturing the Gains* was funded by the UK's Department for International Development (DFID) between 2010 and 2013, and the project's publications, working papers, policy briefs, and other activities are listed on the Capturing the Gains website, http://www.capturingthegains.org/.

3. This normative dimension is particularly important in place-based industrial clusters, where underlying phenomena like the communitarian ethos, a distinctive trait of the Marshallian industrial districts, facilitate mutual trust between people and the transfer and co-production of knowledge (De Marchi and Grandinetti, 2014).

4. This may be emerging not only in the Bangladesh garment industry, with its unprecedented multi-stakeholder coalition of global retailers and brands that have pressured both the Bangladesh government and local factory owners to change legislation and business practices that have led to dangerous and degrading workplace conditions, but also in manufacturing powerhouses like China, where synergistic governance also forced changes by Foxconn and Apple in the electronics sector (Mayer, 2014).

5. Social upgrading can be subdivided into two components (Barrientos and Smith, 2007; Elliott and Freeman, 2003): measurable standards, which include the type of employment (regular or irregular), wage level, social protection, and working hours; and enabling rights, or less quantifiable aspects of social upgrading, such as freedom of association, the right to collective bargaining, non-discrimination, voice, and empowerment.

6. While not directly addressed in this chapter, we view environmental upgrading as an important corollary of economic and social upgrading in the expanded GVC research agenda we discuss here.
7. See more on the Better Work program at its website, http://betterwork.org/global.
8. In one such example in Brazil, labor inspectors not only enforced the labor law but also actively engaged in devising local arrangements such as employers' consortia and prompted producers to make their work practices safer (Coslovsky, 2014: 210). Similarly, labor inspectors in the Dominican Republic, in addition to their conventional role of law enforcement, took a proactive approach to labor regulation and engaged in educating workers about their rights and reconciling disputes between employers and workers (Amengual, 2010).
9. As Coslovsky and Locke (2013) point out, such complementarity may not require explicit communication and coordination between private and public governance actors to make each other's actors effective (see also Amengual, 2010).

References

Altenburg, Tilman and Jorg Meyer-Stamer. 1999. 'How to Promote Clusters: Policy Experiences from Latin America.' *World Development* 27(9): 1693–1713.

Amengual, Matthew. 2010. 'Complementary Labor Regulation: The Uncoordinated Combination of State and Private Regulators in the Dominican Republic.' *World Development* 38(3): 405–414.

Bair, Jennifer and Gary Gereffi. 2001. 'Local Clusters in Global Chains: The Causes and Consequences of Export Dynamism in Torreon's Blue Jeans Industry.' *World Development* 29(11): 1885–1903.

Barrientos, Stephanie. 2013. 'Corporate Purchasing Practices in Global Production Networks: A Socially Contested Terrain.' *Geoforum* 44: 44–51.

Barrientos, Stephanie, Gary Gereffi, and Dev Nathan. 2012. 'Economic and Social Upgrading in Global Value Chains: Emerging Trends and Pressures.' Capturing the Gains Summit Briefing, University of Manchester. Available at http://www.capturingthegains.org/pdf/CTG-GVC.pdf.

Barrientos, Stephanie, Gary Gereffi, and Arianna Rossi. 2011. 'Economic and Social Upgrading in Global Production Networks: A New Paradigm for a Changing World.' *International Labour Review* 150(3–4): 319–340.

Barrientos, Stephanie and Andreinetta Kritzinger. 2004. 'Squaring the Circle: Global Production and the Informalization of Work in South African Fruit Exports.' *Journal of International Development* 16(1): 81–92.

Barrientos, Stephanie and Sally Smith. 2007. 'Do Workers Benefit from Ethical Trade? Assessing Codes of Labour Practice in Global Production Systems.' *Third World Quarterly* 28(4): 713–729.

Barrientos, Stephanie and Margareet Visser. 2012. 'South African Horticulture: Opportunities and Challenges for Economic and Social Upgrading in Value Chains.' Capturing the Gains Working Paper 2012/12, University of Manchester. Available at http://www.capturingthegains.org/publications/workingpapers/wp_201212.htm.

Bartley, Tim. 2005. 'Corporate Accountability and the Privatization of Labor Standards: Struggles over Codes of Conduct in the Apparel Industry.' *Research in Political Sociology* 14: 211–244.

Bernhardt, Thomas and William Milberg. 2011. 'Economic and Social Upgrading in Global Value Chains: Analysis of Horticulture, Apparel, Tourism and Mobile Telephones.' Capturing the Gains Working Paper 2011/06. Available at http://www.capturingthegains. org/publications/workingpapers/wp_201106.htm.

Carr, Marilyn and Martha Chen. 2004. 'Globalization, Social Exclusion and Work: With Special Reference to Informal Employment and Gender.' Geneva: International Labour Office. Available at http://www.ilo.org/dyn/dwresources/docs/625/F1146925582/ gender%20and%20globalisation.pdf.

Carswell, Grace and Geert De Neve. 2013. 'Labouring for Global Markets: Conceptualising Labour Agency in Global Production Networks.' *Geoforum* 44: 62–70.

Cattaneo, Olivier, Gary Gereffi, Sébastien Miroudot, and Daria Taglioni. 2013. 'Joining, Upgrading and Being Competitive in Global Value Chains: A Strategic Framework.' World Bank Policy Research Working Paper 6406. Washington, DC: World Bank.

Chiarvesio, Maria, Eleonora Di Maria, and Stefano Micelli. 2010. 'Global Value Chains and Open Networks: The Case of Italian Industrial Districts.' *European Planning Studies* 18(3): 333–350.

Contreras, Oscar F., Jorge Carrillo, and Jorge Alonso. 2012. 'Local Entrepreneurship within Global Value Chains: A Case Study in the Mexican Automotive Industry.' *World Development* 40(5): 1013–1023.

Coslovsky, Salo V. 2014. 'Flying Under the Radar? The State and the Enforcement of Labour Laws in Brazil.' *Oxford Development Studies* 42(2): 190–216.

Coslovsky, Salo V. and Richard Locke. 2013. 'Parallel Paths to Enforcement: Private Compliance, Public Regulation, and Labor Standards in the Brazilian Sugar Sector.' *Politics and Society* 41(4): 497–526.

Crow, Michael and Michael B. Batz. 2006. 'Clean and Competitive? Small-Scale Bleachers and Dyers in Tirupur, India.' In *Small Firms and the Environment in Developing Countries— Collective Action and Collective Impacts*, edited by Allen Blackman, 147–170. Washington, DC: REF Press.

Damodaran, Sumangala. 2010. 'Upgradation or Flexible Casualization? Exploring the Dynamics of Global Value Chain Incorporation in the Indian Leather Industry.' In *Labour in Global Production Networks in India*, edited by Anne Posthuma and Dev Nathan, 231–250. New Delhi, New York: Oxford University Press.

De Marchi, Valentina, Eleonora Di Maria, and Stefano Ponte. 2014. 'Multinational Firms and the Management of Global Networks: Insights from Global Value Chain Studies.' In *Orchestration of the Global Network Organization*, edited by Torben Pedersen, Markus Venzin, Timothy M. Devinney, and Laszlo Tihanyi, 463–486. Bingley, UK: Emerald Group Publishing Limited.

De Marchi, Valentina and Roberto Grandinetti. 2014. 'Industrial Districts and the Collapse of the Marshallian Model: Looking at the Italian Experience.' *Competition and Change* 18(1): 70–87.

De Neve, Geert. 2014. 'Fordism, Flexible Specialisation and CSR: How Indian Garment Workers Critique Neoliberal Labour Regimes.' *Ethnography* 15(2): 184–207.

Dolan, Catherine S. and Maggie Opondo. 2005. 'Seeking Common Ground – Multistakeholer Processes in Kenya's Cut Flower Industry.' *Journal of Corporate Citizenship* 18: 87–98.

Doner, Richard F. and Ben R. Schneider. 2000. 'Business Associations and Economic Development: Why Some Associations Contribute More than Others.' *Business and Politics* 2(3): 261–288.

Elliott, Kimberley A. and Richard B. Freeman. 2003. 'The Role Global Labor Standards Could Play in Addressing Basic Needs.' In *Global Inequalities at Work*, edited by Jody Heymann, 299–327. New York: Oxford University Press.

European Commission. 2011. 'A Renewed EU Strategy 2011–2014 for Corporate Social Responsibility.' Brussels: European Commission. Available at http://eurlex.europa.eu/ LexUriServ/LexUriServ.do?uri=COM:2011:0681:FIN:EN:PDF.

Gallagher, Mary E. 2014. 'China's Workers Movement and the End of the Rapid-growth Era.' *Daedalus* 143(2): 81–95.

Gereffi, Gary. 1994. 'The Organization of Buyer-driven Global Commodity Chains: How US Retailers Shape Overseas Production Networks.' In *Commodity Chains and Global Capitalism*, edited by Gary Gereffi and Miguel Korzeniewicz, 95–122. Westport, CT: Greenwood Press.

———. 1999. 'International Trade and Industrial Upgrading in the Apparel Commodity Chains.' *Journal of International Economics* 48(1): 37–70.

———. 2005. 'The Global Economy: Organization, Governance, and Development.' In *The Handbook of Economic Sociology*, 2nd edition, edited by Neil J. Smelser and Richard Swedberg, 160–182. Princeton, NJ: Princeton University Press.

———. 2014. 'Global Value Chains in a Post-Washington Consensus world.' *Review of International Political Economy* 21(1): 9–37.

Gereffi, Gary and Karina Fernandez-Stark. 2011. *Global Value Chain Analysis: A Primer*. Durham, NC: Duke Global Value Chains Center. Available at http://www.cggc.duke.edu/ pdfs/2011-05-31_GVC_analy sis_a_primer.pdf.

Gereffi, Gary, John Humphrey, and Timothy J. Sturgeon. 2005. 'The Governance of Global Value Chains.' *Review of International Political Economy* 12(1): 78–104.

Gereffi, Gary and Joonkoo Lee. 2012. 'Why the World Suddenly Cares about Global Supply Chains.' *Journal of Supply Chain Management* 48(3): 24–32.

Gereffi, Gary and Timothy J. Sturgeon. 2013. 'Global Value Chain-oriented Industrial Policy: The Role of Emerging Economies.' In *Global Value Chains in a Changing World*, edited by Deborah K. Elms and Patrick Low, 329–360. Geneva: World Trade Organization, Fung Global Institute and Temasek Foundation Centre for Trade and Negotiations.

Gibbon, Peter, Jennifer Bair, and Stefano Ponte. 2008. 'Governing Global Value Chains: An Introduction.' *Economy and Society* 37(3): 315–338.

Greenhouse, Steven. 2013. 'US Retailers Decline to Aid Factory Victims in Bangladesh.' *New York Times*, November 23. Available at http://www.nytimes.com/2013/11/23/business/ international/us-retailers-decline-to-aid-factory-victims-in-bangladesh.html.

Humphrey, John and Olga Memedovic. 2006. 'Global Value Chains in the Agrifood Sector.' United Nations Industrial Development Organization Working Paper, Vienna. Available at http://www.unido.org/fileadmin/user_media/Publications/Pub_free/Global_value_ chains_in_the_agrifood_sector.df.

Humphrey, John and Hubert Schmitz. 2002. 'How Does Insertion in Global Value Chains Affect Upgrading in Industrial Clusters?' *Regional Studies* 36(9): 1017–1027.

ILO (International Labour Organisation). 1999. *Decent Work: Report of the Director-General to the 89th Session of the International Labour Conference.* Geneva: ILO. Available at http://www.ilo.org/public/libdoc/ilo/P/09605/09605(1999-87).pdf.

Jenkins, Rhys O., Ruth Pearson, and Gill Seyfang. 2002. *Corporate Responsibility and Labour Rights: Codes of Conduct in the Global Economy.* London: Earthscan.

Justice, Dwight W. 2005. 'The Corporate Social Responsibility Concept and Phenomenon: Challenges and Opportunities for Trade Unionists.' Presented at the ITC-ILO/ACTRAV Course A3-50909: Trade Union Training for Global Union Federations in Asia and the Pacific Region on Globalization, Workers' Rights and Corporate Social Responsibility (CSR), Kuala Lumpur, Malaysia.

Kaplinsky, Raphael and Masuma Farooki. 2010. 'Global Value Chains, the Crisis, and the Shift of Markets from North to South.' In *Global Value Chains in a Postcrisis World: A Development Perspective,* edited by Olivier Cattaneo, Gary Gereffi, and Cornelia Staritz, 125–153. Washington, DC: World Bank.

Kaplinsky, Raphael, Anne Terheggen, and Julia P. Tijaja. 2011. 'China as a Final Market: The Gabon Timber and Thai Cassava Value Chains.' *World Development* 39(7): 1177–1190.

Ketels, Christian H. and Olga Memedovic. 2008. 'From Clusters to Cluster-based Economic Development.' *International Journal of Technological Learning, Innovation and Development* 1(3): 375–392.

Khara, Navjote and Peter Lund-Thomsen. 2012. 'Value Chain Restructuring, Work Organization and Labour Outcomes in Football Manufacturing in India.' *Competition and Change* 16(4): 261–280.

Knorringa, Peter. 2011. 'Value Chain Responsibility in the Global South.' In *South-South Globalization: Challenges and Opportunities for Development,* edited by Syed M. Murshed, Pedro Goulart, and Leandro Serino, 194–208. New York: Routledge.

Knorringa, Peter and Lee Pegler. 2007. 'Integrating Labour Issues in Global Value Chains Analysis: Exploring Implications for Labour Research and Unions.' In *Trade Union Responses to Globalisation: A Review by the Global Unions Research Network,* edited by Verena Schmidt, 35–51. Geneva: ILO.

Kolk, Ans and Rob van Tulder. 2004. 'Ethics in International Business: Multinational Approaches to Child Labor.' *Journal of World Business* 39(1): 49–60.

Lee, Joonkoo, Gary Gereffi, and Janet Beauvais. 2012. 'Global Value Chains and Agrifood Standards: Challenges and Possibilities for Smallholders in Developing Countries.' *Proceedings of the National Academy of Sciences of the United States of America* 191(31): 12326–12331.

Locke, Richard M. 2013. *The Promise and Limits of Private Power: Promoting Labor Standards in a Global Economy.* Cambridge, New York: Cambridge University Press.

Locke, Richard M., Matthew Amengual, and Akshay Mangla. 2009. 'Virtue Out of Necessity? Compliance, Commitment, and the Improvement of Labor Conditions in Global Supply Chains.' *Politics and Society* 37(3): 319–351.

Lund-Thomsen, Peter and Adam Lindgreen. 2014. 'Corporate Social Responsibility in Global Value Chains: Where are We Now and Where are We Going?' *Journal of Business Ethics* 123(1): 11–22.

Lund-Thomsen, Peter and Khalid Nadvi. 2010a. 'Clusters, Chains and Compliance: Corporate Social Responsibility and Governance in Football Manufacturing in South Asia.' *Journal of Business Ethics* 93(2): 201–222.

————. 2010b. 'Global Value Chains, Local Collective Action and Corporate Social Responsibility: A Review of Empirical Evidence.' *Business Strategy and the Environment* 19(1): 1–13.

Lund-Thomsen, Peter and Renginee G. Pillay. 2012. 'CSR in Industrial Clusters: An Overview of the Literature.' *Corporate Governance* 12(4): 568–578.

Mayer, Frederick. 2014. 'Leveraging Private Governance for Public Purpose: Business, Civil Society and the State in Labour Regulation.' In *Handbook on the International Political Economy of Governance*, edited by Anthony Payne and Nicola Phillips, 344–360. Cheltenham, UK: Edward Elgar.

Mayer, Frederick and Gary Gereffi. 2010. 'Regulation and Economic Globalization: Prospects and Limits of Private Governance.' *Business and Politics* 12(3): 1–25.

Mezzadri, Alessandra. 2014. 'Indian Garment Clusters and CSR Norms: Incompatible Agendas at the Bottom of the Garment Commodity Chain.' *Oxford Development Studies* 42(2): 238–258.

Nadvi, Khalid. 2014. ''Rising powers' and Labour and Environmental Standards.' *Oxford Development Studies* 42(2): 137–150.

Nadvi, Khalid and Stephanie Barrientos. 2004. 'Industrial Clusters and Poverty Reduction: Towards a Methodology for Poverty and Social Impact Assessment of Cluster Development Initiatives.' Vienna: United Nations Industrial Development Organization. Available at http://www.unido.org/fileadmin/user_media/Services/PSD/Clusters_and_Networks/publications/industrial ClustersandpovertyـNADVI.pdf.

Nathan, Dev and Sandip Sarkar. 2011. 'Blood on Your Mobile Phone? Capturing the Gains for Artisanal Miners, Poor Workers and Women.' *Capturing the Gains* Briefing Note 2. Available at http://www.capturingthegains.org/publications/briefingnotes/bp_02.htm.

Neilson, Jeff and Bill Pritchard. 2009. *Value Chain Struggles: Institutions and Governance in the Plantation Districts of South India*. Malden, MA: Wiley.

————. 2010. 'Fairness and Ethicality in their Place: The Regional Dynamics of Fair Trade and Ethical Sourcing Agendas in the Plantation Districts of South India.' *Environment and Planning A* 42(8): 1833–1851.

O'Rourke, Dara. 2003. 'Outsourcing Regulation: Analyzing Nongovernmental Systems of Labor Standards and Monitoring.' *Policy Studies Journal* 31(1): 1–29.

————. 2006. 'Multi-stakeholder Regulation: Privatizing or Socializing Global Labor Standards?' *World Development* 34(5): 899–918.

Palpacuer, Florence. 2008. 'Bringing the Social Context Back In: Governance and Wealth Distribution in Global Commodity Chains.' *Economy and Society* 37(3): 393–419.

Piore, Michael J. and Charles F. Sabel. 1984. *The Second Industrial Divide*. New York: Basic Books.

Polaski, Sandra. 2003. 'Protecting Labor Rights through Trade Agreements: An Analytical Guide.' *UC Davis Journal of International Law and Policy* 10(1): 13–25.

————. 2006. 'Combining Global and Local Forces: The Case of Labor Rights in Cambodia.' *World Development* 34(5): 919–932.

Ponte, Stefano and Peter Gibbon. 2005. 'Quality Standards, Conventions and the Governance of Global Value Chains.' *Economy and Society* 34(1): 1–31.

Ponte, Stefano and Timothy J. Sturgeon. 2014. 'Explaining Governance in Global Value Chains: A Modular Theory-building Effort.' *Review of International Political Economy* 21(1): 195–223.

Porter, Michael E. 1998. 'Clusters and the New Economics of Competition.' *Harvard Business Review* 76(6): 77–90.

Posthuma, Anne. 2008. 'Seeking the High Road to Jepara: Challenges for Economic and Social Upgrading in Indonesian Wood Furniture Clusters.' In *Upgrading Clusters and Small Enterprises in Developing Countries: Environmental, Labor, Innovation and Social Issues*, edited by Jose A. Puppim de Oliveira, 23–43. Burlington, VT: Ashgate.

————. 2010. 'Beyond 'Regulatory Enclaves': Challenges and Opportunities to Promote Decent Work in Global Production Networks.' In *Labour in Global Production Networks in India*, edited by Anne Posthuma and Dev Nathan, 57–80. New York: Oxford University Press.

Posthuma, Anne and Dev Nathan, eds. 2010. *Labour in Global Production Networks in India*. New York: Oxford University Press.

Puppim de Oliveira, Jose A. 2008a. 'Introduction: Social Upgrading among Small Firms and Clusters.' In *Upgrading Clusters and Small Enterprises in Developing Countries: Environmental, Labor, Innovation and Social Issues*, edited by Jose A. Puppim de Oliveira, 1–21. Burlington, VT: Ashgate.

————. 2008b. *Upgrading Clusters and Small Enterprises in Developing Countries: Environmental, Labor, Innovation and Social Issues*. Burlington, VT: Ashgate.

Pyke, Frank S., Giacomo Becattini, and Werner Sengenberger, eds. 1990. *Industrial Districts and Inter-Firm Co-operation in Italy*. Geneva: International Institute for Labour Studies.

Rodríguez-Garavito, César A. 2005. 'Global Governance and Labor Rights: Codes of Conduct and Anti-Sweatshop Struggles in Global Apparel Factories in Mexico and Guatemala.' *Politics and Society* 33(2): 203–333.

Ruwanpura, Kanchana N. and Leanne Roncolato. 2006. 'Child Rights: An Enabling or Disabling Right? The Nexus between Child Labor and Poverty in Bangladesh.' *Journal of Developing Societies* 22(4): 359–378.

Ruwanpura, Kanchana N. and Neil Wrigley. 2011. 'The Costs of Compliance? Views of Sri Lankan Apparel Manufacturers in Times of Global Economic Crisis.' *Journal of Economic Geography* 11(6): 1031–1049.

Schmitz, Hubert. 1995. 'Collective Efficiency: Growth Path for Smallscale Industry.' *Journal of Development Studies* 31(4): 529–566.

————. ed. 2004. *Local Enterprises in the Global Economy: Issues of Governance and Upgrading*. Cheltenham, UK: Edward Elgar.

————. 2006. 'Learning and Earning in Global Garment and Footwear Chains.' *European Journal of Development Research* 18(4): 546–571.

Schmitz, Hubert and Peter Knorringa. 2000. 'Learning from Global Buyers.' *Journal of Development Studies* 37(2): 177–205.

Schmitz, Hubert and Khalid Nadvi. 1999. 'Clustering and Industrialization: Introduction.' *World Development* 27(9): 1503–1514.

Selwyn, Ben. 2013. 'Social Upgrading and Labour in Global Production Networks: A Critique and an Alternative Conception.' *Competition and Change* 17(1): 75–90.

Sturgeon, Timothy J. 2003. 'What Really Goes On in Silicon Valley? Spatial Clustering and Dispersal in Modular Production Networks.' *Journal of Economic Geography* 3(2): 199–225.

———. 2009. 'From Commodity Chains to Value Chains: Interdisciplinary Theory Building in an Age of Globalization.' In *Frontiers of Commodity Chain Research*, edited by Jennifer Bair, 110–135. Stanford, CA: Stanford University Press.

Sturgeon, Timothy J., Johannes Van Biesebroeck, and Gary Gereffi. 2008. 'Value Chains, Networks and Clusters: Reframing the Global Automotive Industry.' *Journal of Economic Geography* 8(3): 297–321.

Suresh, T. G. 2010. 'Cost Cutting Pressures and Labour Relations in Tamil Nadu's Automobile Components Supply Chain.' In *Labour in Global Production Networks in India*, edited by Anne Posthuma and Dev Nathan, 251–271. New York: Oxford University Press.

Tewari, Meenu and Poonam Pillai. 2005. 'Global Standards and the Dynamics of Environmental Compliance in India's Leather Industry.' *Oxford Development Studies* 33(2): 245–267.

van Tulder, Rob. 2009. 'Chains for Change.' Position Paper for the Third Max Havelaar Lecture. Available at http://www.maxhavelaarlecture.org/downloads/max_havelaar_lectures_2009_booklet.pdf.

Part III

Policy Issues and Challenges

Global Value Chain Analysis

A Primer

Second Edition[1]

Gary Gereffi and Karina Fernandez-Stark

I. Importance of Global Value Chains

The global economy is increasingly structured around global value chains (GVCs) that account for a rising share of international trade, global gross domestic product, and employment. The evolution of GVCs in diverse sectors, such as commodities, apparel, electronics, tourism, and business service outsourcing, has significant implications in terms of global trade, production and employment, and how developing country firms, producers and workers integrate in the global economy. GVCs link firms, workers, and consumers around the world and often provide a stepping-stone for firms and workers in developing countries to participate in the global economy. For many countries, especially low-income countries, the ability to effectively insert into GVCs is a vital condition for development. This supposes an ability to access GVCs, to compete successfully and to 'capture the gains' in terms of national economic development, capability building and generating more and better jobs to reduce unemployment and poverty. Thus, it is not only a matter of whether to participate in the global economy, but how to do so gainfully.

The GVC framework allows one to understand how global industries are organized by examining the structure and dynamics of different actors involved in a given industry. In today's globalized economy with very complex industry interactions, the GVC methodology is a useful tool to trace the shifting patterns of global production, link geographically dispersed activities and actors within a single industry, and determine the roles they play in developed and developing countries alike. The GVC framework focuses on the sequences of value added within an industry, from conception to production and end use. It examines the job descriptions, technologies, standards, regulations, products, processes, and markets in specific industries and places, thus providing a holistic view of global industries both from the top-down and the bottom-up.

The comprehensive nature of the framework allows policy makers to answer questions regarding development issues that have not been addressed by previous paradigms. Additionally, it provides a means to explain the changed global-local dynamics that have emerged within the past 20 years (Gereffi and Korzeniewicz, 1994). As policy makers and researchers alike have come to understand the pros and cons of the spread of globalization, the GVC framework has gained importance in tack ling new industry realities such as the role of emerging economies like China, India, and Brazil as new drivers of global value chains, the importance of international product and process certifications as preconditions of competitive success for export-oriented economies, the rise of demand-driven workforce development initiatives as integral to dynamic economic upgrading, and the proliferation of private regulations and standards (Lee, 2010; Mayer and Gereffi, 2010), while also proving useful in the examination of social and environmental development concerns. A range of institutions and governments have commissioned GVC studies to understand global industries and to guide the formulation of new programs and policies to promote economic development.

II. What Are Global Value Chains?

The value chain describes the full range of activities that firms and workers perform to bring a product from its conception to end use and beyond. This includes activities such as research and development (R&D), design, production, marketing, distribution, and support to the final consumer. The activities that comprise a value chain can be contained within a single firm or divided among different firms (Global Value Chains Initiative, 2011). In the context of globalization, the activities that constitute a value chain have generally been carried out in inter-firm networks on a global scale. By focusing on the sequences of tangible and intangible value-adding activities, from conception and production to end use, GVC analysis provides a holistic view of global industries—both from the top-down (for example, examining how lead firms 'govern' their global-scale affiliate and supplier networks) and from the bottom-up (for example, asking how these business decisions affect the trajectory of economic and social 'upgrading' or 'downgrading' in specific countries and regions).

There are six basic dimensions that GVC methodology explores that are divided in global (top-down) and local (bottom-up) elements (see Figure 11.1). The first set of dimensions refers to international elements, determined by the dynamics of the industry at a global level. The second set of dimensions explains how individual countries participate in GVCs. These six dimensions are: (1) an input-output structure, which describes the process of transforming raw materials into final products; (2) the geographic scope, which explains how the industry is globally dispersed and in what countries the different GVC activities are carried out; and (3) a governance structure, which explains how the value chain is controlled by firms. The local dimensions are: (4) upgrading, which describes the dynamic movement within the value chain by examining how producers shift between different stages of the chain (Gereffi, 1999; Humphrey and Schmitz, 2000); (5) an institutional context in which the industry value chain is embedded in local economic and social elements (Gereffi, 1995); and (6) industry stakeholders, which describe how the different local actors of the value chain interact to achieve industry upgrading.

Figure 11.1 Six Dimensions of GVC Analysis

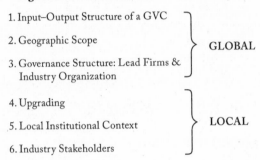

1. Input–Output Structure of a GVC

2. Geographic Scope

3. Governance Structure: Lead Firms & Industry Organization

GLOBAL

4. Upgrading

5. Local Institutional Context

6. Industry Stakeholders

LOCAL

Source: Fernandez-Stark et al., 2013.

The GVC approach analyzes the global economy from these two contrasting vantage points: 'top-down' or global and 'bottom-up' or local. 'Governance' of global value chains, a key concept of the top-down view, focuses mainly on lead firms and the organization of international industries. Upgrading, the main concept for the bottom-up perspective, focuses on the strategies used by countries, regions, and other economic stakeholders to maintain or improve their positions in the global economy.

III. Dimensions of GVC Analysis

Six dimensions constitute global value chain analysis. They are discussed below from the researcher's perspective.

1. Input–Output Structure

a. Identify the Main Activities/Segments in a Global Value Chain

A chain represents the entire input-output process that brings a product or service from initial conception to the consumer's hands. The main segments in the chain vary by industry, but typically include: research and development, design, inputs, production, distribution and marketing, and sales, and in some cases the recycling of products after use. This input-output structure involves goods and services, as well as a range of supporting industries. The input-output structure is typically represented as a set of value chain boxes connected by arrows that show the f lows of tangible and intangible goods and services, which are critical to mapping the value added at different stages in the chain, and to layering in information of particular interest to the researcher (e.g., jobs, wages, gender, and the firms participating at diverse stages of the chain).

In order to understand the entire chain, it is crucial to study the evolution of the industry, the trends that have shaped it, and its organization. Based on general knowledge about the industry, segments of the chain can be identified and differentiated by the value they add to the product or service. The researcher further develops this chain using secondary data and interviews. The role of the researcher is to link these pieces of information and create a united and self-explanatory chain that includes the principal activities of the industry. The segments of the chain illustrate how different value-adding processes contributed to the product or service, and in turn, the differing returns netted for the chain actors behind them.

Diagrams are extremely useful to illustrate the findings. For example, the fruit and vegetables global value chain is comprised of the following segments:

Figure 11.2 Fruit and Vegetables Global Value Chain Segments

| Inputs | Production for Export | Packing & Cold Storage | Processing | Distribution & Marketing |

Source: Fernandez-Stark et al., 2011d.

b. Identify the Dynamics and Structure of Companies Under Each Segment of the Value Chain

Each of the segments identified in the previous step has specific characteristics and dynamics, such as particular sourcing practices or preferred suppliers. For example, in the fruits and vegetable value chain, the inputs for the 'processing' segment may come from fruits that were intended for export but did not meet the quality controls or it may come from production grown exclusively for processing. It is important to identify the type of companies involved in the industry and their key characteristics: global or domestic; state-owned or private; large, medium, or small; etc. Identifying the firms that participate in the chain will help to understand its governance structure (this dimension will be explained later).

Under the production, distribution and marketing segments, the main producers of fresh produce and the final buyers in the chain are listed in Figure 11.3.

Figure 11.3 Fruit and Vegetables Global Value Chain

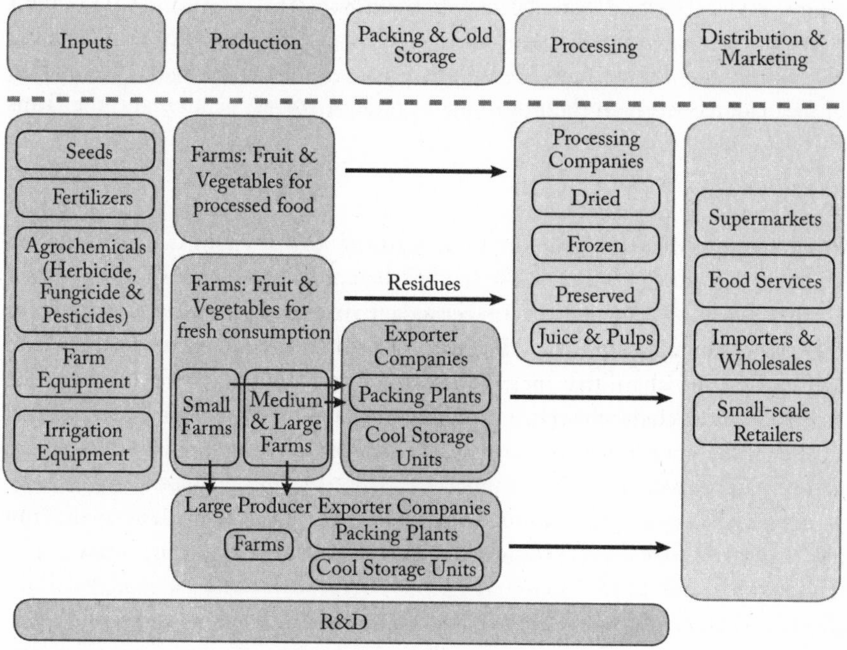

Source: Fernandez-Stark et al., 2011d.

2. Geographic Scope

The globalization of industries has been facilitated by improvement in transportation and telecommunications infrastructure and driven by demand for the most competitive inputs in each segment of the value chain. Today, supply chains are globally dispersed and different activities are usually carried out in different parts of the world. In the global economy, countries participate in industries by leveraging their competitive advantages in assets. Usually developing countries offer low labor costs and raw materials, while rich nations, with highly educated talent, are behind R&D and product design. As a result, firms and workers in widely separated locations affect one another more than they have in the past (Global Value Chains Initiative, 2011).

Geographical analysis is first based on the analysis of global supply and demand. This is done by analyzing the trade flows at each stage of the value chain using international trade statistics databases such as United Nations Comtrade and information compiled using secondary sources of firm-level data, industry publications and interviews with industry experts.

One of the main contributions of GVC analysis has been to map the shifts in the geographic scope of global industries. However, GVCs operate at different geographic scales (local, national, regional, and global) and they continue to evolve. New evidence suggests there may be a trend toward a regionalization of GVCs in response to a variety of factors, including the growing importance of large emerging economies and regional trade agreements (Gereffi, 2014).

3. Governance

Governance analysis allows one to understand how a chain is controlled and coordinated when certain actors in the chain have more power than others. Gereffi (1994: 97) defined governance as 'authority and power relationships that determine how financial, material and human resources are allocated, and f low within a chain'. Initially in the global commodity chains framework, governance was described broadly in terms of ' buyer-driven' or 'producer-driven' chains (Gereffi, 1994). Analysis of buyer-driven chains highlights the powerful role of large retailers, such as Walmart and Tesco, as well as highly successfully branded merchandisers (e.g., Nike, Reebok), in dictating the way the chains operate by requiring suppliers to meet certain standards and protocols, despite limited or no production capabilities. In contrast, producer-driven chains are more vertically integrated along all segments of the supply chain and leverage the technological or scale advantages of integrated suppliers. Understanding governance and how a value chain is controlled facilitates firm entry and development within global industries. In practice, governance analysis requires identification of the lead firms in the sector, their location, how they interact with their supply-base, and their source of inf luence and power over suppliers (e.g. standards compliance).

A more elaborate typology of five governance structures has been identified in the GVC literature: markets, modular, relational, captive, and hierarchy (see Figure 11.4). These structures are measured and determined by three variables: the complexity of the information shared between actors in the chain; how the information for production can be codified; and the level of supplier competence (Frederick and Gereffi, 2009; Gereffi et al., 2005).

Market: Market governance involves transactions that are relatively simple. Information on product specifications is easily transmitted, and suppliers can make products with minimal input from buyers. These arm's-length exchanges require little or no formal cooperation between actors and the cost of switching to new partners is low for both producers and buyers. The central governance mechanism is price rather than a powerful lead firm.

Modular: Modular governance occurs when complex transactions are relatively easy to codify. Typically, suppliers in modular chains make products to a customer's specifications and take full responsibility for process technology using generic machinery that spreads investments across a wide customer base. This keeps switching costs low and limits transaction-specific investments, even though buyer-supplier interactions can be very complex. Linkages (or relationships) are more substantial than in simple markets because of the high volume of information f lowing across the inter-firm link. Information technology and standards for exchanging information are both key to the functioning of modular governance.

Relational: Relational governance occurs when buyers and sellers rely on complex information that is not easily transmitted or learned. This results in frequent interactions and knowledge sharing between parties. Such linkages require trust and generate mutual reliance, which are regulated through reputation, social and spatial proximity, family and ethnic ties, and the like. Despite mutual dependence, lead firms still specify what is needed, and thus have the ability to exert some level of control over suppliers. Producers in relational chains are more likely to supply differentiated products based on quality, geographic origin, or other unique characteristics. Relational linkages take time to build, so the costs and difficulties required to switch to a new partner tend to be high.

Captive: In these chains, small suppliers are dependent on one or a few buyers that often wield a great deal of power. Such networks feature a high degree of monitoring and control by the lead firm. The power asymmetry in captive networks forces suppliers to link to their buyer under conditions set by, and often specific to, that particular buyer, leading to thick ties and high switching costs for both parties. Since the core competence of the lead firms tends to be in areas outside of production, helping their suppliers upgrade their production capabilities does not encroach on this core competency, but benefits the lead firm by increasing the efficiency of its supply chain. Ethical leadership is important to ensure suppliers receive fair treatment and an equitable share of the market price.

Hierarchy: Hierarchical governance describes chains characterized by vertical integration and managerial control within lead firms that develop and manufacture products in-house. This usually occurs when product specifications cannot be codified, products are complex, or highly competent suppliers cannot be found. While less common than in the past, this sort of vertical integration remains an important feature of the global economy.

The form of governance can change as an industry evolves and matures, and governance patterns within an industry can vary from one stage or level of the chain to another. In addition, recent research has shown that many GVCs are characterized by multiple and interacting governance structures, and these affect opportunities and challenges for economic and social upgrading (Dolan and Humphrey, 2004; Gereffi et al., 2009).

Figure 11.4 Five Global Value Chain Governance Types

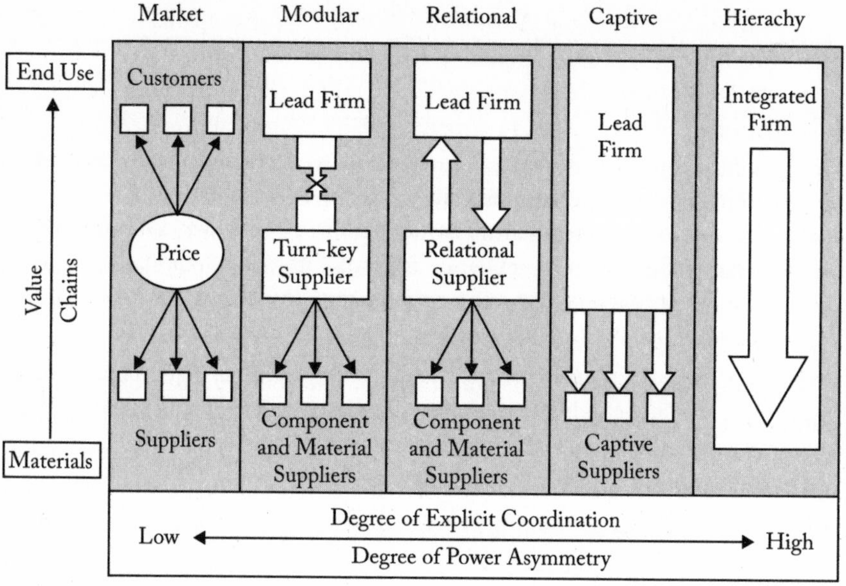

Source: Gereffi et al., 2005: 89.

4. Upgrading

Economic upgrading is defined as firms, countries, or regions move to higher-value activities in GVCs in order to increase the benefits (e.g., security, profits, value-added, capabilities) from participating in global production (Gereffi, 2005a: 171).

Diverse mixes of government policies, institutions, corporate strategies, technologies, and worker skills are associated with upgrading success. Within the GVC framework, Humphrey and Schmitz (2002) identified four types of upgrading:

- *process upgrading*, which transforms inputs into outputs more efficiently by reorganizing the production system or introducing superior technology;
- *product upgrading*, or moving into more sophisticated product lines;
- *functional upgrading*, which entails acquiring new functions (or abandoning existing functions) to increase the overall skill content of the activities; and

- *chain or inter-sectoral upgrading,* where firms move into new but often related industries.

Furthermore, Fernandez-Stark et al. (2014) identified several additional types of upgrading:

- *entry in the value chain,* where firms participate for the first time in national, regional, or global value chains. This is the first and one of the most challenging upgrading trajectories;
- *backward linkages upgrading,* where local firms (domestic or foreign) in one industry begin to supply tradable inputs and/or services to companies—usually multinational corporations (MNCs) that are located in the country and are already inserted in a separate GVC; and
- *end-market upgrading,* which can include moving into more sophisticated markets that require compliance with new, more rigorous standards or into larger markets that call for production on a larger scale and price accessibility.

Upgrading patterns differ by both industry and country based on the input-output structure of the value chain and the institutional context of each country. Certain industries require linear upgrading and countries must gain expertise in one segment of the value chain before upgrading into the next segment, as shown below for countries involved in the horticulture value chain (see Figure 11.5).

Figure 11.5 Upgrading Stages of Selected Countries in the Fruit and Vegetables Value Chain

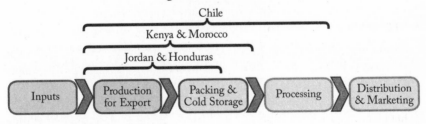

Source: Fernandez-Stark et al., 2011d.

The apparel industry is a classic case that has been used to illustrate different upgrading and downgrading trajectories, since a large number of countries have been significant apparel exporters from the 1970s until the present (Gereffi, 1999; Gereffi and Frederick, 2010). Apparel suppliers in Torreon, Mexico initially entered the blue jeans industry[2] in the assembly stage of the value chain, but they quickly developed expertise in providing trim and labels, and distinct washes and finishes. By 2000, operations based in Torreon had also developed expertise in distribution by shipping their product directly to the point of sale. Figure 11.6 illustrates the region's upgrading trajectory into new higher value added segments of the apparel value chain between 1993 and 2000.

Figure 11.6 US–Torreon Apparel Value Chain: Activities and Location

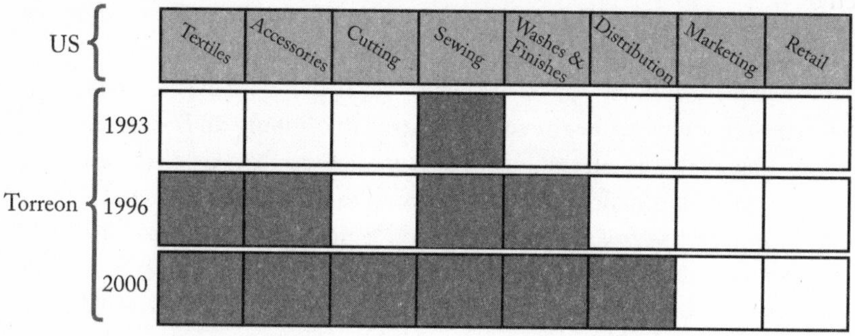

Source: Bair and Gereffi, 2001: 1894.

In 1993, only four US manufacturers—Farah, Sun Apparel, Wrangler, and Levi Strauss and Co.—had a significant presence in Torreon. By 2000, the number of export customers grew to more than two dozen. In the early 1990s, the assembly plants on the Mexican side of the border received cut parts from US manufacturers or brokers. These cut parts were sewn into garments and then re-exported to the United States under the 'maquila' regime, which allowed tariff-free inputs to be sent from the United States to Mexico as long as they were included in Mexican production for re-export to the United States. Brand marketers and retailers 'pulled' Mexican firms to increase their production volumes and the range of activities performed.

Upgrading thus occurred at the firm level in Torreon, in conjunction with the increasing demands of US buyers for full-package production. However, the full-package model did not guarantee long-term success. Blue jean exports from Torreon slumped with the decline in US export demand after 2000, and apparel employment in Torreon, which rose from 12,000 jobs in 1993 to an estimated 75,000 jobs in 2000, declined to 40,000 in 2004. Maintaining a role in the US market in the face of stiff competition from China and other international suppliers required Torreon's blue jeans cluster to continue to upgrade beyond OEM to the OBM and ODM[3] stages of the value chain through the development of local brands, regional marketing directly to US buyers, and the establishment of a local design center in the region (Gereffi, 2005b).

The challenge of economic upgrading in GVCs is to identify the conditions under which developing and developed countries and firms can 'climb the value chain' from basic assembly activities using low-cost and unskilled labor to more advanced forms of 'full package' supply and integrated manufacturing. However, increasingly many of the highest value activities are located in pre- and post-production manufacturing services, which challenge host countries to adopt appropriate workforce development strategies to supply these services locally. As seen in Figure 11.7, developed countries usually have a presence in high value added activities, while developing countries concentrate in lower value added activities.

Figure 11.7 Smile Curve of High-Value Activities in Global Value Chains

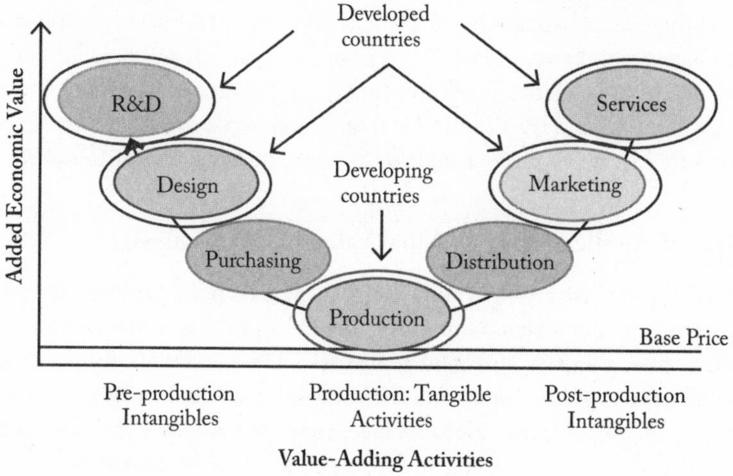

Source: Authors based on Baldwin et al., 2014; Shih, n.d.

5. Local Institutional Context

The local institutional framework identifies how local, national and international conditions and policies shape a country's participation in each stage of the value chain (Gereffi, 1995). GVCs are embedded within local economic, social, and institutional dynamics. Insertion in GVCs depends significantly on these local conditions. Economic conditions include the availability of key inputs: labor costs, available infrastructure, and access to other resources such as finance; social context governs the availability of labor and its skill level, such as female participation in the labor force and access to education; and finally institutions include tax and labor regulation, subsidies, and education and innovation policies that can promote or hinder industry growth and development.

Because global value chains touch down in many different parts of the world, the use of this framework allows one to carry out more systematic comparative (cross-national and cross-regional) analysis to identify the impact of different features of the institutional context on relevant economic and social outcomes.

6. Stakeholder Analysis

Analysis of the local dynamics in which a value chain is embedded requires examination of the stakeholders involved. All the industry actors are mapped in the value chain and their main role in the chain is explained. The most common stakeholders in the value chain are: companies, industry associations, workers, educational institutions, government agencies including export promotion and investment attraction departments, ministries of foreign trade, economy and education amongst others. In addition, it is important to consider how relations between these actors are governed at the local level and which institutions are in a position to drive change. Thus, this type of analysis is critical to identify the key players in the value chain. It became especially relevant for industry upgrading recommendations and the development of an industry growth strategy in which each stakeholder plays a role to contribute in the development of the sector.

IV. Recent Applications of Global Value Chain Analysis

Originally GVC analysis was limited to research on competitiveness in manufacturing industries. Nowadays, this analysis has expanded in several directions to encompass emergent industries such as offshore services, inform industrial policy, guide opportunities to insert small and medium enterprises (SMEs) in the regional and global value chains, and embrace the links between economic and social upgrading such as workforce development. This section includes several examples of the increasingly diverse application of GVC analysis.[4]

1. SME Participation in Regional and Global Value Chains in Agro Industries[5]

The insertion of small- and medium-sized producers in national, regional, and global high-value agriculture value chains has important consequences for poverty alleviation in rural areas of developing countries due to their potential to increase incomes and create employment (Weinberger and Lumpkin, 2007). However, smallholders in developing countries face a series of constraints that often limit their ability to participate competitively in these chains, and there has been considerable concern that these producers are being excluded from important growth opportunities.

The model outlined by the Duke Global Value Chain Center (Duke GVCC) is intended to contribute to the international development community's understanding of how interventions can be more effectively designed to ensure sustainable inclusion of these small- and medium-size producers in the sector. Based on extensive primary and secondary research, with a focus on Inter-American Development Bank Multilateral Investment Fund (IDB-MIF) initiatives in Latin

America, four major constraints were identified that limit the competitiveness of small- and medium-sized producers and their sustainable entry into value chains. A more detailed report (Fernandez-Stark et al., 2012) explains how project interventions can improve competitiveness factors and ensure that producers' inclusion in the value chain is based on a viable business case, rather than corporate social responsibility. Figure 11.8 summarizes a 'holistic' model for inclusion that every intervention should consider.

Figure 11.8 Model for Sustainable Smallholder Inclusion in High-Value Agro-food Chains

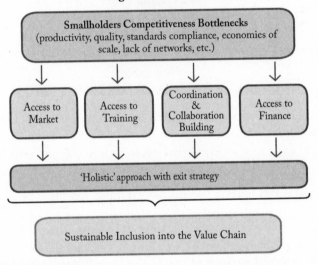

Source: Fernandez-Stark et al., 2012.

Four-Pillars Model for Sustainable Inclusion of Small- and Medium-Sized Producers in the Value Chain

Based on a global value chain analysis, Duke GVCC proposes a holistic model that includes four key 'pillars' that address the major constraints that small- and medium-sized producers face: (1) Access to market; (2) access to training; (3) collaboration and cooperation building; and (4) access to finance.

This model is applicable to all levels of development. Beneficiaries with low capability levels will need longer interventions and usually all four pillars must be included in the intervention. Beneficiaries with higher levels of expertise may need support only in two of these areas as they already have managed to overcome constraints related to the other two areas. A summary of the four pillars model is presented in Figure 11.9. This model was developed for agricultural value chain;

however it can be used in other industries since SMEs in different sectors face similar challenges.

Figure 11.9 Four Pillars Model for SME Participation in GVCs

- Linkages
- Preferences
- Certifications & standards

- Technical
- Entrepreneurial
- Financial literacy
- Soft skills

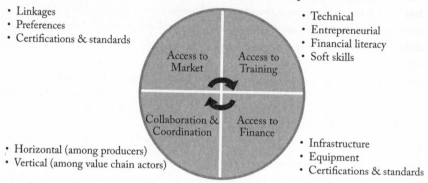

- Horizontal (among producers)
- Vertical (among value chain actors)

- Infrastructure
- Equipment
- Certifications & standards

Source: Fernandez-Stark et al., 2012.

a. Access to Market

Access to market is broadly relevant to inclusion in value chains. In the context of this model, it refers specifically to the presence of value chain linkages between producers and buyers and how they can be established. Traditionally, spot markets in agro-food sectors meant that no direct relationship was required between the producer and the buyer, and the producer sold his/her harvest to the highest bidder. However, the transformation of these sectors and the emphasis on food safety has heightened the need for specific product characteristics, control over production and traceability. Governance of the sector shifted from an arm's length interaction to a much closer relationship with the buyer dictating exactly what product is produced and under what conditions (Lee et al., 2012). The first stage of an intervention therefore requires establishing the link between producers and buyers. This connection requires educating buyers or lead firms regarding the business potential of sourcing from small producers, as well as facilitating interactions until the small producers are in a position to sustainably manage the relationship independently.

b. Access to Training

While many small producers may have worked in agriculture their entire lives, specific training is often required to improve productivity and product quality, introduce new technologies and plant varieties, and comply with food safety and other certification requirements that govern entry into the national, regional and international value chains. Agro-food value chains today are very sophisticated and crops grown with traditional methods often do not meet the international market requirements. Skills development in agro-food value chains, however, has been generally underestimated in the past and the focus on training at the commercial level has only recently emerged. Rural education levels in many developing countries are low and technical assistance run by the government are often understaffed and inadequately prepared to cater to the needs of increasingly demanding buyers (Fernandez-Stark et al., 2011a).

c. Coordination and Collaboration Building

Coordination and collaboration building should occur at two levels. First, horizontal coordination amongst producers facilitates the formation of producer groups or associations, not only to reach needed economies of scale but also to provide opportunities to add value to their products (upgrading). Second, vertical coordination and collaboration involves interactions with other actors of the chain to establish linkages, find synergies, and share information in order to improve the performance of the chain as a whole. Sustainable inclusion in value chains for small producers thus requires some form of organization in an ongoing way to achieve economies of scale.

Horizontal Coordination

Small- and medium-sized producers need economies of scale in order to compete in the marketplace. By definition, they lack the scale required to produce large quantities of any crop. The transaction costs of dealing with individual producers are high and it is not cost-effective or profitable for the buyer to work with producers on an individual basis. Self-organization is a difficult task to achieve for small- and medium-sized producers. Producers' commitment remains critical to successful engagement in a cooperative. Thus they often need the encouragement and support of external actors to understand and appreciate the payoffs of collective action and to establish themselves as formal, legal organizations.

Vertical Coordination

Coordination and collaboration amongst the chain stakeholders is crucial for chain performance and upgrading (Gereffi et al., 2011a). Chain stakeholders include all the actors that play a role in the development of the industry, including: producers, input providers, intermediaries, buyers, industry associations, training institutions, industry services providers, finance institutions, government agencies focused on the industry development, export promoting agencies, and regulatory institutions. Promoting dialogue and public and private alliances have been very beneficial not only for resolving information asymmetries for smallholders, but also for industry advancement at local and country levels. These alliances provide insight into challenges and opportunities faced by the sector with the ultimate goal of coordinating and defining a common industry development strategy.

d. Access to Finance

Entry into the value chain requires certain investments to cover infrastructure, equipment and obtaining certifications. Small producers, however, often face liquidity and credit constraints and have no access to formal finance channels, both of which limit their potential to make the required investments. Credit for small producers is constrained for a number of reasons, including high risk, asymmetrical information, lack of guarantees, dispersion in rural areas, and unfavorable economic policies. These credit constraints prevent small producers from investing in necessary equipment, such as irrigation systems, greenhouses or cold storage, to achieve productivity improvements, to develop unused portions of their land or to upgrade into higher value products, thereby limiting their potential to participate in coordinated value chains. Interventions can facilitate access to finance through various models.

2. Globalizing Service Sectors in the World Economy: Offshore Services[6]

The global value chain methodology has proven quite useful in the analysis of services. While the actual sequence of events from production to consumption of a service is short, GVC analysis allows for the incorporation of all of the services supplied within an industry, ranging from very simple tasks to highly sophisticated interactions in one chain. The example of offshore services illustrates how the GVC framework provides insight into a complex industry and serves as a guide for potential upgrading trajectories.

Offshore Services

Structural changes in the world economy during the past decade facilitated the global outsourcing of MNCs, thereby creating the offshore services industry, a new and rapidly growing sector in developing countries (Gereffi and Fernandez-Stark, 2010b: 1). Information technology (IT) now allows for quick and easy information transfers. Companies looking to improve their efficiency, reduce costs and increase flexibility often unbundle their corporate functions, such as

Figure 11.10 The Offshore Services Global Value Chain

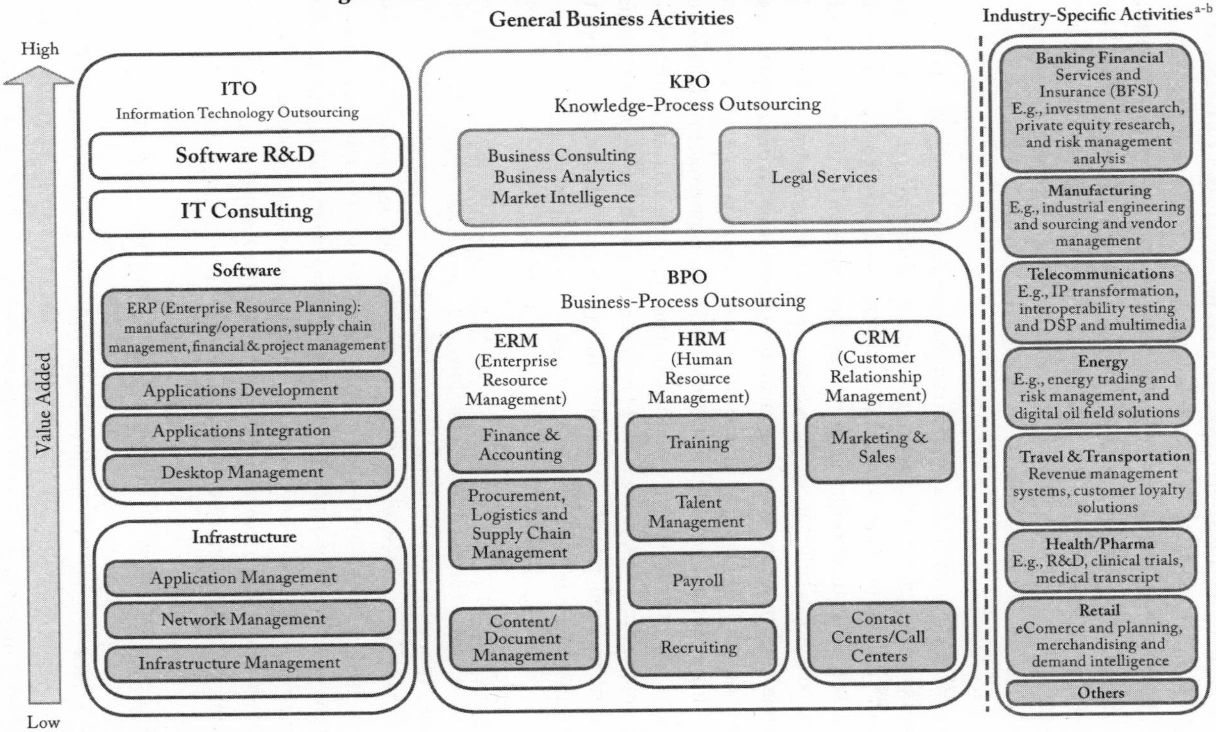

General Business Activities

ITO
Information Technology Outsourcing

- Software R&D
- IT Consulting

Software
- ERP (Enterprise Resource Planning): manufacturing/operations, supply chain management, financial & project management
- Applications Development
- Applications Integration
- Desktop Management

Infrastructure
- Application Management
- Network Management
- Infrastructure Management

KPO
Knowledge-Process Outsourcing

- Business Consulting
  Business Analytics
  Market Intelligence
- Legal Services

BPO
Business-Process Outsourcing

ERM (Enterprise Resource Management)
- Finance & Accounting
- Procurement, Logistics and Supply Chain Management
- Content/Document Management

HRM (Human Resource Management)
- Training
- Talent Management
- Payroll
- Recruiting

CRM (Customer Relationship Management)
- Marketing & Sales
- Contact Centers/Call Centers

Value Added: High → Low

Industry-Specific Activities[a-b]

- **Banking Financial Services and Insurance (BFSI)**
  E.g., investment research, private equity research, and risk management analysis
- **Manufacturing**
  E.g., industrial engineering and sourcing and vendor management
- **Telecommunications**
  E.g., IP transformation, interoperability testing and DSP and multimedia
- **Energy**
  E.g., energy trading and risk management, and digital oil field solutions
- **Travel & Transportation**
  Revenue management systems, customer loyalty solutions
- **Health/Pharma**
  E.g., R&D, clinical trials, medical transcript
- **Retail**
  eCommerce and planning, merchandising and demand intelligence
- **Others**

Source: Gereffi and Fernandez-Stark, 2010a.

Notes:
a. Industry specific: Each industry has its own value chain. Within each of these chains, there are associated services that can be offshored. This diagram captures the industries with the highest demand for offshore services.
b. This graphical depiction of industry-specific services does not imply value levels. Each industry may include ITO, BPO, and advanced activities.

human resource management, customer support, accounting and finance, and procurement operations, and 'offshore' these activities (Gospel and Sako, 2008; Sako, 2006). This reduces the burden of support activities and allows firms to focus on their core business. The increasing participation of developing countries in this new industry highlights the growing capabilities of the global South, not only at the production level but also in creating the knowledge behind products. For example, Chile exports engineering services related to mining, India exports pharmaceutical R&D to lead MNCs, and Uruguay exports sophisticated expertise on cattle traceability.

Duke GVCC has analyzed skill level and work experience to create an offshore services value chain, presented in Figure 11.10. The first categorization refers to three broad types of offshore services that can be provided across all industries (general business services): information-technology outsourcing (ITO), business-process outsourcing (BPO), and knowledge-process outsourcing (KPO). The second categorization refers to services that are industry specific. Firms providing general business services tend to be process-oriented, while those in the vertical chains must have industry-specific expertise and their services may have limited applicability in other industries. For general business services, all activities are related to supporting generic business functions, such as network management, application integration, payroll, call centers, accounting, and human resources. In addition, they include higher-value services, such as market intelligence, business analytics, and legal services (referred to as KPO). Within these services, ITO contains a full spectrum of low-, middle- and high-value activities of the offshore services chain; BPO activities are in the low and middle segments, while KPO activities are in the highest-value segment of the chain.

Within the GVC framework, adapting this scheme to our case evidence, five principal upgrading trajectories can be identified from the 10 country case studies: entry into the value chain; upgrading within the BPO segment; offering full package services; the expansion of IT firms into KPO services; and the specialization of firms in vertical industries. These five upgrading trajectories are presented in Figure 11.11.

These upgrading trajectories show different country strategies to move into higher value-added activities. These trajectories are not mutually exclusive and several of them can happen at the same time. The first trajectory shows how countries have typically entered the value chain, in particular in Latin America, where a common strategy has been to begin offering call center services. The second trajectory refers to countries that are able to offer more sophisticated business operations beyond call and contact centers. In trajectory three, providers move into the provision of knowledge activities that require a considerable degree of analysis. These analytical services demand a more qualified labor force. The fourth upgrading trajectory usually occurs when large operations are set up in a country and are able to offer a broad spectrum of services ranging from low value-added to high value services. These operations offer a 'one-stop shop' for clients and reduce overall transaction costs, but depend on the availability and cost-competitiveness of a large number of workers to serve different stages of the chain. Finally, the industrial specialization upgrading trajectory shows the movement to niche activities for specific industries. This expertise reduces vulnerability to competition from other low-cost locations.

Figure 11.11 Examples of Upgrading Trajectories in the Offshore Services Value Chain

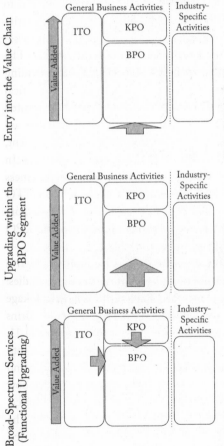

Entry into the Value Chain

- Common way to enter the offshore services value chain is through the establishment of call center operations.
- Opportunity for low-income countries to enter into the knowledge economy.

Recent examples of countries entering the value chain through call centers include **El Salvador** (Dell, Sykes and Teleperformance), **Nicaragua** (Sitel), **Panama** (HP and Caterpillar) and **Guatemala** (Exxon Mobil, ACS and 24/7 Customer) (Gereffi, Castillo & Fernandez-Stark, 2009).

Upgrading within the BPO Segment

- Companies expand their BPO services within the segment.
- Improving and expanding call centers operations or specialization in certain areas.

South Africa has been an important destination for BPO services currently employing around 87,000 people and growing at 33% per year. South Africa is actively working in expanding their BPO activities.

Broad-Spectrum Services (Functional Upgrading)

- Companies positioned in the ITO and KPO segments may opt to provide a more comprehensive range of activities and include BPO services.
- Acquisitions of smaller BPO firms and/ or creating a new business unit within the company.

India has seen a number of firms in the IT and consulting (KPO) segment expand to the BPO sector. This is true for both big domestic firms like Infosys, Wipro and also foreign firms located in India like IBM and Accenture among others.

Cont'd.

Cont'd.

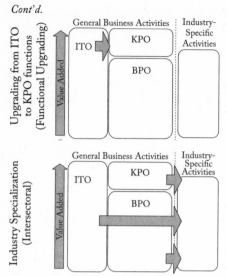

- IT service firms include KPO activities in their portfolio.
- IT companies engage customers to find solutions for unsolved business problems. For example, between 2002 and 2005, **Indian** firms Infosys, Wipro, TCS and WNS, amongst others, developed and launched business consulting services practices.

- Companies offering some ITO, BPO and KPO services for a wide range of industries start specializing and focus on key industries to develop expertise. The **Czech Republic**, which entered into the offshore services industry through the establishment of BPO shared services activities, has quickly upgraded into R&D segments of vertical industries, particularly in the automotive, aerospace and IT areas.

Source: Fernandez-Stark et al., 2011c.

3. Workforce Development and Global Value Chains

Another illustration of new applications of the GVC analysis is the topic of workforce development. The International Labor Organization used the GVC framework to understand the dimensions of production and employment during their 2016 convention (ILO, 2016). Duke GVCC has been a pioneer introducing the skills dimension into GVC analysis in the multi-industry study 'Skills for Upgrading'.[7]

The participation of workers in GVCs can be viewed through the lens of job categories defined by skill level in order to understand the conditions of the workers in these chains and the challenges they face. Each skill level can be loosely associated with stages of the value chain (Gereffi et al., 2011b).

Table 11.1 distinguishes five main types of jobs:[8]

a. Informal Small and Micro-Enterprise or Household-Based Work

Work in informal small and micro-enterprises or households can be found in many GVCs in developing countries and particularly in agriculture and light industries such as apparel. Production takes place in or around the household, with limited separation between commercial productive activity (i.e., making saleable goods) and unpaid reproductive activity (e.g., household subsistence and childcare). Income derived from these activities is generally low, and production involves both paid and unpaid family labor, often including child labor. Education levels vary, but often are very low. Long working hours or health and safety conditions can be precarious. In addition, fragmentation of the labor force across a large number of small firms weakens the potential for any collective activity (Bamber and Fernandez-Stark, 2013).

Table 11.1 Types of Work in Global Value Chains

Job Category	Examples of Conditions of Work	Education Level	Examples
Informal SME or household work	May or may not be compensated; precarious conditions; unregulated work hours	Low; often less than primary education	Small producers in agricultural supply chains
Low skilled labor-intensive work	Formal; job insecurity, low wages, weak organization due to subcontracting	Low; often primary education or less	Workers on apparel or electronic assembly lines
Moderate skilled work	Formal; increased job security, potentially poor working hours	Completed secondary education	Procurement and logistics handling jobs in apparel and automobile chains
High skilled technology-intensive work	Formal; high job security, higher paid work, working hours and work-life balance challenges	Post-secondary technical education	Specialized component production and assembly in aerospace and medical devices chains
Knowledge-intensive work	Formal; potentially freelance, higher paid work, working hours and work-life balance challenges	Completed university education, including advanced degrees	Accounting, engineering and design jobs

Source: Gereffi et al., 2016.

b. Low-Skilled Labor-Intensive Work

Labor-intensive production uses waged labor in a formal setting. It involves a relationship between an employer (who may be the producer or an agent) and a worker, based on a wage. This relationship may be temporary or permanent based on a work contract. In this type of work, it is not uncommon for a core workforce to be on permanent contracts, complemented by temporary workers (often women and migrants) who are hired according to fluctuations in demand (Barrientos et al., 2011; Lee and Gereffi, 2015). The engagement of temporary workers through sub-contracting arrangements in part fragments this group of workers, making organization of labor difficult (Barrientos, 2013). Workers engaged in these stages of value chains typically have up to six years of education. Access to low-cost labor for labor-intensive production was one of the primary drivers of early offshoring, and accounts for a very large share of global employment in value chains.

c. *Moderate-Skilled Work*

Moderate-skilled work is associated with production that requires specific technical knowledge, such as machine operators and pattern makers, often in capital- and technology-intensive supply chains, such as automobiles and electronics. Work is typically formal in nature, and these workers usually have completed secondary education. Depending on skills supply in the specific labor market, these workers may hold permanent contracts due to investment that must be made by the firm in training on specific equipment required to perform core operations. A skills shortage can lead to long working hours. Unionization and other collective action are dependent on the local institutional context.

d. *High-Skilled Technology-Intensive Work*

The offshoring of high-skilled, technology-intensive work emerged in the 1980s and 1990s. Lead firms in capital- and technology-intensive sectors, such as automobiles and electronics, set up international production networks not only to assemble their finished goods, but also to develop a supply-base for key intermediate items and sub-assemblies. Due to the capital- and technology-intensive nature of this work, it accounts for a smaller share of employment in GVCs. At the uppermost tiers of these production networks, the suppliers tend to concentrate 'good' jobs in relatively few locations. Skill scarcity can contribute to improved wages and employment terms, but may also involve long working hours and poor work-life balance. Workers in these activities generally have completed at least post-secondary technical education.

e. *Knowledge-Intensive Work*

Knowledge-intensive work opportunities have been created by a new wave of offshoring in services (Gereffi and Fernandez-Stark, 2010). Knowledge-intensive service jobs include advanced business services, such as finance, accounting, software, medical services and engineering, and are increasingly seen as an opportunity for developing economies to attain both economic and social benefits, with technological learning, knowledge spillovers and higher income. Workers in this category may choose freelance work over permanent contracts to provide them with flexibility, but with lower levels of social protection. On average, the size of employment in this work category is relatively small considering the requirements for high skills and advanced degrees. Skills surplus in this category in developing countries can lead to loss of motivation at work and 'brain drain' (OECD, 2013).

Figure 11.12 shows graphically how these five types of work and skill levels are distributed across different GVCs.

Figure 11.12 Workforce Composition Across Different GVCs

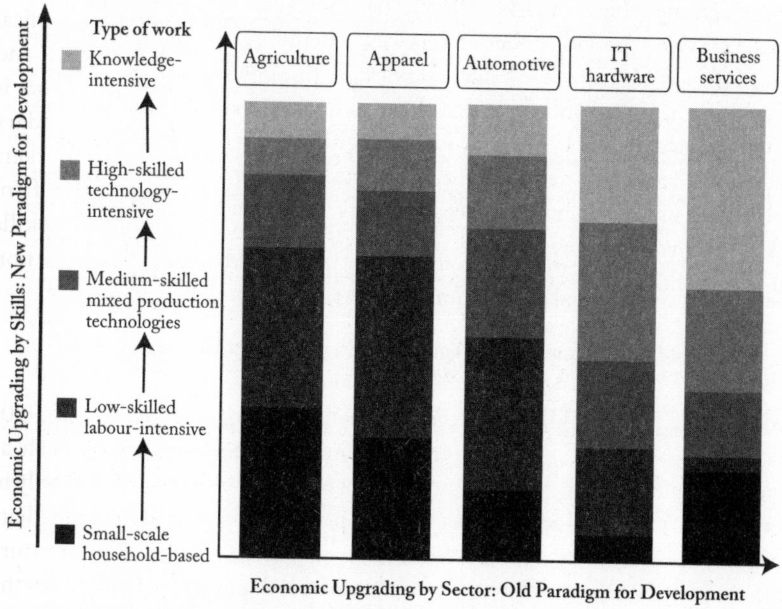

Economic Upgrading by Sector: Old Paradigm for Development

Source: Adapted from Barrientos et al., 2011: 328.

The composition of a country's workforce in GVCs changes as it undergoes economic upgrading. Two dimensions of economic upgrading can be highlighted: traditional development paradigms that stress 'structural transformation' from primary projects to manufacturing and service jobs in the economy (shifting from left to right on the figure); and the new 'GVC paradigm' of upgrading to higher value activities within any specific industry (moving from the bottom to top of each column) (Gereffi et al., 2011; Taglioni and Winkler, 2016).

In the past five years, Duke GVCC has been working to understand workforce development issues using the GVC methodology. This undertaking incorporated a multi-industry and multi-country analysis of upgrading trajectories and workforce initiatives that helped to drive these shifts. The sectors and countries selected in a pioneer study conducted by Duke GVCC were: (1) fruit and vegetables (Chile, Kenya, Morocco, Jordan, and Honduras); (2) apparel (Turkey, Sri Lanka, Bangladesh, Nicaragua, and Lesotho); (3) offshore services (India, the Philippines,

Chile, and Central American countries); and (4) tourism (Costa Rica, Vietnam, and Jordan) (Gereffi et al., 2011b).

In each segment of these value chains, Duke GVCC found that workers required specific skills that frequently are regulated by global rather than local actors. As an illustration, Figure 11.13 below summarizes workforce development implications in the offshore services value chain. Developing countries in offshore services are engaging in market-driven development—acquiring capabilities to upgrade services (providing better services, expanding the number of services, or/and offering higher value-added services)—through significant investments in workforce training and managerial capabilities, provided initially by private offshore service providers but now increasingly supported by an expanded range of public, private, and multi-sector initiatives. Far from a race to the bottom, involvement in the offshore services industry has provided developing country workers, firms, and governments with an attractive opportunity to build the skill-based competencies required to meet the demands of global service markets.

Figure 11.13 Examples of Workforce Development Initiatives in the Offshore Services Value Chain

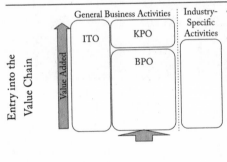

- Call centers hire people with high school diplomas or bachelor's degrees.
- Further skills training is provided by the company.

In **Guatemala**, inter-institutional alliances were created to promote call center and BPO skills training. Intecap, a technical training institution funded through a 1% levy on salaries, has been central to these initiatives (ECLAC, 2009).

Type of skills preparation	Institutions involved
• Short training	• Private sector
	• Government

- Skills development is carried out by the private sector, either through in-house or contracted training programs.
- Educational institutions and governments help to develop course content and provide scholarships.

In **South Africa**, the government created the BPO Support Program to generate more jobs. The program includes training for 35,000 direct jobs and 4,000 in middle management.

Type of skills preparation	Institutions involved
• Short Training	• Private sector
• Formal education (degree required)	• Government
	• Tertiary education

Cont'd.

Contd.

Full-Package Services (Functional Expansion)

General Business Activities | Industry-Specific Activities

ITO   KPO

BPO

Value Added

- Expansive hiring process targets candidates with high school diploma and/or colleges graduates to work in this industry.
- New hires must first complete BPO training programs to guarantee quality services. This refers to the same training offered in the 'Upgrading within the BPO segment.'

In the early 2000s in **India**, there was a significant push into the BPO segment by ITO and KPO firms. Recruiting was the central aspect to this expansion, and firms focused particularly on hiring women from middle class background.

Type of skills preparation
- Short training
- Formal education (degree required)

Institutions involved
- Private sector
- Government

Upgrading from ITO to KPO Functions (Chain Upgrading)

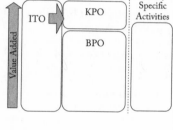

General Business Activities | Industry-Specific Activities

ITO   KPO

BPO

Value Added

- Personnel with higher education qualifications recruited. Typically MBA graduates and workers with business experience. These workers must have sharp analytical skills.

Legal Process Outsourcing requires qualified lawyers. By 2015, LPO will employee 17,000 professionals. These lawyers undergo similar training as in the US.

Type of skills preparation
- Formal education (degree required)

Institutions involved
- Tertiary educational institutions

Vertical Specialization (Chain Upgrading)

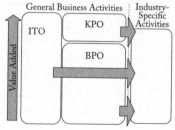

General Business Activities | Industry-Specific Activities

ITO   KPO

BPO

Value Added

- Companies hire area experts to sustain their competitive advantage in specific areas.
- For example, a BPO company providing medical trainscrption services must hire nurses and doctors to ensure accurate service provision.

In the **Czech Republic**, the government has been incentivizing advanced degress suchs as Masters and PhD degrees. Masters students accounted for 40% of the university student population. Today there are more than 73,000 technical university students engaged in R&D in different areas.

Type of skills preparation
- Formal education (degree required)
- Usually MA and PhD degrees

Institutions involved
- Tertiary educational institutions

Cont'd.

Contd.

• Companies undertake process improvements to upgrade their global capabilities. For example, Siemens has specific strategies for organizational training on CMMI (one of the most popular process improvement certification in this industry). The strategy consists in defining the job skills necessary, assess who need the training, train workers with skill gaps, record progress and monitor new skill gaps.

Type of skills preparation	**Institutions involved**
• Internal training	• Private sector
	• Certification institutes (on-site or online)

Source: Fernandez-Stark et al., 2011d.

4. Assisting Governments to Design Industrial Policies

Global value chain analysis has proven to be an effective tool to advise country governments on economic development and specific policies for industry upgrading regarding productive capacity, infrastructure and services, business environment, trade and investment policies, and industry institutionalization. This methodology is widely used by nations in all regions of the globe to identify the various local factors that affected the capacity of developing countries to meet GVC requirements (Bamber et al., 2013).

Duke GVCC has conducted a number of GVC studies commissioned by country governments in all major regions of the world. For example, the Costa Rica government commissioned a GVC study with the objective to provide a set of recommendations to the country to enhance the participation and upgrading in selected industries: medical devices (Bamber and Gereffi, 2013b), electronics (Frederick and Gereffi, 2013), aerospace (Bamber and Gereffi, 2013a) and offshore services (Fernandez-Stark et al., 2013).[9] To that end, the GVC framework is used to understand the changing dynamics of these industries at a global level, to identify Costa Rica's position in these chains, and to highlight potential competitiveness opportunities.

Understanding how GVCs operate is essential for a country such as Costa Rica, which relies significantly on export-oriented foreign direct investment (FDI) for economic growth. The evolution of these GVCs has significant implications in terms of global trade, production and employment, and how developing countries integrate into the global economy. By gaining access to developed country markets, participation in GVCs offers emerging economies an opportunity to add value to their local industries. Insertion and sustained participation in GVCs can be paramount for economic growth, particularly in developing nations, due to accompanying job creation potential, inflow of foreign currency, contributions to poverty reduction, and more recently, access to the global knowledge economy. Understanding these chains is critical for attracting foreign investment and also supporting the competitive growth of local firms. These firms must compete with a growing number of foreign firms not only for the local market, but also for international clients and thus are forced to improve the efficiency and quality of their operations. Below we present a summary of two industries analyzed in the Costa Rica study: medical devices and offshore services.

a. Costa Rica and the Medical Devices Global Value Chain[10]

As part of Costa Rica's economic diversification efforts, the medical devices cluster is arguably the most successful industry that has been developed in the country under this FDI-driven, high-tech export strategy. The Costa Rican medical devices industry dates to 1985, when the first device company established operations in the country. By 2014, exports had reached US$1.4 billion. Accounting for 12% of the country's total exports, medical devices became the largest export industry in the country (UN Comtrade, 2015). In 2015, more than 50 firms were participating in the medical device supply chain in Costa Rica, with an additional 16 companies providing packaging and support services. Over half (60%) of these firms were from the United States and less than 30% were Costa Rican. Companies in the sector are concentrated in the production segments of the value chain, with 70% of them manufacturing components or assembling final goods (Bamber and Gereffi, 2013b).

The growth of the medical devices sector created approximately 17,500 jobs in manufacturing between 2000 and 2015, with approximately 2,000 jobs being added each year since 2012. This job creation has provided opportunities for both men and women; 45.6% of the workforce is male and 54.4% female (CINDE, 2012b). The medical devices industry relies on a highly skilled workforce. By 2012, 10%–20% of the workforce was comprised of engineers and 10%–15% technicians. The remaining 60% –80% of direct production workers initially drew from the unskilled labor pool that had served the apparel sector (Bamber and Gereffi, 2013b).

Costa Rica's export performance in medical devices between 1998 and 2011 shows a very steady and significant growth in the overall quantity of exports from just under US$400 million in 2002 to nearly $1.2 billion in 2011 (Figure 11.14). In terms of upgrading dynamics, the country has undertaken functional upgrading and developed backward linkages. However, the most intriguing story is about product upgrading, shifting the composition of Costa Rica's medical device exports in terms of their technological content. In 2002, about 90% of Costa Rica's medical device exports were in the low-tech disposables category, but by 2011, the other three higher tech medical device categories accounted for more than half of the country's exports. Its main product segments vary considerably in technological complexity:

- *Disposables*: single use-products, such as bandages, catheters, and surgical gloves, which are cost-driven.
- *Medical Instruments*: multi-use products like forceps and surgical scissors that are sterilized between uses with different patients.
- *Therapeutic Devices*: highly diverse products that may be implanted in the human body (e.g., orthopedic implants, pacemakers, hearing aids, etc.), which are subject to very high levels of international health and safety regulation and quality standards.
- *Capital Equipment*: large, long-term investments for complex, single-purchase machines that can be used repeatedly over the years, such as magnetic resonance imaging (MRI) equipment.

Figure 11.14 Costa Rica Medical Exports by Product Category, 1998–2011

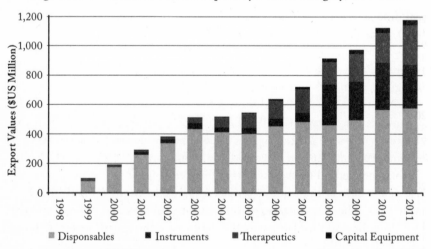

Source: Bamber and Gereffi, 2013.

As the technological content of exports evolved, the MNCs that have established operations in the country have also changed. Table 11.2 disaggregates the firms that entered Costa Rica's medical devices sector into four waves: pre-2000, 2001–2004, 2005–2008, and 2009–2012.[11] A very clear pattern of FDI succession emerges: the companies that invested in Costa Rica pre-2000 were predominantly in the low-tech, cost-driven disposables product category. In each successive time period, companies with higher-level technology entered Costa Rica. When companies were asked during interviews why they came to Costa Rica, two factors were repeatedly mentioned: (a) latecomers were encouraged by the positive experiences of the earlier investors; and (b) the capabilities of Costa Rican managers, as well as skills upgrading by Costa Rican employees and local suppliers, made the country increasingly attractive to high-technology firms.

Table 11.2 Firms in Costa Rica's Medical Devices Sector

Entry Year	Firm Characteristics	Main Product Export Category	Core Market Segments	Product Examples	Select Firms
Up to 2000 24 firms: 8 US 15 CR 1 German	4 OEMs 8 Components 1 Input distributor 7 Packaging 1 Finishing 3 Support services	Disposables	Drug delivery; Women's health	Intravenous tubing (I) Mastectomy bra (I)	Hospira; Baxter; Amoena; Corbel
2001–2004 13 firms: 9 US 3 CR 1 Colombian	3 OEMS 6 Components 1 Finishing 1 Logistics provider 2 Support services	Instruments	Endoscopic surgery	Biopsy forceps (II)	Arthrocare; Boston Scientific; Oberg Industries
2005–2008 8 firms: 7 US 1 Puerto Rico	2 OEM 4 Components 1 Packaging 1 Finishing	Therapeutics	Cosmetic surgery; Women's health and urology	Breast implants (III) Minimally invasive devices for uterine surgery (II)	Allergan; Tegra Medical; Specialty Coating Systems
2009–2012 21 firms: 16 US 1 CR 1 Ireland 1 Japan 2 Joint ventures (US-CR)	5 OEMS 7 Components 2 Non-OEM assemblers 1 Input distributor 2 Sterilization 2 Packaging	Therapeutics Disposables Instruments	Cardiovascular Drug delivery	Heart valves (III) Dialysis catheters (III) Guide wires (III) Compression socks (I)	Abbott Vascular; St. Jude Medical; Covidien; Moog; Synergy Health; Volcano Corp.

Source: Bamber and Gereffi, 2013.
Note: Roman numerals refer to FDA regulatory categories of products.

b. Costa Rica in the Offshore Services Global Value Chain

Costa Rica is a pioneer in attracting offshore services to Latin America. Since the mid-1990s the country has been a preferred location for MNCs looking to reduce costs and take advantage of the country's unique combination of draws, including its location in the US Central Time Zone, largely bilingual population, and relatively safe and stable security environment. MNCs have set up both captive centers and third-party service providers in Costa Rica, with the latter allowing companies to use the country as a platform to export competitively priced services. Costa Rica entered the industry ahead of other countries in Latin America. This strategy gave the country an important 'first mover advantage', allowing it to position itself as a key reference for offshore services in Latin America. As can be seen in Figure 11.15 below, selected companies with presence in Costa Rica are mapped in the offshore services GVC.

**Figure 11.15 Offshore Services Industry in Costa Rica:
MNC Participation by Segment, 2011**

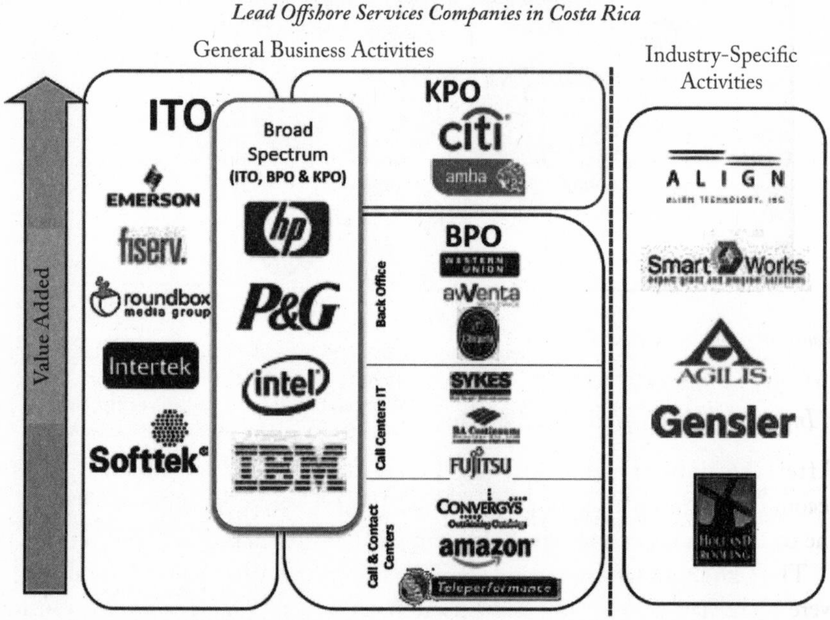

Lead Offshore Services Companies in Costa Rica

Source: Fernandez-Stark et al., 2013.

In 2005, there were 33 MNCs firms employing 10,802 people and exporting around US$387 million. These figures tripled by 2011, when there were close to

100 offshore services MNCs operating in the country, employing 33,170 workers and exporting US$1,390 million[12] (CINDE, 2012a). Since its entry into the offshore GVCs in the late 1990s, Costa Rica has both expanded its participation and upgraded through the value chain, providing increasingly sophisticated services. Figure 11.16 below shows exports and number of employees in the different segments of the offshore services global value chain.

Figure 11.16 Offshore Services Industry in Costa Rica: US Exports and Number of Employees by Segment, 2011

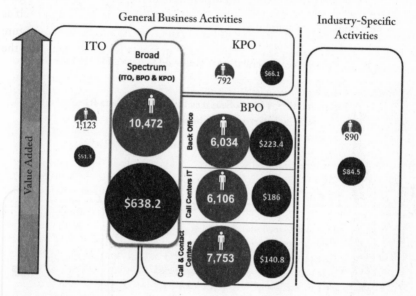

Source: Fernandez-Stark et al., 2013.

c. Industrial Policy Recommendations

After the industry analysis, the Duke GVCC team provided a set of recommendations per sector analyzed and also transversal recommendations for the country. Some of the general recommendations are listed in Figure 11.17.

Through this analysis, several common factors requiring policy interventions were identified across these industries. A transversal policy approach can be implemented to address these factors and to facilitate growth in all sectors analyzed. These themes align with the working groups in Costa Rica's Presidential Council for Competitiveness, and task groups could provide leadership in the following areas:

- Industry institutionalization
- Attraction of foreign direct investments
- Development of local firms
- Human capital development
- Improvements to the business environment
- Infrastructure upgrading

This set of recommendations was also complemented by country comparisons in which best practices were highlighted. These country cases illustrated examples of key policies to support industry upgrading. Best practices for this type of analysis are typically selected from countries that face related challenges and are in a similar stage of economic development.

Figure 11.17 Policy Recommendations: Medical Devices and Offshore Services

Medical Devices

- The high margin industry with a strong emphasis on quality is a good match for Costa Rica's more expensive but quick learning workforce.
- Upgrade into higher value capital equipment products.
- Prepare the workforce for future upgrading into incremental R&D and marketing stages of the chain
- Attract FDI in capital equipment and therapeutics.
- Identify and support high potential domestic firms with proven capabilities to supply products and services to MNCs located in the country.

Offshore Services

- Due to the small size of the labor pool and its corresponding constraints on the number of qualified labor, the country should focus on niche services.
- Costa Rica has a reputation as an enviornmental friendly coutry. One niche area to explore is exporting environmental services.
- Prepare the labour force in the key niche areas. This will require the creation of special training programs and the modification of the curricula in technical schools and universities.
- Attract MNCs in high value added services; especially in the niche services identified as high potential for Costa Rica.

Sources: Fernandez-Stark et al., 2013; Bamber and Gereffi, 2013.

Conclusion

Globalization has given rise to a new era of international competition that is best understood by looking at the global organization of industries and how countries rise and fall within these industries. The GVC framework has evolved from its academic origins to become a major paradigm used by a wide range of country governments and international organizations, including the World Bank, the International Labor Organization, the UK Department for International Development, and the US Agency for International Development. Global value chain analysis highlights how new patterns of international trade, production, and employment shape the prospects for development and competitiveness, using core concepts like 'governance' and 'upgrading'.

On the governance side, GVC are becoming more consolidated (Cattaneo et al., 2010). Large multinational manufacturers, retailers, and marketers who manage global sourcing networks are proclaiming that they want fewer, larger and more capable suppliers, and they will operate in a reduced number of strategic locations around the world. This is likely to promote a higher degree of regional sourcing, with suppliers located close to the major consumer markets in North America, Western Europe, and East Asia. In terms of upgrading, this offers some hope for small regional suppliers, but organizing efficient and sustainable value chains at the regional level remains challenging.

Today we are at a historic juncture. Decision-makers concerned with the role that GVCs play in promoting development face diff iculties in adjusting to a world in which the primary drivers in global production and trade are emerging economies. Until recently, trade integration and growth in many developing countries were fueled by the insertion of local producers in GVCs feeding into high-income markets, in particular North America, Europe and Japan, and in chains led by firms from high-income economies. Recently, however, low growth or stagnation in the historically dominant Northern economies, along with sustained growth in emerging countries, in particular China and India, have spurred a shift in the primary trade and growth drivers with crucial implications for global demand, structures of production and innovation. In some cases, the shift in global demand to emerging economies has forced developing country suppliers to sell final goods at cheaper prices and lower level of processing than in the past, which amounts to downgrading in terms of their participation in the global economy (Kaplinsky and Farooki, 2011).

These new developments represent a potential change in the center of gravity for economic growth, with significant implications for GVCs, employment and innovation, and the strategy of governments and firms in developing countries. Globalization's benefits will continue to be unevenly distributed, with its gains going to those with more education, skills, wealth, and power. However, the inclusion of large emerging economies like China, India, Brazil, and Mexico among those who are benefitting, at least in part, is a qualitative shift in the process. But it does not necessarily improve the chances for smaller countries in the global economy unless they devise policies to enhance their own capabilities to foster development.

Notes

1. The first edition of the *GVC Primer* was released in May 2011. This is the second edition of the *GVC Primer* that was released online on July 2016 and contains totally new material.
2. For more details see Bair and Gereffi (2001).
3. OEM: Original Equipment Manufacturer; OBM: Original Brand Manufacturer; and ODM: Original Design Manufacturer.
4. For a broader mix of industries, see projects listed on the Duke GVCC website: https://gvcc.duke.edu/overview-of-work/.
5. To obtain more information see: Fernandez-Stark and Bamber, 2012a, 2012b; Fernandez-Stark et al., 2012 or the following link https://gvcc.duke.edu/cggcproject/inclusive-development/.
6. For more information see Fernandez-Stark et al., 2011b. Additional information can be found on the CGGC website: https://gvcc.duke.edu/cggcproject/offshore-services-2/.
7. *Skills for Upgrading.* Available at https://gvcc.duke.edu/cggcproject/skills-for-upgrading/.
8. This scheme is based on Barrientos et al. (2011) and Gereffi, Fernandez-Stark et al. (2011). This classification scheme is not intended to refer to all jobs in the global economy; rather, it only applies to jobs linked to the offshore production of goods and services.
9. Costa Rica GVC studies can be found at https://gvcc.duke.edu/cggcproject/comex-costa-rica/. For other studies see the Duke GVCC website. Some recent reports include Peruvian GVCs analysis: Table grapes (Fernandez-Stark et al., 2016b), mining equipment (Bamber et al., 2016) and high quality cotton textiles and apparel (Fernandez-Stark et al., 2016a).
10. The study 'Costa Rica in the Medical Devices Global Value Chain', can be found at https://g vcc.duke.edu/wp-content/uploads/2013-08-20_Ch2 _Medical_Devices.pdf. This study was also highlighted in a World Free Zones Organization bulletin (Gereffi, 2016).
11. This data was gathered from an analysis of FTZ statistics in Costa Rica and firm-level interviews by the authors of the Duke GVCC study.
12. This information is from MNCs operating in a free trade zone (FTZ) regime that represents around 80% of the total companies. According to CINDE, the Costa Rican Central Bank estimates that in 2011 the offshore services industry employed 37,049 and exported almost US$1.6 billion. In this report we use the data from companies operating under the FTZ regime due to the data availability

References

Bair, Jennifer and Gary Gereffi. 2001. 'Local Clusters in Global Chains: The Causes and Consequences of Export Dynamism in Torreon's Blue Jeans Industry.' *World Development* 29: 1885–1903.

Baldwin, Richard, Tadashi Ito, and Hitoshi Sato. 2014. 'The Smile Curve: Evolving Sources of Value Added in Manufacturing.' Available at http://www.uniba.it/ricerca/dipartimenti/dse/e.g.i/egi2014-papers/ito.

Bamber, Penny and Karina Fernandez-Stark. 2013. 'Global Value Chains, Economic Upgrading and Gender in the Horticulture Industry.' In *Global Value Chains, Economic Upgrading and Gender: Case Studies of the Horticulture, Tourism, and Call Center Industries*, edited by Cornelia Staritz and José G. Reis, 11–42. Washington, DC: World Bank. Available at https://gvcc. duke.edu/wp-content/uploads/GVC_Gender_Report_web_2013.pdf

Bamber, Penny, Karina Fernandez-Stark, and Gary Gereffi. 2016. 'Peru in the Mining Equipment Global Value Chain: Opportunities for Upgrading.' Washington, DC: World Bank. Available at https://gvcc.duke.edu/wp-content/uploads/2016-Duke-CGGC-Mining-Equipment-GVC-Report-Peru.pdf

Bamber, Penny, Karina Fernandez-Stark, Gary Gereffi, and Andrew Guinn. 2013. 'Connecting Local Producers in Developing Countries to Regional and Global Value Chains.' Paris: OECD.

Bamber, Penny and Gary Gereffi. 2013a. 'Costa Rica in the Aersopace Global Value Chain: Opportunities for Entry and Upgrading.' Durham, NC: Duke Global Value Chains Center. Commissioned by the Costa Rican Ministry of Foreign Trade. Available at https://gvcc. duke.edu/wp-content/uploads/2013_08_20_Ch4_Aerospace.pdf

———. 2013b. 'Costa Rica in the Medical Devices Global Value Chain: Opportunities for Upgrading.' Durham, NC: Duke Global Value Chains Center. Commissioned by the Costa Rican Ministry of Foreign Trade. https://gvcc.duke.edu/wp-content/uploads/2013-08-20_ Ch2_Medical_Devices.pdf

Barrientos, Stephanie. 2013. '"Labour Chains": Analysing the Role of Labour Contractors in Global Production Networks.' *The Journal of Development Studies* 49(8): 1058–1071.

Barrientos, Stephanie, Gary Gereffi, and Arianna Rossi. 2011. 'Economic and Social Upgrading in Global Production Networks: A New Paradigm for a Changing World.' *International Labour Review* 150(3–4): 319–340.

Cattaneo, Olivier, Gary Gereffi, and Cornelia Staritz, eds. 2010. *Global Value Chains in a Postcrisis World: A Development Perspective*. Washington, DC: World Bank.

CINDE (Costa Rican Investment Promotion Agency). 2012a. Offshore Services Data Industry. San José: CINDE.

———. 2012b. Sector Brief: Life Science in Costa Rica. San José: CINDE.

Dolan, Catherine and John Humphrey. 2004. 'Changing Governance Patterns in the Trade in Fresh Vegetables between Africa and the United Kingdom.' *Environment and Planning* 36: 491–509.

ECLAC (Economic Commission for Latin America and the Caribbean). 2009. 'Foreign Direct Investment in Latin American and the Caribbean.' Santiago: ECLAC.

Fernandez-Stark , Karina and Penny Bamber. 2012a. 'Assessment of Five High-Value Agriculture Inclusive Business Projects Sponsored by the Inter-American Development Bank in Latin America.' Durham, NC: Duke Global Value Chains Center. Available at https://gvcc.duke.edu/wp-content/uploads/CGGC-IDB_Assessment_of_Five_High-Value_Agriculture_Inclusive_Business_Projects_Sponsored_by_the_Inter-American_ Development_Bank_in_Latin_America-_May_1_2012.pdf.

———. 2012b. 'Basic Principles and Guidelines for Impactful and Sustainable Inclusive Business Interventions in High-Value Agro-Food Value Chains.' Durham, NC: Duke

Center on Globalization, Governance and Competitiveness. Available at https://gvcc. duke.edu/wp-content/uploads/CGGC-IDB_-Basic_Principles_and_Guidelines_for_ Impactful_and_Sustainable_Inclusive_Business_Interventions_in_High-Value_Agro-Food_Value_Chains_May_1_2012.pdf.

Fernandez-Stark, Karina, Penny Bamber, and Gary Gereffi. 2011a. 'The Fruit and Vegetable Global Value Chain: Workforce Development and Economic Upgrading.' Durham, NC: Duke Global Value Chains Center.

————. 2011b. 'The Offshore Services Value Chain: Upgrading Trajectories in Developing Countries.' *International Journal of Technological Learning, Innovation and Development* 4(1): 206–234.

————. 2011c. 'Workforce Development in the Fruit and Vegetable Global Value Chain.' In *Skills for Upgrading: Workforce Development and Global Value Chains in Developing Countries*, edited by Gary Gereffi, Karina Fernandez-Stark, and Phil Psilos. Durham, NC: Duke Global Value Chains Center and Research Triangle Institute International.

————. 2011d. 'The Offshore Services Industry: Economic Upgrading and Workforce Development.' In *Skills for Upgrading: Workforce Development and Global Value Chains in Developing Countries*, edited by Gary Gereffi, Karina Fernandez-Stark, and Phil Psilos. Durham, NC: Duke Global Value Chains Center and Research Triangle Institute International.

————. 2012. 'Inclusion of Small- and Medium-Sized Producers in High-Value Agro-Food Value Chains.' Durham, NC: Duke Global Value Chains Center for the Inter-American Development Bank Multilateral Investment Fund. Available at https:// gvcc.duke.edu/wp-content/uploads/2012-05_DukeCGGC_InclusiveBusiness_and_ HighValueAgricultureValueChains_v2.pdf.

————. 2013. 'Costa Rica in the Offshore Services Global Value Chain: Opportunities for Upgrading.' Durham, NC: Duke Global Value Chains Center. Commissioned by the Costa Rican Ministry of Foreign Trade. Available at http://www.cggc.duke.edu/pdfs/2013-08-20_Ch5_Offshore_Services.pdf.

————. 2014. 'Global Value Chains in Latin America: A Development Perspective for Upgrading.' In *Global Value Chains and World Trade: Prospects and Challenges for Latin America*, edited by René Hernández, Jorge M. Martínez-Piva, and Nanno Mulder, 79–106. Santiago: ECLAC.

————. 2016a. 'Peru in the High Quality Cotton Textile and Apparel Global Value Chain: Opportunities for Upgrading.' Washington, DC: World Bank. Available at https://gvcc. duke.edu/wp-content/uploads/2016-Jan-Duke-CGGC-High-Quality-Cotton-GVC-Report-Peru.pdf.

————. 2016b. 'Peru in the Table Grape Global Value Chain: Opportunities for Upgrading.' Washington, DC: World Bank. Available at https://gvcc.duke.edu/wp-content/ uploads/2016-Duke-CGGC-Grape-GVC-Report-Peru.pdf.

Frederick, Stacey and Gary Gereffi. 2009. *Value Chain Governance*. Washington, DC: USAID. Available at https://gvcc.duke.edu/wp-content/uploads/Frederick_Gereffi_ ValueChainGovernance_USAID_BriefingPaper_Feb2009.pdf.

————. 2013. 'Costa Rica in the Electronics Global Value Chain: Opportunities for Upgrading.' Durham, NC: Duke Global Value Chains Center. Commissioned by the

Costa Rican Ministry of Foreign Trade. Available at https://gvcc.duke.edu/wp-content/uploads/2013-08-20_Ch3_Electronics.pdf.

————. 2016. 'Global Value Chains and Upgrading: Export promotion in FTZs.' Available at https://gvcc.duke.edu/wp-content/uploads/2016_May_World_FZO-Bulletin_Gereffi_GVCs_Upgrading_Export_Promotion_FTZs.pdf.

Gereffi, Gary. 1995. 'Global Production Systems and Third World Development.' In *Global Change, Regional Response: The New International Context of Development*, edited by Barbara Stallings, 100–142. Cambridge, New York, and Melbourne: Cambridge University Press.

————. 1999. 'International Trade and Industrial Upgrading in the Apparel Commodity Chain.' *Journal of International Economics* 48(1): 37–70.

————. 2005a. 'The Global Economy: Organization, Governance and Development.' In *The Handbook of Economic Sociology*, 2nd edition, edited by Neil J. Smelser and Richard Swedberg, 160-182. Princeton, NJ: Princeton University Press.

————. 2005b. 'Export-Oriented Growth and Industrial Upgrading: Lessons from the Mexican Apparel Case.' Study commissioned by the World Bank, January 31.

————. 2014. 'Global Value Chains in a Post-Washington Consensus World.' Review of International Political Economy 21(1): 9-37.

Gereffi, Gary, Penny Bamber, and Karina Fernandez-Stark. 2016. 'Promoting Decent Work in Global Supply Chains in Latin America and the Caribbean: Key Issues, Good Practices, Lessons Learned and Policy Insights.' Commissioned by the International Labour Organisation, Lima, Peru.

Gereffi, Gary, Mario Castillo, and Karina Fernandez-Stark. 2009. 'The Offshore Services Industry: A New Opport unity for Latin A merica.' Report for the Inter-A merican Development Bank. Policy Brief #IDB-PB-101. Durham, NC: Duke Global Value Chains Center. Available at https://gvcc.duke.edu/wp-content/uploads/EZSHARE-1728116555-713.pdf.

Gereffi, Gary and Karina Fernandez-Stark. 2010a. 'The Offshore Services Industry: A Global Value Chain Approach.' Durham, NC: Duke Global Value Chains Center. Commissioned by CORFO. Available at https://gvcc.duke.edu/wp-content/uploads/CGGC-CORFO_The_Offshore_-Services_Global_Value_Chain_March-1_2010.pdf.

————. 2010b. 'The Offshore Services Value Chain: Developing Countries and the Crisis.' In *Global Value Chains in a Postcrisis World*, edited by Olivier Cattaneo, Gary Gereffi, and Cornelia Staritz. Washington, DC: World Bank.

Gereffi, Gary, Karina Fernandez-Stark, Penny Bamber, Phil Psilos, and Joe DeStefano. 2011a. 'Meeting the Upgrading Challenge: Dynamic Workforces for Diversified Economies.' In *Skills for Upgrading: Workforce Development and Global Value Chains in Developing Countries*, edited by Gary Gereffi, Karina Fernandez-Stark, and Phil Psilos. Durham, NC: Duke Global Value Chains Center and Research Triangle Institute.

Gereffi, Gary, Karina Fernandez-Stark, and Phil Psilos. 2011b. *Skills for Upgrading: Workforce Development and Global Value Chains in Developing Countries*. Durham, NC: Duke Global Value Chains Center.

Gereffi, Gary and Stacey Frederick. 2010. 'The Global Apparel Value Chain, Trade and the Crisis: Challenges and Opportunities for Developing Countries.' In *Global Value Chains in* a *Postcrisis World: A Development Perspective*, edited by Olivier Cattaneo, Gary Gereffi, and Cornelia Staritz. Washington, DC: World Bank.

Gereffi, Gary and Miguel Korzeniewicz., eds. 1994. *Commodity Chains and Global Capitalism.* Praeger.Publishers.

Gereffi, Gary, Joonkoo Lee, and Michelle Christian. 2009. 'US-based Food and Agricultural Value Chains and their Relevance to Healthy Diets.' *Journal of Hunger and Environmental Nutrition* 4(3): 357–374.

Global Value Chains Initiative. 2011. Available at: https://globalvaluechains.org/.

Gospel, Howard and Mari Sako. 2009. 'The Unbundling of Corporate Functions: The Evolution of Shared Services and Outsourcing in Human Resource Management'. *Industrial and Corporate Change* 19: 1367–1396.

Humphrey, John and Hubert Schmitz. 2002. 'How Does Insertion in Global Value Chains Affect Upgrading in Industrial Clusters?' *Regional Studies* 36(9): 1017–1027.

ILO (International Labour Organization). 2016. *Decent Work in Global Supply Chains.* Geneva: ILO.

Kaplinsky, Raphael and Masuma Farooki. 2011. 'What are the Implications for Global Value Chains When the Market Shifts from the North to the South?' *International Journal of Technological Learning, Innovation and Development* 4(1-3): 13–38.

Lee, Joonkoo and Gary Gereffi. 2015. 'Global Value Chains, Rising Power Firms and Economic and Social Upgrading.' *Critical Perspectives on International Business* 11(3/4): 319–339.

Lee, Joonkoo, Gary Gereffi, and Janet Beauvais. 2012. 'Global Value Chains and Agrifood Standards: Challenges and Possibilities for Smallholders in Developing Countries.' *Proceedings of the National Academy of Sciences* 109(31): 12326–12331.

OECD (Organisation for Economic Co-operation and Development). 2013. 'Upgrading Skills for Current and Future Needs.' In *Perspectives on Global Development 2013: Industrial Policies in a Changing World.* Paris: OECD Development Centre.

Sako, Mari. 2006. 'Outsourcing and Offshoring: Implications for Productivity of Business Services.' *Review of Economic Policy* 22(4): 499–512.

Shih, Stan. n.d. *Millennium Transformation: Change Management for New Acer.* Available at http://www.stanshares.com.tw/StanShares/upload/tbBook/1_20100817144639.pdf.

Taglioni, Daria, and Deborah Winkler. 2016. *Making Global Value Chains Work for Development.* Washington, DC: World Bank.

UN Comtrade. 2015. *United Nations Commodity Trade Statistics Database.* New York: United Nations Statistics Division.

Weinberger, Katinka and Thomas A. Lumpkin. 2007. 'Diversification into Horticulture and Poverty Reduction: A Research Agenda.' *World Development* 35(8): 1464–1480.

Global Value Chains, Development, and Emerging Economies

Global Value Chains and International Competition

Globalization has given rise to a new era of international competition that is best understood by looking at the global organization of industries and the ways in which countries rise and fall within these industries (Gereffi, 2011). Using core concepts like 'governance' and 'upgrading', global value chains (GVCs) highlight the ways in which new patterns of international trade, production, and employment shape prospects for development and competitiveness. GVC analysis documents the international expansion and geographic fragmentation of contemporary production networks and focuses primarily on the issues of industry (re)organization, coordination, governance, and power in the chain (Gereffi and Lee, 2012). Its concern is to understand the causes and consequences of the organizational reconfiguration taking place in global industries.[1] The GVC approach also explores the broader institutional context of these linkages, including trade policy, regulation, and standards.

In the past two decades, profound changes in the structure of the global economy have reshaped global production and trade and have altered the organization of industries and national economies (Gereffi, 2014). As supply chains became global in scope, more intermediate goods were traded across borders, and more imported parts and components were integrated into exports (Krugman, 1995; Feenstra, 1998). In 2009, world exports of intermediate goods exceeded the combined export values of final and capital goods for the first time, representing 51% of non-fuel merchandise exports (WTO and IDE-JETRO, 2011: 81). Because of the unique ability of the GVC framework to show how international supply chains link economic activities at global, regional, national, and local levels within particular industries, international organizations such as the United Nations Conference on Trade and Development (UNCTAD), the Organisation for Economic Co-operation and Development (OECD), the World Bank, and the World Economic Forum are utilizing the GVC approach to structure new donor initiatives and data collection programs on global trade and development (UNCTAD, 2013; OECD, 2013; Cattaneo et al., 2010; World Economic Forum, 2013).

Emerging economies are playing significant and diverse roles in GVCs (Gereffi and Sturgeon, 2013). During the 2000s, they became major exporters of intermediate and final manufactured goods (China, South Korea, and Mexico) and primary products (Brazil, Russia, and South Africa). However, market growth in emerging economies has also led to shifting end markets in GVCs, as more trade has occurred between developing economies (often referred to as South-South trade in the literature), especially since the 2008–2009 economic recession (Staritz et al., 2011: 1–12). China has been the focal point of both trends: it is the world's leading exporter of manufactured goods and the world's largest importer of many raw materials, thereby contributing to the primary product export boom.

The Rise of GVCs

In the 1970s and 1980s, US retailers and global brands joined manufacturers in the search for offshore suppliers of most categories of consumer goods. This led to a fundamental shift from what had been 'producer-driven' commodity chains, which include capital- and technology-intensive industries like automobiles and electronics, to 'buyer-driven' chains, which include a broad range of consumer products like apparel, footwear, toys, and sporting goods (Gereffi, 1994a). The geography of these chains expanded from regional production-sharing arrangements to full-fledged global supply chains, with a growing emphasis on East Asia (Gereffi, 1996). In the 1960s and 1970s, large, vertically integrated transnational corporations dominated the landscape in most international industries (Vernon, 1971), and the prevailing development strategy was import-substituting industrialization (ISI). Well established in Latin America, Eastern Europe, and parts of Asia since the 1950s, ISI was a state-led effort to build domestic industries by requiring foreign manufacturers to replace imports with locally made products, beginning with the assembly of final goods and working back to key components, in return for guaranteed market access (Gereffi, 1994b). These domestic industrial policies were intended to nurture a set of full-blown national industries in key sectors that could significantly reduce, if not fully eliminate, imports from the industrialized nations (Baldwin, 2011).

The death knell for ISI, especially in Latin America, came from the oil shock of the late 1970s and the severe debt crisis that followed it (Urquidi, 1991). The ISI approach was creating large and persistent trade deficits because the manufacturing sectors in ISI countries were simply importing intermediate goods rather than reducing imports altogether, and escalating debt service payments led to a net outflow of foreign capital that crippled economic growth in the 1980s.

Under pressure from the International Monetary Fund (IMF) and the World Bank, many developing countries made the transition from ISI to export-oriented industrialization (EOI) during the 1980s (Gereffi and Wyman, 1990; Haggard, 1990). This new outward-oriented development model focused on exports to the global market by local firms, and it removed the state requirement that foreign firms had to produce for protected domestic markets, which mainly benefitted larger developing economies. There was an equally profound reorientation in the strategies of transnational corporations (Grunwald and Flamm, 1985). The rapid expansion of industrial capabilities and export propensities in a diverse array of newly industrializing economies in Asia and Latin America encouraged transnational companies to accelerate their own efforts to outsource relatively standardized activities to lower-cost production locations worldwide. Precisely this change in the strategies of transnational companies enabled the transition from ISI to EOI in developing economies, and it corresponds with the shift from producer-driven to buyer-driven commodity chains at the level of global industries (Gereffi, 1994a: 97–100).

The rise of GVCs occurred in a period of falling trade barriers, the emergence of the World Trade Organization (WTO), and the policy prescriptions associated with the 'Washington Consensus'—i.e., that governments had only to provide a strong set of 'horizontal' policies (such as education, infrastructure, and macroeconomic stability) and be open to trade in order to succeed (Gore, 2000). Of course, many observers noted that the dynamic emerging economies did much more than establish a set of economy-wide enabling institutions for growth. They frequently also targeted key domestic industries for support, under either ISI or EOI policies that tended to alternate over time in both Latin American and East Asian nations (Gereffi and Wyman, 1990; Haggard, 1990).

Today, industrial policy is on the upswing (OECD Development Centre, 2013; Crespi et al., 2014; Salazar-Xirinachs et al., 2014). WTO accession often comes with allowances for selective industrial policies (e.g., trade promotion, local content rules, taxes, tariffs, and more indirect programs that drive local production) to remain in force for specified periods. Bilateral trade agreements can supersede such allowances under WTO rules, and a handful of relatively large and advanced emerging economies (such as those in the G-20) that have more clout in the institutions of global governance are using them to create policy space to design and implement activist industrial policies.

The organization of global industries into GVCs in which production and trade networks are spread across many countries and regions has reinvigorated industrial policy debates (Baldwin, 2011). There is not likely to be a return to the ISI and EOI policies of old, however. Domestic industries in both industrialized and developing countries no longer stand alone, competing mainly through arm's-length trade. Instead, they have become deeply intertwined through complex, overlapping business networks created through recurrent waves of foreign direct investment and global sourcing. Companies, localities, and entire countries have come to occupy specialized niches within GVCs. Because of this, today's industrial policies have a different character and generate different outcomes than before. Intentionally or not, governments currently engage in GVC-oriented industrialization when targeting key sectors for growth (Gereffi and Sturgeon, 2013).

New governance structures reinforce the organizational consolidation occurring within GVCs and the geographic concentration associated with the growing prominence of emerging economies as key economic and political actors (Gereffi, 2014: 15–17). After 1989, the breakup of the Soviet Union, the opening of China to international investment and trade, and the liberalization of India brought a number of very large economies onto the global stage, known initially as BRICs (Brazil, Russia, India, and China).[2] This resulted in what Richard Freeman called 'the great doubling' of the global labor pool from about 1.5 billion workers to 3 billion workers (Freeman, 2008). The rise of the BRICs spurred the globalization process, as GVCs began to focus their investment and sourcing operations in big and dynamic emerging economies that offered abundant raw materials, large pools of low-wage workers, highly capable manufacturers, and rapidly growing domestic markets.

Faced with slow growth at home, large transnational lead firms in GVCs rushed to set up operations in BRIC countries, especially China, in an effort to carve out brand recognition and market share in rapidly expanding consumer markets and to cut costs on goods produced for export back to home markets (Naughton, 1997; Ross, 2006). In producer-driven chains, the lead firms that to a large degree defined the structure of these industries were largely global manufacturers like General Motors, Ford, IBM, and HP. In buyer-driven chains, the lead firms were a mix of retailers (like Walmart, J. C. Penney, and Carrefour), global marketers (such as Nike, Liz Claiborne, and Polo/Ralph Lauren), and supermarkets and food multinationals (like Tesco, Sainsbury's, Kraft Foods and Nestlé) (Gereffi, 1994a). The lead firms in buyer-driven chains were particularly influential in the globalization process because they accelerated the process of 'global sourcing' based on orders from developed countries, which relied almost entirely on production carried out in developing economies (Gereffi, 1999; Dicken, 2011).

As retailers and branded manufacturers in wealthy countries became more experienced with global sourcing, developing countries enhanced their infrastructure, and suppliers in those countries upgraded their capabilities in response to larger orders for more complex goods.[3] In the 1990s, many US- and Europe-based manufacturers quickly became huge global players, with facilities in scores of locations around the world (e.g., Siemens, Valeo, Flextronics) (Sturgeon, 2002; Sturgeon and Lester, 2004). A handful of elite East Asian suppliers (e.g.,

Pou Chen, Quanta, Foxconn) and trading companies (e.g., Li and Fung[4]) also took on more tasks for multinational affiliates and global buyers (Appelbaum, 2008). These firms expanded production throughout Asia and more recently in Africa, Eastern Europe, and Latin America (Morris et al., 2011; Pickles and Smith, 2011; Smith et al., 2014; Hernández et al., 2014).

Lead firms themselves are getting bigger and increasing their global market shares through mergers, acquisitions, and the decline of many rivals (Gereffi, 2014: 16). This has been coupled with a growing recognition of the strategic vulnerabilities of global supply chains, linked to the risk of single-source relationships and the danger of lead firms losing access to critical inputs and raw material supplies (Lynn, 2005). This is particularly apparent in the agrifoods sector, in which consumer goods firms such as Cadbury, Coca-Cola, and Unilever are expanding their direct involvement in the procurement and sustainability of the raw material sides of their value chains, such as those involving cocoa, coffee, and sugar (Barrientos and Asenso-Okyere, 2008; Oxfam, 2011). This is also evident in the automobile and electronics industries, in which concern about the availability of raw materials such as lithium and coltan (Nathan and Sarkar, 2011), respectively, are spurring greater engagement between GVC lead firms and host country suppliers and governments (Sturgeon and Van Biesebroeck, 2011; Sturgeon and Kawakami, 2011). These examples suggest that a number of GVCs, especially in natural resource-based industries, are giving greater attention to strategic collaboration as a counterweight to the long-term trend toward specialization and fragmentation of supply chains.

Governance and Upgrading in GVCs

The GVC framework focuses on globally expanding supply chains and how value is created and captured therein (Gereffi and Lee, 2012). By analyzing the full range of activities that firms and workers perform to bring a specific product from its conception to its end use and beyond, the GVC approach provides a holistic view of global industries from two contrasting vantage points: top-down and bottom-up (Gereffi and Fernandez-Stark, 2011). The key concept for the top-down view is the 'governance' of global value chains, which focuses mainly on lead firms and the organization of global industries; and the main concept for the bottom-up perspective is 'upgrading', which focuses on the strategies used by countries, regions, and other economic stakeholders to maintain or improve their positions in the global economy (Gereffi, 2011: 39–40).

The concept of governance is the centerpiece of GVC analysis. It examines the ways in which corporate power can actively shape the distribution of profits and risk in an industry and the actors who exercise such power through their activities.

Power in GVCs is exerted by lead firms. In the governance typology outlined in Figure 12.1, the market and hierarchy poles of the GVC governance continuum are driven by price and ownership within vertically integrated firms, respectively. The remaining three categories are stable forms of network governance (modular, relational, and captive), in which different kinds of GVC lead firms control to a large degree the ways in which global supply chains operate and the main winners and losers within these chains (Gereffi et al., 2005).

Figure 12.1 Five Types of Global Value Chain Governance

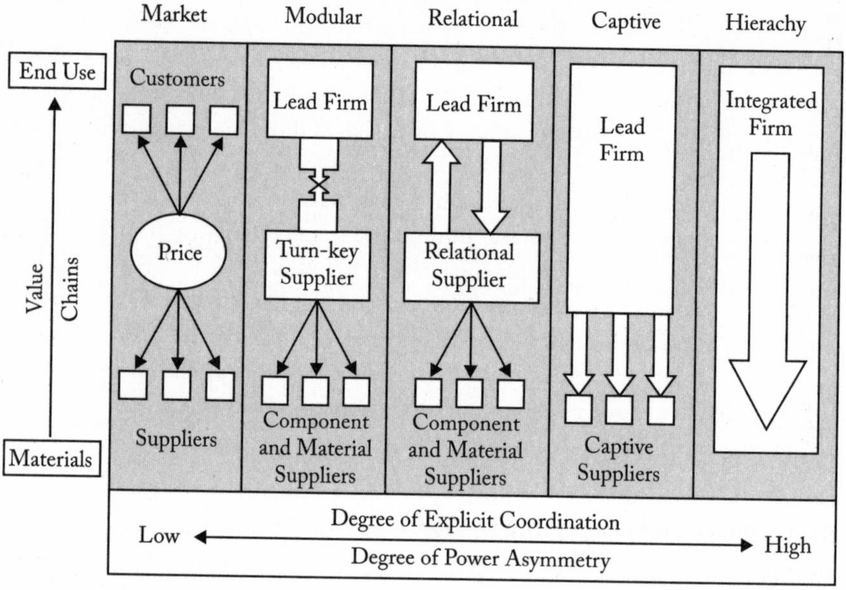

Source: Gereffi et al., 2005: 89.

While governance issues have attracted a good deal of attention among GVC scholars, the research on economic upgrading has been at least as important because many of the people who use the GVC framework have a very strong development focus. 'Economic upgrading' is defined as the process by which economic actors—firms and workers—move from low-value to relatively high-value activities in GVCs (Gereffi, 2005: 171). The challenge of economic upgrading in GVCs is to identify the conditions under which developing and developed countries and firms can 'climb the value chain' from basic assembly activities using low-cost and unskilled labor to more advanced forms of 'full package' supply and integrated manufacturing.

Connecting GVCs to Economic Development

GVCs matter for economic development in several ways, since the ability of countries to prosper depends on their participation in the global economy, which is largely a story about their role in GVCs (Gereffi and Lee, 2012). Connecting countries to GVCs involves both investment and trade, which rely heavily on efficient global supply chains in order to contribute to growth.[5] A key factor in such efficiency is infrastructure development, which enables global trade though the construction and improvement of the physical facilities that link national economies: ports and canals, airports, roads, and a wide range of information and communication technologies (Dicken, 2011: 400–406; WTO and IDE-JETRO, 2011: 28, 30). Improving trade flows at the border can be enhanced by infrastructure investments inside the border (i.e., in roads and facilities that connect rural regions and small firms to larger domestic markets), and also by investments beyond the border, especially in infrastructure facilities that connect a country to its nearby neighbors in regional supply chains (Mayer and Milberg, 2013). These regional markets are often unappreciated because of the importance given to developed country markets in the 1990s and early 2000s, but in the current era, regional value chains are becoming a new focus for investment planning by development banks and international organizations (Gereffi and Lee, 2012: 28–29).

GVC studies are pervasive in academic publications that examine a wide range of global industries.[6] The framework has also been adopted by many of the most important international organizations concerned with economic development, such as the WTO, UNCTAD, the OECD, the World Bank, and the World Economic Forum.[7] The international institutions that have provided the underpinning for the Washington Consensus (such as the World Bank, the IMF, and the WTO) and major bilateral donors (such as the US Agency for International Development (USAID) and the UK's Department for International Development (DFID) have embraced new models of development thinking, with an emphasis on sectoral analysis that links macro issues such as international trade and investment more closely with the micro development issues of employment, gender dynamics, and sustainable livelihoods (M4P, 2008; Staritz and Reis, 2013; Milberg and Winkler, 2013). In addition, new alliances have emerged among diverse UN and other international agencies (such as the World Bank and the ILO) to promote joint research agendas that explore the links between economic and social upgrading, explicitly using the GVC framework (Cattaneo et al., 2010; Barrientos et al., 2011; Rossi et al., 2014).

This is an area in which GVC analysis and supply chain management research can be mutually beneficial. Sophisticated value chain data disaggregated by business functions can complement existing country-level trade statistics and industry-level input-output data, providing a clear picture of who is gaining and losing in GVCs (Sturgeon and Gereffi, 2009). When combined with data on employment, they will greatly advance our understanding of both economic and social development opportunities in the global economy.

Today virtually all major bilateral and multilateral donor agencies use value chain analysis as an instrument of private-sector development (Gereffi, 2014). According to Altenburg (2007), there are two principal reasons for the increasing popularity of the GVC approach within the international donor community since the end of the 1990s: first, the accumulating evidence of a link between economic growth driven by the private sector and poverty reduction; and second, the fact that global integration of trade and production through GVCs transmits the pressures of global competition to domestic markets in developing economies, leaving less space for local firms to design, produce, and market on their own. Given the pervasiveness of GVCs, the question for many is not if, but how, to integrate into value chains in a balanced way that addresses both competitiveness and equity issues and that allows for the incorporation of a growing proportion of the workforce while increasing productivity and output.

There is no simple way to connect GVC analysis to private-sector development, given that the firms in a value chain range from transnational corporations to micro-enterprises, and the institutional context and geographic scope of value chains vary enormously. Generally, however, donor interventions have four objectives: strengthening the weakest link to address potential bottlenecks; improving flows of knowledge and resources to make all firms in the chain more productive; working on specific links between firms to improve efficiency; and creating new or alternate links in the chain to promote diversified outcomes (Humphrey and Navas-Alemán, 2010).

Much of this research and theoretical work has focused on how lead firms in specific GVCs have driven this process in various ways. Decisions about outsourcing and offshoring are, after all, strategic decisions made by managers. But such decisions are not made in a vacuum. The policies and programs of countries and multilateral institutions set the context for corporate decision-making, and there has been an evolution in the form and effects of industrial policy along with the evolution of the business networks that comprise GVCs.

Today, the organization of the global economy is entering a new phase—what some have referred to as a 'major inflection point' (Fung, 2011)—that could have dramatic implications for firms and workers in emerging and industrialized countries. As world trade rebounds from the 2008–2009 economic crisis, emerging economies have become a major engine of growth.

Developing Economies in GVCS: Upgrading Experiences in Diverse Sectors

Many examples could be provided to illustrate how developing countries are participating in GVCs. For purposes of this chapter, we will focus on three aspects of GVCs particularly relevant to economic upgrading and inclusive development goals: (1) building export capabilities—the cases of coffee, apparel, and automobiles; (2) leveraging services to build knowledge capabilities and move to high-value niches in GVCs—the cases of a traceability system for the cattle industry in Uruguay and environmental services in Costa Rica; and (3) the role of public-private partnerships to narrow the human capital gap in India and Latin America, and to develop the aerospace industry in Mexico.

Promoting Growth and Upgrading in Export-Oriented GVCs

The Coffee Value Chain in Central America and East Africa

The world coffee market is large, with retail sales of US$70 billion and demand growing steadily at about 2.5% annually.[8] The biggest global producers are Brazil and Vietnam, followed by Colombia and Indonesia. The United States is the largest consumer market, spending an estimated $30 billion in 2009. Within the coffee GVC, there are important quality distinctions that translate into significant price variations for coffee producers as well as distinct market segments for large branded manufacturers in the coffee sector. The two main varieties of coffee are arabica (higher quality) and robusta (lower quality). These correspond to segmentation at the retail end of the GVC: there is a commercial grade segment (e.g., Folgers), which sells large volumes at relatively low prices; and a specialty or high/quality gourmet segment (e.g., Starbucks, Illy coffee), which sells in niche markets and commands premium prices. Within the United States, the specialty coffee market has grown rapidly, with a number of boutique and super high grade coffees, and this offers great potential for growth by developing country coffee producers (Ponte, 2002).

Central America is recognized as one of the world's leading specialty coffee producers. In most countries of the region, over half of their production is classified as premium coffee (i.e., above commercial grade). Guatemala and Honduras are perhaps the best established Central America coffee suppliers in global markets, with Nicaragua and Panama rapidly gaining market share in the specialty coffee segment. In 2010, Guatemala's coffee exports were valued at $718 million, involving more than 171,000 producers; Nicaragua exported $351 million of coffee produced by nearly 90,000 growers (World Bank, 2012: 19). Whereas specialty coffee accounted for just 20% of Guatemala's coffee exports in 1980s, it now accounts for over 80%.

Most specialty coffee in Central America comes from small producers, and the challenge is how to provide them with a sustainable niche in the specialty coffee GVC. The potential economic, social, and environmental upgrading gains of specialty coffee are not in question. Smallholders growing for the specialty market can sell their coffee at premiums significantly higher than certified coffee and receive a larger share of the retail price. For example, compared to the 2014 minimum price established for fair trade, organic certified coffee, $1.90 per pound, the average price specialty coffee growers received during the first nine months of 2014 was $2.72, and as high as $3.60 (Farmers to 40, 2014). Consumers tend to prefer single-origin coffee with an emphasis on new and unique varietals[9] and source authenticity (like premium wine), and there is a high value attached to socially and environmentally sustainably grown coffee as well.

There are various difficulties, however, in capturing these price premiums within Central America. The specialty coffee value chain is typically dominated by a few large exporters, along with roasters who are located near the final consumers in North America, Europe, and increasingly East Asia. Infrastructure investments are required to build the wet processing plants to assure the quality of premium coffee. For smallholders, it is usually not economical to have washing stations on the farm, and thus they are built at the cooperative level or by private firms.[10] Given infrastructure needs and the relatively high cost of inputs (e.g., fertilizer), inadequate short-term financing for Central American smallholders is a major obstacle in the specialty coffee segment. In addition, given the importance of quality control, branding and coordination across the chain, the creation of strong national or regional coffee associations could provide a major boost to export producers in Central America.

The coffee value chain is considered an important sector for economic upgrading of smallholder farmers in other regions of the world, including South America, Asia, and sub-Saharan Africa (Talbot, 2004; Daviron and Ponte, 2005). Within East Africa, coffee represents a significant share of agricultural exports in Ethiopia, Kenya, Uganda, Rwanda, Tanzania, and Burundi. Despite nearly ideal growing conditions for the arabica coffee needed to produce specialty coffee, production in the Rwandan coffee sector declined sharply in the 2000s. Struggling to regain its economic growth after the 1994 Rwandan genocide, many of Rwanda's smallholders had abandoned coffee production, leaving about 400,000 still committed to the sector in 2002 (Abdulsamad et al., 2015: 31).

In 2000, USAID initiated several projects to help smallholder coffer growers in Rwanda to improve the quality of their coffee to meet specialty status, which substantially increased shareholder revenues. To ensure the sustainability of these gains, USAID implemented a development alliance made up of US and Rwandan universities, enterprises, and non-governmental organizations, which over a 10-year period proved highly successful.[11] The positive outcomes for smallholders required the establishment of cooperatives and coffee washing stations to create a local processing infrastructure that permitted smallholders to partner with specialty roasters in the coffee value chain.[12] This established some balance of power between smallholders and large international coffee buyers, and allowed specialty roasters to introduce the prestigious Cup of Excellence coffee competition to Rwanda in 2008, the first such competition ever held in Africa (Abdulsamad et al., 2015: 36). As in Central America, Rwandan smallholders growing coffee for the specialty market sold their coffee at higher price premiums than certified coffee and for a larger share of the retail price, without having to pursue a costly certification process (Abdulsamad et al., 2015: 39–40).

Nicaragua, Lesotho, and Swaziland in the Apparel Manufacturing Global Value Chain

The Nicaraguan apparel industry's exports nearly doubled from US$716 million in 2005 to $1.36 billion in 2011 (Bair and Gereffi, 2014: 256). Nicaragua mainly participates in the low-value 'cut-make-trim' stage of the apparel value chain (see Figure 12.2). Leveraging the country's competitive wage advantage (Portocarrero Lacayo, 2010), the industry employed more than 51,300 people in 2010 (ILO and IFC, 2010).[13] In 2009, 89% of Nicaraguan apparel exports were destined for the United States. The country is still considered a small regional supplier, but since 2004 it has steadily gained US market share in certain segments, such as woven pants and cotton shirts, as a result of its preferential trade status within the Dominican Republic-Central American Free Trade Agreement (Bair and Gereffi, 2014). Apparel manufacturers in Nicaragua focus on trousers, mainly denim jeans and twill pants, as well as t-shirts.

The industry consists of a large proportion of foreign-owned firms, with very few locally owned companies. Among the foreign firms, Korean and US ownership dominates, with the remainder coming from El Salvador, Honduras, Mexico, and Taiwan. A significant proportion of these firms are part of larger global or regional networks; particularly in Central America, this structure allows global firms to provide full-package services for their clients by leveraging the interactions of multiple country operations. Knit-based firms sell to buyers such as Walmart, Target, and Polo/Ralph Lauren. Woven apparel firms are more regionally focused, with operations in neighboring countries such as Guatemala, Honduras, and Mexico, and leading buyers include Levi Strauss, Cintas, and Kohl's.

Figure 12.2 Curve of Value-Added Stages in the Apparel Global Value Chain: Nicaragua

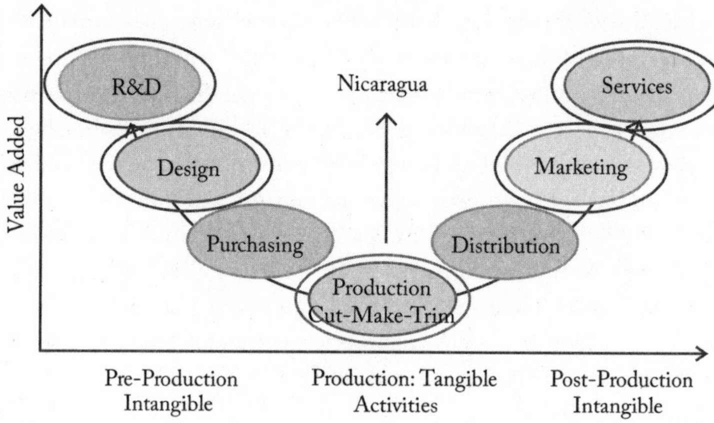

Source: Author.

Between 2005 and 2010, the volume of Nicaragua's apparel exports grew by 8.6%, but despite this increase, Nicaragua has had limited success in moving up the apparel value chain and mainly competes through low-cost apparel assembly. The country's apparel exporters have not achieved significant product upgrading; the value of exports only increased by 4.5% (PRONicaragua, 2010). Rather, this period was characterized by an increase in the production of t-shirts and knitwear, which are low-value-added product segments. Prior to the economic crisis, the country had seen increases in the value of its exports in woven trousers, but due to the economic slowdown in the United States, 2009 exports fell back to their 2006 levels.

Nicaragua remains vulnerable in terms of economic upgrading because its apparel exports are dependent on US trade policy (specifically, the Tariff Preference Level or TPL exception offered to Nicaragua that allowed it to import textiles from East Asia). However, the country has shown advances in social upgrading, due in large part to the efforts of the tripartite National Free Trade Zones Commission to join the interests of workers, the private sector, and government. It also has become part of the Better Work program by the International Labor Organization (Bair and Gereffi, 2014).

The trade-policy dependency of Nicaragua and other Central America Free Trade Agreement (CAFTA) countries on the US market is paralleled by the similar dynamics found in sub-Saharan Africa's apparel-exporting economies that are covered by the African Growth and Opportunity Act (AGOA), such as Lesotho and Swaziland (Morris et al., 2011). As with Nicaragua, apparel exports by Lesotho and Swaziland are concentrated on the US market, which absorbs over 98% of clothing exports from both countries. However, the phase out of the Multi-Fibre Arrangement (MFA) in 2004, which ended the apparel quota system, and the 2008–2009 global economic crisis prompted a sharp drop in clothing exports by both countries to the United States. Many of the Taiwanese firms that concentrated on supplying the US market left in the wake of the crisis.

However, sub-Saharan Africa had a different dynamic that buffered Lesotho and Swaziland from the global economic recession. A new type of investor— South African clothing manufacturers—moved into Lesotho and Swaziland not as a production base to take advantage of AGOA preferences for access to the US market, but rather because of their lower labor costs in comparison to South Africa as a new export market. The South African Customs Union provides duty-free access for apparel produced in member countries (which include Lesotho and Swaziland), which allows South African retailers to maintain low prices and a growing market share (Morris et al., 2011: 98). Furthermore, South African-owned firms are far more likely than their Taiwanese counterparts to utilize local production, supervisory and management skills in their apparel operations in Lesotho and Swaziland, thus promoting additional upgrading prospects in these countries. Sustaining these advantages, however, would require more active government policies to incentivize added skill development within local clothing manufacturers in both countries (Morris et al., 2011: 115–117).

Automobiles in Mexico and Brazil

The automobile industry typifies the sharp contrast in patterns of GVC participation found within Latin America's manufacturing sector.[14] Beginning in the 1980s and accelerated by Mexico's entry into the North American Free Trade Agreement (NAFTA) in 1994, Mexico shifted from an import-substitution strategy to an export-oriented model in its automotive sector, which relied on low-cost Mexican workers and extensive foreign direct investment (FDI) from the United States, Europe, and Japan, interested in establishing a strong network of carmakers and autoparts suppliers that could turn Mexico into a world-class export hub, focused on sales to the US market. On the basis of its strategic proximity to the United States and its trade agreements with over 40 countries, Mexico has become one of the top automotive export countries in the world. While this has created significant job opportunities, the relatively low level of wages has not kept pace with Mexico's growing productivity, and the industry still has relatively weak linkages with local suppliers.

The model of GVC participation in Brazil's automotive sector is quite different. The Brazilian strategy is to emphasize sales to its large internal market and regional connections with its Mercosur partners (mainly Argentina, but also Paraguay, Uruguay, and Venezuela), using high tariffs on automotive products imported from outside of Mercosur to increase the technological capabilities of Brazilian affiliates of foreign carmakers. In addition, Brazil has introduced various incentives for exports, higher levels of local content, and investment in new plants in the country.

Both Brazil and Mexico attract significant amounts of FDI into the automotive sector.[15] However, the role played by transnational corporations (TNCs) is different. In Brazil the exports are lower, but local suppliers are more fully integrated into the operations of the TNCs, with higher levels of local innovation and research and development (R&D) capabilities. In Mexico, the range of activities in the automotive value chain is more diverse, since it supplies the needs of Japanese, German, and American automakers, in both Mexico and the US market. The automotive GVC has created more jobs in Mexico, but higher skill levels and technological capabilities in Brazil. The current development policies in each country related to autos are intended to fill in the gaps left by their current strategies.

Leveraging Local Knowledge to Add Value in Resource-Based GVCs

Creating Knowledge: A Traceability System for the Cattle Industry in Uruguay

With over 12 million head of cattle in Uruguay, cows outnumber people by four to one and beef is Uruguay's leading export. In 2010, Uruguay exported U$1.1 billion in bovine beef products (UN Comtrade, 2012). The global beef industry, however, is extremely vulnerable to health and food safety problems. Uruguay has not been immune to these difficulties; a 2000 outbreak of foot-and-mouth disease led to a multi-year ban on exports to the United States and the European Union, as well as numerous other countries including Chile, Israel, and South Korea. In order to mitigate the impact of these challenges on key export revenues, Uruguay embarked on the development of a sophisticated bovine traceability system, which would allow the country to quickly and efficiently track the source of and contain potential problems, and maintain consumer and regulatory confidence of their products in the developed world.

The livestock traceability system was developed through a collaborative multi-stakeholder initiative bringing together producers, local governments, transport personnel, the private sector, information technology companies, and the central government (the Ministry of Agriculture, in particular). Today, this is the only system in the world with real-time monitoring of 100% of the national cattle herd. A chip implanted in each cow's ear at birth allows the system to keep centralized and accurate information regarding the animal from birth through to sales and distribution points. Approximately 2.5 million new animals are registered on an annual basis (Crescionini, 2012; SONDA, 2012).

Uruguay has a great opportunity to capitalize on its knowledge and experiences, exporting these services to other countries that face similar issues. Indeed, Colombia has already begun to roll out this information system for its cattle herd. This means that Uruguay can participate in different segments of the cattle value chain. In addition to continued beef exports, Uruguay now has the potential to export advanced services not only for the beef industry, but the broader livestock sector as well. In the face of rising concerns in meeting increasingly strict global food safety standards, this is a tremendous competitive advantage for the country.

Environmental Services Offshoring: An Opportunity for Costa Rica

Costa Rica is recognized worldwide for its unique approach to environmental protection and is a leader in the field among both developing and developed countries alike. As a result of conservation incentives put in place in the 1980s, today tropical forest covers more than half of the country. Illegal farming is down to just 15% and farmers are paid to manage and protect their natural surroundings (Conservation International, 2012). To date, however, this know-how has been used principally to support domestic priorities. Experts work for national non-governmental organizations (NGOs) and foundations, and the country has not yet seized the opportunity to commercialize the significant expertise it has built over many years. With the rising prominence of climate change on the global development agenda, there is significant demand for services in these areas.

Due to its critical mass of qualified human capital to sustain this niche (Chassot, 2012; Rodriguez, 2012), Costa Rica is in an excellent position to export high-demand environmental services, such as natural resources management, environmental impact studies, threatened and endangered species assessments, protected areas evaluations, and environmental education and training, among many others. More than 18 other countries, including China, have consulted Costa Rica to learn about its conservation policies (Conservation International, 2012). As with many developing countries, however, limited knowledge of potential markets and undeveloped entrepreneurship skills undermine the potential for translating these consulting opportunities into profitable service exports (Chassot, 2012) The promotion of this industry will require the internationalization of local firms, on one hand, and the attraction of foreign environmental firms, on the other, to use Costa Rica as a platform to export environmental services. Linking these two types of firms will be critical for the development of this niche activity.

Skills for Upgrading

Public–Private Partnerships to Narrow the Human Capital Gap in India and Latin America

National 'finishing schools' represent a promising tool to narrow the gap between the human capital needs of GVCs and the skills supplied by national education systems. The finishing school model has been tested in India and the Philippines, and recently applied in Latin America with the support of the Inter-American Development Bank (IDB). These schools help recent graduates and workers develop high-demand skills, making them more employable. In turn, by increasing workforce employability, finishing schools can help a country improve its position in the value chain.

Finishing schools build upon the fundamental skills acquired in academic institutions, filling in specific gaps in knowledge and soft skills. These gaps are determined by the skill sets needed by a particular industry, as compared with the workforce's current skills. In India, the most effective finishing schools were those that collaborated with companies to identify the desired skill sets, and match trainings to these gaps (Tholons, 2012). In the global services industry, these skills often include technical (IT) skills, English abilities, and soft skills such as relational skills, confidence, and presentation skills. Programs at finishing schools that train workers for careers in IT services can run from five weeks to up to one year in duration (Tholons, 2012: 14). Often, these schools target youths who have recently graduated from high school or university, but they can also play a role in re-training adult workers (IDB, 2012).

Public–private partnerships are central to creating effective financing and governance mechanisms to support finishing school programs in developing countries. Although in India, finishing schools may be run by either the government or a private institution, in Latin America there is increasing recognition that collaborative policies and institutions provide the most effective support to finishing school initiatives.[16]

The public–private model offers two key advantages: (1) such partnerships create opportunities for co-financing, reducing the cost burden borne by any one sector; and (2) the content of the programs is determined by the employers themselves, ensuring that the skills developed match industry needs (IDB, 2012). Thus, the finishing school model recognizes the role of all stakeholders, 'the State, the academe, and industry—in shaping the capabilities of the labor pool towards in delivering information technology and business process outsourcing services' (Tholons, 2012: 14).

The Aerospace Industry in Querétaro, Mexico[17]

The aerospace industry in Querétaro has grown rapidly. Bombardier—one of the leading companies in the sector, based in Canada—arrived to the area in 2006, marking the entry of Querétaro into the aerospace GVC. The French group Safran and Spanish airframe manufacturer Aernnova quickly followed suit, establishing operations in 2007. Under the leadership of the Secretariat for Sustainable Development, Querétaro's aerospace cluster has since become one of the four leading locations in Mexico. By 2012, there were over 30 foreign firms operating in the state, with projected employment of over 6,000, about 20% of the country's aerospace workforce. Mexico's exports in the sector had reached US$4.5 billion by 2011, up from US$1.3 billion in 2004.

Growth was supported by a clear commitment to the development of the industry by the state government, including the creation of the National Aeronautics University of Querétaro (UNAQ) in 2007, which housed several technical programs developed in public-private initiatives and created the first aerospace engineering program in the country. State investments in UNAQ amounted to US$21 million by 2009. In addition to training teaching staff in both Canada and Spain, UNAQ drew teachers from aerospace firms working in the region. By 2012, there were 488 technical and professional students at UNAQ. UNAQ's contributions to human capital development in the state added to an already strong engineering training base. In 2009, engineering graduates accounted for 41% of undergraduate degrees, while 65% of master's degree programs available in the state were in engineering fields (Casalet et al., 2011).

Additionally, in 2007 an aircraft maintenance program was established in Querétaro by the National Mexican Technical Training Institute, which graduates 90 technicians annually. This has supported the ongoing development of the state's maintenance and repair operations capacity, and helped capture large investments, including the 2012 Delta-Aeromexico deal to establish a US$50 million maintenance, repair and overhaul (MRO) facility in Querétaro with seven production lines to serve both airlines.

The Heterogeneity of Emerging Economies and Their Export Profiles

Focusing on a set of seven contemporary emerging economies—China, India, Brazil, Mexico, Russia, South Korea, and South Africa—will give a broader sense of the role of GVCs and development policies in the developing world. They are all centrally involved in distinct types of GVCs in agriculture, extractive industries (mining, oil, and gas), manufacturing, and services (Gereffi and Sturgeon, 2013). Together, these seven emerging economies account for 45% of the world's population, 25% of global exports, and 24% of gross domestic product (GDP) in 2013, and their GDP growth rates are substantially higher than the world average (3.2% versus 2.2%) (see Table 12.1). The economic and social characteristics of these countries are quite diverse, however. The specific roles of these countries in the global economy vary according to their openness to trade and foreign investment; their endowments of natural, human, and technological resources; their geopolitical relationships to the world's most powerful countries; and the characteristics of their immediate neighbors.

As GVCs have expanded in scope and complexity, emerging economies have clearly benefitted, surging ahead of the advanced industrial countries in terms of export performance. Between 1995 and 2007, the global export market shares of the United States and Japan fell by 3.8% and 3.7%, respectively, while China more than doubled its market share from 4% in 1995 to 10.1% in 2007, making it the world's export leader (ahead of Germany, the United States, and Japan). South Korea, Mexico, Turkey, South Africa, and the former transition countries in central Europe also increased their export market shares during this period. Even more surprising, emerging economies made their most significant gains in high and medium-technology industries, which previously were the stronghold of OECD countries. This phenomenon was mainly driven by processing exports from China, whose share of high technology exports soared by 13.5% in the period 1995–2007, moving it ahead of the United States as the world's largest exporter of electronics (Beltramello et al., 2012: 9–10).

Although collectively these seven nations have considerable economic clout, China is the global pacesetter of the group. While China and India are the most populous countries in the world, with 1.36 and 1.25 billion inhabitants, respectively, China is the undisputed export leader, with $2.2 trillion in exports in 2013. China's export total is greater than that of Russia, South Korea, India, Brazil, Mexico, and South Africa combined ($2.14 trillion), and its GDP has grown by over 9% per year for over 30 years. It is now the second-largest economy in the world (after only the United States) and has overtaken Germany as the world's largest exporter (Beltramello et al., 2012: 9). Notwithstanding its rapid economic growth, however, its GDP per capita in US dollars was the third-lowest among these emerging economies in 2013 ($6,807), well ahead of India ($1,498) and a little larger than South Africa ($6,618), but only 60% that of Brazil ($11,208), less than half the per capita income of Russia ($14,611), and just over one-quarter that of South Korea ($25,977). On average, the GDP per capita of these seven emerging economies was about 18% above the world average in 2013, using purchasing power parity (PPP) indicators.

The export profiles of these emerging economies indicate the roles that they play in GVCs. Using a classification scheme that categorizes traded goods according

Table 12.1 Seven Selected Emerging Economies in Comparative Perspective, 2013

Country	Population (Millions)[1]	Exports ($Billions)[2]	GDP ($Billions)[1]	GDP/capita (USD)[1]	GDP/capita (PPP)[1]	GDP growth YoY (%)[1]	% of GDP[3]		
							Agriculture	Industry	Services
China	1,357	$2,209	$9,240	$6,807	$11,906	7.7	10	44	46
South Korea	50	$560	$1,305	$25,977	$33,140	3.0	3	39	58
Russia	143	$527	$2,096	$14,611	$24,114	1.3	4	38	58
Mexico	122	$380	$1,261	$10,307	$16,463	1.1	4	36	60
India	1,252	$337	$1,877	$1,498	$5,412	5.0	17	26	57
Brazil	200	$242	$2,246	$11,208	$15,038	2.5	6	26	68
South Africa	53	$95	$351	$6,618	$12,507	1.9	3	29	68
Total or Avg.	3,177	$4,350	$18,376	$11,004	$16,940	3.2	7	34	59
World Total	7,125	$17,635	$75,593	$10,610	$14,397	2.2			
% of World Total	45%	25%	24%	104%	118%	146%			

Sources:

1. World Bank, World Development Indicators: http://data.worldbank.org.
2. UN Comtrade, International Trade Center: http://comtrade.un.org/.
3. CIA World Factbook, Country Profiles: https://www.cia.gov/library/publications/the-world-factbook/.

Table 12.2 Export Profiles of Emerging Economies, 2000–2013

	Share of exports by sector in 2013*						Total Export Value ($Billions)	Change in total export value, 2000–2013	percentage point change in share of exports by sector, 2000–2013				
	Primary Products	Resource Based	Low-Tech	Medium-Tech	High-Tech				Primary Products	Resource Based	Low-Tech	Medium-Tech	High-Tech
China	3%	8%	32%	23%	34%		2,209	786%	-4	0	-10	4	11
South Korea	2%	17%	9%	43%	28%		560	226%	0	6	-8	10	-8
Russia	55%	29%	2%	8%	2%		527	412%	6	10	-3	-3	-2
Mexico	16%	8%	9%	42%	22%		380	129%	3	3	-6	4	-6
India	14%	38%	20%	18%	8%		337	702%	0	9	-19	7	3
Brazil	33%	33%	5%	21%	4%		242	340%	13	6	-7	-4	-8
South Africa	25%	31%	6%	27%	3%		95	265%	8	1	-3	1	-1

Legend: $x \leq -6$ $-5 \leq x < 0$ $0 \leq x < 9$ $x \geq 10$

*Exports totals do not include uncategorized exports, and therefore they may not equal 100%.

Sources: United Nations Comtrade, SITC Rev. 2.

to primary products plus four types of manufactured exports (resource-based, low-tech, medium-tech, and high-tech) (Lall, 2000), Table 12.2 highlights some of the differences between the export profiles of these countries in 2013. Three of the emerging economies are heavily oriented toward primary product or resource-based exports: Russia (84%), Brazil (66%), and South Africa (56%). Over half of India's exports are resource oriented, and another 20% are low-tech (primarily apparel products) manufactured goods.[18] China, South Korea, and Mexico, by contrast, are heavily involved in manufacturing GVCs. About 90% of China's exports are manufactured goods, while a preponderance of the exports of South Korea (71%) and Mexico (64%) are medium-tech (automotive, machinery) and high-tech (mainly electronics) exports.

China's export success has been a particular challenge for Latin America's two largest economies, Brazil and Mexico. In 2010, China was Brazil's largest trading partner, accounting for about 15% of Brazil's exports and imports. Between 2000 and 2010, Brazil's exports to China increased almost thirty-fold, and since 2002, imports have grown sixteen fold. Although the Lula administration in Brazil was keen to develop a strong economic partnership with China, concern has arisen due to both the composition of Brazil's exports to China (the 'primarization' of Brazilian exports), and their concentration in a relatively small number of products and exporting firms. About 70% of Brazil's global exports in 2011 were primary products or resource-based manufactures. Furthermore, these two categories accounted for just over 60% of Brazilian exports to countries other than China in 2009, compared to almost 90% to China (Sturgeon et al., 2013: 29-30). Brazil's exports to China are concentrated in a very limited number of products, with iron ore and soybeans alone accounting for over two-thirds of the total in 2009.[19]

What is particularly notable about Brazil's trading relationship with China is that it is skewed to the export of products (both primary commodities and manufactured goods) with a very low level of processing, while imports tend to be technology-intensive components and machinery. The soybean value chain is a good example of the former. About 95% of Brazil's soybean exports to China in 2009 were unprocessed beans. In contrast, there were virtually no exports of soybean meal, flour or oil to China. In order to pursue its strategy of promoting the Chinese soybean processing industry, China imposed a tariff of 9% on soybean oil imports, while the tariff on unprocessed soybean imports was only 3%. More processed imported soybean products also paid a higher value-added tax rate in China than unprocessed beans. This same protectionist policy of tariff and non-tariff barriers imposed by the Chinese government to protect its domestic producers was applied to a range of other primary and processed intermediate products from Brazil, including leather, iron and steel, and pulp and paper (Jenkins, 2012: 28–29).

On the import side, Brazil has also been influenced by China's structure of international trade. In 1996, low-technology products accounted for 40% of Brazil's imports from China, while high-technology products accounted for 25%. By 2009, the pattern was nearly reversed: high-technology products were 41.4% of the total, and low-technology products were 20.8%. If we look at this trend in terms of the end use of imports, consumer-goods imports from China to Brazil fell from 44% to 16% between 1996 and 2009, while the imports of capital goods and their parts doubled (Jenkins, 2012: 29–31). Thus, Brazil has been subordinated to occupy the lowest rungs of the value-added ladder in its trade with China in recent decades, which poses long-term structural imbalances for Brazil if the situation doesn't change.

From a GVC perspective, which focuses on the location of value added in global production systems, high-technology imports from mainland China are most often driven by the products and strategies of firms based in OECD countries, along with their business partners (e.g., trading companies, contract manufacturers, and component producers) based elsewhere in the world, especially Taiwan, Hong Kong, and Singapore. Thus, the historic reliance of Brazil on the 'global North' for technology-intensive products has in essence remained, even as China's importance as a trading partner has risen. In other words, China has become a major conduit for technology from the global North.

Notwithstanding the unprecedented momentum of China's rise in the global economy, these competitiveness problems for Brazil can be ameliorated or even reversed. Mexico, which is Latin America's second-largest economy, appears to be in the midst of a remarkable turnaround, based on a little publicized manufacturing revolution that is allowing the country to become a credible competitor to China, after losing US market share to China for more than a decade (Gereffi, 2009). Mexico currently exports more manufactured products than the rest of Latin America combined, and it has begun to diversify its export profile, with exports to the United States falling from 90% of total exports a decade ago to less than 80% today.

The main elements of Mexico's success include a very high degree of trade openness—it has free trade agreements with 44 countries, which is more than twice as many as China and four times more than Brazil. Rising wages and fuel prices have made it increasingly expensive to export from China to the US market. Mexico's wages, which used to be nearly four times higher than China's a decade ago, are just 29% higher today. Also, while Mexico still has an abundance of cheap labor (more than half of its population of 112 million is under 29), its workers are also becoming more skilled, with growing proportions of graduates in engineering, architecture, and other professions (Thomson, 2012). Furthermore, Mexico's geographical proximity to the United States allows shorter supply chains, lower transport costs for bulky items, and quicker delivery times in the context of increasingly popular 'fast fashion', 'just in time', and other 'rapid response' business models. However, this turn-around is not based on the success of domestic firms. As with China, Mexico is a platform for multinational enterprises seeking to locate labor-intensive aspects of GVCs (including both manual and knowledge work) in a country that is both low-cost and close to the huge United States market.

The Role of Industrial Policies in GVCs

Industrial policies that take the new realities of GVCs into account include traditional measures to regulate links to the global economy, especially the regulation of trade, foreign direct investment, and the exchange rates used in ISI and EOI policies that sought to elevate the position of 'national champions' (Salazar-Xirinachs et al., 2014). Today, GVC-oriented industrial policy focuses to a greater extent than in the past on the intersection of global and local actors, and it takes the interests, power, and reach of lead firms and global suppliers into account, accepts international (and increasingly regional) business networks as the appropriate field of play, and responds to pressures from international NGOs (OECD Development Center, 2013; Crespi et al., 2014).

There are three distinguishable types of industrial policies: 'horizontal' policies that affect the entire national economy; 'selective' (or 'vertical') industrial policies targeted at particular industries or sectors; and GVC-oriented industrial policies that leverage international supply chain linkages or dynamics to improve a country's role in global or regional value chains (Gereffi and Sturgeon, 2013: 342–343). 'Horizontal' policies focus on the basic building blocks of competitive national economies, such as education, health, infrastructure, and R&D expenditures. Although these areas all provide attractive opportunities for private investors, the public sector typically plays a role in providing widespread access to these factors as public goods. Domestic industrial policies tend to be 'selective' or 'vertical' because they are associated with prioritizing particular industries or activities at the national level. GVC-oriented industrial policies go beyond the domestic economic focus of ISI-style policy regimes, which try to recreate entire supply chains within a national territory. Given the expansion of international production networks associated with GVCs, this new type of industrial policy explicitly utilizes extraterritorial linkages that affect a country's positioning in global or regional value chains.

Several major features highlight the distinctive nature of GVC-oriented industrial policies (Gereffi and Sturgeon, 2013: 353–354). One is the role of global suppliers. GVC-oriented industrial policies require an increasingly sophisticated understanding of the global-scale patterns of industrial organization that have come to the fore in GVCs since at least the 1990s. Lead firms are relying on global suppliers and intermediaries for an array of processes, specialized inputs, and services, and demanding that their most important suppliers have a global presence. Hence suppliers, not lead firms, are making many of the new investments that developing countries are seeking to capture. In many cases, suppliers generate the bulk of exports as well. The capability to serve multiple customers also takes on heightened importance.[20] Thus, it is no accident that Brazil sought investments from Foxconn, rather than Apple, in its desire for iPhones and iPads to be produced in the country for domestic consumption and export elsewhere in Latin America.

A second feature of industrial policies in the GVC era is global sourcing and value chain specialization. Policies that promote linkages to GVCs have very different aims than traditional industrial policies that intend to build full-blown, vertically integrated domestic industries (Baldwin, 2011).

Policies can target specialized niches in GVCs. These can be higher-value niches suited to existing capabilities, or they can be generic capabilities pooled across foreign investors. Either of these can serve both domestic and export markets. This sort of value chain specialization assumes an ongoing dependence on imported inputs and services. Global sourcing means that the entire value chain may never be captured, but it also assures ongoing involvement in leading-edge technologies, standards, and industry best practices.

Third, firms in emerging economies like China and Brazil are seeking to move to the head of GVCs, regionally if not globally. Encouraging global suppliers to establish facilities within a country has long-term advantages. Local lead firms can rely on global suppliers in their midst and on broader GVCs for a wide range of inputs and services, from design to production to logistics to marketing and distribution. This can lower risk and barriers to entry for local firms, provide access to capabilities and scale that far outstrip what is available domestically, and ensure that products and services are up to date.

The use of industrial policies by emerging economy policy makers should not come as a big surprise. Both developed and developing countries have deployed these policies in the past, often with considerable sophistication, as in the case of East Asian economies such as Japan, South Korea, Singapore, Taiwan, and now China. Looking towards the future, the traditional rulemaking and finance-oriented international organizations of the Washington Consensus era, such as the WTO, the International Monetary Fund, and the World Bank, face the challenge of constructing a new global economic order that aligns with the shifting roles of both the emerging and developed economies. A stable foundation for sustainable development will require both bold vision and a flexible pragmatism to guide a new generation of inclusive growth policies and institutional arrangements within the global economy.

Conclusions and Policy Implications

Economic globalization is a byproduct of international production and trade networks organized by transnational firms, and it is embedded in various kinds of regulation, including rules of the game established by international institutions, national government policies, and various forms of private governance that non-state actors use to manage activities in GVCs (Mayer and Gereffi, 2010). Public governance will likely 'be called upon to play a stronger role in supplementing and reinforcing corporate codes of conduct, product certifications, process standards, and other voluntary, non-governmental types of private governance that have proliferated in the last two decades, and multi-stakeholder initiatives involving both public and private actors will arise to deal with collective action problems' (Gereffi, 2014: 29).

The challenge is to link economic and social upgrading of both material work conditions and the quantity and quality of jobs created in contemporary GVCs (Barrientos et al., 2011). For developing countries, the trade, investment, and knowledge flows that underpin GVCs provide mechanisms for rapid learning, innovation, and industrial upgrading (Staritz et al., 2011). GVCs can provide local firms with better access to information, open up new markets, and create opportunities for fast technological learning and skill acquisition. Because transactions and investments associated with GVCs typically come with quality control systems and prevailing global business standards that exceed those in developing countries, enterprises and individuals in developing countries can acquire new competencies and skills by participating in GVCs.

Still, GVCs are not a panacea for development. Very rapid or 'compressed' GVC-driven development can create a host of new economic and social policy challenges in areas such as health care and education (Whittaker et al., 2010). GVCs can create barriers to learning and drive uneven development over time, even as they trigger rapid industrial upgrading, because of the geographic and organizational disjunctures that often exist between innovation and production. There is considerable evidence that greater profits accrue to those 'lead firms' in the value chain that control branding and product conception (e.g., Apple) and to the 'platform leaders' that provide core technologies and advanced components (e.g., Intel). At the same time, contract manufacturers and business process outsourcing service providers (e.g., call centers) tend to earn slim profits and may never develop the autonomy or capabilities needed to develop and market their own branded products. Typically, firms that provide routine assembly tasks and other simple services within GVCs earn less, pay their workers less, and are more vulnerable to business cycles, not least because they are required to support large-scale employment and fixed capital (Lüthje, 2002).

As developing economies have become key players in GVCs, a new set of issues has emerged regarding how countries can maximize their upgrading opportunities in the global economy. Central to this challenge is how countries can move up the value chain by engaging local firms, assimilating new knowledge, and improving employment conditions, with appropriate policies and institutions to facilitate economic, social, and environmental upgrading. The various examples of GVC participation reviewed in this chapter highlight a variety of options that countries would be wise to consider in trying to improve their international competitiveness. Several targeted recommendations are provided below that highlight what developing countries can do to improve their positions in GVCs.

Infrastructure: Large-scale infrastructure development projects involving roads, shipping terminals, and airports are a major focus of development banks and national governments in their efforts to modernize economies and improve their access to global markets. Increasingly, China and other emerging economies are stepping in to fill what they perceive as a significant infrastructure gap for developing economies.[21] However, our GVC case studies reveal that more specific forms of infrastructure can be highly beneficial to upgrading local economies. As the coffee cases in Central America and East Africa illustrated, sector-specific infrastructure like coffee washing stations that permit wet milling are essential for smallholder farmers to attain the quality needed for specialty coffee exports. For many of the higher value services, world-class information technology infrastructure is essential, which increases connectivity for small and large users alike.

Trade Policy: A prominent feature of the global economy in the last several decades has been the rapid growth of regional trade agreements (e.g., NAFTA, CAFTA-DR and Mercosur in Latin America, AGOA in sub-Saharan Africa, and ASEAN in Asia), and the proliferation of bilateral trade agreements as well (e.g., Mexico has over 40 such agreements and Chile more than 20). While these policies have greatly facilitated the access of developing economies to world-class imports and key export markets, regional agreements can also have a restrictive impact in terms of their country-of-origin requirements. In Nicaragua's apparel industry, for example, the country was able to negotiate a 10-year TPL agreement with the United States to give them access to non-US fabrics (mainly from Asia) for their apparel exports. However, the expiration of the TPLs in 2014 has created considerable uncertainty among foreign investors, and could lead to an outflow of FDI that could cripple the country's apparel exports (Frederick et al., 2014).

Developing countries should be wary of building up their competitive advantage in GVCs on the basis of short-term trade policy advantages. Many of the preferential trade agreements have market access aspects that are of limited duration. Countries should view these as 'windows of opportunity' that permit the development of capabilities that could lead to more sustainable niches in specific GVCs. Often this involves the creation of backward or forward linkages, like textiles in apparel and cold-storage facilities in the fresh fruit value chain. Global buyers in GVCs prefer 'one-stop shopping'. If these capabilities cannot be built at a national level in terms of scale or cost constraints, then another option would be to develop the capabilities that could permit functional upgrading in the GVC with nearby countries in the region.

Industrial Policy: There has been a long history of industrial policy in developing economies, built around the ISI strategy of the 1950s to 1970s, especially in Latin America and East Asia (Gereffi and Wyman, 1990). From the 1980s through the early 2000s, state-led industrial policy fell out of favor, and the 'Washington Consensus' championed by the World Bank and the IMF advocated export-oriented industrialization based on the East Asian model. Due to a variety of factors, including the global economic recession of 2008–2009 and the rise of large emerging economies such as China, India, and Brazil, the Washington Consensus is now in disarray and industrial policy is back (Gereffi, 2014). However, as a result of economic globalization and the predominance of GVCs, a return to traditional ISI industrial policy based on protected domestic markets, local content requirements, mandatory joint ventures, and other measures from the ISI toolkit is unlikely to be effective.

Industrial policy in the GVC era needs to recognize that many of the MNCs that act as lead firms in GVCs are streamlining their supply chains from hundreds or even thousands of suppliers spread across dozens of countries in every continent of the world,[22] to a much smaller number (perhaps just 20–30) of larger, more capable and strategically located manufacturers. In addition, there is also considerable geographic concentration, in which a few countries are controlling larger shares of global output in each industry (Gereffi, 2014). These shifts imply a much greater concentration of industrial production within the global South, higher levels of South-South trade, and the rise of emerging economy TNCs that play a far more significant role in GVCs.

In this context, there are several key features of GVC-oriented industrial policy that are likely to become more significant in developing economies (Gereffi and Sturgeon, 2013): (1) GVC-oriented industrial policies may want to target global suppliers or contract manufacturers that make significant investments in developing economies, rather than the branded lead firms in GVCs;[23] (2) value-chain specialization heightens the importance of joining rather than building GVCs (Baldwin, 2012; Cattaneo et al., 2013), and the policies that promote linkages to GVCs are very different from those intended to build vertically integrated domestic industries; (3) industrial policies should seek to identify GVC lead firms and global contractors that have an interest in partnering with and developing the capabilities of local firms; and (4) in a GVC-oriented world, the industrial policies among emerging economies are increasingly likely to be in conflict, with China often finding itself in the middle of these controversies.

Workforce Development: A skilled workforce is an essential ingredient of GVC upgrading, especially for high-value services, which case studies show can add value to virtually every kind of industry: extractive, agricultural, manufacturing, professional services and even tourism. In the context of GVCs, however, the skills required for upgrading must be oriented to highly dynamic global demand, as defined by key private sector actors. Therefore, workforce development programs should involve a combination of basic education and more specialized training, with private companies supplementing the role played by public agencies (Gereffi et al., 2011; Wadhwa et al., 2008).

Standards and Certifications: Global production must meet very high international standards for quality and safety, especially for industries related to food, health, and with a potentially big environmental impact (like oil and mining). A dizzying array of industry standards and product certifications are linked to GVCs. While there are often significant price premiums for producers of qualifying products, acquiring appropriate certifications can be costly and complex, especially for small firms. Financing to support certifications is likely to facilitate entry by small and medium enterprises (SMEs) into GVCs, but the gains from certification aren't guaranteed unless the global demand and prices for these products continue to be high.[24] Therefore, complying with standards and certifications is best seen as a necessary but not sufficient condition for economic upgrading, which is most likely to affect SMEs.

Public–Private Partnerships: Given the key role played by the private sector in GVCs, international donors and development agencies have shown a great deal of interest in supporting public-private partnerships in developing countries (UNGC, 2011; Bella et al., 2013; USAID, 2014). Since private capital and trade flows in the global economy dwarf official donor assistance, these global flows in GVCs have heightened concerns over how to make sure that positive development trajectories are related not only to economic but also social and environmental objectives. Thus, multilateral and bilateral donors have engaged the private sector to take on a variety of pro-poor development roles. While public-private partnerships can positively impact growth at the industry level through increased investment, output, exports, and employment, the economic gains do not automatically translate to smallholders, SMEs and local households due to the power asymmetries that are embedded in many GVC relationships (Mayer and Milberg, 2013). Therefore, the wide variety of 'Aid for Trade' schemes and other forms of public-private partnerships should seek to assure that SMEs and other targeted beneficiaries of inclusive development projects acquire the productive capabilities needed to respond to dynamic markets through appropriate financing of required infrastructure, affordable certification, technical assistance, improved information flows, and mechanisms to enhance bargaining power to protect worker rights and community development objectives.

There is no magic bullet to improve international competitiveness in GVCs, given the great diversity of experiences and interests within Latin America. However, by acknowledging and addressing the new realities of the global economy, countries in the region can improve their ability to define manageable goals and capture a greater share of the gains in GVCs.

Notes

1. The seminal publication is *Commodity Chains and Global Capitalism*, which applied the global commodity chain (GCC) concept for the first time to a broad range of contemporary industries (Gereffi and Korzeniewicz, 1994). In the early 2000s, the GCC research agenda helped spawn the closely related GVC and global production network approaches (for comprehensive literature reviews, see Bair, 2005; 2009, chapter. 1; Lee, 2010; Gereffi, 1994b, 2005).

2. Jim O'Neill (2011), the Goldman Sachs executive who coined the term BRICs in the early 1990s, now argues that there are a much larger number of 'growth economies' (BRICs plus 11) that fall into this category, including South Korea, Mexico, Turkey, and Indonesia, among others.

3. See Hamilton and Gereffi (2009: 153–159), who describe how US, European, and Japanese buyers worked with suppliers in South Korea and Taiwan to create the necessary conditions for expanding and diversifying exports of a broad array of consumer goods in both economies.

4. Li & Fung, the largest trading company in the world, has about 30,000 suppliers globally and operates in 40 countries (Fung, 2011).

5. According to a recent study, reducing supply chain barriers to trade could increase gross domestic product up to six times more than could removing tariffs (World Economic Forum, 2013: 13).

6. Nearly 1,100 GVC publications and more than 780 researchers are listed on the Global Value Chains website (https://globalvaluechains.org/publications), which is maintained at Duke University, as of July 27, 2018.

7. Illustrative publications include: Cattaneo et al., 2010; OECD, 2013; UNCTAD, 2013; World Bank-IDE-JETRO, 2011; World Economic Forum, 2013. Many more publications and interviews with members of international organizations that have utilized the GVC framework are available at the website for the Duke Global Summit (see https://dukegvcsummit.org/). This conference was held at Duke University on

October 29-November 1, 2014 and brought together 30 organizations and more than three dozen academic and practitioner participants who are actively involved in GVC programs and research. They explored topics related to development, economic and social upgrading in GVCs, advances in GVC metrics related to value creation and value capture, and the future of global governance.

8. The material for this section is drawn primarily from the World Bank (2012: 19–32).

9. Guatemala alone produces seven distinct varietals of specialty coffee due to its diverse geography.

10. In Guatemala, estimates for larger producers show the following distribution of costs across the coffee value chain: 15% for producers with wet mills (who buy from small farmers who do not possess wet mills, which reduces their share of the value chain), 13% for traders, and 72% for the roasters (World Bank, 2012: 25).

11. For a detailed analysis of the varied public-private partnerships in Rwanda's coffee sector, see Abdulsamad et al. (2015).

12. Between 2000 and 2010, the number of coffee washing stations in Rwanda increased from 2 to 187, and the fully washed coffee value chain grew from exporting 32 tons of coffee in 2002 and 5,800 tons in 2010 (Oehmke at al., 2011). An audit conducted in 2010 estimated that these partnership projects delivered 82% higher incomes for beneficiaries, as well as a 17% lower incidence of poverty by 2010 (Abdulsamad, 2015: 37).

13. The industry reached a peak in employment in 2007 with 88,700 employees. However, pressures from the economic crisis forced layoffs and closures during 2008 and 2009.

14. This section draws on the discussion of these two industries in UNCTAD (2014: 67–69).

15. In Brazil, FDI to the automobile industry (assembly and auto parts) soared from an annual average of $116 million in 2007–2010 to $1.6 billion in 2011–2012 (UNCTAD, 2013: 61). Between 2007 and 2012, the automotive industry in Mexico had an influx of $3.6 billion in announced FDI (PwC Mexico, 2013.)

16. The IDB replicated the public-private partnership models developed in India to its first pilot projects in Uruguay and Colombia.

17. The description of this case is drawn from Fernandez-Stark et al. (2014).

18. Lall's categories only cover goods, however, and India is also the world leader in exports of offshore services with 45% of the global total. See Fernandez-Stark et al. (2011), which defines and analyzes recent trends in the offshore services industry using a GVC approach.

19. This is reflected in Brazil's top 10 exports in 2011, where the top seven items are primary products or processed intermediates (Sturgeon et al., 2013; Table 3).

20. Multiple customers provide global suppliers with sufficient business to justify capital-intensive investments that may have high minimum-scale requirements, such as electronic displays and automated production lines.

21. China has taken the lead in launching a new Asian Infrastructure Investment Bank, with appears to be winning the support of US allies not just in Asia (such as Australia, New Zealand, South Korea, Singapore, and Thailand) but in Europe as well (Britain, France, Germany, and Italy have all expressed interest in joining the bank as founding shareholders). China is also a central player in the new 'BRICS' Development Bank

(with Brazil, Russia, India, and South Africa), and a proposed Silk Road development fund to boost connectivity with its neighbors in Central Asia (*The Economist*, 2015).

22. In 2011, for example, Nike's products were made in 930 factories in 50 countries, employing more than one million workers. However, Nike itself had just 38,000 direct employees, most of whom work in the United States. All of the other workers in Nike's global supply chain were employed by subcontractors based in developing economies (Locke, 2013: 48). Over 80% of Wal-Mart's more than 60,000 suppliers are located in China alone (Gereffi and Christian, 2009: 579).

23. Foxconn Technology Group, the largest electronics contract manufacturer in the world, has its home office in Taiwan, but its production and exports for leading brand name multinationals like Apple are concentrated in mainland China, where it employs more than one million workers, making it by far the largest private employer in the country. Li & Fung, the largest trading company in the world, is headquartered in Hong Kong but does most of its sourcing from China, and it has extensive operations in the Americas (Fung, 2011).

24. As we saw in the coffee case, the price for specialty coffee could be double that for certified organic or fair trade coffee.

References

Abdulsamad, Ajmal, Shawn Stokes, and Gary Gereffi. 2015. 'Public-private Partnerships in Global Value Chains: Can they Actually Benefit the Poor?' Report 8. Report Prepared for USAID (United States Agency for International Development), LEO (Leveraging Economic Opportunity). February. Available at http://www.cggc.duke.edu/pdfs/201502_PublicPrivatePartnerships_in_GVCs_Can_they_actually_benefit_the_poor_LEO_report508.pdf.

Altenburg, Tilman. 2007. 'Donor Approaches to Supporting Pro-poor Value Chains.' Report Prepared for the Donor Committee for Enterprise Development, Working Group on Linkages and Value Chains. Available at www.enterprise-development.org/page/download?id=38.

Appelbaum, Richard P. 2008. 'Giant Transnational Contractors in East Asia: Emergent Trends in Global Supply Chains.' *Competition and Change* 12(1): 69–87.

Bair, Jennifer. 2005. 'Global Capitalism and Commodity Chains: Looking Back, Going Forward.' *Competition and Change* 9(2): 153–180.

————, ed. 2009. *Frontiers of Commodity Chain Research*. Stanford, CA: Stanford University Press.

Bair, Jennifer and Gary Gereffi. 2014. 'Towards Better Work in Central America: Nicaragua and the CAFTA context.' In *Towards Better Work: Understanding Labour in Apparel Global Value Chains*, edited by Arianna Rossi, Amy Luinstra, and John Pickles, 251–275. Basingstoke, UK: Palgrave Macmillan and the International Labour Office.

Baldwin, Richard. 2011. 'Trade and Industrialisation after Globalisation's 2nd Unbundling: How Building and Joining a Supply Chain are Different and Why it Matters.' Cambridge, MA: National Bureau of Economic Research Working Paper 17716, December. Available at http://www.nber.org/papers/w17716.

Barrientos, Stephanie and Kwadwo Asenso-Okyere. 2008. 'Mapping Sustainable Production in Ghanaian Cocoa: Report to Cadbury.' Institute of Development Studies (University of Sussex) and the University of Ghana. Available at http://www.bwpi.manchester. ac.uk/medialibrary/research/ResearchProgrammes/businessfordevelopment/mappping_ sustainable_production_in_ghanaian_cocoa.pdf.

Barrientos, Stephanie, Gary Gereffi, and Arianna Rossi. 2011. 'Economic and Social Upgrading in Global Production Networks: A New Paradigm for a Changing World.' *International Labour Review* 150(3–4): 319–340.

Bella, Jose Di, Alicia Grant, Shannon Kindornay, and Stephanie Tissot. 2013. 'Mapping Private Sector Engagement in Development Cooperation.' Ottawa: The North-South Institute. Available at http://www.nsi-ins.ca/wp-content/uploads/2013/09/Mapping-PS-Engagment-in-Development-Cooperation-Final.pdf.

Beltramello, Andrea, Koen De Backer, and Laurent Moussiegt. 2012. 'The Export Performance of Countries within Global Value Chains.' OECD Science, Technology and Industry Working Papers, February 2012. OECD Publishing. Available at http://www.ecb.europa. eu/home/pdf/research/compnet/Beltramello_DeBacker_Moussiegt_2012.pdf.

Casalet, Mónica, Edgar Buenrostro, Federico Stezano, Rubén Oliver, and Lucía Abelenda. 2011. 'Evolución y complejidaden el desarrollo de encadenamientos productivos en México: Los desafíos de la construcción del cluster aeroespacialen Querétaro.' Santiago: CEPAL.

Cattaneo, Olivier, Gary Gereffi, and Cornelia Staritz, eds. 2010. *Global Value Chains in a Postcrisis World: A Development Perspective.* Washington, DC: World Bank.

Chassot, Olivier. 2012. 'Servicios medioambientales.' Personal Communication with Karina Fernandez-Stark. November 2.

Conservation International. 2012. Costa Rica. Available at http://www.conservation.org/where/ north_america/costarica/Pages/costarica.aspx.

Crescionini, Eduardo. 2012. 'Sistema de trazabilidad bovina en Uruguay.' Monteverde: Ministerio de Ganadería, Agricultura y Pesca. Available at http://www.imaginar.org/taller/ agrotic/eduardo_crescioni_ministerio_agricultura_uruguay.pdf

Crespi, Gustavo, Eduardo Fernández-Arias, and Ernesto Stein, eds. 2014. *Rethinking Productive Development: Sound Policies and Institutions for Economic Transformation.* Washington, DC: Inter-American Development Bank.

Daviron, Benoit and Stefano Ponte. 2005. *The Coffee Paradox: Global Markets, Commodity Trade and the Elusive Promise of Development.* London: Zed Books.

Dicken, Peter. 2011. *Global Shift: Mapping the Changing Contours of the World Economy*, 6th edition. New York: Guilford.

Farmers to 40. 2014. 'Analyzing Fair Trade Proof Data.' Available at http://www.farmersto40. com/blog/.

Feenstra, Robert C. 1998. 'Integration of Trade and Disintegration of Production in the Global Economy.' *Journal of Economic Perspectives* 12(4): 31–50.

Fernandez-Stark, Karina, Penny Bamber, and Gary Gereffi. 2011. 'The Offshore Services Value Chain: Upgrading Trajectories in Developing Countries.' *International Journal of Technological Learning, Innovation and Development* 4(1–3): 206–234.

———. 2014. 'Global Value Chains in Latin America: A Development Perspective for Upgrading.' In *Global Value Chains and World Trade: Prospects and Challenges for Latin*

America, edited by René A. Hernández, Jorge M. Martínez-Piva, and Nanno Mulder, 79–106. Santiago: UN Economic Commision for Latin America and the Caribbean and German Cooperation (GIZ).

Frederick, Stacey, Jennifer Bair, and Gary Gereffi. 2014. 'Nicaragua and the Apparel Value Chain in the Americas: Implications for Regional Trade and Employment.' Duke Global Value Chains Center, 18 March. Available at http://www.cggc.duke.edu/pdfs/2014-03-25a_DukeCGGC_Nicaragua_apparel_report.pdf.

Freeman, Richard. 2008. 'The New Global Labor Market.' *Focus* 26(1): 1–6. Available at http://www.irp.wisc.edu/publications/focus/pdfs/foc261.pdf.

Fung, Victor K. 2011. 'Global Supply Chains – Past Developments, Emerging Trends.' Speech to the Executive Committee of the Federation of Indian Chambers of Commerce and Industry, 11 October. Available at http://www.fungglobalinstitute.org/en/global-supply-chains-%E2%80%93-past-developments-emerging-trends.

Gereffi, Gary. 1994a. 'The Organization of Buyer-driven Global Commodity Chains: How US Retailers Shape Overseas Production Networks.' In *Commodity Chains and Global Capitalism*, edited by Gary Gereffi and Miguel Korzeniewicz, 95–122. Westport, CT: Praeger Publishers.

————. 1994b. 'The International Economy and Economic Development.' In *The Handbook of Economic Sociology*, edited by Neil Joseph Smelser and Richard Swedberg, 206–233. Princeton, NJ: Princeton University Press.

————. 1996. 'Commodity Chains and Regional Divisions of Labor in East Asia.' *Journal of Asian Business* 12(1): 75–112.

————. 1999. 'International Trade and Industrial Upgrading in the Apparel Commodity Chain.' *Journal of International Economics* 48(1): 37–70.

————. 2005. 'The Global Economy: Organization, Governance, and Development.' In *The Handbook of Economic Sociology*, 2nd edition, edited by Neil Joseph Smelser and Richard Swedberg, 160. Princeton, NJ: Princeton University Press.

————. 2009. 'Development Models and Industrial Upgrading in China and Mexico.' *European Sociological Review* 25(1): 37–51.

————. 2011. 'Global Value Chains and International Competition.' *Antitrust Bulletin* 56(1): 37–56.

————. 2014. 'Global Value Chains in a Post-Washington Consensus World.' *Review of International Political Economy* 21(1): 9–37.

Gereffi, Gary and Michelle Christian. 2009. 'The Impacts of Wal-Mart: The Rise and Consequences of the World's Dominant Retailer.' *Annual Review of Sociology* 35: 573–591.

Gereffi, Gary and Karina Fernandez-Stark. 2011. 'Global Value Chain Analysis: A Primer.' Durham, NC: Duke Global Value Chains Center. Available at http://www.cggc.duke.edu/pdfs/2011-05-31_GVC_analysis_a_primer.pdf.

Gereffi, Gary, Karina Fernandez-Stark, and Phil Psilos. 2011. *Skills for Upgrading: Workforce Development and Global Value Chains in Developing Countries*. Durham, NC: Duke Global Value Chains Center and the Research Triangle Institute. Available at http://www.cggc.duke.edu/gvc/workforce-development/.

Gereffi, Gary, John Humphrey, and Timothy J. Sturgeon. 2005. 'The Governance of Global Value Chains'. *Review of International Political Economy* 12(1): 78–104.

Gereffi, Gary and Miguel Korzeniewicz, eds. 1994. *Commodity Chains and Global Capitalism.* Westport, CT: Praeger.

Gereffi, Gary and Joonkoo Lee. 2012. 'Why the World Suddenly Cares about Global Supply Chains.' *Journal of Supply Chain Management* 48(3): 24–32.

Gereffi, Gary and Timothy J. Sturgeon. 2013. 'Global Value Chains and Industrial Policy: The Role of Emerging Economies.' In *Global Value Chains in a Changing World*, edited by Deborah K. Elms and Patrick Low, 329–360. Geneva: World Trade Organization, Fung Global Institute and Termasek Foundation Centre for Trade and Negotiations.

Gereffi, Gary and Donald L. Wyman, eds. 1990. *Manufacturing Miracles: Paths of Industrialization in Latin America and East Asia.* Princeton, NJ: Princeton University Press.

Gore, Charles. 2000. 'The Rise and Fall of the Washington Consensus as a Paradigm for Developing Countries.' *World Development* 28(5): 789–804.

Grunwald, Joseph and Kenneth Flamm. 1985. *The Global Factory: Foreign Assembly in International Trade.* Washington, DC: The Brookings Institution.

Haggard, Stephan. 1990. *Pathways from the Periphery: The Politics of Growth in the Newly Industrializing Countries.* Ithaca, NY: Cornell University Press.

Hamilton, Gary G. and Gary Gereffi. 2009. 'Global Commodity Chains, Market Makers, and the Rise of Demand-responsive Economies.' In *Frontiers of Commodity Chain Research*, edited by Jennifer Bair, 136–161. Stanford, CA: Stanford University Press.

Hernández, René A., Jorge M. Martínez-Piva, and Nanno Mulder, eds. 2014. *Global Value Chains and World Trade: Prospects and Challenges for Latin America.* Santiago: United Nations Economic Commission for Latin America and the Caribbean and German Cooperation.

Humphrey, John and Lizbeth Navas-Alemán. 2010. 'Value Chains, Donor Interventions and Poverty Reduction: A Review of Donor Practice.' IDS Research Report 63. Brighton, UK: Institute of Development Studies, University of Sussex.

Humphrey, John and Hubert Schmitz. 2002. 'How Does Insertion in Global Value Chains Affect Upgrading in Industrial Clusters?' *Regional Studies* 36(9): 1017–1027.

Inter-American Development Bank. 2012. 'What is the Inter-America Development Bank Doing About BPO Labor in Latin America?' Available at http://www.nearshoreamericas.com/interamerica-development-bank-bpo-labor-latin-america/.

Jenkins, Rhys. 2012. 'China and Brazil: Economic Impacts of a Growing Relationship.' *Journal of Current Chinese Affairs* 41(1): 21–47.

Krugman, Paul. 1995. 'Growing World Trade.' *Brookings Papers on Economic Activity* 1: 327–377.

Lall, Sanjaya. 2000. 'The Technological Structure and Performance of Developing Country Manufactured Exports, 1985–98.' *Oxford Development Studies* 28(3): 337–369.

Lee, Joonkoo. 2010. 'Global Commodity Chains and Global Value Chains.' In *The International Studies Encyclopedia*, edited by Robert A. Denemark, 2987–3006. Oxford: Wiley-Blackwell.

Locke, Richard M. 2013. *The Promise and Limits of Private Power: Promoting Labor Standards in a Global Economy.* New York, Cambridge: Cambridge University Press.

Lüthje, Boy. 2002. 'Electronics Contract Manufacturing: Global Production and the International Division of Labor in the Age of the Internet.' *Industry and Innovation* 9(3): 227–247.

Lynn, Barry C. 2005. *End of the Line: The Rise and Coming Fall of the Global Corporation.* New York: Doubleday.

Making Markets Work Better for the Poor. 2008. *Making Value Chains Work Better for the Poor: A Toolbook for Practitioners of Value Chain Analysis*. London: UK Department of International Development.

Mayer, Frederick and Gary Gereffi. 2010. 'Regulation and Economic Globalization: Prospects and Limits of Private Governance.' *Business and Politics* 12(3): Article 11.

Mayer, Frederick and William Milberg. 2013. 'Aid for Trade in a World of Global Value Chains: Chain Power, the Distribution of Rents, and Implications for the Form of Aid. *Capturing the Gains*, Working Paper 34. Available at http://www.capturingthegains.org/publications/workingpapers/wp_201334.htm.

Milberg, William and Deborah Winkler. 2013. *Outsourcing Economics: Global Value Chains in Capitalist Development*. New York, Cambridge: Cambridge University Press.

Morris, Mike, Cornelia Staritz, and Justin Barnes. 2011. 'Value Chain Dynamics, Local Embeddedness, and Upgrading in the Clothing Sectors of Lesotho and Swaziland.' *International Journal of Technological Learning, Innovation and Development* 4(1–3): 96–119.

Nathan, Dev and Sandip Sarkar. 2011. 'Blood on Your Mobile Phone? Capturing the Gains for Artisanal Miners, Poor Workers and Women.' *Capturing the Gains* Briefing Note 2. Available at http://www.capturingthegains.org/pdf/ctg_briefing_note_2.pdf.

Naughton, Barry, ed. 1997. *The China Circle: Economics and Technology in the PRC, Taiwan, and Hong Kong*. Washington, DC: The Brookings Institution.

OECD (Organisation for Economic Cooperation and Development). 2013. *Interconnected Economies: Benefitting from Global Value Chains*. Paris: OECD. Available at http://www.oecd-ilibrary.org/science-and-technology/interconnected-economies_ 9789264189560-en.

OECD Development Centre. 2013. *Perspectives on Global Development 2013: Industrial Policies in a Changing World*. Paris: OECD. Available at http://www.oecd.org/development/pgd/pgd2013.htm.

Oehmke, James F., Alexandre Lyambabaje, Etienne Bihogo, Charles B. Moss, Jean Claude Kayisinga, and Dave D. Weatherspoon. 2011. 'The Impact of USAID Investment on Sustainable Poverty Reduction among Rwandan Smallholder Coffee Producers: A Synthesis of Findings.' Available at http://www.jfoehmke.com/uploads/9/4/1/8/9418218/rwanda_synthesis_document_final_draft_oct_2011.pdf.

O'Neill, Jim. 2011. *The Growth Map: Economic Opportunity in the BRICs and Beyond*. New York: Penguin.

Oxfam. 2011. 'Exploring the Links between International Business and Poverty Reduction: The Coca-Cola/SABMiller Value Chain Impacts in Zambia and El Salvador.' *Oxfam Policy and Practice: Private Sector*. Available at http://www.oxfamamerica.org/static/oa3/files/coca-cola-sab-miller-poverty-footprint-dec-2011.pdf.

Pickles, John and Adrian Smith. 2011. 'Delocalization and Persistence in the European Clothing Industry: The Reconfiguration of Trade and Production Networks.' *Regional Studies* 45: 167–185.

Ponte, Stefano. 2002. 'The "Latte Revolution"? Regulation, Markets and Consumption in the Global Coffee Chain.' *World Development* 30(7): 1099–1122.

Portocarrero, Lacayo, Ana Victoria. 2010. 'El sector textil y confección y el desarrollosostenibleen Nicaragua.' Geneva: International Centre for Trade and Sustainable Development. January.

PRONicaragua. 2010. 'Investment Opportunities: Textiles and Apparel.' Available at http://www.pronicaragua.org/index.php?option=com_content&view=article&id=35&Itemid=98&lang=en.

PwC Mexico. 2013. 'Doing Business in Mexico: Automotive Industry.' May. Available at http://www.pwc.com/mx/doing-business-automotive.

Rodriguez, Carlos Manuel. 2012. 'Servicios medioambientales.' Personal Communication with Karina Fernandez-Stark. August 22.

Ross, Andrew. 2006. *Fast Boat to China: Corporate Flight and the Consequences of Free Trade.* New York: Pantheon Books.

Rossi, Arianna, Amy Luinstra, and John Pickles, eds. 2014. *Towards Better Work: Understanding Labour in Apparel Global Value Chains.* New York: Palgrave Macmillan and International Labour Office.

Salazar-Xirinachs, José M., Irmgard Nübler, and Richard Kozul-Wright. 2014. *Transforming Economies: Making Industrial Policy Work for Growth, Jobs and Development.* Geneva: ILO and UNCTAD.

Smith, Adrian, John Pickles, Milan Buček, Rudolf Pástor, and Bob Begg. 2014. 'The Political Economy of Global Production Networks: Regional Industrial Change and Differential Upgrading in the East European Clothing Industry.' *Journal of Economic Geography* 14(6): 1023–1051.

SONDA. 2012. 'Un sistema de trazabilidad para el ganadobovino de Uruguay que aseguracalidad sanitaria.' Available at http://www.sonda.com/caso/10/.

Staritz, Cornelia, Gary Gereffi, and Olivier Cattaneo, eds. 2011. *International Journal of Technological Learning, Innovation and Development* 4(1–3). Special Issue on 'Shifting End Markets and Upgrading Prospects in Global Value Chains.'

Staritz, Cornelia, and José Guilherme Reis, eds. 2013. *Global Value Chains, Economic Upgrading, and Gender: Case Studies of the Horticulture, Tourism and Call Center Industries.* Washington, DC: World Bank. Available at http://www.capturingthegains.org/pdf/GVC_Gender_Report_web.pdf.

Sturgeon, Timothy J. 2002. 'Modular Production Networks: A New American Model of Industrial Organization.' *Industrial and Corporate Change* 11(3): 451–496.

Sturgeon, Timothy J. and Gary Gereffi. 2009. 'Measuring Success in the Global Economy: International Trade, Industrial Upgrading, and Business Function Outsourcing in Global Value Chains.' *Transnational Corporations* 18(2): 1–36.

Sturgeon, Timothy J., Gary Gereffi, Andrew Guinn, and Ezequiel Zylberberg. 2013. 'O Brasil nas cadeiasglobais de valor: implicações para a política industrial e de comércio.' *Revista Brasileira de Comércio Exterior* 115: 26–41.

Sturgeon, Timothy J. and Momoko Kawakami. 2011. 'Global Value Chains in the Electronics Industry: Characteristics, Crisis, and Upgrading Opportunities for Firms from Developing Countries.' *International Journal of Technological Learning, Innovation and Development* 4(1–3): 120–147.

Sturgeon, Timothy J. and Richard K. Lester. 2004. 'The New Global Supply Base: New Challenges for Local Suppliers in East Asia.' In *Global Production Networking and*

Technological Change in East Asia, edited by Shahid Yusuf, M. Anjum Altaf, and Kaoru Nabeshima, 35–87. Washington, DC: World Bank and Oxford University Press.

Sturgeon, Timothy J. and Johannes Van Biesebroeck. 2011. 'Global Value Chains in the Automotive Industry: An Enhanced Role for Developing Countries?' *International Journal of Technological Learning, Innovation and Development* 4(1–3): 181–205.

Talbot, John M. 2004. *Grounds for Agreement: The Political Economy of the Coffee Commodity Chain*. Lanham, MD: Rowman and Littlefield.

The Economist. 2015. 'The Infrastructure Gap: The Asian Infrastructure Investment Bank.' March 21, 32.

Tholons. 2012. 'Outsourcing and National Development in Latin America.' New York: Tholons. Available at http://www.google.com/url?sa=t&rct=j&q=&esrc=s&source=web &cd=1&cad=rja&ved=0CD0QFjAA&url=http%3A%2F%2Fwww.tholons.com%2Fnl_ pdf%2FTholons_Whitepaper_Tholons_Outsourcing_and_National_Development_ Whitepaper_February_2012.pdf&ei=eAi5UK3pIJSw8ATChoHYCQ&usg=AFQjCNG zetmK9aZXhHlKjKXOk7ROE9Y_Gw&sig2=n4Rj-utYcgJ5bCnpMUo8Fw.

Thomson, Adam. 2012. 'Mexico: China's Unlikely Challenger.' *Financial Times*, September 19.

UN Comtrade. 2012. United Nations Commodity Trade Statistics Database. Available at http://comtrade.un.org/.

UNCTAD (United Nations Conference for Trade and Development). 2013. *World Investment Report, 2013 – Global Value Chains: Investment and Trade for Development*. Geneva: UNCTAD.

————. 2014. *World Investment Report, 2014 – Investing in the SDGs: An Action Plan*. Geneva: UNCTAD.

UNGC (United Nations Global Compact). 2011. 'Partners in Development: How Donors can Better Engage the Private Sector for Development in LDCs.' United Nations Global Compact, United Nations Development Program, and Bertelsmann Stiftung. Available at https://www.unglobalcompact.org/docs/issues_doc/development/Partners_in_ Development.pdf.

Urquidi, Victor L. 1991. 'The Prospects for Economic Transformation in Latin America: Opportunities and Resistances.' *LASA Forum* 22(3): 1–9.

USAID (United States Agency for International Development). 2014. 'Global Development Alliances.' Washington, DC: USAID. Available at http://www.usaid.gov/gda.

Vernon, Raymond. 1971. *Sovereignty at Bay: The Multinational Spread of US Enterprises*. New York: Basic Books.

Wadhwa, Vivek, Una Kim de Vitton, and Gary Gereffi. 2008. 'How the Disciple Became the Guru: Workforce Development in India's R&D Labs.' Report Prepared for the Ewing Marion Kauffman Foundation, July 23. Available at http://papers.ssrn.com/sol3/papers. cfm?abstract_id=1170049.

Whitttaker, D. Hugh, Tianbiao Zhu, Timothy J. Sturgeon, Mon Han Tsai, and Toshie Okita. 2010. 'Compressed Development.' *Studies in Comparative International Development* 45: 439–467.

World Bank. 2012. 'Unlocking Central America's Export Potential – 2. Unlocking Potential at the Sector Level: Value Chain Analyses.' Available at http://documents.worldbank.

org/curated/en/2012/10/17211219/unlocking-central-americas-export-potential-vol-2-4-unlocking-potential-sector-level-value-chain-analyses.

WEF (World Economic Forum) in collaboration with Bain and Company and the World Bank. 2013. *Enabling Trade: Valuing Growth Opportunities*: Available at http://www3.weforum. org/docs/WEF_SCT_EnablingTrade_Report_2013.pdf.

WTO and IDE-JETRO. 2011. 'Trade Patterns and Global Value Chains in East Asia: From Trade in Goods to Trade in Tasks.' Geneva and Tokyo: World Trade Organization and Institute of Developing Economies. Available at http://www.ide.go.jp/English/Press/pdf/20110606_news.pdf.

13

Risks and Opportunities of Participation in Global Value Chains

Gary Gereffi and Xubei Luo

Introduction

For millennia, the ancient agrarian cycle based on crops and livestock controlled the fortunes of the world. Then came the Industrial Revolution in the mid-19th century. 'For the first time in history, the living standards of the masses of ordinary people have begun to undergo sustained growth', notes Nobel laureate and economist Robert E. Lucas, Jr. 'Nothing remotely like this economic behavior has happened before' (Lucas, 2002: 109–110). More recently, in the context of integration and modernization, waves of technology improvement since the first industrial revolution have been changing the boundary of production and redefining the spectrum of the role of state. Participation in global value chains (GVCs), which highlight the ways in which new patterns of international trade, production, and employment shape prospects for development and competitiveness, creates opportunities and risks to enterprises. On the one hand, it creates new opportunities for profits and expands the market horizon; and on the other hand, it exposes the enterprise sector to risks previously shielded from market boundaries and geographic distance, and increases the degree of potential information asymmetry. Various forces interact in different directions, exacerbating or mitigating the dynamics of risks.

Risk implies the possibility of loss. The upside of risk, or the possibility of gain, is opportunity. Risk (or opportunity) can be imposed from outside or taken on voluntarily in the pursuit of opportunities. Enterprises are facing a wide range of risks on a day-to-day basis. Due to continual changes in technology, production frontiers are pushing outwards and higher efficiency becomes the norm for survival (for example, personal computers). Demand changes as new tastes and preferences create niches for new products, and the higher profit mark-up from innovation becomes an engine of growth (for example, the iPad). There are also catastrophic risks from unexpected events such as global economic crises and natural disasters.

The information and communication technology revolution has not only sharply increased productivity, but also reinterpreted the function of time and distance. Billions of activities are linked with 'one-click' and new demands become effective with 'just-in-time' delivery. The world is increasingly interconnected. The largely unforeseen changes in the global arena—from the collapse of the dot.com boom in the early 2000s, to the burst of housing bubbles in 2008, and to the ongoing Euro-zone turmoil—have had systemic implication on the survival and growth of firms in different corners of the world, even before reactions were taken to try to disentangle the links. Shocks in access to financing and to commodities were magnified at an unprecedented scale.

To a considerable extent, participating and competing in GVCs have become inevitable. Even if a firm is not export-oriented, it will be competing against imports made in the global economy unless there are protectionist barriers against imports. This chapter looks at the risks and opportunities firms and their workers face in GVCs. First, it examines the risk-sharing mechanisms that firms provide from the national and global perspectives; second, it takes a closer look at the new opportunities and challenges for firms and individuals in the global arena; third, it discusses the role of economic upgrading and social upgrading; and finally it sheds light on how the government can help people manage risks and reap the benefits of participation in GVCs.

This chapter draws from an extensive literature on GVCs, much of which has been based on country- and industry-specific field studies by interdisciplinary researchers. The GVC studies reviewed here span a wide range of extractive, agricultural, manufacturing, and service sectors, with an emphasis on trends during the past 10–15 years. Our objective is to reframe the findings from this literature on the global economy to useful generalizations about risks and opportunities of participating in GVCs.

Firms as a Vehicle of Risk Sharing

Nobel laureate Ronald Coase has argued that firms emerged as a form of social institution to overcome the constraint of transaction costs inherent in direct exchanges: the costs associated with searching for, communicating, and bargaining with possible trading partners (Coase, 1937). Through efficient resource allocation, firms are capable of generating higher income than households alone can do by providing self-produced goods and services directly to the market. Sharing with another party the burden of loss or the benefit of gain from a risk is a common measure of risk management. Importantly, multi-person firms provide the mechanism of risk sharing among workers, firm owners, and between workers and firm owners:

- When risk is shared among workers, if a worker falls sick, others can share the workload to keep the firm going. Also, the risk-sharing mechanism that multi-person firms make possible allows workers to specialize and increase productivity together. Investing in specialized skills is a risky undertaking. By sharing the costs of training or increasing the expected returns of acquiring skills, the enterprise sector can shift the skill distribution in the workforce toward specialization (Acemoglu and Pischke, 1999; Lam and Liu, 1986).

- When risk is shared among owners of capital, for example, with limited liability, investors can take on more creative risk with a given level of expected risk through diversifying their portfolio. As the *Economist* magazine noted in its millennium issue, 'The modern world is built on two centuries of industrialization. Much of that was built by equity finance which is built on limited liability' (The *Economist*, 1999).' With the required legal and institutional frameworks, the contractual arrangements of limited liability limit the down-side risk of investments, allowing investors to separate personal liability from the debt of the production unit. It also enables them to own small pieces of many firms and diversify their investment portfolio, which reduces risk if some of their investments drop in value. Limited liability also led to the development of the stock market, facilitated corporate capital accumulation, and enabled the exploitation of economies of scale.

- When risk is shared between workers and owners of capital, for example, through labor contracts, firms can provide insurance to workers who accept a lower wage in exchange for stable income. Firms can provide a steadier stream of wage income to labor owners by isolating some risks related to production. Through labor contracts, workers can relocate risks in the production process to firms and limit excessive fluctuations in employment and income to maximize welfare. To maximize profit, firms try to minimize the cost of labor as well as the cost of other inputs. To maximize welfare, workers prefer jobs not only with higher but also more stable income. Firms, which are less risk-averse than workers, care more about the average labor cost than its volatility, and thus can offer labor contracts with less volatility in pay (for example, a fixed wage) to compete for workers in exchange for a lower average level of remuneration. By leveraging the two aspects explicitly or implicitly contained in labor contracts—the level and the volatility of the remuneration—both firms and workers could be better off through risk sharing. On the other hand, workers can offer a form of insurance to firms in which they agree to reductions in wages or cutback in work hours during temporary shocks in exchange for higher wages in normal times.

Risk sharing and diversification have encouraged risk taking and increased productivity on a massive scale. Higher income allows individuals to increase savings, purchase market insurance, improve access to finance, invest in nutrition and health, and obtain more knowledge from educational investment. Take savings, for example. If individuals are struggling to meet their current needs, saving for the future will be a slow process. Around the world, as income levels rise, savings rates also rise (Schmidt-Hebbel et al., 1992). In developing countries, a doubling of income per capita is estimated to raise the long-run private savings rate by 10 percentage points of disposable income (Loayza et al., 2000).

However, with the division of labor and diversification of ownership of firms, new risks also emerge. The ways the enterprise sector functions and manages risk affect the risks people face and the risk-management measures they employ. Firms may take risk irresponsibly at the brink of bankruptcy, creating negative externalities for society. The management of the firm, which is often in the hands of professionals who have special managerial skills, may have different interests than its owners.

If the enterprise sector fails to function smoothly or if it shifts its own risks to people, it can be a source of risks to households, communities, and even the financial sector and national government. When business shrinks or technology becomes obsolete, the enterprise sector may generate income-related risks (channeled through loss of jobs and loss of capital returns) and asset-related risks (channeled through loss of investments). Both can further translate into risks related to social inclusion, ranging from loss of insurance and other benefits provided through employment (such as health insurance and pension), to loss of connection with the professional community, loss of social status and involuntary changes in life styles. Regulation and incentive systems need to be in place to ensure that the interests of various stakeholders are protected.

In a globalized world, characterized by lower transport and transaction costs, the interconnectedness across firms or sectors linked through supply networks or financial linkages multiply and intensify. Global value chains include two main types of firms: 'lead firms', which are typically transnational corporations (TNCs) headquartered in the advanced industrial countries, who control and define the main activities in terms of price, delivery, and performance in both producer-driven and buyer-driven GVCs; and the supplier companies who produce the goods and services in GVCs, generally located in developing countries. Thus, the GVC 'enterprise sector' links both developed and developing countries into a common global supply chain (Gereffi and Sturgeon, 2013).

From the GVC point of view, enterprise sectors in national economies are part of the supply-base for lead firms in GVCs. This has two concrete implications: (1) external actors (specifically, GVC lead firms) are a potentially significant form of 'external risk' in national enterprise sectors; and (2) national enterprise sectors are nested within larger regional and global enterprise sectors, which are connected to GVCs. The global enterprise sector, as a series or set of industry-specific GVCs, has the potential to affect people's risk management through the same risk-sharing mechanisms that are operating at a larger scale. It can be advantageous or detrimental to national enterprise sectors and affect firms differently according to their size and industries.

Opportunities and Challenges in the Global Arena

Firms face new opportunities and challenges in the global market. They have the opportunities of supplying much larger global demand, which eliminates the scale and purchasing power limitations of the domestic market in developing economies. There also are many more upgrading opportunities because the quality and price parameters have wider variation, allowing for more extensive product and process upgrading options. There is higher risk as well because international standards for price, quality, and delivery schedules are much less forgiving. Firms typically need a relatively large scale of production to participate in global markets, or have a special technological edge to enter global market niches. There is also a risk from intensified competitive pressures, as everyone can compete with exporters in terms of lower prices or higher quality, so only the best can succeed in GVCs.

The presence of scale economies favors the concentration of production, which tends to minimize costs, leading to higher profits for enterprises and possibly lower prices for consumers. The higher concentration of production yields benefits of large-scale clustering and agglomeration, but also generates new risks for the economy. Shocks in one location can easily spread to the rest of the network, generating cascade effects. If the supply network is highly interconnected, low productivity in one sector can potentially affect the entire economy, as downstream sectors will also suffer (Acemoglu et al., 2010).

The effects of the 2011 earthquake in Japan on the automobile industry worldwide demonstrate the vulnerability of the system to shock (Box 13.1). However, greater openness to international trade and capital can also have a large impact on macroeconomic volatility. When an economy is highly concentrated in certain productive activities, such as Nokia (whose worldwide sales in 2003 represented over one-quarter of Finland's GDP) and Samsung (which accounted for 23% of the Republic of Korea's exports and 14% of its GDP), firm-specific idiosyncratic shocks can generate significant shocks that affect GDP (Di Giovanni and Levchenko, 2009). In the United States, the largest and most diversified economy in the world, a one-time increase in the dividend of one company (Microsoft, for $32 billion) boosted growth in personal income from 0.6% to 3.7% in December 2004 (Bureau of Economic Analysis, 2005).

While firms are exposed to new challenges in an increasingly integrated world, international trade and financial linkages, remittances, and diaspora communities have the potential to serve as safety nets for individuals, families, and communities to absorb and cope with risks to shocks that are not global in nature.

Foreign direct investment can affect the volatility of enterprise performance in times of crisis in different ways. The ability of multinationals to shift production across countries can increase volatility, and market diversification can lend stronger stability to local subsidiaries. For instance, after the recent global financial crisis, multinational subsidiaries linked to parents with strong vertical production and financial linkages fared better on average than local counterparts. The demand from parent firms can help absorb the negative demand shock in the host country, while the performance of subsidiaries linked horizontally with parent firms might become more volatile as the multinationals shifts more production back home (Alfaro and Chen, 2011).

Box 13.1 From One Shock to Another: The 2011 Earthquake in Japan Rattled the Auto Industry Worldwide

Supply chain management, backed by tight vertical connections among enterprises, has resulted in a high level of competitiveness for the automobile industry. Car makers at the top of a chain can procure meticulously customized, high-quality components from firms further down the chain (resulting in differentiated, high-quality cars), collect information to continuously predict the appropriate amount of outputs, and minimize inventory and associated costs.

The high degree of customization and just-in-time production practice, two key drivers of success, also expose the automobile industry to worldwide shocks (Canis, 2011). In March 2011, an earthquake struck eastern Japan. The disruption of production of automotive parts generated immediate impacts. Since automotive parts are highly customized, replacement from other suppliers is almost impossible. In April 2011, Nissan closed plants in Mexico for five days and plants in the United States for six days. Output at eight of Honda's Canadian, Indian, UK, and US plants was cut by half. The US car maker, General Motors, closed its assembly plant in Louisiana because of a shortage of vehicle parts, which in turn led to short layoffs at its New York plant, where the engines are made. Ford closed assembly plants in Belgium and the United States for one week, and plants in China, the Philippines, Taiwan, China, and South Africa for two weeks.

Source: Bunkley, 2011.

The internal capital markets and investment flows in TNCs from parents to subsidiaries can lower subsidiaries' dependence on host-country credit conditions and hence lower their performance volatility when host countries experience credit crunches (Antras et al., 2009). In Poland, for example, during the recent global economic crisis, foreign ownership appears to have provided a higher degree of resilience to affiliates facing external credit constraints through intra-group lending mechanisms (Kolasa et al., 2010).

For individuals, communities, and national economies, remittances of foreign earnings tend to be stable and often counter-cyclical. Migrants are likely to send home more resources to help their families when the home country has experienced an economic downturn or crisis. For example, during the financial crises in Mexico in 1995 and in Indonesia and Thailand in 1998, remittances increased sharply, which not only helped households smooth consumption, but also provided the needed resources to overcome credit constraints for local entrepreneurs, alleviating their risks (World Bank, 2005). Beyond remittances, diasporas can provide assistance in normal times by assisting in philanthropic activities, fostering the exchange of knowledge, and increasing trade links; in time of stress, they are more likely than average investors to finance infrastructure, housing, health, and education projects in their countries of origin. Diaspora bonds have raised over $35 billion in India and Israel, including periods when the home country was suffering a liquidity crisis (Ratha, 2010).

In terms of GVCs, the 'rationalization' that has been going on in terms of shrinking the size of supply chains was accelerated as a result of the 2008–2009 global economic recession. As consumption declined in most advanced industrial countries, which were the main markets for GVCs, the size of GVC supply chains sharply contracted as a result of the recession. Recent studies have highlighted significant new trends in how GVCs are organized in the current period, which alter the nature of risks that national enterprise sectors will confront (see Gereffi, 2014, for a summary of these changes):

- GVCs are becoming geographically more consolidated, which reflects the rise of large emerging economies after 1989. Known initially as BRICs (Brazil, Russia, India, and China), the emerging economies now include a diverse array of 'growth economies' such as Mexico, South Korea, Turkey, Indonesia, the Philippines, and Vietnam, which offer seemingly inexhaustible pools of relatively low-wage workers, highly capable export-oriented manufacturers, abundant raw materials, and sizeable domestic markets (O'Neill, 2011). Emerging economies are now major production centers worldwide, although their specific roles in GVCs vary according to their openness to trade and foreign investment, and other strategic considerations.

- GVCs are also organizationally more concentrated, as the transnational lead firms in GVCs seek to shrink their global supply chains from 500–1,000 suppliers in the heyday of economic globalization in the 1990s and early 2000s to 25–30 key suppliers (or less) in the current era. These new supplier firms are expected to be bigger, more capable (technologically as well as in modern models of supply-chain management), and strategically located to access large regional and national markets. Coupled together, the trends of GVCs toward geographic consolidation and organizational concentration place greater competitive pressures and economic risks on the majority of countries and firms in the global economy that don't have the scale, size, strategic location, or skills to rise to the top in contemporary GVCs.

The global economic recession of 2008–2009 has reinforced some of the pre-existing trends in GVCs, but also introduced new patterns in the global economy that affect the distribution of risk and vulnerability in national enterprise sectors. A study by the World Bank concludes that GVCs have proven resilient in the face of the recent economic crisis, which has accelerated two long-term structural trends in the global economy: the aforementioned consolidation of GVCs, and the growing salience of markets in the developing world (Cattaneo et al., 2010: 6). As world trade is bouncing back from the 2008–2009 global recession, emerging economies are becoming a main engine of world economic recovery. Given stagnant consumer demand in the developed world, GVCs are shifting to supply new end markets in the developing world, which include a renewed emphasis on the domestic markets of large emerging economies and the regionalization of what were previously global supply chains (Staritz et al., 2011).

In the case of the global apparel industry, China's share of global apparel exports increased from 22% to 41%, between 1995 and 2009, and export sales increased from US$32.9 billion to $122.4 billion. Countries whose market shares declined most abruptly during this period, which included the phase out of the Multi-Fiber Arrangement (MFA) in 2005 that guaranteed export quotas for many smaller countries in US and European Union markets, were Mexico, Central America and the Dominican Republic, Thailand, the Philippines, Romania, and Poland (Frederick and Gereffi, 2011). However, even in China, a clear winner in aggregate terms, thousands of apparel factories were shuttered and millions of workers in apparel plants lost their jobs as the industry was streamlined in the late 1990s and early 2000s (when many state-owned apparel firms were closed), and then again in the late 2000s as the recession further reduced export-oriented sales.

In short, the economic crisis has not reversed globalization; international production and consumption have remained central features of the global economy. The role of the developing world compared with that of the developed countries has grown, but inequalities among developing countries in terms of how they are positioned in GVCs are rising as well. In producer-driven chains, the lead firms that to a large degree defined the structure of these industries were mainly global manufacturers like General Motors, Ford, IBM, and HP. In buyer-driven chains, the lead firms were a mix of retailers (like Walmart, J. C. Penney, and Carrefour), global marketers (such as Nike, Liz Claiborne, and Polo/Ralph Lauren), and supermarkets and food multinationals (like Tesco, Sainsbury's, Kraft Foods, and Nestlé) (Gereffi, 1994). The lead firms in buyer-driven chains were particularly influential in the globalization process because they accelerated the process of 'global sourcing' based on orders from developed countries, which relied almost entirely on production carried out in developing economies (Gereffi, 1999; Dicken, 2011). The dominant role of the lead firms (largely from the developed world) could generate additional sources of inequality and potential crises in the future.

Economic Upgrading and Social Upgrading

The distribution of risks and opportunities is closely related to the positioning of an enterprise within a value chain and to the nature of this value chain. Figure 13.1 illustrates this proposition for value chains associated, respectively, with five different industry groups. Economic and social upgrading (or downgrading) of firms and workers can take place in multiple trajectories (Barrientos et al., 2011).

The concept of social upgrading refers to improvements within a specific enterprise (or associated group of enterprises) in the terms of employment, remuneration, worker rights, and workplace safety and employee insurance arrangements (Barrientos et al., 2011). Social upgrading is central to this examination of household risks and enterprises within value chains. Social upgrading by enterprises helps reduce risks for worker households and removes some of the volatility they would otherwise face. The extent and type of social upgrading that is possible are usually related to (but not solely determined by) the economic upgrading in place, which highlights improvements in various aspects of economic performance within GVCs. Other institutional factors and actors, including the extent and nature of worker organization, civil society actions, government legislation and its enforcement, can also make a difference.

Each GVC in Figure 13.1 is represented as a vertical silo, with lower segments signifying the approximate share of less-skilled types of work carried out within the value chain. All value chains include economic activities that span a broad range of skill levels. Consider agriculture, for example. At the lowest level—the farm, typically—this value chain involves a relatively large proportion of small scale and low-skill labor. Higher in the value chain, particularly at the points of processing and marketing, the skill level of workers rises progressively. The same is true for each of the other four GVCs. Skill levels rise as one moves from lower to higher value activities in the chain; the proportion of highly skilled workers at the top of each value chain, who carry out knowledge-intensive activities, vary according to the type of GVC we are examining. In agriculture, for example, this segment tends to be relatively small, while in business services, the proportion of knowledge workers is relatively large The likelihood of enforceable standards also rises as one moves up value chains toward more formal and skill-intensive work. It is not enough merely to specify decent work standards; they must be capable of enforcement at low cost, in the ideal situation being self-enforcing. The prospects of having measurable and enforceable standards typically rise as skill levels and technology increase within value chains.

Figure 13.1 Industry Groups, GVCs, and Economic Upgrading

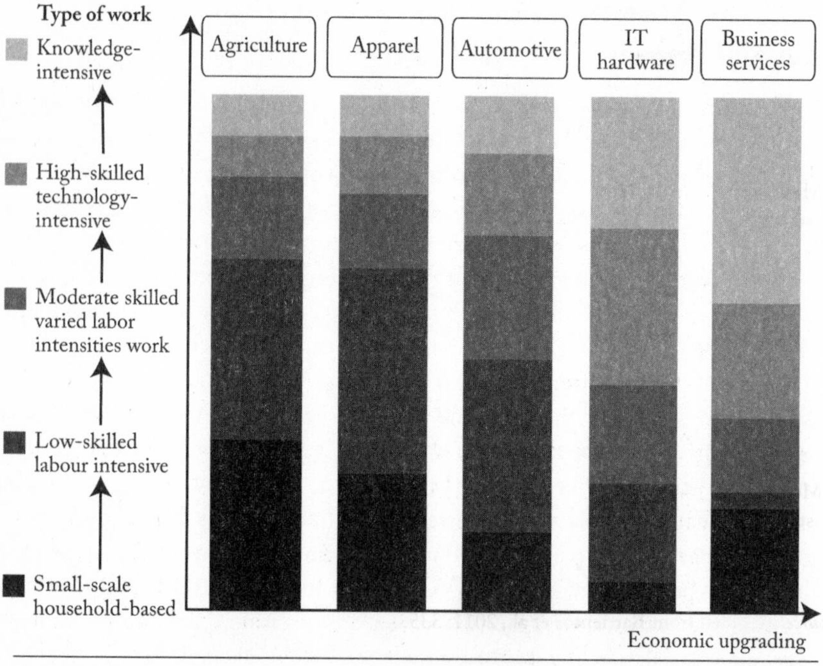

Source: Adapted from Barrientos et al., 2011: 328.

Social upgrading can be achieved through various means, involving different combinations of: (a) economic upgrading: as enterprises move up value chains, the share of skilled workers typically increases; and (b) deliberate actions to introduce enforceable standards—minimum wages, paid time off, workplace safety, insurance, and so on—for those workers whose skill levels remain low, who are more easily replaced, and who for these reasons may be badly treated. The scope for such actions widens considerably as the array of actors is expanded in GVCs. Using illustrative examples of successful social upgrading, we develop an analytical framework to assess possibilities for action.

Alternative pathways for social upgrading are available, as Figure 13.2 shows with the help of three examples. The first example, Pathway A, depicts a situation in which no significant economic upgrading has occurred. Instead, risks to workers were reduced because of deliberate actions that introduced enforceable standards. This could be the situation, for instance, of an enterprise that produced t-shirts branded with the logo of some US university. Actions by concerned student groups resulted in a slew of reforms: doing away with child labor, reducing the length of the work day, improved lighting and other work conditions, and so on.

Figure 13.2 Different Pathways to Social Upgrading

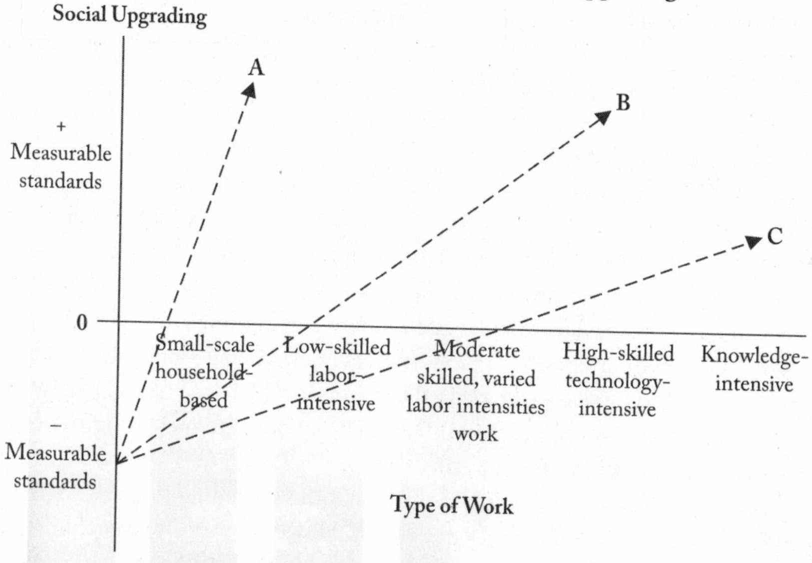

Source: Adapted from Barrientos et al., 2011: 335.

Alternatively, social upgrading can occur along Pathway C, where almost the entire burden is borne by economic upgrading. In this case, risks for workers are reduced as small-scale household work gets turned over into high-tech and knowledge-intensive work, for instance, as in the case when a weaver of traditional rugs takes to computerized design and manufacturing. In the intermediate case of Pathway B, social upgrading within labor-intensive industries like apparel can be achieved with lower risks to workers if outside institutions like the Better Work program run by the International Labor Organization are involved to help certify standards (Rossi et al., 2014).

When the enterprise sector gravitates toward more technology- or knowledge-intensive industries—for example from agriculture to apparel, and to business services—the share of skilled workers typically increases. As a result, labor productivity grows and more jobs of higher quality are created. However, economic upgrading does not always lead to social upgrading in the form of better wage and working conditions. On the one hand, unskilled workers in many developing countries can be excluded from the desirable job opportunities provided by technology-intensive or knowledge-intensive work, which tends to concentrate in more developed countries. On the other hand, workers in the same enterprises can face very different opportunities for social upgrading; regular workers can have better statutory employment protection and benefit from labor standards, while irregular workers, often over-represented among women, youth, minority, and other vulnerable groups, can suffer discrimination.

In many enterprises in the developing world, hiring irregular workers directly or through third-party contractors to perform the most time-sensitive task in the low (unskilled) segment of the production chain, is often a way for firms to reduce costs in response to last-minute orders from outsourcing companies. While this creates new employment opportunities for many low-skilled workers, it also allows firms to shift the risks of production related to fluctuations in demand to workers. Regulations need to be in place to protect workers.

To a considerable extent, as we contend below, reducing risk for workers/households is associated with social and economic upgrading at the enterprise (or industry) level. Since a significant proportion of international production and trade now takes place through coordinated value chains in which lead firms globally and locally play a dominant role, possibilities for upgrading are increasingly defined by firms' locations within these chains.

Firms in GVCs have opportunities for economic upgrading through engaging in higher value production within value chains. However, they also face challenges meeting the commercial demands and quality standards required by buyers, which smaller and less efficient producers find hard to meet (Gereffi and Lee, 2012; Gereffi, 2014). The GVC approach focuses heavily on this notion of inter-firm networks, which exist within corporate supply chains, and international trade and production networks. Adopting a GVC approach to a considerable extent changes the focus of our analysis: instead of looking at individual, self-contained enterprises, we need to examine how firms are positioned within chains having different structures.

Adopting a GVC analytical framework opens the door, therefore, to an additional cast of economic actors and stakeholders who can act as agents of change. In addition to governments and enterprise management, national industry associations, and trade unions, positive change in working conditions can be brought about at the initiatives also of buyers' associations, consumer groups, and international certification and inspection agencies, increasingly employed by buyers wary of their international human rights image (Mayer and Gereffi, 2010).

The expansion of global production, especially in labor-intensive industries, has been an important source of employment generation. Many jobs have been filled by women and migrant workers who previously had difficulty accessing this type of waged work, and they have provided new income sources for poorer households (Oxfam International, 2004; Barrientos et al., 2003). Where this is regular employment that generates better rights and protection for workers, it can enhance social upgrading and decent work. The demand for rising standards often requires the skilling of at least some workers and provision of better employment conditions.

But for many workers, this is not the outcome. Much employment is insecure and unprotected, and there are significant challenges to ensuring decent work for more vulnerable workers. Irregular and low-skilled jobs—which are also low paying, thereby representing limited prospects for upward mobility—are as easily eliminated as brought into being. New risks are introduced, even as some old ones abate. Along with the risk of dismissal (or work reduction) that especially lower-skilled workers (and suppliers) of enterprises face, another significant downside risk accompanying these engagements involves the enhanced probability of injury and illness. Unsafe and unsanitary work conditions are often associated with low-skilled work in the enterprise sector. Labor safety regulations are non-existent or they are routinely flouted, more so at some points within GVCs (Rossi et al., 2014).

Poorer individuals' engagements with the enterprise sector thus produce situations that can be, and often are, volatile. A simple logic for why volatility can be greatest for the worst off in these relationships is provided by Barrientos et al. (2011: 332):

> challenges ... remain significant for irregular workers ... New activities taken on by the factory may well ... lead to social upgrading for regular workers—through the development of more skills and training for new capabilities—but irregular workers continue to be needed in order to respond to buyers' requirements in terms of low cost, short lead times and high flexibility; their very status impedes their social upgrading.

Not all developing countries face similar options in the context of these changes. The shift to Southern markets and the growth in South-South trade have created more possibilities for entry and upgrading in GVCs, but they also present new challenges, particularly for the least-developed countries. GVC consolidation poses opportunities as well, especially for countries and firms with rising capabilities. However, it too threatens to leave many countries and firms that don't possess the required advantages on the periphery of GVCs.

In a more promising vein, the GVC literature shows that value chains oriented to different end markets entail distinct upgrading opportunities (Staritz et al., 2011; Gereffi, 2014). For example, the demand in lower-income countries for less sophisticated products with regard to quality and styles may confront lower entry barriers and less stringent product and process standards, which can facilitate participation and make it easier for developing-country firms to engage in higher value-added GVC activities (such as product development, design, and branding) (Kaplinsky et al., 2011). With more intimate knowledge of local and regional markets than multinational firms, they can generate 'frugal' innovations that are suitable to resource-poor environments (Clark et al., 2009). On the other hand, relying exclusively on low-income markets can lock suppliers into slimmer margins and cut-throat competition, which heightens economic risks.

Rossi's (2011) case study of garment factories in Morocco led by fast-fashion buyers shows that functional upgrading in GVCs can bring about social upgrading and downgrading simultaneously, for regular and irregular workers, respectively. On the one hand, factories supplying a finished product and overseeing packaging, storage and logistics for their buyers offer stable contracts and better social protection to their high-skilled workers to ensure a continuous relationship as well as full compliance with buyers' codes of conduct. On the other hand, in order to be able to respond quickly to buyers' frequently changing orders and to operate on short lead times, they simultaneously employ irregular workers on casual contracts, especially in the final segments of the production chain (such as packaging and loading), often imposing excessive overtime as well as discriminating against them on the basis of wages and treatment (Rossi, 2011).

In agri-food GVCs, private quality standards set by highly concentrated European and US supermarkets and food manufacturers have a direct impact on risks faced by consumers as well as farmers, with conflicting implications for safety and upgrading (Lee et al., 2012). On the one hand, stringent food safety and quality standards imposed by large food retailers and manufacturers, which generally have extensive global sourcing networks, protect consumers against social and environmental risks. However, these tend to marginalize small farmers unable to comply because of high costs and a lack of required skills and facilities (e.g., cold chains to store, distribute, and ship fresh produce). On the other hand, higher standards can be a catalyst for participation in high-value-added chains, such as the role played by smallholders who successfully supply niche markets for organic or Fair Trade-certified products (Gereffi and Lee, 2012: 28).

In both developed and developing countries, the economic gains of participating in global supply chains do not necessarily translate into good jobs or stable employment and, in the worst case, economic upgrading typified by a number of successful export economies, especially in low-income countries, may be linked to a significant deterioration of labor conditions and other forms of social downgrading (Rossi et al., 2014).

A recently concluded three-year research program funded by the United Kingdom's Department for International Development, called 'Capturing the Gains' (UK DFID, 2013), has a website containing many of the research findings in working papers and policy briefs. One of the main conclusions of this project is that GVCs can be a key policy tool for sustained poverty reduction. However, facilitating the upgrading of workers and smallholders also requires public-private-civil society partnerships, as well as regional partnerships involving countries and firms that lead international production networks based in Asia, Africa, and Latin America, which are key to future upgrading of the South (Lee et al., 2011). These partnerships reflect novel forms of risk sharing and strategic collaboration among key value chain actors to address the challenge of promoting widespread and sustainable development.

Various examples of novel partnerships for risk sharing, innovation and upgrading are identified in the Summit Briefings for the Cape Town, South Africa meeting of 'Capturing the Gains' held in December, 2012. A few of these are found in Barrientos et al. (2012: 3–4). For example, over recent decades, the cocoa-chocolate value chain has undergone concentration in processing and manufacturing. Cocoa farmers have received limited support, often have low yields and are poorly remunerated. Media attention has highlighted issues of child labor, and many younger innovative farmers are leaving the sector for better options elsewhere. Consumption of chocolate has grown steadily, especially in emerging economies, with predictions of future cocoa shortages. Leading chocolate manufacturers are working with civil society, donors, and governments to support farmers and their communities. Social upgrading is now recognized as critical to economic upgrading—and ensuring the future resilience of the cocoa-chocolate value chain.

Policy Implications

Overall, the government can provide a critical supportive environment in terms of infrastructure to help exporters, local communities, and small producers trying to access national and international markets, education and training to build a skilled labor force, and sensible regulations to lower the uncertainties.

Firms benefit most from participation in GVCs if they are relatively large, technologically advanced, professionally managed, and have diversified export markets (both in terms of products and countries). Suppliers also benefit from relatively close relationships with their buyers, which can facilitate learning how to upgrade to meet the standards of global markets. These findings accommodate current GVC trends, since TNCs seek to reduce transaction costs by requiring 'one-stop shops' with larger and more capable suppliers. Contract manufacturers and business process outsourcing service providers, and firms that provide routine assembly tasks and other simple services within GVCs, earn slimmer profit and provide less to their workers (Lüthje, 2002).

Workers benefit most from participation in GVCs if their conditions of work are relatively formalized (e.g., wages, length of work day and work week, defined benefits) and if they have higher skills (closely correlated with more advanced education) that allow them to carry out better remunerated tasks. The government can play a key role to address the downside risks for workers—dismissal, debt, injury, illness—and assist in enhancing the upward mobility simultaneously. Enforcing sound regulations dealing with labor conditions is crucial to protect the vulnerable segment of the labor force.

Global buyers (retailers, brands, supermarkets) typically don't pay suppliers to undertake the upgrading required to remain competitive in GVCs. Therefore, supportive government policies are an asset (e.g., helping firms to meet international standards and certification requirements, or providing loans or access to finance capital required for purchasing new or better equipment).

The policy implications for upgrading in terms of different end markets are not clear cut. Facilitating access for export producers to multiple end markets through preferential trade agreements (multilateral or bilateral) would increase the flexibility for suppliers in developing countries to engage in upgrading. However, this will also expose them to greater competitive pressures through low-cost imports. More fundamentally, government policy makers don't know enough about the intricacies of global industries to spur specific forms of innovation in GVCs.

There is no magic bullet to improve international competitiveness in GVCs. What government policy can do is to facilitate the development of human capital, including collaborations with universities and private firms to ensure demand-responsive forms of workforce development. In addition, government can foster global collaboration by making it easier for small- and medium-sized firms to gain the information they need about global markets, and to sponsor local trade fairs or external trade missions to encourage global match-making.

Acknowledgments

This chapter was prepared as a background paper of the *World Development Report 2014: Risk and Opportunity*. The findings, interpretations, and conclusions expressed here are entirely those of the authors. They do not necessarily represent the views of their affiliated organizations. The authors would like to thank Anirudh Krishna for valuable discussions and comments.

References

Acemoglu, Daron, Asuman Ozdaglarand, and Alireza Tahbaz-Salehi. 2010. 'Cascades in Networks and Aggregate Volatility.' Mimeo.

Acemoglu, Daron and Jorn-Steffen Pischke. 1999. 'The Structure of Wages and Investment in General Training.' *Journal of Political Economy* 107(3): 539–572.

Alfaro, Laura and Maggie Chen. 2011. 'Surviving the Global Financial Crisis: Foreign Ownership and Establishment Performance.' Available at http://home.gwu.edu/~xchen/crisis_MNC.pdf.

Antras, Pol, Mihir Desai, and Fritz C. Foley. 2009. 'Multinational Firms, FDI Flows and Imperfect Capital Markets.' *Quarterly Journal of Economics* 124(3): 1171–1219.

Barrientos, Stephanie, Catherine Dolan, and Anne Tallontire. 2003. 'A Gendered Value Chain Approach to Codes of Conduct in African Horticulture'. *World Development* 31(9): 1511–1526.

Barrientos, Stephanie, Gary Gereffi, and Dev Nathan. 2012. 'Economic and Social Upgrading in Global Value Chains: Emerging Trends and Pressures.' *Capturing the Gains* Summit Briefing, December. Available at http://www.capturingthegains.org/ pdf/CTG-GVC.pdf.

Barrientos, Stephanie, Gary Gereffi, and Arianna Rossi. 2011. 'Economic and Social Upgrading in Global Production Networks: A New Paradigm for a Changing World.' *International Labour Review* 150(3–4): 319–340.

Bunkley, Nick. 2011. 'Piecing Together a Supply Chain.' *New York Times*, May 13.

Bureau of Economic Analysis. 2005. 'Like the Personal Income Numbers. Thank Microsoft.' January 31. Available at http://macroblog.typepad.com/macroblog/2005/01/like_the_person.html.

Canis, Bill. 2011. 'The Motor Vehicle Supply Chain: Effects of the Japanese Earthquake and tsunami.' Congressional Research Service Report for Congress, R41831.

Cattaneo, Olivier, Gary Gereffi, and Cornelia Staritz, eds. 2010. *Global Value Chains in a Postcrisis World: A Development Perspective*. Washington, DC: World Bank.

Clark, Norman, Joanna Chataway, Rebecca Hanlin, Dinar Kale, Raphael Kaplinsky, Lois Muraguri, Theo Papaioannou, Peter Robbins, and Watu Wamae. 2009. 'Below the Radar: What Does Innovation in the Asian Driver Economies Have to Offer Other Low Income Economies?' INNOGEN Working Paper 69. UK: Milton Keynes. Available at http://oro.open.ac.uk/15241/.

Coase, Ronald H. 1937. 'The Nature of the Firm.' *Economica* New Series 4(6): 386–405.

Di Giovanni, Julian and Andrei A. Levchenko. 2009. 'International Trade and Aggregate Fluctuations in Granular Economies'. University of Michigan Working Paper. Available at http://crei.cat/files/filesActivity/34/di%20giovanni.pdf.

Dicken, Peter. 2011. *Global Shift: Mapping the Changing Contours of the World Economy*, 6th edition. New York: Guilford.

Frederick, Stacey and Gary Gereffi. 2011. 'Upgrading and Restructuring in the Global Apparel Value Chain: Why China and Asia are Outperforming Mexico and Central America'. *International Journal of Technological Learning, Innovation and Development* 4(1–3): 67–95.

Gereffi, Gary. 1994. 'The Organization of Buyer-driven Global Commodity Chains: How US Retailers Shape Overseas Production Networks.' In *Commodity Chains and Global Capitalism*, edited by Gary Gereffi and Miguel Korzeniewicz, 95–122. Westport, CT: Praeger Publishers.

————. 1999. 'International Trade and Industrial Upgrading in the Apparel Commodity Chain.' *Journal of International Economics* 48(1): 37–70.

————. 2014. 'Global Value Chains in a Post-Washington Consensus world'. *Review of International Political Economy* 21(1): 9–37.

Gereffi, Gary and Joonkoo Lee. 2012. 'Why the World Suddenly Cares about Global Supply Chains.' *Journal of Supply Chain Management* 48(3): 24–32.

Gereffi, Gary and Timothy J. Sturgeon. 2013. 'Global Value Chains and Industrial Policy: The Role of Emerging Economies.' In *Global Value Chains in a Changing World*, edited by Deborah K. Elms and Patrick Low, 329–360. Geneva: World Trade Organization, Fung Global Institute and Termasek Foundation Centre for Trade and Negotiations.

Kaplinsky, Raphael, Anne Terheggen, and Julia P. Tijaja. 2011. 'China as a Final Market: The Gabon Timber and Thai Cassava Value Chains.' *World Development* 39(7): 1177–1190.

Kolasa, Marcin, Michal Rubaszek, and Daria Taglioni. 2010. 'Firms in the Great Global Recession: The Role of Foreign Ownership and Financial Dependence.' *Emerging Markets Review* 11(4): 341–357.

Lam, Kit-Chun and Pak-Wai Liu. 1986. 'Efficiency and Sharing of Investment in Specific Human Capital Under Risk Aversion.' *Economics Letters* 20(1): 83–87.

Lee, Joonkoo, Gary Gereffi, and Stephanie Barrientos. 2011. 'Global Value Chains, Upgrading and Poverty Reduction.' Capturing the Gains Briefing Note 3. November. Available at http://www.capturingthegains.org/pdf/ctg_briefing_note_03.pdf.

Lee, Joonkoo, Gary Gereffi, and Janet Beauvais. 2012. 'Global Value Chains and Agrifood Standards: Challenges and Possibilities for Smallholders in Developing Countries'. Proceedings of the *National Academy of Sciences of the United States of America* 109(31): 12326–12331.

Loayza, Norman, Klaus Schmidt-Hebbel, and Luis Serven. 2000. 'What Drives Private Saving around the World?' Policy Research Working Paper Series 2309. Washington, DC: World Bank.

Lucas, Robert E., Jr. 2002. *Lectures on Economic Growth*. Cambridge: Harvard University Press.

Lüthje, Boy 2002. 'Electronics Contract Manufacturing: Global Production and the International Division of Labor in the Age of the Internet.' *Industry and Innovation* 9(3): 227–247.

Mayer, Frederick and Gary Gereffi. 2010. 'Regulation and Economic Globalization: Prospects and Limits of Private Governance.' *Business and Politics* 12(3): Article 11.

O'Neill, Jim 2011. *The Growth Map: Economic Opportunity in the BRICs and Beyond*. New York: Penguin.

Oxfam International. 2004. *Trading Away Our Rights: Women Working in Global Supply Chains*. Oxford: Oxfam International.

Ratha, Dilip. 2010. 'Diaspora Bonds for Development Financing During a Crisis.' Available at http://blogs.worldbank.org/peoplemove/node/1303.

Rossi, Arianna. 2011. 'Economic and Social Upgrading in Global Production Networks: The Case of the Garment Industry in Morocco'. DPhil Dissertation, Institute of Development Studies at Sussex University, Brighton.

Rossi, Arianna, Amy Luinstra, and John Pickles, eds. 2014. *Towards Better Work: Understanding Labour in Apparel Global Value Chains*. Geneva: International Labour Organization and Palgrave Macmillan.

Schmidt-Hebbel, Klaus, Steven B. Webb, and Giancarlo Corsetti. 1992. 'Household Saving in Developing Countries: First Cross-Country Evidence.' *The World Bank Economic Review* 6(3): 529–547. The World Bank Group.

Staritz, Cornelia, Gary Gereffi, and Olivier Cattaneo, eds. 2011. Special Issue on 'Shifting End Markets and Upgrading Prospects in Global Value Chains'. *International Journal of Technological Learning, Innovation and Development* 4(1/2/3).

The Economist. 1999. 'The Key to Industrial Capitalism: Limited Liability.' 31 December. Millennium issue. Available at https://www.economist.com/node/347323.

United Kingdom, Department for International Development. 2013. *Capturing the Gains*. Available at www.capturingthegains.org.

World Bank. 2005. *Global Economic Prospects 2006: Economic Implications of Remittances and Migration*. Washington, DC.

14

Global Value Chains in a Post-Washington Consensus World

Viewing the Global Economy Through a Value-Chain Lens

Globalization has given rise to a new era of international competition that is reshaping global production and trade and altering the organization of industries (Gereffi, 2011). Since the 1960s, international companies have been slicing up their supply chains in search of low-cost and capable suppliers offshore. The literature on 'the new international division of labor ' traced the surge of manufactured exports from the Third World to the establishment of labor-intensive export platforms set up by multinational firms in low-wage areas (Fröbel et al., 1981). This was typified by the American production-sharing or 'twin plant' program with Mexico and the German export-processing zones for apparel assembly in Central and Eastern Europe. The pace of offshore production soon accelerated dramatically and took new organizational forms (Dicken, 2011). In the 1970s and 1980s, US retailers and brand-name companies joined manufacturers in the search for offshore suppliers of most categories of consumer goods, which led to a fundamental shift from what had been 'producer-driven' commodity chains to 'buyer-driven' chains. The geography of these chains expanded from regional production-sharing arrangements to full-fledged global supply chains, with a growing emphasis on East Asia (Gereffi, 1994, 1996).

In the 1990s and 2000s, the industries and activities encompassed by global supply chains grew exponentially, covering not only finished goods, but also components and sub-assemblies, and affecting not just manufacturing industries, but also energy, food production, and all kinds of services, from call centers and accounting to medical procedures and research and development (R&D) activities of the world's leading transnational corporations (Engardio et al., 2003; Engardio and Einhorn, 2005; Wadhwa et al., 2008). Since the early 2000s, the global value chain (GVC) and global production network (GPN) concepts gained popularity as ways to analyze the international expansion and geographical fragmentation of contemporary supply chains (Gereffi et al., 2001; Dicken et al., 2001; Henderson et al., 2002; Gereffi, 2005).

There are numerous reviews of the distinctive features of the global commodity chain (GCC) and the GVC and GPN approaches to analyzing global supply chains.[1] In general, they all characterize the global economy as consisting of complex and dynamic economic networks made up of inter-firm and intra-firm relationships. However, it is equally true that there are national and international political underpinnings to the shifts in global supply chains that have taken place over the past four decades. In the 1960s and 1970s, the key players in most international industries were large, vertically integrated transnational corporations (Vernon, 1971) and their link to the growing markets of developing countries was primarily via the import-substituting industrialization (ISI) model of growth that had been well established in Latin America, Eastern Europe, and parts of Asia since the 1950s. The 'East Asian Miracle' (World Bank, 1993), based on the rapid economic advance of Japan and the so-called East Asian tigers (South Korea, Taiwan, Hong Kong, and Singapore) since the 1960s, highlighted a contrasting development model: export-oriented industrialization (EOI) (Gereffi and Wyman, 1990). Buttressed by the neoliberal thrust of the Reagan and Thatcher governments in the US and the UK, respectively, export-oriented development became the prevailing orthodoxy for developing economies around the world. This model came to be known as the 'Washington Consensus,' and EOI was lauded for giving many small economies in the developing world the opportunity to benefit from scale economies and to learn from exporting to much larger trade partners, thereby overcoming the bias of the ISI model toward the limited number of developing countries with large domestic markets.

The death knell for ISI, especially in Latin America, came from the oil shock of the late 1970s and the severe debt crisis that followed it (Urquidi, 1991). The ISI approach had devised no way to generate the foreign exchange needed to pay for increasingly costly imports, and escalating debt service payments led to a net outflow of foreign capital that crippled economic growth. When many developing countries, under pressure from the IMF and the World Bank, made the transition from ISI to EOI during the 1980s (Gereffi and Wyman, 1990), there was an equally profound reorientation in the strategies of transnational corporations. The rapid expansion of industrial capabilities and export propensities in a diverse array of newly industrializing economies in Asia and Latin America allowed transnational corporations to accelerate their own efforts to outsource relatively standardized activities to lower-cost production locations worldwide. It is precisely this change in the strategies of transnational companies that enabled the shift from ISI to EOI in developing economies, and it corresponds to the shift from producer-driven to buyer-driven commodity chains at the level of global industries (Gereffi and Korzeniewicz, 1994).[2]

However, the development story for East Asia and other newly industrializing economies cannot be captured solely through a contrast of the ISI and EOI models, since the shift from ISI to EOI was not total or uncontested in either East Asia or Latin America. Indeed, elements of both strategies were intertwined since countries tended to move from relatively easy to more difficult phases of both ISI and EOI over time (Gereffi and Wyman, 1990). In addition, the growth of GPNs has been linked to rising levels of income inequality, within and between countries, which can be explained in large measure by the dynamics of rents in GVCs, which are increasingly determined by intangible assets (such as copyrights, brand names, and design) as more tangible barriers to entry in manufacturing have tended to fall (Kaplinsky, 2000). In the wake of the 2008–2009 global economic crisis, the rapid growth of productive capabilities in China, India, and other large emerging economies has created a profound shift in global demand, for both finished goods and intermediates from North to South, with both positive and negative implications for developing country exporters (Kaplinsky and Farooki, 2011).

Today, the organization of the global economy is entering a new phase, or what some have referred to as a 'major inflection point' (Fung, 2011), which could have dramatic implications for economic and social upgrading and downgrading among countries, firms, and workers. The role of the 'Washington Consensus' as a paradigm for developing countries has been severely weakened (Gore, 2000) and no alternative development strategy has taken its place. Thus, our analysis of GVCs in this post-Washington Consensus world must not only take account of changes in the organization of production and trade on a global scale, but also examine the role of emerging economies as new sources of demand and production competencies in the global economy. The increasing importance of GVCs in the current era challenges the traditional way of measuring countries' export performance and international competitiveness, and it suggests that the post-crisis futures of advanced industrial and developing economies are interdependent to a hitherto unprecedented degree.

The remaining sections of this chapter are organized as follows. First, recent trends in GVC governance reveal a growing consolidation in the supply-base among both countries and firms, and we argue that geographic consolidation is facilitating the co-evolution of more concentrated lead firms, suppliers, and intermediaries in GVCs. Second, the evolution of GVCs has altered our basic notion of how and where economic development occurs, which is illustrated by the growing importance of value-added trade and shifting end markets for GVCs, which are giving rise to new patterns of regionalization in the global economy. Third, the GVC framework has become increasingly prominent in the development agendas of a diverse array of bilateral and multilateral donor organizations, which is leading to a greater focus on showing how vertically coordinated trade and investment patterns in the global economy can be linked to employment outcomes and a renewed concern with social upgrading. Conclusions will be drawn about how these interrelated changes are likely to shape economic and social welfare in emerging models of global development.

Governance Structures and Increasing Concentration in Global Value Chains

The GVC framework focuses on globally expanding supply chains and how value is created and captured therein. By analyzing the full range of activities that firms and workers perform to bring a specific product from its conception to its end use and beyond, the GVC approach provides a holistic view of global industries from two contrasting vantage points: top-down and bottom-up. The key concept for the top-down view is the 'governance' of GVCs, which focuses mainly on lead firms and the organization of global industries; the main concept for the bottom-up perspective is 'upgrading,' which focuses on the strategies used by countries, regions, and other economic stakeholders to maintain or improve their positions in the global economy (Gereffi and Fernandez-Stark, 2011). Recent trends related to GVC governance will be discussed in this section of the chapter, and the links between economic and social upgrading and new forms of value-added trade and shifting end markets in GVCs will be the focus of the next section.

Governance is a centerpiece of GVC analysis. It shows how corporate power can actively shape the distribution of profits and risks in an industry, and it identifies the actors who exercise such power. Within the chain, power at the firm level can be exerted by lead firms or suppliers. In 'producer-driven' chains, power is held by final-product manufacturers and is characteristic of capital-, technology- or skill-intensive industries. In 'buyer-driven' chains, retailers and marketers of final products exert the most power through their ability to shape mass consumption via dominant market shares and strong brand names.[3] They source their products from a global network of suppliers in cost-effective locations to make their goods. The most notable form of 'supplier power ' comes via platform leadership (e.g., firms that exhibit marketing or technological dominance, which allows them to set standards and get higher returns for their products), although, supplier power typically is not associated with the explicit coordination of buyers or other downstream value chain actors (Frederick and Gereffi, 2009; Sturgeon, 2009).

The role played by lead firms is highlighted in various typologies of GVC governance. The initial distinction between producer-driven and buyer-driven commodity chains was introduced in the mid-1990s in order to mark the rise of global buyers in the 1970s and 1980s as retailers and brand marketers began to set up international sourcing networks to procure consumer goods directly from offshore suppliers, mainly in East Asia (Gereffi, 1994, 1999). These 'full-package' production networks based on local suppliers supplanted many of the assembly-oriented production networks initially set up by multinational manufacturers based in the developed economies (Bair and Gereffi, 2001). However, as the case studies of GVCs proliferated, and more industries and countries were incorporated into the analysis, it was clear that the dichotomous categories of buyer-driven and producer-driven commodity chains were too broad to capture the full complexity of the GVC governance structures that were emerging in the world.

In addressing this challenge, a new typology of GVC governance structures was elaborated, which sought both to describe and explain in a parsimonious way the significant differences between various types of value chains. Between the two extremes of classic markets and hierarchies (i.e., vertical integration), three network forms of governance were identified: modular, relational, and captive (Gereffi et al., 2005). In these network forms of GVC governance, the lead firm exercises varying degrees of power through the coordination of suppliers without any direct ownership of the firms (Figure 14.1).

Figure 14.1 Five Types of Global Value Chain Governance

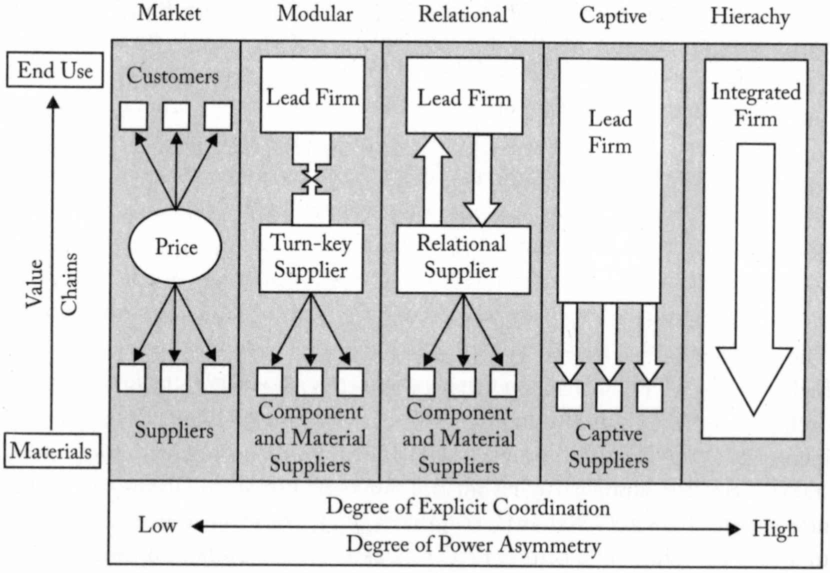

Source: Gereffi et al., 2005: 89.

The fivefold typology of GVC governance published by Gereffi et al. (2005) has been very widely utilized and extensively cited, and it has become a mainstay of our conceptual toolkit on GVC governance. One of the reasons for the popularity of this approach is that it allows us to show quite easily how the form of governance can change as an industry evolves and matures, and indeed how governance patterns within an industry can vary from one stage or level of the chain to another. For example, in the offshore services value chain, all five types of GVC governance structures identified in the typology coexist, but their role in upgrading varies according to the characteristics of suppliers in developing countries, the requirements of lead firms, and the kinds of international professional standards utilized in these chains (Fernandez-Stark et al., 2011). The impact of multiple and shifting forms of GVC governance on the ability of local producers to upgrade within global chains has been particularly notable in the agrifood sector (Dolan and Humphrey, 2004; Gereffi et al., 2009; Lee et al., 2012), although the phenomenon exists in other industries as well (Gereffi and Fernandez-Stark, 2011; Gereffi et al., 2011).

Today, we are entering a very different era. By the mid-2000s, the Washington Consensus development model was already beginning to unravel. US hegemony was eroding and the large emerging economies, led by China and India, were altering the organization of production and how rules were made that affected the global economy. Consolidation was growing at both the country and supply-chain levels in a number of hallmark global industries, such as apparel (Frederick and Gereffi, 2011; Staritz and Frederick, 2012), automobiles (Sturgeon et al., 2008; Sturgeon and Van Biesebroeck, 2011), and electronics (Sturgeon and Kawakami, 2011; Brandt and Thun, 2011). When the global economic recession hit in 2008–2009, this ended all prospects of a return to the old order. As the consumption of advanced industrial economies was curtailed, developing countries around the world began to look for alternatives to declining or stagnant northern markets. Large emerging economies turned inward and redirected production to their domestic markets and regional neighbors, and industrial policy became more prominent.

In this context, the governance structures of GVCs are changing as well. The problem is no longer one of coordinating far-flung, fragmented, and highly specialized global supply chains through triangular production networks orchestrated by East Asian intermediaries (Gereffi, 1999). The question increasingly posed by the transnational lead firms of GVCs is, 'How can we "rationalize" our supply chains from 300–500 suppliers to 25–30 suppliers?' The new suppliers are expected to be bigger, more capable, and strategically located to access large markets. In this new environment, the extreme asymmetries of power in favor of lead firms that characterized the buyer-driven and producer-driven chains are shifting in many cases toward the top manufacturers located in emerging economies such as China, India, Brazil, and Turkey. These countries have well-organized domestic supply-bases and they have moved up the value chain to incorporate key input suppliers, as well as pre-production (design, R&D and purchasing) and post-production (logistics, marketing, and branding) services.

Even in this post-Washington Consensus world, the established GVC governance structures from prior decades still exist and they will continue to play an important role in shaping development agendas. However, new governance structures are being created that reflect the realities of GVCs today. This can be seen in the links between the organizational consolidation occurring within GVCs and the geographic concentration associated with the growing prominence of emerging economies as key economic and political actors.

After 1989, the breakup of the Soviet Union, the opening of China to international investment and trade and the liberalization of India brought a number of very large economies onto the global stage initially known as BRICs (Brazil, Russia, India, and China).[4] This influenced the globalization process as GVCs began to concentrate in these giant countries that offered seemingly inexhaustible pools of low-wage workers, capable manufacturers, abundant raw materials, and sizeable domestic markets. Thus, China became the 'factory of the world', India the world's 'back office', Brazil had a wealth of agricultural commodities, and Russia possessed enormous reserves of natural resources plus the military technologies linked to its role as a Cold War superpower. These emerging economies became major production centers worldwide, although their specific role in GVCs varied according to their openness to trade and foreign investment, and other strategic considerations.

Since 2000, the shift in production from North to South in the global economy has accelerated and an expanding number of high-growth economies are playing prominent roles in a wide variety of industries as exporters and also new markets (Staritz et al., 2011). This reflects multiple factors, including the growing significance of emerging economies, the decline in export orders due to the global economic crisis of 2008–2009, and the explicit efforts of GVC lead firms to rationalize their supply chains in order to deal with smaller numbers of highly capable and strategically located suppliers.

One noteworthy consequence of global consolidation is the growth of big GVC producers and intermediaries, which tend to offset to some degree the power of global buyers. China became the world's dominant supplier of apparel, footwear and consumer electronics products, especially after the termination of the Multi-Fibre Arrangement (MFA) for apparel in 2005, and giant contract manufacturers and traders (such as Foxconn in electronics, Yue Yuen in footwear, and Li and Fung in apparel) have considerable clout. India and Brazil have also generated their own manufacturing multinationals such as Tata and Embraer.

Lead firms themselves are getting bigger through mergers, acquisitions and the decline of many rivals and, thereby, they are also increasing their global market shares.[5] At the same time, there is growing awareness of the strategic vulnerabilities of global supply chains in terms of the access of lead firms to critical raw material supplies (Lynn, 2005). This is particularly apparent in the agrifoods sector, where consumer goods firms such as Cadbury, Coca-Cola, Unilever and others are expanding their direct involvement in the procurement and sustainability of the raw material sides of their value chains, such as cocoa, coffee and sugar. This is also evident in autos and electronics, where concern over the availability of raw materials, such as lithium and coltan (Nathan and Sarkar, 2011), respectively, are introducing greater engagement between GVC lead firms and host-country suppliers and governments. Thus, the long-term trend toward specialization and fragmentation in GVCs is being supplanted by a greater emphasis on strategic collaboration.

In summary, concentration is growing across different segments of GVCs, and this co-evolution of concentrated actors appears to have two main implications for GVC governance: in at least some cases, a shift of bargaining power toward large domestic producers vis-à-vis global buyers; and an affinity between geographic concentration in large emerging economies, such as China and India, and organizational consolidation in GVCs. Novel patterns of industrial organization in emerging economies seem to fit this pattern, including China's supply chain cities, which integrate all aspects of GVCs from input suppliers to final goods manufacturers, and design centers to showrooms, for global buyers within specialized production locations (Gereffi, 2009); India's pioneering workforce development strategies to train local engineers and information technology specialists for global R&D hubs (Wadhwa et al., 2008); and Brazil's 'industrial condominium' and 'modular consortium' concepts for automobile production that recruit GVC lead firms and their top suppliers to set up coordinated manufacturing facilities in the same factory complex, such as Volkswagen's truck and bus chassis plant in Resende (Neto and Pires, 2010).

Economic Upgrading and the New Geography of Global Production and Trade

While governance issues have attracted a good deal of attention among GVC scholars, the research on economic upgrading has been at least as important because many of the people who use the GVC framework have a very strong development focus. The GVC paradigm links scholarly research on globalization with the concerns of international organizations, policy makers and social activists who are trying to harness the potential gains of globalization to the pragmatic goals of economic growth, including more and better jobs and improved competitiveness for numerous regions, countries, and social groups that feel increasingly vulnerable in the global economy. In both developed and developing countries, there is growing concern that the economic gains of participating in global supply chains do not necessarily translate into good jobs or stable employment and, in the worst case, economic upgrading may be linked to a significant deterioration of labor conditions and other forms of social downgrading. A key research question is: Under what conditions can participation in GVCs contribute to both economic and social upgrading in developing countries? (Barrientos et al., 2011a, 2011b; Lee et al., 2011).

The emergence of GVCs has redefined how we conceptualize economic development. For most early industrializers, including the US, Germany, and Japan, industrialization meant building relatively complete supply chains at home. The core idea was that no nation could become globally competitive without a broad and deep industrial base, and thus considerable effort was dedicated to bring together the capital, technology, and labor needed to create new industries. The ISI model of development, as previously noted, attempted to replicate the feat of these initial industrializers by enlisting transnational corporations in producer-driven GVCs to build modern industries in relatively big developing countries, step by step, working from final products back to key components and sub-assemblies (such as engines in cars) under the watchful eye of interventionist developmental states.

The current era of export-oriented industrialization, which is sometimes called 'globalization's second unbundling' (Baldwin, 2011), has opened up a radically new development path. Today, nations seek to industrialize by simply joining a supply chain to assemble final goods or make specialized inputs; they no longer try to build single-nation supply chains from scratch. For Baldwin, globalization's first unbundling was that railroads and steamships made it feasible to spatially separate production and consumption, and once the separation was feasible, scale economies and comparative advantage made it inevitable. The second unbundling was linked to the information and communication technology revolution, which allowed production stages that were previously performed in close proximity to be geographically dispersed in order to reduce production costs. The spatial scale of the second unbundling is not fixed, however; it could be regional or global, and thus the geographical configuration of GVCs can and does change over time.

In short, while industrialization under the EOI model became easier and faster (countries could just 'join' supply chains by performing specialized tasks, rather than 'build' them), it may also be less meaningful. If countries are only engaged in the simplest forms of EOI, such as assembling imported parts for overseas markets in export-processing zones, then they would develop neither the institutions, nor the know-how, nor the consumer markets needed to create and sustain entire industries. Indeed, for many of the small and least developed countries in the global economy, the gains associated with traditional forms of industrialization in terms of high-income jobs, forward and backward linkages, and wealth creation and innovation have been limited and uneven at best under the EOI model. Furthermore, there is growing concern that the extensive global outsourcing associated with globalization's second unbundling may have alarming implications for innovation and the international competitiveness of even the advanced industrial economies.[6]

The challenge of economic upgrading in GVCs, therefore, is precisely to identify the conditions under which developing as well as developed countries and firms can 'climb the value chain' from basic assembly activities using low-cost and unskilled labor to more advanced forms of 'full package' supply and integrated manufacturing. 'Economic upgrading' is defined as the process by which economic actors—firms and workers—move from low-value to relatively high-value activities in GVCs (Gereffi, 2005: 171). Within the GVC framework, four types of upgrading have been identified (Humphrey and Schmitz, 2002):

- *Product upgrading*, or moving into more sophisticated product lines;
- *Process upgrading*, which transforms inputs into outputs more efficiently by reorganizing the production system or introducing superior technology;
- *Functional upgrading*, which entails acquiring new functions (or abandoning existing functions) to increase the overall skill content of the activities; and
- *Chain upgrading*, in which firms move into new but often related industries.

The ability or inability of countries and firms to upgrade in these various ways has been the focal point of numerous GVC studies, but novel aspects related to the upgrading process have been introduced in the post-Washington Consensus era. First, there has been growing interest by the World Trade Organization (WTO), the Organisation for Economic Co-operation and Development (OECD) and other international organizations to establish new metrics of value-added trade that will clarify the extent to which successful export-oriented economies use domestic or imported inputs to fuel their growth. Second, in the wake of the 2008–2009 global economic crisis, economic diversification through shifting end markets appears to be reconfiguring the growth opportunities for GVCs in ways that may shift their orientation toward the domestic markets of large emerging economies and toward more regionally oriented, rather than global, supply-chains. We will consider each topic below.

A New Metric for GVC Analysis: Value-Added Trade

In a world characterized by a predominance of GVCs, exports of final products are increasingly composed of imports of intermediate inputs. As supply chains go global, therefore, more intermediate goods are traded across borders, and more parts and components are imported for use in exports (Feenstra, 1998). In 2009, world exports of intermediate goods exceeded the combined export values of final and capital goods, representing 51% of non-fuel merchandise exports (WTO and IDE-JETRO, 2011: 81). Governments and international organizations are taking notice of this emerging pattern of global trade, which is called a shift from 'trade in goods' to 'trade in value added', 'trade in tasks' and 'trade in capabilities'[7] (OECD, 2011; WTO and IDE-JETRO, 2011).

Emerging economies have clearly improved their position in GVCs, surging ahead of the advanced industrial countries in terms of export performance. Between 1995 and 2007, the global export market shares of the US and Japan fell by 3.8 and 3.7 percentage points, respectively, while China more than doubled its market share from 4% in 1995 to 10.1% in 2007, making it the world export leader (ahead of Germany, the US, and Japan). South Korea, Mexico, Turkey, South Africa, and the former transition countries in central Europe also increased their export market shares during this period (Beltramello et al., 2012: 9–10). Potentially more impressive is the fact that emerging economies made their most significant gains in high- and medium-technology industries, which were previously the stronghold of OECD countries.[8] This phenomenon was mainly driven by China, whose share of exports of goods in high-tech industries soared by 13.5 percentage points during the period of 1995–2007, moving it ahead of the US as the world's largest exporter of high-tech products (Beltramello et al., 2012: 10).

While most intermediate goods are still traded within large regional economic blocks, such as the European Union, rather than across them (OECD, 2011), Asia's linkages to the European Union and North America represented the two highest inter-regional import flows of intermediate goods in 2008. Asia imported more intermediate goods than it exported, indicating the region's high level of integration within global supply chains (WTO and IDE-JETRO, 2011: 83–85). The geographical concentration of supply chains is also obvious at the country level. In 2000–2008, China accounted for 67% of the world's processing exports,[9] followed by Mexico with 18% (WTO and IDE-JETRO, 2011: 21).

China has benefited greatly from this form of participation in global supply chains. One-third of China's imports are destined for export-processing zones, which account for almost half of the country's exports (WTO and IDE-JETRO, 2011: 21). China's 'supply chain cities' are a perfect illustration of how China is turning scale-driven specialization into a persistent competitive advantage for the country. From foreign direct investment-driven clusters in Guangdong to single-product clusters in Zhejiang, China's sheer size has allowed it to set up broad manufacturing clusters at the regional level. These specialized clusters are linked, on the one hand, to East Asian suppliers of key parts and components and, on the other hand, to global buyers to bring Chinese products to the world market (Gereffi, 2009).

Paradoxically, China does not create or capture most of the value generated through its value chain exports. In fact, as more types of intermediate goods are traded within global supply chains, the discrepancy is growing between where final goods are produced and exported and where value is created and captured. For example, Apple's iPhones are entirely assembled in China by a Taiwanese contract manufacturer (Foxconn) and exported to the US. When a traditional measure is used, which assigns the gross export value of the product to the exporting country, the unit export value of iPhones from China is $194.04. Of this, only $24.63 is imported content from the US, meaning that every iPhone imported into the US results in a US balance-of-payments deficit of $169.41 (Figure 14.2). However, this does not mean that China benefits from a trade surplus of $169.41 for each iPhone it exports, since the value added in China is only $6.54 per phone. The balance of China's iPhone production costs is made up of imports from South Korea ($80.05), Germany ($16.08), and diverse other countries.[10]

Figure 14.2 US Bilateral Trade Balance with China for One Unit of iPhone4 (US$)

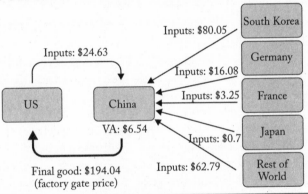

US Trade Balance with	China	S. Korea	Germany	France	Japan	ROW	World
Gross	−169.41	0	0	0	0	0	−169.41
Value added	−6.54	−80.05	−16.08	−3.25	−0.7	−62.79	−169.41

Source: OECD, 2011: 40.

These advances in GVC metrics related to value creation and value capture are a propitious development for policy-oriented research (OECD, 2011; WTO and IDE-JETRO, 2011; UNCTAD, 2013). As showcased by the iPhone study, existing trade statistics are unable to grasp the changing patterns of global production and trade. This is an area where GVC analysis and supply chain management research can be mutually beneficial.[11] Sophisticated value chain data disaggregated by business functions can complement existing country-level trade statistics and industry-level input-output data, providing a clear picture of who is gaining and losing in GVCs (Sturgeon and Gereffi, 2009). When combined with data on employment, they will greatly advance our understanding of both economic and social development opportunities in the global economy.

Shifting End Markets and the Regionalization of GVCs

As world trade bounces back from the 2008–2009 economic crises, emerging economies are becoming a main engine of world economic recovery. Tepid growth in the global North since the mid-1980s was slowed even further by the latest crisis, whereas demand is quickly growing in the global South, particularly in large emerging economies such as China, India, and Brazil (Staritz et al., 2011). Over the period of 2005–2010, the merchandise imports of the European Union and the US increased by 27% and 14%, respectively, while emerging economies expanded their merchandise imports much faster: Brazil (147%), India (129%), China (111%), and South Africa (51%). In 2010, 52% of Asia's manufactured exports were destined for developing countries (WTO, 2011), indicating shifting end markets in the global economy.

The dramatic decline of world merchandise trade as a result of the economic crisis of 2008–2009 has been described as 'the great trade collapse' (Baldwin, 2009). After more than six years of positive trade growth, all OECD countries registered a decline in exports and imports exceeding 10% between 2008 and 2009, reaching a record negative growth of -37% in April 2009 (Beltramello et al., 2012: 27). The trade collapse was much larger in intermediates than in final consumption goods, which underscores the existence of a 'bullwhip' effect in GVCs—namely, lower demand for final consumption goods (downstream) is amplified in more dramatic demand reductions for intermediates that are upstream in the value chain (Altomonte et al., 2012).

The 'great trade collapse' accelerated the shift in end markets from the North to the South in GVCs (Kaplinsky and Farooki, 2011) and it also encouraged lead firms from developing countries to regionalize their supply chains. In sub-Saharan Africa, for instance, the recent entry of South African clothing manufacturers in neighboring countries such as Lesotho and Swaziland has led to the rise of regional value chains driven by South African retailers. Compared to the US buyer-driven chain, these regional chains focus on shorter production runs and quick response with higher fashion content, and are based on direct relationships to large South African clothing retailers (Morris et al., 2011). Similarly, South African supermarkets are expanding via regional supply chains and spearheading the rise of supermarkets across sub-Saharan Africa (Weatherspoon and Reardon, 2003).

The GVC literature shows that value chains oriented to different end markets often entail distinct upgrading opportunities (Palpacuer et al., 2005; Gibbon, 2008). For example, the demand in lower-income countries for less sophisticated products with regard to quality and variety can have major upgrading implications (Kaplinsky et al., 2011). On the one hand, lower entry barriers and less stringent product and process standards in emerging markets can facilitate the participation of developing-country firms in global supply chains. They can engage in higher value-added activities, such as product development and design, which they would have little chance to do in the global chains. With more intimate knowledge of local and regional markets vis-à-vis multinational firms, they can generate 'frugal' innovations that are suitable to resource-poor environments (Clark et al., 2009). On the other hand, solely focusing on low-income markets could lock suppliers into slimmer margins and cut-throat competition. Their knowledge advantage in local markets often evaporates quickly when multinational firms catch up in learning the markets, as found in the Chinese mobile phone industry (Brandt and Thun, 2011).

The Impact of GVC Analysis on the Development Agendas of International Donors

GVC studies are pervasive in academic publications that examine a wide range of global industries,[12] and the framework has been adopted by many of the major international donors and peak organizations concerned with economic development, including the World Bank (Webber and Labaste, 2009; Cattaneo et al., 2010), the WTO (WTO and IDE-JETRO, 2011), the OECD (OECD, 2011; Beltramello et al., 2012), the International Labor Organization (ILO) (Gereffi, 2006), the US Agency for International Development (USAID, 2012), the US International Trade Commission (USITC, 2011), the World Economic Forum (WEF, 2012), and the UN Conference on Trade and Development (UNCTAD, 2013).

The international institutions that have provided the underpinning for the Washington Consensus, such as the World Bank, the IMF, and the WTO, along with major bilateral donors, such as USAID and the UK's Department for International Development (DFID),[13] have embraced new heterodox models of development thinking, with an emphasis on sectoral analysis that allows macro issues such as international trade and investment to be linked more closely with the micro development issues of employment, gender dynamics, and sustainable livelihoods (M4P, 2008). In addition, new alliances have emerged among diverse UN and other international agencies (such as the World Bank and the ILO) to promote joint research agendas that explore the links between economic and social upgrading, explicitly using the GVC framework (Cattaneo et al., 2010; Barrientos et al., 2011a).

Unlike most social science theories and paradigms, which have only a limited impact on specific international organizations and development policy settings, the GVC framework is unusual in that it has diffused very rapidly during the past decade and been adopted by a wide range of economic, social, and cultural organizations, as well as action-oriented non-governmental organizations (NGOs) in the labor and environmental arenas. Table 14.1 identifies some of these international donor organizations and recent projects or studies that are informed by the GVC approach.

While this topic merits a far more detailed discussion, two aspects of the use of GVC analysis in these organizations will be touched on below. First, what are the similarities and differences in how GVC analysis is used in these organizations? For example, most of these international donors have development programs that emphasize pro-poor growth, the protection of small and medium enterprises and local stakeholders, and a private sector-oriented, market-led model. However, they differ in other respects, such as the weight given to economic growth in relation to poverty reduction as well as geographic regions and sectors of particular interest. Second, what are the other development models or frameworks that are being used in each organization and to what degree are these complementary or antagonistic with the GVC approach? One of the key reasons for the turn to GVC and GPN approaches may be that their emphasis on global industries offers a meso-level, sectoral and actor-oriented approach to the global economy, which provides multi-scalar options to link global and local levels of analysis, in contrast to macro models, which focus on general economic trends and broad policy prescriptions, or the micro and localized approach of clusters, which aren't connected to the broader structures at the national, regional or global levels.

Value chain analysis is used widely today as an instrument of private-sector development by virtually all major bilateral and multilateral donor agencies. Altenburg (2007) highlights two main reasons for the increasing popularity of the GVC approach within the international donor community since the end of the 1990s: first, the accumulating evidence of a link between economic growth driven by the private sector and poverty reduction; and second, the fact that global integration of trade and production through GVCs transmits the pressures of global competition to domestic markets in developing economies, leaving less space for local firms to design, produce, and market on their own. As Altenburg (2007: 4) puts it, 'The question is thus not *if*, but *how* to integrate in value chains in a way that allows for incorporation of a growing number of the workforce and increasing levels of productivity and outcomes. This calls for a balanced approach which takes both competitiveness and equity issues into account'.

There is no simple way to connect GVC analysis to private sector development, since the firms in a value chain range from transnational corporations to micro-

Cont'd.

Table 14.1 Use of Global Value Chain Analysis in Selected International Organizations

Organization	Illustrative GVC Publications	Content Description	2012						
			GVC	LED	Clusters	PSD	TVET	Poverty	Micro
World Bank	Cattaneo et al. (2010)	This book uses a GVC perspective to analyze the impact of the global financial crisis of 2008–2009 on global trade, production and demand in several sectors. Particular attention is paid to opportunities for developing countries to enter into GVCs post-crisis.	x		x	x		x	x
IDB	Flores and Vaillant (2011)	This paper compares the upgrading performance of Latin American countries in terms of export sophistication in a variety of industries.	x	x	x	x		x	x
DFID	Capturing the Gains (2012)	This three-year research project brings together an international network of experts to gain information on the employment and well-being of workers and small producers in GVCs.	x		x	x		x	
USAID	Value Chain Development Wiki (2012)	This website gathers information from various projects and draws on research conducted under USAID's Microenterprise Development Team to codify good practice in value chain development, with an eye to linking SMEs into global, national and local value chains.	x		x	x	x		x
GTZ/GIZ	Will (2011)	This manual considers information from GTZ-funded pilot projects in developing countries in order to draw lessons about the various processes by which smallholders can receive GLOBALGAP certification, which is required by many European food retailers.	x	x		x	x	x	

Cont'd.

Organization	Illustrative GVC Publications	Content Description	2012						
			GVC	LED	Clusters	PSD	TVET	Poverty	Micro
WTO	WTO (2011)	This publication uses a GVC framework to consider changing trade patterns in East Asia. It proposes a new trade statistic—trade in value added—to complement traditional trade statistics.	x						
OECD	OECD (2011)	This report to the OECD Working Party on Globalization of Industry and the Committee on Innovation, Industry and Entrepreneurship uses the GVC framework to provide policy advice to OECD countries with a focus on maintaining competitiveness and identifying new sources of growth.	x		x	x			
ILO	Herr and Muzira (2009)	This guide for development practitioners, governments and private actors outlines strategies for upgrading within value chains while maintaining or improving labor standards for workers.	x	x			x	x	

Source: Author.

Notes:

GVC: The Global Value Chain framework focuses on the placement of firms and localities within the global organization of trade and production within particular sectors or industries.

LED: The Local Economic Development framework focuses on initiatives geared towards the local or sub-national public sector as an enabler or instigator of economic development.

Clusters: The Cluster framework focuses on initiatives geared towards the local or sub-national private sector.

PSD: Private Sector Development strategies focus on the concept of 'making markets work.'

TVET: Technical and Vocational Education and Training strategies focus on improving the quality and quantity of workers' marketable skills through vocational training initiatives.

Poverty: Poverty Alleviation programs are those that seek the reduction, alleviation or eradication of poverty.

Micro: Microfinance programs make very small 'microloans' to entrepreneurs or households that are otherwise unable to access financial markets under favorable terms.

enterprises, and the institutional context and geographic scope of value chains vary enormously. In order to provide some guidance for interventions by donors, Humphrey and Navas-Alemán (2010) distinguish four different objectives of donor interventions: strengthening the weakest link to address potential bottlenecks; improving flows of knowledge and resources to make all firms in the chain more productive; working on specific links between firms to improve efficiency; and creating new or alternate links in the chain to promote diversified outcomes.

An alternative to this bottom-up approach to value chain development is targeting lead firms rather than local suppliers—i.e., working with the strongest link in the chain, rather than the weakest. This lead-firm-centered, top-down GVC approach has been used effectively for very different purposes, whether it be the World Bank's revitalized 'Aid for Trade' initiative, which sees the private sector as the engine that powers global trade and urges GVC lead firms to play a greater role in building trade capacity in developing countries (World Bank, 2011), or the confrontational stance of NGOs such as Oxfam (2004), which mobilizes international campaigns against lead firms to improve the conditions of women workers in global supply chains.

The reality is that most bilateral and multilateral donors use GVC analysis in combination with other diagnostic tools they have tried in the past (Table 14.1) to address a variety of broad development goals, including poverty reduction, economic growth, employment creation and income generation, enterprise development, and environmental stability and cleaner production (UNIDO, 2011). One of the most comprehensive reviews of the approaches of seven UN agencies to value chain development concludes, however, that there is considerable 'fuzziness' about how the concept is adopted:

> ... [value chain]-related activities sometimes seem to be rather the outcome of 're-labelling' former private sector development interventions. In other cases, activities that could clearly be subsumed under the value chain approach are not labeled accordingly .... These observed shortcomings in knowledge management, transparency and the lack of defined unique selling positions make inter-agency cooperation in [value chain] promotion difficult (Stamm and von Drachenfels, 2011: 30).

In short, much of the literature that uses the GVC moniker misses the point and doesn't apply the framework consistently.

The widespread adoption of the GVC framework by international donors during the past decade represents a remarkable convergence around a single paradigm, notwithstanding the differing emphases across UN and bilateral agencies. Skeptics might argue that the neoliberal fundamentals of the Washington Consensus model of development remain entrenched in many of these organizations (Neilsen, 2014), even if GVC analysis is rooted in assumptions that are highly critical of the neoliberal paradigm (see Gereffi and Korzeniewicz, 1994; Kaplinsky, 2005; Bair, 2009; Hamilton and Gereffi, 2009; Sturgeon, 2009; Lee, 2010). The counterargument made throughout this chapter is that the GVC perspective highlights the power dynamics in global industries, embodied in the role of lead firms and the institutions that underpin the global economic order, and this introduces broader and more heterodox views of development that challenge the mainstream.

During the past decade, the global economy has seen a transfer of production, technological capabilities, growth potential, consumption and political clout from the North to the South. One of the major reasons for the popularity of the GVC framework is that it allows us to analyze many of these shifts with greater precision than prior paradigms. While interpretations of the direction and impact of these trends will vary, the contributions of GVC analysis should not be discounted because the donor organizations have multiple and sometimes discordant agendas. Furthermore, as more international organizations employ the GVC paradigm, its methodological rigor and policy relevance are likely to increase.

Conclusion

What will replace the globalization model? This is the question posed in a recent newspaper article, which contends: 'The globalization model of the past 30 years is cracking up. And there appears to be no new model to replace it' (Smick, 2012). While we concur that globalization as we know it is undergoing a series of fundamental shifts, many elements of the future system are there for us to see. The international competitiveness of advanced industrial economies has gradually been eroded, at least in terms of traditional measures of export performance. Emerging economies now play a more prominent role in international trade, and they have expanded their export market shares of high-technology and medium-technology products, with China playing a particularly prominent role (Beltramello et al., 2012). The emergence of GVCs cautions against an overreliance on simple export measures of competitiveness, however, and this chapter has sought to unpack various insights from the GVC perspective to better understand some of the new features of the post-Washington Consensus global economy.

The Washington Consensus model of development, which held sway from the mid-1980s through the mid-2000s, is a nation-state-centered view of the global economy, in which countries are the primary units of analysis in international production and trade. The main topics of debate involved the extent to which economic policies were 'market-friendly' or overly interventionist (World Bank, 1993), and the nature of the stabilization programs and market access agreements that would be imposed on recalcitrant developing economies by the IMF, the World Bank and other international financial and trade institutions to bring them in line with the dominant model.

The GVC framework fundamentally challenges this view of the global economy and it provides a different interpretation of the key drivers of change over the past four decades. The sector-based approach of the GVC perspective is premised on the structural diversity of global industries, which are major entry points for developing nations in the global economy. The major analytical categories used to examine global value chains include:

- The role of *lead firms* in setting performance requirements and standards that condition entry and mobility within GVCs
- The evolving nature of *production and trade networks* that link large and small suppliers to the global economy as well as to domestic economies
- Trajectories of social and economic *upgrading and downgrading*, and patterns of *access and exclusion*, which help describe the connections between the development of firms and countries within the international system
- Multiple *governance structures* (international and domestic; public and private; chain-based and civic) that link different components of the system together
- The shift from trade in goods to *trade in value added, tasks and business functions* in looking at key economic activities related to upgrading and competitiveness and
- *Interventions and pressure points* that allow for change in this system

Economic globalization is a byproduct of international production and trade networks organized by transnational firms and it is embedded in various kinds of regulation, including rules of the game established by international institutions, national government policies, and varied forms of private governance used by non-state actors to manage activities in GVCs (Mayer and Gereffi, 2010). One potential outcome of the current situation is that public governance will be called upon to play a stronger role in supplementing and reinforcing corporate codes of conduct, product certifications, process standards and other voluntary, non-governmental types of private governance that have proliferated in the last two decades, and that multi-stakeholder initiatives involving both public and private actors will arise to deal with collective action problems.

While the contours of a new international economic order are still in flux, several features are already having an impact on development agendas. The most dynamic growth poles in the global economy are constituted by an expanding number of rising powers that combine relatively large domestic markets, skilled workforces, capable producers, and a push toward indigenous innovation. These include the original BRIC countries as well as South Korea, Mexico, Turkey, and Indonesia, among others (O'Neill, 2011). As the EOI development strategy is replaced by more inward-looking approaches focusing on domestic and regional markets, industrial policy in the leading economies of the South is likely to become more significant. While policy priorities at the macro level of the global economy seek new ways to channel trade and investment patterns toward more robust employment outcomes (OECD, 2012), the challenge will be to link economic upgrading and social upgrading in terms of both material conditions of work and the quantity and quality of jobs created in contemporary GVCs (Barrientos et al., 2011a, 2011b).

Acknowledgments

The author would like to thank Andrew Guinn, Rebecca Schultz, and Jackie Xu for their research assistance on this chapter.

Notes

1. For recent reviews of GCC and GVC literature, see Bair (2009), Lee (2010), and Gereffi and Lee (2012).
2. In the original 1994 article that introduced the concepts of producer-driven and buyer-driven GCCs, there is a section on 'The Role of State Policies in Global Commodity Chains,' which makes the link between GCCs and development strategies very clear:

   An important affinity exists between the ISI and EOI strategies of national development and the structure of commodity chains. Import substitution occurs in the same kinds of capital and technology-intensive industries represented by producer-driven commodity chains [...] In addition, the main economic agents in both cases are [transnational corporations] and state-owned enterprises. Export-oriented industrialization, on the other hand, is channelled through buyer-driven commodity chains where production in labor-intensive industries is concentrated in small to medium-sized private domestic firms located mainly in the Third World. Historically, the export-oriented development strategy of the East Asian [newly industrializing countries] and buyer-driven commodity chains emerged together in the early 1970s, suggesting a close connection between the success of EOI and the development of new forms of organizational integration in buyer-driven industrial networks (Gereffi, 1994: 100).

3. Knowing if the lead firm in a chain is a buyer or a producer can help to determine the most likely upgrading opportunities for suppliers. For example, buyer-driven chains tend to provide more opportunities to their suppliers in product and functional upgrading because the core competence of the buyers is in marketing and branding, not production; whereas lead firms in producer-driven chains often require varied forms of process upgrading and international certifications among their suppliers due to strict quality and performance standards that affect the entire chain.

4. Jim O'Neill (2011), the Goldman Sachs executive who coined the catchy acronym BRIC in 2001 to refer to Brazil, Russia, India, and China, now argues that there is a much larger number of 'growth economies' (BRICs plus 11) that fall into this category. These include the MIST nations (Mexico, Indonesia, South Korea, and Turkey), and other periodic high-performers such as Bangladesh, Egypt, Pakistan, the Philippines, and Vietnam (Martin, 2012). The original BRIC classification was extended to BRICS with the addition of South Africa in 2010. For purposes of this chapter, the origin of these acronyms is less important than the collective effect of this set of so-called emerging economies, which are reshaping both supply and demand in many GVCs.

5. Li & Fung, the largest trading company in the world, has around 30,000 suppliers globally and operates in 40 countries (Fung, 2011).

6. Pisano and Shih (2009), for example, argue that the US is in danger of losing its 'industrial commons,' which includes not just suppliers of advanced materials, production equipment, and components, but also R&D know-how, engineering and processing skills, and a wide range of other manufacturing competencies. Because manufacturing is closely tied to the capacity for innovation, offshore manufacturing can undermine the capabilities of the US economy to remain competitive in existing high-tech industries, which often depend in critical ways on the industrial commons of mature sectors, and also impede its ability to move into new industries. This helps explain why Apple does not manufacture its iPhone in the US. While labor costs are obviously much lower and a certain class of skilled workers more abundant in China where all US-sold iPhones are assembled, perhaps the biggest limitation is that the vast majority of suppliers needed to make the hundreds of parts that go into every iPhone are located in East Asia, and not North America. This could hinder the ability of US companies to remain innovative (see Duhigg and Bradsher, 2012; Pisano and Shih, 2012; Shih, 2009).

7. There are conceptual difficulties, however, in using individual tasks or capabilities as a unit of analysis in determining how easy it is to fragment and relocate work in GVCs. It is more likely that larger sets of activities associated with 'business functions' will be outsourced, rather than individual jobs and capabilities (Sturgeon and Gereffi, 2009).

8. Since these figures refer to gross exports, we need more detailed information about the degree of domestic or foreign value added to assess the extent to which these numbers reflect the local assembly of high-tech imports or significant national technology content.

9. Processing exports refer to exports that use duty-free imports for subsequent processing and re-exports.

10. This is not an uncommon pattern in China. Domestic content accounts for only about half of China's manufacturing exports and it is even smaller (18%) in its processing exports, mostly done by foreign-owned firms (Koopman et al., 2008).

11. Note that the iPhone study and other similar studies (Dedrick et al., 2010; Linden et al., 2009) are based on tear-down analysis generated by supply chain management consultancies such as iSuppli.

12. Nearly 1,100 publications and more than 780 authors were listed on the Global Value Chains website (https://globalvaluechains.org/publications) as of July 27, 2018.

13. DFID changed the name of its bilateral economic aid program to the UK Agency for International Development (UK Aid) in 2012.

References

Altenburg, Tilman. 2007. 'Donor Approaches to Supporting Pro-Poor Value Chains.' Report prepared for the Donor Committee for Enterprise Development, Working Group on Linkages and Value Chains. Available at www.deza.admin.ch/ressources/resource_en_162916.pdf.

Altomonte, Carlo, Filippo Di Mauro, Gianmarco Ottaviano, Armando Rungi, and Vincent Vicard. 2012. 'Global Value Chains During the Great Trade Collapse: A Bullwhip Effect?' European Central Bank, Working Paper Series 1412. Available at https://papers.ssrn.com/sol3/papers.cfm?abstract_id=1973497.

Bair, Jennifer, ed. 2009. *Frontiers of Commodity Chain Research*. Stanford, CA: Stanford University Press.

Bair, Jennifer and Gary Gereffi. 2001. 'Local Clusters in Global Chains: The Causes and Consequences of Export Dynamism in Torreon's Blue Jeans Industry.' *World Development* 29(11): 1885–1903.

Baldwin, Richard. 2009. 'The Great Trade Collapse: What Caused It and What Does It Mean?' In *The Great Trade Collapse: Causes, Consequences and Prospects*, edited by Richard Baldwin, 1–14. London: Centre for Economic Policy Research.

———. 2011. 'Trade and Industrialisation after Globalisation's 2nd Unbundling: How Building and Joining a Supply Chain are Different and Why it Matters.' Working Paper 17716, December. Cambridge, MA: National Bureau of Economic Research. Available at http://www.nber.org/papers/w17716.

Barrientos, Stephanie, Gary Gereffi, and Arianna Rossi. 2011a. 'Economic and Social Upgrading in Global Production Networks: A New Paradigm for a Changing World.' *International Labour Review* 150(3–4): 319–40.

Barrientos, Stephanie, Frederick Mayer, John Pickles, and Anne Posthuma. 2011b. 'Decent Work in Global Production Networks: Framing the Policy Debate.' *International Labour Review* 150(3–4): 299–317.

Beltramello, Andrea, Koen De Backer, and Laurent Moussiegt. 2012. 'The Export Performance of Countries within Global Value Chains (GVCs).' OECD Science, Technology and Industry Working Papers, 2012/02. OECD Publishing. Available at http://dx.di.org/10.1787/5k9bh3gv6647-en.

Brandt, Loren and Eric Thun. 2011. 'Going Mobile in China: Shifting Value Chains and Upgrading in the Mobile Telecom Sector.' *International Journal of Technological Learning, Innovation and Development* 4(1–3): 148–180.

Capturing the Gains. 2012. 'Programme Overview'. Available at http://www.capturingthegains.org/about/index.htm.

Cattaneo, Olivier, Gary Gereffi, and Cornelia Staritz, eds. 2010. *Global Value Chains in a Postcrisis World: A Development Perspective*. Washington, DC: World Bank.

Clark, Norman, Joanna Chataway, Rebecca Hanlin, Dinar Kale, Raphael Kaplinsky, Lois Muraguri, Theo Papaioannou, Peter Robbins, and Watu Wamae. 2009. 'Below the Radar: What Does Innovation in the Asian Driver Economies Have to Offer Other Low Income Economies?' INNOGEN Working Paper 69. Milton Keynes, UK. Available at http://oro.open.ac.uk/15241/.

Dedrick, Jason, Kenneth L Kraemer, and Greg Linden. 2010. 'Who Profits from Innovation in Global Value Chains? A Study of the iPod and Notebook PCs.' *Industrial and Corporate Change* 19(1): 81–116.

Dicken, Peter. 2011. *Global Shift: Mapping the Changing Contours of the World Economy*, 6th edition. New York: Guilford.

Dicken, Peter, Philip F. Kelly, Kris Olds, and Henry Wai-chung Yeung. 2011. 'Chains and Networks, Territories and Scales: Towards a Relational Framework for Analyzing the Global Economy.' *Global Networks* 1(2): 89–112.

Dolan, Catherine and John Humphrey. 2004. 'Changing Governance Patterns in the Trade in Fresh Vegetables between Africa and the United Kingdom.' *Environment and Planning A* 36(3): 491–509.

Duhigg, Charles and Keith Bradsher. 2012. 'How the US Lost Out on iPhone Work.' *The New York Times*, 21 January. Available at http://www.nytimes.com/2012/01/22/business/apple-america-and-a-squeezed-middle-class.html?_r=1&src= me&ref=general.

Engardio, Pete, Aaron Bernstein, and Manjeet Kripalani. 2003. 'Is Your Job Next?' *Business Week*, February 3, 50–60.

Engardio, Pete and Bruce Einhorn. 2005. 'Outsourcing Innovation.' *Business Week*, March 21, 47–53.

Feenstra, Robert C. 1998. 'Integration of Trade and Disintegration of Production in the Global Economy.' *Journal of Economic Perspectives* 12(4): 31–50.

Fernandez-Stark Karina, Penny Bamber, and Gary Gereffi. 2011. 'The Offshore Services Value Chain: Upgrading Trajectories in Developing Countries.' *International Journal of Technological Learning, Innovation and Development* 4(1–3): 206–234.

Flores, Manuel and Marcel Valliant. 2011. 'Global Value Chains and Export Sophistication in Latin America.' *Integration and Trade* 32(15): 35–48.

Frederick, Stacey and Gary Gereffi. 2009. 'Value Chain Governance.' US-AID Briefing Paper. Available at http://microlinks.kdid.org/library/value-chain-governance-briefing-paper.

———. 2011. 'Upgrading and Restructuring in the Global Apparel Value Chain: Why China and Asia are Outperforming Mexico and Central America.' *International Journal of Technological Learning, Innovation and Development* 4(1–3): 67–95.

Fröbel, Folker, Jürgen Heinrichs, and Otto Kreye. 1981. *The New International Division of Labour*. New York: Cambridge University Press.

Fung, Victor. 2011. 'Global Supply Chains – Past Developments, Emerging Trends.' Available at http://www.fungglobalinstitute.org/publications/speeches/global-supply-chains–past-developments-emerging-trends-193.html.

Gereffi, Gary. 1994. 'The Organization of Buyer-Driven Global Commodity Chains: How US Retailers Shape Overseas Production Networks.' In *Commodity Chains and Global Capitalism*, edited by Gary Gereffi and Miguel Korzeniewicz, 95–122. Westport, CT: Praeger.

———. 1996. 'Commodity Chains and Regional Divisions of Labour in East Asia.' *Journal of Asian Business* 12(1): 75–112.

———. 1999. 'International Trade and Industrial Upgrading in the Apparel Commodity Chain.' *Journal of International Economics* 48(1): 37–70.

————. 2005. 'The Global Economy: Organization, Governance, and Development.' In *The Handbook of Economic Sociology*, 2nd edition, edited by Neil J. Smelser and Richard Swedberg, 160–182. Princeton, NJ: Princeton University Press.

————. 2006. *The New Offshoring of Jobs and Global Development*. ILO Social Policy Lectures. Geneva: International Institute for Labour Studies and International Labour Organisation.

————. 2009. 'Development Models and Industrial Upgrading in China and Mexico.' *European Sociological Review* 25(1): 37–51.

————. 2011. 'Global Value Chains and International Competition.' *The Antitrust Bulletin* 56(1): 37–56.

Gereffi, Gary and Karina Fernandez-Stark. 2011. 'Global Value Chain Analysis: A Primer.' Duke Global Value Chains Center. Durham, NC: Duke University. Available at http://www.cggc.duke.edu/pdfs/2011-05-31_GVC_analysis_a_primer.pdf.

Gereffi, Gary, Karina Fernandez-Stark, and Phil Silos, eds. 2011. *Skills for Upgrading: Workforce Development and Global Value Chains in Developing Countries*. Duke Global Value Chains Center. Durham, NC: Duke University. Available at http://www.cggc.duke.edu/gvc/workforce-development/.

Gereffi, Gary, John Humphrey, Raphael Kaplinsky, and Timothy J. Sturgeon. 2001. 'Introduction: Globalisation, Value Chains and Development.' *IDS Bulletin* 32(3): 1–8.

Gereffi, Gary, John Humphrey, and Timothy J. Sturgeon. 2005. 'The Governance of Global Value Chains.' *Review of International Political Economy* 12(1): 78–104.

Gereffi, Gary and Miguel Korzeniewicz, eds. 1994. *Commodity Chains and Global Capitalism*. Westport, CT: Praeger.

Gereffi, Gary and Joonkoo Lee. 2012. 'Why the World Suddenly Cares about Global Supply Chains.' *Journal of Supply Chain Management* 48(3): 24–32.

Gereffi, Gary, Joonkoo Lee, and Michelle Christian. 2009. 'US-Based Food and Agricultural Value Chains and Their Relevance to Healthy Diets.' *Journal of Hunger and Environmental Nutrition* 4(3–4): 357–374.

Gereffi, Gary and Donald L. Wyman, eds. 1990. *Manufacturing Miracles: Paths of Industrialization in Latin America and East Asia*. Princeton, NJ: Princeton University Press.

Gibbon, Peter. 2008. 'Governance, Entry Barriers, Upgrading: A Re-Interpretation of Some GVC Concepts from the Experience of African Clothing Exports.' *Competition and Change* 12(1): 29–48.

Gore, Charles. 2000. 'The Rise and Fall of the Washington Consensus as a Paradigm for Developing Countries.' *World Development* 28(5): 789–804.

Hamilton, Gary G. and Gary Gereffi. 2009. 'Global Commodity Chains, Market Makers, and the Rise of Demand-Responsive Economies.' In *Frontiers of Commodity Chain Research*, edited by Jennifer Bair, 136–161. Stanford, CA: Stanford University Press.

Henderson, Jeffrey, Peter Dicken, Martin Hess, Neil Coe, and Henry Wai-chung Yeung. 2002. 'Global Production Networks and the Analysis of Economic Development.' *Review of International Political Economy* 9(3): 426–464.

Herr, Matthias L. and Tapera J. Muzira. 2009. *Value Chain Development for Decent Work: A Guide for Private Sector Initiatives, Governments and Development Organizations*. Geneva: ILO.

Humphrey, John and Lizbeth Navas-Aleman. 2010. 'Value Chains, Donor Interventions and Poverty Reduction: A Review of Donor Practice.' *IDS Research Report* 63. Brighton, UK: Institute of Development Studies, University of Sussex.

Humphrey, John and Hubert Schmitz. 2002. 'How Does Insertion in Global Value Chains Affect Upgrading in Industrial Clusters?' *Regional Studies* 36(9): 1017–1027.

Kaplinsky, Raphael. 2000. 'Globalisation and Unequalisation: What Can be Learned from Value Chain Analysis?' *Journal of Development Studies* 37(2): 117–146.

—————. 2005. *Globalization, Poverty and Inequality: Between a Rock and a Hard Place.* Malden, MA: Polity Press.

Kaplinsky, Rapahel and Masum Farooki. 2011. 'What are the Implications for Global Value Chains when the Market Shifts from the North to the South?' *International Journal of Technological Learning, Innovation and Development* 4(1–3): 13–38.

Kaplinsky, Raphael, Anne Terheggen, and Julia P. Tijaja. 2011. 'China as a Final Market: The Gabon Timber and Thai Cassava Value Chains.' *World Development* 39(7): 1177–1190.

Koopman, Robert, Wang Zhi, and Wei Shang-Jin. 2008. 'How Much of Chinese Exports is Really Made in China? Assessing Domestic Value-Added when Processing Trade is Pervasive.' Working Paper 14109. Cambridge, MA: National Bureau of Economic Research. Available at http://www.nber.org/papers/w14109.

Lee, Joonkoo. 2010. 'Global Commodity Chains and Global Value Chains.' In *The International Studies Encyclopedia*, edited by Robert A. Denemark, 2987–3006. Oxford: Wiley Blackwell.

Lee, Joonkoo, Gary Gereffi, and Stephanie Barrientos. 2011. 'Global Value Chains, Upgrading and Poverty Reduction.' *Capturing the Gains*, Briefing Note 3. November. Available at http://www.capturingthegains.org/pdf/ctg_briefing_note_3.pdf.

Lee, Joonkoo, Gary Gereffi, and Janet Beauvais.2012. 'Global Value Chains and Agrifood Standards: Challenges and Possibilities for Smallholders in Developing Countries.' *Proceedings of the National Academy of Sciences of the United States of America* 109(31): 12326–12331.

Linden, Greg, Kenneth L. Kraemer, and Jason Dedrick. 2009. 'Who Captures Value in a Global Innovation Network? The Case of Apple's iPod.' *Communications of the ACM* 52(3): 140–144.

Lynn, Barry C. 2005. *End of the Line: The Rise and Coming Fall of the Global Corporation.* New York: Doubleday.

Martin, Eric. 2012. 'Move over, BRICs. Here Come the MISTs.' *Business Week*, August 9. Available at http://www.businessweek.com/articles/2012-08-09/move-over-brics-dot-here-come-the-mists.

Making Markets Work Better for the Poor. 2008. *Making Value Chains Work Better for the Poor: A Toolbook for Practitioners of Value Chain Analysis.* London: UK Department of International Development.

Mayer, Frederick and Gary Gereffi. 2010. 'Regulation and Economic Globalization: Prospects and Limits of Private Governance.' *Business and Politics* 12(3): Article 11.

Morris, Mike, Cornela Staritz, and Justin Barnes. 2011. 'Value Chain Dynamics, Local Embeddedness, and Upgrading in the Clothing Sectors of Lesotho and Swaziland.' *International Journal of Technological Learning, Innovation and Development* 4(1–3): 96–119.

Nathan, Dev and Sandip Sarkar. 2011. 'Blood on Your Mobile Phone? Capturing the Gains for Artisanal Miners, Poor Workers and Women.' *Capturing the Gains*. Briefing Note 2. February. Available at http://www.capturingthegains.org/ pdf/ctg_briefing_note_2.pdf.

Neilson, Jeffrey. 2014. 'Value chains, Neoliberalism and Development Practice: The Indonesian Experience.' *Review of International Political Economy* 20(1): 38–69.

Neto, Mario S. and Silvio R. I. Pires. 2010. 'Modular Consortium and Industrial Condominium: Analyzing Two Contemporary Forms of Inter-Firm Governance in the Brazilian Automotive Industry.' Gerpisa Colloquium, Berlin. Available at http://gerpisa.org/en/print/677.

OECD (Organization for Economic Cooperation and Development). 2011. 'Global Value Chains: Preliminary Evidence and Policy Issues.' DSTI/IND(2011)3. Paris: OECD. Available at http://www.oecd.org/dataoecd/18/43/47945400.pdf.

———. 2012. *Policy Priorities for International Trade and Jobs*, edited by Douglas Lippoldt. Available at www.oecd.org/trade/icite.

O'Neill, Jim. 2011. *The Growth Map: Economic Opportunity in the BRICs and Beyond*. New York: Penguin.

Oxfam. 2004. *Trading Away Our Rights: Women Working in Global Supply Chains*. Oxford: Oxfam International.

Palpacuer, Florence, Peter Gibbon, and Lotte Thomsen. 2005. 'New Challenges for Developing Country Suppliers in Global Clothing Chains: A Comparative European Perspective.' *World Development* 33(3): 409–430.

Pisano, Gary P. and Wily C. Shih. 2009. 'Restoring American Competitiveness.' *Harvard Business Review* 87(7/8): 114–125.

———.2012. 'Does America Really Need Manufacturing? Yes, When Production Is Closely Tied to Innovation.' *Harvard Business Review* 90(3): 94–102.

Shih, Willy C. 2009. 'The US Can't Manufacture the Kindle and That's a Problem.' *Harvard Business Review*. Available at http://blogs.hbr.org/hbr/restoring-american-competitiveness/2009/10/the-us-cant-manufacture-the-ki.html.

Smick, David M. 2012. 'What will Replace the Globalization Model?' *The Washington Post*, October 16. Available at http://articles.washingtonpost.com/2012-10-16/opinions/35500171_1_global-trade-chinese-banks-euro-zone.

Stamm, Andreas and Christian von Drachenfels. 2011. 'Value Chain Development: Approaches and Activities by Seven UN Agencies and Opportunities for Interagency Cooperation.' Geneva: ILO. Available at http://www.ilo.org/wcmsp5/groups/public/---ed_emp/---emp_ent/---ifp_seed/documents/publication/wcms_170848.pdf.

Staritz, Cornelia and Stacey Frederick. 2012. 'Summaries of the Country Case Studies on Apparel Industry Development, Structure, and Policies.' In *Sewing Success? Employment, Wages, and Poverty Following the End of the Multi-Fibre Arrangement*, edited by Gladys Lopez-Acevedo and Raymond Robertson, 211–497. Washington, DC: World Bank.

Staritz, Cornelia, Gary Gereffi, and Olivier Cattaneo, eds. 2011. Special Issue on 'Shifting End Markets and Upgrading Prospects in Global Value Chains.' *International Journal of Technological Learning, Innovation and Development* 4(1–3).

Sturgeon, Timothy J. 2009. 'From Commodity Chains to Value Chains: Interdisciplinary Theory Building in an Age of Globalization.' In *Frontiers of Commodity Chain Research*, edited by Jennifer Bair, 110–135. Stanford, CA: Stanford University Press.

Sturgeon, Timothy J. and Gary Gereffi. 2009. 'Measuring Success in the Global Economy: International Trade, Industrial Upgrading, and Business Function Outsourcing in Global Value Chains.' *Transnational Corporations* 18(2): 1–36.

Sturgeon, Timothy J. and Momoko Kawakami. 2011. 'Global Value Chains in the Electronics Industry: Characteristics, Crisis, and Upgrading Opportunities in Firms from Developing Countries.' *International Journal of Technological Learning, Innovation and Development* 4(1–3): 120–147.

Sturgeon, Timothy J. and Johannes Van Biesebroeck. 2011. 'Global Value Chains in the Automotive Industry: An Enhanced Role for Developing Countries?' *International Journal of Technological Learning, Innovation and Development* 4(1–3): 181–205.

Sturgeon, Timothy J., Johannes Van Biesebroeck, and Gary Gereffi. 2008. 'Value Chains, Networks and Clusters: Reframing the Global Automotive Industry.' *Journal of Economic Geography* 8(3): 297–321.

UNCTAD (United Nations Conference on Trade and Development). 2013. 'Global Value Chains and Development: Investment and Value Added Trade in the Global Economy – A Preliminary Analysis.' Geneva: UNCTAD. Available at http://unctad.org/en/ PublicationsLibrary/diae2013d1_en.pdf.

UNIDO (United Nations Industrial Development Organization). 2011. *Diagnostics for Industrial Value Chain Development: An Integrated Tool*. Vienna: UNIDO. Available at http://www. unido.org/fileadmin/ user_media/MDGs/IVC_Diagnostic_Tool.pdf.

Urquidi, V. L. 1991. 'The Prospects for Economic Transformation in Latin America: Opportunities and Resistances.' *LASA Forum* 22(3): 1–9.

USAID (United States Agency for International Development). 2012. 'Value Chain Development.' MicroLINKS wiki. Available at .

USITC (United States International Trade Commission). 2011. *The Economic Effects of Significant US Import Restraints: Seventh Update 2011*. Special Topic: Global Supply Chains. Publication 4253. Washington, DC: USITC.

Vernon, Raymond. 1971. *Sovereignty at Bay: The Multinational Spread of US Enterprises*. New York: Basic Books.

Wadhwa, Vivek, Una K. De Vitton, and Gary Gereffi. 2008. 'How the Disciple Became the Guru: Workforce Development in India's R&D Labs.' Report prepared for the Ewing Marion Kauffman Foundation. Available at .

Weatherspoon, Dave. D and Thomas Reardon. 2003. 'The Rise of Supermarkets in Africa: Implications for Agrifood Systems and the Rural Poor.' *Development Policy Review* 21(3): 333–355.

Webber, C. Martin and Patrick Labaste. 2009. *Building Competitiveness in Africa's Agriculture: A Guide to Value Chain Concepts and Applications*. Washington, DC: World Bank.

WEF (World Economic Forum). 2012. 'The Shifting Geography of Global Value Chains: Implications for Developing Countries and Trade Policy.' Global Agenda Council on the Global Trade System, WEF. Available at http://www3.weforum.org/docs/WEF_GAC_ GlobalTradeSystem_Report_2012.pdf.

Will, Margret. 2011. 'Integrating Smallholders into Global Supply Chains.' GTZ Division Economic Development and Employment and Division Agriculture, Fisheries and Food.

April. Available at http://www.giz.de/Themen/ en/dokumente/gtz2010-en-globalgap-group-certification.pdf.

World Bank. 1993. *The East Asian Miracle*. Oxford: Oxford University Press.

————. 2011. *The Role of International Business in Aid for Trade: Building Capacity for Trade in Developing Countries*. Washington, DC: World Bank.

WTO (World Trade Organisation). 2011. *International Trade Statistics 2011*. Geneva: WTO.

WTO and IDE-JETRO. 2011. 'Trade Patterns and Global Value Chains in East Asia: From Trade in Goods to Trade in Tasks.' Geneva and Tokyo: WTO and Institute of Developing Economies. Available at http://www.ide.go.jp/English/Press/pdf/20110606_news.pdf.

15

Protectionism and Global Value Chains

These are extremely unsettled times in the global economy. In a referendum on June 23, 2016, the British electorate voted to leave the European Union (Brexit), and on November 8, 2016, Donald Trump won the US presidential election on the basis of an 'America First' doctrine that could potentially undermine a broad range of economic, political, and military partnerships that previous US administrations have been building since the end of the Second World War. Taken together, Brexit and the election of Donald Trump portend to some 'the end of the Anglo-American order' (Buruma, 2016), a grand alliance that presumed that a Pax Americana, along with a unified Europe, would keep the democratic world safe and capitalist economies prosperous. Instead of the triumph of Anglo-American exceptionalism, the current 'taking back our country' mantra of both English and American nationalists signals a retreat from the world that Anglo-Americans envisioned after 1945.

Meanwhile, just a few days before the inauguration of newly elected US president Trump, China's President Xi Jinping was at the World Economic Forum's annual meeting in Davos, Switzerland, proclaiming himself the new champion of free trade and globalization. Klaus Schwab, the founder of the World Economic Forum, endorsed China's willingness to take over this mantle from an apparently faltering US in introducing President Xi: 'In a world marked by great uncertainty and volatility, the international community is looking to China' (Mishra, 2018). China's spectacular ascent from a relatively isolated, agrarian economy at the end of the 1970s to the world's leading exporter and second-largest economy (after the US) today is a complex story of globalization with Chinese characteristics. Xi's state-controlled market economy has almost none of the openness associated with classic notions of free trade. Instead, China has embraced a style of 'nationalistic mercantilism' that shares many similarities with earlier East Asian success stories like Japan, South Korea, and Singapore (Prestowitz, 2017). But China's unique claim to fame may have been its ability to shift from a labor-intensive, low-cost export strategy ('a race to the bottom') to a high-tech, innovation-driven strategy ('a race to the top') at an unprecedented speed and scale that disrupted the hitherto dominant economies in the West.

To understand the current protectionist moment in the global economy, and indeed, the rapidly evolving development strategies of both the US and China, one needs to examine not only the interplay between interventionist and market forces, but also the shifting patterns of organization in the global economy. This analysis involves several intertwined narratives. The first narrative outlines the institutional origins of the contemporary trade-oriented global value chain (GVC) economy. Although the postwar Anglo-American system espouses the principles of free trade, the shift to an export model of industrialization following the debt crisis of the 1980s also involved activist states and assorted protectionist policies. The second narrative highlights the roles of leading international organizations in the United Nations (UN) development regime, particularly the World Trade Organization (WTO) and the World Bank, in accelerating the adoption of the GVC approach to counter the perceived protectionist threat stemming from the 2008–2009 global economic crisis. Finally, the third narrative focuses on the new era of economic nationalism and protectionism associated with phenomena such as Brexit and the presidency of Donald Trump. In fact, the escalating competition between the world's two economic superpowers, the US and China, goes far beyond tariff disputes. Rather, it involves a strategic battle over who will control the digital economy and the advanced technologies associated with it. This contest features a new generation of corporate and political actors utilizing cutting-edge technologies and yet to be finalized rules of the game that are redefining the future of manufacturing, the nature of work, and where and how value is being created and captured in the global economy.

Emergence of the GVC Economy

The roots of contemporary economic globalization go back to the end of the Second World War and a distinctive Anglo-American vision of an open international economy. The regime set up at the end of World War II has been characterized as 'embedded liberalism' (Ruggie, 1982), where US hegemony took the form of a multilateralism that buffered the US and its main allies against the socially disruptive domestic adjustment costs of the new international order centered around global trade and investment. The pillars of this postwar regime were three Bretton Woods institutions that anchored the US-led system: the General Agreement on Tariffs and Trade (GATT), set up in 1947 to promote multilateralism in trade; the International Monetary Fund (IMF), designed to manage international balance of payments using fixed exchange rates pegged to the US dollar (which in turn was pegged to gold); and the World Bank, established in 1944 with the mission of financing the reconstruction of European nations devastated by World War II, but whose mandate was subsequently expanded to foster economic growth and eradicate poverty in less developed countries. These three organizations undergirded a postwar capitalist system in which foreign direct investment by transnational corporations (TNCs) and international trade thrived in the Cold War era.

In the late 1960s and 1970s, the center of gravity for the global manufacturing system set up by TNCs began to shift to the developing world. Fröbel et al. (1980) likened the surge of manufactured exports from labor-intensive export platforms in low-wage economies to a 'new international division of labor' that used modern transport and communication technologies to establish a global segmentation of production. Initially, these offshore processing programs were regional in nature and set up with neighboring countries, typified in the 1960s by the US production-sharing or 'twin plant' program with Mexico (Grunwald and Flamm, 1985), as well as German export-processing zones for apparel assembly in Central and Eastern Europe (Fröbel et al., 1980). But with the proliferation of free trade agreements in the 1980s and 1990s, the fall of the Berlin Wall in 1989, subsequent market openings in Eastern Europe, and China's decision to join the WTO in 2001 and prioritize export promotion, offshoring became a pervasive global phenomenon.

In retrospect, the assembly-oriented export production in the newly industrializing countries was merely an early stage in the transformation of the global economy into 'a highly complex, kaleidoscopic structure involving the *fragmentation* of many production processes, and their *geographical relocation* on a global scale in ways which slice through national boundaries' (Dicken, 2003: 9). In the 1990s and 2000s, the industries and activities encompassed by global supply chains grew exponentially, covering not only finished goods but also components and subassemblies, and affecting not just manufacturing industries (Engardio et al., 2003), but also agriculture and food production (Fold and Pritchard, 2004) as well as a broad range of simple (back-office) and complex (knowledge-oriented) services (Engardio and Einhorn, 2005; Wadhwa et al., 2008; Fernandez-Stark et al., 2011).

The GVC economy is structurally different from its predecessors. Whereas in earlier periods international trade was largely in finished goods, today almost 60% of world trade consists of intermediate goods and services that are incorporated in GVCs (UNCTAD, 2013: 122). A consequence is that the import content of exports has grown dramatically in a GVC world: in 1990, the import content of exports was 20%; by 2010, it was 40%; and in 2030, it is expected to be about 60% (Lamy, 2013). Moreover, the developing-country share in global value-added trade doubled from 20% to 40% between 1990 and 2010 (UNCTAD, 2013: 133–135). Two decades ago, 60% of world trade was between developed countries (North–North), 30% involved developed and developing nations (North–South), and just 10% was South–South. By 2020, these three patterns of global trade are likely to be split equally.

Economic Crises and the Neoliberal Turn

Investment and trade in the global economy expanded rapidly in the postwar era until a spike in oil prices in 1973 and again in the late 1970s led to a debt crisis for developing countries that engaged in heightened borrowing, lured by low-interest loans offered by private banks with an influx of funds from oil-rich countries that believed sovereign debt was a safe investment. Latin America was particularly hard hit, and the debt crisis of 1982[1] was the most severe in the region's history, resulting in what some have called the 'lost decade' in Latin American development. In order to avoid default on their loans, debtor countries accepted the intervention of the IMF, but restructuring came at a steep price: the IMF forced Latin American and other debtor nations to adopt fiscal austerity programs and deep structural adjustment reforms that favored free-market capitalism but aggravated poverty and social inequalities (Felix, 1990).

The debt crisis of the 1980s ushered in a marked turn away from state-centered approaches such as the import-substitution industrialization (ISI) model popular in Latin America and elsewhere in the developing world (Gereffi and Wyman, 1990) to the market-oriented 'neoliberal' policies of privatization, deregulation, and free trade known as the 'Washington Consensus' (Williamson, 1990). This neoliberal turn in the early 1980s, associated most vividly with President Ronald Reagan in the US and Prime Minister Margaret Thatcher in the United Kingdom, gave rise to a 'market fundamentalism' that delegitimized the interventionist policies of development economics and the ISI model in the 1950s and 1960s (Krugman, 2006). It became fashionable to dismiss any effort by the government to pursue structural transformation of the economy, and 'industrial policy took a backseat to Washington Consensus policies' (Stiglitz et al., 2013: 6).[2]

This ideological and policy shift thrust the Bretton Woods organizations squarely into the development arena. There was an unprecedented centralization of authority and restriction of development policy space by the World Bank and the IMF, which engaged in coordinated lending programs[3] that underpinned the policy prescriptions and conditionality endorsed by the Washington Consensus (Babb, 2013). Yet, even at its most dominant, the Washington Consensus met resistance from developing countries frustrated with their lack of 'policy space' (Wade, 2003). There was a growing chorus of civil society opposition, and even within the WTO, emerging economies of the South—most notably China, India, and Brazil, but also middle powers such as Indonesia, South Africa, and the Philippines—demanded trade policies more aligned to their circumstances. The opportunities for 'strategic compliance' (Chorev, 2013) in combating the external pressures of neoliberalism actually were enhanced by the spread of GVCs linking TNC lead firms with legions of developing country suppliers (Gereffi, 2014).

The financial crisis that began in late 2007 with the catastrophe of the subprime mortgage market in the US metastasized into a full-blown international banking crisis with the collapse of the investment bank Lehman Brothers on September 15, 2008. Excessive risk-taking by banks such as Lehman Brothers magnified the impact of the crisis globally and led to massive bail-outs of financial institutions to prevent a possible crash of the world financial system. The financial crisis prompted a global economic downturn, the Great Recession of 2008-2009, which precipitated 'the great trade collapse': between the third quarter of 2008 and the second quarter of 2009, world trade experienced the steepest fall in recorded history and the deepest since the Great Depression (Baldwin, 2009). The interconnected nature of global supply chains amplified the sudden, severe and synchronized drop in trade since almost every nation's imports and exports fell at the same time. Even though world trade bounced back relatively quickly after its dramatic decline in 2008–2009, for many the crisis revealed the end of the neoliberal moment. UK Prime Minister Gordon Brown famously declared an 'end to the Washington Consensus' at the 2009 G20 meeting (Babb, 2013: 285).

Adoption of GVC Analysis by WTO and the World Bank

For the WTO, the economic crisis of 2008 presented something of an existential threat.[4] Spurred by criticism from developing nations that the Uruguay Round of multilateral trade negotiations that led to the creation of the WTO in 1995 was tilted toward the wealthier countries, the WTO in 2001 orchestrated an enormous global negotiation dubbed the 'Doha Development Agenda' (launched in Doha, Qatar). The talks dragged on for seven years, but by the summer of 2008 there was great optimism around the WTO's Geneva headquarters that the round could be concluded later that year. It was not to be. When the economic crisis hit, already skittish nations balked. For the advanced industrial economies, the rapid rise in unemployment made the domestic politics of supporting trade agreements impossible. For developing countries, free trade as an engine of development suddenly looked like an empty promise.

The concern in Geneva was not only that the Doha talks could fail, but also that many countries would be tempted to adopt protectionist measures that would undo years of progress towards freer global trade. *The Economist* (2008) summed up the mood, 'Rich countries collectively face the severest recession since the Second World War ... This news is bad enough in itself; but it also poses the biggest threat to open markets in the modern era of globalization. There is a risk that in their discomfort governments turn to an old, but false, friend: protectionism'. With the erosion of confidence in the nostrums of neoliberalism, free trade advocates needed a fresh framework with new language to make the case for trade.

Pascal Lamy, who was Director-General of the WTO from 2005 to 2013, had served as the European Union's chief trade negotiator for the first years of the Doha negotiation. He witnessed the rocky start to the negotiations, knew all the main players, and arrived confident that he could bring the negotiations to a successful conclusion. When the negotiations broke down in the fall of 2008, however, Lamy was forced to reassess. As the financial abyss deepened and the specter of protectionism grew, Lamy searched for a novel way to demonstrate the importance of maintaining open markets. 'The WTO needed to provide a different narrative, which was a consequence of the 2008 failure,' he remembered (Lamy, 2014). Almost overnight, Lamy became a champion of the GVC concept, seeing in it a way to explain why it was imperative to maintain free trade. 'If you are importing over 50% of your exports, then imposing measures to protect producers is decreasingly logical,' he later explained (Lamy, 2014). If you raised trade barriers to limit imports, you were just making yourself less competitive.

The WTO's embrace of GVC analysis under Lamy's leadership is illustrated by the recasting of its 'Aid for Trade' initiative, a partnership with the Organization for Economic Cooperation and Development (OECD) intended to foster trade among developing, and particularly least-developed, countries. Prior to the financial debacle, there was little attention to GVCs in the discourse on Aid for Trade at either OECD or the WTO. As stated in the introduction to the first biennial Aid for Trade report in 2007, the goal of aid for trade was to 'better harness trade for development,' but there was not a single reference to value chains (WTO/OECD, 2007). The 2011 biennial report referenced GVCs 15 times and reported that GVCs had become a growing priority for countries responding to the survey, and we see the first indication of value chains as part of national strategies (WTO/OECD, 2011: 32). By 2013, GVCs were the central focus of the biennial review (WTO, 2013). A huge banner at the WTO's headquarters in Geneva announced the theme of the meeting: 'Aid for Trade in Review: Connecting to Global Value Chains.'

By the summer of 2013, the language of GVCs was central to the discourse about Aid for Trade at the OECD and the WTO. Less clear, however, is whether the actual pattern of aid had changed as much as the rhetoric. Mayer and Milberg (2013) found that a substantial portion of Aid for Trade was essentially 'old wine in new bottles' and that only a small portion of aid truly used GVC analysis to help connect firms to GVCs.

The story of the World Bank's uptake of the GVC approach parallels that of the WTO and OECD. The World Bank largely ignored GVCs prior to the onset of the financial crisis; the Great Recession spurred demand for a new way of thinking about the nexus of trade and development, and the GVC framework met this need. But in other ways, the World Bank story is quite distinct. This is perhaps not surprising given the much larger scale of the Bank, its sprawling organization and its more complex mission. Whereas at the WTO top leaders embraced GVCs in the immediate aftermath of the global economic recession of 2008–09 and launched major initiatives that drove change within those organizations, at the World Bank, the story is more bottom-up than top-down—a story that begins with a handful of policy entrepreneurs located in a sub-unit within the organization who first recognized the significance of GVCs as a useful analytic tool for promoting development through trade.

Prior to the crisis, value chains do not figure in any of the reports issued by the World Bank's International Trade Unit, part of the Poverty Reduction and Economic Management (PREM) division that provided policy advice and technical assistance to developing countries. When the 2008 financial crisis hit, the first reaction of top economists in the trade unit was along the same lines as those at WTO and the OECD: fear of rising protectionism. The titles of two publications raced out in the first year of the financial crisis illustrate the point: *The Fateful Allure of Protectionism: Taking Stock for the G8* (Evenett et al., 2009a) and *Effective Crisis Response and Openness: Implications for the Trading System* (Evenett et al., 2009b). Both sought to make the case for continuing on the path towards global free trade and warned that a protectionist response would make matters worse.

But the financial crisis also created an opening for a non-traditional way of thinking, both because the old rationale for free trade had less credence than before and, curiously, because within a year the pressures for protectionism were a great deal less than expected. In 2010, the World Bank's public adoption of the GVC approach was heralded in a new book, *Global Value Chains in a Postcrisis World: A Development Perspective* (Cattaneo et al., 2010). This publication, which featured a number of leading GVC researchers, highlighted the resilience of a global economy organized around GVCs due in large part to the growing importance of supply chains linking producers and markets in South–South trade, as well as more traditional North–South trade and investment.

The Protectionist Threat Redux: Trump and NAFTA

After the 2008–2009 global economic slump, fears of a sustained trade slowdown abated, buoyed by the strong growth performance of the major emerging economies, especially China. Large-scale negotiations centered around two mega-regional trade agreements: the Trans-Pacific Partnership (TPP) and the Transatlantic Trade and Investment Partnership (TTIP). Beyond simply increasing trade ties, mega-regional deals are deep integration partnerships that seek to improve regulatory compatibility and provide a rules-based framework for ironing out differences in investment and business climates. The significance of TPP and TTIP was their size and scope: they aimed to achieve extensive liberalization of both goods and services encompassing at least a quarter of world trade (TPP: 26.3%; TTIP: 43.6%) and augment foreign direct investment as well (World Economic Forum, 2014).

Fulfilling one of his signature campaign pledges, President Trump's initial executive order in his first full day in office on January 23, 2017 was to withdraw from TPP negotiations, the sweeping 12-nation trade deal accounting for 40% of global gross domestic product that Trump railed against as a US jobs killer (Aleem, 2017). Although Trump's fulminations to junk TTIP, the European counterpart of the TPP, have thus far not been realized, talks between the US and the European Union remain stalled since Trump's election (Bravo and Chatterley, 2018). US and Mexico talks on the North American Free Trade Agreement (NAFTA), however, have been much more active and contentious.

On April 27, 2017, after panicked calls from Canadian Prime Minister Justin Trudeau and Mexican President Enrique Peña Nieto, President Trump backed away from his threat to issue an executive order withdrawing from NAFTA. 'I was all set to terminate,' said Trump, 'I looked forward to terminating. I was going to do it' (Parker et al., 2017).[5] The calls might have helped. But apparently what really changed his mind was a map that showed the parts of the country that would be hurt badly if the US withdrew. In 2016, the US exported $2.7 billion worth of maize to Mexico and Canada. More than a quarter of American maize exports go to Mexico, also one of the leading importers of US soybeans. American farmers would be hit hard if the US dismantled NAFTA and Trump knew it.

Actually, US manufacturers also stood to absorb significant losses because of the intertwined nature of North American supply chains: If you make it harder for the US to import parts, it becomes more difficult for US manufacturers to export finished and intermediate goods that include these imported inputs. The North American automotive industry is a striking example. US exports of cars and components total about $100 billion; in 2015, Canada was the largest export market for US automotive parts ($22 billion) and Mexico was a close second ($20.2 billion). A large share of US parts exports return to the US as imports in finished vehicles and sub-assemblies (e.g., wiring harnesses or brake systems) from our NAFTA neighbors. Thus, US automotive imports from Mexico contain 40% US content, and imports from Canada are 25% US content by value. By contrast, for goods imported from China, only 4% of their value is US-made (Center for Automotive Research, 2017: 2, 9). Thus, US suppliers are far more likely to be hurt by a protectionist response to NAFTA partners than to China. In sum, not all imports are created equal in terms of their potential impact on US producers, workers, and consumers.

Much has changed since the signing of NAFTA more than two decades ago. Today a nationalistic approach to trade may have unintended consequences that serve neither global nor national interests. To see why, let's take a look at the main reasons the Trump administration has proposed for rethinking trade relations: bringing jobs back, reducing trade deficits, and punishing nations who don't play fair.

Bringing Jobs Back

The US administration is considering measures to 'bring jobs back to America' by cutting corporate taxes and eliminating regulations, but also by raising tariffs and trade barriers. These proposals are a response to the decision of many US companies, especially in consumer goods industries, to move part of their production abroad to reduce costs. It happened first to simple products like apparel, footwear, and toys. Later it happened to automobiles, ships, aircraft, and electronics (Engardio et al., 2003; Engardio and Einhorn, 2005).

When these industries moved offshore, they generally transferred the relatively labor-intensive stages of production. Some of those industries may return to the US—either in response to new US policies or, more likely, because production technology has become more automated. This is the case for smartphones and electronics, and even consumer appliances like refrigerators and microwave ovens (Immelt, 2012). But even if the same companies that left the US now return, they will bring back far fewer jobs than when the work was first done in the US. Besides, the new jobs will not help most of the people who lost them.

A well-known and relatively dramatic example is the Apple iPhone. Apple Inc., the world's largest information technology firm by revenue and the top company in terms of market capitalization (over $800 billion in 2017),[6] manufactures virtually all of its products overseas. The vast majority are made in China by Taiwanese manufacturing giant Foxconn, the world's biggest electronics contract manufacturer. In 2012 Apple had about 43,000 employees in the US; Foxconn employed over one million people in China alone in factory complexes like Foxconn City (near Shenzhen) where the iPhone is assembled, which has 230,000 employees, many working six days a week for up to 12 hours a day (Duhigg and Bradsher, 2012). Another Foxconn 'factory city' is located in Zhengzhou in central China, which can employ up to 350,000 workers, many of whom earn about $1.90 an hour doing final assembly, testing and packaging of iPhones, among other products. About half of all iPhones are now made in the huge Zhengzhou hub, which can produce 500,000 iPhones a day (roughly 350 a minute) in an assembly process of about 400 steps to make an iPhone (Barboza, 2016).

It is instructive to compare Foxconn's operations for Apple in China with a new plant that it plans to set up in the US. On July 26, 2017, President Trump announced that Foxconn will build a $10 billion flat-screen TV manufacturing facility in Wisconsin. Foxconn officials claim this investment will create up to 13,000 new jobs in Wisconsin, but the deal is being criticized for the $3 billion in taxpayer-funded incentives the company will receive and various environmental concessions offered to Foxconn. In addition, there is evidence that previous Foxconn commitments to construct new facilities in Pennsylvania, Brazil, and elsewhere have fizzled or fallen short of expectations (Barboza, 2017). While the jury is still out on whether Foxconn will actually make more of its products in the US, Foxconn is indeed shifting large-scale production operations beyond China, with recent factories in India, Vietnam, Brazil, Mexico, the Czech Republic, Hungary, and Slovakia. However, Foxconn's newer plants are increasingly automated,[7] suggesting that job creation may be an elusive goal (Glaser, 2017).

Hurting Trade Partners—and National Interests

Since the mid-1960s, the US had encouraged developing countries to adopt export-oriented industrialization. Most of its allies did just that. South Korea, Taiwan, Mexico, and other countries opened their doors to foreign direct investment and began to export to the US and other developed economies (Gereffi and Wyman, 1990). Now the Trump administration is proposing to tax these imports, which would hurt these export nations' major sources of growth. The same was true for poorer, later reformers like Cambodia, China, and Vietnam.

Americans may not consider some of these countries allies, but protectionist policies would not necessarily help US companies or workers. Many of the medium- and high-tech US manufacturing companies have set up regional and global supply chains to make finished products using imported parts. This is obvious for automobiles, but it is also true for medical devices, electronics, and aircraft. If tariffs are raised on imported parts, the companies that make the final products in global supply chains become less competitive. They would have to either raise their prices on final products, or buy all the needed parts from domestic sources—a virtual impossibility in today's cross-border supply-chain world.

Relying on Regional Value Chains

Trump has labeled China a currency manipulator and accused friends and foes alike of unfair trade practices. In some cases, these charges are being dialed down. We should try talking with our trade partners across the world who have benefited from access to US markets. We have done this before. But the negotiators would do well to remember that success in such talks would generally lead to more trade, not less. During the early 1980s, the US dealt with trade imbalances with Japan through voluntary export restraints (VERs). In 1981, for example, VERs limited Japanese auto imports to 1.7 million cars (Benjamin, 1999). VERs remained in place until the mid-1990s. This policy had the effect of requiring many of the Japanese automakers (later also European and Korean companies) to build plants in the US. It also revitalized US automotive supply chains. US protectionist policies encouraged inward foreign direct investment in higher technology industries; this created US jobs as well.[8]

Today, international competition is based on region competing with region, not simply country competing with country. Again, take the US automobile industry. It is really a North American industrial complex spread across Canada, the US, and Mexico (Sturgeon et al., 2008). The same is true of the European automobile industry or the consumer electronics sector in East Asia. China's success in electronics is the consequence of an intricately organized East Asian electronics ecosystem. China's final goods exports rely on imported components from Japan, South Korea, Taiwan, Singapore, and other East Asian neighbors (Grimes and Sun, 2016; Sun and Grimes, 2016; 2018). In much the same way, many US exports rely on components made in Canada and Mexico, and other Central and South American neighbors.

In all of these cases, regional value chains are competing with each other. North America is competing with Europe and East Asia, rather than the US competing with Germany and China. The national approach is an outdated framework from the economic standpoint (Baldwin, 2011). Regional and global supply chains require a new calculus of winners and losers involving workers and companies, as well as consumers[9] (Gereffi and Lee, 2012). If one thinks about trade this way, the US should be figuring out ways to expand NAFTA, not a plan to end it.

The United States and China: It Looks a Lot Like a Trade War

In March and April of 2018, the US administration initiated a new round of import tariffs, but with a more specific focus on China, the country deemed to pose the biggest threat to US jobs and industries. On March 8, President Trump imposed a 25% tariff on steel imports and a 10% tariff on aluminum imports, with exemptions for Canada and Mexico, ostensibly to protect US national security (Baker and Swanson, 2018; US Department of Commerce, 2018). In early April, Trump ratcheted up the trade war rhetoric with China, listing more than 1,300 imported goods from China that would face a 25% US tariff. These products, worth about $50 billion, included flat-screen televisions, medical devices, and aircraft parts. China immediately struck back at the US with its own tariffs, also worth $50 billion, on 106 types of American goods with a heavy focus on agricultural products, including soybeans, corn, cotton, beef, frozen orange juice, tobacco, and whiskey, which come largely from Republican-dominated states that form Trump's core political base in the US (Bradsher and Myers, 2018).

What is going on here? Is this confrontation likely to lead to an all-out trade war between the US and China, whose bilateral trade was valued at $650 billion in 2016? That seems unlikely.

The current trade dispute between the US and China is actually the harbinger of a much deeper strategic competition between the world's two largest and most dynamic economies at the outset of the 21st century. The focus of this competition is not primarily trade in manufactured and agricultural goods, bilateral trade balances, or even the number of US jobs affected by trade. It is about the technologies of the future and the contending development strategies in the US and China used to bolster each country's national, regional and global interests.

Clashes between the US and China must be interpreted with a foreward-looking perspective. The link between US trade policies and broader national interests is clearly articulated by Peter Navarro, Director of the Office of Trade and Manufacturing Policy in the Trump administration:

> Basically what we have here is a situation where every American understands that China is stealing our intellectual property. They are forcing the transfer of our technology when companies go to China, and by doing that they steal jobs from America, they steal factories from America, and we run an unprecedented $370 billion a year trade deficit in goods. This is an unsustainable situation…What is at stake here are the industries of the future: artificial intelligence, robotics, quantum computing. And what is at stake is not just our economic prosperity; it's also our national security because many of these industries of the future have profound military implications (*NBC News*, 2018).

In instituting his latest round of tariffs against China, President Trump cited Beijing's government-driven efforts to retool its economy by building up high-tech industries through the country's ambitious 'Made in China 2025' program (Perlez et al., 2017). Unveiled in 2015, Beijing's 'Made in China 2025' is a national industrial policy that aims to pioneer state-of-the-art technologies for industries like aerospace, maritime and rail transport, power and agricultural equipment, new-energy vehicles, and biopharma products. Many US and European companies fear the program will sponsor state-supported competitors, and it extends long-standing Chinese policies that require foreign companies to hand over technology or take on domestic joint-venture partners as the price for doing business in China. This strategic battle is still in its early stages. However, the tools of GVC analysis remain central to understand how the technological revolution connected to the emerging digital economy is structured, where the lead companies are located, and how value creation and innovation will take place. A preliminary sketch of a few of these issues is provided below with a focus on the two world leaders in this arena, the US and China.

Beyond Protectionism: GVCs and Innovation in the Digital Economy

The rise of the digital economy and its potential impact on trade, productivity and jobs in both developed and developing countries is a hot topic. From the perspective of GVCs, there is strong interest in identifying the companies that are most active in the digital economy, including their business models and internationalization strategies, as well as likely changes in the organization and governance of GVCs. Other concerns include the implications of the digital economy for advanced manufacturing, the future of work, and how the nature of innovation might alter who creates and captures value in the global economy.

Digital Economy Lead Firms in the US and China

New firms are leading the charge in the digital economy. The *2017 World Investment Report* on the digital economy published by UNCTAD (2017) lays out what it calls 'the architecture of the digital economy' in its classification of six types of digital and ICT multinational enterprises (MNEs)[10] (see Figure 15.1).

Figure 15.1 The Architecture of the Digital Economy

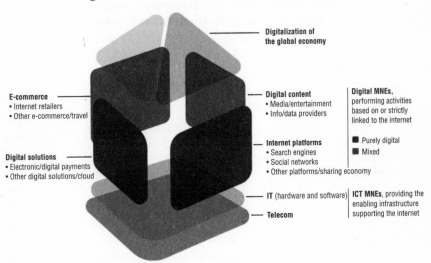

Source: UNCTAD, 2017: 167.

- In the *digital MNE* group, characterized by the central role of the internet in their operating and delivery model, are four types of companies: (a) internet platforms (e.g., Google, Baidu, Facebook and eBay); (b) digital solutions (e.g., PayPal); (c) E-commerce (e.g., Amazon, Alibaba, Expedia); and (d) digital content (e.g., Tencent, Time Warner, Netflix).

- In the *ICT MNE* group are the IT companies selling hardware and software, as well as telecom firms that provide the infrastructure that makes the internet accessible to individuals and businesses: (e) IT MNEs (e.g., Apple, Samsung, Foxconn, Intel, Microsoft, SAP, Wipro); and (f) telecom MNEs (e.g., AT&T, China Mobile).

A different set of business models in the digital economy is provided in a book called *The Network Imperative* (Libert et al., 2016: 14-15). Instead of outlining the full digital economy ecosystem, as UNCTAD does, the typology offered by Libert et al. highlights different roles that shape the strategies of companies in the digital economy: (a) *asset builders* deliver value through the use of physical goods (physical capital); (b) *service providers* deliver value through skilled people (human capital); (c) *technology creators* deliver value through ideas (intellectual capital); and (d) *network orchestrators* deliver value through their connectivity (network capital).

A more fundamental concept that underpins many digital-economy firms is the rise of 'the platform economy' where the application of big data, powerful algorithms and cloud computing change the nature of work and basic supply-chain relationships in the economy (Kenney and Zysman, 2016). These platform-based markets are built on an infrastructure enabled by the internet and related information-technology services, which permit online companies like Amazon, Alibaba, Etsy, Facebook, Google, Uber, and Airbnb to thrive. The propensity of 'platform companies' to use digital technologies to remain asset light but create enormous returns to scale through their ubiquitous supply-chain presence helps to explain the remarkable fact that the top five US companies by market capitalization are all internet-based firms: Apple ($807 billion); Alphabet/Google ($677 billion); Microsoft ($608 billion); Facebook ($497 billion); and Amazon ($467 billion) (CNBC, 2017).

Companies located in the US and China are key drivers in the digital economy. US and Chinese firms are particularly well positioned in the most dynamic digital-economy markets:

- Google and Baidu—the world's largest online search companies
- Amazon and Alibaba—the world's largest internet retailers
- Facebook and Tencent—the world's largest social network providers

In addition, of the world's 262 global 'unicorns' (defined as startups valued at $1 billion or above), many of which are linked to the digital economy, nearly one-half (47%) are located in the US, one in three (34%) are in China, and one in five (19%) in the rest of the world (MGI, 2017: 2).

China has built a unique digital ecosystem around its giant BAT internet companies (as Baidu, Alibaba, and Tencent are collectively known). Baidu accounts for over 80% of the online search-engine market share in China and is shifting its strategic focus to mobile services and artificial intelligence, with commercial applications in various sectors like autonomous vehicle technology. Tencent's social media services include WeChat, a messaging app first released in 2011 that has more than 900 million active users in 2017 (MGI, 2017: 9).

For the Alibaba Group, Wu (2018) found that over the course of its history in China, Alibaba actually encompasses all four types of digital MNEs mentioned in UNCTAD's *World Investment Report* (2017: 165–168): (1) the Alibaba group itself, created in 1999, is listed as China's largest e-commerce firm; (2) the launching of Taobao.com in 2003 helped push eBay out the China market, and eBay is listed by UNCTAD as an 'internet platform' company; (3) the creation of Alipay in 2004, like PayPal, would be a 'digital solutions' company in UNCTAD's scheme; and (4) the creation of Alibaba Cloud, which was set up in 2009 and is involved in data mining and analytics, exemplifies a 'digital content' company. Thus, the evolving business strategy of an internet lead firm like Alibaba requires us to combine many of the categories used by UNCTAD to describe the digital economy.

In their discussion of the BAT companies in China's ICT sector, Sun and Grimes (2018: 116–120) show that all of these internet giants are aggressively diversifying their business portfolios in China and beyond from their initial monopolized position in search engines (Baidu), instant messaging (Tencent) and e-commerce (Alibaba): Tencent and Baidu are seeking to enter the e-commerce field; Alibaba wants to enter the social network and entertainment sectors; and Baidu is forging inroads into the social networking arena.[11]

A similar pattern can be observed for competition between leading US digital-economy firms like Amazon, and traditional legacy retailers like Walmart. Amazon's decision to buy the high-end grocery chain Whole Foods as well as physical bookstores signifies a shift from 'network orchestrator' to 'asset builder', while Walmart is moving in the opposite direction by strengthening its online ordering channels (Irwin, 2017). This hybridization of business models between e-commerce and traditional physical retailers suggests that it is a mistake to simply pit the old (goods-oriented) economy versus the new (digital) economy. Instead the internet can be used by established leaders in both producer-driven and buyer-driven GVCs to increase productivity, and create a durable edge for large companies that can use sophisticated supply-chain management and new technologies to keep prices lower than niche players and entrench their competitive advantage (Gereffi, 2001a).

How Will the Digital Economy Affect the Governance of GVCs?

The increasing digitization of supply chains and the emergence of dynamic internet-based lead firms signals a new era in the global economy. The question from a GVC governance standpoint is whether digital-economy MNEs will complement or displace incumbent lead firms (Gereffi, 2001a; 2001b; Rehnberg and Ponte, 2017). Three scenarios are possible (Brun et al., 2017).

The first option is a *complementarity scenario* in which digital-economy MNEs add dramatically to value creation in the global economy, enhancing existing levels of employment and investment across industries, but they do not replace established lead firms. In this situation, the digital firms create products, employment and investment that augment the existing structure of trade, investment and development alongside the traditional lead firms in physical goods-based GVCs.

Second, a *displacement scenario* could occur in which digital-economy MNEs disrupt existing industries and challenge established lead-firm business models. Displacement could be rapid or gradual. In the rapid-displacement version, technology change alters the traditional firm's business model to such an extent that it does not have time to undergo the organizational changes needed to adapt. In the gradual displacement version, digital MNEs become increasingly powerful connection points or 'digital hubs' between the customer, manufacturer and supplier due to their ability to use Industry 4.0 technologies to synchronize purchasing, manufacturing, and delivery. Due to their ability to achieve global sales with reduced foreign assets, digital MNEs in this scenario eventually displace the 'heavier' asset-based lead firms.

Finally, a *hybridization scenario* could occur in which Industry 4.0 technologies are successfully adopted by the existing lead firms to improve their efficiency and competitiveness. This appears to be a likely outcome in many industries for two reasons. First, social media and online services now touch nearly every aspect of consumers' lives, and established manufacturers and retailers either incorporate these services or they lose business. Second, some of the largest digital companies like Amazon, Google and Microsoft are making significant investments in infrastructure, like cloud computing services and physical distribution outlets, or they develop applications for their new technologies in physical goods industries like transportation or food services. Therefore, hybridization can be a win-win scenario for leading firms in both real-economy and digital-based supply chains.

For Innovation, Manufacturing Still Matters

Notwithstanding the advantages of the GVC economy in lowering costs, reaching new markets and tapping into global talent pools, the outsourcing of manufacturing capabilities can be deleterious to innovation. Pisano and Shih (2009) document the loss of US manufacturing capacity for many high-tech products, including semiconductors, electronic displays, energy storage, clean-energy production, computing and telecommunications equipment, and advanced materials used in sporting goods, aerospace and wind-energy applications.

The case of Amazon's Kindle 2 e-reader is fairly typical. The controller board, lithium-polymer battery and highly polished injection-molded case are made in China, the wireless card comes from South Korea, and the screen utilizing 'electronic ink' (the tiny microcapsule beads used in its electrophoretic display) comes from Taiwan. Although Amazon designed the Kindle in California, some of its key components were also originally developed and manufactured in the US, like the 'ink' made by E Ink, a company based in Cambridge, Massachusetts. However, the special silicon-coated glass used to turn the beads black or white when a voltage is applied was only made in Asia because US companies failed to keep up in the LCD flat-panel-display industry. As a result, the US company E Ink was sold to its Taiwanese rival, which further consolidated Kindle's supply base in Asia.

To deal with the ongoing loss of US competitive advantage in a wide variety of industries, Pisano and Shih (2009, 2012) stress the importance of rebuilding the country's 'industrial commons' – the collective research and development (R&D), engineering and manufacturing capabilities that sustain innovation. This is a joint responsibility of both business and government. Collaborative R&D initiatives, as well as large-scale infrastructure investments, require significant government support to tackle society's big problems. And companies must revisit and overhaul the management practices and internal and external governance structures that have contributed to the exodus of manufacturing from the US. Destructive outsourcing and faltering investments in research and infrastructure will threaten the ability of US firms to innovate the high-tech goods and services essential to compete globally, unless making and developing these new products can be co-located with R&D, design and marketing activities locally.

Conclusion

In the postwar era, the overall expansion of global trade and investment has been punctuated by recurrent economic crises and bouts of protectionism. These cycles resulted in part from shifting balances of power between developed and developing economies, as different blocs sought to leverage their position in the system for financial and political gains. The oil price shocks of the 1970s led by the Organization of Petroleum Exporting Countries precipitated the debt crisis of the 1980s in Latin America and elsewhere. In turn, the debt crisis was exploited by the IMF and the World Bank to impose strict conditionality over debtor countries, whereby new loans were conditioned on structural adjustment programs that mandated fiscal austerity, privatization and deregulation in the domestic economy, and the reduction of external trade barriers. This Washington Consensus model emphasized export-oriented industrialization as a recipe for large and small economies alike.

The financial crisis of 2007 triggered the Great Recession of 2008–2009 and a dramatic slump in world trade that prompted fears of protectionism that could put the entire global economic order at risk. While international trade eventually rebounded, confidence in the Washington Consensus model was shattered, and large emerging economies such as China, Brazil and South Africa began to fashion alternative development strategies that focused more on their domestic economies, industrial policies to build the capabilities of local firms, indigenous innovation, South-South trade and investment, and regional value chains (Gereffi and Sturgeon, 2013).

The current protectionist episode differs from the others in a few respects. First, the architects of the Anglo-American postwar economic system seem to be leading the charge. US President Trump has been particularly acerbic in denouncing the folly of American efforts to prop up the multilateral system of alliances, trade agreements and treaties previous US administrations worked so assiduously to create.

Second, the populist and nativist rhetoric of President Trump seems particularly ill suited to the times. In a GVC world driven by interconnected economies, advanced manufacturing, digitization and the search for global talent, Trump's emphasis on America First, preserving industries of the past, tethering American TNCs to national borders, and restrictions on high-skilled immigrants who could contribute most to the burgeoning knowledge economy appears self-defeating.

Third, China poses a unique threat as a global economic competitor. It not only has an abundance of natural and human resources that make it a formidable challenger in terms of its comparative economic advantages; China also has an institutional advantage in its ability to devise and carry out extremely ambitious national plans. On the domestic front, 'Made in China 2025' is a blueprint to transform the country into a high-tech powerhouse that will dominate cutting-edge industries like robotics, artificial intelligence, clean energy, and electric cars. On the international front, China's 'Belt and Road Initiative' is a massive infrastructure program proposed by the Chinese government in late 2013 that will encompass over 65 countries along several land corridors and the maritime silk road primarily in Asia and Europe, but also including Oceania and East Africa, at a total cost estimated at $4 to $6 trillion (*The Economist*, 2017; Brînză, 2018).

In this context, President Trump might be using the bluster of protectionism as a bargaining chip with China and other nations, rather than as a determined US strategy. This could be consistent with the goal of achieving more 'balanced trade' to moderate the ballooning US trade deficits (Prestowitz, 2017), but it would not address the strategic challenges posed by the need to harness the potential of the digital economy and Industry 4.0. Trump gave some credence to protectionism as a form of 'deal making' when he dangled the possibility that the US might rejoin TPP in response to the China-US trade disputes (Swanson, 2018), but he continues to reiterate his preference for bilateral deals where the US retains greater leverage.

A final issue to consider are the implications of protectionism and the weakening of the Anglo-American order on the ability of international organizations to maintain stable forms of global governance. In the words of Richard Baldwin, Professor of International Economics at the Graduate Institute of International and Development Studies in Geneva, Switzerland:

> If regional trade agreements and their power asymmetries take over, there is a risk that the WTO would go down in future history books as a 70-year experiment where world trade was rules-based instead of power-based. It would, at least for a few more years, be a world where rich nations write the new rules of the road in settings marked by vast power asymmetries. This trend should worry all world leaders (cited in World Economic Forum, 2014).

The international community is at a critical juncture in leadership within the global economy. Traditionally UN agencies assumed responsibility for making and implementing rules that guided not only the most powerful nations, but also gave poorer and marginal countries a stake in the system. The need for global governance is a collective challenge and responsibility, and a rules-based system probably offers the best chance for sustainable and inclusive development for large and small economies alike.

Notes

1. After August 1982, when Mexico's Finance Minister Silva Herzog declared that Mexico would no longer be able to service its debt, most commercial banks significantly reduced or halted new lending to Latin America.
2. Debates over the role of states versus markets in the global economy are in full display in discussions of the World Bank's *East Asia Miracle* report (1993). The success of the high-performing Asian economies, such as Japan and the 'four tigers' (South Korea, Taiwan, Hong Kong, and Singapore), elicited divergent explanations: the 'neoclassical' view attributed East Asian success to limited government intervention and an export-oriented trade strategy; the 'revisionist' view argued that East Asian governments actively 'led the market' in critical ways via industrial policy; and the 'market-friendly' view

eventually advocated by the Bank acknowledged the significance of selective government interventions that did not contravene market fundamentals (see Gereffi, 1995).

3. The IMF had engaged in policy leverage since the 1950s in terms of 'macroeconomic' issues (e.g., cutting government spending and raising interest rates). However, this shifted to a new level in the 1980s when the IMF required its borrowers to engage in 'structural' reforms such as privatizing state-owned enterprises and lifting trade barriers (Babb and Chorev, 2016: 89).

4. This section draws from Mayer and Gereffi (forthcoming).

5. This section draws from Gereffi (2017).

6. As of October 24, 2017, Apple's market capitalization was $807 billion (CNBC, 2017).

7. Foxconn boasted in 2016 that it replaced 60,000 workers with robots at a single plant in China (Glaser, 2017).

8. The apparel industry is another case where the US-supported imposition of production quotas through the Multi-Fiber Arrangement (MFA) led to a rapid expansion of US apparel imports via an ever-growing set of developing country exporters from the 1970s until the termination of the MFA system in 2005 (Gereffi, 1999).

9. In his classic article 'Who Is Us?', Robert Reich (1990) made this same point in the early 1990s.

10. In UNCTAD's 'Technical Annex: The Top 100 Digital MNEs', data are provided on the total sales, total assets and the foreign-asset 'lightness ratio' (i.e., ratio between the share of foreign assets and the share of foreign sales) for the top 100 digital MNEs and the top 100 ICT MNEs in the world.

11. For additional company examples in China's ICT sector, see Sun and Grimes (2016); Grimes and Sun (2016).

References

Aleem, Zeeshan. 2017. 'Trump Just Pulled Out of the TPP Free Trade Deal.' *Vox*, January 23. Available at https://www.vox.com/policy-and-politics/2017/1/23/14356398/trump-pull-out-tpp-nafta.

Babb, Sarah. 2013. 'The Washington Consensus as Transnational Policy Paradigm: Its Origins, Trajectory and Likely Successor.' *Review of International Political Economy* 20(2): 268–297.

Babb, Sarah and Nitsan Chorev. 2016. 'International Organizations: Loose and Tight Coupling in the Development Regime.' *Studies in Comparative International Development* 51(1): 81–102.

Baker, Peter and Ana Swanson. 2018. 'Trump Authorizes Tariffs, Defying Allies at Home and Abroad.' *New York Times*, March 8.

Baldwin, Richard. 2009. 'The Great Trade Collapse: What Caused It and What Does It Mean?' November 27. Available at https://voxeu.org/article/great-trade-collapse-what-caused-it-and-what-does-it-mean.

————. 2011. 'Trade and Industrialisation After Globalisation's 2nd Unbundling: How Building and Joining a Supply Chain Are Different and Why It Matters.' National Bureau of Economic Research, Working Paper 17716. December. Available at http://www.nber.org/papers/w17716.

Barboza, David. 2016. 'An iPhone's Journey, from the Factory Floor to the Retail Store (And Why the Product Costs More in China).' *New York Times*, December 29.

————. 2017. 'Before Wisconsin, Foxconn Vowed Big Spending in Brazil. Few Jobs Have Come.' *New York Times*, September 20.

Benjamin, Daniel K. 1999. 'Voluntary Export Restraints on Automobiles.' *PERC Reports* 17(3). Available at https://www.perc.org/1999/09/01/voluntary-export-restraints-on-automobiles/.

Bradsher, Keith and Steven L. Myers. 2018. 'China Strikes Back at the U.S. with Plans for Its Own Tariffs.' *New York Times*, April 4.

Bravo, Richard and Julia Chatterley. 2018. 'Trump is Willing to Reopen TTIP Amid EU-US Trade Dispute, Ross Says.' Bloomberg, March 29. Available at: https://www.bloomberg.com/news/articles/2018-03-29/trump-willing-to-reopen-ttip-amid-eu-u-s-trade-spat-ross-says.

Brînză, Andreea. 2018. 'Redefining the Belt and Road Initiative.' *The Diplomat*, March 20. Available at https://thediplomat.com/2018/03/redefining-the-belt-and-road-initiative/.

Brun, Lukas, Gary Gereffi, and James Zahn. 2017. 'The "Lightness" of Industry 4.0 Lead Firms: Implications for GVCs.' Paper presented at the International Conference on Globalisation, Human Capital, Regional Growth and the 4th Industrial Revolution, Bologna, Italy, October 20.

Buruma, Ian. 2016. 'The End of the Anglo-American Order.' *New York Times*, November 29.

Cattaneo, Olivier, Gary Gereffi, and Cornelia Staritz, eds. 2010. *Global Value Chains in a Post-Crisis World: A Development Perspective*. Washington, DC: World Bank.

Center for Automotive Research. 2017. 'NAFTA Briefing: Trade Benefits to the Automotive Industry and Potential Consequences of Withdrawal from the Agreement.' January. Available at http://www.cargroup.org/wp-content/uploads/2017/01/nafta_briefing_january_2017_public_version-final.pdf.

Chorev, Nitsan. 2013. 'Restructuring Neoliberalism at the World Health Organization.' *Review of International Political Economy* 20(4): 627–666.

CNBC. 2017. 'The Top 10 US Companies by Market Capitalization.' October 24. Available at: https://www.cnbc.com/2017/03/08/the-top-10-us-companies-by-market-capitalization.html#slide=6.

Dicken, Peter. 2003. *Global Shift: Reshaping the Global Economic Map in the 21st Century*, 4th edition. London: Sage.

Duhigg, Charles and Keith Bradsher. 2012. 'How the U.S. Lost Out on iPhone Work.' *New York Times*, January 22.

Engardio, Peter, Aaron Bernstein, and Manjeet Kripalani. 2003. 'Is Your Job Next?' *Business Week*, February 3, 50–60.

Engardio, Pete and Bruce Einhorn. 2005. 'Outsourcing Innovation.' *Business Week*, March 21.

Evenett, Simon, Bernard Hoekman, and Olivier Cattaneo, eds. 2009a. *The Fateful Allure of Protectionism: Taking Stock for the G8*. London: Centre for Economic Policy Research.

————. 2009b. *Effective Crisis Response and Openness: Implications for the Trading System*. London: Centre for Economic Policy Research.

Felix, David. 1990. 'Latin America's Debt Crisis.' *World Policy Journal* 7(4): 733–771.

Fernandez-Stark, Karina, Penny Bamber, and Gary Gereffi. 2011. 'The Offshore Services Value Chain: Upgrading Trajectories in Developing Countries.' *International Journal of Technological Learning, Innovation and Development* 4(1–3): 206–234.

Fold, Niels and Bill Pritchard, eds. 2004. *Cross-Continental Agro-Food Chains: Structures, Actors and Dynamics in the Global Food System*. London: Routledge.

Fröbel, Folker, Jürgen Heinrichs, and Otto Kreye. 1980. *The New International Division of Labor.* Cambridge, UK: Cambridge University Press.

Gereffi, Gary. 1995. 'State Policies and Industrial Upgrading in East Asia.' *Revue d'économie industrielle* 71: 79–90.

————. 1999. 'International Trade and Industrial Upgrading in the Apparel Commodity Chain.' *Journal of International Economics* 48(1): 37–70.

————. 2001a. 'Beyond the Producer-driven/Buyer-driven Dichotomy: The Evolution of Global Value Chains in the Internet Era.' *IDS Bulletin* 32(3): 30–40.

————. 2001b. 'Shifting Governance Structures in Global Commodity Chains, with Special Reference to the Internet.' *American Behavioral Scientist* 44(10): 1616–1637.

————. 2014. 'Global Value Chains in a Post-Washington Consensus World.' *Review of International Political Economy* 21(1): 9–37.

————. 2017. 'NAFTA and Global Value Chains.' Brookings Future Development blog, April 28. Available at https://www.brookings.edu/blog/future-development/2017/04/28/understanding-trade-relations-in-a-value-chain-linked-world/.

Gereffi, Gary and Joonkoo Lee. 2012. 'Why the World Suddenly Cares About Global Supply Chains.' *Journal of Supply Chain Management* 48(3): 24–32.

Gereffi, Gary and Timothy J. Sturgeon. 2013. 'Global Value Chain-Oriented Industrial Policy: The Role of Emerging Economies.' In *Global Value Chains in a Changing World*, edited by Deborah K. Elms and Patrick Low, 329–360. Geneva: World Trade Organization, Fung Global Institute, and Temasek Foundation Centre for Trade & Negotiations.

Gereffi, Gary and Donald L. Wyman, eds. 1990. *Manufacturing Miracles: Paths of Industrialization in Latin America and East Asia.* Princeton, NJ: Princeton University Press.

Glaser, Amy. 2017. 'The New Wisconsin Foxconn Plant Will Probably Be Staffed by Robots— If It Ever Gets Built.' *Future Tense*, July 27. Available at http://www.slate.com/blogs/future_tense/2017/07/27/the_wisconsin_foxconn_plant_will_be_staff_by_robots.html.

Grimes, Seamus and Yutao Sun. 2016. 'China's Evolving Role in Apple's Global Value Chain.' *Area Development and Policy* 1(1): 94–112.

Grunwald, Joseph and Kenneth Flamm. 1985. *The Global Factory: Foreign Assembly in International Trade.* Washington, DC: The Brookings Institution.

Immelt, Jeffrey R. 2012. 'The CEO of General Electric: On Sparking an American Manufacturing Revival.' *Harvard Business Review* (March): 43–46.

Irwin, Neil. 2017. 'The Amazon-Walmart Showdown That Explains the Modern Economy.' *New York Times*, June 16.

Kenney, Martin and John Zysman. 2016. 'The Rise of the Platform Economy.' *Issues in Science and Technology* 32(3): 61–69.

Krugman, Paul. 2006. 'The Rise and Fall of Development Economics.' Online archives. Available at http://www.pkarchive.org/theory/dishpan1.html.

Lamy, Pascal. 2013. 'Global Value Chains, Interdependence, and the Future of Trade.' December 18, *Vox*. EU. Available at http://www.voxeu.org/article/global-value-chains-interdependence-and-future-trade.

————. 2014. 'A Conversation with Pascal Lamy,' conducted by Gary Gereffi and Frederick Mayer, *Duke Global Summit* (https://dukegvcsummit.org/). Available at https://www.youtube.com/watch?v=D_rjQ3SJrWA&feature=youtu.be.

Libert, Barry, Megan Beck, and Jerry Wind. 2016. *The Network Imperative: How to Survive and Grow in the Age of Digital Business Models*. Boston, MA: Harvard Business Review Press.

Mayer, Frederick and Gary Gereffi. Forthcoming. 'International Development Organizations and Global Value Chains.' In *Handbook on Global Value Chains*, edited by Gary Gereffi, Stefano Ponte and Gale Raj-Reichert. Cheltenham, UK: Edward Elgar Publishing.

Mayer, Frederick and William Milberg. 2013. 'Aid for Trade in a World of Global Value Chains: Chain Power, the Distribution of Rents and Implications for the Form of Aid.' *Capturing the Gains* Working Paper 34: 1–23. Available at http://www.capturingthegains.org/pdf/ctg-wp-2013-34.pdf.

MGI (McKinsey Global Institute). 2017. 'China's Digital Economy: A Leading Global Force,' by Jonathan Woetzel, Jeongmin Seong, Kevin Wei Wang, James Manyika, Michael Chui, and Wendy Wong. August. Available at https://www.mckinsey.com/global-themes/china/chinas-digital-economy-a-leading-global-force.

Mishra, Pankav. 2018. 'The Rise of China and the Fall of the "Free Trade" Myth.' *New York Times*, February 7.

NBC News. 2018. Interview of Peter Navarro by Chuck Todd on 'Meet the Press,' April 8. Available at https://www.nbcnews.com/meet-the-press/meet-press-april-8-2018-n863726.

Parker, Ashley, Philip Rucker, Damian Paletta, and Karen DeYoung. 2017. '"I Was All Set to Terminate": Inside Trump's Sudden Shift on NAFTA.' *Washington Post*, April 27.

Perlez, Jane, Paul Mozur, and Jonathan Ansfield. 2017. 'China's Technology Ambitions Could Upset the Global Trade Order.' *New York Times*, November 7.

Pisano, Gary P. and Willy C. Shih. 2009. 'Restoring American Competitiveness.' *Harvard Business Review* (July–August): 114–125.

———. 2012. 'Does America Really Need Manufacturing?' *Harvard Business Review* (March): 94–102.

Prestowitz, Clyde. 2017. 'The New Shape of Globalization.' *American Affairs* 1(1): 50–61.

Rehnberg, Martha and Stefano Ponte. 2018. 'From Smiling to Smirking? 3D Printing, Upgrading and the Restructuring of Global Value Chains.' *Global Networks* 18(1): 57–80.

Reich, Robert B. 1990. 'Who Is Us?' *Harvard Business Review* (January–February): 53–64.

Ruggie, John G. 1982. 'International Regimes, Transactions and Change: Embedded Liberalism in the Postwar Economic Order.' *International Organization* 36(2): 379–415.

Stiglitz, Joseph E., Justin Yifu Lin, and Célestin Monga. 2013. 'The Rejuvenation of Industrial Policy.' The World Bank, Policy Research Working Paper 6628. Washington, DC: The World Bank.

Sturgeon, Timothy J., Johannes Van Biesebroeck, and Gary Gereffi. 2008. 'Value Chains, Networks and Clusters: Reframing the Global Automotive Industry.' *Journal of Economic Geography* 8(3): 297–321.

Sun, Yutao and Seamus Grimes. 2016. 'China's Increasing Participation in ICT's Global Value Chain: A Firm Level Analysis.' *Telecommunications Policy* 40(2): 210–224.

———. 2018. *China and Global Value Chains: Globalization and the Information and Communications Technology Sector*. Abingdon, UK: Routledge.

Swanson, Ana. 2018. 'Trump Proposed Rejoining Trans-Pacific Partnership.' *New York Times*, April 12.

The Economist. 2008. 'Fare Well, Free Trade: With the Global Economy Facing Its Worst Recession in Decades, Protectionism Is a Growing Risk.' December 18. Available at https://www.economist.com/node/12815617.

———. 2017. 'What Is China's Belt and Road Initiative?' May 15. Available at https://www.economist.com/blogs/economist-explains/2017/05/economist-explains-11.

UNCTAD (United Nations Conference for Trade and Development). 2013. *World Investment Report, 2013 — Global Value Chains: Investment and Trade for Development*. Geneva: UNCTAD.

———. 2017. *World Investment Report, 2017 — Investment and the Digital Economy*. Geneva: UNCTAD.

US Department of Commerce. 2018. 'U.S. Department of Commerce Announces Steel and Aluminum Tariff Exclusion Process.' March 18. Available at www.commerce.gov/news/press-releases/2018/03/us-department-commerce-announces-steel-and-aluminum-tariff-exclusion.

Wade, Robert H. 2003. 'What Strategies Are Viable for Developing Countries Today? The World Trade Organization and the Shrinking of "Development Space".' *Review of International Political Economy* 10(4): 621–644.

Wadhwa, Vivek, Una Kim De Vitton, and Gary Gereffi. 2008. 'How the Disciple Became the Guru: Workforce Development in India's R&D Labs.' Report prepared for the Ewing Marion Kauffman Foundation. Available at http://papers.ssrn.com/sol3/papers.cfm?abstract_id=1170049.

Williamson, John. 1990. 'What Washington Means by Policy Reform.' In *Latin American Adjustment: How Much Has Happened?* edited by John Williamson, 5–20. Washington, DC: Institute for International Economics.

World Bank. 1993. *The East Asian Miracle: Economic Growth and Public Policy*. New York: Oxford University Press.

World Economic Forum. 2014. 'What Are Mega-Regional Trade Agreements.' July 9. Available at https://www.weforum.org/agenda/2014/07/trade-what-are-megaregionals/.

WTO (World Trade Organization). 2013. *Fourth Global Review of Aid for Trade: 'Connecting to Value Chains' — Summary Report*. Geneva: WTO.

WTO, OECD (Organisation for Economic Co-operation and Development). 2007. *Aid for Trade at a Glance 2007: 1st Global Review*. Geneva, Paris: WTO and OECD.

———. 2011. *Aid for Trade at a Glance 2011: Showing Results*. Geneva, Paris: WTO and OECD.

Wu, Xinyi. 2018. 'Business Model and Global Competitiveness of Amazon and Alibaba.' April. Masters paper for Asian Pacific Studies Institute, Duke University, Durham, NC.

Co-authors

Jennifer Bair is Associate Professor of Sociology at the University of Virginia. Her research interests in global political economy include labor standards in global value chains. She is the editor of *Frontiers of Commodity Chains Research* (Stanford, 2009), and has published in numerous journals including *World Development*, *Economy and Society*, and *Signs*.

Stephanie Barrientos is Professor of Global Development at the University of Manchester. She has published widely on gender, employment, agribusiness and ethical trade in global value chains. She has advised companies, NGOs, government and international organizations.

Karina Fernandez-Stark is Senior Research Analyst at the Duke University Global Value Chains Center. She has led numerous research projects related to economic development and competitiveness in Latin America and other regions of the world, providing recommendations to country governments.

John Humphrey is Honorary Professor at the Department of Business and Management at Sussex University. He has researched and published extensively on global value chains, contributing both theoretical and empirical papers, with a particular focus on food production retailing and private food safety standards.

Joonkoo Lee is Assistant Professor of Organization Studies at the School of Business at Hanyang University, Seoul, South Korea. His research interests include globalization and development, global value chains, political economy in Asia, and cultural and creative industries.

Xubei Luo is Senior Economist at the World Bank Group. She has published over 40 articles on poverty, growth, labor market, spatial economy, global value chains, business environment, and results chains. She holds a Ph.D. in Economics from International Development Research Center, University of Auvergne, France.

Frederick Mayer is Professor of Public Policy, Political Science, and Environment and Associate Dean for Strategy and Innovation at Duke University's Sanford School of Public Policy. He teaches courses on the political economy of public policy, globalization and governance, political analysis, and leadership. He is the director of POLIS: The Center for Political Leadership, Innovation and Service.

Arianna Rossi is Senior Research and Policy Specialist for the ILO-IFC Better Work Programme. Her work covers policy research, impact assessment, and gender equality. She holds a PhD from the Institute of Development Studies at Sussex University, an MSc from the London School of Economics and a degree in Economics from the University of Ferrara, Italy.

Timothy J. Sturgeon is Senior Researcher at the Industrial Performance Center at Massachusetts Institute of Technology. He has made significant contributions to global value chain theory, and is working to improve the metrics and methods available for globalization research.

Index

Subject Index

accessibility
  to finance, 320, 382, 384
  to labor, 326
  to market, 15, 92, 116, 128, 189, 268, 318,
    344, 355, 368, 388, 396, 405, 418
  to training, 318–319
Acer, 91, 160, 243
African Growth and Opportunity Act
  (AGOA), 286, 354–355
agriculture value chains
  private quality standards, 394
  SME participation in, 316–317
Alibaba, 442–443
Amazon (the firm), 442–444
Amazon's Kindle, 445
'America First' doctrine, 429
Anglo-American exceptionalism, 429
anti-globalization movement, 162–165
anti-sweatshop movement, 263–264
Aoyama Trading, 81
apparel commodity chain, 18–19, 49–52
  backward and forward linkages in
    production process, 51–52, 65
  entry barriers, 78
  evolution in Asia, 90–99
  'higher-order' advantages, 50
  'lower-order' competitive advantage, 50
  North American, 99, 101–103
  organizational succession in, 88–89
  standardized and fashion-oriented
    garments, 50–51
  textile manufacturers and garment
    producers, 49–50

trade shifts and industrial upgrading in,
  83–90
apparel industry, 120–121, 313
  from captive to relational value chains,
    120–121
  global production networks, 156–159
  wages in Mexico, 200n12
Apple, 295n4, 367
  Apple's iPhones, 366, 411, 421n6, 437
  market capitalization, 442, 448n6
Armani, 68n26
Asda, 122
Asian apparel sourcing, 81, 104n7
Asian apparel value chain, 157–158
Asian Infrastructure Investment Bank,
  372n21
assembly-oriented production model, 75, 120
Associated Merchandising Corporation
  (AMC), 68n20, 68n22, 97
Australia, 153, 372n21
automobile industry, 355–356, 439
  2011 earthquake in Japan, effect of,
    385–386
  'industrial condominium' and 'modular
    consortium' concepts for
    automobile production, 407

Baidu, 441–443
Bangladesh, 48, 58, 94, 101, 157, 246, 266–
  267, 328, 421n4
  Bangladesh garment industry, 286, 295n4
Battle of Seattle, 162
Benetton, 55

Berkeley Roundtable on the International
    Economy (BRIE), 30n43
bicycle industry, 119–120
'Big Three' Asian apparel producers, 83, 86
Bombardier, 359
branded apparel manufacturers, 82–83
branded marketers, 81–82. *See also*
    manufacturers without factories
Brazil, 3–4, 10, 12–14, 23, 26n9, 32n56, 48,
    58, 179, 207, 209, 255, 261, 266–267,
    281, 291, 296n8, 337, 344, 346, 351,
    366, 372n15, 372n19, 373n21, 387,
    405–407, 412, 421n4, 432, 438, 446
    automobile industry, 355–356, 407
    export profile, 359–365
    trading relationship with China, 363–364
Bretton Woods system, 1, 140, 432
BRICs, 1, 406, 420
Burundi, 352
business groups, 154–155
business process outsourcing (BPO), 322
    Czech Republic, 324, 330
    Guatemala, 329
    India, 323–324, 329
    South Africa, 323, 329
business systems, 154, 168n24
buyer-driven global commodity chains,
    18–20, 52, 73, 90, 112, 230, 280–281,
    420n3
    definition, 46, 77
    economic agents, 56–58
    flexible specialization perspectives, 47
    global sourcing strategies, 58–62
    organizational features of, 43–44
    original equipment manufacturer (OEM)
        arrangements, 46
    producer-driven commodity chains *vs*,
        44–47, 75–78
    profitability, 47, 77
    retail revolution, 52–56
buying offices, 96–97

Cadbury, 407
Calvin Klein, 67n13, 187, 195
Cambodia, 86, 266, 268, 288, 438

Cambodian Garment Manufacturers
    Association (CGMA), 288
Canada, 6, 24, 79–80, 86, 95, 105n14, 145,
    153, 156, 200n4, 237, 436
    aerospace, 359
    automotive, 439
captive value chains, 113, 117–118, 121
Capturing the Gains research program, 21,
    32n57
Carrefour, 267, 346, 389
cattle industry, Uruguay, 356–357
Celestica, 161, 237
Central America Free Trade Agreement
    (CAFTA), 353–354
child labor, 235, 277, 287, 291, 395
Chile, 3, 6, 26n6, 27n16, 81, 166n8, 207, 209,
    322, 328, 356, 368
China , 1, 58, 61–62, 64, 92, 157, 182, 429–
    430, 439–440
    Chinese Contract Labor Law, 267
    cluster cities, 222
    digital economy, 441–443
    exports to United States, 2000–2014,
        214–218
    exports to world market, 1990–2014,
        212–213
    export profile, 359–365
    industrial organization in, 20
    iPhone production, 411
    labor costs, 213
    MFN status, 64, 69n35
    special economic zones, 48
    supply chain cities, 219–222, 407, 410
    third-party production in, 62
    trading relationship with Brazil, 363
China's development model, 20, 209–212
    annual FDI flows in, 210–211
    growth of R&D centers, 210
    reliance on FDI and private property, 211
Chinese-led clusters, 222
Clean Clothes Campaign (CCC), 164
cluster-driven path (of social upgrading), 291
cluster firms, in developing economies, 279
cluster governance, 287

Coca-Cola, 347, 407
codification of information, 124–126
coffee value chain, Central America and East
    Africa, 351–353
Cold War, 13, 24, 431
collective efficiency, 78, 279, 285
Colombia, 351, 357, 372n16
commercial subcontracting. *See* original
    equipment manufacturing (OEM)
commodity-chain dynamics, 9, 72–73
    developmentalist turn, 15
    internationalization of production, 92–95
    triangle manufacturing, 95–97
concept stores, 83
contract manufacturing, 58, 68n27, 112, 123
coordinated market economies, 153
coordination and collaboration building,
    319–320
corporate social responsibility (CSR), 22, 253,
    269, 276–277, 279, 282–284
    CSR-driven path (of social upgrading),
    289
Costa Rica, 102, 144, 164, 328
    environmental services offshoring, 357
    export performance in medical devices,
    1998–2011, 332
    GVCs in, 328–331, 338n9
    industrial policy recommendations,
    335–336
    medical devices industry, 331–333
    offshore services GVC, 334–335
    Presidential Council for Competitiveness,
    335
Czech Republic, 438

Daewoo, 91–92
Dayton Hudson, 53, 66n9, 79, 104n4
dependency theory, 2–3, 11, 152
    developing economies and, 11
    limitations of, 8
    measures of dependency, 25n4
development models
    in Latin America, 206–209
    in China, 209–212
development strategies, 11–13

de-verticalization of production, 82–83
digital economy, 441–445
    impact of GVC governance, 444
    strategies of companies in, 442
discount retail chains, 53, 67n12
Disney, 83, 258
doctrinaire market fundamentalism, 12, 432
Dominican Republic, 58, 63, 94, 96, 101–102,
    293, 296n8, 388
    Dominican Republic-Central America
        Free Trade Agreement, 353
Donna Karan, 68n26, 104n7, 187
Dubai, 81
Duke University Global Value Chain Center
    (Duke GVCC), 22, 316, 322, 328

East Asia
    industrial growth and development
        strategies in, 11–13
East Asian Miracle, 72, 146, 159, 401, 447n2
East Asian NICs. *See* newly industrialized
    countries (NICs) of East Asia
Eastern Europe
    industrial growth, 11
economic globalization, 141, 209, 253,
    255–257, 419
economic neoliberalism in Latin America,
    207–209
Egypt, 421n4
El Salvador, 61, 102, 353
electronic data interchange (EDI), 66n7,
    67n15
electronics sector
    impact of GVC governance, 123–125
    global production networks and, 159–161
embedded liberalism, 162, 256, 269, 430
Embraer, 406
emerging economies, export profile of,
    359–365
environmental services offshoring, 357
Episode, 69n34, 91
'essential drugs' programs, 10
Ethical Trading Initiative (ETI), 288
Ethiopia, 352

Europe, 1, 6, 63–64, 66n9, 68n20, 80, 82–83,
90–92, 99, 128, 139, 141, 154, 156,
237, 337, 352, 355, 372n21, 439, 446
Central Europe, 244, 255, 360, 400, 410,
431
certification institutions in Europe, 164
collapse of communism in Europe, 255
Eastern Europe, 48, 73, 82, 99, 144, 244,
255–256, 344, 347, 400–401, 431
European Community, 95
European Union, 79. 87, 99, 130n14, 137,
166n10, 356, 410, 412, 429, 434,
436
social democracy in Europe, 162
Western Europe, 67n18, 83, 86, 99, 244,
337
explicit coordination, 121–123, 127
export-oriented industrialization (EOI),
12–13, 28n25, 48, 401–402, 408–409

Facebook, 441–442
Fair Labor Association (FLA), 164
Fair Trade movement, 164, 258
Fair Trade coffee, 254, 261, 269, 352,
373n24
Fang Brothers Group, 69n34, 91, 121
Farah, 187, 314
fashion-oriented segment of apparel
commodity chain, 50–51
fashion-oriented clothing companies, 46
fashion-oriented retailers, 58, 88
wholesale value of domestic apparel
production, 51
Fayva Shoes, 67n12
Federated Department Stores, 66n9
filière approach, 151
finishing school model, 358
firms
opportunities in global market, 385–389
policy implications, 395–396
role in risk sharing, 382–385
flexible specialization perspectives/flexibly
specialized forms of production,
30n40, 47, 52
Flextronics, 161, 283, 346

'flying geese' model of Asian development,
168n27
Foot Locker chain, 56, 67n13, 67n18
footwear cluster, Brazil's Sinos Valley, 179
footwear industry
athletic footwear companies, 46
East Asian footwear exports, 29n32–33
footwear commodity chain, 14
footwear-exporting countries, 14, 29n31
US footwear imports, 29n31
foreign-led clusters, 222
Forest Stewardship Council (FSC)
certification, 163, 254, 260–261
Ford, 346, 389
four-pillars model for sustainable SMEs,
317–318
Foxconn, 234, 237, 295n4, 347, 366, 406, 411,
442, 448n7
Foxconn's factory cities, 437
proposed manufacturing facility in
Wisconsin, 437–438
Foxconn Technology Group, 373n23
France, 58, 79, 88, 165n2, 372n21
Fruit of the Loom, 50
fresh vegetables trade
impact of GVC governance, 121–123
global production networks and, 161–162
global value chain, 308–309
full-package production, 73–75, 88, 101,
104n1, 120–121, 130n13, 159, 203,
233, 236, 243–244, 403–404. *See also*
OEM production
in Torreon's blue-jeans cluster, 181, 187–
194, 198–199, 314

The Gap, 46, 53, 61, 67n14, 75, 156, 230, 257,
260, 262, 267
gender bias, 240, 284
General Agreement on Tariffs and Trade
(GATT), 140–141
General Motors, 346, 386, 389
Germany, 79, 153, 165n2, 168n24, 360,
372n21, 408, 410–411, 439
German export-processing zones in
Central and Eastern Europe, 431

Giordano, 91
global commodity chain (GCC), 2, 13–15,
    111, 150–151, 177, 180
    activities in, 26n13
    core-peripheral activities, 26n13
    governance structure of, 45
    ISI and EOI strategies of national
        development, 48
    main dimensions of, 44–45
    producer-driven and buyer-driven. *See*
        buyer-driven global commodity
        chains; producer-driven
        commodity chains
    role of state policies in, 47–49
    triangle manufacturing in, 19, 62–63, 65,
        95–97. *See also* newly industrialized
        countries (NICs) of East Asia
global economy, 137–138, 266, 309
    chain analysis of, 150–151
    contenporary, 141–144
    fragmentation, coordination, and
        networks in, 108–111
    governance in, 151–155
    international trade and production
        networks, 147–151
    macro level, 137
    meso level, 138
    micro level, 138
    'neoliberal' policies and, 432–433
    origin of, 139–140
    pattern of competition, 149
    reorganization of production and trade in,
        144–151
    value-chain perspective, 400–403
global 'governance deficit,' 254
global industries, 8–11
globalization, 139, 142–144, 147–148, 151,
    155
    backlash, 162–165
    industrial clusters and, 278–280
global pharmaceutical industry, 9–10
global production networks (GPNs), 21, 228,
    400–401
    changing patterns of trade, production
        and employment, 229–232

comparison of varieties of capitalism and,
    153
economic and social analysis of labor,
    231–232
global apparel industry, 156–159
    high-skilled, technology-intensive work
        in, 237
    knowledge-intensive work in, 237–238
    low-skilled, labor-intensive work in,
        235–236
    medium-skilled, mixed production
        technologies work in, 236
    small-scale, household-based work in, 235
    workers in, 230–231
global sourcing strategies, 58–62, 78–83
global value chain governance, 108, 111–113.
    See also governance in clusters and
    GVCs
    apparel industry, 120–121
    bicycle industry, 119–120
    dynamics, 119, 125–126
    fresh vegetables trade, 121–123
    key determinants of, 117
    key variables, 116
    operational theory of, 113–118
    US electronics industry, 123–125
global value chains (GVCs), 2, 15–18, 151,
    229–230, 276. *See also* global value
    chain governance
    application of, 316–336
    basic dimensions of, 306–316
    building blocks, 5–13
    in developing countries, 351–359
    development and emerging economies,
        22–23
    for economic development, 349–350
    GVC economy, 430–431
    geographical analysis, 309–310
    geographic consolidation of production
        in, 281–282
    governance and upgrading in, 19, 27n20,
        280–282, 310–315, 347–348,
        403–405
    industrial clusters and, 278–280
    industrial policies, role of, 365–366,
        369–370

infrastructure development, 368
input-output structure, 307–309
international competition and, 343–344
international donors and peak
    organizations, impact on, 413–418
leveraging local knowledge in, 356–357
local institutional context, 315
post-Washington Consensus era, 23
recommendations for developing
    countries, 368–371
regionalization of, 412–413
reorganization of production and trade
    in, 20
rise of, 344–347
risks and opportunities of participation in
    , 23, 382–396
SME participation in, 316–318
stakeholders, 316
standards and certifications, 370
trade policies, role of, 368
value-added trade, 409–412
workforce development, 324–328, 370
Goldstar, 91
Google, 441–442, 444
governance , in clusters and global value
    chains (GVCs), 284–294, 307,
    310–312, 402–407, 419, 441, 444–447.
    See also private governance, public
    governance, social governance,
    synergistic governance
captive governance, 116–118, 311–312
hierarchical governance, 116–118,
    311–312
horizontal (cluster) governance, 284
modular governance, 116–118, 311–312
relational governance, 116–118, 311–312
Greece, 81
Guatemala, 58, 63, 94, 96, 102, 351–353,
    372n9, 372n10

Haiti, 268
Hang Ten, 91
Hewlett-Packard (HP), 161, 346, 389
high-skilled, technology-intensive work, 237,
    326

high-value agro-food chains, 317
Honduras, 94, 101–102, 328, 351, 353
Hong Kong, 12, 61–63, 68n22, 68n28, 72–73,
    82–83, 86, 101, 146, 364, 401, 447n2
clothing companies, 91
establishing giant factories and foreign-
    led clusters in China, 221–222
internationalization of textile and apparel
    companies, 93–94
OBM production, 91, 157
OEM production, 90–92
transition from an entrepôt to a
    manufacturing-based economy,
    95–96
horizontal (cluster) governance, 284
horizontal coordination and collaboration
    building, 319
Horticultural and Ethical Business Initiative
    (HEBI), 288
human capital gap, in Latin America and
    India, 358
Hungary, 438
Hyundai, 91

IBM, 120, 123, 237, 346, 389
import-substituting industrialization (ISI),
    11, 13, 28n25, 48, 401–402, 432
India, 3–4, 48, 58, 94, 121, 228, 246, 255,
    266–267, 306, 337, 346, 351, 358–363,
    369, 387, 402, 405–406
    business process outsourcing (BPO),
        323–324, 329
    garment industry in, 239
    Jalandhar football cluster, 287, 289
    trading companies, 96
Indonesia, 58, 62–64, 69n35, 81, 94–96, 121,
    157, 159, 262–263, 281, 351, 371n2,
    387, 420, 421n4, 432
industrial clusters in developing countries,
    178–181
industrial commons, 421n6
industrial districts, 178, 180
industrial policies, role in GVCs, 365–366,
    369–370

horizontal, 365
vertical, 365
industrial upgrading, 73–75, 83–90, 280–282.
    See also upgrading
    apparel suppliers in Asia, 83–90
    chain upgrading, 233, 283, 313, 409
    functional upgrading, 233, 283, 312, 409
    global production networks and, 155–162
    in China, 212–219
    in Mexico, 189–192, 212–219
    in the Asian apparel value chain, 157–158
    levels of analysis, 87
    organizational learning, 73–74, 87–88
    organizational succession, 74–75, 88–89
    process upgrading, 232
    product upgrading, 232
    skills for upgrading, 358–359
    types of, 312–313
industry 'scouts,' 58, 62, 90
informal small and micro-enterprises or
    household-based work, 324–325
information technology outsourcing (ITO),
    322
Intel, 127, 367, 442
Inter-American Development Bank (IDB),
    358
Inter-American Development Bank
    Multilateral Investment Fund (IDB-
    MIF) initiatives in Latin America,
    316
international competition in GVCs, 343–344
international economy and development,
    perspectives, 2–5
International Labor Organization (ILO),
    137, 231, 256, 278, 288, 324, 337, 413
    adoption of the GVC framework, 349,
    413
    ILO's Better Work program, 268, 288,
    354, 391–392
    ILO's Decent Work Agenda, 233, 283
International Monetary Fund (IMF), 137,
    140–141, 162, 199, 255, 257, 345, 366,
    369, 401, 413, 419, 430
    restructuring of Latin American debt
    crisis, 432, 446, 448n1

international subcontracting, 68n27, 82, 257
Israel, 356, 387
Italy, 29n31, 29n32, 30n40, 55, 58, 79, 88,
    165n2, 178, 372,n21

J. C. Penney, 54, 56, 68n22, 75, 79, 88, 96,
    267, 389
J. C. Penney's private-label lines, 80–81
Jamaica, 63, 96, 102
Japan, 29n31, 58, 63, 69n31, 72–73, 78, 88,
    91, 95, 101, 120, 141, 146, 153, 219,
    337, 355, 360, 366, 385–386, 401, 408,
    410, 429, 439, 447n2
    economic growth rate, 12
    in the Asian apparel value chain, 157–158
    in the electronics value chain, 159–160
    Japanese automotive production system,
    46, 77
    Japanese model of 'lean production', 148,
    178
    Large Retail Store Law, 79
    migration of textile and apparel
    production to Japan, 83, 86
    revaluation of the yen, 86
    sogo shosha, 62, 95, 155
    third-party production in, 62
    voluntary export restraints in, 438–439
Jordan, 268, 328
just-in-time production, 78, 178

Kenya, 3, 121–123, 130n14, 161–162, 288,
    290, 328, 352
Kmart, 53–54, 59–60, 64, 67n12, 67n15,
    67n19, 68n22, 75, 79, 88, 96–97, 187
    Kmart-Liverpool, 103
knowledge-intensive work, 237–238,
    326–328
knowledge process outsourcing (KPO), 322
Kraft Foods, 346, 389

L. A. Gear, 46, 68n26
labor, economic and social analysis of, 231
labor-centered path (of social upgrading),
    290–291
Laos, 63, 86

Latin America, 432
  'essential drugs' programs in, 10
  export-oriented assembly in, 102
  human capital gap in, 358
  industrial growth and development
    strategies in, 11–13
Latin American development model
  import-substituting industrialization
    (ISI), 206–207
  neoliberalism, 207–209, 432–433
Laura Ashley, 55
legal process outsourcing (LPO), 324, 330
Lehman Brothers collapse, 433
Lesotho, 268, 328, 354–355, 412
Levi Strauss and Co., 50, 61, 67n14, 83, 260,
  267, 314, 353
Li and Fung, 121, 347, 371n4, 373n23, 406,
  421n5
liberal market economies, 153
The Limited, 46, 53, 61, 67n14, 75, 97, 104n6,
  156
livestock traceability system, 356
Liz Claiborne, 46, 50, 60, 67n13, 67n14,
  68n21, 69n34, 75, 80, 91, 104n6, 156,
  164, 187, 257, 346, 389
  early years in Asian apparel sourcing, 81
low-skilled, labor-intensive work, 235–236,
  325–326

Macao, 93, 222
Macy's, 60, 66n5, 68n22, 96–97
Malaysia, 58, 63–64, 93, 96, 159
manufacturers without factories, 81, 150, 256.
  See also branded marketers
manufacturing miracles, concept of, 12–13
maquiladora program (Border
    Industrialization Program), 165n4. *See
    also* Mexico, *maquiladora* sector
market-based global value chain governance,
  115, 118
  fresh vegetables trade, 121–123
market-driven path (of social upgrading),
  288–289
market governance, 310, 312
Marks and Spencer, 79, 156, 267

mass merchandising chains, 53, 66n11
Mast Industries, 97
Mauritius, 58, 63, 93, 96
May Department Stores, 66n9, 67n19,
  68n22, 97
medium-skilled, mixed production
  technologies work, 236
Mexico, 1, 4, 6–7, 12–13, 23–24, 48, 58, 73, 75,
    81–82, 86, 92, 94, 121, 144, 255, 266,
    344, 371n2, 386, 388, 410, 420, 421n4.
    See also Torreon blue jeans cluster
  aerospace industry, 359
  apparel commodity chain of, 101–104
  automobile industry, 355–356, 372n15,
    439
  bilateral trade agreements, 368
  exports to United States, 2000–2014,
    214–218
  exports to world market, 1990–2014,
    212–213
  export profile, 359–365
  financial crises, 387, 447n1
  foreign direct investment in, (1995–2015),
    211
  industrial upgrading in, 212–219
  Korean-owned Kukdong factory, 164
  maquilada sector, 66n4, 68n29, 102, 143,
    165n4, 184, 199n3, 236
  NAFTA impact, 20, 24, 159
  OEM production, 158
  pharmaceutical industry in, 10
  production sharing with US (also called
    'twin plant' program), 82, 104n5,
    400, 431
  talks with US President Trump, 436, 438
  US apparel sourcing, 101–103
Mexico's development model, 20, 209–212
Microsoft, 127, 386, 442, 444
Mitac Corporation, 91–92, 243
Mitsubishi, 29n32, 68n23
moderate-skilled work, 326
modernization theory, 2–3
modular product architectures, 78, 112, 114,
  130n11

modular value chains, 115, 117–118, 125–126
Montgomery Ward, 64, 66 n11, 68n22, 96–97
Morocco, 328, 394
    Moroccan garment industry, 21, 229,
        238–239, 242, 246, 247n3
Multi-Fiber Arrangement (MFA), 86, 121,
    158, 355, 388, 406
multinational corporations (MNCs), 2, 313,
    333. *See also* transnational corporations
    (TNCs)
    pharmaceutical industry, 7, 10
    power and global reach of, 5–8
Multinational Enterprise Project, Harvard
    Business School, 6–7, 145
multi-stakeholder initiative (MSI), 289–290
multi-stakeholder path (of social upgrading),
    289–290
Myanmar, 58, 90, 94

neoliberalism, economic, 207–209, 211, 223,
    432–433
Nestlé, 346, 389
New Zealand, 372n21
newly industrialized countries (NICs) of
    East Asia, 43, 48, 58, 61, 65, 72–73,
    87–88, 96
    apparel industry, 99–104
    non-quota markets for, 99
    northern tier, 87
    OBM production, 90–92, 157
    OEM production, 90–92, 157
    offshore sourcing by, 92–95
    preferred countries for new factories, 96
    third-party production, 62
    three Ds, 69n31
    triangle manufacturing, 62–63, 95, 157 .
        See also global commodity chain
        (GCC)
Nicaragua, 328, 351, 353–354, 368
    Nicaraguan apparel industry, 353–355
Nigeria, 3–4, 26n7
Nike, 46, 68n21, 68n26, 81, 83, 156, 164,
    230, 257–258, 260–262, 267, 310, 346,
    373n22, 389

Nokia, 234, 385
North American Free Trade Agreement
    (NAFTA), 20, 24, 87, 103, 137,
    159, 176–177, 184, 208, 271n5, 286,
    435–439
    maquila networks, 181, 199n3, 200n4
North Korea, 63

offshore services value chain, 320–323, 328
Organisation for Economic Co-operation
    and Development (OECD), 343
organizational features of global industries,
    16, 43–44
original brand manufacturing (OBM), 19,
    73–74, 88, 155–156
    in East Asia, 90–92
    reversals in experience, 91–92
original design manufacturing (ODM), 19,
    155–156
original equipment manufacturing (OEM),
    19, 63, 65, 73–75, 88, 155–156
    in East Asia, 90–92
outward processing arrangements (OPA), 82,
    93, 128
outward processing trade (OPT), 82, 244
overseas buying offices (of US retailers), 57,
    96–98

Pagoda Trading Company, 68n19, 68n23
Pakistan, 26n6, 166n8, 291, 421n4
Pan-American Health Organization
    (PAHO), 7, 10
Panama, 351
Payless ShoeSource, 67n12, 67n19, 68n24
pharmaceutical industry
    in Mexico, 7
    UNCTC report, 10
the Philippines, 58
Phillips-Van Heusen, 61, 83
Plaza Agreement, 86
Polo/Ralph Lauren, 68n26, 156, 187, 346,
    353, 389
    Polo, 104n7, 195
Portugal, 81
private governance, 21–22, 163, 268–270,
    285, 292

branded products, impact on, 261–262
demand for, 255–257
effective, 262–264
evolving pattern of, 268–270
functions of, 270n2
innovations in, 253
interaction between public governance and, 254
potential impact and scope, 259–260
six hypotheses about, 259–268
social or environmental concerns, 264–265
social responses and, 257–259
private-label (or store-brand) programs, 58, 67n14, 68n21, 69n34, 75, 80–81, 88, 96, 200n8
process upgrading, 282, 312, 409
producer-driven commodity chains, 18–20, 73, 112, 230, 280–281, 420n3
buyer-driven commodity chains *vs*, 44–47, 75–78
capital- and technology-intensive, 52
definition, 46, 76
East Asian division of labor, 46
Japanese and US car companies, 46
mass production, 47
profitability, 77
production networks in global economy, 147–151
product upgrading, 282, 312, 409
protectionism and global value chains (GVCs), 24, 49, 86–87, 429–430, 433–435, 437–438
public governance, 22, 266–267, 269–270, 284–286
public-governance path (of social upgrading), 292
public-private partnerships, 358, 370–371

quasi-hierarchical relationships, 112
quotas, 49, 51, 64–65, 86, 147
in triangle manufacturing, 62–63
in East Asia's apparel commodity chain, 92–95, 157–158
non-quota markets, 95, 99

US import quotas established by the MFA, 121, 156, 388, 448n8

RCA, 123
Reebok, 46, 68n26, 81, 164, 257, 310
regional value chains, 438–439
relational value chains, 113, 118, 121
apparel industry, 120–121
rents, 78, 104n2, 144, 402
types of (brand name, organizational, relational, technology, trade policy), 78
retailers, 56–57, 80–81
across European Union, 79
and global sourcing strategies, 58–62
private-label programs, 80–81
scope for 'family shopping,' 53
retail sector in the United States, 52–56
re-verticalization of brands and stores, 83
risk sharing, firms' role in, 382–385
Romania, 159, 388
Russia, 23, 144, 344, 346, 359–363, 387, 406, 421n4
Rwanda, coffee sector, 352–353, 372n11, 372n12

Sainsbury's, 122, 346, 389
Saipan, 58, 63
Samsung, 91, 126, 385, 442
Sara Lee Corporation, 50, 82–83, 103, 200n7
Sears Roebuck, 53, 64, 66n11, 68n22, 75, 79, 96
Shimano, 119–120, 127
Singapore, 12, 63, 68n22, 72, 81, 95–97, 101, 146, 156, 219, 364, 366, 372n21, 401, 429, 439, 447n2
OEM production, 90–92
Slovakia, 244, 438
small and medium enterprises (SMEs), 316–318
small-scale, household-based work, 235
Social Accountability 8000 (or SA 8000), 163–164
social governance, 22, 284–286
Solectron, 123–124, 161
Sony, 126

South Africa, 4, 23, 32n57, 144, 239, 243, 281, 344, 359–363, 373n21, 386, 395, 410, 412, 421n4, 432, 446
  boycotts, 255
  South African clothing manufacturers and retailers, 355, 412
South Korea, 3–4, 12–13, 60, 63, 68n28, 83, 86, 101, 146, 356, 366, 372n21, 401, 429, 438–439, 447n2
  apparel exports, 86
  finished consumer goods exports, 58
  in the electronics value chain, 160
  internationalization of textile and apparel firms, 94
  orderly marketing agreements in footwear, 66n3
  OBM production, 91, 157
  OEM production, 90–92
Spain, 29n31, 29n32, 168n23, 247n3, 359
Sri Lanka, 58, 61–63, 83, 94, 157, 246, 328
SSRC working group, 6–7, 26n9
Standard International Trade Classification (SITC), 166n11, 224n1
Starbucks, 164, 258, 261, 351
state policies, role in global commodity chain (GCC), 47–49
store-within-a-store boutiques, 67n13
strategic interviews, 4, 25n3, 185, 203–204
Sun Apparel, 314
supermarkets, 121–122, 161–162, 256, 260, 276, 346, 389, 394, 412
supply chain cities, 219–222
supply chain management, 122, 160, 221, 276, 294, 349, 386, 411, 443
Swaziland, 354–355, 412
Sweden, 165n2
synergistic governance, 22, 293

Taiwan, 3–4, 12–13, 60–61, 63, 68n28, 83, 86, 101, 146, 353, 364, 366, 401, 438–439, 447n2
  apparel exports, 86, 105n11
  establishing giant factories and foreign-led clusters in China, 221–222
  finished consumer goods exports, 58
  in the electronics value chain, 160

internationalization of textile and apparel firms, 94–95
  investments in the PRC, 69n33
  OBM production, 91, 157
  OEM production, 90–92
  orderly marketing agreements in footwear, 66n3
  quota markets, 94–95
  US retail buying offices, 97–98
Tanzania, 352
Target, 53, 67n12, 75, 104n4, 156, 187, 353
Tata, 406
Tencent, 442–443
Tesco, 122, 230, 267, 288, 310, 346, 389
Texas Instruments, 123
Thailand, 58, 64, 104n7, 372n21
third-party labor contractors, 239
Third World, 2–3, 48–49, 91, 400, 420n2
Tommy Hilfiger, 75, 104n7, 156, 187, 195, 267
Torreon blue jeans cluster, 20, 181–184, 313–314
  apparel industry indicators for, 183
  commodity-chains perspective, 197–199
  full-package networks, 189
  labor market, 193–197
  main clients of, 187
  NAFTA-era networks, 186–189
  on-site research in, methodology, 184–185, 203–204
  success and limitations, 189–197
  top 10 apparel manufacturers in, 192
  upgrading of industry, 189–192
  value of a commodity-chains perspective, 197–199
  vertical network structure and hierarchical organization, 192–193
total quality management, 178
trade liberalization, 179
trading companies, 57
Transatlantic Trade and Investment Partnership (TTIP), 435–436
transnational business networks, 155
transnational corporations (TNCs), 46, 139, 144–147, 165, 166n12, 356, 396.

See also multinational corporations (MNCs)

German, 168n24

internal capital markets and investment flows in, 387

transnational economic linkages, 11, 28n23

Trans-Pacific Partnership (TPP), 435–436

triangle manufacturing, 19, 62–63, 65, 95–98

Trump, Donald, 24, 429, 435–440, 446–447

Turkey, 121, 159, 266, 328, 360, 371n2, 387, 405, 410, 420, 421n4

turn-key supplier, 112

UCSD's Center for US-Mexican Studies, 13, 28n26

Uganda, 352

UN Centre on Transnational Corporations (UNCTC), 7, 9, 27n16, 27n18, 27n19

Unilever, 407

United Arab Emirates, 81

United Kingdom, 6, 55, 79, 93, 121–123, 145–146, 153, 168n30, 239, 395, 432

United Nations Conference on Trade and Development (UNCTAD), 26n6, 27n16, 343, 349, 441–443

United Nations Economic Commission for Latin America, 11

United Nations Global Compact, 163, 268

United States (US)

apparel sourcing, 100–104

'bring jobs back to America,' 437–438

digital economy, role of, 441–442

electronics industry, 123–125

exports of cars and components, 436

global sourcing by retailers, 60

import tariffs, 438–439

mass market, 53, 66n11

807/9802 program or 'production sharing' in, 82. *See also* Mexico, production sharing with US

quick response (QR) programs, 78, 104n3

retailers overseas production networks, 18

retail sector in, 52–56, 79–81

shifts in regional structure of US apparel imports, 1986–1996, 89

trading relationship with China, 411

trend in apparel imports, 84–86

Trump's policies, 435–439

upgrading , economic and social, 21–22, 277, 282–284, 389–391. *See also* industrial upgrading

defining economic and social upgrading, 232–234, 295n5

distribution of risks and opportunities, 389–395

global production and trade, role in, 407–413

key drivers of economic and social upgrading/downgrading, 240–242, 293

status of workers, 238–240

trajectories of economic and social upgrading/downgrading, 242–246, 391–392

types of, 312–315

typology of work, 235–238

upgrading in diverse GVCs, 282–284, 351–356

Uruguay, 207, 209, 322, 351, 356–357, 372n16

Uruguay Round of multilateral trade negotiations, 433

value-added chain, 167n14

value-added trade, 409–412

varieties of capitalism, 128, 138–139, 152–153

vertical coordination and collaboration building, 167n18, 319–320

vertical (GVC) governance, 284

vertical-specialization-based-trade, 129n3, 148

VF Corporation, 50, 103, 200n7

Vietnam, 58, 62–63, 83, 86, 92, 94–95, 99, 157, 159, 214, 266, 268, 328, 351, 387, 421n4, 438

voluntary export restraints (VERs), 438

Walmart (*also* Wal-Mart), 53–54, 59–60, 64, 75, 79, 97, 156, 230, 254, 258, 310, 346, 353, 389, 443

Walmart's Sustainability Consortium, 260

'dolphin safe' labeling, 261
'greening' the value chain, 265
Washington Consensus, 1, 20, 141, 166n7,
    207, 345, 349, 369, 401–402, 417–419,
    432–433
    post-Washington Consensus era, 23,
        405–406, 418, 446
Whole Foods, 271n8, 443
Woolworth Corporation, 54, 56, 66n11,
    67n13, 67n18, 68n22, 97
Workers Rights Consortium (WRC), 164
worker-training programs, 92
workforce development and global value
    chains (GVCs), 324–328, 370
World Bank, 137, 141, 257, 343, 345, 349,
    366, 388, 401
    adoption of GVC analysis, 434–435
    'Aid for Trade' initiative, 417
    analysis of GVCs, 433–435
    view of East Asian success, 12, 166n7

world-systems theory, 8–9, 14, 29n37, 139, 152
World Trade Organization (WTO), 1, 137,
    141, 163, 199, 219, 255, 257, 345, 349,
    366, 409, 413, 430, 432, 447
    1999 protests against WTO trade talks,
        162
    2005 phase-out of the MFA by the
        WTO, 158, 219
    adoption of GVC analysis, 433–435
    China's 2001 accession to the WTO, 209,
        431
Worldwide Responsible Apparel Production
    (WRAP), 164
Wrangler, 314

Yap, 63
Yue Yuen (footwear), 224n4, 406

Zara, 126, 247n3, 267
Zimbabwe, 161–162

Author Index

Abdulsamad, Ajmal, 352–353, 372
Acemoglu, Daron, 383, 385
Aglietta, Michel, 148, 152
Akamatsu, Kaname, 168
Albaladejo, Manuel, 219
Aleem, Zeeshan, 436
Alfaro, Laura, 386
Allen, Michael, 164
Altenburg, Tilman, 279, 350, 414
Altomonte, Carlo, 412
Amable, Bruno, 153
Amengual, Matthew, 292–293, 295–296
Amin, Samir, 3
Amsden, Alice H., 11–12, 152
Antras, Pol, 387
Aoyama, Yuko, 30
Appelbaum, Richard P., 31, 95, 101, 180, 219,
    224, 347
Arndt, Sven W., 109, 147
Arrighi, Giovanni, 4, 8–9, 15, 27–29, 140,
    143, 165

Asenso-Okyere, Kwadwo, 347
Auld, Graeme, 260, 263
Ayres, Robert L., 141

Babb, Sarah L., 207–208, 432–433, 448
Bain, Joe, 7
Bair, Jennifer, 14, 25, 27, 30, 102–103, 143,
    159, 168, 189, 195, 230, 232, 236, 256,
    276–277, 338, 353–354, 371, 404, 418,
    420
Baker, Peter, 439
Baldwin, Carliss Y., 114, 129–130, 344–345,
    433, 439
Baldwin, Richard, 315, 366, 369, 408, 447
Bamber, Penny, 325, 328, 331–333, 336, 338
Barboza, David, 214, 219, 221, 236, 437–438
Barff, Richard, 46
Barnet, Richard J., 5, 145–146
Barrett, Richard E., 11
Barrientos, Armando, 231, 278
Barrientos, Stephanie, 17, 228, 230–231, 234,

239–240, 242, 247, 277, 279–280,
283–284, 286, 290–291, 293–295,
326–327, 338, 347, 349, 367, 389–391,
393, 408, 413, 420
Bartley, Tim, 258, 260, 262–263, 293
Batz, Michael B., 292
Becker, David, 3
Bella, Jose Di, 370
Beltramello, Andrea, 360, 410, 418
Bendix, Reinhard, 3
Benjamin, Daniel K., 439
Bennett, Douglas C., 3, 8, 26
Berger, Peter L., 11
Berger, Suzanne, 93–94, 128, 152
Bergsten, C. Fred, 146
Bernard, Mitchell, 86
Bernhardt, Thomas, 284
Beviglia Zampetti, Americo, 166
Bhagwati, Jagdish, 144
Biersteker, Thomas J., 3
Birnbaum, David, 82, 90
Block, Fred, 165
Bluestone, Barry, 51, 53, 67
Bonacich, Edna, 120
Bonnen, Arturo R., 126
Bornschier, Volker, 25
Borrus, Michael, 30, 77, 128, 159–160
Boyer, Robert, 152, 199
Bradshaw, York W., 3
Bradsher, Keith, 421, 437, 439
Brandt, Loren, 210, 405, 413
Branstetter, Lee, 209
Bravo, Richard, 436
Brenner, Robert, 25
Bresky, Bart, 104
Brewer, Benjamin D., 29
Brînză, Andreea, 446
Brown, Drusilla K., 242
Brun, Lukas, 444
Buitelaar, Rudolf M., 184
Bunkley, Nick, 386
Buruma, Ian, 1, 429
Büthe, Tim, 21, 258, 262, 270

Cafaggi, Fabrizio, 271
Campbell, John L., 152
Cañas, Jesus, 143, 165
Canis, Bill, 386
Caporaso, James, 3, 7–8, 25–26
Cardoso, Fernando Henrique, 3, 8, 152
Carlsen, Laura, 209
Carr, Marilyn, 284
Carrillo, Jorge, 143, 184, 196, 236
Carroll, William K., 155
Carswell, Grace, 290
Casalet, Mónica, 359
Castells, Manuel, 155
Cattaneo, Olivier, 23, 266, 276, 281, 337, 344,
349, 369, 388, 413, 435
Chase-Dunn, Christopher, 25
Chassot, Olivier, 355
Chatterley, Julia, 436
Chazen, Jerome A., 81–82
Chen, Maggie, 386
Chen, Martha, 284
Chen, Xiangming, 61
Chiarvesio, Maria, 277
Chirot, Daniel, 25
Chorev, Nitsan, 432, 448
Christian, Michelle, 254, 261, 373
Clark, Kim B., 114, 129–130
Clark, Norman, 394, 413
Clelland, Donald A., 29
Clemons, Eric K., 129
Coase, Ronald, 382
Coe, Neil, 230
Collins, Jane Lou, 240
Contreras, Oscar F., 276
Coronado, Roberto, 143, 165
Coslovsky, Salo V., 292, 296
Crescionini, Eduardo, 357
Crespi, Gustavo, 365
Crow, Michael, 292
Cumbers, Andy, 230–231

Damodaran, Sumangala, 284
David, Paul A., 125
Daviron, Benoit, 352

de Andrade Baltar, Paulo Eduardo, 267
De Coster, Jozef, 93
Dedrick, Jason, 421
De la Garza, Enrique, 177, 196
De Marchi, Valentina, 278, 281, 295
De Neve, Geert, 283, 290
de Oliveira, Puppim, 281, 283–284, 288–289,
    291–293
Deyo, Frederic C., 12
Diaz-Alejandro, Carlos, 6
Dicken, Peter, 28, 44, 111, 129, 139, 143, 145,
    167, 255–256, 346, 349, 400, 431
Dickerson, Kitty G., 74, 79–80
Dillon, Sam, 200
Dobbin, Frank, 165
Dolan, Catherine S., 17, 30, 112, 130, 168,
    230, 236, 256, 260, 283, 286, 288, 290,
    312
Donaghu, Michael T., 46
Doner, Richard F., 5, 46, 77, 279, 291
Dore, Ronald, 128, 152
Dos Santos, Theotonio, 3
Downie, Andrew, 261
Downs, Anthony, 264
Drangel, Jessica, 4, 9, 15, 27–28, 143
Duhigg, Charles, 421, 437
Dunaway, Wilma A., 29
Dunning, John H., 6, 145
Dussel Peters, Enrique, 176–177, 208
Duvall, Raymond D., 8

Egan, Edmund, 30
Einhorn, Bruce, 400, 431, 437
Elliott, Kimberley A., 234, 295
Ellner, Steve, 208
Elson, Diane, 240
Emerson, Richard M., 8
Encarnation, Dennis, 3
Engardio, Peter, 143, 400, 431, 437
Ernst, Dieter, 30, 160
Esbenshade, Jill, 258
Evans, Peter B., 3, 8–9, 26, 146, 152, 165, 253
Evenett, Simon, 435
Evgeniev, Evgeni, 244
Ewert, Joachim, 244

Faletto, Enzo, 3, 8, 152
Farooki, Masuma, 289, 337, 402, 412
Farrell, Diana, 223
Feenstra, Robert C., 19, 109, 148, 155, 165–
    166, 235, 343, 410
Felix, David, 432
Felmingham, Bruce, 219
Fennema, Meindert, 155
Fernandez-Kelly, Patricia, 183
Fernandez-Stark, Karina, 27–28, 237, 266,
    277, 309, 313, 317–321, 324–326, 328,
    330, 334–336, 338, 347, 372, 403, 405,
    431
Fine, Charles H., 110, 126
Finnie, Trevor A., 79
Fitter, Robert, 17, 164
Flamm, Kenneth, 345, 431
Fleury, Afonso, 17, 30
Fleury, Maria Tereza, 17
Florida, Richard, 77, 126, 128, 148
Fold, Niels, 27, 431
Fourcade-Gourinchas, Marion, 207–208
Frank, Andre Gunder, 3
Frederick, Stacey, 28, 266, 310, 313, 368, 388,
    403, 405
Fredriksson, Torbjörn, 166
Freeman, Richard B., 210, 234, 295, 346
Freyssenet, Michel, 199
Fröbel, Folker, 142, 400, 431
Fuchs, Doris, 256, 259, 270
Fung, Archon, 163–164
Fung, Victor K., 350, 373, 421

Galvin, Peter, 119, 130
Gao, Bai, 210
Garretón, Manuel Antonio, 163
Gereffi, Gary, 3–5, 7–10, 12–17, 23, 25–32,
    43–44, 47, 61, 69, 73–74, 83, 88, 90,
    95, 97, 101–103, 105, 111–112, 121,
    129, 143, 146, 150–151, 154–157, 159,
    163–164, 166, 168, 180, 184, 189, 207,
    212, 219, 229–230, 232, 235–236, 241,
    243–244, 254, 256–257, 260–261, 266,
    270–271, 276–277, 280–281, 292–293,
    295, 306–307, 310, 312–314, 319–321,

324–328, 331–333, 336, 338, 343,
345–350, 353–354, 359, 364–365, 367,
369, 371, 373, 384, 387–389, 392–393,
400–404, 407, 410, 413, 418–420, 432,
438–439, 443–444, 446, 448
Gibbon, Peter, 30, 129, 281–282, 413
Glaser, Amy, 438, 448Godfrey, Shane, 240
Gold, Thomas B., 3
Goodman, Louis Wolf, 6
Goodman, Peter S., 214
Gore, Charles, 141, 207, 345, 402
Gospel, Howard, 322
Gourevitch, Peter, 28
Grandinetti, Roberto, 278, 295
Granitsas, Alkman, 91
Granovetter, Mark, 111, 154, 165
Green, Jessica F., 258, 262
Greenhouse, Steven, 286
Grieco, Joseph, 3
Grimes, Seamus, 439, 443, 448
Grunwald, Joseph, 345, 431
Guillén, Mauro F., 168
Güler, Esra, 241
Gusfield, Joseph R., 3

Haggard, Stephan, 12, 345
Hale, Angela, 231, 240
Hall, Peter A., 152
Hall, Thomas D., 25
Hamel, Gary, 111
Hamilton, Gary G., 31, 155, 235, 371, 418
Hammer, Nikolaus, 260
Harris, Nigel, 43
Harrison, Bennett, 45, 67, 199
Held, David, 140, 142, 255
Henderson, Jeffrey, 5, 46, 77, 111, 230, 400
Hernández, René A., 347
Herzenberg, Stephen, 143, 184
Hess, Martin, 230
Hill, Richard C., 46, 77
Hilowitz, Janet, 163
Hochstetler, Kathryn, 267
Hollingsworth, Joseph R., 152
Holmes, John, 68
Hopkins, Rose, 260

Hopkins, Terence K., 5, 14–15
Hu, Albert G. Z., 210
Hualde, Alfredo, 143
Huang, Fuping, 211
Huang, Yasheng, 211
Huber, Evelyne, 165, 207, 209
Hughes, Alexandra, 111, 260
Hummels, David, 129, 148
Humphrey, John, 17, 27, 30, 112, 126, 130,
    151, 168, 178, 181, 230, 236, 256, 260,
    276–277, 282, 307, 312, 350, 409, 417
Humphrey, Peter, 30
Huntington, Samuel P., 3
Iglesias Prieto, Norma, 183

Inglehart, Ronald, 267
Irwin, Neil, 443

Janczuk, Agnieszka, 271
Jarillo, Carlos J., 110
Jefferson, Gary H., 210
Jenkins, Rhys O., 26, 283, 363–364
Johnson, Chalmers, 12
Jones, Jackie, 80, 104
Jordan, Mary, 200
Jordhus-Lier, David C., 230
Justice, Dwight W., 292

Kahn, Gabriel, 221, 224
Kahn, Joseph, 211
Kalfagianni, Agni, 256, 259, 270
Kaplinsky, Raphael, 17, 30, 78, 104, 129, 144,
    151, 164, 199, 230, 255, 282, 289, 337,
    394, 402, 412–413, 418
Katz, Jorge, 6
Kawakami, Momoko, 27, 266, 347, 405
Keck, Margaret E., 267
Keesing, Donald B., 114
Kenney, Martin, 77, 128, 442
Keohane, Robert, 255
Ketels, Christian H., 279
Khanna, Sri Ram, 83, 93, 95
Khanna, Tarun, 211
Khara, Navjote, 279, 285, 289
Kidder, Thalia, 231
Kierzkowski, Henryk, 109, 147

Kim, Eun Mee, 47
King, Larry, 165
Kitschelt, Herbert, 152
Klein, Naomi, 162, 258
Knorringa, Peter, 112, 200, 230, 234, 283, 288–289
Kogut, Bruce, 109, 148–149, 167
Köhler, Horst, 168
Kolasa, Marcin, 387
Kolk, Ans, 258, 269
Koopman, Robert, 421
Korzeniewicz, Miguel E., 4–5, 14, 18, 29–30, 44, 111, 150–151, 180, 256, 306, 371, 401, 418
Korzeniewicz, Roberto Patricio, 28
Kritzinger, Andrienetta, 231, 240, 242, 284
Krugman, Paul, 72, 105, 141, 147, 166–167, 343
Kuptsch, Christiane, 240
Kusterbeck, Staci, 221

Labaste, Patrick, 413
Lall, Sanjaya, 9, 114, 219, 224, 363
Lam, Kit-Chun, 383
Lamy, Pascal, 431, 434
Langlois, Richard N., 110, 114
Lardner, James, 46, 50
Lardy, Nicholas, 209
Lash, Scott, 149
Lee, Ji-Ren, 30, 112, 130, 219
Lee, Joonkoo, 32, 280, 285, 306, 318, 326, 343, 347, 349, 392, 394–395, 408, 418, 420, 439
Legomsky, Joanne, 53–54, 56
Leslie, Deborah, 127
Lester, Richard K., 93–94, 130, 237, 261, 266, 346
Leung, Hon-Chu, 96
Libert, Barry, 442
Lim, Eun Mie, 30
Lim, Hyun-Chin, 3
Linden, Greg, 30, 421
Lindgreen, Adam, 22, 277–278, 282–283, 288, 290
Liu, Pak-Wai, 383

Loayza, Norman, 384
Locke, Richard M., 240, 242, 258, 260, 265, 268–269, 283, 286, 289, 292, 294, 296, 373
Lora, Eduardo, 208
Lorenz, Edward H., 110
Love, Joseph L., 11
Lowden, Pamela, 206, 208
Lucas, Jr., Robert E., 381
Luen Thai, 221
Lukas, Karin, 268
Lumpkin, Thomas A., 316
Lund-Thomsen, Peter, 22, 277–279, 282–292
Lundvall, Bengt-Ake, 152
Lüthje, Boy, 222, 367, 396
Lynch, Teresa, 30, 128
Lynn, Barry C., 347, 407

Maertens, Miet, 244
Magretta, Joan, 121
Malmberg, Anders, 127
Mandle, Jay R., 264
Martin, David, 26
Martin, Eric, 421
Martin, Philip, 239
Maskell, Peter, 127
Mattli, Walter, 259
Mayer, Frederick W., 247, 270–271, 277, 286, 292–293, 295, 306, 349, 367, 371, 393, 419, 434, 448
McCormick, Dorothy, 30, 231, 235
McFate, Katherine, 30
McGrew, Anthony, 255
Memedovic, Olga, 27, 121, 168, 260, 276, 279
Meng, Xiaochen, 209, 219
Menkhoff, Thomas, 113
Meyer, John W., 155
Meyer-Stamer, Jorg, 279
Mezzadri, Alessandra, 284
Milberg, William, 243, 247, 284, 349, 371, 434
Miller, Annetta, 67
Miller, Doug, 231
Miller, James P., 83
Mishra, Pankav, 429

Mitchell, Russell, 67
Mody, Ashoka, 50
Moore, David, 26
Moran, Theodore H., 3, 8
Morgan, Glenn, 168
Morkel, Andre, 119, 130
Morris, Mike, 30, 347, 354–355, 412
Mosley, Layna, 30
Müller, Ronald E., 5, 145–146
Myers, Steven L., 439

Nadvi, Khalid, 30, 129, 178, 277, 279–280,
    284–285, 287, 289–292
Nasar, Sylvia, 67
Nathan, Dev, 284–285, 347, 407
Naughton, Barry, 346
Navarro, Peter, 440
Navas-Alemán, Lizbeth, 350, 417
Nee, Victor, 165
Neilson, Jeffrey, 282, 284, 287, 289, 292, 417
Nelson, Richard R., 152
Neto, Mario S., 407
Newfarmer, Richard, 3, 7, 26, 146
Nolan, Peter H., 211, 223
Nye, Joseph, 255

Ocampo, Jose A., 255, 257
Oehmke, James F., 372
Offe, Claus, 149
Olson, Mancur, 263
O'Neill, Jim, 371, 387, 420–421
Opondo, Maggie, 283, 286, 288, 290
O'Riain, Seán, 30
O'Rourke, Dara, 286, 288, 290, 292
Orsato, Renato J., 269
Ortega, Bob, 81
Özveren, Eyüp, 29

Palley, Thomas I., 212
Palpacuer, Florence, 30, 129, 282, 413
Pan, Mei-Lin, 30, 97, 105
Pang, Carmen, 221
Parker, Ashley, 436
Pathasarathy, Balaji, 30
Pay, Ellen, 269
Pearson, Ruth, 240

Pegler, Lee J., 230, 234, 283
Pelizzon, Sheila, 29
Penrose, Edith, 110
Peres, Wilson, 176
Pérez, Ramón Padilla, 184
Perlez, Jane, 440
Pickles, John, 244, 247, 347
Pillai, Poonam, 292
Pillay, Renginee G., 277, 279, 286–287
Piore, Michael J., 47, 278
Pires, Silvio R. I., 407
Pisano, Gary P., 421, 445
Pischke, Jorn-Steffen, 383
Plank, Leonhard, 247
Polanyi, Karl, 253–254
Polaski, Sandra, 286, 288, 293
Ponte, Stefano, 31, 164, 244, 281–282,
    351–352, 444
Poon, Teresa Shuk-Ching, 160
Porter, Michael, 31, 50, 61, 74, 149, 167, 278
Portes, Alejandro, 3, 207–208
Portocarrero Lacayo, Ana Victoria, 353
Posthuma, Anne, 280, 284, 291
Powell, Walter W., 110
Prahalad, Coimbatore K., 111
Prebisch, Raúl, 11
Prestowitz, Clyde, 429, 447
Pritchard, Bill, 282, 284, 287, 289, 292, 431
Pyke, Frank, 178, 199, 278

Rabach, Eileen, 47
Rabellotti, Roberta, 179
Ragin, Charles, 25
Raikes, Philip, 151
Raj-Reichert, Gale, 31
Ranis, Gus, 6
Ratha, Dilip, 387
Rauch, James E., 19
Ravenhill, John, 30, 86, 160
Raworth, Kate, 228, 231, 240, 242
Rawski, Thomas G., 210
Reardon, Thomas, 260, 412
Reich, Robert B., 47, 167
Reimer, Suzzane, 127
Reinhardt, Nora, 176

Reis, José Guilherme, 349
Rhee, Yung W., 74, 105
Richards, John, 30
Riisgaard, Lone, 260
Ritzer, George, 162
Robertson, Paul L., 110, 114
Robinson, William I., 177
Rodríguez-Garavito, César A., 293
Rodriguez, Carlos Manuel, 355
Rodrik, Dani, 162, 219
Rogaly, Ben, 239
Rohter, Larry, 102
Romis, Monica, 258, 268
Roncolato, Leanne, 287
Ross, Andrew, 346
Ross, Robert J. S., 44
Rossi, Arianna, 229–230, 233, 238, 242–243, 246–247, 349, 392, 394–395
Rostow, Walt W., 2
Rothstein, Richard, 51
Rubinson, Richard, 25
Rudolf, John C., 26
Ruggie, John G., 162–163, 253, 256, 268–269, 430
Rugman, Alan M., 6, 145
Ruwanpura, Kanchana N., 279, 287–288

Sabel, Charles F., 47, 278
Sack, Karen J., 53, 56
Safarian, A. Edward, 6, 145
Sako, Mari, 322
Salazar-Xirinachs, José M., 345, 365
Sampson, Anthony, 5, 27, 145
Saporito, Bill, 54
Sarkar, Sandip, 285, 347, 407
Sassen, Saskia, 155
Scheffer, Michael, 80
Scherer, Frederic M., 7
Schilling, Melissa A., 114, 130
Schmidt-Hebbel, Klaus, 384
Schmitter, Philippe C., 149
Schmitz, Hubert, 17, 27, 30, 32, 112, 151, 178–179, 198, 200, 231, 235, 276–277, 279, 282, 285, 288, 307, 312, 409
Schneider, Ben R., 279, 291

Scott, Allen J., 127
Seidman, Gay, 163, 165
Selwyn, Ben, 286, 291
Selwyn, Michael , 91–92
Sen, Amartya, 231, 233
Sengenberger, Werner, 178, 199
Shaiken, Harley, 143, 184
Sharpe, Kenneth E., 3, 8, 26
Sheperd, Andrew, 260
Shepherd, Phillip, 26
Shifter, Michael, 209
Shih, Stan, 315
Shih, Willy C., 421, 445
Sklair, Leslie, 143, 155, 183
Skocpol, Theda, 25
Smelser, Neil J., 19, 165
Smick, David M., 418
Smith, Adam, 140
Smith, Adrian, 347
Smith, Sally, 234, 240, 279, 286, 290, 295
Solt, Fred, 207, 209
Sonobe, Tetsuki, 219, 222
Soskice, David, 128, 152
Spencer, Jennifer, 30
Staritz, Cornelia, 23, 27, 230, 344, 349, 388, 405–406, 412
Starobin, Shana, 263–264, 271
Steensma, H. Kevin, 114, 130
Stiglitz, Joseph E., 432
Storper, Michael, 45, 125, 127
Streeck, Wolfgang, 128
Strom, Stephanie, 66
Sturgeon, Timothy J., 16–17, 23, 27, 30–31, 112, 114, 126, 128, 130, 148, 161, 219, 237, 261, 266, 276, 279, 281, 346–347, 350, 359, 363, 365, 372, 384, 403, 405, 418, 439, 446
Sun, Yutao, 439, 443, 448
Sunkel, Osvaldo, 8, 146, 166
Suresh, T. G., 280, 284
Swanson, Ana, 439, 447
Swedberg, Richard, 19, 165
Swinnen, Joe, 244

Tabuchi, Hiroko, 236

Taglioni, Daria, 327
Talbot, John M., 352
Tam, Tony, 73
Taplin, Ian M., 49
Tarrow, Sidney, 271
Tewari, Meenu, 17, 31, 292
Theron, Jan, 240
Tholons, 358
Thompson, Ginger, 200
Thomson, Adam, 364
Thorelli, Hans, 110
Thorp, Rosemary, 206, 208
Thun, Eric, 405, 413
Tong, Xin, 219, 221–222
Trachte, Kent C., 44

Ulrich, Karl, 130
Urquidi, Victor L., 166, 344, 401
Urry, John, 149

Van Biesebroeck, Johannes, 347, 405
Vanhamme, Joelle, 22
van Tulder, Rob, 258, 269, 276, 283
Vargas Llosa, Alvaro, 208–209
Vernon, Raymond, 6–7, 145, 158, 344, 401
Visser, Margareet, 291
Vogel, David J., 257, 259, 262, 264–265, 268, 271

Wade, Robert H., 12, 141–142, 152, 432
Wadhwa, Vivek, 370, 400, 407, 431
Waldinger, Roger, 51
Walker, Richard, 127
Wallerstein, Immanuel, 4–5, 14–15, 26, 139–141, 152
Wältring, Frank, 129
Wang, Jici, 219, 221–222
Wang, Mark Y., 209, 219

Warfield, Carol, 81, 83
Weatherspoon, Dave. D, 412
Webber, C. Martin, 413
Weber, Samuel, 66
Weinberger, Katinka, 316
Weinthal, Erika, 263–264, 271
West, Peter, 26
Weyland, Kurt, 207, 209
Wheeler, David, 50
Whiting, Jr., Van, 26
Whitley, Richard, 154
Whittaker, D. Hugh, 367
Whyte, Martin King, 11
Whytock, Christopher A., 259
Williams, Oliver F., 163
Williamson, John, 432
Williamson, Oliver E., 109, 116
Wills, Jane, 231, 240
Winkler, Deborah, 243, 247, 327, 349
Wolfensohn, James D., 165
Womack, James P., 148
Woods, Ngaire, 259
Worthen, Ben, 266
Wrigley, Neil, 279, 288
Wu, Xinyi, 443
Wyman, Donald L., 12–13, 28, 47, 166, 345, 369, 401–402, 432, 438

Yeats, Alexander J., 109, 147
Yeung, Henry Wai-chung, 155, 230
Young, Alwyn, 72

Zeitlin, Jonathan, 199
Zeng, Douglas Zhihua, 236
Zhang, Qing, 219
Zhang, Zhiming, 219, 221–222
Zysman, John, 442